The

CALENDAR

of Modern Letters

VOLUME I

THE CALENDAR OF MODERN LETTERS

March 1925 — July 1927

Edited by

Edgell Rickword and Douglas Garman

New Impression with a Review in Retrospect by
Malcolm Bradbury

VOLUME I

March — August 1925

Routledge
Taylor & Francis Group

LONDON AND NEW YORK

First published in 1925 by Frank Cass & Co. Ltd.
First edition   1925-27
New impression   1966

This edition published 2013 by Routledge
2 Park Square, Milton Park, Abingdon, Oxfordshire OX14 4RN
711 Third Avenue, New York, NY 10017

First issued in paperback 2014

*Routledge is an imprint of the Taylor & Francis Group,
an informa business*

ISBN 13: 978-0-7146-2104-3 (hbk)
ISBN 13: 978-0-415-76107-9 (pbk)

A REVIEW IN RETROSPECT

by

MALCOLM BRADBURY

A REVIEW IN RETROSPECT*

THE three great literary reviews of the 1920s were *The Criterion*, *The Adelphi* and *The Calendar of Modern Letters*. Of these, the last-mentioned was in many ways much the best, yet it is certainly the least remembered. In 1933 Dr F. R. Leavis edited a selection from its pages, entitled *Towards Standards of Criticism*; he remarked, in his introduction, that the review had commanded the services of 'half a dozen really distinguished critics, each one better than any that finds frequent employment in existing periodicals' and he compared the review with *The Criterion*, remarking on its superior liveliness and its greater critical excellence. Moreover, there was in the founding, in 1932, of *Scrutiny* a strong and conscious debt to *The Calendar*, and perhaps it was the sense of the gap left by the demise of the paper that stirred *Scrutiny* into life. When *The Calendar* died there was left no periodical concerned for the moral and cultural enrichment of literature and none devoted to the exposition of serious critical principles. *The Criterion*, while the most serious and intelligent of contemporary journals, did not seem to the editors of *Scrutiny* to be performing the service required of a literary periodical at this time, and indeed that review never consolidated the distinguished statements on critical matters which Eliot had contributed to its pages early in its career. Thus *The Calendar*, which appeared between March 1925 and July 1927, was able to spread its influence much more widely than its present lack of reputation would suggest. It had much to do with the growth of the modern movement in criticism.

On the whole, the significant activity in the little magazines of the previous decade had been that of accomplishing a literary revolution. The tone of the important journals was *avant garde;* their circulation was small; they were addressed largely to a bohemian-intellectual reading public. Such criticism as appeared in these magazines tended to be written by literary practitioners, like Pound and Eliot, Ford Madox Hueffer and F. S. Flint, and was very much devoted to what Pound called Making It New.

* This essay first appeared in *The London Magazine*, October, 1961.

It was reformatory rather than considered; but it offered many
critical insights that subsequent critics sought to pursue with
greater precision. The twenties were a period of *critical* revolution. Indeed, it is, perhaps, the development of criticism that
forms the most *visible* advance that has been made in the pages
of the twentieth-century literary periodical. By the beginning
of the century the play of criticism as a serious discipline that
had prevailed in the reviews and magazines of the early nineteenth century had almost disappeared. 'Time is ripe for the
forging of a weapon of criticism, and for the emphatic assertion
of literary standards,' declared Harold Monro in the first number of *The Poetry Review* in January 1912, and elsewhere in the
same issue of the same periodical the point was made again:

> Criticism is always with us, yet it has achieved no consis-
> tent method by which the true artist can be distinguished
> from the false with any reliability . . . no standard of taste
> has yet proved sufficiently comprehensive to essay correctly
> the merit of a new poet and relegate him, as the critics still
> futilely attempt to do, to a fitting rank and station among his
> peers.

These comments, by Arthur K. Sabin, now seem dated; they
seem so not because they no longer apply but because they pre-
scribe, with such freshness, the attempt. Nowadays there is no
lack of emphatic assertions of literary standards, and there are
enough 'consistent methods' and 'comprehensive standards of
taste' to require critical study themselves.

But the criticism of the early years of the century was not, by
and large, disposed to treat such problems, or to talk of scientific approaches to criticism; it was all a matter of taste. Some had
it and some didn't; this was the implication. It was towards the
end of the Great War that signs of development appeared. *The
Egoist* began to print criticism and, more importantly at the
time, discussion of criticism by Eliot and Pound; *The Athenaeum*,
in a final burst of glory under the editorship of John Middleton
Murry, presented its readers with a succession of book reviews
and articles on literature by many of the best minds of the time.
With the foundation of reviews like *The Criterion* and *The
Calendar of Modern Letters*, which not only criticized but sub-
mitted to searching examination the positions from which
critical standpoints were made, the critical revival was estab-

lished, and by 1932 it was possible for a review, *Scrutiny*, to appear whose main concern was the revaluation of the whole body of English literature from a central carefully presented critical viewpoint, which had developed under the stimulus of the critical gains of Eliot, Pound, Murry, Richards and the group of *Calendar* critics.

By 1920, the old literary establishment had been more or less ousted by the younger generation that had been coming into prominence since about 1910. Lawrence, Eliot, Pound, Joyce, Katherine Mansfield, Norman Douglas, Wyndham Lewis, Middleton Murry and many others had established themselves over this period; and in 1924 there appeared in print T. E. Hulme's posthumous volume of essays. *Speculations*, which consolidated many ideas which had been active among writers over the previous two decades. In *The Criterion* (XVI, 65) for July 1937, T. S. Eliot remarked, in one of his 'Commentaries':

> The period which may be said to have begun about 1910 had its own critical requirements which were not those of a general assessment of the literatures of the past. What was needed was a critical activity to revise creative writing, to introduce new material and new technique from other coun-tries and other times. The accomplishment of the Imagist movement in verse seems to me, in retrospect, to have been critical rather than creative; and as criticism, very important.

But, he adds, the period after the war seems to him one of less lively interest in the problems of creative writing, one more concerned with esthetics in general, and with psychology. 'For this period, the psychological subtleties of Mr I. A. Richards, and the more general and increasingly political aesthetics of Mr Read seem to provide what is desired.'

The catch-word of the post-war period was Hulme's word, 'classical', with its distrust of the metaphysical attitude and the infinite view. *The Criterion, The Calendar of Modern Letters* and *Scrutiny* were all classical in tone, opposed to the Roman-ticism of Murry's *The Adelphi* and the Dionysianism of Jack Lindsay's *London Aphrodite*. For *The Calendar*, the word 'classicism' had a specific context—'the characteristics of a healthy criticism' wrote Bertram Higgins 'are invariably "classic", tending towards an ever greater rigidity of principle, organizations more explicit, and the canalization of the wide, shallow stream of taste'. But it was not classicism as the *Criterion* meant it; the same critic complained that in Eliot's review 'neo-classicism' was being used as a repressive instrument of literary criticism, in which religious and ethical preoccupations held too much place. Criticism in *The Calendar* was more carefully poised, but geared always toward some general critical agreement, some implied consent. This was a period concerned to clarify and define; a 'period of consolidation' after the establishment of the modern movement at the beginning of the century. Its spirit *was* distinctively modern. But it was a period concerned to establish a tradition and to develop a sound relationship with other arts and sciences; it was concerned too with the development of what Eliot called 'the European mind'—a whole, wide-ranging cultural responsibility. And this extension of interests paved the way for the political interests of the writers of the 1930s.

II

The Calendar of Modern Letters first appeared in March 1925 as a monthly literary review. Its editor was Edgell Rickword; and Douglas Garman, and later Bertram Higgins, was its assistant editor. It published twelve numbers in monthly form and then, with the issue for April 1926, it became a quarterly, increasing its price by one shilling to half a crown. In this form it continued until it ended its short life with volume four, number two, dated July 1927. During that short period of existence, it published some of the best criticism to appear in any literary review since the decline of the great politico-literary reviews of the nineteenth century. Moreover, it was criticism informed by theory; on the strength of a very small number of articles, clearer formulation of critical ideas was made available to that small body of readers which the review reached (its circulation, according to Edgell Rickword, began at 7–8,000 and dropped over the first year to 2–3,000; it then became a quarterly and its circulation dropped to 1,000).

The circumstances of its foundation, as Edgell Rickword recollected them for me, were these: the paper was the project of a loosely-knit group of young writers feeling their way in London literary journalism. Two of them, Rickword and

Bertram Higgins, who met as undergraduates at Oxford soon after the War, had been publishing verse and criticism in various journals for some years. They were joined in 1923 or 4 by Douglas Garman, a slightly younger friend just down from Cambridge. These three had a good deal in common, including, which was most relevant at this point, a profound dissatisfaction with the current literary scene—particularly so, as Eliot's *Criterion* was, they thought, failing to achieve the critical precision they had expected of it under an editor of such acute critical power. After many discussions, they sketched out an alternative platform for a literary journal.

There the matter might have remained had not a common friend, Ernest Wishart, keenly interested in contemporary literature, undertaken to provide the necessary financial backing.

It began with rigorous standards and, even when at the end of its life it seemed it might continue by foregoing some of its strictness, it preferred to fail with its intentions uncompromised. In its last number a statement, entitled 'Valediction Forbidding Mourning', suggests what those intentions were:

> The most natural step for a review to take, if it wishes to survive, is to adopt a 'political' attitude (one, that is, which implies a tendency to judge by expediency) and, though we realize that such an attitude may be almost essential to the achievement of a sound economic status, we cannot consider it as less than an abuse of function. For, in taking such a step, the freedom to exercise an independent judgement on contemporary work will be lost—not in so gross a sense as by commercial obligation, but by the more subtle and more obnoxious distortions required for the continued support of one's own platform. One can have little respect for the periodical which flaunts a pretension to philosophical righteousness and yet makes as many blunders with regard to the actual works of poetry or literature before it as the most unenlightened of its Georgian predecessors.

The value of a review, the article went on, must be judged by its attitude to the living literature of the time, which includes such works of the past as can be absorbed into the contemporary sensibility. A magazine with such standards should be able to draw, in its more regular contributors, on a homogeneity of view—but a vital homogeneity and not 'the placid acceptance of a body of dogma or prejudices of one superior mind (legitimate only to itself) by some unindividualized members of the *intelligentzia*'. The consensus of *The Calendar* was vital enough, and it seems to have been contemporary also, since many of the opinions expressed passed into critical lore. On the other hand, however, this final editorial did admit a suspicion that its own synthesis had not been in every respect adequate, and it explained that it was partly because of this suspicion that the review was ceasing to function:

> There comes a moment in the creation of a work of art when a new conception interposes itself and makes further revision impossible. A review has quite different functions from a work of art but the parallel may serve to explain the unwillingness of those most closely associated with *The Calendar* to continue it in its present form. . . .

What this new conception was was never made clear, though the appearance of one of the editors in the *The Left Review* in due course may be something of an explanation.

That *The Calendar* was assertive enough about 'standards of criticism' may be gathered from this editorial tone, and some of its aims as a periodical may be clarified by a review it gave to *The New Criterion*—as *The Criterion* was at this period called —in February 1926, in which the question of an organizing principle for a magazine is debated—'not even the bulkiest review can be boundlessly eclectic, and as soon as the element of choice is introduced the question of a principle or a programme becomes paramount'. The reviewer remarks of *The Criterion* that Mr Eliot's 'colours' are 'very faintly painted in' and identifies his position with the intellectualist reaction against 'the intuitionalist debauch'. Bertram Higgins later elaborated the point by remarking that Eliot's 'neo-classicism' ·was the literary version of a reactionary Latin philosophy, neo-Thomism, which was adapted into a repressive instrument of criticism, whose main aspects were a 'verbal sobriety which disguised its positivism, its calm and socialized demeanour in the midst of the revolutionary concepts by which we are surrounded, and its genuine but exaggerated docility to the world of learning'. *The Calendar* went in for fresher and more pragmatic style, advancing its standards warily and in action. It announced in its first issue:

We lay down no programme as to *The Calendar's* perfor- mance, nor prophecy as to its character, since these things can- not interest our readers till they have a tangible existence, and then we shall be ready to join our own criticism with theirs. A conviction of the value of spontaneous growth (or growth which seems spontaneous to the watching mind) and of unpoliced expression. . . .

It aimed to be of value to those readers who 'wish to keep in touch with the literature which reflects the spirit of the present day', and it promised a series of critical articles entitled 'Scrutinies' which would 'examine the reputations of certain writers who are the object of somewhat indiscriminate admira- tion'.

The cageyness about standards didn't mean that the paper could claim none, as was evident when the series of 'Scrutinies' began. The series (which is reprinted with revision in the first of two volumes of *Scrutinies: Critical Essays* (edited by Edgell Rickword) (London, 1928) is perhaps the main achievement of the review; it demonstrated, by the use of close critical analysis and with a higher skill in exegesis than had been commonly found up to now in any critical paper, positive literary deficien- cies in works that had up to the time been held in high esteem. The articles were the first full scale attempt for many years to achieve by close and exacting criticism a scrupulous and con- sidered evaluation of a work of art. The series gave *Scrutiny* its name and something of its method, and may be compared with the series in *Scrutiny* called 'Revaluations', which went on to examine reputations even more soundly established, and to address itself to the task of reconsidering the whole tradition of English literature. *The Calendar* was concerned primarily with the main figures of twentieth-century literature as they appeared at that time. With the rise of Eliot, Pound and the survivors of the Imagist movement, a number of poets and novelists of the earliest part of the century had been challenged. But unlike many magazines intent upon establishing a new era, it did not dismiss easily, working through its argument by close and exacting analysis. Thus the first of the series, an examination by Edgell Rickword of Sir James Barrie, noted 'an essential dramatic deficiency in [Barrie's] failure to separate his figures from his own emotional attitude towards them, a failure to complete the objectification of feeling which is the condition of art', an observation we would take for granted today but which was far from being familiar in 1925. Rickword's final conclusions elaborate his standard:

> At the end of the play, comedy or tragedy, if it is what we call successful, the level of desirable emotion has been heightened in those characters with whom the writer has decided that we shall identify our sympathies; others are inevitably the poorer. Barrie's peculiar trick, and that which prevents one from receiving any genuine stimulation from his plays, is a confusion of emotional perspective: by this means, emotions or loss and deprivation are made equivalent in value to those of fruition. . . .

This is practical criticism, concerned with technicalities, and concerned with solving artistic problems about design of works of art and the relations of parts to wholes. However, there is also a moral note struck, a willingness to challenge an artist's whole view of life, as when Douglas Garman, in the second of the series, speaks, in discussing Walter de la Mare, of 'the falsity of the values which he supports'. In the third, Bertram Higgins, considering the poetry of John Masefield, hits a note rather like Rickwords', analysing

> the emotional intention which, in all imperfect poetry, perceptibly accompanies the aesthetic achievement. The careless reader is only too likely to mistake the first for the second, and in Masefield this game of substitution assumes the proportions of downright bluff. . . .

C. H. Rickword, in the fifth of the series, pointed out that Bernard Shaw was rather an evangelist than a serious writer; and he pointed out that the artistic consequence of his belief in, and use of, the Life Force was that his plays 'far from attempting a reconciliation of life in the classical manner, are purely romantic flights from reality'. These analyses represent the standpoint of the review; they involve a clear idea of the full dramatic organization of the play, or the artistic organization of the novel, and an awareness of the traits which emasculate the general effect, in terms of failures to answer structural problems thrown up by a work of this kind. The method might be descri-bed as Aristotelian, since it presupposes that each work throws up its own rules and probabilities as it advances, and that offences against these expectations are failures in working. There is also the moral observation, always rooted closely in the literary judgement; when Douglas Garman picks out, in the work of Walter de la Mare, certain lines that 'approximate to the effect he intends but are almost nonsense', he shows the technique at its best—precise and exacting with an awareness of the effect of the whole work on its parts and the effect of the writer's emotional attitude toward his material.

Outside this series *The Calendar* printed a number of articles of high critical importance. There were studies of Poe, James Joyce and—tackling another field ready for criticism, criticism itself—Kenneth Burke. Robert Graves and Laura Riding wrote on anthologies. In an important article, 'The Re-Creation of Poetry' (*Calendar* I, 3, May 1925), Edgell Rickword addressed the problem of analysing the sources of the poetic emotion, observing that 'a poem must, at some point or other, release, enable to flow back to the level of active life, the emotions caught up from life and pent in the aesthetic reservoir', a view that raises evident critical consequences. Perhaps, from the historical point of view, an even more important article was John Crowe Ransom's essay, 'Thoughts on Poetic Discontent' (*Calendar* I, 6, August 1925), one of the earliest salvoes of the American 'new criticism'. Ransom addressed himself to considering irony as a form of poetic control—'Irony may be regarded as the ultimate mode of great minds—it presupposes the others.' Another important issue, the relation of a writer to his society, was aired profoundly by Edwin Muir in an essay on 'The Zeit-Geist' (*Calendar* II, 8, October 1925); Muir argued that the power most solidly obnoxious to the artist is not the public but the intelligentsia. It is the calibre of his resistance to the values and standards presented there that give an artist's work its quality, and the *zeitgeist* nowadays not only encourages that resistance but also 'gives him a new inspiration, once the resistance has been vitally pierced'. Wyndham Lewis was another important contributor, appearing several times; of particular interest is his argument in 'The Dithyrambic Spectator' (*Calendar* I, 2, April 1925 and *Calendar* I, 3, May 1925) where he puts the case (which reappears in his *The Diabolical Principle* (1931)) that the Arts today exist where the need for them is absent, and they are perpetuated for their own sake. D. H.

Lawrence appeared several times, contributing poems, reviews and the essay 'Morality and the Novel'. Both Lawrence and Lewis were solicited for contributions because of the intrinsic value of their work, not because they supported the 'programme' of the review. The editors had also sought a contribution from James Joyce, but when it arrived (an extract from 'Anna Livia Plurabelle') were frustrated by the quite excessive (even for those days) prudery of their printers, and had to retreat discomfited.*

In this way, and gradually, the review built up a body of opinion, centred around Edgell Rickword, his cousin C. H. Rickword, Bertram Higgins and Douglas Garman, but widening out to include and support Lewis, Lawrence and Edwin Muir, which had a coherent sense to it, a conviction about literature as a field worthy of close exegetical study and yet open to larger issues about its social background and its moral content. Perhaps the best example of the spirit, and the practical success, of the review's thinking and its effect upon those who took the opportunity of the running debate it offered is to be found in two discussions by C. H. Rickword of the criticism of fiction. The occasion of the first discussion was Elizabeth Drew's book, *The Modern Novel*, which C. H. Rickword reviewed (*Calendar* III, 2, July 1926) and which gave him the chance to observe that the critical terminology we had been applying to novels was unreal and dangerous. He gave as an example the singling out of 'character' as a part of the novel:

> . . . whereas rhythm [in poetry] corresponds to an actual excitement in the reader's mind that can be traced to its source in the means employed, character corresponds to nothing so definite. Rhythm is a property of words, character a product that needs analysis before a satisfactory account of its effect can be given in terms of its constituents, and a product, moreover, that invites extra-literary scrutiny. Such scrutiny is fatal to criticism, for, though it may be that the critic's ultimate concern is with the conception of life (the 'values') of which the novel is a vehicle, yet he is only so concerned in so far as that conception is made active through art.

Critics tend moreover to regard character 'as a portrait of an imagined human being' and to prefer the writer who provides the deeper illusion. But, though Raskolnikov is 'deeper' than

Tom Jones, in that more of his interior is directly exposed, he is
a figure of different and not great significance. Character is
merely the term by which the reader alludes to 'the pseudo-
objective image he composes of his responses to the author's
verbal arrangements'; and once this image has been composed
it can be criticized from many angles and regarded for its political, social or religious significance, as though it possessed actual
objectivity. This article is further developed in the next issue of
The Calendar, when under the title of 'A Note on Fiction'
(*Calendar* III, 3, October 1926), C. H. Rickword postulates a
more 'organic' approach to fiction. The form of a novel only
exists as a balance of response on the part of the reader. 'Only
as precipitates from the memory are plot or character tenable;
yet only in solution have either any emotional valency.' Such
effects are technical devices, effects produced by the novelist;
the techniques of the novel are just as symphonic as the technique of the drama and depend upon the dynamic devices of
articulation and control of narrative tempo. Thus plot and
character exist in solution. Modern opinion has inclined to the
view, says Rickword, that plot be determined by, or arise out of,
character. It is, he declares, evident however that character
arises out of narrative. Further, novels in which character does
not seem to dominate give aesthetic satisfaction and one has
to look for this by noting a common quality in all great works
of literature:

> It is a unity among the events, a progressive rhythm that
> includes and reconciles each separate rhythm. As manifested
> in the novel, it resolves, when analysed, chiefly into character
> and plot in a secondary, schematic sense—qualities that are
> purely fictitious. Neither is an active element in the whole
> work in the way that melody and harmony are elements in a
> piece of music. Perhaps it would be less ambiguous to desig-
> nate this basic, poetic quality by some such term as rhythm
> or development; on the other hand, plot or story do indicate
> its nature—that it is primarily a sequence of events develop-
> ing in accordance with an inner necessity.

The recognition of this inner necessity (which Rickword uses
much as Aristotle uses the notion of plot or myth) constitutes
the recognition of value—and it springs ultimately from the

writer's conception of life and the adequacy of his vehicle in presenting that conception.

The article is clearly a seminal one not only for *The Calendar* but for modern criticism generally, both in England and the United States, where the paper circulated. Many modern attitudes toward the criticism of fiction are concentrated in it. There is the assumption that novels are 'wholes', unified conceptions; that they are not just life rendered on the page but verbal constructs with their own laws and their own ways of producing effects on the reader; and that the quality of the author's conception of life plays a substantial part in his invention. While, clearly, there *are* novels invented in terms of that conception of 'plot' and 'character' that Rickword challenges, our reading is richer if we acknowledge that inventions in the novel do usually work to a pattern like the one Rickword describes.

The Calendar's record in creative work is also impressive, though, for obvious reasons, it could not always uphold the standards set by the criticism. It felt a responsibility to do justice to writers of promise who deserved the encouragement of publication and it sought to be of value to those readers who wished to keep in touch 'with literature which reflects the spirit of the present age'. The review had in fact no reason to be modest on this account; the standard was very high indeed. The opening numbers serialized D. H. Lawrence's story 'The Princess', and there were stories from Pirandello, A. E. Coppard, Liam O'Flaherty, Leonid Leonov, William Gerhardi, Stephen Hudson, Douglas Garman and others. Chekov's comedy *The Wood Demon* was serialized. The poetry came from Robert Graves, Siegfried Sassoon. Edgell Rickword, Edmund Blunden, Bertram Higgins and others. There were, too, critical essays which lay rather outside the general theory of the review and are yet of real importance—such essays as E. M. Forster's on 'Anonymity', Samuel Hoare's on Rimbaud and Edwin Muir's on *Ulysses*. One aspect of the review deserves particular attention—it was among the earliest papers to draw attention to the younger American poets and critics who were coming into prominence at this time. Thus there is John Crowe Ransom's essay on irony, and Gorham B. Munson's study of the criticism of Kenneth Burke. In addition the work of three important

young American poets—John Crowe Ransom, Hart Crane and
Allen Tate—appeared in its pages.

It is strange, considering its record and its historical importance,
that *The Calendar* has not been more widely remembered and,
one might add, imitated. There is still room for a review of its
sort—eclectic yet with a high critical sophistication and exigence
—at the present time. Its blood brothers are in fact American
reviews like *The Kenyon Review*; and it is interesting to note
that the review did have a strong impact in America, and is still,
it seems, better remembered there. Nonetheless, there have
always been a few critics and writers who remembered the
paper with gratitude. To some minds the paper was over-
austere; thus H. P. Collins, reviewing the second volume of
Scrutinies, spoke of a group of critics, mostly unknown, 'who
possess a detachment and capacity for subtle differentiation and
analysis which would have been incomprehensible a dozen years
ago' together with 'a new degree of sophistication more formidable than the old 'superiority' of the ultra-artistic, a sophistication rather bloodless and probably deplorable, but arising
from a mature, if not a deep, culture' (*Criterion* X, 41, July
1931). He was worried by its intellectualism—'at once the
apotheosis of Bloomsbury and the dissolvent of Bloomsbury'—
and the fact that its criticism was not creative, not concerned
even with the society in which art grows. Today we are not so
apt to find intellectuality so worrying, and a fresh look at
The Calendar would show it to be surprisingly modern and
enduring.

* See Sylvia Beach, Shakespeare and Company. (Faber, 1960)

CONTENTS

INDEX TO CONTRIBUTORS

CONTENTS

COMMENTS AND REVIEWS

A page number in parenthesis means that the reference is to a note only.

BOOKS REVIEWED

CONTENTS

CONTENTS

LIST OF REVIEWERS

The CALENDAR
of Modern Letters

VOLUME I   MARCH
NUMBER I   1925

The Princess

BY D. H. LAWRENCE.

TO her father, she was The Princess. To her Boston aunts and uncles she was just *Dollie Urquhart, poor little thing.*

Colin Urquhart was just a bit mad. He was of an old Scottish family, and he claimed royal blood. The blood of Scottish kings flowed in his veins. On this point, his American relatives said, he was just a bit " off." They could not bear any more to be told *which* royal blood of Scotland blued his veins. The whole thing was rather ridiculous, and a sore point. The only fact they remembered was that it was not Stuart.

He was a handsome man, with a wide-open blue eye that seemed sometimes to be looking at nothing, soft black hair brushed rather low on his low, broad brow, and a very attractive body. Add to this a most beautiful speaking voice, usually rather hushed and diffident, but sometimes resonant and powerful like bronze, and you have the sum of his charms. He looked like some old Celtic hero. He looked as if he should have worn a greyish kilt and a sporran, and shown his knees. His voice came direct out of the hushed Ossianic past.

For the rest, he was one of those gentlemen of sufficient but not excessive means, who, fifty years ago, wandered vaguely about, never arriving anywhere, never doing anything, and never definitely being anything, yet well received and familiar in the good society of more than one country.

He did not marry till he was nearly forty, and then it was a wealthy Miss Prescott, from New England. Hannah Prescott at twenty-two was fascinated by the man with the soft black hair not yet touched by grey, and the wide, rather vague blue eyes. Many women had been fascinated before her. But Colin Urquhart, by his very vagueness, had avoided any decisive connection.

Mrs. Urquhart lived three years in the mist and glamour of her husband's presence. And then it broke her. It was like living with a fascinating spectre. About most things he was completely, even ghostlily oblivious. He was always charming, courteous, perfectly gracious in that hushed, musical voice of his. But absent. When all came to all, he just wasn't there. " Not all there," as the vulgar say.

He was the father of the little girl she bore at the end of the first year. But this did not substantiate him the more. His very beauty and his haunting musical quality became dreadful to her after the first few months. The strange echo : he was like a living echo ! His very flesh, when you touched it, did not seem quite the flesh of a real man.

Perhaps it was that he was a little bit mad. She thought it definitely the night her baby was born.

" Ah, so my little princess has come at last ! " he said, in his throaty, singing Celtic voice, like a glad chant, swaying absorbed.

It was a tiny, frail baby, with wide, amazed blue eyes. They christened it Mary Henrietta. She called the little thing *My Dollie*. He called it always *My Princess*.

It was useless to fly at him. He just opened his wide blue eyes wider, and took a childlike, silent dignity there was no getting past.

Hannah Prescott had never been robust. She had no great desire to live. So when the baby was two years old she suddenly died.

The Prescotts felt a deep but unadmitted resentment against Colin Urquhart. They said he was selfish. Therefore they discontinued Hannah's income a month after her burial in Florence, after they had urged the father to give the child over to them, and he had courteously, musically, but quite finally refused. He treated the Prescotts as if they were not of his world, not realities to him : just casual phenomena, or gramophones, talking-machines that had to be answered. He answered them. But of their actual existence he was never once aware.

They debated having him certified unsuitable to be guardian of his own child. But that would have created a scandal. So they did the simplest thing, after all—washed their hands of him. But they wrote scrupulously to the child, and sent her modest presents of money at Christmas, and on the anniversary of the death of her mother.

To The Princess her Boston relatives were for many years just a nominal reality. She lived with her father, and he travelled continually, though in a modest way, living on his moderate income. And never going to America. The child changed nurses all the time. In Italy it was a *contadina* ; in India she had an *ayah*; in Germany she had a yellow-haired peasant girl.

Father and child were inseparable. He was not a recluse. Wherever he went he was to be seen paying formal calls, going out to luncheon or to tea, rarely to dinner. And always with the child. People called her Princess Urquhart, as if that were her christened name.

She was a quick, dainty little thing with dark gold hair that went a soft brown, and wide, slightly prominent blue eyes that were at once so candid and so knowing, She was always grown up ; she never really grew up. Always strangely wise, and always childish.

It was her father's fault.

" My. little Princess must never take too much notice of people and the things they say and do," he repeated to her. " People don't know what they are doing and saying. They chatter-chatter, and they hurt one another, and they hurt themselves very often, till they cry. But don't take any notice, my little Princess. Because it is all nothing. Inside everybody there is another creature, a demon which doesn't care at all. You peel away all the things they say and do and feel, as cook peels away the outside of the onions. And in the middle of everybody there is a green demon which you can't peel away. And this green demon never changes, and it doesn't care at all about all the things that happen to the outside leaves of the person, all the chatter-chatter, and all the husbands and wives and children, and troubles and fusses. You peel everything away from people, and there is a green, upright demon in every man and woman ; and this demon is a man's real self, and a woman's real self. It doesn't really care about anybody, it belongs to the demons and the primitive fairies, who never care. But, even so, there are big demons and mean demons, and splendid demonish fairies, and vulgar ones. But there are no royal fairy women left. Only you, my little Princess. You are the last of the royal race of the old people ; the last, my Princess. There are no others. You and I are the last. When I am dead there will be only you. And that is why, darling, you will never care for any of the people in the world very much. Because their demons are all dwindled and vulgar. They are not royal. Only you are royal, after me. Always remember that. And always remember, it is a *great secret*. If you tell people, they will try to kill you, because they will envy you for being a Princess. It is our great secret, darling. I am a prince, and you a princess, of the old, old blood. And we keep our secret between us, all alone. And so, darling, you must treat all people very politely, because *noblesse oblige*. But you must never forget that you alone are the last of Princesses, and that all others are less than you are, less noble, more vulgar. Treat them politely and gently and kindly, darling. But you are the Princess, and they are commoners. Never try to think of them as if they were like you. They are not. You will find, always, that they are lacking, lacking in the royal touch, which only you have—."

The Princess learned her lesson early—the first lesson, of absolute reticence, the impossibility of intimacy with any other than her father ; the second lesson, of naïve, slightly benevolent politeness. As a small child, something crystallised in her character, making her clear and finished, and as impervious as crystal.

"Dear child!" her hostesses said of her. "She is so quaint and old-fashioned ; such a lady, poor little mite!"

She was erect, and very dainty. Always small, nearly tiny in physique, she seemed like a changeling beside her big, handsome, slightly mad father. She dressed very simply, usually in blues or delicate greys, with little collars of old Milan point, or very finely-worked linen. She had exquisite little hands, that made the piano sound like a spinet when she played. She was rather given to wearing cloaks and capes, instead of coats, out of doors, and little eighteenth-century sort of hats. Her complexion was pure apple-blossom.

She looked as if she had stepped out of a picture. But no-one, to her dying day, ever knew exactly the strange picture her father had framed her in, and from which she never stepped.

Her grandfather and grandmother and her Aunt Maud demanded twice to see her, once in Rome and once in Paris. Each time they were charmed, piqued, and annoyed. She was so exquisite and such a little virgin. At the same time so knowing and so oddly assured. That odd, assured touch of condescension, and the inward coldness, infuriated her American relations.

Only she really fascinated her grandfather. He was spellbound ; in a way, in love with the little faultless thing. His wife would catch him brooding, musing over his grandchild, long months after the meeting, and craving to see her again. He cherished to the end the fond hope that she might come to live with him and her grandmother.

" Thank you so much, grandfather. You are so very kind. But Papa and I are such an old couple, you see, such a crotchety old couple, living in a world of our own."

Her father let her see the world—from the outside. And he let her read. When she was in her teens she read Zola and Maupassant, and with the eyes of Zola and Maupassant she looked on Paris. A little later she read Tolstoi and Dostoevsky. The latter confused her. The others, she seemed to understand with a very shrewd, canny understanding, just as she understood the Decameron stories as she read them in their old Italian, or the Nibelung poems. Strange and *uncanny*, she seemed to understand things in a cold light perfectly, with all the flush of fire absent. She was something like a changeling, not quite human.

This earned her, also, strange antipathies. Cabmen and railway-porters, especially in Paris or Rome, would suddenly treat her with brutal rudeness, when she was alone. They seemed to look on her with sudden violent antipathy. They sensed in her curious impertinence, an easy, sterile impertinence towards the things *they* felt most. She was so assured, and her flower of maidenhood was so scentless. She could look at a lusty, sensual Roman cabman as if he were a sort of grotesque, to make her smile. She knew all about him, in Zola. And the peculiar condescension with which she would give him her order, as if she, frail, beautiful thing, were the only reality, and he, coarse monster, were a sort of Caliban floundering in the mud on the margin of the pool of the perfect lotus, would suddenly enrage the fellow, the real Mediterranean who prided himself on his *beauté mâle*, and to whom the phallic mystery was still the only mystery. And he would turn a terrible face on her, bully her in a brutal, coarse fashion —hideous. For to him she had only the blasphemous impertinence of her own sterility.

Encounters like these made her tremble, and made her know she must have support from the outside. The power of her spirit did not extend to these low people, and they had all the physical power. She realised an implacability of hatred in their turning on her. But she did not lose her head. She quietly paid out money and turned away.

Those were dangerous moments, though, and she learned to be prepared for them. The Princess she was, and the fairy from the North, she could never understand the volcanic phallic rage with which coarse people could turn on her in a paroxysm of hatred. They never turned on her father like that. And quite early she decided it was the New England mother in her whom they hated. Never for one minute could she see with the old Roman eyes, see herself as sterility, the barren flower taking on airs and an intolerable impertinence. This was what the Roman cabman saw in her. And he longed to crush the barren blossom. Its sexless beauty and its authority put him in a passion of brutal revolt.

When she was nineteen her grandfather died, leaving her a considerable fortune in the safe hands of responsible trustees. They would deliver her her income, but only on condition that she resided for six months in the year in the United States.

" Why should they make me conditions ? " she said to her father. " I refuse to be imprisoned six months in the year in the United States. We will tell them to keep their money."

6

THE PRINCESS

"Let us be wise, my little Princess, let us be wise. No, we are almost poor, and we are never safe from rudeness. I cannot allow anybody to be rude to me. I hate it, I hate it!" His eyes flamed as he said it. "I could kill any man or woman who is rude to me. But we are in exile in the world. We are powerless. If we were really poor, we should be quite powerless, and then I should die. No, my Princess. Let us take their money, then they will not dare to be rude to us. Let us take it, as we put on clothes, to cover ourselves from their aggressions."

There began a new phase, when the father and daughter spent their summers on the Great Lakes, or in California, or in the South-West. The father was something of a poet, the daughter something of a painter. He wrote poems about the lakes or the red-wood trees, and she made dainty drawings. He was physically a strong man, and he loved the out-of-doors. He would go off with her for days, paddling in a canoe and sleeping by a camp-fire. Frail little Princess, she was always undaunted; always undaunted. She would ride with him on horseback over the mountain trails till she was so tired she was nothing but a bodiless consciousness sitting astride her pony. But she never gave in. And at night he folded her in her blankets on a bed of balsam-pine twigs, and she lay and looked at the stars unmurmuring. She was fulfilling her rôle.

People said to her as the years passed, and she was a woman of twenty-five, then a woman of thirty, and always the same virgin dainty Princess, "knowing" in a dispassionate way, like an old woman, and utterly intact:

"Don't you ever think what you will do when your father is no longer with you?"

She looked at her interlocutor with that cold, elfin detachment of hers:

"No, I never think of it," she said.

She had a tiny, but exquisite little house in London, and another small, perfect house in Connecticut, each with a faithful housekeeper. Two homes, if she chose. And she knew many interesting literary and artistic people. What more?

So the years passed imperceptibly. And she had that quality of the sexless fairies, she did not change. At thirty-three she looked twenty-three.

7

Her father, however, was ageing, and becoming more and more queer. It was now her task to be his guardian in his private madness. He spent the last three years of life in the house in Connecticut. He was very much estranged, sometimes had fits of violence which almost killed the little Princess. Physical violence was horrible to her; it seemed to shatter her heart. But she found a woman a few years younger than herself, well educated and sensitive, to be a sort of nurse-companion to the mad old man. So the fact of madness was never openly admitted. Miss Cummins, the companion, had a passionate loyalty to the Princess, and a curious affection, tinged with love, for the handsome, white-haired, courteous old man, who was never at all aware of his fits of violence once they had passed.

The Princess was thirty-eight years old when her father died. And quite unchanged. She was still tiny, and like a dignified, scentless flower. Her soft brownish hair, almost the colour of beaver fur, was bobbed, and fluffed softly round her apple-blossom face, that was modelled with an arched nose like a proud old Florentine portrait. In her voice, manner and bearing she was exceedingly still, like a flower that has blossomed in a shadowy place. And from her blue eyes looked out the Princess's eternal laconic challenge, that grew almost sardonic as the years passed. She was the Princess, and sardonically she looked out on a princeless world.

She was relieved when her father died, and at the same time, it was as if everything had evaporated around her. She had lived in a sort of hot-house, in the aura of her father's madness. Suddenly the hot-house had been removed from around her, and she was in the raw, vast, vulgar open air.

Quoi faire ? What was she to do ? She seemed faced with absolute nothingness. Only she had Miss Cummins, who shared with her the secret, and almost the passion for her father. In fact the Princess felt that her passion for her mad father had in some curious way transferred itself largely to Charlotte Cummins during the last years. And now Miss Cummins was the vessel that held the passion for the dead man. She herself, the Princess, was an empty vessel.

An empty vessel in the enormous warehouse of the world.

THE PRINCESS

Quoi faire? What was she to do? She felt that, since she could not evaporate into nothingness, like alcohol from an unstoppered bottle, she must *do* something. Never before in her life had she felt the incumbency. Never, never had she felt she must *do* anything. That was left to the vulgar.

Now her father was dead, she found herself on the *fringe* of the vulgar crowd, sharing their necessity to *do* something. It was a little humiliating. She felt herself becoming vulgarised. At the same time she found herself looking at men with a shrewder eye: an eye to marriage. Not that she felt any sudden interest in men, or attraction towards them. No. She was still neither interested nor attracted towards men vitally. But *marriage*, that peculiar abstraction, had imposed a sort of spell on her. She thought that *marriage*, in the blank abstract, was the thing she ought to *do*. That *marriage* implied a man she also knew. She knew all the facts. But the man seemed a property of her own mind rather than a thing in himself, another being.

Her father died in the summer, the month after her thirty-eighth birthday. When all was over, the obvious thing to do, of course, was to travel. With Miss Cummins. The two women knew each other intimately, but they were always Miss Urquhart and Miss Cummins to one another, and a certain distance was instinctively maintained. Miss Cummins, from Philadelphia, of scholastic stock, and intelligent but un-travelled, four years younger than the Princess, felt herself immensely the junior of her "lady." She had a sort of passionate veneration for the Princess, who seemed to her ageless, timeless. She could not see the rows of tiny, dainty, exquisite shoes in the Princess's cupboard without feeling a stab at the heart, a stab of tenderness and reverence, almost of awe.

Miss Cummins also was virginal, but with a look of puzzled surprise in her brown eyes. Her skin was pale and clear, her features well modelled, but there was a certain blankness in her expression, where the Princess had an odd touch of Renaissance grandeur. Miss Cummins' voice was also hushed almost to a whisper; it was the inevitable effect of Colin Urquhart's room. But the hushedness had a hoarse quality

9

The Princess did not want to go to Europe. Her face seemed turned west. Now her father was gone, she felt she would go west, westwards, as if for ever. Following, no doubt, the March of Empire, which is brought up rather short on the Pacific coast, among swarms of wallowing bathers.

No, not the Pacific coast. She would stop short of that. The South-West was less vulgar. She would go to New Mexico.

She and Miss Cummins arrived at the Rancho del Cerro Gordo towards the end of August, when the crowd was beginning to drift back east. The ranch lay by a stream on the desert some four miles from the foot of the mountains, a mile away from the Indian *pueblo* of San Cristobal. It was a ranch for the rich ; the Princess paid thirty dollars a day for herself and Miss Cummins. But then she had a little cottage to herself, among the apple-trees of the orchard, with an excellent cook. She and Miss Cummins, however, took dinner at evening in the large guest-house. For the Princess still entertained the idea of *marriage*.

The guests at the Rancho del Cerro Gordo were of all sorts, except the poor sort. They were practically all rich, and many were romantic. Some were charming, others were vulgar, some were movie people, quite quaint and not un-attractive in their vulgarity, and many were Jews. The Princess did not care for Jews, though they were usually the most interesting to *talk* to. So she talked a good deal with the Jews, and painted with the artists, and rode with the young men from College, and had altogether quite a good time. And yet she felt something of a fish out of water, or a bird in the wrong forest. And *marriage* remained still completely in the abstract. No connecting it with any of these young men, even the nice ones.

The Princess looked just twenty-five. The freshness of her mouth, the hushed, delicate-complexioned virginity of her face gave her not a day more. Only a certain laconic look in her eyes was disconcerting. When she was *forced* to write her age, she put twenty-eight, making the figure two rather badly, so that it just avoided being a three.

Men hinted marriage at her. Especially boys from college suggested it from a distance. But they all failed before the look of sardonic ridicule in the Princess's eyes. It always seemed to her rather preposterous, quite ridiculous, and a tiny bit impertinent on their part.

The only man that intrigued her at all was one of the guides, a man called Romero—Domingo Romero. It was he who had sold the ranch itself to the Wilkiesons, ten years before, for two thousand dollars. He had gone away, then reappeared at the old place. For he was the son of the old Romero, the last of the Spanish family that had owned miles of land around San Cristobal. But the coming of the white man and the failure of the vast flocks of sheep, and the fatal inertia which overcomes all men, at last, on the desert near the mountains, had finished the Romero family. The last descendants were just Mexican peasants.

Domingo, the heir, had spent his two thousand dollars, and was working for white people. He was now about thirty years old, a tall, silent fellow, with a heavy closed mouth and black eyes that looked across at one almost sullenly. From behind he was handsome, with a strong, natural body, and the back of his neck very dark and well-shapen, strong with life. But his dark face was long and heavy, almost sinister, with that peculiar heavy meaninglessness in it, characteristic of the Mexicans of his own locality. They are strong, they seem healthy. They laugh and joke with one another. But their physique and their natures seem static, as if there were nowhere, nowhere at all for their energies to go, and their faces, degenerating to misshapen heaviness, seem to have no *raison d'être*, no radical meaning. Waiting either to die or to be aroused into passion and hope. In some of the black eyes a queer, haunting mystic quality, sombre and a bit gruesome, the skull-and-crossbones look of the Penitentes. They had found their *raison d'être* in self-torture and death-worship. Unable to wrest a *positive* significance for themselves from the vast, beautiful, but vindictive landscape they were born into, they turned on their own selves, and worshipped death through self-torture. The mystic gloom of this showed in their eyes.

But as a rule the dark eyes of the Mexicans were heavy and half-alive, sometimes hostile, sometimes kindly, often with the fatal Indian glaze on them, or the fatal Indian glint.

Domingo Romero was *almost* a typical Mexican to look at, with the typical heavy, dark, long face, clean-shaven, with an almost brutally heavy mouth. His eyes were black and Indian-looking. Only, at the centre of their hopelessness was a spark of pride, of self-confidence, of dauntlessness. Just a spark in the midst of the blackness of static despair.

But this spark was the difference between him and the mass of men. It gave a certain alert sensitiveness to his bearing and a certain beauty to his appearance. He wore a low-crowned black hat, instead of the ponderous head-gear of the usual Mexican, and his clothes were thinnish and graceful. Silent, aloof, almost imperceptible in the landscape, he was an ad-mirable guide, with a startling quick intelligence that antici-pated difficulties about to arise. He could cook, too, crouching over the camp-fire and moving his lean, deft brown hands. The only fault he had was that he was not forthcoming, he wasn't chatty and cosy.

"Oh, don't send Romero with us," the Jews would say. "One can't get any response from him."

Tourists come and go, but they rarely *see* anything, in-wardly. None of them ever saw the spark at the middle of Romero's eye, they were not alive enough to see it.

The Princess caught it one day, when she had him for a guide. She was fishing for trout in the canyon, Miss Cummins was reading a book, the horses were tied under the trees, Romero was fixing a proper fly on her line. He fixed the fly and handed her the line, looking up at her. And at that moment she caught the spark in his eye. And instantly she knew that he was a gentleman, that his "demon," as her father would have said, was a fine demon. And instantly her manner towards him changed.

He had perched her on a rock over a quiet pool, beyond the cotton-wood trees. It was early September, and the canyon already cool, but the leaves of the cotton-woods were still green. The Princess stood on her rock, a small but perfectly-formed figure, wearing a soft, close grey sweater and neatly-cut grey riding breeches, with tall black boots, her fluffy brown hair straggling from under a little grey felt hat. A woman? Not quite. A changeling of some sort, perched in outline there on the rock, in the bristling wild canyon. She knew perfectly well how to handle a line. Her father had made a fisherman of her.

Romero, in a black shirt and with loose black trousers pushed into wide black riding boots, was fishing a little further down. He had put his hat on a rock behind him; his dark head was bent a little forward, watching the water. He had caught three trout. From time to time he glanced upstream at the Princess, perched there so daintily. He saw she had caught nothing.

Soon he quietly drew in his line and came up to her. His keen eye watched her line, watched her position. Then, quietly, he suggested certain changes to her, putting his sensitive brown hand before her. And he withdrew a little, and stood in silence, leaning against a tree, watching her. He was helping her across the distance. She knew it, and thrilled. And in a moment she had a bite. In two minutes she had landed a good trout. She looked round at him quickly, her eyes sparkling, the colour heightened in her cheeks. And as she met his eyes a smile of greeting went over his dark face, very sudden, with an odd sweetness.

She knew he was helping her. And she felt in his presence a subtle, insidious male *kindliness* she had never known before, waiting upon her. Her cheek flushed, and her blue eyes darkened.

After this, she always looked for him, and for that curious dark beam of a man's kindliness which he could give her, as it were, from his chest, from his heart. It was something she had never known before.

A vague, unspoken intimacy grew up between them. She liked his voice, his appearance, his presence. His natural language was Spanish; he spoke English like a foreign language, rather slow, with a slight hesitation, but with a sad, plangent sonority lingering over from his Spanish. There was a certain subtle correctness in his appearance; he was always perfectly shaved; his hair was thick and rather long on top, but always carefully groomed behind. And his fine black cashmere shirt, his wide leather belt, his well-cut, wide black trousers going into the embroidered cowboy boots had a certain inextinguishable elegance. He wore no silver rings or buckles. Only his boots were embroidered and decorated at the top with an inlay of white *suède*. He seemed elegant, slender, yet he was very strong.

And at the same time, curiously, he gave her the feeling that death was not far from him. Perhaps he too was half in love with death. However that may be, the sense she had that death was not far from him made him " possible " to her.

Small as she was, she was quite a good horsewoman. They gave her at the ranch a sorrel mare, very lovely in colour, and well-made, with a powerful broad neck and the hollow back that betokens a swift runner. Tansy, she was called. Her only fault was the usual mare's failing, she was inclined to be hysterical.

So that every day the Princess set off with Miss Cummins and Romero, on horseback, riding into the mountains. Once they went camping for several days, with two more friends in the party.

" I think I like it better," the Princess said to Romero, " when we three go alone."

And he gave her one of his quick, transfiguring smiles.

It was curious no white man had ever showed her this capacity for subtle gentleness, this power to *help* her in silence across a distance, if she were fishing without success, or tired of her horse, or if Tansy suddenly got scared. It was as if Romero could send her *from his heart* a dark beam of succour and sustaining. She had never known this before, and it was very thrilling.

Then the smile that suddenly creased his dark face, showing the strong white teeth. It creased his face almost into a savage grotesque. And at the same time there was in it some-thing so warm, such a dark flame of kindliness for her, she was elated into her true Princess self.

Then that vivid, latent spark in his eye, which she had seen, and which she knew he was aware she had seen. It made an inter-recognition between them, silent and delicate. Here he was delicate as a woman in this subtle inter-recognition.

And yet his presence only put to flight in her her *idée fixe* of " marriage." For some reason, in her strange little brain, the idea of *marrying* him could not enter. Not for any definite reason. He was in himself a gentleman, and she had plenty of money for two. There was no actual obstacle. Nor was she conventional.

No, now she came down to it, it was as if their two " demons " could marry, were perhaps married. Only their two *selves*, Miss Urquhart and Señor Domingo Romero, were for some reason incompatible. There was a peculiar subtle intimacy of inter-recognition between them. But she did not see in the least how it would lead to marriage. Almost she could more easily marry one of the nice boys from Harvard or Yale.

The time passed, and she let it pass. The end of September came, with aspens going yellow on the mountain heights, and oak-scrub going red. But as yet the cotton-woods in the valley and canyons had not changed.

" When will you go away ? " Romero asked her, looking at her fixedly, with a blank black eye.

" By the end of October," she said. " I have promised to be in Santa Barbara at the beginning of November."

He was hiding the spark in his eye from her. But she saw the peculiar sullen thickening of his heavy mouth.

She had complained to him many times that one never saw any wild animals, except chipmunks and squirrels, and perhaps a skunk and a porcupine. Never a deer, or a bear, or a mountain lion.

" Are there no bigger animals in these mountains ? " she asked, dissatisfied.

" Yes," he said. " There are deer—I see their tracks. And I saw the tracks of a bear."

" But why can one never see the animals themselves ? " She looked dissatisfied and wistful like a child.

" Why, it's pretty hard for you to see them. They won't let you come close. You have to keep still, in a place where they come. Or else you have to follow their tracks a long way."

" I can't bear to go away till I've seen them : a bear, or a deer—"

The smile came suddenly on his face, indulgent.

" Well, what do you want ? Do you want to go up into the mountains to some place, to wait till they come ? "

" Yes," she said, looking up at him with a sudden naïve impulse of recklessness.

And immediately his face became sombre again, responsible.

" Well," he said, with slight irony, a touch of mockery of her. " You will have to find a house. It's very cold at night now. You would have to stay all night in a house."

" And there are no houses up there ? " she said.

" Yes," he replied. " There is a little shack that belongs to me, that a miner built a long time ago, looking for gold. You can go there and stay one night, and maybe you see something. Maybe ! I don't know. Maybe nothing come."

" How much chance is there ? "

" Well, I don't know. Last time when I was there I see three deer come down to drink at the water, and I shot two raccoons. But maybe this time we don't see anything."

" Is there water there ? " she asked.

" Yes, there is a little round pond, you know, below the spruce trees. And the water from the snow runs into it."

" Is it far away ? " she asked.

" Yes, pretty far. You see that ridge there "—and turning to the mountains he lifted his arm in the gesture which is somehow so moving, out in the West, pointing to the distance —" that ridge where there are no trees, only rock "—his black eyes were focussed on the distance, his face impassive, but as if in pain—" you go round that ridge, and along, then you come down through the spruce trees to where that cabin is. My father he bought that place, claim from a miner who was broke, but nobody ever found any gold or anything, and nobody ever goes there. Too lonesome ! "

The Princess watched the massive, heavy-sitting, beautiful bulk of the Rocky Mountains. It was early in October, and the aspens were already losing their gold leaves ; high up, the spruce and pine seemed to be growing darker; the great flat patches of oak-scrub on the heights were red like gore.

" Can I go over there ? " she asked, turning to him and meeting the spark in his eye.

His face was heavy with responsibility.

" Yes," he said, " you can go. But there'll be snow over the ridge, and it's awful cold, and awful lonesome."

" I should like to go," she said, persistent.

" All right," he said. " You can go if you want to."

She doubted, though, if the Wilkiesons would let her go ; at least alone with Romero and Miss Cummins.

Yet an obstinacy characteristic of her nature, an obstinacy tinged perhaps with madness, had taken hold of her. She wanted to look over the mountains into their secret heart. She wanted to descend to the cabin below the spruce trees, near the tarn of bright green water. She wanted to see the wild animals move about in their wild unconsciousness.

" Let us say to the Wilkiesons that we want to make the trip round the Frijoles canyon," she said.

The trip round the Frijoles canyon was a usual thing. It would not be strenuous, nor cold, nor lonely : they could sleep in the log house that was called an hotel.

Romero looked at her quickly.

" If you want to say that," he replied, " you can tell Mrs. Wilkieson. Only I know she'll be mad with me if I take you up in the mountains to that place. And I've got to go there first with a pack-horse, to take lots of blankets and some bread. Maybe Miss Cummins can't stand it. Maybe not. It's a hard trip."

He was speaking, and thinking, in the heavy, disconnected Mexican fashion.

" Never mind ! " The Princess was suddenly very decisive and stiff with authority. " I want to do it. I will arrange with Mrs. Wilkieson. And we'll go on Saturday."

He shook his head slowly.

" I've got to go up on Sunday with a pack-horse and blankets," he said. " Can't do it before."

" Very well ! " she said, rather piqued. " Then we'll start on Monday."

She hated being thwarted even the tiniest bit.

He knew that if he started with the pack on Sunday at dawn he would not be back until late at night. But he consented that they should start on Monday morning at seven. The obedient Miss Cummins was told to prepare for the Frijoles trip. On Sunday Romero had his day off. He had not put in an appearance when the Princess retired on Sunday night, but on Monday morning, as she was dressing, she saw him bringing in the three horses from the corral. She was in high spirits.

THE CALENDAR

The night had been cold. There was ice at the edges of the irrigation ditch, and the chipmunks crawled into the sun and lay with wide, dumb, anxious eyes, almost too numb to run.

" We may be away two or three days," said the Princess.

" Very well. We won't begin to be anxious about you before Thursday, then," said Mrs. Wilkieson, who was young and capable : from Chicago. " Anyway," she added, " Romero will see you through. He's so trustworthy."

The sun was already on the desert as they set off towards the mountains, making the greasewood and the sage pale as pale-grey sands, luminous the great level around them. To the right glinted the shadows of the adobe *pueblo*, flat and almost invisible on the plain, earth of its earth. Behind lay the ranch and the tufts of tall, plumy cottonwoods, whose summits were yellowing under the perfect blue sky.

Autumn breaking into colour in the great spaces of the South-West.

But the three trotted gently along the trail, towards the sun that sparkled yellow just above the dark bulk of the ponderous mountains. Sideslopes were already gleaming yellow, flaming with a second light, under the coldish blue of the pale sky. The front slopes were in shadow, with submerged lustre of red oak-scrub and dull-gold aspens, blue-black pines and grey-blue rock. While the canyon was full of a deep blueness.

They rode single file, Romero first, on a black horse. Himself in black, he made a flickering black spot in the delicate pallor of the great landscape, where even pine-trees at a distance take a film of blue paler than their green. Romero rode on in silence past the tufts of furry greasewood. The Princess came next, on her sorrel mare. And Miss Cummins, who was not quite happy on horseback, came last, in the pale dust that the others kicked up. Sometimes her horse sneezed,' and she started.

But on they went, at a gentle trot. Romero never looked round. He could hear the sound of the hoofs following, and that was all he wanted.

For the rest, he held ahead. And the Princess, with that black, unheeding figure always travelling away from her, felt strangely helpless, withal elated.

THE PRINCESS

They neared the pale, round foot-hills, dotted with the round dark piñon and cedar shrubs. The horses clinked and clattered among stones. Occasionally a big round grease-wood held out fleecy tufts of flowers, pure gold. They wound into blue shadow, then up a steep stony slope, with the world lying pallid away behind and below. Then they dropped into the shadow of the San Cristobal canyon.

The stream was running full and swift. Occasionally the horses snatched at a tuft of grass. The trail narrowed and became rocky, the rocks closed in, it was dark and cool as the horses climbed and climbed upwards, and the tree-trunks crowded in in the shadowy, silent tightness of the canyon. They were among cottonwood trees that ran up straight and smooth and round to an extraordinary height. Above, the tips were gold, and it was sun. But away below, where the horses struggled up the rocks and wound among the trunks, there was still blue shadow by the sound of waters, and an occasional grey festoon of old-man's-beard, and here and there a pale, dipping cranesbill flower among the tangle and the debris of the virgin place. And again the chill entered the Princess's heart as she realised what a tangle of decay and despair lay in the virgin forests.

They scrambled downwards, splashed across stream, up rocks and along the trail on the other side. Romero's black horse stopped, looked down quizzically at the fallen trees, then stepped over lightly. The Princess's sorrel followed, carefully, But Miss Cummins's buckskin made a fuss, and had to be got round.

In the same silence, save for the clinking of the horses and the splashing as the trail crossed stream, they worked their way upwards in the tight, tangled shadow of the canyon. Sometimes, crossing stream, the Princess would glance upwards, and then always her heart caught in her breast. For high up, away in heaven, the mountain heights shone yellow, dappled with dark spruce firs, clear almost as speckled daffodils against the pale turquoise blue lying high and serene above the dark-blue shadow where the Princess was. And she would snatch at the blood-red leaves of the oak as her horse crossed a more open slope, not knowing what she felt.

They were getting fairly high, occasionally lifted above the canyon itself, in the low groove below the speckled, gold-sparkling heights which towered beyond. Then again they dipped and crossed stream, the horses stepping gingerly across a tangle of fallen, frail aspen stems, then suddenly floundering in a mass of rocks. The black emerged ahead, his black tail waving. The Princess let her mare find her own footing ; then she too emerged from the clatter. She rode on after the black. Then came a great frantic rattle of the buckskin behind. The Princess was aware of Romero's dark face looking round, with a strange, demon-like watchfulness, before she herself looked round, to see the buckskin scrambling rather lamely beyond the rocks, with one of his pale buff knees already red with blood.

"He almost went down ! " called Miss Cummins.

But Romero was already out of the saddle and hastening down the path. He made quiet little noises to the buckskin, and began examining the cut knee.

"Is he hurt ? " cried Miss Cummins anxiously, and she climbed hastily down.

"Oh, my goodness ! " she cried, as she saw the blood running down the slender buff leg of the horse in a thin trickle. "Isn't that *awful* ? " She spoke in a stricken voice, and her face was white.

Romero was still carefully feeling the knee of the buckskin. Then he made him walk a few paces. And at last he stood up straight and shook his head.

"Not very bad ! " he said. "Nothing broken."

Again he bent and worked at the knee. Then he looked up at the Princess.

"He can go on," he said. "It's not bad."

The Princess looked down at the dark face in silence.

"What, go on right up here ? " cried Miss Cummins. "How many hours ? "

"About five," said Romero simply.

"Five hours ! " cried Miss Cummins. "A horse with a lame knee ! And a steep mountain ! Why-y ! "

"Yes, it's pretty steep up there," said Romero, pushing back his hat and staring fixedly at the bleeding knee. The buckskin stood in a stricken sort of dejection. "But I think he'll make it all right," the man added.

"Oh!" cried Miss Cummins, her eyes bright with sudden passion of unshed tears. "I wouldn't think of it. I wouldn't ride him up there, not for any money."

"Why wouldn't you?" asked Romero.

"It *hurts* him."

Romero bent down again to the horse's knee.

"Maybe it hurts him a little," he said. "But he can make it all right, and his leg won't get stiff."

"What! Ride him five hours up the steep mountains?" cried Miss Cummins. "I couldn't. I just couldn't do it. I'll lead him a little way and see if he can go. But I *couldn't* ride him again. I couldn't. Let me walk."

"But Miss Cummins, dear, if Romero says he'll be all right?" said the Princess.

"I know it hurts him. Oh, I just couldn't bear it."

There was no doing anything with Miss Cummins. The thought of a hurt animal always put her into a sort of hysterics.

They walked forward a little, leading the buckskin. He limped rather badly. Miss Cummins sat on a rock.

"Why, it's agony to see him!" she cried. "It's *cruel*!"

"He won't limp after a bit, if you take no notice of him," said Romero. "Now he plays up, and limps very much, because he wants to make you see."

"I don't think there can be much playing up," said Miss Cummins bitterly. "We can *see* how it must hurt him."

"It don't hurt much," said Romero.

But now Miss Cummins was silent with antipathy.

It was a deadlock. The party remained motionless on the trail, the Princess in the saddle, Miss Cummins seated on a rock, Romero standing black and remote near the drooping buckskin.

"Well!" said the man suddenly at last. "I guess we go back, then."

And he looked up swiftly at his horse, which was cropping at the mountain herbage and treading on the trailing reins.

"No!" cried the Princess. "Oh no!" Her voice rang with a great wail of disappointment and anger. Then she checked herself.

Miss Cummins rose with energy.

"Let me lead the buckskin home," she said, with cold dignity, "and you two go on."

This was received in silence. The Princess was looking down at her with a sardonic, almost cruel gaze.

"We've only come about two hours," said Miss Cummins. "I don't mind a bit leading him home. But I *couldn't* ride him. I *couldn't* have him ridden with that knee."

This again was received in dead silence. Romero remained impassive, almost inert.

"Very well, then," said the Princess. "You lead him home. You'll be quite all right. Nothing can happen to you, possibly. And say to them that we have gone on and shall be home to-morrow—or the day after."

She spoke coldly and distinctly. For she could not bear to be thwarted.

"Better all go back, and come again another day," said Romero—non-committal.

"There will never *be* another day," cried the Princess. "I want to go on."

She looked him square in the eyes, and met the spark in his eye.

He raised his shoulders slightly.

"If you want it," he said. "I'll go on with you. But Miss Cummins can ride my horse to the end of the canyon, and I lead the buckskin. Then I come back to you."

It was arranged so. Miss Cummins had her saddle put on Romero's black horse, Romero took the buckskin's bridle, and they started back. The Princess rode very slowly on, upwards, alone. She was at first so angry with Miss Cummins that she was blind to everything else. She just let her mare follow her own inclinations.

(To be continued next month.)

Poems

By ROBERT GRAVES.

The Clipped Stater.

He, Alexander, had been deified
By loud applause of the Macedonian phalanx,
By sullen groans of the wide worlds he had vanquished.
Who but a God could have so hacked down their pride ?

He would not take a Goddess to his Throne
In the elder style, remembering those disasters
That Juno's jealous eye brought on her Consort.
Thäis was fair ; but he must hold his own.

Nor would he rank himself a common god
In fellowship with those of Ind or Egypt
Whom he had shamed : even to Jove his father
Paid scant respect (as Jove stole Saturn's Nod).

Now meditates " No land of all known lands
Has offered me resistance, none denies me
Infinite power, infinite thought and knowledge :
What now awaits the assurance of my hands ? "

He weeps : the occasion, documented well,
Begins my now for the first time recorded
And philosophic tale of *The Clipped Stater*
(Though how it came to me, I must not tell).

Alexander in a fever of mind
Reasons " Omnipotence by its very nature
Is infinite possibility and purpose,
Which must embrace, *that it can be confined.*"

Then Finity is true Godhead's final test,
Nor does it shear the grandeur from Free Being ;
" I must fulfil my self by self-destruction."
The curious phrase renews his conquering zest.

THE CALENDAR

He assumes man's flesh. Djinn catch him up and fly
To a land of yellow men beyond his knowledge,
And that he does not know them, he takes gladly
For surest proof he has put his Godhead by.

In Macedonia shortly it is said
" Alexander, our God, has died of a fever :
Demi-gods parcel out his huge dominions."
So Alexander, as God, is duly dead.

But Alexander the Man, whom yellow folk
Find roving naked, armed with a naked cutlass,
Has Death, which is the strangers' fate, excused him.
Joyfully he submits to the alien yoke.

He is enlisted for the frontier guard
With gaol-rogues and the press-gang's easy captures ;
Where captains who have felt the Crown's displeasure
But have thought suicide too direct and hard,

Teach him a new tongue and the soldier's trade
To which the trade *he* taught has little likeness,
So that he glories in his limitations :
At every turn his hands and feet are stayed.

" Who was your father, friend ? " He answers " Jove,"
" His father ? " " Saturn." " And *his* father ? " " Chaos."
" And *his* ? " Thus Alexander loses honour
Ten fathers is the least that a man should prove.

Stripes and bastinadoes, famine and thirst,
All these he suffers, never in resolution
Wavering, nor in his heart enquiring whether
God can be by his own confines accursed.

And he grows grey and eats his frugal rice ;
Endures his watch on the fort's icy ramparts,
Staring across the uncouth wildernesses,
And cleans his leather and steel ; and shakes the dice.

He will not dream Olympicly, nor stir
To enlarge himself with comforts or promotion,
Nor evade punishment when, sour of temper,
He has pulled the corporal's nose and called him " cur."

His comrades mutinously demand their pay.
" We have had none since the Emperor's Coronation.
At one gold piece a year there are fifteen owing.
One-third that sum would bribe us free," say they.

The pay-sack came at length, when hope was cold,
But much reduced in bulk since the first issue
By the Royal Treasurer ; and he, be certain,
Kept back a half of the silver and all the gold.

Every official hand had dipped in the sack
And the frontier captains, themselves disappointed
Of long arrears took every doit remaining,
But from good feelings put a trifle back.

Telling their men " since no pay has come through
We will advance from our too lavish purses
To every man of the guard, a piece of silver.
Let it be repaid when you have your overdue."

The soldiers grumbling but much satisfied
By thoughts of a drink and a drab, accept the favour,
And Alexander advancing to the pay-desk
Salutes and takes his earnings with no pride.

The coin is bored, to string with the country's bronze
On a cord, one side is scraped to glassy smoothness
And the Head, clipped of its hair and neck, bears witness
That it had a broad, more generous mintage once.

And Alexander gazing at it then
Knows it well for a Silver Alexander
Coined from the bullion taken at Arbela.
How is it current among these slant-eyed men ?

He stands in a troubled reverie of doubt
Till a whip stings his shoulders and a voice bellows
" Are you dissatisfied, you scum of the ditches ? "
So he salutes again and turns about.

But he cannot fathom what the event may mean.
Was his lost Empire, then, not all-embracing ?
And how does the stater, though defaced, owe service
To a God that is as if he had never been ?

Is he still God ?   No, truly.   Then all he knows
Is he must keep the course he has resolved on ;
He spends the coin on a feast of fish and almonds,
And back to the ramparts briskly enough he goes.

Essay on Knowledge.

Be assured, the Dragon is not dead,
Who once more from the pools of peace
Shall rear his fabulous green head.

The flowers of innocence shall cease
And like a harp the wind shall roar
And the clouds shake an angry fleece.

" Here, here is certitude," you swore,
" Below this lightning-blasted tree.
Where once it strikes, it strikes no more."

(Fool !) And you sang " Here is a Three
And in this Three love lives unshaken
As now, so must it always be."

You sang with harsh notes to awaken
That ancient toad who sits immured
Within your hearth-stone, light-forsaken.

He knows that limits long endured
Must open out in vanity.
That gates by bolts of gold secured
Must open out in vanity.

That thunder bursts from the blue sky,
That gardens of the mind fall waste.
That age-established brooks run dry.
That age-established brooks run dry.

A Letter from Wales.

Richard Rolls to his friend, Captain Abel Wright. *

This is a question of identity
Which I can't answer. Abel, I'll presume
On your good-nature, asking you to help me.
I hope you will, since you too are involved
As deeply in the problem as myself.
Who are we ? Take down your old diary, please,
The one you kept in France, if you *are* you
Who served in the Black Fusiliers with me.
That is, again, of course, if I am I—
This isn't Descartes' philosophic doubt
But as I say a question of identity
And practical enough.—Turn up the date,
July the twenty-fourth, nineteen-sixteen,
And read the entry there.
                              " To-day I met
Meredith, transport-sergeant of the Second.
He told me that Dick Rolls had died of wounds.
I found out Doctor Dunn, and he confirms it ;
Dunn says he wasn't in much pain, he thinks."

Then the first draft of a verse-epitaph
Expanded later into a moving poem.
" Death straddled on your bed : you groaned and tried
To stare him out, but in that death-stare died."

Yes, died, poor fellow, the day he came of age.
But then appeared a second Richard Rolls
(Or that's the view that the facts force on me)
Showing Dick's features to support his claim
To rank and pay and friendship, Abel, with you.
And you acknowledged him as the old Dick,
Despite all evidence to the contrary,
Because, I think, you missed the dead too much.
You came up here to Wales to stay with him
And I don't know for sure, but I suspect

---

*The characters and incidents are unhistorical.

THE CALENDAR

That you were dead too, killed at the Rectangle
One bloody morning of the same July,
The time that something snapped and sent you Berserk :
You ran across alone, with covering fire
Of a single rifle, routing the Saxons out
With bombs and yells and your wild eye ; and stayed there
In careless occupation of the trench
For a full hour, reading, by all that's mad,
A book of pastoral poems ! Then, they say,
Then you walked slowly back and went to sleep
Without reporting ; that was the occasion,
No doubt, they killed you : it was your substitute
Strolled back and laid him down and woke as you
Showing your features to support his claim
To rank and pay and friendship, Abel, with me.
So these two substitutes, yours and my owns
(Though that's an Irish way of putting it
For the I now talking is an honest I
Independent of the I's now lost,
And a live dog's as good as a dead lion),
So, these two friends the second of the series
Came up to Wales pretending a wild joy
That they had cheated Death : they stayed together
At the same house and ate and drank and laughed
And wrote each other's poems, much too lazy
To write their own, and sat up every night
Talking and smoking almost until dawn.
Yes, they enjoyed life, but unless I now
Confound my present feelings with the past*
They felt a sense of unreality
In the proceedings—yes, that's good, *proceedings*—
It suggests ghosts. Well, then I want to ask you
Whether it really happened. Eating, laughing,
Sitting up late, writing each other's verses,
I might invent all that, but one thing happened
That seems too circumstantial for romance.
Can you confirm it ? Yet, even if you can
What does that prove ? for who are you ? or I ?

---

*A reminiscence from Wordsworth's " Nutting."

POEMS

Listen, it was a sunset. We were out
Climbing the mountain eating blackberries ;
Late afternoon, the third week in September.
The date's important : it might prove my point,
For unless Richard Rolls had really died
Could he have so recovered from his wounds
As to go climbing less than two months later ?
And if it comes to that, what about you ?
How had you come on sick-leave from the Line ?
I don't remember you as ill or wounded.
Anyhow . . . . We were eating blackberries
By a wide field of tumbled boulderstones
Hedged with oaks and nut-trees. Gradually
A glamour spread about us, the low sun
Making the field unreal as a stage,
Gilding our faces with heroic light ;
Then oaks and nut-boughs caught this golden flood
Sending it back in a warm flare of green . . . . .
There was a mountain ash among the boulders
But too full-clustered and symmetrical
And highly coloured to convince as real.
We stopped blackberrying and someone said
(Was it I or you ?) " It is good for us to be here."
The other said " Let us build Tabernacles."
(In honour of a new Transfiguration ;
It was that sort of moment) ; but instead
I climbed up on the massive pulpit-stone,
An old friend, but unreal with the rest,
And prophesied—not indeed of the future,
But declaimed poetry, and you climbed up too
And prophesied. The next thing I remember
Was a dragon scaly with fine-weather clouds
Poised high above the sun, and the sun dwindling
And then the second glory.
                                        You'll remember
That we were not then easily impressed
With pyrotechnics whether God's or Man's.
We had seen the sun rise daily, weeks on end,
And watched the nightly rocket-shooting, varied
With red and green, and livened with gun-fire

And the loud single-bursting overgrown squib
Thrown from the minen-werfer : and one night
From a billet-window some ten miles away
We had watched the French making a mass-attack
At Notre Dame de Lorette, in a thunderstorm.
That was a grand display of all the Arts,
God's, Man's, the Devil's : in the course of which
So lavishly the piece had been stage-managed,
A Frenchman was struck dead by a meteorite,
That was the sort of gala-show it was !
But this Welsh sunset, what shall I say of it ?
It ended not at all as it began,
An influence rather than a spectacle
Raised to a strange degree beyond all wonder.
And I remember that we looked and found
A region of the sky below the dragon
Where we could gaze behind all time and space
And see as it were the colour of pure thought,
The texture of emptiness, and at that sight
We came away, not daring to see more ;
Death was the price, we knew, of such perfection ;
And walking home . . . . .
                                        fell in with Captain Todd,
The Golf-Club Treasurer ; he greeted us
With "*Did* you see that splendid sunset, boys ?
Magnificent, was it not ?   I wonder now,
What writer could have done real justice to it
Except, of course, my old friend Walter Pater ?
Ruskin perhaps ?   Yes, Ruskin might have done it."

Well, *did* that happen, or am I just romancing ?
And then again, one has to ask the question
What happened after to that *you* and *me ?*
I have thought lately that they too got lost.
My representative went out once more
To France, and so did yours, and yours got killed,
Shot through the throat while bombing up a trench
At Bullecourt ; if not there, then at least
On the thirteenth of July, nineteen eighteen,
Somewhere in the neighbourhood of Albert,

POEMS

When you took a rifle bullet through the skull
Just after breakfast on a mad patrol.
But still you kept up the same stale pretence
As children do in nursery battle-games
" No, I'm not dead. Look, I'm not even wounded."
And I admit I followed your example,
Though nothing much happened that time in France.
I died at Hove after the Armistice,
Pneumonia, with the doctor's full consent.

I think the *I* and *you* who then took over
Rather forgot the part we used to play ;
We wrote and saw each other often enough
And sent each other copies of new poems,
But there was a constraint in all our dealings,
A doubt, unformulated, but quite heavy
And not too well disguised. Something we guessed
Arising from the War, and yet the War
Was a forbidden ground of conversation.
Now *why*, can you say *why*, short of accepting
My substitution view ? Then yesterday
After five years of this relationship
I found a relic of the second Richard,
A pack-valise marked with his name and rank . . . .
And a sunset started, most unlike the other,
A pink-and-black depressing sort of show
Influenced by the Glasgow School of Art.
It sent me off on a long train of thought
And I began to feel badly confused
Being accustomed to this newer self ;
I wondered whether you could reassure me.
Now I have asked you, do you see my point ?
What I'm asking really isn't " Who am I ? "
Or, " Who are you ? " (you see my difficulty ?)
But a stage before that, *how am I to put*
The question that I'm asking you to answer ?

Poe's Analysis of Inspiration

By Douglas Garman.

NO one realised more fully than Poe the gulf of æsthetic understanding which separated him from his American contemporaries, yet even he could not have foreseen that, by an unusual and paradoxical fate, his genius would be adopted by the French before it was handed back, recognised, to his countrymen and to us. The result of this vicarious recognition has been a tendency for us to see in him only the author of *Tales of Mystery and Imagination* and a harsh critic who considered a long poem to be a contradiction in terms. From his own poetry we turn too lightly aside, forgetting that Baudelaire found it "*profonde et plaintive . . . transparente et correcte comme un bijou de crystal,*" that Mallarmé was at pains to translate it, that in the opinion of Remy de Gourmont it contained Poe "*tout entier.*" To find the reason for such unstinted admiration it is not sufficient for us to consider his poetry ; we must also examine the poetic theories which hampered his achievement at the same time that they freed him from those false conceptions of poetry abounding during his lifetime.

Poe was not a great poet in his practice of verse. His poems (with two or three exceptions) are not intrinsically beautiful, for unless they are read through the veil of his theories, their latent beauty escapes us. But, since he was a poetical genius, to understand him it is exactly thus that they should be read.

"I would define, in brief, the Poetry of words as *The Rhythmical Creation of Beauty.*" This is the fundamental, incontrovertible axiom from which he sets out, whether to criticise or to create, and to it he adds a definition of beauty and an explanation of rhythm. Having decided that a poem "deserves its title only inasmuch as it excites, by elevating the soul," he maintains that this can only be done through that sense of the Beautiful which is an immortal instinct in the spirit of man ; and by beautiful he does not denote the "mere appreciation of the Beauty before us—but a wild effort to reach the Beauty above." For the moment—that is to say in *The Poetic Principle*—he does not further discuss the nature of Beauty, but turns to a consideration of Truth and Duty, the two abstracts which teased 19th Century poetry almost to death.

"Dividing the world of mind into its three most immediately obvious distinctions, we have the Pure Intellect, Taste, and the Moral Sense," he says; "we find the *offices* of the trio marked with a sufficient distinction. Just as the Intellect concerns itself with Truth, so Taste informs us of the Beautiful, while the Moral Sense is regardful of Duty. Of this latter, while Conscience teaches the obligation, and Reason the expediency, Taste contents herself with displaying the charms: waging war upon Vice solely on the ground of her deformity—her disproportion—her animosity to the fitting, to the appropriate, to the harmonious—in a word, to Beauty." Nor does he stop here. He goes on to elaborate the relationship of these three distinctions with a clarity and completeness which leave no opportunity for quibbling. He does not make the mistake, too common in the theory of his followers, of underrating the intimacy of that relationship. "It by no means follows, however, that the incitements of Passion, or the precepts of Duty, or even the lessons of Truth, may not be introduced into a poem, and with advantage . . . but the true artist will always continue to tone them down in proper subjection to that *Beauty* which is the atmosphere and the real essence of the poem." That is to say that, though poetry may result from the perception of the harmony existing in a truth, the effect obtained is "referable to the harmony alone, and not in the least degree to the truth which merely served to render the harmony manifest."

At this time the truth and originality of this doctrine are not so startling as when it was first expounded, for the way to our acceptance of it has been paved by a body of poetic achievement of which the worth cannot be denied. Baudelaire, at once the most positively creative and fruitfully influential poet of the latter half of the 19th Century, accepted these theories with no other amendment than that which his genius enforced. He found in Poe an affinity of soul, and the reason for this affinity arose from Poe's uncompromising search for the ideal beauty. Later we shall try to explain the comparative failure of Poe's poetry, but first of all we must investigate the meaning of the other half of his definition of poetry—of the word "rhythmical."

From *The Poetic Principle* much cannot be learned of the meaning he attributed to this word, but already there are

33

signs of that overstressing of music, "in its various modes of metre, rhythm and rhyme," which was one of the causes of the disparity between his poetic intention and achievement. He goes further than merely to emphasise the importance of music : he adds that in it, perhaps, "the soul most nearly attains the great end for which, when inspired by the poetic sentiment, it struggles—the creation of supernal Beauty." There is truth in this statement, for music is the factor common to all poetry and that which is, since its appeal is the most directly sensuous one made by language, essential. It is the quality of verse which most readily triumphs over the idiosyncratic use of words and phrasing : but it is not the only essential, and Poe was in danger, in practice more than in theory, of losing sight of the face-value of language as a means of materialising thought.

Apart from this, much of what he says concerning the less essential methods of creating rhythm shows a surprisingly prescient sensitiveness to the possible uses of language. Synæresis, or "blending," he unequivocally condemns (in *The Rationale of Verse*), and gives as his reason, that there is "no absolute necessity for adhering to the precise number of syllables, provided the time required for the whole foot is preserved inviolate." But though "in all rhythms the prevalent or distinctive feet may be varied at will, and nearly at random, by the *occasional* introduction of equivalent feet," he insists that "it is the business of the poet so to construct his line that the intention *must* be caught *at once*." This is the most important of his purely prosodical innovations, but he adds much that is of great value as to the use of alliteration, of "unusual and unanticipated" rhyme, and of refrains, and most emphatically denies the right of the poet to inversion. One other saying, this time from the *Marginalia*, is to be remarked as further evidence of the degree to which modern poetry has been unwittingly influenced by Poe. Emphasising the intolerableness of inversion, he says : "In short, as regards verbal construction, the *more prosaic* a poetical style is the better."

So far we have considered Poe only as a theorist ; but there are other reasons than the opinion of critics, notably Frenchmen, for our considering him as a poet. Baudelaire has shown that, insomuch as a poet has need of a Poetic, the theories developed by Poe are sufficient for the creation of the greatest poetry. Yet the theorist himself only reached that standard on very rare occasions. He was, it is true, continually hampered by the necessity, which he was under all his life, to earn his living by journalism. That balance of mental and physical health which creative work demands was denied him, and the continual obligation to criticise poetry for which he felt but little respect, exacerbated unduly the analytical tendency of his mind. He was quite right in his scornful denial of the fallacy that poets " compose by a species of fine frenzy " : to disprove it, he wrote *The Philosophy of Composition*. But in asserting that his design was " to render it manifest that no one point in its composition [he was speaking of *The Raven*] was referable either to accident or intuition," he lost sight, momentarily, of a fact to which in another place he had drawn attention. One of the *Marginalia* shows that he believed the perception of that beauty " supernal to the human nature "—that is to say, the supernal beauty which alone affords the proper scope for poetry—to be but an " instantaneous intuition." When, in the same note, he goes on to say that from experiments he could " be sure, when all circumstances were favourable, of the supervention of the condition " governing that perception, he does not deny that the perception is an " instantaneous intuition "—that is to say, involuntary—for he adds, " the favourable circumstances are, however, rare—else had I compelled, already, the heaven into the earth." Yet in tracing the growth of *The Raven*, he maintains that he has done this very thing, and the truth of his assertion can be gauged by the absence, in that poem, of the inspirational quality which alone could give it the true poetic life. Here, then, is one cause for his comparative failure as a poet, and it leads immediately to another—his increasing tendency to limit the meaning of Beauty.

So intent was he on discovering the essential, the ideal beauty, that he set up for himself a criterion which excluded, more and more, any mode of perception other than that induced by the poetic mood. And this mood was not, for him —as it was for Baudelaire—a crucible in which *any* experience might be transmuted to the ideal, for he would only admit the

poetic potentiality of a certain range of experience. Beginning
with the conviction that " the naked senses sometimes see too
little—but then *always* they see too much," he grew to rely,
almost entirely, on his power of ensuring the supervention of
the condition which would allow him to assimilate those
fancies, or " psychal impressions," having the " absoluteness
of novelty." In practice he failed to perceive that through
passion and truth harmonies might be manifested which,
before, were not apparent. The sphere of his poetic consciousness was shifted from that wherein he had conceived
such poems as *The Coliseum*, the two poems *To Helen*, *The
Sleeper* and *The City in the Sea*, to the ethereal, unreal world of
Ulalume and *The Raven*. Following his theories, he turned
aside from much which he showed in the Tales to have the true
poetic quality. The result was a sort of barren coldness,
the danger of which he foresaw when he wrote : " There *are*
artists, however, who fancy only the *finest* material, and who,
consequently, produce only the *finest* ware. It is generally
very transparent and excessively brittle."

To anyone, however, who has read Poe's poetry, there will
be another, and more obvious, cause for dissatisfaction. It
lies in his application of technique. In *The Rationale of Verse*
he designated verse as " an inferior or less capable music " ;
a faulty definition to which attention has already been drawn.
But though this over-emphasis of the musical element of verse
dictated lines like " In my most immemorial year," it was
also responsible for some of his finest poetry.

> "Lo ! Death has reared himself a throne
> In a strange city lying alone
> Far down within the dim West,
> Where the good and the bad and the worst and the best
> Have gone to their eternal rest."

Here the first three lines are perfect and inevitable *because*
of their music. Later this intuitive rhythm degenerated into
the mechanism of *The Bells* or *The Raven*, but even these poems
do not discount the truth of his prosodical doctrine ; they
suffer only from its excessive practice.

These quotations are sufficient to show that Poe, though
he was not a great poet, was one of the greatest poetical
geniuses of the last century, and that occasionally his practice

and theory attained the superb balance which could create true poetry, in spite of the small quantity of verse that he wrote. With Baudelaire he shares the honour of having instigated a new poetic era, and the influence which he exerted has not yet had its full effect either in his own country or in England. It would have been easy to have shown him as a poet in a more positive light, had it not been our intention to explain the discrepancy between his intention and his achievement. "It too often happens," he said, "that to reflect analytically upon Art is to reflect after the fashion of the mirrors in the temple of Smyrna, which represent the fairest images as deformed"; but then he also wrote: "To say that the critic could not have written the work which he criticises is to put forth a contradiction in terms."

Scrutinies

By EDGELL RICKWORD.

(1) Sir James Barrie

THE discussion begins in Thrums, a mountain-village north of the Tweed. *The Little Minister*, from the ethnologist's point of view, is a useful compilation of the habits, customs and superstitions of the tribe which inhabits Thrums. The story is told, as everyone knows, through the Dominie, a character who possesses the germ of that trick of observation which Barrie afterwards turned to account, and also the quality of secular piety which suffuses the whole of Barrie's work. Though he is not entirely Barrie, the Dominie is clearly a rough draft, and his relation to the tribe is very much like Barrie's relation to metropolitan society. The tribesmen of Thrums regarded their little Minister just as primitive peoples look on their medicine-men and witch-doctors. He is the intermediary between them and the Big Man who makes the crops grow. In order that his petitions may be efficacious, he must possess certain virtues, must keep the traditional taboos with a strictness not essential in the lay tribesman. When he becomes polluted, as Gavin was by his affair with Babbie, he is likely to be dismissed in favour of a more scrupulous or cautious one ; he is in danger even of mutilation : " The very women is cursing him, and the laddies has begun to gather stones."

Naturally, the personal property of the witch-doctor is a fetish, invested with the virtues which belong to his vocation :

" This was not the only time Jean had been asked to show the minister's belongings. Snecky Hobart, among others, had tried on Gavin's hat in the manse kitchin, and felt queer for some time afterwards. Women had been introduced on tip-toe to examine the handle of his umbrella."

The Dominie, it will be gathered, was more intelligent than most of the community ; at least, he was able to observe them with that astuteness, within the distorted image of reality Barrie gives us, which is one of the positive virtues of his plays. So, when he came to describe a more sophisticated society, Barrie sometimes introduced a little trenchant maxim, almost a cynicism; a tiny mischievous wriggle not meant to be taken too seriously by the Big Man of Thrums, who, of course, had an eye on a stalk like a snail's for wandering tribesmen. So Barrie, or that other self M'Connachie, who, he tells us, writes his plays, has only been able to conceive a perfected action by an escape into fantasy. He has never had, like the Southerner Hardy, the audacity to state the indifference of the Universe. Though his plays are admirably free from didacticism, one is generally aware of a pendulous Benevolence from which their characters suck a comforting resignation. The lack of emancipation from theological concepts reacts on his attitude to sex. Though he outgrew the extreme idealisation of women which the maudlin Dominie expressed—" all that is carnal in me is my own, and all that is good I got from her"—the sweet and capable creature who appears so monotonously in the plays, was turned out of the same mould. Barrie's eyes are keen enough to have seen deeper had he wished to follow the ramifications of the desire *d'etre un peu l'Homme avec la Femme*, yet his men and women have the tendency to fall into the relationship of mother and child. He has expressed with a distasteful accuracy the furtive sex-interest of the unemancipated male.

" They are two bachelors who all their lives have been afraid of nothing but Woman. David in his sportive days—which continue—has done roguish things with his arm when taking a lady home under an umbrella from a *soirée*, and has both chuckled and been scared on thinking of it afterwards."

The skill with which Barrie handles the half-human material he selects for use on the stage, to some extent dazzles the spectator into accepting a sleight-of-hand. It is only on coming closer that one can see the cotton thread running from the puppet's breeches to the showman's heart, for it is Barrie's heart which pumps into them whatever vitality they possess. He loves them and wants them to be loved so very much. The way in which, in the printed text, he insinuates his people on to the stage, shows an evident anxiety to win ·sympathy for them at the outset. He and Shaw are back to back on the circumference of a circle, for Shaw, by his diagrammatic preliminary directions, and the aggressive shove with which he pitches his people into their opening lines, seems to repel any sentimental inclination from the audience. The real dramatist's attitude to his creations is paternal ; he watches them with curiosity and passion ; he does not intervene in the destiny which his impulse has set in motion. His fertility is everything, the objects of his fertility nothing, to him. Barrie, on the other hand, has a maternal solicitude in protecting his characters, not only from Consequence, but from the criticism of the audience. He darts here and there like the showman with his duster in *Boutique Fantasque*, petting his characters and displaying their good points to the best advantage. Alice's maternal instinct requires fresh attention (for he has rather emphasised her gay, flirtatious nature), so when she finds her daughter in the cupboard in a man's chambers he puts in parenthesis, " It has been the great shock of Alice's life." Maggie, a prominent politician's wife, must be rehabilitated as a *cliché* of Scotch industry and domestic virtue, so she resumes her knitting. What has been hailed as a triumph of dramatic *volte-face*, the ballroom scene between Valentine Brown and Phœbe, in *Quality Street*, is brought about by the author's prejudice in favour of spinsterdom, by forcing a ten-year-old sentiment into a position of supremacy over the natural attraction towards physical youth and vitality.

There is an essential dramatic deficiency in this failure to separate his figures from his own emotional attitude towards them, a failure to complete the objectification of feeling which is the condition of art. It has prevented him from presenting any real conflict of character, which is the mainspring of comedy, as his belief in the friendliness of destiny would have prevented his success in tragedy, which springs from a sense of the hostility of destiny to the hero. No dramatist, of course, has been able to create a character absolutely antipathetic to himself ; but a dramatist of the narrowest sympathies might construct a very fine play if he could imagine the one essential, an antipathy among the characters themselves. This need not involve an ethical hostility, for hero and villain have long since been relegated to the melodrama, but it must involve a temperamental conflict. Since all Barrie's characters are so closely attached to himself, they all swim in the sweet oily liquor of universal pathos which is his philosophy of life. A dramatist may deny a fact of circumstance at his own risk ; he can only contradict a spiritual fact at the expense of extinction. The law which Barrie has violated is that of the conservation of spiritual energy. Whatever access of passionate life we receive is at the expense of some other individual ; if we give it out again it can only be in a lower form. We tear the spirits of our friends for emotional food as unconsciously, and as inevitably, as we ravage land and sea for our dinner, and with as little animosity. At the end of a play, comedy or tragedy, if it is what we call successful, the level of desirable emotion has been heightened in those characters with whom the writer has decided that we shall identify our sympathies ; others are inevitably the poorer. Barrie's peculiar trick, and that which prevents one from receiving any genuine stimulation from his plays, is a confusion of the emotional perspective; by this means, emotions of loss or deprivation are made equivalent in value to those of fruition. One feels that the M'Connachie who writes Barrie's plays would give up his mistress to a rival with more pleasure than he would embrace her ; the necessary compensation is derived through a system of social values at the root of which may be found the Edict of Thrums against the satisfaction of impulses. No one could be less of a Calvinist than Barrie, for he is what is left of a man when Calvinism has done its worst. Frighten a man out of doing wrong, of offending God and his neighbour, and you have the most amenable piece of sentimentality which any pusillanimous populace could desire. To go and see a Barrie play is like going to see a sheep in a cage in the Zoo ; the bars, the "drama," are merely a device to encourage mutual self-esteem.

It would not matter that there are no villains in Barrie's work ; villains are a relic of an obsolete ethical dualism. The most favourable critic, I suppose, would not assert that Lord Rintoul, in *The Little Minister*, was anything but a literary machine, a naughty English lord from a *feuilleton*, a foil to a God-fearing monogamous Scot. Lady Sybil (also English) is so film-like a vampire that she can be thrown aside when she has played the part of temptress long enough to " bring together " John and Maggie Shand. Captain Hook is the nearest thing to a villain Barrie has ever dared to imagine ; he is the shadow of reality troubling Barrie's fantasy, and because he is admitted, even as a fantastic shadow derived from Stevenson's romantic shadow, *Peter Pan* has a vitality which the plays of experience lack. In the language of psycho-analysis, Peter Pan is a symbol of the libido, wandering in the asexual infantile world from which it has never been able to escape. The pirates represent that glimmering sense of the hostility of reality which Barrie has so consistently denied in his other work. The ease with which the pirates are defeated by the Lost Boys gives away, perhaps, the secret of Barrie's failure as an artist ; his ingenuity of fancy has always found a way round an experience, along pre-established lines, so easily. We cannot accept Peter Pan as a valid symbol of Joy. He is the boy who would not grow up, but that is the freak of an adult who cannot face the responsibility of adult life. It is middle-age, much more than youth, that the play represents. The boy is actually in a ferment to grow up, to shed his dependences and ignorances. As Mr. Desmond MacCarthy said of Barrie's attitude to young people : " Judging him as an artist, he strikes me in general as beautifully unshockable, most wisely indulgent ; but there is one thing I think would shock him artistically—a youth who did not take an enthusiastic, trusting attitude towards the world, who was discontented, though not personally persecuted, sceptical, self-withdrawn, world-questioning, disillusioned. I cannot approve Sir James Barrie as a lover of youth, because I have never yet seen in his work that sympathy with pimpled and sullen spiritual gawkishness, which, it seems to me, youth's true lover must also possess." The play reveals better than any other what the critic of a great paper described as the " infinitely various cleverness with which he reveals his loveableness." But I think the fantasy coarse beside that of Lewis Carroll, and the romance weak after that of Stevenson. The loveableness remains, but that is purchased at the price Barrie usually asks one to pay, the surrender of all conflict, which is really the surrender of all values. Even here there are specimens of that terrible insensitiveness to human nature which results from a refusal to face the grossness of its pain.

"When was I born, Mummy ?
At midnight, dear.
I hope I didn't wake you, Mummy."

Such a *calembour* in sentiment, if dashed out, might pass for a lapse of genius ; produced with such a consummate air,

to be flashed on the screen as a sub-title, it can only indicate the absence of understanding. It is done with
a smile, as if he did Nature a favour by pretending
not to notice her whilst she was making up — that
grim and indelicate process. Faced with a char-
woman's bonnet, which it would be difficult to make
effectively of the Barrie atmosphere by a description in terms
of fusty gimp and jet, he slips off at a familiar emotional tan-
gent : " Such a kind old bonnet that it makes you laugh at
once ; I don't know how to describe it, but it is trimmed with
a kiss, as bonnets should be when the wearer is old and frail."

" Trimmed with a thimble " Pan would have said, and the
conventions of the fantastic would have condoned what is
intolerable in a scene of actuality.

A few years ago, in a Rectorial Address at St. Andrew's
University, Sir James Barrie anticipated a criticism of the
older by the younger generation, whom he imagines saying
that the older generation's "avoidance of frankness in life and
in the arts is often, but not so often as you think, a cowardly
way of shirking unpalatable truths." Surely no young man
would have the self-complacency to accuse Sir James Barrie of
doing any of these things, even as often as he might, it seems, be
willing to admit to them. In any case, " cowardly " is a word
of no significance in the context. It must be plain to any reader
that Barrie has transcribed what he felt in life with great
fidelity. It is this transcript, not the personality behind it,
which is the subject of criticism ; its irrelevance to the world
as we see it deprives us of a pleasure which our elders
undoubtedly enjoyed.

Dostoevsky and Pauline Souslov

TRANSLATED BY S. S. KOTELIANSKY.

The following letter written by Dostoevsky to Mlle. Apollinaria Pankratievna Souslov was quite recently found in Golziev's archives in Moscow, and published in Russia.

Dostoevsky's daughter, Aimée, in her book on her father, which originally appeared in German, in 1920, and was translated into English and published here a couple of years ago, has for the first time given a somewhat lurid account of her father's love affair with Mlle. Souslov—" Pauline," as Aimée D. calls her. From Dostoevsky's letters to his brother Michael, as well as from Mlle. Souslov's diaries and letters, we learn many interesting details of their travels and adventures abroad in 1863, some time before the death of Dostoevsky's first wife, Marie Dmitrievna Issayev.

F. M. DOSTOEVSKY'S LETTER TO MLLE. SOUSLOV.

DRESDEN, *April 23-May 5*, 1867.

Your letter, my precious friend, was handed over to me at Basunov's (the bookseller) very late, just before I left for abroad ; and as I was in an awful hurry, I could not manage to answer it. I left Petersburg on Good Friday (April 14, I believe) ; my journey to Dresden took a fairly long time, with stops, and I have, therefore, only now found time to have a chat with you.

And so, my dear, you know nothing about me, at any rate you knew nothing when you sent me your letter ? I married last February. According to my contract with Stelovsky [the publisher] I was bound to deliver to him by November 1st of last year a *new novel*, of not less than ten folios of ordinary print ; otherwise I was liable to a terrible fine. Meanwhile I was writing a novel for the *Russky Vestnik**. I had written twenty-four folios, but there remained another twelve to be done. And then, I had also to write the ten folios for Stelovsky. It was the fourth of October, and I had not yet begun. Milyukov advised me to engage a stenographer to whom I could dictate the novel, which would speed up the

---

* *Crime and Punishment*, published in NN 1, 2, 4, 6, 8, 11-12 of Katkov's review, *Russky Vestnik* for 1886.

DOSTOEVSKY AND PAULINE SOUSLOV

work four times. Olkhin, the professor of stenography, sent me his best pupil, a young lady, whom I engaged. And on October 4 we commenced. My stenographer, Anna Gregorievna Snitkin, is a young and rather pretty girl of twenty, of a good family, who passed her school examinations with honours, and is of an extraordinarily kind and bright disposition. The work went off superbly. On November 28 my novel *The Gambler* (just published) was finished in twenty-four days. Towards its completion I noticed that my stenographer was sincerely fond of me, although she had never said a single word about it ; and I went on liking her more and more. As since my brother's death* I have grown terribly weary and find life a burden, I have proposed to her. She has agreed, and now we are married. The difference in years is terrible (she twenty and I forty-four), but I am becoming more and more convinced that she will be happy. She has a heart and she can love.

Now about my position generally. You are partly aware that after the death of my brother I lost my health completely through the worry caused by his review† ; but, exhausted in my struggle with the indifference of the public and so on and so on, I dropped it. Again, the three thousand roubles (which I received from the sale of my works to Stelovsky) I spent on the review, on my brother's family, and on paying the creditors. The result was that I piled up new debts in connection with the review, which, together with my brother's unpaid debts, amounted to over fifteen thousand roubles. That was the state of my affairs when I left for abroad in 1865, having on me altogether forty Napoleons. Abroad I made up my mind that only by relying on myself should I be able to pay those 15,000 roubles. Besides, with the death of my brother, who was *everything* to me, I have become very sick of life. I still thought of finding a heart that would respond to mine, but I did not find it. Then I plunged into work and began writing a novel. Katkov paid me more than the others, and I gave him the novel. But thirty-seven folios of the novel and another ten folios for Stelovsky turned out to be too much for me, though I have completed both books. My epilepsy became aggravated disgustingly, but after all I diverted myself and also saved

* Michael Dostoevsky died June 10, 1864.
† "*Epocha*," stopped publication in 1865.

45

myself from prison. The novel (published in the review and in book form) brought me as much as 14,000 roubles, on which I lived, and also paid back twelve thousand of my fifteen thousand debt. Now my debts are altogether about three thousand roubles. But these three thousand are the wickedest. The more you pay back, the more impatient and more stupid creditors become. Mark you, had I not taken over those debts, the creditors would not have received a penny, and they know it themselves, for they had begged me to take them over *out of pity* to them, promising not to touch me. But the repayment of the 12,000 aroused the cupidity of those whose bills had not yet been paid. Now I shall have no money till the new year, and that only if I finish the work on which I am now engaged. But how am I going to finish it if they give me no peace ? That is why I went (with my wife) abroad. Again, by living abroad I expect my epilepsy to be relieved, for in Petersburg, lately, it has become almost impossible for me to work. I could no longer work at night, for every time I had a fit. And so I want to recover my health and to finish my work. From Katkov I received money in advance. They gave it willingly. They pay excellently. From the very first I declared to Katkov that I was a Slavophile, and that I did not agree with certain views of his. This improved and smoothed our relations considerably. As a man, he is the noblest fellow on earth. I did not know him at all before. His immense self-love is awfully damaging to him. But who is without immense self-love ?

During my last days in Petersburg I met Mme. Brylkin, and paid her a visit. We spoke a great deal about you. She is fond of you. She told me she was very sad about my being happy with another woman. I shall write to her. I like her.

Your letter left a sad impression on me. You say that you are very sad. I have not known your life for the last year, and what has been in your heart, but judging from all I know about you, it is difficult for you to be happy. Oh, my dear, I do not call you to cheap, *necessary* happiness. I respect you (and always respected you) for your exacting nature, and I indeed know that your heart can't help demanding life, but you yourself consider people either infinitely glorious, or—at once

DOSTOEVSKY AND PAULINE SOUSLOV

—scoundrels and banal. I judge from facts. Draw the conclusion yourself.

Au revoir, my eternal friend ! I am afraid this letter will not find you in Moscow. Know at any rate that from May 8 (old style) I shall still be in Dresden (that is in any case ; I may stay on longer), and therefore, if you wish to answer me, do so immediately on receipt of this letter. (*Poste restante*, Dostoevsky, Dresden, Sax.). My further addresses I will communicate to you. Good-bye, my friend. I press and kiss your hand.

Your F. DOSTOEVSKY.

The following article, written by Leonid Grossman, which contains a good deal of new and valuable information relating to the character of Mlle. Souslov, has recently appeared in a Petersburg literary monthly.

One of Dostoevsky's greatest infatuations goes back to the beginning of the sixties. The young girl Apollinaria Pankratievna Souslov left a most profound trace on the creative activity of Dostoevsky's later period.

From Aimée Dostoevsky's book on her father we can gather only a few facts concerning " Pauline." She arrived in Petersburg from the provinces, and became a student at the University. Although in the beginning of the sixties Dostoevsky only rarely appeared at students' literary evenings, and was not at all so popular with the students and public as he was at the end of the seventies, we take it that Mlle. Souslov had made his acquaintance at one of those evenings. In the existing Dostoevsky archives Apollinaria's first love-letter to him is not to be found, yet we can accept Aimée Dostoevsky's assurance that he had actually received such a letter, and that it moved him by its sincerity, *naïveté*, and romantic tone : the tone of a young girl dazed by the genius of the great writer, and expressing her admiration for him.

At any rate, there is no doubt whatever that in 1863 the love affair between Dostoevsky and Apollinaria was at its height. That summer Dostoevsky travelled abroad in the company of Mlle. Souslov. In his letters to his brothers he quite frankly speaks of the happiness of travelling with his beloved. It is true, however, that his habitual distrust and disposition to gloom, and, chiefly, his losses at roulette, clouded his first European tour in the company of his beloved.

" We have lots of adventures," writes Dostoevsky to his brother, " yet I feel awfully dissatisfied, in spite of A. S[ouslov]. Even happiness I take with pain, for I have separated myself from all those I have hitherto loved and suffered for many a time. And although I have given up everything for the sake of happiness, even matters in which I could be of use—my egotism and the thought of this are now poisoning my happiness (if indeed it exists at all)."

Dostoevsky's companion suffered because of his gambling losses ; she pawned her ring, she experienced together with him the anxieties of a sudden impecuniosity, was afraid of being presented with the hotel bill which could not be met. The history of their relations, evidently complicated by various love incidents, is quite clearly reflected in Dostoevsky's *The Gambler*. Mlle. Souslov's Diary makes it possible to re-establish the history of their personal relations, and it also throws much light on Dostoevsky's method of transforming the raw material of experience into a work of art.

Dostoevsky's relations with Mlle. Souslov did not run smooth ; there seem to have been ruptures, reconciliations, violent misunderstandings, and withal a constant mutual attraction. Their correspondence, too, seems to have been interrupted for long intervals, and yet it did not cease even after Dostoevsky's second marriage. On the 5th of May, 1867, that is, two months after his marriage to Anna Gregorievna Snitkin, Dostoevsky sent Mlle. Souslov a detailed letter about the change in his life. [See D.'s letter to Mlle. Souslov published in full above.]

From the Diary of Anna Gregorievna [Dostoevsky's second wife] we learn that she was extremely distressed by the frequent correspondence between her husband and Mlle. Souslov. This is how Mme. D. describes the reading by her husband of a letter from Mlle. Souslov, received on May 27, 1867, whilst they were staying at Dresden.

"All the time he was reading that letter I watched the expression of his face. He read and re-read the first page for a long time as if he could not make out what was written there ; then, at last, he read it through and blushed scarlet. His hands seemed to tremble. I pretended not to know from whom the letter was, and asked him what Soniechka [a relation of D.] was writing about. He said that the letter was not from Soniechka, and gave a bitter smile. I have never yet seen such a smile on his face. It was a smile either of contempt or of pity —indeed, I do not know, but it was a pitiable, lost smile. Afterwards he became awfully distrait, and he hardly could make out what I was saying."

We are inclined to think that Apollinaria Souslov was the object of Dostoevsky's greatest passion. A woman of extremes, ever disposed to unbounded sensations, to psychological polarities, she demanded a great deal from life. Her inclination to divide people only into saints or villains is as characteristic of her passionate, emotional nature as her constant infatuations, her directness, imperiousness, resoluteness. Her heart, moved to noble impulses of pity and loving-kindness (as, for instance, her tears on hearing of the illness of Dostoevsky's brother), was no less inclined to blind, riotous impulses of passion and persecution. Her sensibility, evidently, did not exclude a certain vein of cynicism. These traits are established beyond doubt from the evidence of V. V. Rosanov, who married Mlle. Souslov the same year in which Dostoevsky died [1881]. It is, however, necessary to bear in mind that Rosanov's account relates to a Pauline no longer young (when he married her she was about forty-five) ; also perhaps his characterisation of her is somewhat unfavourably biassed. Nevertheless, Rosanov's evidence is of great value, and it also coincides with other evidence from different sources.

" I married her," says Rosanov, " when I was an undergraduate at the University, a year before I took my degree. But after six years of our married life, she left me, having fallen in love with a young Jew." Then, in his application to the Synod, Rosanov gives the following information about his first wife : " Apollinaria, née Souslov, left her husband, V. V. Rosanov, in 1886, giving as a reason that her husband, in violation of his promise to her, continued to meet a certain young man, a Jew, Goldovsky, who looked after the distribution of Rosanov's books in the bookshops." But, from all the evidence at hand, it seems that she, having fallen in love with that Goldovsky, but having met with no response on his part, persecuted him abominably, and by indescribable quarrels she compelled her husband to break completely with the man. Goldovsky comes of an excellent Jewish family, and is an excellent young man : Apollinaria herself had invited him to spend the summer with the Rosanovs. On the whole, this was one of Apollinaria's most absurd and monstrous actions.

Having settled as teacher at Eletz, Rosanov goes on to say, he asked his wife to return to him, in the hope that in a new place, amongst new people and new surroundings, they would settle down. But she refused. " Thousands of husbands," she replied, " are in the same position as you (*i.e.*, deserted by their wives) and yet they do not whine—men aren't dogs."

Apollinaria's father, to whom Rosanov wrote asking him to use his influence with his daughter and to urge her to return to her husband, wrote to him as follows : " The enemy of the human race [*i.e.*, his daughter] is settled here in my house, and I can no longer remain here myself."

A friend of Rosanov's told me the following. In the nineties Rosanov's life became very miserable owing to Apollinaria's flat refusal to divorce him. In 1902 the late Rosanov sent a friend of his to Sebastopol, where A. resided at that time, to plead with her and to persuade her to divorce him. Apollinaria was over sixty then; she lived quite alone in her own house, on which was the inscription, " Mrs. V. V. Rosanov's House." The house was extraordinarily clean and tidy ; she herself produced on me the impression of an active and energetic woman. In her conversation with her husband's messenger she remained inflexible. No arguments could change her mind. Of Rosanov she spoke with extreme bitterness, and despite the messenger's persistence, refused to make any concession.

In reply to some questions put to him about his first wife, Mlle. Souslov, by A. S. Volzhsky, a personal friend of his and a student of Dostoevsky's works, Rosanov wrote the following extremely valuable letter :—

" I met Apollinaria for the first time in the house of my pupil, Mlle. A. M. Scheglov (I was 17, Sheglov 20 or 23, Apollinaria 37). Apollinaria was dressed all in black; her face bore 'traces of former (remarkable) beauty ' ; she was a Russian *légitimiste* waiting for the triumph of the Bourbons in France, where she had left her *best* friends, for in Russia she had none. Here she loved only what was aristocratic. With the look of an 'experienced coquette,' she understood that she had 'hit' me —she spoke coldly, indifferently. In a word, she was a kind of Catharine de Medici. Indeed, she looked like de Medici. A crime she would commit coldly, and would assassinate with too much indifference. . . . Generally speaking, A. was indeed superb. I know that people (and a friend of hers, Anna Osipovna G., fifteen years her senior) were absolutely charmed by her. I have never seen such a Russian woman. In the *style of her soul* she was a perfect Russian, and as a Russian she might have been a *raskolnik* of the 'Universal Harmony' sect, or, better still, a 'Mother of God' of the Khlysts' sect.

"She had had a liaison with Dostoevsky, and lived with him. I once asked her, 'Why did you part from him?'

"'Because he did not want to divorce his [first] wife, who was consumptive and dying,' she said.

"'But she was dying?'

"'Yes, she was. She died six months later. But I had by that time already ceased to love him,' she said.

"'Why did you cease to love him?'

"'Because he did not want to divorce her.' And after a silence, she added:

"'I had given myself to him in love, without questioning, without reasoning. And he, too, ought to have acted likewise. He failed to do so, and I left him.'

"This is her 'style'; the conversation is almost literally correct."

Rosanov asserts that Apollinaria possessed an almost unique fascination, an imperious, captivating "style" of femininity. Coldly sensuous, she remained a "tormentor" even in love, showing deviations from the normal, and perverse traits of a complicated character. Looking back thirty years, Rosanov still remembered, with profound agitation and keenest admiration, the fascination of that strange woman—the Catharine de Medici or the Khlysts' Mother of God.

Rosanov compares Apollinaria to Dostoevsky's heroines. Dounia, Raskolnikov's sister (in *Crime and Punishment*), he says, and Aglaia (in *The Idiot*) are like her. But as to Groushenka (of *The Brothers Karamasov*)—no, nothing of the kind. Groushenka is an obscene Russian, but in Apollinaria there was nothing coarse or obscene."

Rosanov thinks that the following fragment from Dostoevsky's *Insulted and Injured* characterises Apollinaria perfectly correctly. The fragment is a description of a certain Countess, given by Prince Valkovsky to Ivan Petrovitch : " She was a first-rate beauty," says the Prince. "What a figure, what a bearing, what a gait ! Her glance was piercing, like that of an eagle, but ever stern and severe. She was majestic and inaccessible. She was reputed to be as cold as icy winter, and she frightened all away by her exalted, by her rigorous virtue. . . . She regarded everyone dispassionately, like an abbess of a mediæval monastery. . . . And, well ? There never was such a voluptuous woman as she was. . . . My lady was so perverse that the Marquis de Sade could have taken lessons from her. . . . Yes, she was the devil incarnate, but an invincibly fascinating devil. . . " In Rosanov's opinion this description is the best characterisation of Apollinaria, although, in fact, it has no reference to her, for *Injured and Insulted* was written by Dostoevsky before he met Apollinaria.

Rosanov's letter throws a great light on the character of Dostoevsky's love affair with Mlle Souslov. The latter furnished D. with certain characteristics for his " proud girls " and " infernal women." In almost all the novels of Dostoevsky's mature period there appears a new type and character of woman, undoubtedly revealed to him by his captivating and unique travelling companion of 1863.

———

Fifty Pounds.

By A. E. COPPARD.

A FTER tea Philip Repton and Eulalia Burnes discussed their gloomy circumstances. Repton was the precarious sort of London journalist, a dark deliberating man, lean and drooping, full of genteel unprosperity, who wrote articles about "Single Tax," "Diet and Reason," "The Futility of this, that, and the other," or "The Significance of the other, that and this"; all done with a bleak care, and signed "P. Stick Repton." Eulalia was brown-haired and hardy, undeliberating and intuitive; she had been milliner, clerk, domestic help, and something in a canteen; and P. Stick Repton had, as one commonly says, picked her up at a time when she was drifting about London without a penny in her purse, without even a purse, and he had not yet put her down.

"I can't understand! It's sickening, monstrous!" Lally was fumbling with a match before the penny gas fire, for when it was evening, in September, it always got chilly on a floor so high up. Their flat was a fourth floor one, and there were—O, fifteen thousand stairs! Out of the window and beyond the chimneys you could see the long glare from lights in High Holborn, and hear the hum of buses. And that was a comfort.

"Lower! Turn it lower!" yelled Philip. The gas had ignited with an astounding thump; the kneeling Lally had thrown up her hands and dropped the matchbox, saying "Damn" in the same tone as one might say "Good morning" to a milkman.

"You shouldn't do it, you know," grumbled Repton. "You'll blow us to the deuce." And that was just like Lally, that was Lally all over, always; the gas, the nobs of sugar in his tea, the way she . . . and the, the . . . O dear, dear! In their early life together, begun so abruptly and illicitly six months before, her simple hidden beauties had delighted him by their surprises; they had peered and shone brighter, had waned and recurred; she was less the one star in his universe than a faint galaxy.

This room of theirs was a dingy room, very small but very high. A lanky gas tube swooped from the middle of the ceiling towards the middle of the table-cloth as if burning to discover whether that was pink or saffron or fawn—and it *was* hard to tell —but on perceiving that the cloth, whatever its tint, was disturbingly spangled with dozens of cupstains and several large envelopes, the gas tube, in the violence of its disappointment, contorted itself abruptly, assumed a lateral bend, and put out its tongue of flame at an oleograph of Monna Lisa which hung above the fireplace.

Those envelopes were the torment to Lally ; they were the sickening, monstrous manifestations which she could not understand. There were always some of them lying there, or about the room, bulging with manuscripts that no editors— they *couldn't* have perused them—wanted ; and so it had come to the desperate point when, as Lally was saying, something had to be done about things. Repton had done all *he* could ; he wrote unceasingly, all day, all night, but all his projects insolvently withered, and morning, noon and evening brought his manuscripts back as unwanted as snow in summer. He was depressed and baffled and weary. And there was simply nothing else he could do, nothing in the world. Apart from his own wonderful gift he was useless, Lally knew, and he was being steadily and stupidly murdered by those editors. It was weeks since they had eaten a proper meal. Whenever they obtained any really nice food now, they sat down to it silently, intently and destructively. As far as Lally could tell, there seemed to be no prospect of any such meals again in life or time, and the worst of it all was Philip's pride—he was actually too proud to ask anyone for assistance ! Not that he would be too proud to accept help if it were offered to him : O no, if it came he would rejoice at it ! But still, he had that nervous shrinking pride that coiled upon itself, and he would not ask ; he was like a wounded animal that hid its woe far away from the rest of the world. Only Lally knew his need, but why could not other people see it—those villainous editors ! His own wants were so modest, and he had a generous mind.

" Phil," Lally said, seating herself at the table. Repton was lolling in a wicker armchair before the gas fire. " I'm not going on waiting and waiting any longer, I must go and get a job. Yes, I must. We get poorer and poorer. We can't go on like it any longer, there's no use, and I can't bear it."

FIFTY POUNDS

" No, no, I can't have that, my dear . . . "

" But I will ! " she cried. " O, why are you so proud ? "

" Proud ! Proud ! " He stared into the gas fire, his tired arms hanging limp over the arms of the chair. " You don't understand. There are things the flesh has to endure, and things the spirit too must endure. . . . " Lally loved to hear him talk like that ; and it was just as well, for Repton was much given to such discoursing. Deep in her mind was the conviction that he had simple access to profound, almost unimaginable, wisdom. " It isn't pride, it is just that there is a certain order in life, in my life, that it would not do for. I could not bear it, I could never rest : I can't explain that, but just believe it, Lally." His head was empty but unbowed ; he spoke quickly and finished almost angrily. " If only I had money ! It's not for myself. I can stand all this, any amount of it. I've done so before, and I shall do again and again I've no doubt. But I have to think of you."

That was fiercely annoying. Lally got up and went and stood over him.

" Why are you so stupid ? I can think for myself and fend for myself. I'm not married to you. You have your pride, but I can't starve for it. And I've a pride, too. I'm a burden to you. If you won't let me work now while we're together, then I must leave you and work for myself."

" Leave ! Leave me now ? When things are so bad ? " His white face gleamed his perturbation up at her. " O well, go, go." But then, mournfully moved, he took her hands and fondled them. " Don't be a fool, Lally ; it's only a passing depression, this ; I've known worse before, and it never lasts long, something turns up, always does. There's good and bad in it all, but there's more goodness than anything else. You see."

" I don't want to wait for ever, even for goodness. I don't believe in it, I never see it, never feel it, it is no use to me. I could go and steal, or walk the streets, or do any dirty thing—easily. What's the good of goodness if it isn't any use ? "

" But, but," Repton stammered, " what's the use of bad, if it isn't any better ? "

" I mean . . . " began Lally.

55

" You don't mean anything, my dear girl."

" I mean, when you haven't any choice it's no use talking moral, or having pride, it's stupid. O, my darling," she slid down to him and lay against his breast, " it's not you, you are everything to me ; that's why it angers me so, this treatment of you, all hard blows and no comfort. It will never be any different, I feel it will never be different now, and it terrifies me."

" Pooh ! " Repton kissed her and comforted her : she was his beloved. " When things are wrong with us our fancies take their tone from our misfortunes, badness, evil. I some-times have a queer stray feeling that one day I shall be hanged. Yes, I don't know what for, what *could* I be hanged for ? At other times I have felt sure that one day I shall come to be— what do you think ?—Prime Minister of this country. You can't reason against such things. I even made a list of the men I would choose for my Cabinet. Yes, oh yes."

But Lally had made up her mind to leave him ; she would leave him for a while and earn her own living. When things took a turn for the better she would join him again. She told him this. She had friends who were going to get her some work.

" But what are you going to do, Lally, I . . . "

" I'm going away to Glasgow," said she.

Glasgow ! He had heard things about Glasgow ! Good Heavens !

" I've some friends there," the girl went on steadily. She had got up and was sitting on the arm of his chair. " I wrote to them last week. They can get me a job almost anywhen, and I can stay with them. They want me to go—they've sent the money for my fare. I think I shall have to go."

" You don't love me then ! " said the man.

Lally kissed him.

" But *do* you ? Tell me ! "

" Yes, my dear," said Lally, " of course."

An uneasiness possessed him ; he released her moodily. Where was their wild passion flown to ? She was staring at him intently, then she tenderly said : " My love, don't you be melancholy, don't take it to heart so. I'd cross the world to find you a pin."

FIFTY POUNDS

"No, no, you mustn't do that," he exclaimed idiotically. At her indulgent smile he grimly laughed too, and then sank back in his chair. The girl stood up and went about the room doing vague nothings, until he spoke again.

"So you are tired of me?"

Lally went to him steadily and knelt down by his chair. "If I was tired of you, Phil, I'd kill myself."

Moodily he ignored that. "I suppose it had to end like this. But I've loved you desperately." Lally was now weeping on his shoulder, and he began to twirl a lock of her rich brown hair absently with his fingers as if it were a seal on a watch chain. "I'd been thinking we might as well get married as soon as things had turned round."

"I'll come back, Phil," she clasped him so tenderly, "as soon as you want me."

"But you are not really going?"

"Yes," said Lally.

"You're not to go!"

"I wouldn't go if . . . if anything . . . if you had any luck. But as we are now I must go away, to give you a chance. You see that, darling Phil?"

"You're not to go, I object. I just love you, Lally, that's all, and of course I want to keep you here."

"Then what are we to do?"

"I . . . don't . . . know. Things drop out of the sky. But we must be together. You're not to go."

Lally sighed: he was stupid. And Repton began to turn over in his mind the dismal knowledge that she had taken this step in secret, she had not told him while she was trying to get to Glasgow. Now here she was with the fare, and as good as gone! Yes, it was all over.

"When do you propose to go?"

"Not for a few days, nearly a fortnight."

"Good God," he moaned. Yes, it was all over then. He had never dreamed that this would be the end, that she would be the first to break away. He had always envisaged a tender scene in which he could tell her, with dignity and gentle humour, that . . . Well, he never had quite hit upon the words he would use, but that was the kind of setting. And now, here she was with her fare to Glasgow, her heart turned towards Glasgow, and she as good as gone to Glasgow ! No dignity, no gentle humour—in fact he was enraged, sullen but enraged ; he boiled furtively. But he said with mournful calm :

"I've so many misfortunes, I suppose I can bear this too." Gloomy and tragic he was.

"Dear darling Phil, it's for your own sake I'm going."

Repton sniffed derisively. "We are always mistaken in the reasons for our commonest actions ; Nature derides us all. You are sick of me, I can't blame you."

Eulalia was so moved that she could only weep again. Nevertheless she wrote to her friends in Glasgow promising to be with them by a stated date.

Towards the evening of the following day, at a time when she was alone, a letter arrived addressed to herself. It was from a firm of solicitors in Cornhill inviting her to call upon them. A flame leaped up in Lally's heart : it might mean the offer of some work which would keep her in London after all ! If only it were so she would accept it on the spot, and Philip would have to be made to see the reasonableness of it. But at the office in Cornhill a more astonishing outcome awaited her. There she showed her letter to a little office boy with scarcely any finger nails and very little nose, and he took it to an elderly man who had a superabundance of both. Smiling affably the long-nosed man led her upstairs into the sombre den of a gentleman who had some white hair and a lumpy yellow complexion. Having put to her a number of questions relating to her family history, and appearing to be satisfied and not at all surprised by her answers, this gentleman revealed to Lally the overpowering tidings that she was entitled to a legacy of eighty pounds by the will of a forgotten and recently deceased aunt. Subject to certain formalities, proofs of identity, and so forth, he promised Lally the possession of the money within about a week.

Lally's descent to the street, her emergence into the clamouring atmosphere, her walk along to Holborn, were accomplished in a state of blessedness and trance, a trance in which life became a thousand times aerily enlarged, movement was a delight, and thought a rapture. She would give all the money to Philip, and if he very much wanted it she would even marry him now. Perhaps, though, she would save ten pounds of it for herself. The other seventy would keep them for . . . it was impossible to say how long it would keep them. They could have a little holiday somewhere in the country together, he was so worn and weary. Perhaps she had better not tell Philip anything at all about it until her lovely money was really in her hand. Nothing in life, at least nothing about money, was ever certain ; something horrible might happen at the crucial moment and the money be snatched from her very fingers. O, she would go mad then ! So for some days she kept her wonderful secret.

Their imminent separation had given Repton a tender sadness that was very moving. " Eulalia," he would say ; for he had suddenly adopted the formal version of her name : " Eulalia, we've had a great time together, a wonderful time, there will never be anything like it again." She often shed tears, but she kept the grand secret still locked in her heart. Indeed, it occurred to her very forcibly that even now his stupid pride might cause him to reject her money altogether. Silly, silly Philip ! Of course, it would have been different if they had married ; he would naturally have taken it then, and really, it would have *been* his. She would have to think out some dodge to overcome his scruples. Scruples were *such* a nuisance, but then it was very noble of him : there were not many men who wouldn't take money from a girl they were living with.

Well, a week later she was summoned again to the office in Cornhill and received from the white-haired gentleman a cheque for eighty pounds drawn on the Bank of England to the order of Eulalia Burnes. Miss Burnes desired to cash the cheque straightway, so the large-nosed elderly clerk was deputed to accompany her to the Bank of England close by and assist in procuring the money.

" A very nice errand ! " exclaimed that gentleman as they crossed to Threadneedle Street past the Royal Exchange. Miss Burnes smiled her acknowledgment, and he began to tell her of other windfalls that had been disbursed in his time —but vast sums, very great persons—until she began to infer that Blackbean, Carp & Ransome were universal dispensers of heavenly largesse.

" Yes, but," said the clerk, hawking a good deal from an affliction of catarrh, " I never got any myself, and never will. If I did, do you know what I would do with it ? " But at that moment they entered the portals of the bank, and in the excitement of the business Miss Burnes forgot to ask the clerk how he would use a legacy, and thus she possibly lost a most valuable slice of knowledge. With one fifty-pound note and six five-pound notes clasped in her handbag she bade good-bye to the long-nosed clerk, who shook her fervently by the hand and assured her that Blackbean, Carp & Ransome would be delighted at all times to undertake any commissions on her behalf. Then she fled along the pavement, blithe as a bird, until she was breathless with her flight. Presently she came opposite the window of a typewriting agency. Tripping airily into its office she laid a scrap of paper before a lovely Hebe who was typing there.

" I want this typed, if you please," said Lally.

The beautiful typist read the words on the scrap of paper and stared at the heiress.

" I don't want any address to appear," said Lally, " just a plain sheet, please."

A few moments later she received a neatly-typed page folded in an envelope, and after paying the charge she hurried off to a District Messenger office. Here she addressed the envelope in a disguised hand to *P. Stick Repton, Esq.*, at their address in Holborn. She read the typed letter through again :

Dear Sir,

 In common with many others I entertain the greatest admiration for your literary abilities, and I therefore beg you to accept this tangible expression of that admiration from a constant reader of your articles, who, for purely private reasons, desires to remain anonymous.

Your very sincere,

WELLWISHER.

Placing the fifty-pound note upon the letter Lally carefully folded them together and put them both into the envelope. The attendant then gave it to a uniformed lad, who sauntered off whistling very casually, somewhat to Lally's alarm—he looked so small and careless to be entrusted with fifty pounds. Then Lally went out, changed one of her five-pound notes and had a lunch—half-a-crown, but it was worth it. O how enchanting and exciting London was! In two days more she would have been gone ; now she would have to write off at once to her Glasgow friends and tell them she had changed her mind, that she was now settled in London. O, how enchanting and delightful! And to-night he would take her out to dine in some fine restaurant, and they would do a theatre. She did not really want to marry Phil, they had got on so well without it, but if he wanted that too she did not mind—much. They would go away into the country for a whole week. What money would do! Marvellous! And looking round the restaurant she felt sure that no other woman there, no matter how well-dressed, had as much as thirty pounds in her handbag.

Returning home in the afternoon she became conscious of her own betraying radiance ; very demure and subdued and usual she would have to be, or he might guess the cause of it. Though she danced up the long flights of stairs she entered their room quietly, but the sight of Repton staring out of the window, forlorn as a drowsy horse, overcame her and she rushed to embrace him crying " Darling ! "

" Hullo, hullo ! " he smiled.

" I'm so fond of you, Phil dear."

" But . . . but you're deserting me ! "

" O no," she cried archly, " I'm not—not deserting you."

" All right." Repton shrugged his shoulders, but he seemed happier. He did not mention the fifty pounds then : perhaps it had not come yet—or perhaps he was thinking to surprise her.

" Let's go for a walk, it's a screaming lovely day," said Lally.

" O, I dunno." He yawned and stretched. " Nearly tea-time, isn't it ? "

" Well, we . . . " Lally was about to suggest having tea out somewhere, but she bethought herself in time. " I suppose it is. Yes, it is."

So they stayed in for tea. No sooner was tea over than Repton remarked that he had an engagement somewhere. Off he went, leaving Lally disturbed and anxious. Why had he not mentioned the fifty pounds ? Surely it had not gone to the wrong address ? This suspicion once formed, Lally soon became certain, tragically sure, that she had misaddressed the envelope herself. A conviction that she had put No. 17 instead of No. 71 was almost overpowering, and she fancied that she hadn't even put London on the envelope—but Glasgow. That was impossible, though, but—O the horror!—somebody else was enjoying their fifty pounds. The girl's fears were not allayed by the running visit she paid to the messenger office that evening, for the rash imp who had been entrusted with her letter had gone home and therefore could not be interrogated until the morrow. By now she was sure that he had blundered ; he had been so casual with an important letter like that ! Lally never did, and never would again, trust any little boys who wore their hats so much on one side, were so glossy with hair-oil, and went about whistling just to madden you. She burned to ask where the boy lived, but in spite of her desperate desire she could not do so. She dared not, it would expose her to . . . to something or other she could only feel, not name ; you had to keep cool, to let nothing, not even curiosity, master you.

Hurrying home again, though hurrying was not her custom, and there was no occasion for it, she wrote the letter to her Glasgow friends. Then it crossed her mind that it would be wiser not to post the letter that night ; better wait until the morning, after she had discovered what the horrible little messenger had done with her letter. Bed was a poor refuge from her thoughts, but she accepted it, and when Phil came home she was not sleeping. While he undressed he told her of the lecture he had been to, something about Agrarian Depopulation it was, but even after he had stretched himself beside her he did not speak about the fifty pounds. Nothing, not even curiosity, should master her, and so she calmed herself, and in time fitfully slept.

At breakfast next morning he asked her what she was going to do that day.

"O," replied Lally offhandedly, "I've a lot of things to see to, you know ; I must go out. I'm sorry the porridge is so awful this morning, Phil, but . . . "

"Awful ?" he broke in. "But it's nicer than usual ! Where are you going ? I thought—our last day, you know— we might go out somewhere together."

"Dear Phil ! " Lovingly she stretched out a hand to be

caressed across the table. "But I've several things to do. I'll come back early, eh ? " She got up and hurried round to embrace him.

"All right," he said. "Don't be long."

Off went Lally to the messenger office, at first as happy as a bird, but on approaching the building the old tremors assailed her. Inside the room was the cocky little boy who bade her "Good Morning " with laconic assurance. Lally at once questioned him, and when he triumphantly produced a delivery book she grew limp with her suppressed fear, one fear above all others. For a moment she did not want to look at it : Truth hung by a hair, and as long as it so hung she might swear it was a lie. But there it was, written right across the page, an entry of a letter delivered, signed for in the well-known hand, *P. Stick Repton*. There was no more doubt, only a sharp indignant agony, as if she had been stabbed with a dagger of ice.

"O yes, thank you," said Lally calmly. "Did you hand it to him yourself ? "

"Yes'm," replied the boy, and he described Philip.

"Did he open the letter ? "

"Yes'm."

"There was no answer ? "

"No'm."

"All right." Fumbling in her bag, she added : "I think I've got a sixpence for you."

Out in the street again she tremblingly chuckled to herself. "So that is what he is like, after all. Cruel and mean ! " He was going to let her go and keep the money in secret to himself ! How despicable ! Cruel and mean, cruel and mean. She hummed it to herself : " Cruel and mean, cruel and mean ! " It eased her tortured bosom. "Cruel and mean ! " And he was waiting at home for her, waiting with a smile for their last day together. It would *have* to be their last day. She tore up the letter to her Glasgow friends, for now she *must* go to them. So cruel and mean ! Let him wait ! A 'bus stopped beside her and she stepped on to it, climbing to the top and sitting there while the air chilled her burning features. The 'bus made a long journey to Plaistow. She knew nothing of Plaistow, she wanted to know nothing of Plaistow, but she did not care where the 'bus took her ; she only wanted to keep moving, and moving away, as far away as possible from Holborn and from him, and not once let those hovering tears down fall.

From Plaistow she turned and walked back as far as the Mile End Road. Thereabouts, wherever she went she met clergymen, dozens of them. There must be a conference, about charity or something, Lally thought. With a vague desire to confide her trouble to some one, she observed them ; it would relieve the strain. But there was none she could tell her sorrow to, and failing that, when she came to a neat restaurant she entered it and consumed a fish. Just beyond her three sleek parsons were lunching, sleek and pink, bald, affable, consoling men, all very much alike.

" I saw Carter yesterday," she heard one say. Lally liked listening to the conversation of strangers, and she had often wondered what clergymen talked about among themselves.

" What, Carter ! Indeed. Nice fellow, Carter. How was he ? "

" Carter loves preaching, you know ! " cried the third.

" O yes, he loves preaching ! "

" Ha ha ha, yes."

" Ha ha ha, oom."

" Awf'lly good preacher, though."

" Yes, awf'lly good."

" And he's awf'lly good at comic songs, too."

" Yes ? "

" Yes ! "

Three glasses of water, a crumbling of bread, a silence suggestive of prayer.

" How long has he been married ? "

" Twelve years," returned the cleric who had met Carter.

" O, twelve years ! "

" I've only been married twelve years myself," said the oldest of them.

" Indeed ! "

" Yes, I tarried very long."

" Ha ha ha, yes."

" Ha ha ha, oom."

" Er . . . have you any family ? "

FIFTY POUNDS

" No."

Very delicate and dainty in handling their food they were, very delicate and dainty.

" My rectory is a magnificent old house," continued the recently married one. " Built originally 1700. Burnt down. Rebuilt 1784."

" Indeed ! "

" Humph ! "

" Seventeen bedrooms and two delightful tennis courts."

" O, well done ! " the others cried, and then they all fell with genteel gusto upon a pale blanc-mange.

From the restaurant the girl sauntered about for a while, and then there was a cinema wherein, seated warm and comfortable in the twitching darkness, she partially stilled her misery. Some nervous fancy kept her roaming in that district for most of the evening. She knew that if she left it she would go home, and she did not want to go home. The naptha lamps of the booths at Mile End were bright and distracting, and the hum of the evening business was good despite the smell. A man was weaving sweetstuffs from a pliant roll of warm toffee that he wrestled with as the athlete wrestles with the python. There were stalls with things of iron, with fruit or fish, pots and pans, leather, string, nails. Watches for use—or for ornament—what d'ye lack ? A sailor told naughty stories while selling bunches of green grapes out of barrels of cork dust which he swore he had stolen from the Queen of Honolulu. People clamoured for them both. You could buy back numbers of the comic papers at four a penny, rolls of linoleum for very little more—and use either for the other's purpose.

" At thrippence per foot, mesdames," cried the sweating cheapjack, lashing himself into ecstatic furies, " that's a piece of fabric weft and woven with triple-strength Andalusian jute, double-hot-pressed with rubber from the island of Pagama, and stencilled by an artist as poisoned his grandfather's cook. That's a piece of fabric, mesdames, as the king of heaven himself wouldn't mind to put down in his parlour—if he had the chance. Do I ask thrippence a foot for that piece of fabric ? Mesdames, I was never a daring chap."

Lally watched it all ; she looked and listened ; then looked and did not see, listened and did not hear. Her misery was not the mere disappointment of love, not that kind of misery alone; it was the crushing of an ideal in which love had had its home, a treachery cruel and mean. The sky of night, so smooth, so be-starred, looked wrinkled through her screen of unshed tears; her sorrow was a wild cloud that troubled the moon with darkness.

In miserable desultory wandering she had spent her day, their last day, and now, returning to Holborn in the late evening, she suddenly began to hurry, for a new possibility had come to lighten her dejection. Perhaps, after all, so whimsical he was, he was keeping his " revelation " until the last day, or even the last hour, when (nothing being known to her, as he imagined) all hopes being gone and they had come to the last kiss, he would take her in his arms and laughingly kill all grief, waving the succour of a flimsy banknote like a flag of triumph. Perhaps even, in fact surely, that was why he wanted to take her out to-day! O, what a blind, wicked, stupid girl she was, and in a perfect frenzy of bubbling faith she panted homewards for his revealing sign.

From the pavement below she could see that their room was lit. Weakly she climbed the stairs and opened the door. Phil was standing up, staring so strangely at her. Helplessly and half-guiltily she began to smile. Without a word said he came quickly to her and crushed her in his arms, her burning silent man, loving and exciting her. Lying against his breast in that constraining embrace, their passionate disaster was gone, her doubts were flown; all perception of the feud was torn from her and deeply drowned in a gulf of bliss. She was aware only of the consoling delight of their reunion, of his amorous kisses, of his tongue tingling the soft down on her upper lip that she disliked and he admired. All the soft wanton endearments that she so loved to hear him speak were singing in her ears, and then he suddenly swung and lifted her up, snapped out the gaslight, and carried her off to bed.

Life that is born of love feeds on love; if the wherewithal be hidden how shall we stay our hunger? The galaxy may grow dim, or the stars drop in a wandering void; you can neither keep them in your hands nor crumble them in your mind.

What was it Phil had once called her? Numskull! After

all it was his own fifty pounds, she had given it to him freely, it was his to do as he liked with. A gift was a gift, it was poor spirit to send money to anyone with the covetous expectation that it would return to you. She would surely go to-morrow.

The next morning he awoke her early, and kissed her.

"What time does your train go?" said he.

"Train!" Lally scrambled from his arms and out of bed.

A fine day, a glowing day. A bright sharp air! Quickly she dressed, and went into the other room to prepare their breakfast. Soon he followed, and they ate silently together, although whenever they were near each other he caressed her tenderly. Afterwards she went into the bedroom and packed her bag; there was nothing more to be done, he was beyond hope. No woman waits to be sacrificed, least of all those who sacrifice themselves with courage and a quiet mind. When she was ready to go she took her portmanteau into the sitting-room; he, too, made to put on his hat and coat.

"No," murmured Lally, "you're not to come with me."

"Pooh, my dear!" he protested, "nonsense."

"I won't have you come," cried Lally with an asperity that impressed him.

"But you can't carry that bag to the station by yourself!"

"I shall take a taxi." She buttoned her gloves.

"My dear!" His humorous deprecation annoyed her.

"O, bosh!" Putting her gloved hands around his neck she kissed him coolly. "Good-bye. Write to me often. Let me know how you thrive, won't you, Phil? And "—a little waveringly—"love me always." She stared queerly at the two dimples in his cheeks; each dimple was a nest of hair that could never be shaved.

"Lally darling, beloved girl? I never loved you more than now, this moment. You are more precious than ever to me."

At that, she knew her moment of sardonic revelation had come—but she dared not use it, she let it go. She could not so deeply humiliate him by revealing her knowledge of his perfidy. A compassionate divinity smiles at our puny sins. She knew his perfidy, but to triumph in it would defeat her own pride. Let him keep his gracious mournful airs to the last, false though they were. It was better to part so, better from such a figure than from an abject scarecrow, even though both were the same inside. And something capriciously reminded her, for a flying moment, of elephants she had seen swaying with the grand movement of tidal water—and groping for monkey-nuts.

Lally tripped down the stairs alone. At the end of the street she turned for a last glance. There he was, high up in the window, waving good-byes. And she waved back at him.

———

A Post Elizabethan Tragedy.

By Siegfried Sassoon.

'Tis Pity She's a Whore ; last acted—Lord
Knows when !   Revived (and played to-night before 'em,)
By the Phœnician Stage Association,
Whose staunch subscribers, eager to applaud
Examples of archaic indecorum,
Combine with this their chaste discrimination.

Though Lamb extolled it, highbrows here allude
(Rapt in a Freudian future) to its " crude
And obsolete psychology." . . . Detractors
Shatter my estimates. I'm disposed to think
(Wandering between the acts in search of drink)
That the audience gets between me and the actors.

They squeeze and smoke ; a jabbering, conscious crowd
Of intellectual fogies, fools, and freaks—
A cultural inferno, parrot-loud,
With *clichés* of accumulated weeks ;
While, here and there, some calmly chatting sage
(Immortalised by Max) exhibits fame
That awes the advertisers of our Age—
Those press-concerned celebrities who came
Intent to shine conspicuous in the stalls.

*   *   *   *   *

'Tis Pity She's a Whore . . . the curtain falls
On a composed but corpse-encumbered stage
Of expiated incest. Curtain calls
Reanimate the agonists of passion.
And I'm aware, half-hostile and confused,
That, much though the Phœnicians were amused,
Old *Mermaid Dramatists* are out of fashion.

Comments and Reviews

A preconceived idea is, as the artist knows, a tyrant dangerous to the proper organisation of the impulse, definable in no other terms than those of the finished work, which compels him to his strange exertion. The same reticence is necessary even in the humble creation of a Review, in which activity, since it is to some degree an æsthetic one, there is virtue not in intentions but in achievement only. We lay down no programme as to THE CALENDAR'S performance nor prophecy as to its character, since these things cannot interest our readers till they have a tangible existence, and then we shall be ready to join our own criticism with theirs. A conviction of the value of spontaneous growth (or growth which seems spontaneous to the watching mind) and of unpoliced expression, is as near as we come to any public challenge or editorial doctrine.

* * * *

Besides, the readers of a paper have their share in the formation of its induaividlity, though it may be designed in the first place with some imagined kind of reader in the foreground. As this hypothesis is corrected by the reality, the balance of sympathies and antipathies is adjusted into an unpredictable harmony.

* * * *

The reader we have in mind, the ideal reader, is not one with whom we share any particular set of admirations and beliefs. The age of idols is past, for an idol implies a herd—to each literary idol a herd of literary worshippers—and for the modern mind the age of herds is past. For some time after the breakdown of the Victorian religion of great men, disconsolate worshippers sought refuge from the rigour of solitary conviction in a succession of literary chapels, each of which claimed its patron as most efficacious to salvation. Scepticism as to the validity of choice has destroyed the comfort of this "exclusiveness" except for a few simple souls. The slang use of "exclusive" was one of the last tremors due to the poison of snobbery, before it was, as it is always in the end, fatal to its devotee. In all seriou. ness, apparently, a novel was advertised recently as "A Romance for a Few People." (*11th Thousand.*) That is making the best of both worlds.

* * * *

To-day there is only the race, the biological-economic environment; and the individual. Between these extremes there is no class, craft, art, sex, sect or other sub-division which, it seems to us, can claim privilege of the rest. It is with the mind of the individual, the queer creature, rather new in geological time, which flaunts agressively or smiles furtively behind the social mask, that literature communicates. Perhaps there are not so many individuals as there are men and women with names and addresses. Perhaps the streams of people in the street are not so dissimilar as autumn leaves, manure for next summer's generations. The artist, who can differ only in degree and in function from the rest of men, by revealing differences, creates realities. It is through him that we can perfect our individuality, our own shape, which under the comparatively crude strokes of actual experience might remain only roughly chipped out on the surface of that rock of ages, the folk-mind.

* * * *

This view of society means the death of dogma. Parson may roar in the pulpit (and the lay preacher is trying hard just now to snatch a share of the old prestige) but the congregation turn round amicably in the pews to discuss the text with their neighbours. Agreement and disagreement are terms which mean little in such circumstances. The aim of writing is not to convince someone else (for that can never happen against the will) but to satisfy oneself. If, as well, the reader's pleasure is aroused by one of the many means which literature has to waken such a response, then the reader may make a gift of his assent or dissent to the conventicles which are founded on those wraiths, for the cycle of expression is complete without them.

In reviewing we shall base our statements on the standards of criticism, since it is only then that one can speak plainly without offence, or give praise with meaning. It is difficult to keep these standards in a little space and still to be just to contemporary work which is perhaps immature. It would be best if our readers would remember that, since we can notice only a few of all the books which are published, our choosing a book at all means that we believe it to merit their attention. The only other books we shall mention will be those whose incompetence has not received sufficient attention in other Reviews. The same reviewers will deal with the same subjects each month, so that their methods of evaluation may become familiar.

* * * *

A monthly review has some difficulty in keeping its notices of books on the heels of publication. A book which is published on the day we go to press has to wait five weeks for notice, by which time everyone has probably read so many reviews of it in daily and weekly papers that they are determined not to read any more. The section " Among New Books " is designed to minimise this inconvenience. Notice of a book in those pages does not preclude a full review in the next issue of THE CALENDAR if its subject is found to demand discussion. It is not a receptacle for the less good books of the month, but for those which can be characterised briefly.

Life in the Middle Ages

Our picture of the middle ages, perhaps even more than that of other periods, has been falsified to suit our own prejudices. Sometimes the picture has been too black, sometimes too rosy. The eighteenth century, which had no doubt of itself, regarded mediæval times as merely barbarous; to Gibbon, the men of those days would have been our " rude forefathers." The reaction against the French Revolution produced the Romantic admiration of absurdity, based upon the experience that reason led to the guillotine. This engendered a glorification of the supposed " age of Chivalry," popularised among English-speaking people by Sir Walter Scott. The average boy or girl is probably still dominated by the Romantic view of the middle ages; he or she imagines a period when knights wore armour, carried lances, said " quotha " and " by my halidom," and were invariably either courteous or wrathful; when all ladies were beautiful and distressed, but were sure to be rescued at the end of the story. There is a third view, quite different, though, like the second, it admires the middle ages: this is the ecclesiastical view, engendered by dislike of the Reformation. The emphasis here is on piety orthodoxy, the scholastic philosophy, and the unification of Christendom by the Church. Like the Romantic view, it is a reaction against reason, but a less naïve reaction, cloaking itself in the forms of reason, appealing to a great system of thought which once dominated the world, and may dominate it again.

In all these views there are elements of truth : the middle ages were rude, they were knightly, they were pious. But if we wish to see a period truly we must not see it contrasted with our own, whether to its advantage or disadvantage: we must try to see it as it was to those who lived in it. Above all, we must remember that, in every epoch, most people are ordinary people, concerned with their daily bread rather than with the great themes of which historians treat. Such ordinary mortals are portrayed in a delightful book by Miss Eileen Power,* which ranges from the time of Charlemagne to that of Henry VII. The only eminent person in her gallery is Marco Polo ; the other five are more or less obscure individuals, whose lives are reconstructed by means of documents which happen to survive. Chivalry, which was an aristocratic affair, does not appear in these democratic annals ; piety is displayed by peasants and British merchants, but is much less in evidence in ecclesiastical circles ; and everybody is much less barbaric than the eighteenth century would have expected. There is, however, in favour of the " barbaric " view, one very striking contrast brought out in the book : the contrast between Venetian art just before the Renaissance, and Chinese art in the fourteenth century. Two pictures are reproduced: one a Venetian illustra-

* Mediæval People. Methuen, 6s.

tion of Marco Polo's embarkation, the other a Chinese fourteenth-century landscape by Chao Meng-fu. Miss Power says: "The one (that by Chao Meng-fu) is obviously the work of a highly-developed and the other of an almost naïve and childish civilisation." No one who compares the two can fail to agree with her.

Another recent book,* by Professor Huizinga of Leiden, gives an extraordinarily interesting picture of the fourteenth and fifteenth centuries in France and Flanders. In this book Chivalry receives its fair share of attention, not from the Romantic point of view, but as an elaborate game which the upper classes inven.ed to beguile the intolerable tedium of their lives. An essential part of Chivalry was the curious courtly conception of love as something which it was pleasant to leave unsatisfied. "When in the twelfth century unsatisfied desire was placed by the troubadours of Provence in the centre of the poetic conception of love, an important turn in the history of civilisation was effected. Courtly poetry . . . makes desire itself the essential *motif*, and so creates a conception of love with a negative ground-note." And again :

"The existence of an upper class whose intellectual and moral notions are enshrined in an *ars amandi* remains a rather exceptional fact in history. In no other epoch did the ideal of civilisation amalgamate to such a degree with that of love. Just as Scholasticism represents the grand effort of the mediæval spirit to unite all philosophic thought in a single centre, so the theory of courtly love, in a less elevated sphere, tends to embrace all that appertains to the noble life."

A great deal of the middle ages may be interpreted as a conflict between Roman and Germanic traditions : on the one side the Church, on the other the State ; on the one side theology and philosophy, on the other chivalry and poetry ; on the one side the law, on the other pleasure, passion, and all the anarchic impulses of very headstrong men. The Roman tradition was not that of the great days of Rome, it was that of Constantine and Justinian ; but even so it contained something which the turbulent nations needed, and without which civilisation could not have re-emerged from the dark ages. Because men were fierce, they could only be curbed by an awful severity ; terror was employed until it lost its effect through familiarity. After describing the Dance of Death, a favourite subject of late mediæval art, in which skeletons dance with living men, Dr. Huizinga proceeds to tell of the church-yard of the Innocents in Paris, where Villon's contemporaries promenaded for pleasure :

"Skulls and bones were heaped up in charnel-houses along the cloisters, enclosing the ground on three sides, and lay there open to the eye by thousands, preaching to all the lesson of equality. . . . Under the cloisters the death dance exhibited its images and its stanzas. No place was better suited to the simian figure of grinning death, dragging along pope and emperor,

*The Waning of the Middle Ages. Arnold, 16s.

monk and fool. The Duke of Berry, who wished to be buried there, had the history of the three dead and the three living men carved on the portal of the church. A century later this exhibition of funeral symbols was completed by a large statue of Death, now in the Louvre, and the only remnant of it all. Such was the place which the Parisians of the fifteenth century frequented as a sort of lugubrious counterpart of the Palais Royal of 1789. Day by day crowds of people walked under the cloisters, looking at the figures and reading the simple verses, which reminded them of the approaching end. In spite of the incessant burials and exhumations going on there, it was a public lounge and a *rendezvous*. Shops were established before the charnel houses, and prostitutes strolled under the cloisters. A female recluse was immured on one of the sides of the church. Friars came to preach, and processions were drawn up there. . . . Even feasts were given there. To such an extent had the horrible become familiar."

As might be expected from the love of the *macabre*, cruelty was one of the most highly prized pleasures of the populace. Mons purchased a brigand solely in order to see him tortured, " at which the people rejoiced more than if a new holy body had risen from the dead." In 1488 some of the magistrates of Bruges, suspected of treason, were repeatedly tortured in the market place for the delectation of the people. They begged to be killed, but the boon was refused, says Dr. Huizinga, " that the people may feast again upon their torments."

Perhaps, after all, there is something to be said for the eighteenth-century view.

Dr. Huizinga has some very interesting chapters on the art of the late middle ages. The exquisiteness of the painting was not equalled in architecture and sculpture, which became florid from the love of magnificence associated with feudal pomp. For example, when the Duke of Burgundy employed Sluter to make an elaborate Calvary at Champmol, the arms of Burgundy and Flanders appeared on the arms of the Cross. ·What is still more surprising is that the figure of Jeremiah. which formed part of the group had a pair of spectacles on its nose ! The author draws a pathetic picture of a great artist controlled by a Philistine patron, and then proceeds to demolish it by suggesting that perhaps " Sluter himself considered Jeremiah's spectacles a very happy find." Miss Power mentions an equally surprising fact : that in the thirteenth century an Italian Bowdler, outdoing Tennyson in Victorian refinement, published a version of the Arthurian legends which omitted all reference to the loves of Lancelot and Guinevere. History is full of queer things, for example, that a Japanese Jesuit was martyred at Moscow in the sixteenth century. I wish some erudite historian would write a book called " facts that have astonished me." In such a book Jeremiah's spectacles and the Italian Bowdler would certainly find a place.

BERTRAND RUSSELL.

Triple Biography

MEMOIRS OF THE FOREIGN LEGION. By M. M. With an Introduction by D. H. LAWRENCE. (Secker, 7s. 6d.)

D. H. LAWRENCE AND MAURICE MAGNUS. By NORMAN DOUGLAS. (Obtainable from the Author, c/o T. Cook and Son, Florence. 5s.)

Imagine that an operation is being performed on a body surrendered by the Morgue of Literature to the will of two eminent artists in surgery. The younger of these doctors is like Caméristus in *La Peau de Chagrin*, a specialist, a doctrinaire experimentalist —some say a dangerous crank ; the elder resembles Brisset, a brilliant practitioner of the old order, ambitious for cures rather than for science, sceptical of panaceas and famous for the success of his *ad hoc* methods. Add two personal complications : the elder doctor discovers that the corpse is known to him, a former friend, and becomes antipathetic to the horrid designs his colleague intends against it ; and the latter alienates him still further from the business by consecrating his scalpel, with distasteful rhetoric, to the unprofessional quest of a " dark god " in the blood of the victim or of the philosopher's stone in the bladder. Imagine the deed done and the subsequent quarrel between the participants, their public controversy on general questions arising from the case, and the revelation of varying taste and temperament in the opinions expressed.

These events would form a rough parallel to the situation which has been brought about by the publication of *Memoirs of the Foreign Legion*, and of Mr. Douglas's pamphlet of protest against the biographical Introduction contributed thereto by Mr. Lawrence. They were both acquainted with Maurice Magnus, the author of the *Memoirs*, during the years of his life in Italy which led up to his suicide in 1920. Magnus seems to have been a fairly typical American *déclassé* idealist straying about the Continent—a sociable, mild-natured adventurer, romantically responsive to the ancient, the royal, the papal, but incapable of preserving *himself* in the naturalistic struggles of the real Old World. This, at any rate, is the impression one gets from his own pages, and there is nothing in either Mr. Lawrence's or Mr. Douglas's account that conflicts radically with such a general estimate of Magnus. The elementary pencilled outline, the factual vision of the outward eye, takes a similar shape in both portraits ; it is in the disposition of colours, the laying on of the pigment, the finalising wrest into form, that the differences are manifested. The criticism of conduct is an exact science only for those who interpret it according to the Absolute of a dogmatic religion, or the fictitious Absolute of Law, and our writers adopt neither of these criteria in their judgments of Magnus's character, or of his petty larcenies. Human personality is a puzzle of Yale locks, and the common-denominator key is kept unused in the safe of the ingenious manufacturer. Perhaps it has been thrown away in a fit of divine anger or mathematical despair. But none of our kind has found it ; and, though hope is illimitable, endeavour is restricted to a contemplation of the mechanism's intricate navel.

Here, then, we have Mr. Lawrence, the novelist, giving a hundred-page biography of his reactions to the personality of Maurice Magnus, and Mr. Douglas, the novelist, being moved to write a protest against Mr. Lawrence's particular narrative and the general method of which it is an example. Magnus's own narrative is worth reading for its description of a famously brutal institution. But the main interest of the tripartite affair is its disclosure, more generalised in Mr. Douglas's pages, of the attitude to human personality of two important writers : their attitude to Magnus, to one another, to themselves, and to the general principles arising from the occasion. It would take a treatise to extricate the matter with any thoroughness ; all that can be done here is to sketch a few points of difference and show up the odder contrasts.

Mr. Lawrence, from the beginning, surrounds his subject with a mass of vivid and suggestive detail, and he does it with an overt passion which we are inclined to attribute to the effort of creation until we remind ourselves that it must be the effort of remembrance. It was Mr. Douglas, " decidedly shabby and a gentleman, with his wicked red face and tufted eyebrows "—it was Mr. Douglas who, one day in Florence, introduced him to Magnus, who makes his first appearance as " a man of about forty, spruce and youngish in his deportment, very pink-faced, and very clean, very natty, very alert, like a sparrow painted to resemble a tom-tit." There is already a hint of instinctive dislike in the language, but the novelist in Mr. Lawrence sets up a reflex action, for " he was just the kind of man I had never met ; little sharp man of the shabby world, very much on the spot, don't you know." From thence-forward, as Mr. Lawrence's relations with Magnus grow more complicated, his observation sharpens, his outspokenness increases, and his *tone* reflects with delightful sensitiveness the state of his *feelings*, which reach a crescendo in the great borrowing scene. It was an embarrassing moment.

> " And again he put his hand on my arm, and the tears began to fall from his upturned eyes. I turned my head aside. Never had the Ionian Sea looked so sickening to me.
> ' I don't want to,' said I."

But, " with bowels full of bitterness," he was drawn deeper into the financial worries which culminated in the suicide of the borrower. This event is the signal for Mr. Lawrence's final change of tone, the notable discord of his Introduction. Like an enthusiastic hunter with his Reynard, our biographer moralises over the kill. " I could, by giving half my money, have saved his life. I had chosen not to save his life. Now, after a year has gone by, I keep to my choice. . . . No, I would not help to keep him alive, not if I had to choose again. . . . He shall and should die, and so should all his sort ; and so they will." And the funeral sermon fades into an hysterical outburst against the War. Mr. Lawrence's mind is a very Gothic edifice, haphazard with saints and gargoyles. His transitional moral consciousness is continuously rich in the creations of an antithetical fancy. It makes melodrama of his vision of mankind—a species of melodrama which, in the intuitive portions of his work, is of a legitimate and thrilling order, for then the extremism of action is transferred to a level on which the events are the symbols of mental life, and enjoy a scope more plausibly independent than external happenings, of the curtailments of space and time. But Mr. Lawrence's introspective intelligence is too feeble to balance this melodramatic fancy in activities which cater for a free play of mind ; and so, since criticism begins at home, his latter-day garment of philosopher and preacher is shot through with the vulgarity of aggressive self-ignorance. And yet, in this Introduction, he has built up for us an unforgettably real figure of a man. He has achieved this by mixed means ; by keeping his eye unremittingly on the object, while grappling with it in a sort of nervous abandonment. Biographical dignity is scrapped : the recording instrument, like a Robot, shudders into humanity and advances towards the stimulating body in a torment of new experience. It is not the usual biographical instrument, a separator with a private leak. It is a revolutionary organism, whose philosophic justification, if it can offer one, is that it substitutes the aim of " reality " for the aim of " truth," and replaces the superficial definitions of formal justice by the autocratic charity of intensive speculation—the gift, whether beneficial to the subject or not, of the author's imaginative partnership.

Mr. Douglas has another name for the distinguishing quality of this new form ; he calls it " the novelist's touch in biography."

"What is this touch ? It consists, I should say, in a failure to realise the profundities and complexities of the ordinary human mind ; it selects for literary purposes two or three facets of a man or woman, generally the most spectacular, and therefore " useful " ingredients of their character, and disregards all the others. . . . The facts may be correct, but there are too few of them ; what the author says may be true, and yet by no means the truth. That is the novelist's touch. It falsifies life."

And he proceeds to enumerate several instances where, in his opinion, Mr. Lawrence has falsified the life of Maurice Magnus. The anecdotes are supported with good reason and tolerance ; we feel that they are a true representation of Magnus ; what we cannot admit is that, except in one or two matters of fact, they destroy the

THE CALENDAR

validity and value of Mr. Lawrence's representation. The structure
of controversy demands positive outlines, but the outlines of Magnus
himself in Mr. Douglas's sketch merge like a complementary
phantom with those of Mr. Lawrence's portrait. This seems to
be due to the fact that both writers present their memories frankly
and with practised clarity. Thus, if the self-deceptive spirit of
Mr. Lawrence's last pages of general comment had governed his
particular narrative ; or if Mr. Douglas had dropped his difficult
sense of humaneness for the fun of idealising ; or if either of them had
emended the *Memoirs* in some integral part of its author's self-
expression, our image of Magnus would be disturbed. As it is,
it would be futile to try and fix one's realisation of him in a number
of generalisations, for such judgments would have to be impossibly
refined not to violate that "uncommunicability" which the
scholastic philosophers considered to be the essential quality of
personality. Through Mr. Douglas's description of Magnus, as
through Mr. Lawrence's, we watch principally the display of his
own faculties and temperament, thrust forward and expanding,
like the head of a snail manœuvring an unexpected stone, in the
curiosity to discover his man in words. Mr. Douglas's "pagan"
lack of nostalgias, that unclouded relish for the inconsistencies of
life which is the explanation of his almost pedantically continuous
humour, the unworried conventional ethic which gives a dilettante
leisure to his exploration of eccentricities ; such personal intimations
rise up and hang like a qualifying mist over the intention of his
narrative. And yet there, beneath the mist, is the outline of
Magnus, untraceable by definition—the same outline that we
realise, under different atmospherics, in the other two narratives.
"Uncommunicability" has been overcome in the only possible way ;
it is Art, founded on the unity in perception, which presents this
object in its singularity. For the *Memoirs*, a primitive document
of formless experience, are the rough material of art ; Mr. Lawrence's
Introduction is art in all its deliberation ; and Mr. Douglas, though
his artist's course is queered by the necessities of controversy, takes
his share in the miracle of this trinity by virtue of the powers of
apprehension which make him an artist.

BERTRAM HIGGINS.

THE THIRTEENTH CÆSAR. By SACHEVERELL SITWELL.
(Grant Richards, 6s.).

Mr. Sacheverell Sitwell is a poet with a very specialized and
consistent vision, and his strange technique is beginning to fit
the body of his poems with an easier individuality and more habitual
grace. His art is as purely decorative as poetry can be ; the poet
seems to be urging his mood towards a second childhood of perception, where words are stripped of their ideal fungus and disclosed
as sensuous and limited objects among the vegetation of experience.

78

> Each of these branches is a ghost I've slain,
> It's rind breathes soft to me, its warm throat sings;
> I have snared these shadow-prisoners,
> Like sun among the branches
> Where the ripe fruit fall;
> I have climbed to the tree's core, plucking them;
> The glass world of metaphor, the wood of metamorphosis,
> Die like a ghost's breath on the leaves.

The last age was one in which the common messages of the senses had become chaotic and colourless; ours is more particularly a period of idea-dissociation, and we have reached a stage at which the desire for a restoration of the primitive functions of mind has revived one half of the energies necessary for a great creative efflorescence. Mr. Sitwell's poetry, therefore, is both characteristic and timely. He is intent on delineating a fresh visual environment for his mind. The effort is sometimes made painfully, with a seriousness too self-wrapt (as in " The Wind as Husbandman "), for his scrutiny is of a scene whose shape is as fickle as water. The consciousness receding from concepts is like a drunken man's; whenever it steadies itself the world reels. This explains the disconcerting speed and apparent wantonness with which objects melt and merge in these poems : we are travelling in an express train through a wide sunny country, and we gaze out of the window at haystacks becoming houses becoming cattle becoming people becoming air; and when night extinguishes the landscape the chain of images is continued in fancy. The unities which give equilibrium to this flux of Nature—this multiplication and refining of pictures—are Nature's own elements; Mr. Sitwell, in his need for " machinery," goes back past the figures of myth to Air, Earth, Fire and Water, of which we ourselves are the tutelary deities.

> If we order every star, the tides,
> And own all the treasure, what have we to fear ?
> God cannot speak to us from off a cloud,
> No longer is He manifest in thunder or the storm ;
> We can hit back at him and keep him far.
> Space becomes a lawn for all the dancing stars. . . .

Such an art, though inexhaustible in subject-matter, is restricted in its range of poetic appeal. It is noticeable that when Mr. Sitwell attempts to change his tone to the dramatic, satirical or elegiac, an unpleasant naivety takes hold of the versification, or an Influence discloses himself through the lines to distract their purpose— Browning in " In a Wine Shop," M. Jean de Bosschère in " On Hearing Four Bands Play at Once in a Public Square," and models as distant but unmistakeable as *Beowulf* and *The Complaint of Deor* in the elegiac passage of " The Poet and the Mirror." And, as a point of form, a comparison between the general effects of " The Venus of Bolsover Castle " and " Bolsover Castle," two of the most beautiful poems in this volume, the first in a strict, the second in a free measure, makes one hope that Mr. Sitwell will not cease to cultivate that side of his poetic personality which seeks a discipline against unmindful obscurity and diffuseness.

B. H.

———

CHARLES BAUDELAIRE, translated by ARTHUR SYMONS. The Casanova Society. 30s.

From the preface to this book we learn that Mr. Symons considers *Les Paradis Artificiels* to be " the most wonderful book Baudelaire ever wrote," and the tribute he pays to it is that, in translating it, he gives an adequate reproduction of the original. Of the two other works here translated so much cannot be said ; they are, in fact, astonishingly bad. Speaking of the *Petits Poèmes en Prose*, he says : " I have tried to be absolutely faithful to the sense, the words and the rhythm." The extent to which he has succeeded will be best appreciated from a few quotations.

No. X. " *Pendant quelques heures*," he translates " during some hours "—this is a gallicism.

No. XI. A man apostrophising " *sa petite maîtresse* " is made to say, " Let us consider carefully, I beg of you " !

No. XVII, for " *Laisse-moi* . . . . *les [cheveux] agiter avec ma main comme un mouchoir odorant*," he gives " Let me agitate thy tresses with my hand like an odorous handkerchief." This may be " in prose," but it is hardly part of a " little poem."

In attempting to translate *Les Fleurs du Mal*, Mr. Symons set himself a still harder task, for not only does he translate them, but he puts them into verse, forgetting, perhaps, that Baudelaire had written : " mais le mal serait encore plus grand dans une singerie rimée." Without discussing the intrinsic merits of Mr. Symons's verse, I would say emphatically that his translation is an unpardonable travesty of Baudelaire's poetry. What right has he to render :

" *Nous volons au passage un plaisir clandestin
Que nous pressons bien fort, comme une vieille orange*,"
by
" We steal our pleasures inside a Brothel's door,
Insidious as the orange-skin one touches." ?

Why, in a poem beginning " *Ce beaux matin d'été si doux*," should he translate

" *Et le ciel regardait la carcasse superbe comme une fleur s'épanouir*,'
by
" This superb carcass was not even blinking under the aching moon " ?

There is scarcely a single poem which is not marred by some such unpardonable licence.

D. M. G.

THE SISTERS' TRAGEDY, and Three Other Plays. By RICHARD HUGHES (Heinemann, 6s.).

IN spite of the title of this volume, the most important play it contains is *A Comedy of Good and Evil*, which was performed at the Royal Court Theatre on July 6, 1924, under the auspices of the Three Hundred Club. It had a mixed, and, on the whole, an unfavourable reception. From the common standpoint it was even a failure. This was not due to any fault in the production. For although the Three Hundred Club is handicapped for want of money ; does not pay its actors, and cannot, therefore, exercise the necessary discrimination in selecting the casts for the plays it produces ; does not, perhaps, sufficiently realise the serious responsibility it undertakes when it puts before the public the work of young authors whose future it may endanger ; yet, on this occasion, the production, if imperfect, was in essentials adequate—owing chiefly to the good work of the producer, Mr. A. E. Filmer, the remarkable performance of Miss Louise Hampton as Minnie, and Mr. Leslie Banks's fine acting as Minnie's husband, Mr. Williams.

The cause of the play's comparative failure lay in the audience, which is a select one characterised by its high standard of education rather than by any gifts of intelligence or imagination. Mr. Hughes' play deals with the theme of good and evil, and bears on its title page an appropriate quotation from *Lao Tse :* " For one must always be careful of distinctions." It may be admitted at once that as an intellectual contribution to the subtle theme of " good and evil," Mr. Hughes's play is not important ; but, on the other hand, it is quite sound intellectually, for if it contributes nothing new, it does not travesty the intelligence—the real intelligence of the age. Of how many plays can one say that ? Of very few indeed ! Where Mr. Hughes's play excels is in the dramatic representation of his theme. The play is of absorbing interest. It holds the spectator from the rise to the fall of the curtain. It is at turns thrilling, poignant and comic. It progresses smoothly from one phase to another. At moments it is almost intolerably exciting. It combines a most adroit and successful handling of the supernatural with a realistic study of Welsh rural life that is absolutely convincing. Nobody with any sense of the theatre could see this play without realising that here was an author with an innate dramatic sense, for this play is full of dramatic inventions—inventions that escape the reader, but delight the spectator. The most remarkable of these is Minnie's artificial leg. The effectiveness of this on the stage has to be seen to be believed, but in itself it stamps Mr. Hughes as a dramatist.

A Comedy of Good and Evil is a remarkable play for a young man of twenty-four to have written, and the other plays in this volume are enough to confirm one's belief that in Mr. Richard Hughes the English theatre is likely to possess a considerable dramatist. Unfortunately, it is not easy to see how Mr. Hughes

is to obtain employment as a dramatist. He, like all our other
young English dramatists, is at the mercy of a convention-ridden
commercial organisation which controls the mechanism of the
theatre. No ordinary West-end management would even dream of
putting on *A Comedy of Good and Evil*, and it is probable that if
it were put on as an isolated production it would fail ; but if Mr.
Hughes and his contemporaries can go on writing plays there will
come a time when some enterprising buccaneer of imagination, some
Diaghlieff of the drama, will raise the necessary capital, take a
theatre, and give a twelve months' season of special plays produced
with the greatest possible perfection, and then Mr. Hughes and our
young English dramatists will come into their own, as Mr. Bernard
Shaw did when Mr. H. Granville-Barker gave his celebrated Court
Theatre season many years ago.   W. J. TURNER.

NOVELS.

THOSE BARREN LEAVES. By ALDOUS HUXLEY. (Chatto
and Windus. 7s. 6d. net.)

When a conjuror produces pigeons from his hat, the success of
the trick depends chiefly on his legerdemain, the animation of the
birds, and their number ; a single pigeon would not surprise, a
dead one would not convince. In *Antic Hay*, Mr. Huxley showed
himself to be a master-conjuror. There, with inimitable virtuosity,
he produced half a dozen characters, all of whom lived with that
degree of restricted, self-conscious animation that one expects of
the best pigeons in the hands of the best conjurors. Occasionally
he sneered at the birds, but for the most part he watched their
sophisticated flight with a smiling, satirical urbanity. Emily
and Gumbril, however, were signs that he was becoming bored
with his own skill, and bored by the pigeons. Their introduction
suggested that the complacent smile with which he faced his audience
was growing wearisome, that he was beginning to distrust it. In
Those Barren Leaves his dissatisfaction is more patent.

Like Chelifer, Mr. Huxley has long been aware of his undeniable
talent for writing, but not content to forward journalistically the
propagation of rabbits, he has used it as Cardan might have done,
to investigate the artificialities and insincerities of life. He has
never been completely anomphaloskeptic, it is true, but in
Those Barren Leaves he considers more reverently and at greater
length than before the possible validity of a transcendental point
of view. It was as though, until now, he had been urged by a
precocity of experience towards an immature scepticism. His
self-consciousness, instead of being confined to the consideration
of his technique, seemed to have vitiated his outlook, and to have
impaired the spontaneity of his inspiration, so that he was left
with a highly-developed means of expression that he was fearful
of using lest he should betray a naïvety which he was accustomed

to mock. This dilemma he tried to solve by attributing his own doubts to all intellectual people, and satirising in them the scepticism which etiolated his own emotions and passions. The result was that he was forced to choose his characters from amongst the artistic and high-brow, and so he wrote *Chrome Yellow* and, more perfectly, *Antic Hay*.

In this latter book the majority of the characters are entertaining, but they have no reality ; without the vitality of Mr. Huxley's wit and cynicism they would collapse like sawdust dummies. Thus, since there is no other standard of life than their own by which to judge them, the satire lacks trenchancy. Emily's part in the story is slight, and Lypiatt, the transcendental artist, is laughed—at times, it is true, with regret—from the stage. When Mr. Huxley wishes to advance a theory of life other than cynical, he protects himself by expressing it through a character who is potentially risible, so that he himself may, if he wishes, escape the responsibility for it.

In *Those Barren Leaves* the tone of the satire is changed, for it is no longer the criticism of a cynic, but of a creative mind. Cardan, it is true, might have come in any of his other books, and Chelifer, Mrs. Aldwinkle and Mary Thriplow are only modifications of former characters, but Calamy represents a new point of view. For the first time in Mr. Huxley's work here is a character who, not content with a sceptical or hedonistic attitude to life, is yet, nevertheless, sanctioned by the fact that he is neither mocked nor condemned. There have been others who felt this same discontent, but they have either been unimportant or ultimately defeated. Calamy, however, is left at the end of the book to contemplate in solitude the problems of existence, and, though he is by no means triumphant, he feels " somehow reassured." It is, perhaps, unfortunate that his character is not more fully developed, for he is important as being the most humanly animated of any of the personalities yet attempted by Mr. Huxley, but the influence of his presence is felt throughout the book, adding to the other characterisation a truer sensibility. Whenever he appears, one is struck by his aloofness from the glib males and insipid females by whom Mrs. Aldwinkle is surrounded, and in the last chapter it is Calamy who, though more perplexed than his two companions, stands out most boldly. He still occasionally laughs at his own aspirations, but he does not sneer at his own earnestness when he says, " I'd like to find some more serious occupation " (than those followed by his associates), and, what is more important, Mr. Huxley shows his sympathy for the man he has created. He is no longer shamefaced at producing a character who thinks that " one might be able to burrow one's way right through the mystery and really get at something—some kind of truth, some explanation."

It is obvious that this review is not an attempt to directly criticise *Those Barren Leaves*, but rather to indicate the tendency

THE CALENDAR

of Mr. Huxley's mind as revealed by his work ; for it is chiefly in as much as it does this that his latest book is interesting. Intrinsically it shows little advance on *Antic Hay :* the language, descriptive power and wit of the former are common to both, the plot is less adroitly handled, and, with one exception, the characterisation is not improved. If, however, one is right in concluding from this exception—and from other hints less obvious—that Mr. Huxley is writing from a richer and better assimilated experience of life, then *Those Barren Leaves* is important. One would be justified in expecting from him a great book ; for up till now he has only written what is brilliant, witty, learned, but of the second or non-creative order.

SERENA BLANDISH, or THE DIFFICULTY OF GETTING MARRIED. By A LADY OF QUALITY (Heinemann, 7s. 6d. net).

In an age when the majority of writers are tiresomely eager to deliver their " message," or to lament with a cynical and confidential sophistication that they have none to announce, it is pleasing to find a Lady of Quality who is too well-bred to regret what she has not, or to dissemble what she has. *Serena Blandish* is a witty and improbable tale, nothing more or less. It is good because it is well written, and because, aiming at no very high achievement, it reaches its mark.

Serena's ingenuous candour is enlivened by her dispassionate contemplation of her lost virginity. In her moments of calmness she listens to the voice of experience warning her that " the poison in her eyes dissolved resolution and honour in men " without obtaining for her an honourable proposal of marriage, but in the presence of a suitor she is too kind-hearted to deny, too generous to demand payment. She occasionally sobs, but the remembrance of her beauty is always sufficient to console her. Even when she is awakened in the middle of her first night in the Countess Flor di Folio's house by the butler's assuring her that he had not come to ruin her, she is not at a loss. Though hardly awake, she replies without perturbation, " I am ruined already." One is glad that in the end she marries a Count, and one's pleasure is not diminished at discovering that he is " the illegitimate son of a Portuguese negress, by her first lover, a Frenchman," for by that time Serena is as cynically temperate in her views as the Lady of Quality. She is a tragic figure, but her reflections on life are so apt and unusual that one does not pity her, and the pert naïvety of her repartee disarms sympathy. In her many encounters with men she is often menaced, but never in danger ; she realises that she cannot lose what she no longer possesses.

84

COMMENTS AND REVIEWS

THE CONSTANT NYMPH. By MARGARET KENNEDY. (Heine-mann, 7s. 6d. net.)

It is not surprising that *The Constant Nymph* should have been so well received by the critics, nor that their acclamation should have been somewhat exaggerated, for within the circumscription of its kind it is undoubtedly a good book. There has, however, been a tendency to mistake the kind, and to overrate its possibilities. Since criticism is continually hampered by its inability to use absolute terms of approbation or condemnation, it is obliged to fall back on the unscientific method of subdivision in order to give a more definite meaning to the words good and bad. So, in this case, one must further qualify *The Constant Nymph* by saying that it is a good *melodramatic* novel, and by adding—perhaps arbitrarily—that if this opinion is correct, the word great is not applicable to it.

The idea which in both her books Miss Kennedy has chiefly considered, is that the differences apparent in the behaviour of the artist and the non-artist are the phenomena of a difference in their essence. Scientific psychology has shown that this idea is fallacious ; Miss Kennedy has shown that it is a fertile source of plots. The shadow of Sanger, and Dodd in the flesh, represent the vital, untameable spirit of art struggling against philistinism and the limitations of existence, and in this lies the weakness of the book. Real feeling is not there, for neither Dodd nor Sanger struggles, but only an idea, a conception, so vague as to be meaningless. Had Dodd been identified with this idea, or had the idea been made concrete, then a problem would have been posed out of which great tragedy might have sprung, for all tragedy is founded on the incompatibility of two ideas, two facts, or a fact and an idea. When either of these is not completely convincing, the tragedy becomes melodramatic, and that is what has happened here. Every incident important to the main story is caused by Dodd's part in it, and he is only convincing if one regards his music as having the significance which he and Miss Kennedy give it. To do this it is not sufficient to assume that the artistic function is an important and engrossing one ; one must be made to believe that it is so in this specific case. But the book has not that effect. It is not sufficient to know that Dodd's conducting was impressive, that his talent was unrecognised and revolutionary, that he was passionate, amoral, callous to anyone's feelings but his own, and irregular in his habits. These are the conventional, ready-made attributes of the artist which could be taken from dozens of second-rate novels ; unless they are made circumstantial they are mere extravaganza.

Where Miss Kennedy has eminently succeeded is in the manipulation of an engrossing and intricate plot, and in the drawing of the minor characters, of whom more than one are amplifications of those in her first novel, *The Ladies of Lyndon*. There is a marked improvement in her style, and the use she makes of language, and the dialogue is less diffuse in *The Constant Nymph* than in its predecessor. Teresa and Florence are both flesh and blood figures. The poignancy of their tragedies is real, for though Dodd himself does not convince, their belief in him and what he stands for is living and cogent. D. M. G.

LIFE OF JAMES ELROY FLECKER. By GERALDINE HODGSON, D.Litt. Blackwell. 12s. 6d.

THE ordinary biographer, as we know him, is an Old Man of the Sea straddling a victim whose stature scarcely exceeds his own ; the commonplace mind is presented with slow-motion by double-exposure photography.

Minor politicians are written up by still more minor politicians, industrial magnates by advertisenemt managers, actresses by salaried husbands, philanthropists by sentimentalists, sporting peers by journalistic touts, exiled princesses by unemployed courtiers, private prodigies by adoring mothers, and God—season after season—by epileptics and rationalists. Biography has become the most formless of forms, outraging literary canons far more importantly than those of taste. The only thing to do about the mass of such books is to class them as sociological phenomena and admit that they add to the fun of life.

Sometimes, however, the subject suffers so badly from the prepossessions or insufficient equipment of the writer that a protest becomes due. James Elroy Flecker, for instance, needs an intelligent biographer : a decade after his death the need becomes vital, for that is the first great testing-period for the reputations of poets. Dr. Geraldine Hodgson's Life is sentimental and prudish in its interpretation of Flecker's personality, conceited and irrelevant in its treatment of his poetry. She is at great pains to exonerate Flecker from charges of " idleness, unpracticalness, untidiness," and of " rioting in the fantastic " (!), and fills half her space with banal details of his unexceptional boyhood. The two most interesting events in his life—his broken engagement and his life in the East— are described scantily, hastily and with camouflage. As for his poetry, Dr. Hodgson considers it to be " not only singular in his generation but in our Literature," and makes that belief an excuse for a stale dissertation on a number of modern French poets, whose affinities with Flecker are less demonstrated than taken for granted. No English poet was ever quite " singular in our Literature " ; certainly Flecker was not ; and it is the business of his critics to give him a name and place in our own tradition. Dr. Hodgson's evaluation leaves him the bastard of two cultures.

B. H.

Among New Books

GRACE AFTER MEAT. By JOHN CROWE RANSOM. Hogarth Press, 4s. 6d.

In Mr. Ransom Mr. Robert Graves has discovered, for England, one of the most accomplished and promising American poets. It is, perhaps, more depressing than surprising that work of such quality, produced over a number of years, should have met with small recognition ; this poetry is rooted too truly in tradition to make a lightning appeal to the gang of literary sensationalists, too serious in originality to endear itself to the wider audience of literary sentimentalists. Certain strands in these poems connect up with the " cerebral " style of Mr. T. S. Eliot, and the astute silver-age pastorals of Mr. Robert Frost, but Mr. Ransom is a poet of deeper reserves than Mr. Eliot, and of wider range than Mr. Frost. We hope that this twenty-poem volume will soon be followed by a larger selection.

POEMS OF THIRTY YEARS. By GORDON BOTTOMLEY. Constable. 21s.

Mr. Bottomley's poetry is among the most original produced by the Edwardian generation. He was aware of a transition in poetic technique, and his attempt to harmonise conflicting elements of rhythm and idiom requires a close examination.

A FOOL I' THE FOREST : A PHANTASMAGORIA By RICHARD ALDINGTON. Allen & Unwin. 5s.

A very vigorous expression of the disorder and unease of the modern mind, in which imaginative gaiety has been killed by savage experiences and the intellect discredited by its naïve credulity towards scientific mumbo-jumbo. Mr. Aldington makes his free-verse a trenchant instrument for satire, but it is hardly organised sufficiently to express the loss of harmony poetically.

THREE FURTHER PLAYS BY LUIGI PIRANDELLO. Translated from the Italian by DR. ARTHUR LIVINGSTON. Dent. 10s. 6d.

By this time the work of Pirandello should need no bush. The three plays are called *Each in His Own Way*, *The Pleasure of Honesty* and *Naked*.

HARVEST IN POLAND. By GEOFFREY DENNIS. Heinemann. 7s. 6d.

Much of Mr. Dennis's creative force is dissipated by the incoherence of his plot ; the incidents at Oxford and in Paris are an uneconomical use of material, which prolongs the story without giving it consistency. That part of the action which takes place in Poland would have gained much in power if the characters of Weronika, Karol and Emile had been better exploited—the leaven of their " sanity " would have thrown into relief the hysteria of the others. As it is, the tension is too great ; an effect in no way relieved by Mr. Dennis's style, which is bad baroque, with coarse and damaged carving. When, however, he is writing of diabolism or the effects of intuitive terror, he is at times surprisingly convincing, though his " chatty " familiarity with the Principles of Good and Evil is often distasteful.

THE LITTLE KAROO. By PAULINE SMITH. Jonathan Cape. 4s. 6d.

Within the limited range of experience of which she writes, Miss Smith shows profound emotional power and a sense of clear representation. Each story stands firmly on its own legs and each character is an individual conception, and this in spite of a common setting and a single method of treatment. The dignity of her prose—undoubtedly influenced by the Bible—saves the sentiment from that mawkishness to which it tends ; the atmosphere is well sustained. It is a simple book, but shows great promise.

THE CALENDAR

MR. TASKER'S GODS. By T. F. Powys. Chatto and Windus. 7s. 6d.

Mr. Powys knows life in the country, and his village setting is admirably done, but his portraits of the inhabitants are discoloured by his preoccupation with the squalid and vicious side of their lives. Mr. Tasker is a dairyman who worships his swine, buys a vicious dog in the hope that it will kill his tramp father, and wakes his daughter by throwing her across the room. Almost all the other characters are similarly actuated by lust or greed or cruelty, the exceptions by loving-kindness. Mr. Powys allows them no middle course, so that their future actions are too easily foreseen and one soon wearies of his distorted point of view.

THE LONDON SPY. By Ned Ward. The Casanova Society. 25s.

A reprint, very well produced, of a journalistic enterprise which has survived because it gives a most vivid picture of the social life of London at the end of the seventeenth century. It stands between the pamphlets of Green and Dekker, on the one hand, and, among later offspring, the " Tom and Jerry " of Pierce Egan. It is not a book for the queasy reader ; Ward had a turn of mind for bawdy humour. He is rather like a plebian Petronius ; his vigour, though nothing else, allows the comparison. His style is an interesting specimen of debased exuberance, though it has infinitely more real literary virtue than most respectable modern journalism.

OLD PINK 'UN DAYS. By J. B. Booth. Grant Richards. 21s.

As a document, this book has a similar value to *The London Spy*, though it will not last so long, for it has less personality and frankness, and less power of expression. It does not evoke the " Bohemian gaiety " of the late Victorian period with the forcefulness with which Ward suggests the squalid vitality of his London. The staff of *The Sporting Times*, to which Mr. Booth belonged, was in touch with everybody and everything that mattered in the world of pleasure—the Stage, the Turf and the Ring.

THE THREAD OF ARIADNE. By Adrian Stokes. Kegan Paul. 6s.

The relativity of truth (even the relativity of that statement) is the theme of Mr. Stokes's divagation. It opens splendidly and is in parts extremely interesting, especially in those parts where he describes the experiences, mental and physical, which came to him on his journey round the world. His attempt to destroy the validity of concepts with conceptual weapons is necessarily tiresome. This is a first book ; we shall see in his next book whether Mr. Stokes realises the importance of his own statement—" as I am fighting your thoughts and words, I need Art."

JOHN KEATS : LIFE AND LETTERS. By Amy Lowell. Jonathan Cape. (2 vols.) 42s.

PRINCIPLES OF LITERARY CRITICISM. By I. A. Richards. Kegan Paul. 10s. 6d.

A remarkable synthetic effort ; Mr. Richards dissociates all the familiar ideas of aesthetic values. He lays down a track which he thinks will lead to a firmer basis for the appraisement of values. A book which will be referred to again.

The CALENDAR
of Modern Letters

VOLUME I
NUMBER 2

APRIL
1925

The Dithyrambic Spectator.
An Essay on the Origins and Survivals of Art.
By WYNDHAM LEWIS.
INTRODUCTION.

IF, in response to an immediate need, some industry requiring great skill comes into existence ; and if the need is then removed, and the industry languishes, there is mostly no excuse for perpetuating the craft, however elaborately that has been developed in the process of meeting this vital demand. Most of the fine Arts are to-day in that position ; only with the difference that their exercise is in itself so enjoyable that their various techniques, it is felt, should be perpetuated *for their own sake.* That is what was realised by the " Æsthete " of the Nineties, who coined the expression *ART for ART'S sake.* The arts had then for a century been in competition with industry, and it had come to be generally recognised that they could not survive, except as a group of privileged activities dissociated from the needs of life, which they no longer met so satisfactorily as many of the industries that had substituted mechanical process for manual dexterity and emotional formulæ. But these ancient and superseded industries were still superstitiously entrenched in men's conceit about their *Civilisation* (their way of referring to the exceptional activities of a handful of their kind, whose efforts their malice delights to embarrass, but the results of which efforts they appropriate) and the devolution of these practically obsolete technical traditions was still in the hands of a specially-trained professional class.

As, however, we recede from the time when these arts were the only substitutes for nature—before machinery went straight to nature and eliminated the middleman, Man—the position of this " professional " nucleus becomes more and more precarious. In the great readjustment in the sensibility of the world which is in progress there are very powerful factors whose instincts will hardly allow the survival of this purely orna-mental human fringe of " professional " *playing*. The human conceit that made it possible for this small privileged guild of specialists to claim the protection of " Civilisation " has received many rebuffs. The scandal of man's " Origins " was the first ; and the scandal of the recent gigantic war is the last scandal, from which it is doubtful if the fair name of " Civilisa-tion " will ever recover. The course that has been taken is not " to live it down," but rather to " brazen it out." " Civilisa-tion " having become brazen in her new role of Whore of Babylon, she has a malignant squint for her traditional retainers and wears her high-brow ornaments with an unconcealed impatience. When she was a Madonna and claimed her descent from Simon Magus, she was the friend of every art. But as a tart she has her living to make ; as she ages she becomes more practical.

The Fine Arts to-day survive on the same basis (or that will soon be the case) as the Art of the hunter or *Sportsman*. Hunting, the supreme art and business of primitive life, sur-vived in our civilisation as the most delightful pastime and a coveted privilege. So the fine arts, corresponding to no present need that a variety of industries cannot answer more effectively, the last survivals of the *hand* against the *machine*, but beaten by the machine in every contest involving a practical issue, must, if they survive at all, survive as a sport and the privilege of the wealthy, negligently indulged in, and not any longer as an object of serious devotion. The sport of hunting either large or small game is the symbol of an idle and strictly useless life ; and to-day the fox-hunter and the painter or poet are in the same category. All that is necessary is for the fox-hunter to take to painting pictures and writing verse and the close association of these two occupations in the public mind will be effected.

Had the primitive hunter been presented suddenly with machine-guns, with which he could mow down his game in droves, he would not have troubled to practise his lonely and difficult art any more. Similarly, had the Peruvian potters been accommodated with the resources of a Staffordshire factory for producing pots, they would have immediately abandoned their archaic wheel. Since men in the aggregate, however, are made by their occupation, both the potter and the hunter would deteriorate, become parasitic on their machines, and on the engineer and inventor. But in neither case would that appear to them as a consideration of an order to appeal to a man or woman of the world.

A business that survives as a sport does so only when it has some pleasure-value or vanity-value. Shooting or trapping other animals has these values ; and also the pictorial representation of objects, the composing of music and performing on musical instruments, singing, literary composition, verbal dexterity, and so forth. In future probably what are now still "artists" by profession (for there are still people who on identity cards describe themselves in that way) will form a class similar to that of gamekeepers, huntsmen, horse trainers, sculptors' ghosts, and printers' devils. They will be the people who will keep the game, but not shoot at it, rear the horse, but not ride it. The actual act of art (whereby a picture is finally produced with delight, or a song sung with unction) will become of the same character as the laying of a foundation-stone, or rather the ceremonious fixing of the last tile on the roof, or the driving of the last rivet in the ship. It will be performed "while you are dressing for dinner." There will have to be, in short, a class of experts in the various arts, non-performers themselves (for there must be no professional competition) to coach and encourage with flattering remarks the wealthy performers. The pleasure-value of such performance will probably be regarded as considerable enough to make it worth while to preserve it. But its money-value (in the sense of its value to the man doing it, its value as an expensive pastime, not, of course, the value of what is produced, which will eventually be openly admitted to be zero) will also assure it the status of an exclusively privileged pastime. Also it will be definitely recognised as a pastime only, with none of that unseemly competition with the agent-principle to which Lord Byron so rightly objected—that adulation lavished in his time on a man of letters (as though he had won a naval engagement) or on a musician (as though he had been the head of a noble house); or that competition that our present-day industrial magnate so justly resents in the Intelligence, as though it were a slight on the beauty of his power, or an insult to Mammon; or of that competition with "life" against which the vitalist philosopher of the egalitarian interregnum finds it his duty to protest. Whether it is your opinion that these Conditions would or would not promote the grandest and severest forms of artistic expression is immaterial, for there is clearly no alternative. In the Civilisation into which we are moving the fine arts can only survive on these terms. And whether in the upshot they should, from your standpoint, deteriorate or improve, they must undergo a very great transformation.

The money value of *leisure*—which is a condition of much artistic production—is now assessed. When the "Man of Genius" was respected by a public more rustic than ours, and who also had no incentive to compete with genius, as its interests were of such an opposite order; a public who never dreamt how their dissimilar interests might be combined to the advantage of the lesser; then the leisure that the "Man of Genius" enjoyed was accepted as part of the natural order of things. But with a better sense of values, people to-day have valued leisure, and they price it very high. Simultaneously they do not regard the fine arts as the preserve of "genius," but as an activity with a pleasure-value and vanity-value by no means negligible, but which up to the present has selfishly been monopolised by "geniuses" and other specialists. Instead of this dirty *professional* workshop (they say), the fine arts should constitute a sort of grown-up nursery where the rich can be kept young, dabbling and dreaming in studios and galleries. In this way these two valuable things, *leisure* and the *satisfaction of artistic performance* should not go begging and waste their sweetness (or rather their money value) on people who already have more genius than they have any right to, or need for, or money to support—that is, who possess something for which they have not paid in hard cash, and who almost unlawfully secrete something that it is impossible to get at, or of which it is impossible to supervise the issue.

" Saint-Amant n'eut du ciel que sa veine en partage,
L'habit qu'il eût sur lui fut son seul héritage."

The heroic immaterial wealth bombastically described by Boileau, with the leisure that it always claimed as other forms of wealth claim leisure, is to-day illegal, for it is a reactionary possession ; and the only thing that is recognised as entitled to put the egalitarian law at defiance in contemporary society is money. No other possession takes that or any other privileges with it. And the spoils of " Genius " in the revolution of our taste is very strictly the perquisite and preserve of the wealthy. None of the furniture or jewellery or other dazzling possessions of " Genius " goes to the crowd, in whose name " Genius " is proscribed and dispossessed. That portion of it that it is impossible to despoil (until Science has discovered some means) must be ignored as far as possible, on the principle that establishes a blind spot in the brain where it is liable to come in contact with those other tricks of nature so disconcerting to the civilised, irreducible standing outrages, such as the lavatory or war. The only difference is that those time-honoured scandals tend to be rescued from obscurity and dishonour, and there is a strong feeling that they have been misunderstood or treated with unnecessary superiority by the ape-like creature who depended on them for his existence or his virility ; whereas those so much vaunted intellectual qualities of his, on whose behalf his more animal functions suffered a prolonged eclipse, are, with the natural tact of revenge, consigned to the oubliettes and dustbins to which formally he banished his " animal " functions. There is, in short, a price on the man-ape's *head ;* and contrariwise, his more specialised organs receive many flattering attentions.

The standard of workmanship when a fine art is one of the " arts of life " is necessarily high and exacting. But to-day none of the pictorial and plastic arts, at least, are any more than an adjunct to the critical and historic faculty. The contemporary audience is essentially an audience of critics,

THE CALENDAR

that is to say, they are as active as the performer, who, indeed, exists chiefly in order that the critic may *act*—as a Critic. The only *rationale* of the professional artist to-day is to provide the critic with material for criticism ; it is no longer to give delight or to serve any useful end. And were it not for this, the whole elaborate pretence that the fine arts are still an effective part of our life would be immediately abandoned. There is, of course, the other motive for clinging to this pretence ; the motive of respectability ; it is felt that the public demise *en masse* of every art would be the crowning scandal of all. The fine arts are the last rags of a by now hardly even laughable respectability. But that is scarcely any longer a serious difficulty. It is unlikely that these rags would be put on every morning and taken off every night, if it were not for the requirements of this critical faculty, this new " professionalism " of the spectator. There would be no " professional " performers if the audience had not become in some sense a " professional " audience.

But already as the technical standard declines (except for a very few privileged star performers) the performers are more often than not recruited directly from the audience, and return to the audience when their summary performances are terminated. The community of the stage and of the auditorium is becoming absolute. And it is hardly any longer correct to refer to this audience as composed of critics ; for the critic is, on the one hand, enough of an amateur performer to take a part, and on the other, enough of a passive and voluptuous spectator to get a thrill of sorts ; always, at all events, too much of both to be unbiased. At the end of this essay this fusion will be seen to bear a strong resemblance to the triumph of the 'εθελονταί, as described by Aristotle ; or, in that contemporary school of anthropology and folk-lore that has given a new lease of life to classical research originating with the work of Sir James Frazer, as traced by Miss Harrison in her popular book, *Art and Ritual*. The *critic* stage is now half way between the spectator and the full effective crowd-performer.

The first part of this essay will briefly expound a recent and brilliant account of the origin of the fine arts, an account with a bias directed to show the supremely vital character of their earliest functions. And from that I will pass to a very different account of their origin, also with a bias—but this time an un-intelligent, doctrinaire, and political bias—in favour of vitalist explanation ; namely, that contained in Miss Harrison's little book.

————

THAT Art started on its long career—or rather that it first started being a substantial factor in human life— as a sort of Elixir, or Life-giver, is what Dr. Elliot Smith's book, *The Evolution of the Dragon*, sets out to show. That it was hand-in-hand not only with magic, but with the doctor and anatomist, that Art made its debut ; that the site of its first serious efforts was Egypt ; and that it began as a purveyor of immortality, he affirms. ("The sculptor who carved the portrait-statues for the Egyptian's tomb was called *sa'nkh*, 'he who causes to live,' and the word 'to fashion' (*ms*) a statue is to all appearance identical with (*ns*) 'to give birth ')." It was hand-in-hand with the Great Mother or with Aphrodite, surrounded by the vulvas of cowrie shells, and assisted by mandrake roots, in the same workshop as the embalmer and primitive physician, that the Artist began his terrestrial career.

" In delving into the remotely distant history of our species we cannot fail to be impressed with the persistence with which, throughout the whole of his career, man (of the species *sapiens*) has been seeking for an elixir of life, to give added ' vitality ' to the dead (whose existence was not consciously regarded as ended), to prolong the days of active life to the living, to restore youth, and to protect his own life from all assaults, not merely of time, but also of circumstance."

The great imaginative interest of this book of Dr. Elliot Smith is further that it shows the statue evolving out of the corpse, and how closely the sculptor's and painter's art was imitational and vitalist in its earliest destiny.

Mummification is picked out as the great fecundating fact of Egyptian life from which world-civilisation has ensued.

In *The Evolution of the Dragon* he sets out to trace the effects throughout the world, wherever the Egyptian influence penetrated, of, this peculiar concrete necromancy, as Diodorus calls it. The past became as important as the future, and these strangely preserved inanimate figures from a distant reality carried in themselves a host of questions. They were a living portrait gallery almost, a waxwork, not an art. The mummy symbolized in fact the extremely vitalist character of the Egyptian view of art's functions.

I suppose that Dr. Elliot Smith's identification of the birth of culture with mummification—or of the birth of the Great Mother with the cowrie shell—would be called a *theory*. But in the sort of historical research in which he is engaged the word *theory* should not be given the same meaning as in a more exact research. Such an identification should probably be regarded as a genial expedient for the effective launching of a more imaginatively fused information. It is with him a habit almost ; and an extremely attractive and unusual one, an almost necessary simplification. You see isolated for you at the beginning of time the EMBALMER, bending over a CORPSE. And from the very simple conjunction of these two figures, representing the function of PRESERVATION and CONTINUITY, you see the whole world, from Ireland to Peru, bursting into cultural bloom.

As another good example of Dr. Elliot Smith's method, the few lines of literary simplification by which the rise of Chinese culture is reduced to a thing as simple as the cowrie shell, or as the mummy, can be cited. Only instead of the cowrie shell or the mummy, it is *jade*.

He is, in his pursuit of the Dragon, considering the *thunder-ball* of the Chinese dragon. It is not a *thunder-ball*, however, he thinks ; but the dragon's ball is the pearl-moon, by swallowing which he is able to supply the fertilising rain. "Was the ball originally also a pearl, not of Buddhism, but of Taoism ? " de Visser has asked.

" In reply to this question I may call attention to the fact that the germs of civilisation were first planted in China by people strongly imbued with the belief that the pearl was the quintessence of life-giving and prosperity-composing powers ; it was not only identified with the moon, but also was itself a particle of moon-substance which fell as dew on the gaping oyster. It was the very people who held such views about pearls and gold who, when searching for alluvial gold and freshwater pearls in Turkestan, were responsible for transferring these same life-giving properties to jade ; and the magical value thus attached to jade was the nucleus, so to speak, around which the earliest civilisation of China was crystallised." So you see Siberian civilisation attaching life-giving properties to *jade,* and the wonderful civilisation of China resulting from the elixir.

Returning to Dr. Elliot Smith's development of everything out of the embalmer's workshop, he reviews the unlikelihood at first sight that such a practice should have had such far-reaching effects as he claims for it. Can this fantastic and unpleasant habit of preserving their dead have had the reverberations in culture, political and social life, in the development of arts and crafts—in short, all that we describe as civilisation ? Nevertheless, he asserts, it had.

The arts and crafts of the carpenter and stonemason, architecture, the shaping of religious belief and ritual practices (developing in connection with the evolution of the temple and the conception of a material resurrection) he enumerates as the direct tributaries of this all-important " gruesome " art.

Furthermore, it was mainly responsible for the maritime initiative of the Egyptians. It was the resins and balsams used in embalming in the funerary practices and in the temples that were the main incentives to their voyages in the Mediterranean and Red Sea. And it was these surprising habits acquired in the service of this corpse and in seeking for the substances required for its preservation, that ultimately induced them to push further afield. Hence the heliolithic culture, and, according to this writer, all our civilization.

There are also " the manifold ways in which the practice of mummification reflected the history of medicine and pharmacy. By accustoming the Egyptians, through thirty centuries, to the idea of cutting the human corpse, it made it possible for Greek physicians of the Ptolemaic and later ages to initiate in Alexandria the systematic dissection of the human body which popular prejudice forbade elsewhere, and especially Greece itself. Upon this formulation the knowledge of anatomy and the science of medicine has been built up."

So Dr. Elliot Smith concludes, " the vague and ill-defined ideas of physiology and psychology, which had probably been developing since Aurignacian times in Europe, were suddenly crystallised into a coherent structure and definite form by the musings of the Egyptian embalmer."

It may be that as a doctor Prof. Elliot Smith was especially disposed to choose this anatomical fact : from that standpoint it may in a sense be a doctor's dream of civilisation growing around the operating-table. His own brilliant theoretic structure has originated in that way : for it was during the period of eleven years as a doctor in a Cairo hospital, no doubt, that all his subsequent research received its original stimulation. It would be natural in that way that he should weave his own destiny into his theories. While there, many desiccated bodies that had been buried five thousand years before, and which had been preserved in the hot Egyptian gravel, were brought to him for dissection. He would find in the intestines of the proto-Egyptian the bones of fish off which he had made his last meal, and would find in the throat of a child the skinned body of a mouse, administered in this way when it was *in extremis* as the supreme remedy for a child in that condition. He lived to that extent in a magically preserved morgue ; and even the atmosphere of the country must have seemed to conspire in the staging of the famous Living Death invented—or formularised—by the Egyptians.

You only have to walk into a museum gallery devoted to Egyptian art to recognise at once that you are walking into a sort of churchyard or very curious sort of undertaker's shop. Thoth, in massive trutination, is weighing life against death : and sure enough the form life takes on this occasion is that of *art*. Indeed, in dynastic Egypt, *art* comes nearer to being *life* than at any other recorded period ; and apparently for the reason that it was *death*.

Plastic or graphic art, indeed, necessarily flourishes in the mortuary. The *living death* that is represented by Egyptian culture is the very place for the sculptor and painter to thrive in. A vivid materialistic life (such as the Egyptian population, no doubt, lived, but which was not allowed to migrate without hushing itself into the tombs and temples), wherever lived, produces, at its best, some coloured easy popular homologue of the Japanese print. At its worst, it produces the feeble gibberish of the contemporary railway bookstall, the designs and stories of the popular magazines. Great art is, for the hurried and unexacting standards of this quick unconscious life, a useless instrument—such life itself resembling a railway station, or railway carriage, the things of which it is specifically composed made for its hurried uses, left on the seat when the train is left, and swept up as rubbish at the terminus.

But the premium or fine paid by great Pharaohs for leases in the other world is put aside in this world for the upkeep of vast imitation establishments peopled by imitation immortals : in other words, for building, sculpting, and recording on a giant scale worthy of eternity. The Egyptian sepulchre and temple is, actually, a building already in another life : and it is replete with all the massive state of an ambitious, and almost endless, continuity.

Into the Egyptian *living death*, again, a good deal of the *rigor mortis* has passed ; and that suits art admirably. It asks nothing better than a corpse, and thrives on bones. Did not Cezanne bellow at his sitter when he fell off the chair, " You're *moving !* Les pommes, ça ne bouge pas! " He preferred apples, in short, not because he otherwise discriminated between men and apples, but because men moved, whereas apples did not.

But there was an even further stroke of luck for the Egyptian craftsman. That was that the corpse or the corpse-statue had to be a particularly *lively* one. This, of course, might go too far : as can be gathered from the account of the naturalism that this life-obsession engendered, especially as regards the eye. This sparkling eye threatened the whole structure of Egyptian art, and probably contributed to its downfall.

The sculptor, always pre-occupied with the *life-like* and nothing else, arrived at last at startlingly natural images in stone or wood of the grandees he was commissioned to immortalise. With paint he improved still further his facsimile. But still there was something lacking, apart from the movement of life, that even he could not give. The EYE was the last thing to resist his ingenuity. But at last he had that shining, coloured and marvellously alive as well. His statue, although so still, now sparkled and lived.

This triumph of the imitative art was not regarded by the Egyptian as a *tour de force*, however—not one of art, or rather not *for* art. The sculptor, he thought, *had made the statue live.* Death's psychic evulsion was reversed, the soul had been put back by this craftsman, into the dead. It was a "living image." The eyes themselves were regarded as one of the chief sources of the vitality which had been conferred upon the statue.

According to the most fanatical canons of art, and according also to many quite temperate canons, these statues are not the best produced in Egypt. These sparkling eyes, had the Egyptians possessed the mechanical equipment, with the centuries of positive research behind them, that we have, would soon have moved. Thereby, from the artist's point of view, they would have come into competition with apples, the advantage remaining heavily on the side of the fruit. But luckily the liaison between art and science had not then been effected. There was a lacuna in human ingenuity on the hither side of which, like an island nation, art prospered.

The information brilliantly presented by Dr. Elliot Smith about all this ferment of creative intelligence around the corpses of Egyptian magnates is of the greatest importance for the understanding not only of Egyptian art, but of art alto-gether. The more you reflect on this information, the more you are convinced how very much to be preferred a dead magnate is to a live one. "There's a great deal to be said for being dead" (or for the incessant contemplation of death) on the part of a person sitting for his or her portrait. These death-masks, mouldings like a diver's scaphander for the *last plunge*, all this work on death's frontiers where only the embalmer and the portraitist stood between some wealthy person and extinction, made these two fine fellows into a kind of death profiteers. Or if they were never allowed to line their pockets, at least they had more work than they have ever had since. What has become of the embalmer? as an artist you cannot help wondering. He has disappeared, only the artist is left. But if the portraitist could meet the embalmer now, what a tale he would have to tell! He would have to say to him, "Things is not what they was! Don't you worry: you're better where you are—though it *is* along of all those Pharaohs—damn their eyes!")

Dr. Elliot Smith goes through all the minutiæ of this inten-sive science developed by the embalmer and the portraitist together. To preserve the actual tissues of the body of the dead man handed over to them intact, and to disturb throughout the processes of evisceration and the ceremonial accompanying it, the living appearance as little as possible—that was the burden of the embalmer's thoughts : and the portraitist was busy with the manufacture of his stone or wooden doubles. The embalmer was the *first* artist, but as it was found that he could not achieve what was desired, during twenty-five centuries this ingenious ghoul wrestled with the refractory human material. Then in the XXIst dynasty he was at last satisfied, and everybody else also, that the trick had been done.

"By means of linen wrappings wound round the body, impregnated with the resinous paste (stucco being alternately used) and moulded in against the limbs, the organs of reproduction especially emphasised and carefully treated, it was sought to preserve in facsimile the living man. On the linen-enveloped head, eyes would be painted to increase the lifelike appearance."

First the " reserve head " of Egyptian archæology, a large stone head, was placed with the mummy in the tomb, and later a life-size statue.

It was, Dr. Elliot Smith thinks, from contemplating these simulacra (the life-size statue and the mummy) that the Egyptian notions of life and death became reinforced and assumed the proportions that they did.

The contemplation of the nature of life and death derived naturally, with the earlier people, from this incessant spectacle of the embalmed dead. What was lacking—they must have asked themselves—in these physically intact bodies, to prevent them from continuing to behave like living beings ?

To regard the image in the mirror, or the thought or image in the mind, as being as real as its original, or the shadow as the substance, has characterised everywhere the primitive mind. "Everything he (the Egyptian) knew or thought of," in Professor Sayce's words, " had its double." The Egyptian Other-world was such a *double*. The *Ka* was a double : and the statue of the portraitist was in the nature of a shadow.

The mortuary philosophy of the Egyptians, in earlier times, found expression in a ritual designed to convey the breath of life to the work of the sculptor. The odour and sweat of the body was represented by unguents. Offerings of blood were supposed to supply the necessary oil for the revivification of the heart of the statue of the deceased in the Ka-house; and incense to supply the odour of human sweat and cosmetics.

In the *Migrations of Early Culture*, Dr. Elliot Smith attributed the making of statues directly to the practice of mummification : and in spite of Dr. Alan Gardiner, he is still disposed to stick to this order—namely, mummy first, statue after : though his distinguished colleague would prefer that they were placed abreast of each other.

" It is clear that this conception of the possibility of a life beyond the grave assumed a more concrete form when it was realised that the body itself could be rendered incorruptible and its distinctive traits could be kept alive by means of a portrait-statue. There are reasons for supposing that primitive man did not realise or contemplate the possibility of his own existence coming to an end. . . . If a corpse were destroyed or underwent a process of natural disintegration, the fact was brought home to him that death had occurred."

The preservation of the body (implying continuance of existence), and the care lavished on it, in this way became intelligible.

But when the statue took over the function of representing the deceased, a dwelling was provided for it above ground. This developed into the temple, where the relatives and friends of the dead came and made the offerings of food which were regarded as essential for the maintenance of posthumous existence. The evolution of the temple was thus the direct outcome of the ideas that grew up in connection with the preservation of the dead. For at first it was nothing more than the dwelling-place of the unanimated dead. The full-fledged temple had its origin in the apotheosis of the dead king. (Osiris, for instance, was a dead king.)

Whether the portraitist or the embalmer are at the bottom of it all, or whether they shared the honours, does not very much matter. The participation of both is proved. And it was when they came to the surface out of the scene of their subterranean activities, and the architect stepped in, that

THE DITHYRAMBIC SPECTATOR

Egyptian art reached its stage of evident and multiform mastery. And it is about that that we are talking.

As I have already mentioned, the sculptor who modelled the portrait-statue was called " he who causes to live," and the word " to fashion " a statue is identical with that which means " to give birth." The god Ptah created man by modelling his form in clay. Similarly the life-giving sculptor made the portrait which was to be the means of securing a perpetuation of existence when it was animated through the mouth-opening, by libations and incense.

The sculptor, the humble incarnation of the god Ptah (who was, of course, a Pharaoh), was only half a god : for the statue, once it was made, had to be brought to life ; and this was effected with considerable ceremony (which was, of course, where the priest came in) by the descent of some animating principle from the sky or elsewhere.

Whether the sculptor ultimately must share with his lugubrious friend, the embalmer, the honour of starting off those varied and superb activities or not, there is one thing that he seems certainly to have been responsible for ; that is, the *ka* or soul. The Egyptian *ka*, the Italian *genius*, the Greek ψῦχή, the Iranian *fravashi* are similar phenomena : so with or without the sculptor they no doubt came into existence in conformity with some bias of the intellect independent of such accidents as the " double " making of the portrait-sculptor. Indeed, Dr. Elliot Smith (again, no doubt, here prompted to obstetric explanations by his training) insists on the placenta theory of psychic origins.

" The *ka* is not simply identical with the breath of life or *animus*, as Burnet supposes," says Dr. Elliot Smith, " but has a wider significance. The adoption of the conception of the *ka* as a sort of guardian angel which finds its appropriate habitation in a statue that has been animated does not necessarily conflict with the view so concretely and unmistakably represented in the tomb pictures that the *ka* is also a double who is born along with the individual."

" The development of the custom of making statues of the dead necessarily raised for solution the problem of explaining the deceased's two bodies, his actual mummy and his portrait stone. During life on earth his vital principle dwelt in the former, except on those occasions when the man was asleep. His actual body also gave expression to the varied attributes of his personality. But after death the statue became the dwelling-place of the manifestations of the spirit of vitality."

It was not by showing men their *kas* or souls that the sculptor produced this result, but merely by providing an ancient superstition with suitable quarters—namely, a life-size duplicate of the body. The idea of the soul originated in the belief of an independent existence of something that is *you* or *I* apart from our bodies, both sleep and death providing their corroborative evidence.

The Roman *genius*, according to Dr. Aust (*Relig. der Römer*), works out as a rather phallic thumbling ; and there is no reason to suppose that the Egyptians (certainly not behind other people in their predilection for symbols of fertility, and in their identification of man's fertility with the earth) would not have made their *ka* on some such analogy. But in one form or another the notion of a " double " is almost ineradicable. As one of the strangest examples of its persistence, Schopenhauer provides us with an example. He would have been as emphatic as a Behaviorist in condemning this particularly pitiable fiction. The man going to him in search of an assurance of *selfhood* would have received little satisfaction. The deluded creature longing for some stupid promise of a perpetuation of *anything* contingent on the *principium individuationis* by whose grace we live, would have received the full weight of his German scorn. Yet in an essay (*On apparent design in the fate of the individual*) he supplies every individual (without being asked) with a *genius* or double. This brother lurks in the unconscious regions of the Will. But he watches over the destiny of his charge with infinite foresight and devotion.

Schopenhauer explains the mechanism of this double in a curious way. He reminds his reader of his dreams, and especially of dreams in which his sex centres are involved. He draws our attention (he always assumes that his readers are men, of course) to the fact that sometimes we compass our wishes, couple with some phantom, and an emission takes place ; whereas at other times, try as we will to achieve this result, some obstacle interposes, and we are unable to do so. That obstacle, he says, is the Will that looks after us ; our little personal Will, who does not think it would be good for us, and so interferes. And similarly in waking life, engaged in incessant struggle with this other type of what we call living phantom, there is a similarly solicitous interested third party, possessing all the resources of the Unconscious, that intervenes, for our good, in our affairs.

If the Egyptian sculptor's work gave rise to the notion of the *ka* or double, or gave it substance, he was certainly availing himself of one of the chief securities of plastic or graphic art. No man, I believe, who has an elaborate portrait painted or sculpted of himself, is without an instinctive sense that an *alter ego* is coming into existence under the painter's or sculptor's hand. It might be said (if a painter were speculating as to whether so-and-so would have his portrait painted or not) that the man whose instinct would favour cremation would *not* have his portrait painted ; whereas the man inclined to burial without cremation, other things being equal, would. But interfering with such deep-seated instincts in " enlightened " people is a very anxious and thankless occupation : and the portraitist to-day, however well paid he is, deserves every penny he gets.

But where this art (equally it appears a child of life and death) was nearest to those conditions most favourable to art was in the nature of the *truth* required. It had its chance of perfection because it was working for *the other world*. The artist could be said indeed to be living as much in one world as in the other. People's small vanities do not transgress death very readily, though their mortal needs were supposed by the Egyptians to accompany them. They do not want so much to be *beautiful*, under such circumstances, as to be *like themselves*, terribly and truly like. And so long as they think that such things as the earlier dynastic sculpture are like them, the artist is at the zenith of his opportunity. (As they become more knowing or mechanical, the art *pari passu* becomes less good.) The art of the *perruquier* or dressmaker, though it has its place, has given way in Egyptian art to the great creative instincts of our kind. To be true rather than false was the function of the Egyptian artist.

Any account of the origins of art given us by Dr. Elliot

Smith necessarily confines us, to begin with, to the banks of the Nile ; for there and nowhere else, he says, all civilisation saw the light. Whether this necessary restriction has given a particular twist to his version—which we have just surveyed —or not, it remains a very interesting one. And whatever the ultimate fate of his theory of Egyptian priority in civilisation, there is nothing *behind* Egypt that has been so far discovered that can be said to interfere with its claim to origination. When we are examining a work of Egyptian art, it is even an assumption that we cannot entirely dispense with that here we may be confronted with the first tremendous human effort, that perhaps we may have been dissipating ever since, and which is unlikely to be repeated. In touch in an organised way with a supernatural world of whose potentialities we can form no conception, the art of Egypt is as rare and irreplaceable a thing as some communication dropped from another planet on our earth would be.

For Dr. Elliot Smith, then, the practice of plastic art, which is one of the most peculiar activities of human beings, developed body to body with the corpses of pharaohonic grandees. It was thus a superhuman effort of *imitation*. Because it was all carried out not in the interests of this life, and its vanities, but for the Other-world, it was able to be *true*. This facsimile truth, imposed on a certain naïf hieratic gaucherie, is all there is to it.

In the first place, had the art of Egypt been nothing but that—and a great deal of it, especially later work, is not much more—we should not have heard so much about it. This *corps-à-corps* imitation of the human form, its translation into a stone or wood facsimile, leaves out of count the great wealth of abstract design, with all its peculiar and untranslatable severity of imagery, which is equally a feature of Egyptian art. Enamelled plates, perfume spoons, vases, amulets, stools, borders and facings of all sorts, every form of applied art, show an almost inhuman wedding of what is a sort of geometric power with a particular æsthetic principle. Then the beauty of the Canopic jars, which are amongst the earliest inventions of Egyptian art (examples dating to the Old Kingdom, we are told), cannot be put down to the practical requirements of evisceration. The wall and ceiling decorations of the mastabas are the reverse of *imitation*. They are as mathematical, intricate, and in contradiction to the disorder of the natural world as musical composition or geometry. If you add to this the superb architectural remains, and the records that we have of their secular building activities, you arrive at a mass of creative work in the midst of which the exact portrait study of the deceased becomes unimportant as *art*. It is no more important to the study of the origin of this instinct than is the singular means taken in the case of the statue of the Pharaoh Mycerinus to ensure its perduration by rooting it in the virgin rock.

This, of course, does not interfere with the theory of how all this extraordinary harvest of intellectual achievement was made possible by the early business association of the sculptor and embalmer. But it reduces this theory of the origin of art in Egypt to a practical question, which has no bearing on the essential function of art. It is an account of the social conditions or accidents that are likely to enable an artist to do his art : not an account of the inner process whereby a person becomes an artist, or what art *is*. *If* there were a man in London who was prepared to pay two thousand pounds to have a large music room and hall, say, or billiard, bathroom, and hall, decorated (instead of buying a Daimler), and *if* such a man had some taste, of a rather severe and unusual nature, then I should be able to indicate to this man where he could find an artist who could be entrusted with this commission. Such a patron does not exist, of course : but Egypt bred such patrons like flies, under the shadow of the Other-world, and with the help of the theory of the immortality of the soul. But that does not tell you anything about *art*, but about the opportunities that bring it to flower. Indeed, the specific examples of Egyptian art that are the closest to this origin in a practical requirement are the least interesting things in that art.

[*The second, and last, part of Mr. Wyndham Lewis's essay, which discusses recent theories on the relation between Art and Ritual in Greek civilisation, will be published next month.*]

Poems

BY PETER QUENNELL.

Leviathan.

I.

Leviathan drives his broad and painted face,
With the surge dumbly rippling round his lips,
Toward the Atlantid shore ;
Not flat and golden like the cherubim,
Or a face round and womanish like the seraphim,
But thick and barbed—the broad, barbed cheeks of Donne.
Beneath he stretched his hands to the sea-forests,
Obscure and thick, with the cool freshes under,
Lifts his surprised brows to the sky's milky light,
New come from the abyss.
While a faint radiance, webbed from the wave's substance,
Clung to his changing limbs and his coiled body,
Reddening, making them darker than the sea,
Or half translucent.
And when the mouths of Atlantean brooks
Struck on his mouth with taste of sudden cold
And wound his shoulders like embracing hands,
He put out both thick palms and felt the shallows.
The salt had scurfed his body with white fire
And knotted the thick hair between his breasts—
And as he rose delicate Atlantis trembled,
Tilting upon the sea's plain like a leaf.
The passionless air hung heavy on Atlantis,
And the inclined spears of the flowering bushes
Smoothly dropped down their loosened, threaded blossoms,
Softening the pathways.
For tideless night had covered her, and sealed
All scent within the narrow throat of flowers,
And sound within the navel of the hills,
And stars in the confusion of the air.
Within her darkness and unconsciousness
She hid all beauty, and her silences

Sounds' measures and sequences,
And the black earth quickened
With oppression of blossom.
Ah ! thief that swims by night—Leviathan,
Rolled blindly in the wave's trough like a rotting thing,
Come to Atlantis' further edge by dark,
Poised over her quietness ;
Measureless drunkard of the bitter sea,
Insatiate—like some slow stain
Creeping on pleasure's face
—Like sudden misery.
For you have built yourself a house, and heaped
Dried foam, and scurf and ruin of the waves,
And crudded thoughts and shapes hardly conceived,
—Thief, boaster.
So foul, so desolate,
That you are crept to seek new life
—Have crossed the water's plain
Desiring and by stealth to gain
For rankness, foolishness and half-conceived beauty
Some perfect shape—an Atlantean body.

II.

A music met Leviathan returning
While the still troubled waters of his passage
Danct every island like a lily head ;
Through all the shadowed throats of the wide forest,
His unnumbered monster children rode to greet him
On horses winged and dappled over like flowers.
Now huddled waves had lulled their bursting foam,
And slight clouds laid their breasts upon the sea ;
The sullen winds head downward from the sky
Solicited his movement on their viols.
And the palm trees, heat weary,
Chafing smooth limbs within a rinded shell,
Spoke of his coming with faint acclamation,
Like watchers long grown tired, languid and sorry ;
" Look, how he comes "—as soft as whispering deer—
" What storm and state he brings."   Then louder voices
The unchaste turtles crying out for pleasure,

And badgers from the earth
Sprawled upon the rocks with animal laughter.
"The Cretan bull ferrying across the sea
Did not bear richer load ;
In the reed forest of Eurotas' bank
That quivering swan, clapping strong wings together,
With harsh, sweet voice called out no keener marriage."
Then shrill response, as seeming from the air,
Invoking joy, summoning desire.
"Hither desires,
Coming as thick and hot as the press and hurry of blood,
Striking the apse of the brain,
Ranging abroad, carrying your torches high,
Running as light and remote as a scattered cast of pearls."
Then antic spirits from the tulip trees ;
"We must have tumblers like a wheel of fire ;
We must have dancers moving their suave hands ;
The tumblers strung backward like a hoop
Till they thrust vermilion cheeks between their knees ;
And the intricacy
Of sweet involving gaiety,
And wine to warm our innocence,
Music to smooth the prickled sense,
Sounding like water or like ringing glass."

.   .   .

The mitred Queen of Heaven stirred on her broad, low throne,
Setting the lattice just so much ajar
That wandering airs from earth should cool the room ;
Peered down on more-than-Leda and smoothed her wrinkled
    snood,
Crying to her Father-Spouse,—"Dear Lord, how sweet she
    looks."
The clumsy hierarchies,
Wearied by their continual task of praise,
Rested wide heifer eyes upon her fallen lids.
Islanded in stars,
Even the keen Intelligences turned away
From the mathematic splendour of the spheres' incessant
    rolling chime.
Himself The Father moved,

Traditional and vast,
Remembering fresher years,
Might have inclined his steeply pinnacled head.
But his more zealous son,
As neat as Thammuz, with smooth, pallid cheeks,
Sensing an evil shut the casement fast.

. . .

But I, remembering Atlantis, wept;
Remembering her paths and their unswept flowers,
Clean beaches patterned by a light sea wrack,
And the ruined halcyon nests that came on shore.
Tears, in their freedom, cloud the eyes,
Drowsing the sense ;
Honey and poppy equally mixed together
They cannot drug away or curtain off with sleep
So many crowding faces,
Such pitiless disharmony of shapes.
Upon Atlantis' plain I walked too long,
As one on a broad stairway hesitant :
" On this hand then to the small arrased room
Or upward climb to the smooth dancing-floor ? "
My pleasures flowed harmonious as water—
As flowing water left so little trace.

The Flight into Egypt

The Guiding Angel to Mary,

Within Heaven's circle I had not guessed at this,
I had not guessed at pleasure such as this,
So sharp a pleasure,
That like a lamp burning in foggy night
Makes its own orb and sphere of flowing gold
And tents itself in light.
Going before you now how many days,
Thoughts—all turned back like birds against the wind—
Wheeled sullenly toward my Father's house,
Considered his blind presence and the gathered bustling pæan,
The affluence of his *sweetness*, his *grace*, and unageing *might*.
My flesh glowed then in the shadow of a loose cloak

THE CALENDAR

And my brightness troubled the ground with every pulse of
    the blood,
My wings lax on the air, my eyes open and grave,
With the vacant pride of hardly less than a God.
We passed thickets that pricked with hidden deer,
And wide shallows dividing before my feet,
Empty plains threaded and between stiff aloes
I took the asses' bridle to climb into mountain pathways.
When cold bit you, through your peasant's mantle,
And my Father filled the air with meaningless stars,
I brought dung and dead white grass for fuel,
Blowing a fire with the breath of the holy word.
Your drudge, Joseph, slept ; you would sit unmoving,
In marble quiet, or by the unbroken voice of a river,
Would sometimes bare your maiden breast to his mouth,
The suckling, to the conscious God balanced upon your knees.
Apart I considered the melodious names of my brothers,
As again in my Father's house, and the even spheres
Slowly, nightlong recalled the splendour of numbers ;
I heard again the voluptuous measure of praise.
Sometimes pacing beneath clarity immeasurable
I saw my mind lie open and desert,
The wavering streams frozen up and each coppice quieted,
A whole valley in starlight with leaves and waters.
Coming at last to these farthest Syrian hills,
Attis or Adon, some ambushed lust looked out ;
My skin grows pale and smooth, shrunken as silk,
Without the rough effulgence of a God.
And here no voice has spoken ;
There is no shrine of any Godhead here :
No grove or hallowed fires,
And Godhead seems asleep.
Only the vine has woven
Strange houses and blind rooms and palaces,
Into each hollow and crevice continually
Dropped year-long irrecoverable flowers.
The sprawling vine has built us a close room ;
Obedient Hymen fills the air with mist ;
And to make dumb our theft,
The white and moving sand that will not bear a print.

Byron : Marginalia.

By DESMOND MacCARTHY.

[As the title indicates, these are detached notes. I have endeavoured to arrange them in such an order that the change of subject may not be more abrupt than is inevitable.]

BIBLIOGRAPHICAL.

Byron's Centenary produced three books of value ; Mr. Harold Nicolson's *Byron : The Last Journey*, Sir John Fox's *The Byron Mystery*, and Professor Chew's *Byron in England ;* the first is an admirable narrative, the second in thoroughness and arrangement resembles a report of a Royal Commission, the third is a most valuable book of reference, indispensable henceforth ; for from it you can discover how Byron's successive works struck his contemporaries, and it contains brief accounts of almost every English book which has been written about him. Professor Chew is impartial except when " The Astarte Question " crops up, when he apparently ceases to weigh evidence. This makes him unfair to Miss Mayne's *Life of Byron*. The Centenary produced no long treatise on Byron's poetry—a sign that much more interest is taken in Byron himself than in his poetry. The late Professor Kerr, Professor Grierson and Professor Garrod each gave a lecture containing admirable criticism. Professor Elton's chapter on Byron in *A Survey of English Literature* (published some years ago) was very good, but Mr. Arthur Symons's beautiful and masterly essay on him in *The Romantic Movement* (Constable, 1909) remains the best criticism of Byron's poetry. The Centenary critics all tell us that we underrate it. They say Byron must be judged in the bulk. At the same time they admit that the great mass of his poetry is poor poetry. These statements do not necessarily cancel each other out, but if both are true, it is unlikely that this generation will read him thoroughly enough to change its estimate. We are more likely, in that case, to admit with a shrug that it may be true we underrate him, and leave it at that. Posterity, however, may not.

THE CALENDAR

ÆSTHETIC FASHIONS.

There are fashions in poetry. These fashions are strong modes of feeling, and it is impossible for the sensibility of the modern reader not to be coloured by them, unless (always possible) he confines his reading to past periods. The leading fashion in poetry is now tolerant of obscurity to a degree exceeding the seventeenth century, and contemptuous of plain, invigorating rhetoric in verse. It is mannered and subtle in the expression of emotion. A dread of the commonplace and lack of faith in common ideas and moral values have driven modern poets upon idiosyncratic associations and subjective themes—upon a shiver of obscure disillusionment, *Hi / Hi / Hi / les amants bizarres*, or upon an equally obscure and sudden mystic exaltation, meaningless to the poet himself in any philosophic sense, or upon an odd collocation of images, suggesting a wonder-world. It will pass. It may return ; and if the present generation throws up in this mode of sensibility a poet as indubitable as Donne, some future generation may rediscover them as they themselves have rediscovered " the metaphysical poets." But the taste for oratorical poetry, for the poetry of sentiment, for the poetry written in relief of feelings and to transmit as much emotion as possible, is also bound to return. Then it will not be so hard to read and judge Byron in the mass.

> So, we'll go no more a roving
>   So late into the night,
> Though the heart be still as loving,
>   And the moon be still as bright.
>
> For the sword outwears its sheath,
>   And the soul wears out the breast,
> And the heart must pause to breathe,
>   And love itself have rest.
>
> Though the night was made for loving,
>   And the day returns too soon,
> Yet we'll go no more a roving
>   By the light of the moon.

It is possible these verses may mean more to mankind (including poets) over a long period of time than most of the best modern love-poems, though they sound now in contemporary ears like a sentimental drawing-room ballad. Is that a test of great poetry ? It does not seem a conclusive one. Which tests are conclusive ? I do not know. It is certainly one test, for we judge poetry by comparing it with poetry which has been remembered, or at least we check and corroborate our judgments by that comparison.

* * *

> Their praise is hymn'd by loftier harps than mine :
> Yet one I would select from that proud throng,
> Partly because they blend me with his line,
> And partly that I did his sire some wrong,
> And partly that bright names will hallow song ;
> And his was of the bravest, and when shower'd
> The death-bolts deadliest the thinn'd files along,
> Even where the thickest of war's tempest lower'd,
> They reach'd no nobler breast than thine, young, gallant
>   Howard !
> There have been tears and breaking hearts for thee,
> And mine were nothing, had I such to give ;
> But when I stood beneath the fresh green tree,
> Which living waves where thou didst cease to live,
> And saw around me the wide field revive
> With fruits and fertile promise, and the Spring
> Came forth her work of gladness to contrive,
> With all her reckless birds upon the wing,
> I turn'd from all she brought to those she could not bring.

That is a noble valediction. It matters little that the diction is worn and stereotyped : "loftier harp," "breaking hearts," "sire," "reckless birds." This unself-conscious docility in the use of conventional phrases seems an integral part of its dignity and universality. The poet's references to himself are becoming here because they are candid, brief, direct. It is not necessary, in order to understand them, to know that the wrong Byron did "Howard's sire" was to refer to that nobleman's poems as "the paralytic pulings of Carlyle." The mood is not one of grief, but of the recognition of sorrow :

> There have been tears and breaking hearts for thee,
> And mine were nothing, had I such to give.

All can feel the poignancy of youthful death and Spring in juxtaposition, and it is out of poignant juxtapositions, sad, gay, or exciting poetry springs. Here, as always, Byron feels and expresses what the ordinary man can feel :

> " I turned from all she brought to those she could not bring."

It is poignantly intelligible and will remain so, however men's thoughts change about death in battle or mortality. But is it poetry ? Who knows what poetry is ? Is *odi et amo et excrutior* poetry ? Is, " To be or not to be " ? Is " After life's fitful fever he sleeps well " poetry ? If so, is it only the four *f*'s which make it so ? Coleridge thought the couplets of Pope were not poetry ; they are certainly not prose. All we know is that men have treasured words which, in expressing thoughts and emotions, remove them from the surrounding pettiness of life. Most often this is accomplished through some subtle music in the words themselves ; but sometimes it seems to be achieved by mere finality in expression, thanks to which emotions have been transmuted into ideas ; sometimes a diction consecrated and unfamiliar has been an essential aid. There are different kinds of poetry ; the poetry of incantation, of bare statement and of august eloquence, and others for which we might find names. One thing is certain, however, that poetry was made for man and not man for a particular kind of poetry. High priests of the Muse may be forgiven for thinking otherwise, but such a blunder is excusable in them only.

THE COLISEUM.

Byron was the most obvious of poets. Confronted by sea, mountains, storms, he reflected upon the helplessness of man ; before tombs, on the vanity of ambition ; among ruins, that Cities and Empires pass away. It is a characteristic he shares with the great poets and the worst. It won for him once the compromising admiration of those who care not for poetry, and it still commands the loyalty of those who honour classical tradition.

> And here the buzz of eager nations ran,
> In murmur'd pity, or loud-roar'd applause,

As man was slaughter'd by his fellow-man.
And wherefore slaughter'd? wherefore, but because
Such were the bloody Circus' genial laws,
And the imperial pleasure.—Wherefore not?
What matters where we fall to fill the maws
Of worms—on battle-plains or listed spot?
Both are but theatres where the chief actors rot.

I see before me the Gladiator lie:
He leans upon his hand—his manly brow
Consents to death, but conquers agony,
And his droop'd head sinks gradually low—
And through his side the last drops, ebbing slow
From the red gash, fall heavy, one by one,
Like the first of a thunder-shower; and now
The arena swims around him—he is gone,
Ere ceased the inhuman shout which hail'd the wretch who
    won.

He heard it, but he heeded not—his eyes
Were with his heart, and that was far away;
He reck'd not of the life he lost nor prize,
But where his rude hut by the Danube lay,
There were his young barbarians all at play,
There was their Dacian mother—he, their sire,
Butcher'd to make a Roman holiday—
All this rush'd with his blood—Shall he expire
And unavenged?—Arise! ye Goths, and glut your ire!

A famous passage, but I doubt if it is really familiar,
though it may seem so, to many readers of this magazine.
Read, perhaps, in childhood, it has never been forgotten, while
afterwards half-mocking quotation has made it hard to listen
to it with fresh susceptibility. But if you read it now, a new
poem here, on this page, what would you think of it? Certainly
you would not forget it. You would feel it was a long time
since a living poet had addressed you with such directness;
no reflection here upon reflection, nothing here between you
and a clear-cut vision of life, a vision, too, requiring from you
no special mood for its appreciation, no preparatory sensitizing
of the mind, and carrying with it a massive, simple emotion

which, though undoubtedly touched by theatricality, might make you wonder how long you had been persuaded that poetry must be a matter of semi-tones of feeling. The passage shows Byron's strength and his weakness. He begins with a commonplace reflection such as occurs to anyone standing in the Coliseum, surrounded by those ruined tiers of empty seats, and, indeed, had that not been his first emotional response the poet might as well have been elsewhere. He then launches out in an untidy, emphatic piece of declamation : brutal as the gladiatorial shows were, there is no call for special indignation, since the whole world is a blood-stained arena. He says this because he knows it is violent and thinks it is fine. But clearly it is not felt. For not only does the poem end with a shout of indignation, but his sympathy with the dying gladiator grows so absorbing that the other gladiator, surely as innocent as he, becomes " the wretch who won " ! This narrowness of emotional focus is characteristic of Byron ; so also is this pretence of regarding indifferently what moves him, from the height of philosophic despair. It is in his response to the thing itself he is magnificent. Examine the diction ; small wonder Arnold, with his faith in the classic quality of strong simplicity, thought Byron must survive :

Consents to death, but conquers agony.

He heard it, but he heeded not—his eyes
Were with his heart, and that was far away.

At one phrase the fastidious might hitch, " his manly brow." Its central significance is perfectly right here, only in use that adjective has acquired accidental bluff-sentimental associations. Byron was insensitive to such surface refractions from words ; he sometimes used words inaccurately, for he was hasty and no scholar, but it was always the definite core of meaning he fastened upon, using words, in his lofty style, as it were, stark from the dictionary. This is why, when he talks in verse (*Beppo*, *Don Juan*), his diction is so much surer. Then, he caught words with all their living inflections from the lips of men. His mind was really too matter-of-fact and impetuous to handle that treacherous instrument, poetic diction. This naturally escapes the foreigner, who would see only a fine suggestion in a phrase like " manly brow." (I am told there is often to a fastidious Frenchman a distressing commonness in the diction of Musset, which certainly escapes me.) Nor can a foreigner appreciate the full horror of what we mean when we say that no poet of equal rank, or anywhere near it, ever had so bad an ear as Byron. These two facts go far to explaining the enormous difference which exists between his reputation at home and abroad. Abroad they feel the energy and animated movement of his verse, the massiveness of his emotional power, the largeness of his conceptions, without being conscious of any of the accompanying drawbacks. No doubt his being one of the few English poets for whom the Continent had a real existence has also had something to do with it. Foreigners have taken far more seriously his abuse of England than Byron did himself.

SWINBURNE AND BYRON.

In 1865 Swinburne wrote a preface to a selection he made from Byron's work. In that preface he asserted that he can only be judged or appreciated in the mass, an assertion which nearly all critics have repeated since. "The greatest of his works was his whole work taken together ; and to know or to honour him aright he must be considered with all his imperfections and with all his glories on his head." "The time has passed," he says, "when all the boys and girls who paddled in rhyme and dabbled in sentiment were wont to adore him with foolish faces of praise. It is of little moment to him or to us that they have long ceased to cackle and begun to hiss. They have become used to better verse and carefuller workmen ; and must be forgiven if, after such training, they cannot at once appreciate the splendid and imperishable excellence which covers all his offences and outweighs all his defects : the excellence of sincerity and strength. Without these no poet can live ; but few have ever had so much of them as Byron. His sincerity is indeed difficult to discover and define ; but it does in effect lie at the root of all his good works : deformed by pretension and defaced by assumption, masked by folly and veiled by affectation ; but perceptible after all, and priceless." In 1881 Matthew Arnold, in the preface to a selection from Byron, quoted with admiration this passage, but urged in his own criticism by "some power not ourselves which makes " for paradox, he proceeded to exalt Byron above such poets as Coleridge, Keats and Shelley, placing him on a double throne above the poets of the nine-teenth century with Wordsworth at his side. This essay enraged Swinburne, and in the most amusing critical tirade he ever wrote (*Under the Microscope* not excepted) Swinburne hurled himself upon Arnold and Byron. His *Wordsworth and Byron* contains, however, one sentence which, like that just quoted, anticipated, if it did not determine, the modern esti-mate of Byron. Swinburne asserts that Byron only discovered himself in *Don Juan, Beppo, The Vision of Judgment :* "Byron was supreme in his turn—a king by truly divine right ; but in a province outside the proper domain of absolute poetry. His is undisputed suzeraine of the debateable border-land to which Berni has given his name : the style called Bernesque might now be more properly called Byronic, after the great master who seized and held it by the right of a stronger hand. If to be great as a Bernesque writer is to be great as a poet, then was Byron assuredly a great poet ; if it be not, then most assuredly he was nothing of the kind." When Byron wrote using " common words in their common places," when realism and satire were uppermost in his dual nature, he rose, as in *Don Juan,* easily into poetry ; when he made poetry his direct aim, though for brief moments he might attain it, he soon fell into unimaginative literalness, disguised by vehement emphasis.

BYRON AS HIS OWN CRITIC.

No one can make out a case for Byron as a critic, though he certainly got the best of the controversy with Mr. Bowles. In criticism, as in everything else, he was a partisan fighter. He held that the age of the heroic couplet was the great age of English poetry, and that Pope was its acme ; he thought the romantic movement a mistake. He regarded the greater part of his own work—nearly all that part of it which had won him popularity—as decadent stuff, and though he had good reason to regard himself as the grand "Napoleon of the realms of rhyme," he was uneasy about the quality of his fame. His expressions of indifference to it, of boredom and exasperation with it, were certainly half sincere. He could not help writing his Giaours, Corsairs, etc. : " But I have lived in far countries abroad," he says, "in the agitating world at home, which was not favourable to study or reflection, so that almost all I have written has been mere passion—passion, it is true, of different kinds, but always passion." He adds in apology, " But then, I did other things besides writing." His own work he compared to " lava whose eruption prevents earth-quake." " To withdraw *myself* from myself—oh, that cursed selfishness —has ever been my sole, my entire, my sincere motive in scribbling at all." He complains that even in that he has failed ; for his own private troubles run through everything he writes. All this shows that, though as a man he was as perplexed by his own character as those who knew him intimately usually were, he understood himself as an author very well. Once he compared himself to a tiger which attains its object at one bound, and if it missed, " goes growling back to its den." It would be impossible to find an apter comparison for his failure and success as a poet.

The Princess (II).

By D. H. LAWRENCE.

The peculiar spell of anger carried the Princess on, almost unconscious, for an hour or so. And by this time she was beginning to climb pretty high. Her horse walked steadily all the time. They emerged on a bare slope, and the trail wound through frail aspen-stems. Here a wind swept, and some of the aspens were already bare. Others were fluttering their discs of pure, solid yellow leaves, so *nearly* like petals, while the slope ahead was one soft, glowing fleece of daffodil yellow; fleecy like a golden foxskin, and yellow as daffodils alive in the wind and the high mountain sun.

She paused and looked back. The near great slopes were mottled with gold and the dark hue of spruce, like some unsinged eagle, and the light lay gleaming upon them. Away through the gap of the canyon she could see the pale blue of the egg-like desert, with the crumpled dark crack of the Rio Grande Canyon. And far, far off, the blue mountains like a fence of angels on the horizon.

And she thought of her adventure. She was going on alone with Romero. But then she was very sure of herself, and Romero was not the kind of man to do anything to her against her will. This was her first thought. And she just had a fixed desire to go over the brim of the mountains, to look into the inner chaos of the Rockies. And she wanted to go with Romero, because he had some peculiar kinship with her; there was some peculiar link between the two of them. Miss Cummins anyhow would have been only a discordant note.

She rode on, and emerged at length in the lap of the summit. Beyond her was a great concave of stone and stark, dead-grey trees, where the mountain ended against the sky. But nearer was the dense black, bristling spruce, and at her feet was the lap of the summit, a flat little valley of sere grass and quiet-standing yellow aspens, the stream trickling like a thread across.

THE PRINCESS

It was a little valley or shell from which the stream was gently poured into the lower rocks and trees of the canyon. Around her was a fairy-like gentleness, the delicate, sere grass, the groves of delicate-stemmed aspens dropping their flakes of bright yellow. And the delicate, quick little stream threading through the wild, sere grass.

Here one might expect deer and fawns and wild things, as in a little paradise. Here she was to wait for Romero, and they were to have lunch.

She unfastened her saddle and pulled it to the ground with a crash, letting her horse wander with a long rope. How beautiful Tansy looked, sorrel, among the yellow leaves that lay like a patina on the sere ground. The Princess herself wore a fleecy sweater of a pale, sere buff, like the grass, and riding breeches of a pure orange-tawny colour. She felt quite in the picture.

From her saddle pouches she took the packages of lunch, spread a little cloth, and sat to wait for Romero. Then she made a little fire. Then she ate a devilled egg. Then she ran after Tansy, who was straying across-stream. Then she sat in the sun, in the stillness near the aspens, and waited.

The sky was blue. Her little alp was soft and delicate as fairy-land. But beyond and up jutted the great slopes, dark with the pointed feathers of spruce, bristling with grey dead trees among grey rock, or dappled with dark and gold, The beautiful, but fierce, heavy, cruel mountains, with their moments of tenderness.

She saw Tansy start, and begin to run. Two ghost-like figures on horseback emerged from the black of the spruce across the stream. It was two Indians on horseback, swathed like seated mummies in their pale-grey cotton blankets. Their guns jutted beyond the saddles. They rode straight towards her, to her thread of smoke.

As they came near, they unswathed themselves and greeted her, looking at her curiously from their dark eyes. Their black hair was somewhat untidy, the long rolled plaits on their shoulders were soiled. They looked tired.

They got down from their horses near her little fire—a camp was a camp—swathed their blankets round their hips, pulled the saddles from their ponies and turned them loose, then sat down. One was a young Indian whom she had met before, the other was an older man.

" You all alone ? " said the younger man.

" Romero will be here in a minute," she said, glancing back along the trail.

" Ah, Romero ! You with him ? Where are you going ? "

" Round the ridge," she said. " Where are you going ? "

" We going down to Pueblo."

" Been out hunting ? How long have you been out ? "

" Yes. Been out five days." The young Indian gave a little meaningless laugh.

" Got anything ? "

" No. We see tracks of two deer—but not got nothing."

The Princess noticed a suspicious looking bulk under one of the saddles—surely a folded-up deer. But she said nothing.

" You must have been cold," she said.

" Yes, very cold in the night. And hungry. Got nothing to eat since yesterday. Eat it all up." And again he laughed his little meaningless laugh. Under their dark skins, the two men looked peaked and hungry. The Princess rummaged for food among the saddle-bags. There was a lump of bacon— the regular stand-back—and some bread. She gave them this, and they began toasting slices of it on long sticks at the fire. Such was the little camp Romero saw as he rode down the slope : the Princess in her orange breeches, her head tied in a blue-and-brown silk kerchief, sitting opposite the two dark-headed Indians across the camp-fire, while one of the Indians was leaning forward toasting bacon, his two plaits of braid-swathed hair dangling as if wearily.

Romero rode up, his face expressionless. The Indians greeted him in Spanish. He unsaddled his horse, took food from the bags, and sat down at the camp to eat. The Princess went to the stream for water, and to wash her hands.

" Got coffee ? " asked the Indians.

" No coffee this outfit," said Romero.

They lingered an hour or more in the warm midday sun. Then Romero saddled the horses. The Indians still squatted by the fire. Romero and the Princess rode away, calling *Adios !* to the Indians, over the stream and into the dense spruce whence the two strange figures had emerged.

When they were alone, Romero turned and looked at her curiously, in a way she could not understand, with such a hard glint in his eyes. And for the first time she wondered if she was rash.

" I hope you don't mind going alone with me," she said.

" If you want it," he replied.

They emerged at the foot of the great bare slope of rocky summit, where dead spruce-trees stood sparse and bristling like bristles on a grey dead hog. Romero said the Mexicans, twenty years back, had fired the mountains, to drive out the whites. This grey concave slope of summit was corpse-like.

The trail was almost invisible. Romero watched for the trees which the Forest Service had blazed. And they climbed the stark corpse slope, among dead spruce, fallen and ash-grey, into the wind. The wind came rushing from the west, up the funnel of the canyon, from the desert. And there was the desert, like a vast mirage tilting slowly upwards towards the west, immense and pallid, away beyond the funnel of the canyon. The Princess could hardly look.

For an hour their horses rushed the slope, hastening with a great working of the haunches upwards, and halting to breathe, scrambling again, and rowing their way up length by length, on the livid, slanting wall. While the wind blew like some vast machine.

After an hour they were working their way on the incline, no longer forcing straight up. All was grey and dead around them, the horses picked their way over the silver-grey corpses of the spruce. But they were near the top, near the ridge.

Even the horses made a rush for the last bit. They had worked round to a scrap of spruce forest near the very top. They hurried in, out of the huge, monstrous, mechanical wind, that whistled inhumanly and was palely cold. So, stepping through the dark screen of trees, they emerged over the crest.

In front now was nothing but mountains, ponderous, massive, down-sitting mountains, in a huge and intricate knot, empty of life or soul. Under the bristling black feathers of spruce nearby lay patches of white snow. The lifeless valleys were concaves of rock and spruce, the rounded summits and the hog-backed summits of grey rock crowded one behind the other like some monstrous herd in arrest.

It frightened the Princess, it was *so* inhuman. She had not thought it could be so inhuman, so, as it were, anti-life. And yet now one of her desires was fulfilled. She had seen it, the massive, gruesome, repellent core of the Rockies. She saw it there beneath her eyes, in its gigantic, heavy gruesomeness.

And she wanted to go back. At this moment she wanted to turn back. She had looked down into the intestinal knot of these mountains. She was frightened. She wanted to go back.

But Romero was riding on, on the lee side of the spruce forest, above the concaves of the inner mountains. He turned round to her and pointed at the slope with a dark hand.

" Here a miner has been trying for gold," he said. It was a grey, scratched-out heap near a hole—like a great badger hole. And it looked quite fresh.

" Quite lately ? " said the Princess.

" No, long ago—twenty, thirty years." He had reined in his horse and was looking at the mountains. "Look ! " he said. " There goes the Forest Service trail—along those ridges, on the top, way over there till it comes to Lucytown, where is the Government road. We go down there—no trail—see behind that mountain—you see the top, no trees, and some grass ? "

His arm was lifted, his brown hand pointing, his dark eyes piercing into the distance, as he sat on his black horse twisting round to her. Strange and ominous, only the demon of himself, he seemed to her. She was dazed and a little sick, at that height, and she could not see any more. Only she saw an eagle turning in the air beyond, and the light from the west showed the pattern on him underneath.

" Shall I ever be able to go so far ? " asked the Princess faintly, petulantly.

" Oh yes ! All easy now. No more hard places."

They worked along the ridge, up and down, keeping on the lee side, the inner side, in the dark shadow. It was cold. Then the trail laddered up again, and they emerged on a narrow ridge-track, with the mountain slipping away enormously on either side. The Princess was afraid. For one moment she looked out, and saw the desert, the desert ridges, more desert, more blue ridges, shining pale and very vast, far below, vastly palely tilting to the western horizon. It was ethereal and terrifying in its gleaming, pale, half-burnished immensity, tilted at the west. She could not bear it. To the left was the ponderous, involved mass of mountains all kneeling heavily.

She closed her eyes and let her consciousness evaporate away. The mare followed the trail. So on and on, in the wind again.

They turned their backs to the wind, facing inwards to the mountains. She thought they had left the trail; it was quite invisible.

" No," he said, lifting his hand and pointing. " Don't you see the blazed trees ? "

And making an effort of consciousness, she was able to perceive on a pale-grey dead spruce stem the old marks where an axe had chipped a piece away. But with the height, the cold, the wind, her brain was numb.

They turned again and began to descend ; he told her they had left the trail. The horses slithered in the loose stones, picking their way downward. It was afternoon, the sun stood obtrusive and gleaming in the lower heavens—about four o'clock. The horses went steadily, slowly, but obstinately onwards. The air was getting colder. They were in among the lumpish peaks and steep concave valleys. She was barely conscious at all of Romero.

He dismounted and came to help her from her saddle. She tottered, but would not betray her feebleness.

" We must slide down here," he said. " I can lead the horses."

They were on a ridge, and facing a steep bare slope of pallid, tawny mountain grass on which the western sun shone full. It was steep and concave. The Princess felt she might start slipping, and go down like a toboggan into the great hollow.

But she pulled herself together. Her eye blazed up again with excitement and determination. A wind rushed past her ; she could hear the shriek of spruce trees far below. Bright spots came on her cheeks as her hair blew across. She looked a wild, fairy-like little thing.

" No," she said. " I will take my horse."

" Then mind she doesn't slip down on top of you," said Romero. And away he went, nimbly dropping down the pale, steep incline, making from rock to rock, down the grass, and following any little slanting groove. His horse hopped and slithered after him, and sometimes stopped dead, with forefeet pressed back, refusing to go further. He, below his horse, looked up and pulled the reins gently, and encouraged the creature. Then the horse once more dropped his forefeet with a jerk, and the descent continued.

The Princess set off in blind, reckless pursuit, tottering and yet nimble. And Romero, looking constantly back to see how she was faring, saw her fluttering down like some queer little bird, her orange breeches twinkling like the legs of some duck, and her head, tied in the blue and buff kerchief, bound round and round like the head of some blue-topped bird. The sorrel mare rocked and slipped behind her. But down came the Princess in a reckless intensity, a tiny, vivid spot on the great hollow flank of the tawny mountain. So tiny! Tiny as a frail bird's egg. It made Romero's mind go blank with wonder.

But they had to get down, out of that cold and dragging wind. The spruce trees stood below, where a tiny stream emerged in stones. Away plunged Romero, zigzagging down. And away behind, up the slope, fluttered the tiny, bright-coloured Princess, holding the end of the long reins, and leading the lumbering, four-footed, sliding mare.

At last they were down. Romero sat in the sun, below the wind, beside some squaw-berry bushes. The Princess came near, the colour flaming in her cheeks, her eyes dark blue, much darker than the kerchief on her head, and glowing unnaturally.

" We make it," said Romero.

" Yes," said the Princess, dropping the reins and subsiding on to the grass, unable to speak, unable to think.

But, thank heaven, they were out of the wind and in the sun.

In a few minutes her consciousness and her control began to come back. She drank a little water. Romero was attending to the saddles. Then they set off again, leading the horses still a little further down the tiny stream-bed. Then they could mount.

They rode down a bank and into a valley grove dense with aspens. Winding through the thin, crowding, pale-smooth stems, the sun shone flickering beyond them, and the disc-like aspen leaves, waving queer mechanical signals, seemed to be splashing the gold light before her eyes. She rode on in a splashing dazzle of gold.

Then they entered shadow and the dark, resinous spruce trees. The fierce boughs always wanted to sweep her off her horse. She had to twist and squirm past.

But there was a semblance of an old trail. And all at once they emerged in the sun on the edge of the spruce-grove, and there was a little cabin, and the bottom of a small, naked valley with grey rock and heaps of stones, and a round pool of intense green water, dark green. The sun was just about to leave it. Indeed, as she stood, the shadow came over the cabin and over herself ; they were in the lower gloom, a twilight. Above, the heights still blazed.

It was a little hole of a cabin, near the spruce trees, with an earthen floor and an unhinged door. There was a wooden bed-bunk, three old sawn-off log-lengths to sit on as stools, and a sort of fireplace ; no room for anything else. The little hole would hardly contain two people. The roof had gone— but Romero had laid on thick spruce-boughs.

The strange squalor of the primitive forest pervaded the place, the squalor of animals and their droppings, the squalor of the wild. The Princess knew the peculiar repulsiveness of it. She was tired and faint.

Romero hastily got a handful of twigs, set a little fire going in the stove grate, and went out to attend to the horses. The Princess vaguely, mechanically, put sticks on the fire, in a sort of stupor, watching the blaze, stupefied and fascinated. She could not make much fire—it would set the whole cabin alight. And smoke oozed out of the dilapidated mud-and-stone chimney.

When Romero came in with the saddle-pouches and saddles, hanging the saddles on the wall, there sat the little Princess on her stump of wood in front of the dilapidated fire-grate, warming her tiny hands at the blaze, while her orange breeches glowed almost like another fire. She was in a sort of stupor

" You have some whisky now, or some tea ? Or wait for some soup ? " he asked.

She rose and looked at him with bright, dazed eyes, half comprehending ; the colour glowing hectic in her cheeks.

"Some tea," she said, "with a little whisky in it. Where's the kettle ? "

"Wait," he said, " I'll bring the things."

She took her cloak from the back of her saddle, and followed him into the open. It was a deep cup of shadow. But above the sky was still shining, and the heights of the mountains were blazing with aspen like fire blazing.

Their horses were cropping the grass among the stones. Romero clambered up a heap of grey stones and began lifting away logs and rocks, till he had opened the mouth of one of the miner's little old workings. This was his cache. He brought out bundles of blankets, pans for cooking, a little petrol camp-stove, an axe, the regular camp outfit. He seemed so quick and energetic and full of force. This quick force dismayed the Princess a little.

She took a saucepan and went down the stones to the water. It was very still and mysterious, and of a deep green colour, yet pure, transparent as glass. How cold the place was ! How mysterious and fearful.

She crouched in her dark cloak by the water, rinsing the saucepan, feeling the cold heavy above her, the shadow like a vast weight upon her, bowing her down. The sun was leaving the mountain tops, departing, leaving her under profound shadow. Soon it would crush her down completely.

Sparks ?—or eyes looking at her across the water ? She gazed, hypnotised. And with her sharp eyes she made out in the dusk the pale form of a bob-cat crouching by the water's edge, pale as the stones among which it crouched, opposite. And it was watching her with cold, electric eyes of strange intentness, a sort of cold, icy wonder and fearlessness. She saw its *musseau* pushed forward, its tufted ears pricking intensely up. It was watching her with cold, animal curiosity, something demonish and conscienceless.

She made a swift movement, spilling her water. And in a flash the creature was gone, leaping like a cat that is escaping ; but strange and soft in its motion, with its little bob-tail. Rather fascinating. Yet that cold, intent, demonish watching ! She shivered with cold and fear. She knew well enough the dread and repulsiveness of the wild.

Romero carried in the bundles of bedding and the camp

outfit. The windowless cabin was already dark inside. He lit a lantern, and then went out again with the axe. She heard him chopping wood as she fed sticks to the fire under her water. When he came in with an armful of oak-scrub faggots, she had just thrown the tea into the water.

"Sit down," she said, "and drink tea."

He poured a little bootleg whiskey into the enamel cups, and in the silence the two sat on the log-ends, sipping the hot liquid and coughing occasionally from the smoke.

"We burn these oak sticks," he said. "They don't make hardly any smoke."

Curious and remote he was, saying nothing except what had to be said. And she, for her part, was as remote from him. They seemed far, far apart, worlds apart, now they were so near.

He unwrapped one bundle of bedding, and spread the blankets and the sheepskin in the wooden bunk.

"You lie down and rest," he said, "and I make the supper."

She decided to do so. Wrapping her cloak round her, she lay down in the bunk, turning her face to the wall. She could hear him preparing supper over the little petrol stove. Soon she could smell the soup he was heating; and soon she heard the hissing of fried chicken in a pan.

"You eat your supper now?" he said.

With a jerky, despairing movement, she sat up in the bunk, tossing back her hair, She felt cornered.

"Give it me here," she said.

He handed her first the cupful of soup. She sat among the blankets, eating it slowly. She was hungry. Then he gave her an enamel plate with pieces of fried chicken and currant jelly, butter and bread. It was very good. As they ate the chicken he made the coffee. She said never a word. A certain resentment filled her. She was cornered.

When supper was over he washed the dishes, dried them, and put everything away carefully, else there would have been no room to move in the hole of a cabin. The oak-wood gave out a good bright heat.

He stood for a few moments at a loss. Then he asked her:

"You want to go to bed soon?"

"Soon," she said. "Where are you going to sleep?"

"I make my bed here—" he pointed to the floor along the wall. "Too cold out of doors."

"Yes," she said, "I suppose it is."

She sat immobile, her cheeks hot, full of conflicting thoughts. And she watched him while he folded the blankets on the floor, a sheepskin underneath. Then she went out into the night.

The stars were big. Mars sat on the edge of a mountain, for all the world like the blazing eye of a crouching mountain lion.· But she herself was deep, deep below in a pit of shadow. In the intense silence she seemed to hear the spruce forest crackling with electricity and cold. Strange, foreign stars floated on that unmoving water. The night was going to freeze. Over the hills came the far sobbing-singing howling of the coyotes. She wondered how the horses would be.

Shuddering a little, she turned to the cabin. Warm light showed through its chinks. She pushed at the rickety, half-opened door.

"What about the horses?" she said.

"My black, he won't go away. And your mare will stay with him.—You want to go to bed now?"

"I think I do."

"All right. I feed the horses some oats."

And he went out into the night.

He did not come back for some time. She was lying wrapped up tight in the bunk.

He blew out the lantern, and sat down on his bedding to take off his clothes. She lay with her back turned. And soon, in the silence, she was asleep.

She dreamed it was snowing, and the snow was falling on her through the roof, softly, softly, helplessly, and she was going to be buried alive. She was growing colder and colder, the snow was weighing down on her. The snow was going to absorb her.

(To be concluded next month.)

Scrutinies

(2) Walter de la Mare.

By DOUGLAS GARMAN.

"HE was clearly the fruit of breeding-in . . . what the dear old evolutionists esteem a *sport* . . . and he had bats in his belfry . . . *extra*-terrestrial bats." In his hands, of course, the firm of Lispet, Lispett & Vaine went bankrupt, but he, Anthony, did not care. He sat alone in his decaying factory, planning a "kind of ludicrous doll's merchandise," content to follow the bidding of the Sylph who had been "evoked by a moment's aspiration and delight out of his own sublime wool-gatherings." Astutely, de la Mare does not present him isolated in his pathetic fatuity, but sets him off against a prosaic audience, the better to show where his own sympathies lie. To him Anthony is the true type of the imaginative mind, the visionary, the sublime. He has escaped completely from the matter-of-fact into the dream world of his own making. De la Mare has not been so successful : scantly he acknowledges the prosaic, though his most typical work is the reflection of a belief in his own emancipation.

From the beginning, de la Mare postulated two independent worlds, Anthony's and reality, not spontaneously, but from necessity born of a distaste for the one in which he found himself. This being the case, he turned to poetry for the *Open Sesame* which would admit him to the former, but his poetry fails because he lacks imagination, the oracle of all pass-words. Fancy, to accept Coleridge's distinction, he has in plenty, and in his essay on Rupert Brooke has written a defence of it. He splits the poetical imagination into two distinct types, "the one visionary, the other intellectual," but he only effects a distinction between the former and *fancy* when he says : "The visionaries . . . have to learn to substantiate their imaginings, to base their fantastic palaces on *terra firma*, to weave their dreams into the fabric of actuality." So he breaks down the contrast between the visionary and the intellectual, for this substantiation of imaginings can only come about through "knowledge and experience"—means which he would appropriate solely to the use of the intellectual imagination. The means by which he would replace it, intuition or divination, are not the antitheses he suggests. They are the components of any imagination; the greater part, in fact, since it is they which enable the mind to fill out and give form to its experience.

In practice he has shown an increasing recognition of the importance of building on *terra firma*, if not in his verse at any rate in his tales. But by excluding from his work humanity, the passions and ethics, he has rashly limited the modes of perceiving beauty to a single factitious aspiration. To a great extent he has the power of inducing a belief in the "poetic state," nebulous and undefined, and the degree to which he is accepted as a poet depends on the susceptibility of the reader to this belief, for without it his poetic consciousness is a world of tinsel, based in no fundamental part of general consciousness. Once the validity of this thaumaturgic power is admitted, de la Mare becomes a magician; if we drink the fairy wine, "then us will *all* be changed into wild swans, Sally, and fly —fly away over the trees to the sea."

Now de la Mare has two ways of administering this wine. Either directly, by the power of words—imagery, metaphor, music—usually in verse; or indirectly, usually in prose. It is not without purpose that his stories are so often repeated or recollected, rather than told: an intermediary is necessary. Nor is it chance that these should be usually monkeys, old people, half-wits, deformities, unchildlike children or fairies, for otherwise they would not serve their purpose. Their abnormal vision prepares the transition of the reader's consciousness from the real to the unreal, and serves as a filter through which the stream of raw life may be strained.

At first the method was an ingenuous one. Mount your hero on Rosinante and let him loose in a dream-world peopled with the ghosts of fiction, romance or allegory, and he is unlikely to be over-troubled with the facts of existence. At the same time his adventures afford unbounded scope for the description of phantastic countrysides and for a flood of diluted, lifeless philosophising. But Mr. de la Mare was not content to ride for ever behind Henry Brocken, or perhaps he just slipped off that emaciated rump on to the hard earth and was awoken. In any case he was undaunted. He set off on a trip with three monkeys—one of whom, of course possessed the Wonder-Stone—to discover Tishnar, that land of happiness from which death is banished. For children— and, ostensibly, the book was written for them—the journey is a success, since its end is attained; but for us, though it contains de la Mare's philosophy, it is a failure, since the appended description of Tishnar ends with the admission that, as everyone can see, he is only chattering about what he cannot understand.

After these two exotic experiences it would seem that the hand of reality began to tug more insistently at the magician's robe, for the action of the next novel takes place in a suburban town. The *timbre* of the book is also changed, losing to a certain extent "that peculiar little bell-peal in the voice which one simply cannot avoid when trying to placate infants, the ailing, and the aged." The approach to phenomena is at once more scientific and direct, and the intermediary is at least a man, albeit mentally deranged. But the bias of the book is still anti-human. The revenant is, by his insanity, endowed with the qualities which enable him to find his way unhampered into the world beyond; he is the fictitious link making unreality plausible. But here the falsity of values which he supports is not blatant while he is partaking of a ghostly life, it is only when he is in contact with his wife or her friends that the fundamental shallowness of the story is revealed. It is as though de la Mare had less faith in Tishnar, and were looking back over his shoulder at the existence from which he was fleeing. Yet, when for a moment he checks the panic of escape, he writes of a world filled with crude wax-works who take part uncouthly in a lifeless melodrama.

And so with ever more frequent backward glances he wrote the *Memoirs of a Midget*. It is a supreme *tour de force*, depending for its value on its characteristics of picturesqueness and pathos. Fanny Bowater alone lives : the other characters are the stock-in-trade of a very accomplished writer, lay figures used as the *décor* for an anæmic drama. The world is distorted by the peevish, debilitated vision of a freak, and the ingenuity with which de la Mare sustains the illusion of two antagonistic modes of life is the measure of his talent. By her nature the Midget is debarred from vital experience, so that her emotional life can, without falsification, take place in a plane of emasculate feelings, remorse and self-pity. It required a great degree of skill to make this perverted relationship of a dwarf and a hunchback tragic, but de la Mare has almost succeeded by the subtle toning-down of emotional value and by presenting the specific limitations of the Midget as general. In all the material details of her existence there is meticulous exactitude, but, since she is psychologically normal, this allows her that very freedom from the body which makes credible de la Mare's postulation of an independent, fantastic world. This is exactly the same fiction as that on which rests his conception of children. They, he maintains, " live in a world peculiarly their own, so much so that it is doubtful if the adult can do more than very fleetingly reoccupy that far-away consciousness. . . . They are not bound in by their groping senses. . . . Between their dream and their reality looms no impassable abyss." This is an unequivocal but arbitrary assumption, based on a neglect of facts or failure to observe them. Yet it is demanded by his point of view. Without some such pretext the theory of an intrinsically poetic attitude would be impossible. In man the animal is too obvious to be denied : children and the abnormal, however, are more feasibly, though quite erroneously, assumed to be free from the taints of an unbroken process of evolution. Without bowels or sexual desire they are apt subjects of, or mediums for, de la Mare's poetic hypnosis.

All poetry is, of course, in a sense hypnotic, since it is its function to produce in the reader a state of mind, an attitude towards life, prescribed by the poet. Its value depends on the nature of this attitude and therefore on the technique by which alone it may be apprehended. So de la Mare's poetry, which forsakes humanity and this world for fairies and Araby, can only be of worth inasmuch as it is woven " into the fabric of reality." But we are like Thumb in *The Three Mulla-Mulgars*, we feel as he did towards Nod : " Have it as you will. It is easy to fear nothing and to see what is not here when you meddle with magic " ; only we cannot admit the potency of the magic. In the past poets had this magic at their disposal, whether as a pagan theogony or as Christianity, but for them there was no need to transmute it : it was reality. To Milton the divinity of Christ was a fact, and Satan was a mighty prince. In writing of them he was writing of a concept which was as actual a part of his consciousness as the mystery of vision or the fact of birth. But we have no such belief, and the poet who would substitute for it a factitious one, in magic or the æsthetic state, is essentially decadent.

And this decadence is at once noticeable in Mr. de la Mare's technique. Poetic differs from scientific expression in its ability to make use of qualities of language other than those which specifically belong to it, but these qualities may be exploited to the detriment of expression, as is the case with de la Mare. His extreme sensibility to the musical value of words often leads to an invertebrate style ; he sacrifices coherence to a meretricious effect. Such lines, for instance, as " *Upon a bank, easeless with knobs of gold,*" or " *Where*on *a small and sanguine sun Floats* in *a mirror on,*" or " *His fangs like spears in him uprose,*" approximate to the effect he intends, but are almost nonsense. His use of inversion has the same result of weakening his meaning by flouting the intellect. " *O restless fingers—not that music make* " ; " *Small at the window looped cowled bat awing* " ; " *And there fell upon his sense . . . the faint shrill sweetness of the birds' throats, Their tent of leaves beneath.*"

Yet, since Mr. de la Mare is an accomplished technician, it would be mere carping to draw attention to the weaknesses of his style, were it not that they all point to an innate degeneracy. The use of archaisms—even such as are conventionally accepted as proper to poetic diction—inevitably destroys the virility of a language, and the coinage of words when not absolutely necessary is evidence of a writer's debility. They result in a windy rhetoric or a fantastic vagueness ; sometimes, as in *In the Dock*, in a melodramatic crudity. The characteristics of Mr. de la Mare's style are the characteristics of his mind—" obviously the fruit of breeding-in." His imagery is seldom drawn from direct sensuous experience, but is taken from books or the storehouse of pale reverie. This is very noticeable in his descriptions. The different facets do not conspire together to give solidity because they are not chosen to satisfy a fundamental sensuous need, but are selected for their derivative or face-value.

The effect of his poems is to produce an atmosphere of romance, or mystery, or simulated childishness. This is the initial stage, corresponding to the intermediary in his prose tales, which tempers the reader's mind to a condition susceptible to de la Mare's point of view. Imagination requires no such preliminary process : it takes the incoherent experiences of life and, by giving them form, creates its own standard of values. Fancy cannot do this. It accepts its values, ready-made, from an extrinsic conception, and can only communicate them by an intermediary process. It results in the divorce of art from life, for the poetry which it dictates is incapable of creating a valid attitude to life and does not, therefore, fulfil its essential function.

The Natural Pander : Leopold Bloom and Others.

By BERTRAM HIGGINS.

THROUGHOUT literature there runs a figure which makes an appeal different in kind from the rest of the literary creation by approaching an identity in its various manifestations. Gargantua, Sancho Panza, The Wife of Bath, Falstaff, Uncle Toby, Pickwick are outstanding examples of a unique confraternity whose birth cannot be explained by the artist's usual process of abstracting objects from the wave-like, subsuming action of experience, and disclosing their unpredictable individuality. When this process of abstraction is unduly simplified, as it is in the mediæval Morality plays, the apprehension of the characters by the audience is restricted to that same portion of the mind which was exerted by their authors. There some single quality of a character is developed to its utmost by the logic of imagination, but—except for certain passages where, inevitably, the genius proved too strong for the intention—this quality is stressed at such expense to the others that, as in a physical organism, the localised vitality sets up a malignant growth to which the whole succumbs. Extremism of simplification is a danger to which the writers of a classic tradition also are exposed : Molière's comedy of Types and Ben Jonson's comedy of Humours are, in plan, only one degree more complex than the spectacle of personified Virtues and Vices, and their superiority as creations is due solely to the poetic power which refined and particularised them in the course of composition, multiplying life in the hardly animate uni-cellular *dramatis personæ* of the original conception. The writers of what is called a romantic tradition are liable to the opposite set of temptations. Their altered vision peoples the world with new forms, and until the arrival of a mature spokesman they cultivate the variety of human nature to a point at which it is snapped off from connection with its roots.

" Hernani " was hissed at, with good reason, for its exaggera
tion and unreality; Byron's dramatic figures disintegrate
when the support of his immediate sentiment is withdrawn;
Balzac and Dickens, even, lavish so much attention on freaks
that we suspect an uncertain principle of life behind their
invention. Take, now, a great artist of a transitional period.
Dostoevsky's rooted dissatisfaction with the conditions of
his time, the reforming ambitions which were imposed upon
him by a transitional environment, laid this embarrassment
on his work, that, finding the actual world slow and unmalle-
able to his realisation of its needs, he was driven to project
his entire scene into an atmosphere of prophecy, in which the
spirit of the characters is always tending to break away from
their flesh and Nature suspends action in a universal yearning
towards futurity. It is Dostoevsky's tremendous artistic
will that keeps his figures upright on this base of shifting sands.
    The ordinary literary creation is as subtly influenced by
such conditions as a human embryo is by the incidents of
pregnancy. But the members of our unique confraternity—
they might be nicknamed the Confraternity of Natural
Panders—are sensitive only to the broad modifications which
approximate them to the ideal of their tribe. An individual
in literature, a Hamlet, is built up by a progression of related
qualities which have no coherence outside his personality;
a type, a Tartuffe, is maintained by the exclusion from his
conduct of all traits save those which illustrate the moral
idea that is his essence. The natural pander, on the other
hand, neither progresses, like the individual, nor simplifies
himself, like the type. He embodies something constant in
human nature, and his embodiment is static. It would be
dogmatic to assert that Falstaff disclosed himself in his fulness
from the hour when he was born " with a white head and
something a round belly " till the moment when they became
" as cold as any stone," for Shakespeare, with right intuition,
produces him middle-aged; but his reproach to the case-
hardened young king, " Banish plump Jack, and banish *all
the world*," impresses us like the word of an Old Testament
prophet revealing his mission. What is the extra-personal
attribute in Falstaff that establishes his identity with the other
natural panders ? It is his role of man purely vegetative and

animal conserving the creation in which he is at home, and dispensing with the whole shadow-world of man ideal. "Can honour set to a leg ? No : or take away the grief of a wound ? No. Honour has no skill as surgery, then ? No. What is honour ? A word. What is that word honour ? What is that honour ? Air. A trim reckoning ! . . Honour is a mere scutcheon : and so ends my catechism."

They are our throw-backs, and we are their monsters. Our aspirations are checked or purified by contact with their vulgar good nature : so valid, indeed, is the test, that their creators use them as impersonal forces, as trustworthy instruments of renewal to be moved up into the slack portions of the play, narrative or poem. " Comic relief " is a true phrase, for laughter is the last resort both of invention and of criticism ; its extraverting energy clears the ground for a resumption of the constructive or of the analytic attempt, where persistent earnestness would only thicken the mists. The formula of the natural panders is the Roman Catholic motto for Ash Wednesday, but with reversed bias: *Memento homo quia pulvis es et in pulverem reverteris*. Their service to us resembles that of the life-revivers in the ancient Dithyrambic Rites and May Festivals. The physical gestures of joy and suppliance with which our ancestors greeted Spring have been transferred to the mind, and modern man gratifies the same impulses when, on the mental level, he turns to the cornucopia of comedy for renewal.

In our age a permanent addition has been made to the ranks of the natural panders in the person of Leopold Bloom, the part-hero of "Ulysses." Mr. Joyce has fashioned the two principal figures of his gigantic exposition in an antithetical form inherited from great writers of the past. The radical opposing concepts of philosophy, matter and mind, intellect and feeling, subject and object, have become flesh in some of the most deliberated works of art, for art realises what thought discovers, and the only act impossible to its nature is the Hegelian synthesis with which philosophy closes shop. Bloom and Stephen Dedalus are perhaps the most logically opposed pair that ever issued from this convention, if we except Sancho Panza and Quixote, who are the creations of a mind untroubled by the strife for new categories. Hazlitt says of "Tristram Shandy" that Sterne "has contrived to oppose, with equal felicity and originality, two characters, one of pure intellect, and the other of pure good nature." Stephen and Bloom are cast into the same elementary mould as My Father and My Uncle Toby; but the differences in their relations are stressed by the dissimilarity of their authors' intentions. Sterne's predominating interest in the affective part of conduct caused him to drag Uncle Toby intermittently from his proper stand of natural pander to gain a sentimental triumph over My Father, and this wilful translation of a natural into a moral force unbalances the book. In "Ulysses," so unwavering is the construction, so disciplined the development, the protagonists are not once perverted from themselves in enslavement to a minor or cursory desire of their author's; the objective scheme is maintained with a pertinacity heroic in a work of such dimensions. Indeed, as we shall see later, Bloom and Stephen are not even allowed mutual comprehension; they pass and repass one another in their odysseys without establishing contact.

Bloom's status is made clear at his first introduction:

"Mr. Leopold Bloom ate with relish the inner organs of beasts and fowls. He liked thick giblet soup, nutty gizzards, a stuffed roast heart, liver slices fried with crustcrumbs, fried hencods' roes. Most of all, he liked grilled mutton kidneys, which gave to his palate a fine tang of faintly-scented urine."

Savages believe that they annex the qualities of animals by eating them. The same instinct is shown in the natural panders, who invariably have a heavy meat diet; and we must remember that the god from whom their name derives won his hoofs by creative devolution. But Bloom is a pander with a difference: all the others are, in varying degrees, uninhibited agents who externalise their whole flow of energy; Bloom is a pander discomfited, like Pan, by the movement of the world away from a state in which his impulses were natural towards one in which it is necessary to repress, moderate, or sublimate them. He cannot even express his case against this alien dispensation in its own terms. The incidental fact that he is a Jew, whose *damnosa hereditas* is homelessness, adds nourishment to the real roots of his indignation:

" — And I belong to a race, too," says Bloom, " that is

hated and persecuted. Also now. This very moment. This very instant.

Gob, he near burnt his fingers with the butt of his old cigar.

— Robbed, says he. Plundered. Insulted. Persecuted. Taking what belongs to us by right. At this very moment, says he, putting up his fist, sold by auction off in Morocco like slaves or cattle.

— Are you talking about the new Jerusalem ? says the citizen.

— I'm talking about injustice, says Bloom. . . . And then he collapses all of a sudden, twisting round all the opposite, as limp as a wet rag.

— But it's no use, says he. Force, hatred, history, all that. That's not life for men and women, insult and hatred. And everybody knows that it's the very opposite of that that is really life.

What ? says Alf.

— Love, says Bloom. I mean the opposite of hatred. I must go now."

This is the explanation of the melancholy that suffuses the whole of his mental life, which Mr. Joyce present in minute detail and in a variety of style that shapes itself intricately round the tiny crises of his day's experience. It is a quality in Bloom which might have been exploited to effect a working sympathy between him and Stephen Dedalus. Bloom's melancholy is the outcome of his thwarted senses, and Stephen's personality is wrapped in a despair that arises from his foiled search for an abstract ideal. Or rather, from his failure to solve the conflict in his nature which keeps him back from self-fulfilment. The problem he detects in Shakespeare is his own : " his unremitting intellect is the hornmad Iago ceaselessly willing that the Moor in him shall suffer." He is bound to the past by what psycho-analysts call an emotional fixation, for his speculative genius, while it flouts, is whirled in a circle round the Jesuitical God of his boyhood, and the victim of his most reckless attempt for liberation paralyses his later endeavours with remorse:

> " Silently, in a dream, his mother had come to him
> after her death, her wasted body within its loose brown
> graveclothes giving off an odour of wax and rosewood,

her breath, that had been upon him, mute, reproachful, a faint odour of wetted ashes."

But Bloom's paternal solicitude for Stephen in the brothel episode, and his doubly paternal attitude in the scene immediately subsequent (he sees in Stephen the man into whom his son Ruby might have grown, had he lived) are not so much as repulsed. Stephen's self-willed inhumanity as a social being seems to endow him with an angelic body which can hold no parley with the human substance ; more truly, he is an intermediate being like the Virgil who guided and guarded Dante in supernatural territory. The only acquaintance who distracts his consciousness into forming a self-defensive concept is Buck Milligan, whose shrewd mocking peasant's mind follows him about like Lear's fool, annotating his thought with affection, pity and derision.

The fate that prevents Bloom and Stephen from pooling any part of their experience is evidenced in the first episodes of "Ulysses"—in which the two streams of consciousness are realized with a minimum of comment—and proved in the long cross-examination section near the end of the book. The superficial conclusiveness of the summaries here is a parody of law-court methods:

> " Did Bloom discover common factors of similarity between their respective like and unlike reactions to experience ?—Both were sensitive to artistic impressions, musical in preference to plastic or pictorial. Both preferred a Continental to an insular manner of life, a cisatlantic to a transatlantic place of residence. Both, indurated by early domestic training and an inherited tenacity of heterodox resistance, professed their disbelief in many orthodox, religious, national, social and ethical doctrines. Both admitted the alternately stimulating and obtunding influence of heterosexual magnetism."

The human mind is in a ceaseless state of becoming ; with each new impression made by an image or an idea it is altered instantaneously and irretrievably, its combinations are reshuffled and the qualifying power of memory is swelled or sifted. Apart from his innovating greatness, as pure writer, in grafting on to prose a new vitalizing gland from poetry (an artificial rejuvenation of which it is in periodic need), Mr. Joyce's method of recording the innermost activities of Bloom and Stephen is a highly original attempt to bring literary art into a more intimate relation with the time factor of mind-processes. On the novelistic side he has found a new angle of impartiality for the delineation of character by disclosing the thread of association on which the mind climbs to its quickly-falling climaxes, where his predecessors have restricted themselves, more or less, to a description and elaboration of the climaxes.

It is like an ordeal of water for Bloom and Stephen, a flooding of their minds to test the weight and volume of the contents. We see Bloom reacting almost exclusively to the practical incidents of his environment ; his selection of objects is like a scavenger's, an aggrandisement of oddments to gratify his stray desires. His perceptions are brought to a head, not by the intimation of a concept or feeling waiting to impose order, but by sudden sensuous memories. Here is a typical passage of his mind :

"Enough of this place. Brings you a bit nearer every time. Last time I was here it was Mrs. Simco's funeral. Poor papa too. The love that kills. And even scraping up the earth at night with a lantern like that case I read of to get at fresh buried females. . . . Gives you the creeps after a bit. I will appear to you after death. . . . Plenty to see and hear and feel yet. Feel live warm beings near you. Let them sleep in their maggoty beds. They are not going to get me this innings. Warm beds."

For Stephen, on the other hand, a thing perceived is like a note struck to suggest a whole symphony of words and ideas, and during the improvisation he resents any further intrusion by the external world :

"She trudges, schlepps, trains, drags, trascines her load. A tide, westering, moondrawn, in her wake. Tides, myriadislanded, within her, blood not mine, *oinopa ponton*, a winedark sea. Behold the handmaid of the moon. In sleep the wet sign calls her hour, bids her rise. Bridebed, childbed, bed of death, ghostcandled. *Omnis caro ad te veniet.* He comes, pale vampire, through storm his eyes, his bat sails bloodying the sea " . . .

THE CALENDAR

The effect of this form of presentation in a prolonged reading is a gradual hypnosis of those faculties which impede the action of (in Ruskin's phrase) " imagination penetrative." The reader's attention is so taken up with the minute parts in which the subject is presented, in order that it may be reconstructed with the minimum of official dogma, that the moment of inactive contemplation, the crisis of aesthetic experience, is in danger of fatal postponement. Whether for this reason or another, Mr. Joyce, while carrying through the experiment, falls back on his technical virtuosity to preserve Bloom and Dedalus from dissolution within the mass of their experience. But for this saving device Bloom would probably have floundered from extension of bulk, and Stephen have been lost to humanity in the essential state to which his consuming daemon refines him.

The Big Drum.

By WILLIAM GERHARDI

THE brass band played *Im Köpfle zwei Äugle*, and it seemed to her that the souls of these men were like notes of this music, crying for something elusive, for something in vain. To blare forth one's love on a brass trumpet ! An earnest of one's high endeavour fallen short through the inadequate matter of brass ; but withal in these abortive notes one felt the presence of the heights the instrument would reach, alas, if it but could !

It touched her to the heart. She would have liked her Otto to play the trumpet instead of the big drum. It seemed more romantic. Otto was not a bit romantic. He was a soldier all right, but he looked more like a man who had started life as a shoemaker's apprentice, had grown old, and was still a shoemaker's apprentice. The band played well— a compact synthetic body—but Otto was a forlorn figure who watched the proceedings with sustained and patient interest and was suffered by them, every now and then, to raise his drumstick and to give a solitary, judicious " Bang ! " And he—a tall gaunt man—seemed as though he were ashamed of his small part. And as she watched him she felt a pang of pity for herself : wedded to him, she would be forgotten, while life, indifferent, strode by ; and no one in the world would care whether she had her share of happiness before she died. And the music brought this out acutely, as if along the hard stone-paved indifference of life it dragged, dragged on excruciatingly its living bleeding soul. It spoke of loneliness, of laughter, of the pathos, pity and futility of life.

She watched them. The bayonets at their side. The military badges of rank. The hard discipline. And the music seemed to say, " Stop ! What are you doing ? Why are you doing this ? " And thoughts flowed into her mind. Of soldiers dreaming on a Sunday afternoon. A fierce old corporal of whom everyone was afraid talking to her of children

and of daisies. Soldiers who, too, had dreams in long waves
—of what ? she did not know—but not this. And the men
who stood up and blew the brass trumpets seemed to say,
and the shining trumpets themselves seemed to say: " We
were not born for the Army ; we were born for something
better—though Heaven only knows what it is !"

That was so. Undeniably so. Yet she wished it were
otherwise. It helped to make allowances for Otto. Whatever
else he lacked, it made her think at least he had a soul. But
to be wedded for life to the big drum ! She did not fancy the
idea. It didn't seem a proper career. But Otto showed no
sign of *wanting* to " get on "—even in the orchestra. The
most exasperating thing about it all was that Otto showed
no sign of even *trying* ! She had asked him if he would not,
in time, " move on " and take over—say, the double-bass.
He did not seem to think it either feasible or necessary. Or
necessary ! He had been with the big drum for close on twelve
years. " It's a good drum," he had said. And that was all.

There was no . . . " go " in him. That was it : no
go. It was no use denying it. As she watched him—gaunt
and spectacled—she wished Otto were more of a man and
less of an old maid. The conductor, a boozer with a fat red
face full of pimples, some dead and dried up, others still
flourishing, was a gallant—every inch a man. He had the
elasticity and suppleness and military alertness of the continental military man. She could not tell his rank from the
stripes on his sleeves, but thought he must be a major. His
heels were high and tipped with indiarubber, and so were
straight and smart, but his trousers lacked the footstrap to
keep them in position—poor dilapidated Austrian Army !
How low it had sunk ! Nevertheless they were tight and
narrow and showed off the major's calves to advantage. He
wore a pince-nez, but a rimless kind, through which gazed a
pair of not altogether innocent eyes. But a man and a leader
of men. While Otto had no rubber on his heels. His heels
looked eaten away. He wore a pair of spectacles through
which he peered from afar at his neighbour's music-stand,
and at the appointed time—not one-tenth of a second too
late or too early—down came the drumstick with the long-
awaited " Bang ! " So incidental, so contemptible was Otto's

part that, in addition to handling the drum, he had to turn the pages for the man who played the cymbals. It seemed to her humiliating. It was very wrong that Otto had no music-stand of his own.

He smiled shyly, and she turned away, annoyed. The little modiste walked on, meeting the stream of people who promenaded the path surrounding the bandstand; a man on high heels, three girls with a pinched look, a famous Tyrolese basso with a long ruddy beard, a *jeune premier* with whiskers and hair like a wig, whose look appeared to imply : " Here am I." Innsbruck looked morose that Sunday morning, and the military band in the park executed music that was tattered, gross, a little common, yet compelling, even like the daily fare of life. Oh, why were there no heroes ? Of course she would have loved to be dominated. That's what men were for. She was a womanly woman. From Vienna. Exalted, brimming over with life. These men of the Tyrol ! And as for Otto ? Why, she could have only waved her hand !

She began to wonder whether she had not really better break it off with him. If men would but realise how little was required from them. Only an outward gesture of romance : a touch sufficed, the rest would be supplied by woman's powerful imagination. Not even so much. A mere abstention from the cruder forms of clumsiness, a surface effort to conceal one's feeblest worst. A mere semblance of mastery, a glimpse of a will. In short, anything at all that would provide the least excuse for loving him as she so wished to do. A minute she stood, thinking. " A minimum. Hardly as much." There passed along the man on high heels, the three girls with the pinched look, the Tyrolese basso with the long ruddy beard, the *jeune premier* with whiskers and hair like a wig, whose look seemed to say, " Here am I " ; then again the man on high heels, the three girls with the pinched look, the Tyrolese singer, and again the " jeune premier " whose look implied, " Here am I." They walked round and round as if the park were a cage and there was nothing to do but walk round—with heads bent, lifeless, sullenly resolute. And again there came along the man on high heels. " The minimum of a minimum. . . ."

The music resumed. She consulted her programme. Item 7. Potpourri from the operette *Die Fledermaus* by Johann Strauss. She returned to the stand, prepared to give her fiancé another chance. Otto's part, as before, was contemptible, more contemptible than before. He was inactive. He smiled shyly. She coloured. And, looking at him, she knew. She knew it was no use, her love could not bridge the chasm. He was despised by the rest of the band. A stick-in-the-mud. Not a man. A poor fish. Not for her. . . .

The potpourri, as if suddenly turning the corner, broke out into a resounding march, and behold, the big drum now led the way. Bang! bang! bang! bang! Clearly he whacked, never once missing the chance ; and the man with the cymbals, as if one heart and brain operated their limbs, clashed the cymbals in astounding unison, the big drum pounding away, pounding away, without cease or respite. And the trumpeters smiled, as who might say : " Good old big drum ! You have come into your own at last ! " Bang! bang! bang! bang! The big drum had got loud and excited. And all the people standing around looked as though a great joy had come into their lives ; and if they had not been a little shy of each other they would have set out and marched in step with the music, taken up *any* cause and, if only because the music implied that all men were brothers, gone forth if need be and butchered another body of brothers, to the tearing, gladdening strains of the march. (Since it is not known from what rational cause men could have marched to the war.) And if in the park of the neighbouring town there were just such a band with just such a drum which played this same music, the people of the neighbouring town would have marched to this music and exterminated this town. The conductor, like a driver who, having urged his horse over the hill, leans back and leaves the rest to the horse, conceded the enterprise to the drummer, as if the hard, intricate work were now over and he was taking it easy ; his baton moved perfunctorily in the wake of the drum, he looked round and acknowledged the greetings of friends with gay, informal salutes of the left hand, his bland smile freely admitting to all that it was no longer himself but the drum which led them to victory. Or rather, the hard fight had already been won and these, behold, were the happy results! Bang! bang! bang! bang! Strangers passed smiles of intimate recognition, old men nodded reminiscently, small boys gazed with rapt eyes, women looked sweet and bright-eyed, ready to oblige with a kiss; while the big drum, conscious of his splendid initiative, pounded away without cease or respite.

"Wonderful! Beautiful!" said the public surrounding them. And thought:

"Noise is a good thing."

The band had described the first circle and was repeating it with added gusto and deliberation. The drum and the cymbals were pounding, pounding their due through the wholly inadequate blazing of brass. But these did not mind: "Every dog has his day"—and they followed the lead of the drum. He led them. He—Otto! Her Otto was leading them. God! Merciful Virgin! What had she done to deserve such happiness? Otto! . . . And she had doubted him, thought there was no "go" in him. No *go*! She burnt red with shame at the mere thought of it. He was all "go." And didn't he make them go, too, the whole lot of them? How he led them! Puffing, the sweat streaming down their purple faces, they blazed away till their cheeks seemed ready to burst, but Otto out-drummed them—annihilated their efforts. He—Otto! O, God! Watching him, people could hardly keep still. But that none of them stirred and all of them wanted to, added piquancy to the illusion of motion. They stood rooted—while the drum carried on for them: Bang! bang! bang! bang!

"Marvellous!" sighed the public around them.

Her Otto—cock of the walk! She could scarcely believe her eyes. Standing in front of the crowd, only a few paces from his side and raising herself on her toes ever so gently in rhythm with the music, so that by the very tininess of her movements she seemed to be sending added impetus into the band, as if, indeed, she were pressing with her little feet some invisible pump, she scanned his face with tenderness, in dumb adoration. And Otto at the drum must have felt it, for, at this turn, he put new life into his thundering whacks: *Bang! bang! bang! bang!* he toiled, and the conductor, as if divining what was afoot, at that moment accelerated the pace of the march.

"Bravo, bravo!" said the people surrounding them.

There was no doubt about it. This was Art. The unerring precision. The wonderful touch. Otto! . . . Otto, as never before, whacked the big drum, whacked it in excitement, in a frenzy, in transcending exaltation. Thundering bangs! And now she knew—what she couldn't have dreamed—she knew it by his face. Otto was a hero. A leader of men. Something fluttered in her breast, as though a bird had flown in, ready to fly out.

"Now it's all over," thought the people, "and we are going home to lunch." And everyone smiled and felt very happy and gay. A sort of prolonged accelerated thundering of the big drum, and then one tremendous BANG!

The thing was over. The conductor raised a bent hand to the peak of his cap, acknowledging the applause. The bird in her fluttered more wildly than ever. She wanted to cry out, but her throat would not obey. She clutched at her heaving breast with trembling fingers. "My love," she thought. "My king! My captain! My lord! My padishah!"

Comments and Reviews

THE Spring publishing season has begun in a quiet way. As far as one can judge from the advance lists, it appears to be a season of not more than average interest. The level of expectation is highest, exceptionally high, among the reprints; a fact to be accepted with resignation. The production of pure literature always appears as a thin stream when we look at what is passing actually beneath our feet.

* * * *

The scarcity of books of verse which show more than the tepid competence of the prevailing manner, continues. The standard of publication is still far too low in the matter of verse, probably because the better kind of publisher feels that a book or two of poems will enhance the dignity of his list—a healthy instinct, if a trifle sentimental. The art and criticism of verse have a long period of discipline still to undergo if poetry is to regain its supremacy over the other forms of literature, a supremacy which is inherent, since verse is capable of a more sensitive organisation than prose. But at present, it must be confessed, verse offers less nourishment to the sophisticated adult than it has done at any time in the last three hundred and thirty years; with one or two individual exceptions, it lacks a general social interest. Like Joseph Hall in 1597, the modern reader cannot be satisfied with "the well-known dainties of the time," when "men rather chuse carelessly to lose the sweet of the kernel, than to urge their teeth with breaking the shell wherein it is wrapped." The real passion of the age seems to be for the sciences allied to anthropology and psychology, especially when the treatment of them tends to speculation. For this taste the Spring brings forth such plums as "Psyche : The Cult of Souls and the Belief in Immortality among the Greeks," by Erwin Rohde (Kegan Paul) ; the third volume of Freud's "Collected Papers" (Hogarth Press) ; and the second volume in that interesting compilation of personal statements, "Contemporary British Philosophy" (Allen and Unwin).

* * * *

In the matter of reprints, the poets are well-represented. The first volume of Milton's Poems, edited by Professor H. J. C. Grierson (Chatto and Windus), will probably stimulate the Milton revival which is about due, and necessary to restore our sense of proportion in the matter of those recent enthusiasms, Donne and Dryden. The poems of Lovelace are to be edited in two volumes by Mr. C. H. Wilkinson (Oxford Press). W. C. Hazlitt's edition was the last, and is by no means satisfactory.

THE CALENDAR

Bishop Henry King is the last of the great Metaphysical poets to find a modern editor. This gap will be filled by Mr. John Sparrow's edition (The Nonesuch Press). The same publishers announce an edition of Blake's writings, containing over fifty collotype plates, which, from the specimen pages we have seen, will be a very beautiful book. What is more important, the text of Blake, which is in a tangled condition, will be re-edited from original sources by Mr. Geoffrey Keynes.

* * * *

Christopher Marlowe is legendarily supposed to have died swearing. Documents have recently been discovered which are said to clear up the mystery of the brawl in which he was killed—generally taken to have been a drunken affair. The matter is not of very great importance, but the new papers, to be published by The Nonesuch Press, may throw some light on Marlowe's character, particularly if his violent death turns out to have been connected with his subversive attitude to religion.

* * * *

The works of the eccentric millionaire, William Beckford, have never been collected. The first two volumes of the " Fonthill " edition of his works are shortly to be published by Mr. Guy Chapman. It is very appropriate that the introduction to the work of this baroque personality should be written by Mr. Sacheverell Sitwell, who is most likely to disengage the essential flavour of Beckford's fascinating style.

* * * *

The great influence of Seneca on the Elizabethan dramatists has never been thoroughly traced. Chapman goes so far as to make Guise refer to Clermont (*The Revenge of Bussy D'Ambois*) as " this Senecal man," a term of supreme praise. The translation with which the dramatists must have been familiar, *Seneca, His Tenne Tragedies*, is to be reprinted in the " Tudor Translations " (Constable), with an introduction by Mr. T. S. Eliot, the critic whose sensitized erudition here meets with a subject which should be particularly congenial to his great gifts.

* * * *

We record with very great regret the death of M. Jacques Rivière, at the age of thirty-nine. M. Rivière succeeded M. André Gide as editor of the *Nouvelle Revue Française* in 1919. He had been actively associated with the paper from its foundation in 1912. We cannot in this place do justice to his great gifts, but those who read the critical studies which he contributed to the *Nouvelle Revue Française* during the last few years will appreciate how rare a mind, in intelligence and in culture, has been lost. The loss is the greater since his later work showed a definite maturing, a

COMMENTS AND REVIEWS

coupling of intuition and judgment, which suggests that even such essays as " De la Sincérité envers Soi-même " or " Sur une crise de la Littérature " do not realise the whole potentiality of his mind.

*　　*　　*　　*

The exhibition of the film, " The Last Laugh," at the Capitol on Thursday, March 19, was adorned rather unnecessarily by the personal appearance of Hr. Emil Jannings, who played the chief part. The story is definitely Victorian, almost Galsworthian. It is about the childishly vain hall-porter of a big hotel who is super-annuated and sent to the basement as lavatory attendant. Hr. Jannings, an actor with many of the qualities of Tree, overdoes the " character " of his part. The pathos of the poor old man sitting in the lavatory while his successor struts in glorious uniform up above was carried over into bathos. With such an unattractive story, it is hardly possible to compare the film to " Destiny " or " Warning Shadows." We understand Hr. Jannings to be an advocate of realism on the screen, and " The Last Laugh " perhaps represents the reaction from " Caligari." But whatever its defects, it has a definite æsthetic superiority to almost all American films. The deliberate slowing-down of the action, though not responsible for this superiority of the German film, helps to make possible the attainment of an æsthetic equivalent to crude realism.

Edward VII.

KING EDWARD VII. A Biography. By Sir Sidney Lee.
Vol. I. From Birth to Accession. (Macmillans, £1. 11s. 6d. net.)

This book is dead. Thousands and thousands of facts are
presented, and facts need not kill a book, but these facts do, because
they are trivial, disconnected, and presented with incredible pom-
posity. Sir Sidney Lee has many valuable qualities : he is accurate,
learned, temperate, he never stoops to sycophancy. But as to the
eternal importance of his theme he has no misgivings. He cannot
be too serious or swell himself out too large when he mentions
royalty, the least sentence he writes must be tumid, gravid,
authoritative, apopletic, apocalyptic. Kings may do wrong like the
Kaiser or come to grief like the Czar, but they may never be presented lightly—that is the sin against the Lord's Anointed—and
when the House of Guelf is concerned, it becomes physically impossible to use too many words.

> Despite the restraints on boyish liberty and the educational
> discipline in which the paternal wisdom chiefly made itself
> visible to the son, the boyish faith in his dead father's exalted
> and disinterested motive lived on.

Such a sentence pops when trodden upon, like seaweed, yet it
would be wrong to say it contains nothing. A diplomatic residuum
survives—something gummy, something as subtle in its way as
literature though it exudes from the opposite end of the pen.
Read the sentence again, and do not try to find out whether the
Prince liked his father or was cowed by him, whether he obeyed him
or disobeyed, for these are not the points. Consider instead the
repetition of the adjective "boyish." It is significant. In
literature a repeated adjective does something, and it does something here too : it helps us to forget that we are reading about a boy.
The five words "boyish," "paternal," "son," "boyish," "father,"
are used with a sort of inverted art. They are used so many nails in the
coffin of reality. They are used without vision, without music,
without feeling, and consequently they leave us with a deep sense
of the abstract importance of royalty. To convey that importance
is the aim of an official biographer, and the achievement of the
volume under review. That's why the book's dead.

What of the facts themselves ? It is the attempt to inflate
them into national events that makes them trivial : they were not
trivial to the Prince. It mattered very much to him in the summer
of 1867 that the Sultan of Turkey should receive a proper decoration.
"I wish you would write to the Queen on the subject as soon as
possible," he told Lord Derby, "as there is no time to be lost."
Lord Derby thought a G.C.S.I. sufficient, but the Sultan let it be
known that only the K.G. would do, and the Prince warmly con-

curred, for he had pleasant memories of his own stay in Constantinople. But Queen Victoria had never been to Constantinople, did not mean to go, had not invited the Sultan to England, was disinclined to do anything that pleased her son, and, finally, did not think it right to confer the Garter, which is a Christian emblem, upon a Moslem ruler's leg. The Prince was in despair. His energy and tact were strained to their utmost, and, continuing to lose no time, he scarcely left the Sultan's side for ten days. All went well, thanks to his assiduity. The Queen relented, there was a lunch at Windsor, a reception at the India Office, and—triumph of triumphs !—the bestowal of the Garter on the deck of the Royal Yacht at Spithead during a howling storm. The Sultan shed tears of gratitude and joy. To him, as to his young host, it must have seemed that an event of international importance had occurred. But before many years had passed, the Sultan was assassinated, and even earlier the Prince turned from Turkey to Russia and was equally flurried over a colonelcy in a Russian regiment, which the Czar offered him and the Queen would not let him accept. "We are more independent without all these foreign honours," wrote the Queen. And so to Ober-Ammergau, which made a "serious impression." He "had never been so struck with anyone in his life" as with the peasant who played the part of Christ, and managed to have a talk with him before proceeding to military manœuvres in Hampshire.

In this constant flittering—which forecasts the still swifter movements of his grandson—the Prince was not the least trivial or inconsistent from his own point of view. His life sprang straight out of his circumstances and character and we shall never think clearly on the urgent subject of royalty until we realise this. If we do sometimes get cynical during eight hundred pages, it is usually the fault of Sir Sidney Lee. He should not imply that trinkets and uniforms, lunches, launches, and railway trains have any value outside the purely human, nor should he state that the subject of his memoir is a "great historic figure."

The Prince was indeed anxious to be a figure, and always clamouring for work, real work. He belonged to the great army of the constitutional unemployed which thronged Europe in the nineteenth century and is only just beginning to thin. The royal families bred abundantly, and there were numerous restless sons. In the fifteenth century these young men would have become condottieri, but they were constitutional, so they had to represent something or other, they didn't much mind what. It is pathetic to see them in their crowded palaces, scanning the political horizons for some form of popular life, and asking to represent it. An Austrian goes to Mexico, a Dane to Greece, and the Prince of Wales, debarred from more distant quests, attempts to be identified with the island of Ireland. His mother refused. She felt—and perhaps rightly—that she was doing all the representing necessary to the Empire and all the work modern royalty can ever do : signing papers, seeing Ministers, opening special boxes.   And she felt, too— and some other observers have agreed with her—that the Prince sought publicity rather than work, and was too impetuous and desultory to make a satisfactory Viceroy.   At any rate, after playing with his hopes for a time, she refused, and Ireland joined the long series of snubs she administered to her son.   For the first fifty years of his life he was scarcely allowed to do anything, or to go anywhere save in a social capacity, and it is therefore impossible that a book dealing with those years can have any historical im- portance.   It is the domestic tragedy that stands out.   As a mother, Queen Victoria behaved very badly.   The boy was over-educated by elderly experts, and when his rather ordinary mind and very normal character did not respond, she put him on a shelf as a failure.   He grew into a middle-aged man, but remained on the shelf—and woe betide him if the sound of breaking glass came to his mother's ears.   It never occurred to her that the Mordaunt and the Baccarat cases and other forbidden sweets could be ascribed to enforced idleness ; or that she herself could be indirectly responsible for them.   She may have been right to shelve him, but she was also cruel and blind.

The last two hundred pages of the book are the best because there is here less disproportion between the facts and the gravity with which they are related.   The squabbles between the Prince and the Kaiser increased the existing mistrust between England and Germany, so that the royal personages managed to represent something at last, and a little to accelerate the outbreak of an European war.   Here is one momentous step towards the cata- strophe :—

> After a short call on the Duke of Gmünden, on leaving Homburg, the Prince on 10th September reached Vienna, where he donned for the first time the resplendent uniform of his new Austro-Hungarian regiment of Hussars—gold-frogged tunic, red breeches, Hessian boots and shako.   From his host's lips he at once learnt to his mortification that his nephew had stipulated that no royal guest save himself should be present at the Viennese Court during his forthcoming stay. No doubt as to the Kaiser's meaning was permissible.

When you have assigned the " his-es " to their proper owners, you will realise that here was indeed an insult.   The Hessian boots had to be pulled off, the red breeches to follow them, and the out- raged and denuded uncle withdrew entirely from Austrian soil, to seek refuge with the King and Queen of Roumania.   In his next volume Sir Sidney will deal with the progress of the feud, and with its pendent, King Edward's cultivation of a particular type of Frenchman.   The volume will probably be more interesting than the present one, but it is sure to show the same deadness of outlook and of style. Sir Sidney is not stupid or uncritical, but officialism has destroyed his scale of values. He has taken neither of the courses open to a responsible biographer. Hessian boots, red breeches, Garters—they can be treated from two points of view : the scientific, when they vanish, and the sympathetic, when they are seen to be of genuine importance to their wearers. But they are not of importance to the universe or even to Europe ; nothing, nothing matters there, except distinction of spirit, and this King Edward VII did not happen to possess.

E. M. FORSTER.

Foundations.

THE MENTALITY OF APES. By W. KÖHLER. Kegan Paul 16s.

This book is not an attempt to prove that the chimpanzee is capable of miracles of thinking. For this reason it is a very valuable document in the study of intelligence, and the claim which, with all modesty, Professor Köhler makes for the chimpanzees, after four years' close and affectionate observation of *untrained* animals at the Teneriffe Anthropoid Station, is that thought definitely enters into their mental processes. The experiments he conducted were of the simplest form, but the problems he set the animals were designed with a nicety which excluded, ultimately, the possibility of solution by an animal such as the behaviourists postulate, a complex of motor reactions. The basic problem set the animals in many different ways was to reach some fruit they desired, which was so placed that they could only get to it, or get it to them, by the invention of a new process. One example must suffice. Sultan, a young and particularly bright chimpanzee, wanted to get a banana which lay outside his cage. He had already taught himself the use of a stick in dragging an object to him, but neither of the two sticks in his cage was long enough, in the present instance, to reach the fruit. He tried each of the sticks in turn, even tried pushing one stick with the other till it touched the fruit, but as they were not joined together this was of no practical use, though it was a good error, from the point of view of rational conduct. At last he admitted that he was baffled and sat back in his cage and played with the sticks, one of which was hollow, and the other thin enough to fit in it. He joined the two sticks together, and immediately turned to the bars and raked in the fruit. Whether the joining was an accident or not does not really matter, for he at once made use of the new stick, so that he must have had in his mind what we should call an idea of length, though only as *long enough* and *not long enough*. The author has a chapter on " Chance and Imitation " to which we refer the sceptical reader.

The ape, like the man, is not continually rational. Most of his life is, no doubt, governed by affective relations. One of the saddest sections of the book confesses that the apes try to solve a problem, which is only superficially the same as an earlier one, by the repetition of inappropriate solutions remembered from earlier problems. Periods of inertia, mental fatigue due to unsuccessful grappling with the problem, laziness, age, and personality, all affect the efficiency of the ape's mental processes just as they do those of human beings. The tendency, particularly strong under certain conditions, to repeat old solutions, whether practicable in the circumstances or not, is a human trait with which the critic of civilisation and culture will be very familiar. Another interesting point is the frequently repeated observation that the elements of the successful solution are associated in a flash ; however much work may have been spent on a problem, the answer comes as an inspiration—a fact also observed by mathematicians (Poincaré is a familiar example) and poets. The apes may serve to remind us that the most intelligent people are those susceptible to " inspiration." They may also remind us that " inspiration," poetic or otherwise, has nothing to do with emotional frenzy, which, when it overtakes the chimpanzees, renders them incapable of a correct solution. Professor Köhler's observations of the social life of the animals are full of interest, and, it must be said, charm. We really begin to accept our relationship to these creatures with some emotional warmth, not as with the vague assent to a hypothesis. Their behaviour as a loose political group is most instructive, and it is a pity that there was no opportunity of observing family relationships. In spite of this, there is enough information in the book to make one say of these particular apes not " how almost human," but " how very human." Actually, of course, millions of our fellow-countrymen go through life without ever solving a problem so difficult, relatively to the achievement of Galileo or Newton, as that of Sultan when he made two short sticks into a long one.

THE ORIGIN OF MAN. MAN AND HIS SUPERSTITIONS.
By CARVETH READ. Second Editions, revised. Cambridge University Press. 5s. and 12s. 6d. respectively.

Although there is undoubtedly a difference in intellectual power between individual apes, on Professor Read's theory we should expect to find it less strongly marked than in civilised man. His hypothesis traces the rise of man from the movement which led the ancestral anthropoid out of the forest and a vegetarian diet to hunt his living meat over lightly wooded plains. It follows that the form of human society developed out of the organisation of the hunting-pack, and this is a view which Professor Read sustains with skill and erudition and a sense of style, and without that forcing of the evidence which so often accompanies hypothetical discussions. It was during the early days of hunting that the utility of leaders became apparent, both to the leader and the led, but it is evident that even in a highly-organised pack there is still almost as great a demand for initiative on the part of subordinate members of it as there is on the leaders. It was probably after the invention of agriculture, which introduced the possibility of living by routine, that the gap between the individual and the mass became seriously wide. And it remained more or less constant until the industrialisation of civilisation, by drawing the arts and crafts (previously the refuge of initiative) into routine production, made life a matter of automatic functioning for almost everybody except the poet and the scientist pure. Society still depends on these two for new modes of feeling and new directions of activity. The apparent leaders, the financiers and commercial magnates, are mere functionaries, organisers of effort with politicians for their subalterns, in whom a remnant of the primitive urge to leadership still survives.

Professor Read's second volume contains a detailed account of the surviving instances of animism and magic as they exist among primitive peoples (and incidentally among ourselves). An examination of the conditions which gave rise to these fallacious, but momentarily useful, explanations of the order of natural phenomena, is of the utmost importance, since through it we can attain to some knowledge of the constitution of the mind of contemporary man. The reader will find Professor Read of the greatest assistance in clarifying his ideas, in giving historical perspective to his conceptions of different levels of culture, and his bold exposure of contemporary barbarisms will attract those who wish to emancipate themselves completely from the no longer acceptable myths of the past. This is not, as it may seem, remote from the subject of literature, nor even poetry. Poetry is not directly concerned with myths, as romantic practice might seem to imply, but only with myths which are capable of symbolising the poet's reactions to the life he actually lives ; that they should be familiar to his audience is, of course, a necessary condition of communication. We believe that the modern poet will tend to a more frequent use of the myths peculiar to our own civilisation, the accepted body of scientific theory (for its absolute truth is neither here nor there), which is bound to replace the theological myths surviving from the last great effort of human intelligence, the scholastic philosophy. For this reason we have drawn attention to these books, which discuss these fundamental matters with integrity, and with the charm which complete sincerity and lack of pretentiousness brings with it. Our readers will, no doubt, be able to bridge the gap between the work of Professor Köhler and Professor Read. To us the path of tradition between the ape Sultan and the modern engineer appears to need only a little clearing done on it to become quite plain, and the fact need be no discredit to the engineer. Whether we shall ever have any but a hypothetical bridge between the ape and the animistic savage is, perhaps, not to be hoped for, but we see a very fruitful field for investigation in the connection between animism and idealistic philosophy, between the savage " soul-stuff " and, for instance, the Kantian " thing-in-itself." It would do no harm at present if the prestige of certain of these metaphysical conceptions which are commonly made the basis for a judgment of poetic values should be diminished.

PRINCIPLES OF LITERARY CRITICISM. By I. A. RICHARDS. Kegan Paul. 10s. 6d.

We are not often privileged to follow so lucid a discussion of the fundamental conditions of aesthetic judgment as that with which the above volume presents us. Its analysis of current methods of evaluating works of art is delicate, destructive, and final ; the mechanism with which it replaces them may not have the same quality of finality, but its adaptation to the needs of our time is so nearly complete that we cannot imagine its essential modification. The tone of the book is astringent, and its comment uncompromising, but it is not dogmatic ; it offers us " not a rock to shelter under or to cling to, rather an efficient aeroplane in which to ride the tempestuous turmoil of change " to which the human mind is native.

It is in definiteness of statement rather than in any novelty of conception that Mr. Richards' preliminary destruction is valuable. Anyone who has already freed himself from the system of values imposed on literature by the Kantian metaphysic, with its categorical imperative of judgment, will have been teased by the unreality of such terms as ideal Beauty or pure Beauty, and its derivative, the specifically aesthetic emotion. This dissatisfaction is the first step to a real appreciation of literature, but it provides no effective instrument for the organisation of the responses evoked by the impact of actual specimens of the literary " stuff." Mr. Richards arrives at a basis for the judgment of value by examining the processes of psychology. He does not differentiate between the kind of stimulus which we receive from raw life and the kind which we receive from the representation of life in the arrangements recognised as artistic forms. He shows, in fact, that there is no basic difference, though there is a difference of degree in the quality of response, which we receive from certain arrangements and not from others ; it is this difference of degree which determines his scale of values. The created work is valuable when the response to the impulses which it sets up is the satisfaction of an appetency or of appentencies which does not involve " the frustration of some equal or *more important* appetency." It is obvious that if this definition of value is to be anything but a dodge round the problem, the critic must particularise the hierarchy of appetencies, must state the positive from which his comparative *more important* is derived. We could wish that Mr. Richards had been more explicit on this point, though, if we understand him rightly, it is a matter which is determined by biological evolution, a fact which naturally follows from his destruction of the absolute point of reference. The physio-psychological entity, the individual, is continually changing under the constant impact of sensations, so that the same work can never evoke the same response; so, " there are specialist and universal poets, and the specialist may be developing in a manner either consistent or inconsistent with general development, a consideration of extreme importance in judging the value of his work." Here is an opportunity for a false syllogism to assert that the poet who is in line with the general development is a better poet than the one who is not, when really all one can deduce from the premises is that he will exist *as a poet* for a longer time.

This existence of poetry *in* the audience is the crucial point in Mr. Richards' theory of value. It has an obvious affinity with the Augustan conception of poetry as the supreme social attitude, and similarly, in spite of his codicils, his reasoning tends to diminish the importance of the solitary illuminant who is the natural outcome of a metaphysical theory of criticism. Mr. Richards admits the possibility of " admirable though utterly eccentric experience," and claims the right to neglect work which may be " admirable in itself " if " a general approximation to it is impossible." He says, too, " what is excellent and what is to be imitated are not necessarily the same," though his criterion of excellence is that which we tend to imitate. His definition of value does not admit of a thing being " admirable in itself." In his anxiety, which we appreciate, to assert the " normality " of the poetic mind, he has inadvertently put in juxtaposition the mentality of " the usual and ordinary man " and that of Blake, Nietzsche and the Apocalypst, and naturally recoils at their incompatibility. Certainly this difference can be only relative, not one of kind, yet Mr. Richards seems to underestimate the gap, and, for the moment, though only for the moment, to threaten us with a dynasty of " occasional " poets.

We should give an inadequate notion of the wealth of ideas in Mr. Richards' book if we neglected to draw attention to the chapters of technical—more particularly literary—criticism. His analysis of the effect of metre, which he concludes to be " for the most difficult and most delicate utterances . . . the all but inevitable means," is an example of the heightened understanding which is reached by his way of approach to the subject :

" Metre adds to all the variously fated expectancies which make up rhythm a definite temporal pattern, and its effect is not due to our perceiving a pattern in something outside us, but to our becoming patterned ourselves. With every beat of the metre a tide of anticipation in us turns and swings, setting up as it does so extraordinarily extensive sympathetic vibrations."

THE CALENDAR

The chapters on "Imagination" and allied subjects are extremely illuminating, and many ideas are set down which should yield very profitably to a fuller exposition. There are a couple of pages on the nature of Tragedy from which we should like to quote, since they are in such contrast to the usual comments which that breeding-ground of sentimentality brings forth.

A suggestive assertion is that " irony is constantly a characteristic of poetry which is of the highest order." Certainly there is a high percentage of irony in the poetry which we most admire at the present time. It would need longer space than a review to discuss such a problem, which as Mr. Richards states it, is made of fundamental importance. Since it is only one of a multitude of fine perceptions, it may, perhaps, stand as a sort of colophon to an appreciation which is far from exhaustive.

EDGELL RICKWORD.

POEMS BY JOHN SKELTON. Edited by RICHARD HUGHES. (Heinemann. 15s.)

Few poets have been more versatile than Skelton, either in their methods or their moods, but his versatility is less the measure of himself than the result of his environment. In 1500 the long period of literary sterility which followed Chaucer had not yet given rise to the efflorescence of the Elizabethans ; the Wars of the Roses had but lately ended ; the Reformation was only foreshadowed. Skelton, though a conservative, could not fail, as an intellectual and enquiring mind, to react to the influences of unrest which surrounded him, and this disquietude is reflected in the preponderantly satiric tone of his poems.

The selection made by Mr. Hughes leaves little to be desired, but one cannot altogether accept his criticism. Writing of *Speke, Parot*, he says that " the extraordinary sense of rhythm, the extraordinary intellectual grasp that not only makes every word significant but every juxtaposition of words, every possible turn and shade of meaning, render it one of those few poems that can be read with increasing admiration, increasing comprehension and delight, year after year." This is the exaggeration of partisanship. Even cutting out the stanzas which are definitely satiric, the poem that remains is a formless congeries of description, learning and facetiousness : its value lies in its metrical skill and its naive vigour :

" With my becke bent, my lyttyl wanton eye,
My fedders fresh as is the emrawde green,
About my neck a circulet like the ryche rubye,
My lyttyl leggys, my feet both fete and clene,
I am a mynyon to wayt uppon a quene."

As a metrist Skelton is always interesting, whether using this unanalysed form of pentameter, or the intricate versification of *Woffully Araid*, or the short, running, frequently-rhymed metre which he usually prefers. He can be as sententious and heavy as Lydgate or Gower, chained to the cumbrous machinery of allegory, and the lifeless iambic, but in his lyrical masterpiece, *Phyllyp Sparowe*, he writes with a fluent vitality which they rarely attain. And in his satiric and descriptive poems, *Colyn Cloute* or *Elynour Rummynge*, this same fluency is evident, breaking down the wearisome decorum, and freeing expression from the turgid rhetoric of his predecessors. This latter poem, far from being " one of the few really abstract poems in the language "—as Mr. Hughes would have it—is a piece of extremely vivid imaginative writing. Its bawdiness and vigoui are as much a part of Skelton as the fragrance of *Phyllyp Sparowe* and the erudition of *Garlande of Laurrel.*

Mr. Hughes has done a valuable service in rescuing Skelton from the scholars and presenting his work with the minimum of impedimenta.

D. M. G.

POEMS OF THIRTY YEARS. By GORDON BOTTOMLEY. (Constable. 21s.)

There is in some of Mr. Bottomley's lyrical poetry a strain of individuality which shows up to better advantage in the small dimensions of the " Chambers of Imagery " than in this collected edition. Roughly between 1902 and 1909, there were indications that Mr. Bottomley had something original to say and that his sensitiveness to words would enable him to find an appropriate technique. The impulse, though strong enough to permit him to write such interesting poems as " Babel," " The Orchard Feast," " The End of the World," " Netted Strawberries," and the Hymns to Form, to Imagination, and to Touch, was not strong enough, or did not last long enough, to enable him to write sustainedly without reliance on literary models. A considerable part of this volume is plainly derivative. The Pre-Raphaelite, or " pictorial " influence from the early Tennyson and Rossetti is self-evident. It is strange that a mind in some ways so fresh should be content with such obvious pastiche as the poems in ballad-form here reprinted ; for this the example of Rossetti and Swinburne is perhaps responsible. The influence of Browning, led sometimes to a deliberate avoidance of euphony, and to an over-free articulation of the terms of expression which resulted in such loose-limbed movements as this :

> but tall small she
> Ruffled a bosom, swung a sleeve,
> Peacocked a skirt swan-yearningly
> As though her body curved to leave
> Itself to dote in worshipry. (1902.)

We do not wish to multiply instances of this forced ingenuity of language, but to show that the above instance is not an isolated one we quote a few lines produced at different periods :

Helen :   the consort's crown
    Of your upthrust hybrid and thrasonic realm . . .

    Sounding delirious and neurotic sistrums. . . .
                                  (1899.)

    Like window-veils in mirrors a hum
    Of little flies waving their feet
    Dims the air like a flicker of heat . . .   (1904.)

    In a hawthorn's light she pondered,
    While dark dew her gleam-feet laundered.   (1909.)

In the last two examples, the desire to be poetic has completely broken down the control of the instrument of expression. It is difficult to see how, with the regard he seems to have towards the English language, Mr. Bottomley could pass such affected and trivial statements as we suppose to be contained in those lines.

When Mr. Bottomley is most nearly original, as in the poems we have named (except " The Orchard Feast," which is a perfectly successful piece in the romantic tradition), it seems that there has been a conscious effort to maintain the integrity of his feeling, and because of that consciousness, the poetic fusion is prevented; when the intuition of rhythm is lost, there is no real organisation, but a setting side by side of rhythmically incompatible masses :

    Blindness and Blake and all primæval things
    (Blindness, that moonlight of the sense's space)
    Contain a primitive order unconfined,
    Depths of denial, wells of might—
    Form without reason, with no explanation by uses : "

What this lacks is not interest of a superficially intellectual kind, but aesthetic cohesion ; the subject has not been felt poetically. This lack we find general in Mr. Bottomley's verse, though its indebtedness to the successes of the past may, we understand, give it a momentary effectiveness. What it means to write from a pure and unprejudiced sense of words we may best exemplify by a stanza from one of the rare poems which make one wonder why Mr. Bottomley has not realised finer things, from " Netted Straw-berries," a poem of a wren :

    Though I alight and swing
    I never reach the things that tumble and crush,
    And if I had such long legs as a thrush
    The web would tangle and cling.
                                   E. R.

JOHN KEATS. By AMY LOWELL. (Jonathan Cape. 2 vols. 42s.)
    In her preface Miss Lowell asserts that the " twentieth century has been silent in regard to Keats." Her two bulky volumes shatter

that silence with a muffled detonation, whose noise will be heard at a great distance. This is unfortunate : for one cannot admit that her contribution to Keats literature adds to our knowledge of him in proportion to the size of her work. As a biography it is, as far as it concerns facts, minute and all-embracing, but Sir Sidney Colvin had already told as much as it was necessary to know. It does not matter that Keats's hair was a fine reddish-gold and not carroty ; nor that when visiting the Snooks, he and Brown, " although they reached the Snooks' house by three, found dinner already over." These are details which obscure rather than clarify a portrait, are as unnecessary and unimportant as the imaginative descriptions of scenery and weather with which Miss Lowell over-burdens an already detailed account. As a psychological study the book is of little more value. Miss Lowell prefers to rely on her own obvious inferences rather than scientific deductions. One is grateful to her, incidentally, for standing up for Fanny Brawne. The letters from her to Fanny Keats after John's death, to which she has had access, go some way to disproving a malignant attitude, unjustified by the facts, which previous historians of Keats have held towards her.

It was, however, the critical sections of the book which were most eagerly awaited, since it was to be expected that a poet would really have something to say. Miss Lowell has talked much, but said little. She has made no attempt to analyse the poems *qua* poems, but has furnished a running commentary on them, interwoven with a minute chronology and motherly suggestions. If only Keats had lived in our enlightened century, science might have saved him from tuberculosis, and at any rate his friends would have been sensible enough to stop him playing cricket when he was already ill, she says. And of the poems she speaks in the same vein :— *St. Agnes' Eve* " is no mere charming tale of love . . . but a profoundly dramatic study of an unplumbed mystery," and, summing up her theory of its counterpoint, " Past death, misunderstanding, the imprisonment of personality, the lovers escape towards life together, not into a live-happy-ever-after kind of existence, but into the stress and storm of a future which at least they face side by side." To *Endymion* she devotes 140 pages, to *Hyperion* but half-a-dozen. Her criticism of the former is prefaced by an ingenious but not valuable attempt to trace a connection between it and Drayton's *Endimion and Phoebe*, and when she turns to deal with the poem itself, she begins : " Book I. So Keats, sitting down at Carisbrooke, either indoors or out, began his poem :

' A thing of beauty is a joy for ever.'

The next line came afterwards—after the briefest of intervals perhaps, but still afterwards," Direct criticism is scanty, but Miss Lowell pads it out with her own hypotheses and a recapitulation of the narrative.

It is in her criticism of *Hyperion*, however, that she breaks down completely. Of the two versions she says, " the one is a failure, the other is too fragmentary to enable us to come to a decision concerning it." She suggests that Keats wrote the second version— usually and, I think, correctly considered to be the first—" to show that he was capable of the grand style if ever poet was." It was, she adds, a work of " sheer cleverness . . . merely a tracing from a pattern of an older age " This shows a complete failure to recognise the continual advance which Keats was making in this poem on the work even of the Odes. As a thinker he was developing and his technique did not lag behind.

But it is impossible to discuss the book in detail. While admitting the value of the biographical part and the interest of those passages in which Miss Lowell has been able to clear up doubtful questions, one cannot accept the book as a whole, for it is written from a misconception of the critic's function. It would be easy to write of it sarcastically, but to do so would be to show a lack of respect for Miss Lowell's devotion to Keats and for the labour which her book must have involved.

D. M. G.

MYRTLE. By STEPHEN HUDSON. (Constable. 6s.)

It is typical of Mr. Hudson's art that the chief character in this book should not appear in person. Myrtle is the book, yet nowhere is she drawn *sur le vif*. She emerges gradually from the shadows of nine personal reactions, gathering from each a new firmness of line and depth of colour, until finally she attains a living solidity. The book is written in nine chapters, each of which, a complete study in the form of a soliloquy, reveals a distinct aspect of Myrtle in respect to an isolated and extraneous incident. The ultimate effect is a cumulative one and, therefore, depends on the intrinsic value of each chapter ; for only in so far as the several characters live is Myrtle's response valid.

It is in the third and last chapters that Mr. Hudson is most successful, though all are but modifications of the same process. In the former it is Sylvia who is speaking. She has appeared previously as Myrtle's favourite sister and the wife of Hildebrand Moreton, so that already, by acquiring an individuality of her own, she has to a certain extent delineated the character of the principal figure. Here she makes Myrtle the confidante of Hildebrand's desertion and her own disillusionment, the nature of which is subtly chosen to heighten the significance of her intimacy with her sister. We are not told what attitude Myrtle takes, or what is the psychological effect of this disclosure of life, but her sympathy is implied, and that her reaction should be allowed to remain tacit is evidence of Mr. Hudson's very fine artistic sense. When Richard Kurt becomes the protagonist, Myrtle's presence is more definite,

COMMENTS AND REVIEWS

but only for moments ; it is still the influence of her personality
which is cogent.   That she should marry Kurt is not the important
point, but rather that she should cause him to revolt from the
tyranny of the loveless marriage which for twenty years had
oppressed him.

The range of Mr. Hudson's sympathy, however, is limited.
He writes convincingly of polite, leisured society, but outside
that field his grasp is less sure.   Marcel and Nanny, and to some
extent Moriarty, are conventional, rather lifeless figures ; the
Vendramin circle, on the other hand, is described with the most
subtle finish.   For the most part, his style is admirable for its nice
lucidity, but there is a tendency for it to become monotonous ;
the *tempo* is so regular that the rhythm is sometimes wearisome.
Yet this economy of language is the counterpart of the stern
emotional restraint which is the most pleasing quality of this
charming and accomplished artist.

D. M. G.

PLAINTE CONTRE INCONNU. Par P. Drieu La Rochelle.
(Nouvelle Revue Française.   7frs. 50.)

The four pieces collected in this volume may be called *tales* though
the term is not very exactly descriptive.   The *conte* has undergone
radical changes since the time of Maupassant even, and absorbed
many of the elements of the essay and the " character."   The
importance of the narrative is reduced to a minimum and the thing
often resolves itself into a study of temperament and manners.

M. Drieu la Rochelle is one of the young post-war writers whose
small volumes of poems INTERROGATIONS and FOND DE CANTINE,
though perhaps evidence of an unusual sensibility rather than of a
specifically poetic gift, are certainly among the most interesting of
contemporary productions.   In the present volume he has extended
his range of expression very considerably, and that part of the
English reading public which is curious as to the work of the younger
French writers and accepts without much discrimination the
reputations which somehow find their way across the Channel,
cannot afford to ignore his work.   M. Drieu la Rochelle has not the
facility, which sometimes degenerates into virtuosity, of contemporaries more familiar among us, like MM. Morand, Giraudoux,
Maurois and Mauriac, he hangs on the trail of his quarry with a
persistence which is sometimes agonising.   So Gonzague, the
objective of *Le Valise Vide*, is followed through a maze of parties,
chance meetings in bars, liaisons, etc., until the pursuer has drained
the last drop from his devitalised soul.   Like M. Morand, M. Drieu
la Rochelle is, and knows himself to be, the observer of a distempered
generation, though there is a reserve, a fastidiousness in the latter's
manipulation of his material, which implies a consciousness more
adult, more detached, than that of his contemporaries.   Even down

to his deliberate sententiousness, he is rather like a man from the eighteenth century surveying the adolescent sensibility which is at the root of almost all recent French literature which is not prematurely senile. He is of the generation which has ceased to flatter itself on its disillusionment, without for that rushing into facile idealism or promiscuous satisfactions.

" Il renfermait une lourde couche d'amour et de foi, il ne voulait pas la livrer aux becs distraits."

The personality of the author is not obtruded, however keenly it makes itself felt. This detachment allows the admirably precise vivisection of *Anonymes* and *Nous fûmes surpris*. Towards the character of Liessies in *Le Pique-Nique*, from which the above quotation is taken, there does seem to be a slight emotional prejudice and the story is unnecessarily complicated with retrospect and digression. But this story has the merit common to the others, that the ordinary social contacts of young men and women are presented with the particularity which marks them definitely of this time and of no other, and yet with a clarity, with an objectification, which ensures their independent existence.

E. R.

MARTIN ARROWSMITH. By Sinclair Lewis. (Jonathan Cape. 7s. 6d.)

Martin Arrowsmith is the story of genius in Main Street ; of Gottlieb, the idealist scientist, and the Men of Measured Merriment. It is vigorous and engrossing and written in a firmer and more solid style than Mr. Lewis has shown before, but it is not always convincing. The distinction between idealism and materialism is too crudely emphasized, although Martin and Leora are robust imaginative creations. They set the tone of the characterisation, but leading, as they do, a real and passionate existence, the Pickerhaughs and Tozers appear as lifeless improvisations ; as caricatures rather than people. The harmony of the book is thus weakened by the too harsh disparity in the texture of negatives and positives.

The same weakness is noticeable in the construction of their peculiar settings. The McGurk Institute is an oasis of reality in a desert of shams ; the social life which surrounds it is pastiche. True, much of the book is satirical and therefore does not demand fairness, but to have its deepest effect, the evils which it attacks or the attitudes which it condemns, must be adequately realised. The monotonous joviality of Clif, the insincerity of Holabird and Joyce's conventional restraint become insipid and wearisome. Indeed the episode with the latter might well have been left out. Her appearance on the plague-stricken island and Martin's momentary infatuation have an obvious dramatic value, but the last 50 pages of the book, after Leora's death, add nothing to one's conception of Martin, and are a tiresome anti-climax.

It is a powerful book chiefly because Mr. Lewis has written it as an American and not as an English immigrant. He has not relied upon an extraneous culture, but has used his own language with its vigorous idiom and frequently vivid slang. Leora and Martin are unsophisticated people ; they are the positive part of a crude civilisation, the " live wires " in a straggling Main Street.

D.M.G.

THREE FURTHER PLAYS OF LUIGI PIRANDELLO. Translated from the Italian by Dr. Arthur Livingston. (J. M. Dent and Sons, Ltd. 10s. 6d.)

None of the three plays contained in this new volume has been produced in England, and of the three plays in the previous volume, two only have been seen on the stage—*Six Characters in Search of an Author*, given by the Stage Society for two performances in London, and *Henry IV.*, of which the Cambridge A.D.C. recently gave a remarkably fine production, filling their theatre for a week with audiences drawn from all over England. Pirandello is, therefore, unknown to the London theatre-goer, but even a reading of his plays is enough to convince one that, apart from Mr. Shaw, we have no dramatist of anything like the same class in this country.

Unfortunately, the new volume is no better translated than the last. Mr. Arthur Livingston, who was responsible in the first volume, for the translation of *Cosi è, se vi pare !*—which he ineptly rendered by the facetious " Right You are ! (If You Think So) " —has this time translated all three plays, and the reader is constantly irritated by such Americanisms as " tea and *cookies*," " *My*, what a row ! " " You will rest *up* a little," " I am *all* tired out," " *light*-haired," etc. Mr. Livingston's want of linguistic tact is such that in a perfectly serious passage he is capable of the following :

> MADDALENA : I know—I know. He *is* mad about her ! And do you know, if he had not been really in love with her, I am sure what has happened would not have happened.
>
> MAURIZIO : Fabio is a good boy.

Nor is Mr. Livingston's power of expression equal to the demands Pirandello makes. Here is an obscure passage :

> BALDOVINO : That is not sufficient. You see, it's this way, Marquis. Inevitably, try as we may, we make ourselves over. Let me explain. I come into this house, and right away—as far as you are concerned—I become the man that I am going to be—the man that I have the possibility of being. I make myself over—that is to say, I present myself to you in a manner adapted to the relation-ship I am about to establish with you, etc.

The " Translator's Note " is all that an introduction should not be. Mr. Livingston seems incapable of clear thinking. He is also incapable of stating a fact.

He gives none of the information we want—neither the dates of the plays, nor the principle on which he has selected them. He tells us nothing about Pirandello, and we do not know whether these three plays represent the work of two or of thirty years— except for a passage which suggests that all Pirandello's plays have been written since 1919. Instead, we get the vaguest nonsense about the " Stream of Life," a stream, we are told, " which Bergson would call the vital urge, and Freud, may be, the Unconscious." It is deplorable that such stuff should be given to the English public by a firm of publishers as respectable as Messrs. J. M. Dent and Sons, Ltd. The paper, typography, and format are all singularly unpleasant ; in fact, this volume, like the first, is a most unattractive book, and it is a relief to find that it was printed in America, and not in England.

Each of these three new plays shows Pirandello's extraordinary gift of dialectic and of psychological analysis. Such is the substance of the plays, and it is exhibited in a dramatic composition of ingenious construction. Our aesthetic pleasure is got from the harmony the plot makes with the theory of the play. But they are plays in two dimensions only, for although the characters are not purely gargoyles through which the author's ideas run out—as are so many of the characters in Mr. Shaw's plays—they have a purely intellectual life, and one cannot imagine anyone of them in a different set of circumstances than that in which the dramatist has presented him. Therefore they are *creatures*, not living men and women. But they are superb creatures, marvellous puppets whose activity we watch with a breathless delight.

W. J. TURNER.

THE PRISONERS OF WAR : A Play in Three Acts. By J. R. ACKERLEY. (Chatto and Windus. 5s.)

Has it any meaning if we say of a book that we think it is extraordinarily well done, but we don't like it ? Very little, if we leave the statement in that bare form, but if we try and analyse our dislike we may be able to find good reasons for it, which will modify our original notion that the book is extraordinarily well done. My first reading of Mr. Ackerley's play made a vivid impression. My first impulse was to cry,." This is superb, magnificent, perfect ! " On reading it again, after an interval, I found that it again held my attention absorbingly, but not so absorbingly that I was unable to say " This is false, distorted, unreal, horrible ! " Is it possible to compose this discrepancy ? I think it is. A diseased foot is not a beautiful sight, but it could be described in such a way as to hold the listener spellbound in horror. This is what

Mr. Ackerley has done, and it demanded a rare gift of writing and a good deal of knowledge, and knowledge of a kind that is not to be found under every bush. However, although the diseased foot admirably described may, if you like, become *qua* description a work of art, it nevertheless remains confined within those limitations which make it a diseased foot. Mr. Ackerley has taken an unpleasant situation—the situation of a group of war prisoners interned in Switzerland, who have got upon one another's nerves. Their enforced idleness, the monotony of their existence, is horrible enough, but Mr. Ackerley introduces into this warped existence an exceptionally narrow and unbalanced personality, the character of Conrad. The combination of Conrad and his environment produces disaster—Conrad becomes mad, and another officer kills himself. The unrelieved gloom and the unpleasantness of the play are not due to the unpleasantness of any one of the features. Unpleasant details are as good as pleasant details, ugly details as good as beautiful details for the purpose of the artist. The depressing aesthetic effect of *Prisoners of War* is due to its leaving one impoverished instead of enriched.

We feel that we have been cheated—although by a very cunning hand—for at the end of the play Conrad, who is the chief and all-important character, is less than Conrad at the beginning of the play. He begins as a man, he ends as a sort of psychological freak. Therefore, we lose interest in him, and we feel the conclusion of the play is false, because intellectual, artificial, and forced into one dimension. Adelby, another of the prisoners, suffers the same diminution, Only Grayle, Tetford, and Rickman remain, but they were, from the beginning, merely cleverly differentiated types in whom we were not asked to take interest. Mr. Ackerley's aim was to create a character, and explore it under given circumstances. But Conrad and his circumstances, taken all together, as a whole, do not make a reality. *The Prisoners of War* remains a melodrama in spite of its unconventional material, but a first-rate melodrama.

W. J. T.

Among New Books

SIXTY-FOUR, NINETY-FOUR. By R. H. Mottram. Chatto & Windus. 7s. 6d.

As a record of the war from an individual point of view, Mr. Mottram's book is often interesting but never arresting. His effort to be dispassionate has robbed his story of vitality, so that a bombardment is no more startling than a rest-camp discussion of tactics. Skene's gradual disillusionment is well set-off by the enthusiasm of the New Armies and the Americans, but his spasmodic passion for Madeleine is commonplace and unconvincing. It is better than many war books, but it does not appease the desire for something more than "Histories, necessarily official, memoirs, necessarily personal, novels, necessarily fiction." Beside such a work as Tolstoy's it is a pale and inadequate representation.

INNER CIRCLE. By Ethel Colburn Mayne. (Constable. 6s.)

Eleven short stories by Miss Mayne furnishes an evening with entertainment that is neither radical nor transient. Her feeling for life accommodates itself neatly to the short story form, and this collection, like her former volume, "Nine of Hearts," is given a unity of impression lacking in most of its kind, by the similarity of its themes. Miss Mayne's outlook and style have been compared with Katherine Mansfield's ; one characteristic which they certainly share is an explorative sympathy for the sexual sensibilities of women. These stories are not altogether free of that exploitation of the sense of pity on which so much distinguished modern fiction reclines, but Miss Mayne's general manner of treatment is a distinct intellectualisation of her delicate perceptions.

CARAVAN. The Assembled Tales of John Galsworthy. Heinemann. 7s. 6d.

A remarkably substantial volume (960 pages), containing, the author says, "all my tales falling short of the novel in length, written between the years 1900 and 1923 inclusive." It confirms us in our opinion of the sentimental origin of most of Mr. Galsworthy's work. The insistent "social pity" which is the main-spring of the majority of these narratives pokes its cloven hoof very obviously through the shorter of these pieces and prevents their reality. In the longer pieces Mr. Galsworthy's virtues as observer and recorder to some extent redeem this radical defect.

TWO PLAYS. By Sean O'Casey. Macmillan. 7s. 6d.

Mr. O'Casey's play, *Juno and the Paycock*, was performed with enormous success at the Abbey Theatre, Dublin, and Mr. James Stephen has declared that Mr. O'Casey is "the greatest dramatic find of modern times." *Juno and the Paycock* does not move us to such language, but it is unquestionably a good play. It deals with life in Dublin during 1922, and shows how an ordinary Irish family suffered in the frenzied political disorders of the time when men and boys were murdered in broad daylight under the eyes of a terrorised population. The characters are well drawn and the dialogue is picturesque and amusing, having a vivacity and a lyricism that distinguishes it from that of the ordinary " good " play.

HALF A MINUTE'S SILENCE AND OTHER STORIES. By Maurice Baring. Heinemann. 8s. 6d. net.

Ten of these stories are Russian, imitated, one cannot help feeling, from Tchekov. Yet, though they contain all the accidents of the model—landowners, sunflower-seed, troikas, and dilapidated country houses—their

AMONG NEW BOOKS

inconsequence is only inconsequence, their slightness has no force of suggestion. *The Police Officer* is good, however, and amongst the others, *Fête Galante* and *The Shadow of Midnight*. A clumsy over-insistence spoils the two longest stories : in both cases an amusing fantasy is too heavily loaded with strings of commonplace deductions, and the same fault, in addition to an anti-climax, destroys the humour of *A Luncheon Party*.

THE CAMBRIDGE BOOK OF PROSE AND VERSE. From the
Beginnings to the Cycles of Romance. Edited by GEORGE SAMPSON.
Cambridge University Press. 10s. 6d.
Illustrative extracts from the poets, chroniclers and theologians dealt with in the corresponding section of the " Cambridge History of English Literature." A dangerous way of scraping acquaintance with literature, but justified in this early period by the general unfamiliarity of the subject. Anglo-Saxon writings are translated, which cuts the knot of a problem to be resolved only by a knowledge of the language. A successful compromise is made with Middle English by printing a glossary beneath the text. Mr Sampson's work has been done well, and if his book habituates the general reader to pre-Chaucerian literature, it will have been magnificently worth doing.

PIERCE PENILESSE. HIS SUPPLICATION TO THE DIVELL. (1592.) By
THOMAS NASH. Lane. 2s. 6d. (paper) and 3s.
This volume and the one below are additions to The Bodley Head Quartos. This series of reprints, well edited and well printed, has now a dozen titles, all of them of uncommon interest and not otherwise accessible to the ordinary reader.
Nash's pamphlet is typical of its author and of Elizabethan journalism at its best. The defence of poetry and of plays, into which he digresses here, helps us to appreciate the attitude of the populace of London to its new literature.

THE ENGLISH ROMAYNE LIFE. (1582.) By ANTHONY MUNDAY.
Lane. 2s. 6d. (paper) and 3s.
A bright account of the corrupt and superstitious practices of the Romans by a staunch Protestant who wormed his way into the English Seminary at Rome. On his return to England he became a spy and helped to bring his former hosts to the gallows.

THE GOLDEN KEYS. By VERNON LEE. The Bodley Head. 7s. 6d.
Most descriptive books of dilatory travel are written, it would seem, for the sake of their purgative effect on the authors. They are a handy means of getting rid of inchoate musings and formless emotions, or for airing opinions in an irresponsible manner. Miss Lee does these things gracefully in a sensitive prose. Her recollections have just the æsthetic value—and not more than that—which she missed in the atmosphere of Venice : " The virtue of paucity, the stimulus of the insufficient and the unfinished, the spell of the fragment forcing us to furnish what it lacks out of our own heart and mind."

CHARLES DICKENS AND OTHER VICTORIANS. By SIR ARTHUR
QUILLER-COUCH. Cambridge University Press. 10s. 6d.
Sir Arthur Quiller-Couch writes about Dickens, Thackeray, Trollope, Gaskell and Disraeli. The two longest sections, on the two first-mentioned novelists, were papers read to a Cambridge literary society, and are similar in tone and treatment to the popular weekly letters of " John O'London." They are likely to perform much the same function—that of converting a wide audience of little natural responsiveness to literature, to a recognition of its moral and civic gratifications. Sir Arthur makes skilful use in his propaganda of such roundabout auxiliaries as patriotism, democracy, history and the sentiment of hearty living, but avoids any sort of frontal attack on his subjects. It is only through lack of a more suitable category that this volume has to be classified under " CRITICISM."

THE PSYCHOLOGY OF RELIGIOUS MYSTICISM. By JAMES H. LEUBA.
   Kegan Paul. 15s.

An exhaustive examination of the pretentions of certain experiences of " rapture " to be means of union with the Infinite. The feeling of intense satisfaction enjoyed in these states is really due to a balance reached within the mind itself, not to any harmony with the outer universe, or any revelation as to its nature. Criticism of the value of these states is hostile to those which do not lead to a more sensitive organisation of responses, and this by no means excludes all mystics from the roll of honour—only their qualifications are not quite those which they thought they were.

The CALENDAR
of Modern Letters

VOLUME I   MAY
NUMBER 3   1925

The First Letter from Heloïse to Abelard.

TRANSLATED FROM THE LATIN BY C. K. SCOTT MONCRIEFF.

Heloïse, formerly Abelard's mistress and then his wife, had, some time before this letter was written, been given by him the charge of the Monastery of Paraclete, which he had founded with the wealth of his disciples. The bodily outrage to which she refers is the castration of Abelard by his enemies, a fact related in his earlier letter to a friend.

TO her master, nay her father, to her husband, nay brother, his handmaid, nay daughter, his spouse, nay sister: to ABELARD, HELOÏSE.

Your letter written to a friend for his comfort, beloved, was lately brought to me by chance. Seeing at once from the title that it was yours, I began the more ardently to read it in that the writer was so dear to me, that I might at least be refreshed by his words as by a picture of him whose presence I have lost. Almost every line of that letter, I remember, was filled with gall and wormwood, to wit those that related the miserable story of our conversion, and thy unceasing crosses, my all. Thou didst indeed fulfil in that letter what at the beginning of it thou hadst promised thy friend, namely

---

Mr. Guy Chapman will shortly publish the first complete translation of these letters.

that in comparison with thy troubles he should deem his own to be nothing or but a little matter. After setting forth thy former persecution by thy masters, then the outrage of supreme treachery upon thy body, thou hast turned thy pen to the execrable jealousy and inordinate assaults of thy fellow-pupils also, namely *Alberic* of Rheims and *Lotulph* the Lombard ; and what by their instigation was done to that famous work of thy theology, and what to thyself, as it were condemned to prison, thou hast not omitted.

From these thou comest to the machinations of thine Abbot and false brethren, and the grave detraction of thee by those two pseudo-apostles, stirred up against thee by the aforesaid rivals, and to the scandal raised by many of the name of Paraclete given to the oratory in departure from custom : and then, coming to those intolerable and still continuing persecutions of thy life, thou hast carried to the end the miserable story of that cruellest of extortioners and those wickedest of monks, whom thou callest thy sons. Which things I deem that no one can read or hear with dry eyes, for they renewed in fuller measure my griefs, so diligently did they express each several part, and increased them the more, in that thou relatedst that thy perils are still growing, so that we are all alike driven to despair of thy life, and every day our trembling hearts and throbbing bosoms await the latest rumour of thy death.

And so in His Name Who still protects thee in a certain measure for Himself, in the Name of Christ, as His handmaids and thine, we beseech thee to deign to inform us by frequent letters of those shipwrecks in which thou still art tossed, that thou mayest have us at least, who alone have remained to thee, as partners in thy grief or joy. For they are wont to bring some comfort to a grieving man who grieve with him, and any burden that is laid on several is borne more easily, or transferred. And if this tempest should have been stilled for a space, then all the more hasten thou to write, the more pleasant thy letter will be. But whatsoever it be of which thou mayest write to us, thou wilt confer no small remedy on us ; if only in this that thou wilt show thyself to be keeping us in mind.

For how pleasant are the letters of absent friends *Seneca*

himself by his own example teaches us, writing thus in a certain passage to his friend *Lucilius :* " Because thou writest to me often, I thank thee. For in the one way possible thou showest thyself to me. Never do I receive a letter from thee, but immediately we are together." If the portraits of our absent friends are pleasant to us, which renew our memory of them and relieve our regret for their absence by a false and empty consolation, how much more pleasant are letters which bring us the written characters of the absent friend. But thanks be to God, that in this way at least no jealousy prevents thee from restoring to us thy presence, no difficulty impedes thee, no neglect (I beseech thee) need delay thee.

Thou hast written to thy friend the comfort of a long letter, considering his difficulties, no doubt, but treating of thine own. Which diligently recording, whereas thou didst intend them for his comfort, thou hast added greatly to our desolation, and while thou wert anxious to heal his wounds hast inflicted fresh wounds of grief on us and made our former wounds to ache again. Heal, I beseech thee, the wounds that thou thyself hast given, who art so busily engaged in healing the wounds given by others. Thou hast indeed humoured thy friend and comrade, and paid the debt as well of friendship as of comradeship ; but by a greater debt thou hast bound thyself to us, whom it behoves thee to call not friends but dearest friends, not comrades but daughters, or by a sweeter and a holier name, if any can be conceived.

As to the greatness of the debt which binds thee to us neither argument nor evidence is lacking, that any doubt be removed ; and if all men be silent the fact itself cries aloud. For of this place thou, after God, art the sole founder, the sole architect of this oratory, the sole builder of this congregation. Nothing didst thou build here on the foundations of others. All that is here is thy creation. This wilderness, ranged only by wild beasts or by robbers, had known no habitation of men, had contained no dwelling. In the very lairs of the beasts, in the very lurking places of the robbers, where the name of God is not heard, thou didst erect a divine tabernacle, and didst dedicate the Holy Ghost's own temple. Nothing didst thou borrow from the wealth of kings or princes, when thou couldst have obtained so much and from so many, that whatsoever was wrought here might be ascribed to thee alone. Clerks or scholars flocking in haste to thy teaching ministered to thee all things needful, and they who lived upon ecclesiastical benefices, who knew not how to make but only how to receive oblations, and had hands for receiving, not for giving, became lavish and importunate here in the offering of oblations.

Thine, therefore, truly thine is this new plantation in the divine plan, for the plants of which, still most tender, frequent irrigation is necessary that they may grow. Frail enough, from the weakness of the feminine nature, is this plantation; it is infirm, even were it not new. Wherefore it demands more diligent cultivation and more frequent, after the words of the Apostle : " I have planted, *Apollos* watered ; but God gave the increase." The Apostle had planted, by the doctrines of his preaching, and had established in the Faith the Corinthians, to whom he wrote. Thereafter *Apollos*, the Apostle's own disciple, had watered them with sacred exhortations, and so by divine grace the increment of virtues was bestowed on them. Thou art tending the vineyard of another's vine which thou didst not plant, which is turned to thine own bitterness, with admonitions often wasted and holy sermons preached in vain. Think of what thou owest to thine own, who thus spendest thy care on another's. Thou teachest and reprovest rebels, nor gainest thou aught. In vain before swine dost thou scatter the pearls of divine eloquence. Who givest so much thought to the obstinate, consider what thou owest to the obedient. Who bestowest so much on thine enemies, meditate what thou owest to thy daughters. And, to say nothing of the rest, think by what a debt thou art bound to me, that what thou owest to the community of devoted women thou mayest pay more devotedly to her who is thine alone.

How many grave treatises in the teaching, or in the exhortation, or for the comfort of holy women the holy Fathers composed, and with what diligence they composed them, thine excellence knows better than our humility. Wherefore to no little amazement thine oblivion moves the tender beginnings of our conversion, that neither by reverence for God, nor by love of us, nor by the examples of the holy Fathers hast thou been admonished to attempt to comfort me, as I waver and am already crushed by prolonged grief, either by speech in thy presence or by a letter in thine absence. And yet thou knowest thyself to be bound to me by a debt so much greater in that thou art tied to me more closely by the pact of the nuptial sacrament ; and that thou art the more beholden to me in that I ever, as is known to all, embraced thee with an unbounded love. Thou knowest, dearest, all men know what I have lost in thee, and in how wretched a case that supreme and notorious betrayal took me myself also from me with thee, and that my grief is immeasurably greater from the manner in which I lost thee than from the loss of thee.

And the greater the cause of grief, the greater the remedies of comfort to be applied. Not, however, by another, but by thee thyself, that thou who art alone in the cause of my grief may be alone in the grace of my comfort. For it is thou alone that canst make me sad, canst make me joyful or canst comfort me. And it is thou alone that owest me this great debt, and for this reason above all that I have at once performed all things that thou didst order, till that when I could not offend thee in anything I had the strength to lose myself at thy behest. And what is more, and strange it is to relate, to such madness did my love turn that what alone it sought it cast from itself without hope of recovery when, straightway obeying thy command, I changed both my habit and my heart, that I might show thee to be the one possessor both of my body and of my mind. Nothing have I ever (God wot) required of thee save thyself, desiring thee purely, not what was thine. Not for the pledge of matrimony, nor for any dowry did I look, nor my own passions or wishes but thine (as thou thyself knowest) was I zealous to gratify.

And if the name of wife appears more sacred and more valid, sweeter to me is ever the word friend, or, if thou be not ashamed, concubine or whore. To wit that the more I humbled myself before thee the fuller grace I might obtain from thee, and so also damage less the fame of thine excellence. And thou thyself wert not wholly unmindful of that kindness in the letter of which I have spoken, written to thy friend for his comfort. Wherein thou hast not disdained to set forth sundry reasons by which I tried to dissuade thee from our marriage, from an ill-starred bed ; but wert silent as to many, in which I preferred love to wedlock, freedom to a bond. I call God to witness, if *Augustus*, ruling over the whole world, were to deem me worthy of the honour of marriage, and to confirm the whole world to me, to be ruled by me for ever, dearer to me and of greater dignity would it seem to be called thy strumpet than his empress.

For it is not by being richer or more powerful that a man becomes better ; one is a matter of fortune, the other of virtue. Nor should she deem herself other than venal who weds a rich man rather than a poor, and desires more things in her husband than himself. Assuredly, whomsoever this concupiscence leads into marriage deserves payment rather than affection ; for it is evident that she goes after his wealth and not the man, and is willing to prostitute herself, if she can, to a richer. As the argument advanced (in *Aeschines*) by the wise *Aspasia* to *Xenophon* and his wife plainly convinces us. When the wise woman aforesaid had propounded this argument for their reconciliation, she concluded as follows : " For when ye have understood this, that there is not a better man nor a happier woman on the face of the earth ; then ye will ever and above all things seek that which ye think the best ; thou to be the husband of so excellent a wife, and she to be married to so excellent a husband." A blessed sentiment, assuredly, and more than philosophic, expressing wisdom itself rather than philosophy. A holy error and a blessed fallacy among the married, that a perfect love should preserve their bond of matrimony unbroken, not so much by the continence of their bodies as by the purity of their hearts. But what error shows to the rest of women the truth has made manifest to me. Since what they thought of their husbands, that I, that the entire world not so much believed as knew of thee. So that the more genuine my love was for thee, the further it was removed from error.

For who among kings or philosophers could equal thee in fame ? What kingdom or city or village did not burn to see thee ? Who, I ask, did not hasten to gaze upon thee when thou appearedst in public, nor on thy departure with straining neck and fixed eye follow thee ? What wife, what maiden did not yearn for thee in thine absence, nor burn in thy presence ? What queen or powerful lady did not envy me my joys and my bed ? There were two things, I confess, in thee especially, wherewith thou couldst at once captivate the heart of any woman ; namely the arts of making songs and of singing them. Which we know that other philosophers have seldom followed. Wherewith as with a game, refreshing the labour of philosophic exercise, thou hast left many songs composed in amatory measure or rhythm, which for the suavity both of words and of tune being oft repeated, have kept your name without ceasing on the lips of all ; since even illiterates the sweetness of thy melodies did not allow to forget thee. It was on this account chiefly that women sighed for love of thee. And as the greater part of thy songs descanted of our love, they spread my fame in a short time through many lands, and inflamed the jealousy of many women against me. For what excellence of mind or body did not adorn thy youth ? What woman who envied me then does not my calamity now compel to pity one deprived of such delights ? What man or woman, albeit an enemy at first, is not now softened by the compassion due to me ?

And though exceeding guilty I am, as thou knowest, exceeding innocent. For it is not the deed but the intention that makes the crime. It is not what is done but the spirit in which it is done that equity considers. And in what state of mind I have ever been towards thee, only thou, who hast knowledge of it, canst judge. To thy consideration I commit all, I yield in all things to thy testimony. Tell me one thing only, if thou canst, why, after our conversion, which thou alone didst decree, I am fallen into such neglect and oblivion with thee that I am neither refreshed by thy speech and presence nor comforted by a letter in thine absence. Tell me, one thing only, if thou canst, or let me tell thee what I feel, nay what all suspect. Concupiscence joined thee to me rather than affection, the ardour of desire rather than love. When therefore what thou desiredst ceased, all that thou hadst exhibited at the same time failed. This, most beloved, is not mine only but the conjecture of all, not peculiar but common, not private but public. Would that it seemed thus to me only, and thy love found others to excuse it, by whom my grief might be a little quieted. Would that I could invent reasons by which in excusing thee I might cover in some measure my own vileness.

Give thy attention, I beseech thee, to what I demand; and thou wilt see this to be a small matter and most easy for thee. While I am cheated of thy presence, at least by written words, whereof thou hast an abundance, present to me the sweetness of thine image. In vain may I expect thee to be liberal in things if I must endure thee niggardly in words. Until now I believed that I deserved more from thee when I had done all things for thee, persevering still in obedience to thee. Who indeed as a girl was allured to the asperity of monastic conversation not by religious devotion but by thy command alone. Wherein if I deserve nought from thee, thou mayest judge my labour to have been vain. No reward for this may I expect from God, for the love of Whom it is well known that I did not anything. When thou hastenedst to God, I followed thee in the habit, nay preceded thee. For as though mindful of the wife of *Lot*, who looked back from behind him, thou deliveredst me first to the sacred garments and monastic profession before thou gavest thyself to God. And for that in this one thing thou shouldst have had little trust in me I vehemently grieved and was ashamed. For I (God wot) would without hesitation precede or follow thee to the Vulcanian fires according to thy word. For not with me was my heart, but with thee. But now, more than ever, if it be not with thee, it is nowhere. For without thee it cannot anywhere exist. But so act that it may be well with thee, I beseech thee. And well with thee will it be if it find thee propitious, if thou give love for love, little for much, words for deeds. Would that thy love, beloved, had less trust in me, that it might be more anxious! But the more confident I have made thee in the past, the more neglectful now I find thee. Remember, I beseech thee, what I have done, and pay heed to what thou owest me. While with thee I enjoyed carnal pleasures, many were uncertain whether I did so from love or from desire. But now the end shows in what spirit I began. I have forbidden myself all pleasures that I might obey thy will. I have reserved nothing for myself, save this, to be now entirely thine. Consider therefore how great is thine injustice, if to me who deserve more thou payest less, nay nothing at all, especially when it is a small thing that is demanded of thee, and right easy for thee to perform.

And so in His Name to whom thou hast offered thyself, before God I beseech thee that in whatsoever way thou canst thou restore to me thy presence, to wit by writing me some word of comfort. To this end alone that, thus refreshed, I may give myself with more alacrity to the service of God. When in time past thou soughtest me out for temporal pleasures thou visitedst me with endless letters, and by frequent songs didst set thy *Heloïse* on the lips of all men. With me every public place, each house resounded. How more rightly shouldst thou excite me now towards God, whom thou excitedst then to desire. Consider, I beseech thee what thou owest me, pay heed to what I demand ; and my long letter with a brief ending I conclude. Farewell, my all.

Poems

By EDGELL RICKWORD.

Introduction.

The only birds to call this city home
Roost on the branching nerves, at every stride
Dig talons deeper through the vein's thin crust
To rip the surface of my life's winding dream—
Such thoughts as these; I carry Time on my wrist,
A weak thong straps that daemon at my side,
He overshadows me, unseen to others
Who only see the hands on a common dial,
And not the hands I linked for my undoing,
Naming Duration, chains of change and decay.
His fingers are ten winds that fan the stars,
Extinguish some and set others glowing;
Mountains are more impermanent and the forests
Wither not much slower than a flower-bed,
Whose deep-grained iron trunks, brittle as stalks
Of dandelions to me, his fingers crumple.
Even the land has that old enemy ocean
Quiet as a cat rubbing the edge of things
And purring on the limits of destruction.
The tragedy of human habitations
Is subject for the eloquence of Gibbon,
I meditate private disasters only,
And among these, Time's treachery to women,
The faint cosmetic mask grain by grain stolen
Till their moon-faces wane and no light fills
With thin romantic foliage lips' dry valleys.

The root of misery is the fact of change
Always anticipated by the mind,
Which, met like Dürer's Death at a street-crossing,
Would shock imagination to create
New shapes of permanence and evolve machines

POEMS

Not anthropomorphic but in power like Spring,
Whence young gods would step down to wound the earth,
Raising like crocus-flocks delicate beings—
As spirits flutter from the gash of pain.

Time the cartographer makes no more quaint maps,
Putting at boundaries where venture failed
A whorlèd Kraken belching blank surmise,
But over all, profaning mysteries,
Lays sleek meridians crossed with parallels ;
So the twin hemispheres, Anger and Love,
With forests feathered and wide ocean eyes
Decoyed at mating like wild sea-birds, glare
In gorgeous ruin from the cuckold's net.

Later causality builds on this foundation
An iron pain and concrete mass of thought,
Such a cuirass as Milton's Satan wanted
Against the coldly bright angelic darts
Insinuating hope, remorse, regret,
Thin dimming poisons in his sparkling veins.
Emotion sprouts slender geometries,
Angular vines and dark festooning cables
Bursting in crackling heads that shed for scent
A sick mauve luminosity in our lanes,
All deathless vegetation frets far-off ;
The arborescent chaos of the blood
Lapping like water the sea-walls of sense ;
The womb of words and grave where naked men,
Not coffined, nailed or shrouded in conceits,
But embryonic corpses of desire,
Rock in the moon-drawn cradle of a sea,
Warm dark salt secret turgid dung-tanged waste.

———

Annihilation.

My cat and dog dream not as I. This room
Is their smooth field, hazardous but not strange ;
Tall flowers stand there biting at the touch,
And half my wisdom hangs upon that bloom.

For when those candles fade we are shut up ;
Sight gone, no sense responds to summons much ;
But darkness is a world the beast may range
And miss no stone the orphic sun built up.

Light gone, my books are dumb for me or cat,
Taste wanes, smell fails, the fingers hardly wake ;
My dog cocks ears at a familiar foot
And greets my love before my brain thinks that.

Dark holds Earth rigid in whose bowl of hills
Silence flows down, a soft reflecting lake
Filled with this velvet, gold-pierced scene whose root
My Thought leans over, sighing as it kills.

Absences.

(i)

In the Solitude of Soul
Not another did I see,
Till my longing in despair
Grew incorporate with Air.

Then, O Shadow, no control
Bounded our twin unity,
And the land grew soft as moss
That gentle thoughts bare-foot might cross.

Guileless figures came and went,
Creating it a place of calm.
Self nor Shadow did not move
In the atmosphere of Love.

One above the other bent
Like willows in a pool of balm.
Air so luminous that Shade
One with her own self was made.

Now is Joy's own image spilled
And the Landscape in Eclipse
Has the crumpled emptiness
Of a fine discarded dress.

Broken mirror Pride had willed !
Her form like water from me slips.
No lake, no glass will now return
The shade with which, lonely, I burn.

(ii)
Now that you lie in lonely pain,
O Moon in no flower-clouded bed,
What shall evoke our Joy again,
O Tears, rain Tears on Pleasure dead.

Under their sharp caressing stroke
The foliage of our love revives,
Though your face pale when anguish broke
Alone on Night's dead sea survives.

Memory.

Dumb forest belts the Mountains of the Moon,
Unverdant, sapless, twilit, bird-deserted ;
The shadow of the heart unvisited,
The grey antithesis of golden noon.
Root-stricken Fancy in an endless swoon
Dies but decays not, to new use perverted ;
Staunch phallic trunks to pretty emblems twisted,
Question the passing of their sun so soon.

Birds might expect the crystal note of dawn
And in shrill cries anticipate the light ;
This vegetation has no way to praise.
The faintest whistle through its stillness drawn,
This weightless fabric sinks to dust and night,
Having once bloomed, for such are natural ways.

Assuagement.

What messages are these the morning brings
My angry city from kind-bosomed fields ?
The cool, soft words of vegetable things
Placating her whose rumour never yields
To the far-blown persuasion of quiet grass ;
Whose wrinkled fever dewfall never cools ;
Now for a moment stilled, as waggons pass,
To faint remembrance of her ancient pools.

The streets of pain and theatres of despair,
The heart's metropolis, this peace dispute,
Matching solidity against permanence ;
Only the moon wears a consistent air,
Watching the clouds answer the wind's thin flute
In azure meadows' poor inheritance.

Covent Garden. Early Morning.

Invocation to Angels.

Angels ! bequeath your tongues of flame
To those who need them more than you,
In Paradise you know no shame
And love blooms not without that dew.

In these pale-leaved suburban groves
We melancholy couples lie,
Whom some uncouth persuasion moves
In one another's arms to die.

Our better nature then proceeds
To sublimation of its dross,
And to ideals from lower needs
Flings a phantasmal bridge across.

Shall we tread proudly, O my love,
This Jacob's Ladder of escape ?
I know you gentler than the dove
Whose timid eyes invite the rape ;

Yet not, I think, so small of mind
As to preen plumage of the Bird
Whose dazzling beauty strikes us blind
Though but abstracted from a word.

The swans in flight through winter dusk
Seem to man fast in Nature's vice,
Emblems of power as pure as musk
And first to pride his thoughts entice.

Yet in our shameful partnerships
Such rarely lovely moments rise,
It must be Impotence equips
A licensed brothel in the skies.

Let eyes reflect like forest lakes
All beasts to ancient comfort led,
Till joy to innocence awakes,
As children hug, in Earth's cold bed.

Chronique Scandaleuse.

Between low walls whose faded paper mocks
With painted blossoms bridals of the air
When lovers lay at will among their flocks,
A common scene stripped love's fresh branches bare.

Out of the ruin an old candour cried
Like a man speaking to a faithless friend,
" Now Hangman Pleasure's triple knot is tied
And we must share one halter till the end.

THE CALENDAR

" So priest and victim in the antique glade
   Felt the peculiar bond compress their heart,
   Gazing in awed communion on the blade
   That binds the creatures it would seem to part.

" My love is like an anchorite who frets
   In ecstasy upon his couch of stone,
   So little in me moves the hate that whets
   The steel of vengeance on a wrong once done.

" The modern crowd that laps up tears for blood
   Takes in such errors with its Sunday milk,
   But there's a dualism in my mood
   And envy tears my anguish like fine silk.

" My soul's a trampled dwelling-ground where Sade,
   The gallant marquis, fences for his life
   Against the invulnerable retrograde
   Masoch, his shade, more constant than a wife."

Farewell to Fancy : or Suburb of Adolescence Re-visited.

The evening villas smoke and doze
Like men from daytime tasks released.
Round each small yard the air is creased
Where a thin boundary paling goes.

Like sick men's thoughts, the narrow strips
Of garden push forth small strange flowers
Sown in long-since vague hours
On curious or on shy girls' lips.

POEMS

The nubile daughters now escape
To any waste or open plot
Where flowers or sweethearts may be got
For decoration or feigned rape.

On building-sites by tall stiff poles
Sweetly their maiden langour droops.
O dandelions and rusty hoops
And low foundations in their souls !

This is the rock on which we build,
Poets or Pierrots, our True Church ;
The Deacon blessing our long search
A boy with amorous mischief filled.

Let us abjure the stately creeds
With mystic glades of conifers,
And all that Eloquence confers
Upon our elemental needs.

We will go with them by the tram
Beyond the city's lamps, and sit
With such emotions as befit
Those borne between the *Plough* and *Ram*.

And afterwards the gramophone
In dusky parlours shall delude
Our mutual insolicitude
With sentiments that mask our own.

We have been snobs or something worse,
Maintaining an elaborate pose,
Like girls with too-pretentious hose,
In a suburban Universe.

Plough and Ram : Emblems of Toil and Procreation.

The Dithyrambic Spectator.

An Essay on the Origins and Survivals of Art.

By WYNDHAM LEWIS.

PART II.

A VERY different book from this exhilarating and adventurous treatise by Dr. Elliot Smith* is the other one that I will arbitrarily associate here with it ; in the hope of arriving, from a consideration of the two together, at something requiring some such historic backgrounds as they provide.   This second book is Miss Harrison's *Ancient Art and Ritual* (Home University Library).

If Dr. Elliot Smith is attracted, through his professional experience, to the physiological antecedents of art, Miss Harrison is temperamentally attracted by the May-pole festivities of the village green of Merry England, and still merrier Greece.   Whereas the truth of which Dr. Elliot Smith makes us so handsome a present has the authentic stamp of the hospital on it, and the appeal of that type of reality ; Miss Harrison is principally indebted to Dr. Frazer for her very interesting evidence, and the anthropological *pugging*, if not the plan, of her theory.   She naturally in *Ancient Art and Ritual* is concerned directly with the philosophy of art ; and she presents her material in an attractive and lucid form.

Her theory of the origin of art reduces itself to this : (1) that the transition of art out of some earlier activity can be studied better in Greek art than elsewhere.   (2) Of the two most important forms of art in Greece, the *drama* and *sculpture :* that (3) the *drama* came out of the ritual and magical practices of the people, or the particular practices associated with the cult of Dionysos ; and that (4) the *statue* is—well, what all statues of gods are, a representation of a deity, which in its turn is the ideal presentment in mud, wood, or stone of a May-King, or Jack-in-the-Green—Dionysos or Apollo.

---

* "The Evolution of the Dragon."   For the first part of Mr. Lewis's essay see Vol. 1, No. 2, pp. 89-107.

THE DITHYRAMBIC SPECTATOR

" The stages, it would seem," she says, " are : actual life with its motor reactions, the ritual copy of life with its faded reactions ; the image of the god projected by the rite ; and, last, the copy of that image, the work of art. We see now why in the history of all ages and every place art is what is called the ' handmaid of religion.' She is not really the ' handmaid ' at all. She springs straight out of the rite, and her first outward leap is the image of the god. Primitive art in Greece, in Egypt, in Assyria, represents either rites, processions, sacrifices, magical ceremonies, embodied prayers, or else it represents the images of the gods who spring from those rites."

Art invariably originated, for Miss Harrison, in a magical rite. Art is ritualistic material converted into secular display or representation : and in many cases arises on the decay of magic. The distinction between religion and magic is therefore a question presenting itself at the outset in her theory. She does not deal with it herself except very briefly, probably for want of space. It is a very involved question indeed on which few people are found to agree. It is really a distinction between a practical activity (that is magic) and a theoretic or abstract activity (religion) : and in that way there would seem to be some analogy between magic and religion on the one side, and ritual and art on the other, as the latter is understood by Miss Harrison.

The belief in magic is the sign of man's persuasion of his identity with nature. As he gradually separates himself from nature and becomes a human personality (as he thinks), and as he sees (as he then believes) that nature is inhuman and indifferent to him, he no longer believes that he can influence events outside himself in the objective mechanism over against which he stands. The fatalism that faces *la pluie et le beau temps* with an equal face since not a drop can be drawn from the sky, or prevented from falling, by any intercession or human coercion, such as formerly had been thought, is the sign of the civilised man who " takes things as they come."

Between this absolute mechanistic fatalism, the latest phase, and the phase of magic and ritual, the earliest, comes *religion*. The sacrificial bull, or bull-god, becomes a man. The " man-like daemon who rose from a real King of the May, must himself be approached and dealt with as a man, bargained with, sacrificed to." In place of the ritual of sympathetic magic, we get the worship of a god. It is no longer attempted to coerce the seasons, or bring back, with little painted suns, the sun, or prevent him from interfering with the rain-clouds, and the crops ; but the seasons are *personified :* " Abstract Fruitfulness " becomes a person—Ceres or Dionysos.

When the Roman State took into its care the superstitions of the people, organised the *jus divinum*, and relieved the private citizen of any obligation for personal anxiety and personal initiative and ingenuity where the various supernatural agencies were concerned, it killed the " religio," thus standardised, in the people. Such a taking over by the State of all the field of magic and superstition (such as the Calendar of Numa witnesses) did not occur apparently in Greece, and irresponsible rites flourished. The Roman gods were rigidly state-gods ; all the observances, lustrations and so forth appropriate for the various phases of the agricultural year or of military service (the Roman year, beginning in the war-month with the activities of the Salii, and a great lustration) were standardised and attended to by the State. Whereas the Greek worship was more individualistic. It was no doubt this certain backwardness (if you look at it from the State standpoint) and individualism that made *art* flourish in Greece, whereas in Rome it hardly existed.

Religion, as we generally understand it, and in the sense in which Miss Harrison uses it, may be regarded as the arrival of something quite new on the scene, caused by the separation of the Subject from the Not-self. It is this first sundering of the subject from its surroundings that produces it. It is something arising to fill in the gap caused by the separation. Just as the order of animal gestation is that two beings by mingling produce a third, so a " god " is produced by their *separation*. But this god is not an amalgam of man and his environment, but rather a new environment created to correspond to needs transcending the scene of his earlier magical operations. It is all that is (1) terrestrially the Not-self ; and (2) yet that to which no visible Not-self properly corresponds. It is to celebrate his divorce from nature that man creates a god.

THE DITHYRAMBIC SPECTATOR

In primitive magic there is at most a *numen* or functional spirit. Dr. Warde Fowler quotes a schema of the evolution of the *numen*, by von Domaszewski, as follows :

" (1) Momentary function of the *numina*, *e.g.* lightning ; (2) elevation of this into a permanent power or function ; (3) consequent limitation of the numen to a special well-marked function ; (4) elevation of the numen to a *deus*, conceived in the likeness of man, and male or female, because man cannot think of power otherwise than on the analogy of male and female creative energy. Lastly, when the *deus* is complete, the functions of the former numen become attributes or qualities, etc."

The *numina* are strictly "metaphoric powers" of animals or things. A *numen* is " a doing," an " activity," a manifestation of will in anything or anybody. It is certainly, in the end, the clearer and clearer conception of the Subject that anthropomorphises this function. At first there is nothing more in it than *itself*. It is just an ability to *do* something, or *be* something, a mechanism, as much an ascertainable and evident part of the world as experienced by men as are the leaves of the tree, a plough, or a piece of firewood. *Forculus* is the spirit of the door, but is nothing more than a door—the significance and use of a door. Similarly *Gardia* is the hinges of the door : it is a spirit that is *hinges* and all that we associate with hinges, and all that they can do, and nothing else. *Janus* was, it seems, a door-spirit. With all these varieties of "power" man regards himself, to begin with, as mixed up. There is an interpenetration of everything, enabling him to influence things as he is influenced by them. The door will fly to and nip his enemy for him : the hinges creak to warn him of an intruder, and so forth : that is if he treats them as he should. They are not anthropomorphic because he is hardly yet *man*. When he realises that these "powers" or functions are independent of him, and independent of his will, they are more menacing than before. For they now are *strange* and of a different substance to him. He redoubles his attentions, but with more respect. At that point comes the period of *pacts*, of religion, and of the legal structure whereby he secures himself.

We can now return to Miss Harrison's theory. In the magical and ritualistic stage men thought that *their* fertility

was the same as the fertility of their crops. When they sprinkled water on the ground, they thought that all water being
one, as it were, this would break the drought. Their sprinkling
was a kind of surgical operation on nature, that would bring
on a miscarriage of the moisture of the sky, and precipitate
the rain they desired. "Among the Omaha Indians of North
America, when the corn is withering for want of rain, the
members of the sacred Buffalo Society fill a large vessel with
water and dance four times round it. One of them drinks some
of the water and spirts it into the air, making a fine spray in
imitation of mist or drizzling rain. Then he upsets the vessel,
spilling the water on the ground ; whereupon the dancers fall
down and drink up the water, getting mud all over their faces.
This saves the corn."

In Eastern Russia on Shrove Tuesday a girl gets into a
hoop, to which leaves, flax, and a bell are attached. She jumps
about vigorously crying "Flax, grow." She *is* the flax. Man
is still, in such cases as that of the Russian peasant or the
Omaha Indian, a part of nature. He can get inside nature,
identify himself with it, and so influence it not from *without*,
as a distant or disconnected suppliant, but as part of it, as the
little toe can make itself felt from head to foot, and get its
way probably.

With an agricultural people the bull is regarded as an
especially fertile object : and the dionysian ritual in Greece
centred round this animal. The long series of sacrificial spring-
time bulls driven in procession eventually became Dionysos ;
just as Janus, who began as a door, would finish as a stately
and bearded man.

It will be necessary for my subsequent argument to give
a summary outline of Miss Harrison's account of the origin
of Greek drama. It is such a familiar theme that the roughest
indication will suffice.

"Tragedy—as also Comedy," Aristotle says, "was at first
mere improvisation—the one (tragedy) originated with the
leaders of the Dithyramb." This statement of Aristotle's
connecting the art of the drama with the dithryamb gives
the art and ritual theory, Miss Harrison believes, a firm
"historical ground." The dithyramb was an excited dance
occurring at the spring festival of Dionysos. This festival

resembled all the April and May-time festivals in any land, ushering in the summer, and all containing some fertility ritual or other, designed to promote the food supply.

In the original dionysian festival a flower-decked bull was driven about in procession by the Graces. It was of this bull that Dionysos was " born," as Plutarch conjectures. There is a record of what happened to this spring-time bull at Magnesia (a Greek city in Asia Minor). Till the following April he was handsomely kept, and then sacrificed. " Why must a thing so holy die ? Why not live out the term of his life ? He dies because he *is* so holy, that he may give his holiness, his strength, his life, just at the moment it is holiest, to his people." So the bull is eaten, each man gets a piece, that he may take into his composition " the strength of the Bull, . . . the luck of the State." But the bull would come to life again, or be resurrected, in another bull, and so on endlessly.

" Year by year in the various villages of Greece was seen an actual holy Bull, and bit by bit from the remembrance of these various holy Bulls, who only died to live again each year, there arose the image of a Bull-Spirit, or Bull-Daimon, and finally, if we like to call him so, a Bull-God."

The long succession of the chorus-leaders of the dithyramb, the Kings of the May, became in retrospect, in the same way, Miss Harrison tells us, *one* King, or Spirit of the Spring. So arises the conception of a God, in this case Dionysos.

So far this is evidently the history of a certain fertility ritual, and is not necessarily *art*, any more than the evolution of words is poetry ; except in so far as all language is a sort of poetry, and all movement a sort of dance.

The transition between the bull and the man-god, and the transition between the dithyramb and the full-fledged drama of Sophocles, is necessarily obscure : and as there is no exact contemporary record (Aristotle being our best, and one of our only, authorities, we learn from Miss Harrison and others engaged in the same investigations) a great deal is left to the imagination, and there is considerable room for alternative theories.

Art " springs straight out of the rite, and the first outward leap is the image of the god." The " leap " of art mentioned by Miss Harrison is like the lightning flash ; we know that such

a flash occurs, and at that we must leave it. At one moment
it is one thing, and then suddenly it is something else.

The transition from the crude dithyramb—the dance and
song occurring at the spring festival of Dionysos, a circular
space being set aside for the final performance, in the centre
of which was placed the altar of the god—to the drama is
another "leap," for the following of which we possess only a
slender illumination " . . . Tragedy—as also Comedy—was
at first mere improvisation," Aristotle tells us. Further he
informs us that " Æschylus first introduced a second actor ;
he diminished the importance of the Chorus and assigned the
leading part to the dialogue. Sophocles raised the number of
actors to three, and added scene-painting. Moreover, it was
not till late that the short plot was discarded for one of greater
compass, and the grotesque diction of the earlier satyric form
for the stately manner of Tragedy. The iambic measure then
replaced the trochaic tetrameter, which was originally employed
when the poetry was of the satyric order, and had greater
affinities with dancing. Once dialogue had come in, Nature
herself discovered the appropriate measure. For the iambics,
of all measures, are the most colloquial . . . "

The researches of Miss Harrison, Messrs. Gilbert Murray,
Cornford, or Cook are *pugging* for the above clear but spare
account found in the Poetics. We see in the passage above,
even, Aristotle's assumption of a common origin for Tragedy
and Comedy. Add to that Miss Harrison's one solid bit of
" ground " for her theory—namely Aristotle's remark that
Tragedy originated with the leaders of the dithyramb, and
you arrive at Mr. Cornford's statement (*The Origin of Attic
Comedy*) that " the ritual drama lying behind Comedy proves
to be essentially of the same type as that in which Professor
Gilbert Murray has sought the origin of Tragedy."

From the point of view of these investigators Aristotle's
account is inadequate (possibly owing to the loss of the second
book of the Poetics, where he might have been more historically
explicit) because he is not interested in the extant book of the
Poetics with the origins of art, but with its philosophy once it is
there. *Imitation* is for him the key to it. But Poetry has its
origin, he tells us, in amateur improvisations. Miss Harrison's
book traces the development of art from this inchoate

existence as amateur contribution to a common magical ritual, into the highly trained professional setting of Attic drama.

As to Comedy, Mr. Cornford writes, "we have no ground for supposing that the folk-play which lay behind Comedy took shape in the *city* of Athens at all. The best tradition that we have connects both Susarion, the reputed founder of Comedy, and Thespis, the founder of Tragedy, not with Athens, but with Ikaria, an outlying centre of Dionysaic worship . . . such processions and mummer's plays are more likely to survive in country villages than in cities." Augustine tells us that the Italian Liberalia were celebrated "in the fields" and *later* brought into Rome itself. So "why should we not accept the tradition that Comedy was imported from Ikaria to Athens ? "

Aristotle's account of the rival claims of the Dorians and the Megarians seems to have something to do with this question. "Tragedy too is claimed by certain Dorians of the Peleponese. In each case they appeal to the evidence of language. The outlying villages they say are by them called κῶμαι, by the Athenians δῆμοι ; and they assume that Comedians were so named not from κωμάζειν, 'to rival,' but because they wandered from village to village (κατὰ κωμας), being excluded contemptuously from that city " (*Butler's translation, Poetics*, chap. iii).

Mr. Cornford concludes that the great Dionysia (in which the Attic dance aıose) was an artificial thing, imported into Athens from the country districts. "The great Dionysia, again, has not the air of a primitive feast at all. It was probably the artificial creation of Peisistratus' desire to have a great musical festival at a season of the year when it was possible for foreigners to be present and enjoy the glories of Athens ; "—Miss Harrison is more disposed to give a rustic, "merry-England " picture of Athens not so metropolitan as Mr. Cornford's. But, when she has to "leap," with art, from the dithyramb to the drama, she naturally allows that it was no doubt Peisistratus who was responsible ; that, in short, Attic drama did not grow, but had to be brought to birth by a "tyrannic " midwife, as a feature of his policy.

The artificial imposition of the Homeric cycle on Athens, the substitution of the hero-cult of the Achaians and the achaian pantheon for the local peasant ritual and agriculturist superstition, was an imposition from without and above. The personal intervention of Peisistratus seems (under correction) to weaken Miss Harrison's theory.

"Athens might, it would seem, but for the coming of Homer, have lain stagnant in a backwater of conservatism, content to go on chanting her traditional Spring Songs year by year. It is wonderful that this city of Athens . . . should have been saved from the storm and stress . . . spared the actual horrors of a heroic age, yet given heroic poetry, given the clear wine-cup poured when the ferment was over."

So Athens is, even in its destiny, made *the perfect artist*. This city, "beloved of the gods," in Miss Harrison's words, is not brought into violent contact with reality, but this heroic reality of the Achaian sagas—when all the fuss and disturbing violence is over—is brought to her in an after-glow of romance ; and the Attic stage blooms, at a safe distance from the devastating demi-gods of which it treats. " The Homeric saga had for an Athenian poet just the remoteness from immediate action which, as we have seen, is the essence of art as contrasted with ritual." But the existence of this saga, its convenient remoteness, the accident of a tyrant with an eye on it for his own purposes, are all obstacles to the smooth running of the theory.

" The main contention of the present book is that ritual and art have, in emotion towards life, a common root, and further, that primitive art develops normally; all over the world it is found that primitive ritual consists, not in prayer and praise and sacrifice, but in mimetic dancing. But it is in Greece, and perhaps in Greece only, in the religion of Dionysos, that we can actually trace, if dimly, the transition steps that led from dance to drama, from ritual to art."

That *art* and *ritual* " have, in emotion towards life, a common root " is what Miss Harrison not only does not, I think, prove : but also it is what, elsewhere, her statements certainly contradict. From the interest of their hunt for sources to enable them to derive the drama from a primitive magical rite, a collective religious activity, it is perhaps only a step that these specialists should wish to drag *art* in, as well, to help them in their attachments, and to round their structure.

Or there may be some other, and emotional reason, at work. But whatever the reason, in Miss Harrison's case, it involves her in a kind of fundamental contradiction which I think it will be useful to point out.

That Mr. Cornford is more conscious than is Miss Harrison of this possible pitfall is proved by various passages in his book (*Origin of Attic Comedy*).

"Anyone who states a theory," he writes in his ninth chapter, "of the historic origin of any form of art is sure to be attacked for neglecting the creative power of individual men of genius, and—something that lies deeper still—the common impulse obscurely felt by the men of a certain society, at a certain time, the common need that their apprehension of life, its laughter and its tears, shall find some expression in art. Such a criticism may be just. This book would deserve it, if I were for a moment to delude myself or the reader with the suggestion that there is nothing in the *Agamemnon* of Æschylus or the *Birds* of Aristophanes, of which the germ is not already present in Punch and Judy. If it is necessary to disclaim anything so absurd, it shall here be set down that our argument does not suppose the original drama, or the degenerate folk-play which may have followed it, to have contained, even in germ, either the wit of Aristophanes or the wisdom of Æschylus, either the comic or the tragic perception of life. It admits, moreover, that all these factors were needed, as independent and original forces, to shape fifth-century drama. But that is a good reason for excluding them, so far as possible, from a scientific discussion of historic origins."

And Mr. Cornford admits also "that there was every reason that Aristotle should exclude a scientific discussion of historic origins" from a treatise on the nature of art. Miss Harrison, however, *confuses* them with considerable gusto.

I should not presume to offer any opinion on these very technical matters if it were not that, in the first place, this question of origins is involved with Miss Harrison's theory of art to such an extent that it is impossible to discuss one without discussing the other : and secondly, it seems clear that the available argument of this group of investigators really hinges on Aristotle's Poetics, and so their *agon* is thus being carried on much nearer to the non-specialist borderland than is often the case.

In Mr. Cornford's book this transpires more clearly than in Miss Harrison's.

"Aristotle quite clearly states that Tragedy had emerged from a phase which he calls 'satyric.' . . . Without going further into the historic problems I will here express the opinion that, if Tragedy had declined to this level, its dignity and stateliness can only have been conferred upon it by the deliberate and conscious effort of individual poets, probably under the direction of Peisistratus. The process may have involved the expurgation of that side of the drama which was most obviously connected with fertility " (p. 214).

" . . . we cannot, I believe, dispense with the supposition of a conscious rescue of Tragedy from its satyric phase—a deliberate expulsion of those elements which distinguish the satyric drama from the tragic plays to which it was so closely linked. The conclusion that concerns our present argument is that there is good reason to believe that, if we could see a tragedy of the time before Æschylus and Peisistratus, we might find that it was a performance not much more serious and dignified than the Old Comedy. . . . In the case of Comedy we have not to suppose any such violent break with the popular tradition of the folk-play as I conjecture to have been deliberately effected for Tragedy " (p. 215).

He ends the book still attached to this doubt. "There is, so far as I can see, nothing in Aristotle's positive statements that is inconsistent with the hypothesis of this book, which I now commend to the reader's judgment."

It is not so much that anything in Aristotle's statements contradicts these theories, as that Aristotle would probably have regarded the historic explanation offered here as beside the point. Further, when employed by Miss Harrison, it becomes more dangerous, as the emotional acceleration occurring as we pass from the admirably argued pages of Mr. Cornford to those of Miss Harrison involves us, we find, in many things with which Aristotle certainly would not have agreed.

It will be easily seen how the statements of Miss Harrison's colleague, Mr. Cornford, weaken her theory. The " deliberate and conscious efforts of individual poets " under the arbitrary directions of Peisistratus ; the arbitrary imposition of the Achaian cycle on the old so different " iambic element " ; the " violent break " whereby this transition from a rude mummery into drama was effected, does not seem, on the face of it, to provide Miss Harrison with a universal law of growth of art out of ritual.

" It is a fact of cardinal importance," Miss Harrison writes, " that their (the Greeks') word for theatrical representation, *drama*, is own cousin to their word for rite, *dromenon* : drama also means ' thing done.' "

She takes these two words, *dromenon* and *drama*, to stand for the two things, " ritual " and " art." " The savage is a man of action," she tells us. " Instead of asking a god to do what he wants done, he does it or tries to do it himself." The savage is a *doer* (as Carlyle's king was " a man able to do.") There are no flies on the savage—he does not allow the grass to grow under his feet. We can surrender ourselves to a study of his practices with the full confidence that we shall be in the presence of " one of ourselves "—a man, in short, that we can respect. Again, " the two great interests of primitive man are food and children " ; more and more like us. We feel that we soon shall be quite at home with the savage.

It is this savage—a Greek savage—who decides to stake his luck on the Spring-time Bull : to regard it as holy, form a procession and so forth, as we have seen. And so (as we have also seen) in due course art makes its " leap," and a god turns up, named Dionysos. This savage spring-time rout invents crude and obscene mummeries to give a little variety to its festive processions. The townsmen are disposed to turn up their noses at these goings-on : but all of a sudden Peisistratus, the crafty tyrant, has an idea, and invites the savages into the town, gives them a circular spot, carefully flattened, to dance and howl on, and he also proposes an entire rehandling of their mummeries ; great town-poets appear, the Homeric cycle is brought forward, and the Attic stage is born. Such, duly foreshortened, is the tale Miss Harrison has to tell—into which I have incorporated Mr. Cornford's emendations. (As far as possible, I will imitate the tone of Miss Harrison's exposition, and respond as the reader envisaged is supposed to respond.)

The history of this circular spot on which the dancing first occurs is a drama in itself. " We have seen that the orchestra (that is the circular spot set apart, with its dancing chorus) stands for ritual, for the stage on which all were worshippers, all joined in a rite of practical intent. We saw further that the *theatre*, the place for the spectators, stood for art. In the orchestra all is life and dancing ; the marble *seats* are the very symbol of rest, aloofness from action, contemplation. The seats for the spectators grow and grow in importance till at last they absorb, as it were, the whole spirit, and give their name *theatre* to the whole structure ; *action is swallowed up in contemplation.*"

So there we have the *artist* (the contemplative spectator, seated on the cold marble) contrasted with the *ritualist* (the savage and practical-minded, actor or " doer " of his *dromenon*). The savage ritualistic dancing mass is gradually overcome by the growing mass of silent spectators, seated on the cold marble of contemplation, on the one hand (in the spectator-place), and the even more formidable innovation of a stage on the other. For the spectators knew that the dancing ritualistic savages were " men-of-action." They knew that " the ritual-dance was a *dromenon*, a thing to be done, not a thing to be looked at." But they were getting cold on the marble seats of contemplation, and wanted something *to look at*. (For in a sense a spectator is a man-of-action too ; only his way of *acting* is to *look*—that is why he is called a spectator, of course.)

" The history of the Greek stage is one long story of the encroachment of the stage on the orchestra. At first a rude platform or table is set up, then scenery is added ; the movable tent is translated into a stone house or temple front. This stands at first outside the orchestra ; then bit by bit the *scene* encroaches till the sacred circle of the dancing place is cut clean across. As the drama and the stage wax, the *dromenon* and the orchestra wane."

So these savage, practical-minded representatives of life —of food and children—are overcome by the spectator and the actor. Why should not the actor also be called an artist, as well as the spectator ? And then there is a third party that must also be let into this new pact against *life*—that is of course the playwright. Since the actor is only *playing* at life he is *looking on* in a sense : also the playwright is probably a contemplative type of man.

That these new and, all said and done, rather strange elements have formed a veritable *pact against life* Miss Harrison makes clear. For she tells us to start with that " primitive man . . . has, it would seem, little sensitiveness to the æsthetic impulse of the beauty of a spring morning, to the pathos of autumn." Or : " It is not that the Australian wonders at and admires the miracle of the spring, the bursting of the flowers and the singing of birds ; it is not that his heart goes out in gratitude to an All-Father who is the giver of all good things ; it is that, obedient to the push of life within him, his impulse is towards *food*. He must *eat*, etc." Or : " It cannot be too often remembered that primitive man has but little, if any, interest in sun and moon and heavenly bodies for their inherent beauty or wonder : he cares for them . . . he performs rites in relation to them when he notes that they bring the seasons, and he cares for the seasons mainly because they bring him *food*."

We are already beginning to feel that the repetition of *food* in connection with the " man-of-action " (to whom we likened ourselves in the earlier stages of the story) is a little unnecessary and overdone. We mentally bridle (what's wrong with *food* ? anyway) and feel we have been deceived.

" Primitive man," again we hear, is " weak . . . in individuality, it is not his private and personal emotions that tend to become ritual, but those that are public, felt and expressed officially, that is by the whole tribe or community."

In the old ritual dance *the individual was nothing*, the choral band, the group, everything, and in this it did but reflect primitive tribal life. Now in the heroic saga *the individual* is everything, the mass of the people, the tribe or the group, is but a shadowy background which throws up the brilliant, clear-cut personality into a more vivid light.

This " shadowy background " we hear more about. We hear that our art to-day, under the impulsion of science, is an art of the background : and that the individual no longer exists.

Still (and pardonably) a little vague as to where we shall issue forth—whether we shall be expected to end practical-minded savages, or spectators glued contemplatively to a cold marble seat—we proceed with Miss Harrison to a consideration of that puzzling individual—the *artist*. (The ritualist we know : he is a "man-of-action," a simple practical chap, and not unlike ourselves.)

"The artist renounces *doing*, in order to practise *seeing*." (So far so good : we never thought he *did* much.) "To understand and still more to contemplate life you must come out from the choral dance of life and stand apart." (That's not so good : for she seems to be suggesting that *we* don't "understand life.")

"Art is a cutting off of motor reactions." "Art, both creation and its enjoyment, is *unpractical*." "Thanks be to God, life is not limited to the practical!" (I liked her way of *putting* that last thing—but mercy, how my head turns !) "Artists . . . . are always late for dinner, they forget to post their letters or return books or even money that is lent them." (I should watch them !) "Art is profoundly connected with life. It is nowise superfluous."

"Art . . . is of sight or hearing. Sight and hearing are the distant senses." (The *spectators'* senses ; they cannot *touch* or *smell* the actors or actresses.) . . . "Taste and touch are too intimate." "In Russian, as Tolstoi has pointed out, the word for beauty (*krasata*) means . . . only *that which pleases the sight*."

"To see a thing, to feel a thing, as a work of art, we must, then, become for the time *unpractical*, must be loosed from the fear and flurry of actual living, must become spectators." (What ! do I enjoy watching a man drink a glass of beer as much as I do drinking it myself ?) "Why can we not live and look at once ?" "If we watch a friend drowning we do not note the exquisite curve made by his body as he falls into the water, nor the play of sunlight on the ripples as he disappears below the surface ; we should be inhuman, æsthetic fiends if we did." "If we want to . . . watch the cumbrous grace of a bear, we prefer that a cage should intervene. The cage cuts off the need for motor reactions ; it interposes the needful physical and moral distance, and we are free for contemplation. . . . A man intent on action is like a horse in blinkers . . ." etc.

THE DITHYRAMBIC SPECTATOR

" By neglecting most of the things we see and hear, we can focus on those which are important for action : we can cease to be potential artists, and become efficient practical human beings, but it is only by . . . a great renunciation as to the things we see and feel. The artist does just the reverse." " The ordinary man often thinks the artist a fool, or, if he does not go so far as that, is made vaguely uncomfortable by him, never really understands him. The artist's focus, all his system of values, is different, his world is a world of images which are his realities."

So *ritual* is a representation " always with a practical end." Art is a representation " cut loose from immediate action." " It may seem strange to some that the decay of religious faith should be an impulse to the birth of art." But all the same it is : and once we have got rid of the notion that stamping about and screaming is going to do any good, half can go and sit down on the marble seats, and, watching the other half, watch in a sense themselves—with profound admiration and astonishment. This is *art*.

The reader at this point will collect his wits. The man of action can neither *understand* nor *feel*. He is too busy. (Quite right ! No : that's not right !) He can't *feel*, because you cannot *feel* and at the same time *act*. Being a man-of-action, he realises that by dancing he will make the corn grow, and by singing make the sun shine, and the mare foal. Next, he ceases to believe that that is likely : he ceases to be a man of action, and becomes an artist. He looks on. (Is this the same man ? What a change !) He appreciates now (as though he were the sun-god watching his own magical dance) how extremely pretty it is : how it *should* have made the sun shine, even if it didn't, and the mare foal again. It is indeed just as good as though it *had*—and he has become a *god* into the bargain. (Oh, this is capital !)

Curtain. Gotterdammerung ! The fun is over.

Space does not allow me to quote Miss Harrison more fully, I would, for the rest, refer the reader to the book itself : but from these few contrasted extracts (with the appropriate comments of the sort of reader envisaged) it will be seen that a certain emotional confusion reigns in the pages of this small, popular, very learned book, and so, it is assumed, in the mind of this very learned would-be *modern* lady. The confusion arises from her desire to reconcile that part of her mind emotionally conforming to the democratic ideals of her time, and that part emotionally snobbish about art. It is, in short, the clash of two snobberies, and the desire to serve two masters, that involves her in the fifty turbid discursive pages of almost inextricable muddle-headedness with which her treatise terminates. Tolstoi becomes Marinetti : artists are implored to rush into the street and squeeze all the motor-horns within reach : art is very nice and respectable, and "life" is first rate too : they do not agree, but that doesn't matter.

"We English are not supposed to be an artistic people, yet art, in some form or another, bulks large in the national life. We have theatres, a National Gallery, we have art-schools, our tradesmen provide for us "art-furniture," we even hear, absurdly enough, of "art-colours." Moreover, all this is not a matter of mere antiquarian interest, we do not simply go and admire the beauty of the past in museums ; a movement towards or about art is all alive and astir among us. We have new developments of the theatre, problem plays, Reinhardt productions, Gordon Craig scenery, Russian ballets. We have new schools of painting treading on each other's heels with breathless rapidity : Impressionists, Post-Impressionists, Futurists. Art—or at least the desire for, the interest in, art —is assuredly not dead.

Moreover, and this is very important, we all feel about art a certain obligation, such as some of us feel about religion. There is an "ought" about it. Perhaps we do not really care much about pictures and poetry and music, but we feel we 'ought to.'"

Art "bulks large" with "we English" : we don't care much about pictures and poetry, but art "bulks large." We go to a picture gallery as we go to church : for we are a people with a conscience, etc., etc.

What is useful in her book is her description of the process of the differentiation of the original dithyrambic mass, whereby *art* is born. The introduction of the Homeric cycle governs the Attic stage. But "A heroic age, happily for society, cannot last long. . . . The world has seen several heroic ages, though it is, perhaps, doubtful if it will ever see another."

THE DITHYRAMBIC SPECTATOR

" Why," however, " was this influx of heroic poetry . . . of such immense influence on, and importance to, the development of Greek dramatic art ? Why had it power to change the old, stiff, ritual dithyramb into the new and living drama ? " *Because* " In the old ritual dance *the individual was nothing*, the choral band, the group everything." But " in the heroic saga *the individual is everything*." That was the reason.

Again : " In the primitive choral dance all three—artist, work of art, spectator—were used, or rather not yet differentiated." Greek art, as seen in the Attic drama, is the history of this differentiation, separating out, of (1) the artist, (2) the work of art, and (3) the spectator. This is *art*.

Ritual on the other hand is as follows :

(1) Ritual is " always collective."

(2) Primitive man is " weak in individuality."

(3) " At the beginning of things " men's impulses were " deeper, vaguer, more emotional."

To-day we have started the return journey *back* to ritual, Miss Harrison tells us. In her *finale* ACTION is uppermost once more—" Thanks be to God."

" For those of us who are not artists or original thinkers the life of the imagination, and even of the emotions, has been perhaps too long lived at second hand, received from the artist ready-made and felt. To-day, owing largely to the progress of science, and a host of other causes social and economic, life grows daily fuller and freer, and every manifestation of life is regarded with a new reverence. With this fresh outpouring of the spirit, this fuller consciousness of life, there comes a need for first-hand emotion and expression. . . . . Art in these latter days goes back as it were on her own steps, recrossing the ritual bridge back to life."

So at the last, having watched with some pain and perplexity the differentiation into artist, spectator, and so forth (with the *terribly* cold marble seats), we are privileged to observe the tide setting back again to those " deeper, vaguer, more emotional regions." Once more the " amateurs " (ἐθελονταί) come crowding back : once more we live *collectively* : all men once more are *actors*.

Now this fusion, or uprising of the audience and return of Everyman into the arena or choral acting-place, is, true enough, occurring universally. But it is not *a return to life*, as a return to a true primitive belief would be. There is a third stage, therefore, with which Miss Harrison does not deal, and of which apparently she is not aware.

Greek humanism is for Miss Harrison, " characteristically a group limitation." " We moderns are in love with the background. Our art is a landscape art." Our art is " the art of a stage, without actors ; a scene which is all background, all suggestion. It is an art given us by sheer recoil from science, which has dwarfed actual human life almost to imaginative extinction." It is science, according to Miss Harrison, that has " given us back a world-soul " : it is also, she says, science that has given us an art of backgrounds, in which the human individual disappears. It is science that is the great democratising force, in short, of the modern world. Science stands for the theory of *collective* life, art for the doctrine of *individual* life : science for the *dromenon*, art for the *drama ;* science for the dithyrambic dance, art for the aloof perfection of the Attic stage.

If it is asked of what *use* art is, it has been put to innumerable uses, and when not interfered with can make a sort of paradise of the world (which, it is unnecessary to say, whenever such a thing has occurred, can no more have been noticed by those privileged to dwell in the midst of it than the abstract beauty of "nature " is experienced, probably, by primitive men). But its great traditional use as a *catharsis* is still its best credential. With religion, magic, or primitive " mystery," usually the crowd has those " backgrounds " just referred to thrown open to it, or there is always a tendency to " fusion " and ecstasy. " The back is knocked out " of the stage. With art men are shown these " backgrounds " too : great art is cut out of the same wild material. But it is as spectators that they survey these terrible truths, with the atmosphere of the distances which art maintains, and the *measure* of its trance, to soften them ; and it is the form, no doubt, in which a community less demented than most, and capable of receiving their purges with fortitude and relative calm, would always receive them. But art ceases to be art, or great art at least, when beneath its seductive exterior these ultimate realities are not found. And it is the most perishable of specifics. It requires great discipline to prefer to watch a game *perfectly* played, rather than kick a ball about clumsily yourself, if you have the option. Very rapidly the banks of spectators turn into a great assembly of "amateurs" (ἐθελονταί) once more. Then comes the phase that Miss Harrison left out : the phase in which a collective " play " is engaged in, in which no " real " or " practical " issues are involved. That is the *bridge* back to primitive life, no doubt : since people cannot " play " and fiddle about for long. The full blind collective ecstasy is not far off when this transition of the *spectators* into *amateurs* has been effected.

Frau Karl Druschki.*

By STEPHEN HUDSON.

HE stopped a moment at a banker's office near the hotel, he knew bankers everywhere, always had the appropriate money and, it seemed, endless quantities of it. I could see him from the carriage talking to the banker, who sat at his table in the window laughing, apparently in genial humour. Presently a servant in shirt sleeves and a white apron came with a bottle and glasses. The banker toasted him, and they both drank. The blazing sun beat down. I watched them under my parasol. The banker had a bald head. He was not old, not more than thirty-seven, and he had good features ; a small man, not in size, for he appeared to be large and stout, but in personality, as he sat opposite him, talking. An instant later they came to the door ; there was a vine growing over it, and a seat that must be inviting in the shade at evenings. He introduced the banker to me: " Madame will be coming to you when she needs money." They smiled and nodded to each other familiarly. Money is a passage to familiarity when both parties possess it. The banker had an ugly baldness at the top of his head like a tonsure ; I always disliked that kind of baldness. He bowed several times, muttering complimentary phrases and, as his client turned to get into the carriage beside me, asked me the usual question with his eyes. Of course, he saw and I was glad he did. I should like to bring discomfort and annoyance to the fat banker, because of his self-complacent expression, his nice well-brushed tail-coat, his stomach and his nasty baldness. He never showed he had noticed the banker's eye, he only looked slightly amused, glanced at me as he put the cushion behind my back, and lit his cigarette. The band was playing on the Casino terrace, and he ordered a table. There were a great many people standing about on the gravel, walking up and down, and fussing about tables. He never fussed ; we got ours at once near the steps, but protected

---

* Frau Karl Druschki is the name of a very beautiful white rose which has neither scent nor thorns.

by the railing so that I could sit in the corner, and he beside me. I was distracted and amused by the crowd. He followed my eyes a moment, and seeing me interested, pulled some letters out of his pocket and put on his glasses. He always did what I wanted at the moment without my asking, I don't know how he guessed. That was the comfort of being with him, and it was a part of his hold on me. I don't think glamour had more than a little to do with it. It pleased me that other women admired him and envied me, but most of them envied me because he was rich and generous, and I had always been with rich and generous men. There was certainly a little fear in it ; I never was certain how much he knew. My silent nature had been an armour, but I did not feel it protected me from him, though he made no sign of seeing. If he had not been what he was in every way I could test, gradually his seeing without showing, his knowing without asking, his answers to unasked questions would, I think, have got on my nerves. He must have understood that also, for, unexpectedly, he sometimes explained a knowledge and in very simple words. He talked very simply to everyone, saying exactly what he meant, and when anyone told him a lie, he smiled. I do not lie with my tongue, I never found it necessary, I could always act one when circumstances required. I had acted one to him from the beginning, a large, consistent, unavoidable lie, for which I had no regret. I could not regret a part of myself. I am what I am, and he was himself. I did not know whether he had yet read that lie. Sometimes I thought so, and I used all the power my subtlety gave me. I wanted to keep him. I could never find another like him. There were no others like him. And if love is not the word, I wanted to give him all that I had to give. I have no smallest notion what he felt for me. He never made a declaration ; his tributes were never in words. He never asked for what he received, he never pleaded his right to any- thing ; he wrung from me more than any other man. But satisfaction was never in his eyes. That is why I was afraid.

A young man dressed in a grey suit with a light blue tie that matched his eyes sat down at the next table. The waiter brought three cocktails and placed them in front of him. He looked at me, but unobservantly, so that I could continue

noticing him. The blue eyes left my face and wandered to
him, then to the crowd, and back again to him reading letters.
It amused me that the young man thought I was being ignored ;
the knowledge that he was so completely wrong pleased me.
He stopped reading and put the letters back in his pocket ;
I knew he had not finished them. He glanced casually at the
next table, but at the cocktails, not at the man, and asked me
if he should remove my wrap. The waiter began serving us.
Behind him, two women, young and fashionably dressed, took
their seats next to each other ; the young man gave his up,
and sat opposite them looking pleased and possessive. They
drank their cocktails ; the *chef d'orchestre* came bowing.
Tosca ? Bohême ? I leant forward a little to see them. The
older one was much powdered, her lips were red, she wore a
pearl necklace and emerald rings to go with her green dress.
She was very blonde. She observed me at once, and I leant
back again so that his body interposed between her and me.
We talked a little in short sentences, requiring no effort, and
while we talked I looked at the other woman. She was a young
girl, not more than nineteen, with very brilliant eyes and teeth
and skin. She had a radiant smile. Her mouth turned up at the
corners, showing the glistening teeth and the pink tongue like
a kitten's. She had a charming, not obviously self-conscious
manner. I knew she was aware that I was looking at her, that it
pleased her, not the less because her companion had noticed my
interest, and stared back at me with suspicious impertinence.
She must be the young man's wife, an American, with experience.

The band struck up " Vissi d'arte " and he glanced for the
first time at them. I knew that the glance, lingering a moment
on the face of the girl, was comprehensive ; I knew as he asked
me what sweet I wanted he was searching my thoughts.   I
changed them determinedly ; they hovered above both tables,
flickered round the dark head of the girl, the blonde of the
woman's, poised a moment on my own hair, *cendré* with a
strain of gold, very fine and silky. Hers was coarse hair, and
the colour artificial, the younger one's a rich brown, curling
naturally behind the ears in delicate kiss-enticing ringlets on
the nape of the neck. They played well, he was saying the
conductor had temperament—he knew him from Carlsbad ; and
he was searching me while he spoke. When coffee was brought,

he turned, asking permission to smoke. I knew it was that he might look at them more closely. " Charming ! " he answered the unspoken comment, " I am not surprised you admire her."

He could make acquaintance very easily—the right word at the moment, the suitable gesture. There was always lightness in his phrase and in his voice. The young man answered with a deeper, heavier sweep of words, with the tongue of a talker, of one accustomed to an easy understanding. It was always an entertainment to observe him with a new acquaintance, mastering knowledge without use of many words, adding up, subtracting, then multiplying to make it pleasanter for both. He did this without an air of knowing, without the smallest object. He simply could not help knowing, because the world for him had always been an easy plaything. He talked about them a little afterwards as we walked to the hotel, a few casual words, suggesting to me that he believed we were likely to meet them soon again.

There was little significance to me about the incident. I think I should not have called it an incident or thought about the people again but for him. Quite unusually, he referred to them during the afternoon. We dined alone in our apartment : I did not feel inclined to go to the Casino after our tiring motor journey. He came back early, as always when he went out alone, and found me reading. He stood by the bedside with his hat under his arm. The silver sides of his hair caught the light, and he held his chin between his finger and thumb, pulling the lower lip down a little so that the strong teeth showed. He stood looking down at me, raised my hand to his mouth, asked me if I felt rested, if the bed was comfortable. There was something in his mind to say; he was waiting for an opening—he did not want to make too much of it. " A devoted husband, dear, appeals to me." " And she ? " " For that I can give you his assurance. Married during the war, saw her little, has been back but a short time from a mission since the peace. They are in this hotel." He paused ; there was more to come, kept till the last deliberately. " He leaves to-morrow." His dark, soft eyes were on mine, searching. They left my eyes, roamed the bed, returned to my book. He envied me being able to read novels—was it interesting ? He lifted my hand again to his mouth slowly; there was a very slight smile in his eyes. " Is there anything more to tell you ? " Ah . . . now it came. " The girl has come for company in his absence." I lay looking up at him, I was not sure I showed no interest, for he had stirred it by his greater certainty of knowledge, had constrained me to look into myself, and looking, I discovered what he may have seen. He went slowly to the door. His movements are always measured, like his speech, he never takes a step too many. I think he was born to make some woman pay for her undoing of men. Do I wish I were the woman I believe, but cannot know he thinks me ? To be loved and to love passionately—or to give without loving ? Can I not offer him more than any woman, though I cannot give that which is not mine to give ? To own a world is worth a lie, a lie against a body born to age for the sake of that which does not age. A world is in my keeping, a world belonging to us two, where no other enters. Is he so much man that he must probe and probe till he pierces a mortal heart ? Is he not so close to my heart that I lie here thinking of him, with my tired body aching for sleep that my fevered brain will not yield ? He knows what I could have from others, and that part was never wanting. All the rest was. It could not be bearable to lose him. I must keep his low voice, his unexpectedness, his serenity. But can I keep him ? Has he read the lie ?

Scrutinies

(3) John Masefield.

By BERTRAM HIGGINS.

WHEN the sea, fabulously attentive to Britannia, cast up Mr. Masefield, it parted with one of its queerest fish—a fish normal in size and shape, but striped and bedizened by tropical waters, and concealing a monstrous roe.   Melville's pioneer message was long since delivered, and Joseph Conrad had disembarked ; but the early Edwardians, amused by the contrast of French naturalism and Irish mysticism, and lazily refusing to relate these importations, had come no closer to their heritage than sniffing the brine at Brighton and dispatching their royalty in peaceful dreadnoughts to see and terrorise the world.

Masefield stepped in with his *Salt-Water Ballads* at the moment when the nation's conscience, too roughly salved by Kipling for the humiliations of the Boer War, was in need of a little warm restorative. The *Ballads* sound a thin trumpet-note of romance, rather boyish-manly, like a Scout's, but the idealism of the sentiment is beaten down by the drum-taps of the borrowed idiom.   Attitude and art are tentative in the next volume, with a falling inclination towards Celtic fatalism, gratified later in the prose rhythms of *A Mainsail Haul* and *A Tarpaulin Muster* : a poem like *Fragments*, defective but personal, is an indication of something valuable under this facility and swerve of style.   And then something happens to Mr. Masefield.   So far, his work is what is called promising : the imitativeness of a young technique is no bar to future achievement unless the failures in the borrowed pattern are on a lower level of vitality than the whole.   Perhaps Masefield does not quite come through this test, but there are signs of an uneasy sensibility and an emotional force which, if directed by the self-criticising faculty (" the artistic conscience ") will be fulfilled in art.   Psychologists tell us that during adolescence incidents which at any other period would be minor in their effect on personality, readily turn into primary ones. " Writer's adolescence " is a period of still more delicate adjustments, because it concerns developments which, being less amenable to the conventions governing conduct, are remediable mainly by inner processes. Masefield's early indecision between two attitudes, as exemplified in his first two volumes of verse, should in the ordinary course have been settled by the emergence of a predominating creative desire, the imaginative equivalent of an effort of will. The drama of his adolescence was the clash between his " heroic " and " æsthetic " tendencies, represented by Kipling and Yeats respectively—a conflict which he could have solved by defining it. That problem was never solved ; and for all his output Masefield to-day remains an adolescent writer.

Consider the general characteristics of his work. The Beauty-hunt to which he spurs himself is a purely reactive ritual, youth's desperate shame for the bodily initiations of puberty. The image he chases over Lollingdon Downs is a tribal fiction with a blurred face ; he never gets near her, and, if he did, personal lineaments are the last thing he would look for in a goddess for whom his feelings are strictly generalised. " She was something too pure and gentle for a wild man like himself. His nature knelt to her." Thus Heseltine and Rhoda in *The Street of To-day*, and Masefield's spirit of reverence has never outgrown its attachment to the crude hypotheses which are society's compromise with nature in the equivocal stages of the individual's development.

" Woman, beauty, wonder, sacred woman,
    Spirit moulding man from brute to human " :
the invocation is ineffectual because it is cast in the terms of an archaic need ; and it comes from a poem called " Imagination." The world goes on unravelling its multiplicity to Roger Naldrett, in *Multitude and Solitude*, but " it was his duty to beat back the world before it fouled his inner vision. If he were not careful he would find that his next work would be tainted with some feverish animosity, some personal bitterness or weakness of contempt. It was his duty as a man and as an artist to prevent that, so that his mind might be as a hedged garden full of flowers, or as a clear, unflawed mirror, reflecting only perfect images." Masefield has perhaps by

now discarded the letter of such an aestheticism, but its spirit persists throughout his work as a determinant of the form in which it is conceived. Experience is piled up in successive books (the "heroic"inclination of the author satisfying itself by an eager-seeming cataloguing of external detail), but the heroes themselves are held back from any vital adjustment by the limitations of the interpretative ideas they bring to bear on it. Sard Harker is a pseudo-naïve, a parody of Conrad's dangerously simplified Lord Jim; his romantic sense of honour, interesting in itself, becomes pitiable when Masefield flourishes it in the face of the tropics as man's strongest weapon against natural evil. Father Garsinton, personifying intellectual evil, is the creation of a mind whose moral uncertainty resents responsible action. The foil to this figure is the little Susan Jones of *Melloney Holtspur*. In this play Masefield entangles the characters in situations which demand a fine sense of good and evil for their proper *dénouement*, and though the scene is filled with prompting spirits and the dialogue lets off a heavy incense of consecration, the shoddiness of the solutions shows how insincere was the assumption of values on which the action depends. Lonny Copshrews, the "ill-living" genius who breaks Melloney's heart, is the prospective victim of the supernatural machinery, but the dramatist, finding himself unable to justify his anathema, calls in little Susan, a sort of "salvation-kid," whose omniscient innocence, backed by a vision of young love, charms away the malice of the ghostly revenge. The muddle of moral cate gories is complete when Lonny's Spirit, before Melloney's Spirit has been appeased, is allowed to turn his apology into self-justification. "For all my wickedness, I cared for truth and beauty and colour; three things which have never let man down. I was taunted and despised. I was ragged and starved. But I called those things noble with all my strength, all my life long." The Spirit of Myrtle West, who was seduced by Lonny's friend, does not need appeasement : "she goes out in ecstasy Front Left."

> "O joy of trying for beauty, ever the same,
> You never fail, your comforts never end ;
> O, balm of this world's way ; O, perfect friend ! "

This is Mr. Masefield addressing us directly through the narrative of *Dauber*. Dauber has a similar ambition ; he goes to sea in search of experience and " copy," but his paintings are ruined by the brutal sailors. Concealing his vexation, he decides to postpone his unpopular habit of staring at the seascape (" My Lord, my God, how beautiful it is ! "), and prove himself a man at the masthead.

> " It's not been done, the sea, not yet been done,
> From the inside by one who really knows ;
> I'd give up all if I could be the one. . .
> This is the art I've come for, and am learning,
> The sea and ships and men and travelling things.
> It is most proud, whatever pain it brings."

He encounters storm and distinguishes himself, but later falls while furling a sail. Before he dies he exclaims, " ' It will go on,' " not knowing his meaning rightly ; and, his canvasses extinct, is buried at sea. Dauber's plight would win our sympathy if his creator, at least, knew his meaning rightly. Set down in the midst of a company whose rough natural ways Mr. Masefield's spleen has perverted into brutalities of Philistinism, his appeal is falsened ; we take sides against the unanalysed prepossession which exalts him and the hysteria with which the claim is enforced. (A similar hysteria persecutes Dick Pargetter in " The Tragedy of Nan " : Masefield's women, Nan and Melloney, can be singularly distasteful when they are made the vessels of it.) *Dauber* has been called a great poem—" great," says one critic, " because of its pictures of the storm, the sea night, the ship entering the calm bay at day-dawn." Such judgments come from a complaisance with the emotional intention which, in all imperfect poetry, perceptibly accompanies the æsthetic achievement. The careless reader is only too likely to mistake the first for the second, and in Masefield this game of substitution assumes the proportions of downright bluff.

> " Then from the hidden waters something surged—
> Mournful, despairing, great, greater than speech,
> A noise like one slow wave on a still beach. . .

' Whales ! ' said the mate.   They stayed there all
    night long
Answering the horn.   Out of the night they spoke,
Defeated creatures who had suffered wrong,
But still were noble underneath the stroke.
They filled the darkness when the Dauber woke ;
The men came peering to the rail to hear,
And the sea sighed, and the fog rose up sheer."

These are average lines from the descriptive passages
which have called forth so much enthusiasm.   It does not
need much alertness to find the cause of their failure : Masefield
may possibly have seen whales, but he has never imagined
them.   " Mournful, despairing, great, greater than speech."
The tritely associative first pair of adjectives provide emo-
tionalised comment where the narrative requires an image,
and the comment is so deficient in vital force as to depress the
curiosity stimulated by the " something " of the preceding
line.   The comparative construction following—indeed, the
whole phrase—is a good example of the substitution process
mentioned above ; a good thing might have been made of the
" speech " idea, but the imageless " greater " aspires to a moral
prestige which will be allowed only by facile victims of a
poetic hypnosis.   In the second half of the fourth line a metrical
foot, at least, is sacrificed to the desire for an easy rhyme-
scheme.   The sentence " Out of the night . . . underneath
the stroke " is obscure in meaning till we realise that, having
nothing to say about the subject he has introduced, the poet
is making the best of a bad job by using words to evoke an
abstract compassion which, with a little luck, may kindle the
reader for reception of the next subject.   What is this whole
lumbering, half-minded passage worth, next to that little
flash in Job ?

" Leviathan maketh a path to shine after him ;
    One would think the deep to be hoary."
Or Milton ?

" There Leviathan
Hugest of living creatures, in the deep
Stretched like a promontory sleeps or swims,

And seems a moving land ; and at his gills
Draws in, and at his breast spouts out the sea."

Or Rimbaud ?

" J'ai vu fermenter les marais, énormes nasses
Où pourrit dans les joncs tout un Léviathan,
Des écroulements d'eaux au milieu des bonaces,
Et les lointains vers les gouffres cataractant ! "

Or the most casual description of " Moby Dick " ?

" From this height the whale was now seen some
mile or so ahead, at every roll of the sea revealing his
high sparkling hump, and regularly jetting his silent
spout into the air."

The poem of Masefield's in which he most nearly discards his second-nature falsity is *The Everlasting Mercy*. It has been hailed as " one more of the world's great sudden original poems and one of the greatest religious poems ever born " ; but the effect of that eulogy is qualified by the critic's report of his reactions—" At first we gasped ' Oh ! ' What blasphemy ! What indecency ! Phew ! Then, dazed and unbelieving, one read the long poem again—and again—and again. . . . A challenge to all that mistakes respectability for righteousness . . . a torrent of ' inspiration,' " etc. The " indecency," of no importance in itself, is noteworthy in so far as it produces many instances, rare in Masefield, of a feeling, immanent not aspirant, prolonged beyond a few lines. The social satire of which Saul Kane is made the mouthpiece, though it is weakened by an alliance with the poet's familiar self-pitying exasperations, is protected, to a degree, against the familiar preciosity by the short-winded metre. The question of greatness need not be raised ; judged as a whole, it is impossible to call *The Everlasting Mercy* a *true* poem : Masefield has never recovered from (what we have conceived to be) the mismanagement of his adolescence.

In *Reynard the Fox*, published in 1919, we saw him reaching a point at which the preference for a completely objective theme might have been expected to assist in his liberation. A re-reading of *Reynard* proves any such hope ill-founded. A fever has passed out of his language, but the ravages of the disease remain.

Behind them rode her daughter Belle,
A strange, shy, lovely girl whose face
Was sweet with thought and proud with race,
And bright with joy of riding there.
She was as good as blowing air,
But shy and difficult to know.
The kittens in the barley-mow,
The setter's toothless puppies crawling,
The blackbird in the apple calling,
All knew her spirit more than we.
So delicate these maidens be
In loving lovely helpless things.

Masefield's style has always been more suggestible than assimilative, and these lines have been likened to Chaucer. If the reader troubles to verify the comparison, he will be let in for a painful experience : the metaphysical horror of animism, of death parodying (and persecuting) life. Far better the vilified, and perhaps incestuous, ballad of the *Lollingdon Downs* volume.

> " His father clubbed
> The girl on the head.
> Young Will upped
> And shot him dead.
>
> ' Now, sister,' said Will,
> ' I've a-killed father,
> As I said I'd kill.
> O my love, I'd rather
>
> A-kill him again
> Than see you suffer.
> O my little Jane,
> Kiss good-bye to your brother.' "

There is vitality in that, protoplasmic as poetry, but genuine. Henry James, with narrow-minded justice, condemned Whitman's work on the ground that it " pretends to persuade the soul while it slights the intellect ; because it pretends to gratify the feelings while it outrages the taste." Substitute " perception " for "taste," and you have the germ of the Masefieldian malady neatly isolated for a test.

The Princess (III).

By D. H. LAWRENCE.

She woke with a sudden convulsion, like pain. She was really very cold; perhaps the heavy blankets had numbed her. Her heart seemed unable to beat, she felt she could not move.

With another convulsion she sat up. It was intensely dark. There was not even a spark of fire, the light wood had burned right away. She sat in thick oblivious darkness. Only through a chink she could see a star.

What did she want? Oh, what did she want? She sat in bed and rocked herself wofully. She could hear the steady breathing of the sleeping man. She was shivering with cold; her heart seemed as if it could not beat. She wanted warmth, protection, she wanted to be taken away from herself. And at the same time, perhaps more deeply than anything, she wanted to keep herself intact, intact, untouched, that no one should have any power over her, or rights to her. It was a wild necessity in her that no one, particularly no man, should have any rights or power over her, that no one and nothing should possess her.

Yet that other thing! And she was so cold, so shivering, and her heart could not beat. Oh, would not someone help her heart to beat?

She tried to speak, and could not. Then she cleared her throat.

"Romero," she said strangely, "It is so cold."

Where did her voice come from, and whose voice was it, in the dark?

She heard him at once sit up, and his voice, startled, with a resonance that seemed to vibrate against her, saying:

"You want me to make you warm?"

"Yes."

As soon as he had lifted her in his arms, she wanted to scream to him not to touch her. She stiffened herself. Yet she was dumb.

And he was warm, but with a terrible animal warmth that seemed to annihilate her. He panted like an animal with desire. And she was given over to this thing.

She had never, never wanted to be given over to this. But she had *willed* that it should happen to her. And according to her will, she lay and let it happen. But she never wanted it. She never wanted to be thus assailed and handled, mauled. She wanted to keep herself to herself.

However, she had willed it to happen, and it had happened. She panted with relief when it was over.

Yet even now she had to lie within the hard, powerful clasp of this other creature, this man. She dreaded to struggle to go away. She dreaded almost too much the icy cold of that other bunk.

" Do you want to go away from me ? " asked his strange voice. Oh, if it could only have been a thousand miles away from her ! Yet she had willed to have it thus close.

" No," she said.

And she could feel a curious joy and pride surging up again in him : at her expense. Because he had got her. She felt like a victim there. And he was exulting in his power over her, his possession, his pleasure.

When dawn came, he was fast asleep. She sat up suddenly.

" I want a fire," she said.

He opened his brown eyes wide, and smiled with a curious tender luxuriousness.

" I want you to make a fire," she said.

He glanced at the chinks of light. His brown face hardened to the day.

" All right," he said, " I'll make it.   "

She hid her face while he dressed. She could not bear to look at him. He was so suffused with pride and luxury. She hid her face almost in despair. But feeling the cold blast of air as he opened the door, she wriggled down into the warm place where he had been. How soon the warmth ebbed, when he had gone !

He made a fire and went out, returning after a while with water.

" You stay in bed till the sun comes," he said. " It's very cold."

"Hand me my cloak."

She wrapped the cloak fast round her, and sat up among the blankets. The warmth was already spreading from the fire.

"I suppose we will start back as soon as we've had breakfast?"

He was crouching at his camp-stove making scrambled eggs. He looked up suddenly, transfixed, and his brown eyes, so soft and luxuriously widened, looked straight at her.

"You want to?" he said.

"We'd better get back as soon as possible," she said, turning aside from his eyes.

"You want to get away from me?" he asked, repeating the question of the night in a sort of dread.

"I want to get away from here," she said decisively. And it was true. She wanted supremely to get away, back to the world of people.

He rose slowly to his feet, holding the aluminium frying-pan.

"Don't you like last night?" he asked.

"Not really," she said. "Why? Do you?"

He put down the frying-pan and stood staring at the wall. She could see she had given him a cruel blow. But she did not relent. She was getting her own back. She wanted to regain possession of all herself, and in some mysterious way she felt that he possessed some part of her still.

He looked round at her slowly, his face greyish and heavy.

"You Americans," he said, "You always want to do a man down."

"I am not American," she said. "I am British. And I don't want to do any man down. I only want to go back, now."

"And what will you say about me, down there?"

"That you were very kind to me, and very good."

He crouched down again, and went on turning the eggs. He gave her her plate, and her coffee, and sat down to his own food.

But again he seemed not to be able to swallow. He looked up at her.

"You didn't like last night?" he asked.

"Not really," she said, though with some difficulty. "I don't care for that kind of thing."

A blank sort of wonder spread over his face at these words, followed immediately by a black look of anger, and then a stony, sinister despair.

" You don't ? " he said, looking her in the eyes.

" Not really," she replied, looking back with steady hostility into his eyes.

Then a dark flame seemed to come from his face.

" I make you," he said, as if to himself.

He rose and reached her clothes, that hung on a peg : the fine linen underwear, the orange breeches, the fleecy jumper, the blue-and-buff kerchief ; then he took up her riding boots and her bead moccasins. Crushing everything in his arms, he opened the door. Sitting up, she saw him stride down to the dark-green pool in the frozen shadow of that deep cup of a valley. He tossed the clothing and the boots out on the pool. Ice had formed. And on the pure, dark green mirror, in the slaty shadow, the Princess saw her things lying, the white linen, the orange breeches, the black boots, the blue moccasins, a tangled heap of colour. Romero picked up rocks and heaved them out at the ice, till the surface broke and the fluttering clothing disappeared in the rattling water, while the valley echoed and shouted again with the sound.

She sat in despair among the blankets, hugging tight her pale-blue cloak. Romero strode straight back to the cabin.

" Now you stay here with me," he said.

She was furious. Her blue eyes met his. They were like two demons watching one another. In his face, beyond a sort of unrelieved gloom, was a demonish desire for death.

He saw her looking round the cabin, scheming. He saw her eyes on his rifle. He took the gun and went out with it. Returning, he pulled out her saddle, carried it to the tarn, and threw it in. Then he fetched his own saddle, and did the same.

" Now will you go away ? " he said, looking at her with a smile.

She debated within herself whether to coax him and wheedle him. But she knew he was already beyond it. She sat among her blankets in a frozen sort of despair, hard as hard ice with anger.

He did the chores, and disappeared with the gun. She

got up in her blue pyjamas, huddled in her cloak, and stood in the doorway. The dark-green pool was motionless again, the stony slopes were pallid and frozen. Shadow still lay, like an after-death, deep in this valley. Always in the distance she saw the horses feeding. If she could catch one ! The brilliant yellow sun was half way down the mountain. It was nine o'clock.

All day she was alone, and she was frightened. What she was frightened of she didn't know. Perhaps the crackling in the dark spruce wood. Perhaps just the savage, heartless wildness of the mountains. But all day she sat in the sun in the doorway of the cabin, watching, watching for hope. And all the time her bowels were cramped with fear.

She saw a dark spot that probably was a bear roving across the pale grassy slope in the far distance, in the sun.

When, in the afternoon, she saw Romero approaching, with silent suddenness, carrying his gun and a dead deer, the cramp in her bowels relaxed, then became colder. She dreaded him with a cold dread.

"There is deer-meat," he said, throwing the dead doe at her feet.

"You don't want to go away from here," he said. "This is a nice place."

She shrank into the cabin.

"Come into the sun," he said, following her. She looked up at him with hostile, frightened eyes.

"Come into the sun," he repeated, taking her gently by the arm, in a powerful grasp.

She knew it was useless to rebel. Quietly he led her out, and seated himself in the doorway, holding her still by the arm.

"In the sun it is warm," he said. "Look, this is a nice place. You are such a pretty white woman, why do you want to act mean to me ? Isn't this a nice place ? Come ! Come here ! It is sure warm here."

He drew her to him, and in spite of her stony resistance, he took her cloak from her, holding her in her thin blue pyjamas.

"You sure are a pretty little white woman, small and pretty," he said. "You sure won't act mean to me—you don't want to, I know you don't."

She, stony and powerless, had to submit to him. The sun shone on her white, delicate skin.

"I sure don't mind hell fire," he said, "after this."

A queer, luxurious good-humour seemed to possess him again. But though outwardly she was powerless, inwardly she resisted him, absolutely and stonily.

When later he was leaving her again, she said to him suddenly :

"You think you can conquer me this way. But you can't. You can never conquer me."

He stood arrested, looking back at her, with many emotions conflicting in his face—wonder, surprise, a touch of horror, and an unconscious pain that crumpled his face till it was like a mask. Then he went out without saying a word, hung the dead deer on a bough, and started to flay it. While he was at this butcher's work, the sun sank and cold night came on again.

"You see," he said to her as he crouched, cooking the supper, "I ain't going to let you go. I reckon you called to me in the night, and I've some right. If you want to fix it up right now with me, and say you want to be with me, we'll fix it up now and go down to the ranch to-morrow and get married or whatever you want. But you've got to say you want to be with me. Else I shall stay right here, till something happens."

She waited a while before she answered :

"I don't want to be with anybody against my will. I don't dislike you ; at least, I didn't, till you tried to put your will over mine. I won't have anybody's will put over me. You can't succeed. Nobody could. You can never get me under your will. And you won't have long to try, because soon they will send someone to look for me."

He pondered this last, and she regretted having said it. Then, sombre, he bent to the cooking again.

He could not conquer her, however much he violated her. Because her spirit was hard and flawless as a diamond. But he could shatter her. This she knew. Much more, and she would be shattered.

In a sombre, violent excess he tried to expend his desire for her. And she was racked with agony, and felt each time she would die. Because, in some peculiar way, he had got hold of her, some unrealised part of her which she never wished tc realise. Racked with a burning, tearing anguish, she felt that the thread of her being would break, and she would die. The burning heat that racked her inwardly.

If only, only she could be alone again, cool and intact! If only she could recover herself again, cool and intact! Would she ever, ever, ever be able to bear herself again?

Even now she did not hate him. It was beyond that. Like some racking, hot doom. Personally he hardly existed.

The next day he would not let her have any fire, because of attracting attention with the smoke. It was a grey day, and she was cold. He stayed around, and heated soup on the petrol stove. She lay motionless in the blankets.

And in the afternoon she pulled the clothes over her head and broke into tears. She had never really cried in her life. He dragged the blankets away and looked to see what was shaking her. She sobbed in helpless hysterics. He covered her over again and went outside, looking at the mountains, where clouds were dragging and leaving a little snow. It was a violent windy, horrible day, the evil of winter rushing down.

She cried for hours. And after this a great silence came between them. They were two people who had died. He did not touch her any more. In the night she lay and shivered like a dying dog. She felt that her very shivering would rupture something in her body, and she would die.

At last she had to speak.

"Could you make a fire? I am so cold," she said, with chattering teeth.

"Want to come over here?" came his voice.

"I would rather you made me a fire," she said, her teeth knocking together and chopping the words in two.

He got up and kindled a fire. At last the warmth spread, and she could sleep.

The next day was still chilly, with some wind. But the sun shone. He went about in silence, with a dead-looking face. It was now so dreary and so like death she wished he would do anything rather than continue in this negation. If now he asked her to go down with him to the world and marry him, she would do it. What did it matter? Nothing mattered any more.

But he would not ask her. His desire was dead and heavy like ice within him. He kept watch around the house.

On the fourth day as she sat huddled in the doorway in the sun, hugged in a blanket, she saw two horsemen come over the crest of the grassy slope—small figures. She gave a cry. He looked up quickly and saw the figures. The men had dismounted. They were looking for the trail.

"They are looking for me," she said.

"Muy bien," he answered in Spanish.

He went and fetched his gun, and sat with it across his knees.

"Oh!" she said. "Don't shoot!"

He looked across at her.

"Why?" he said. "You like staying with me?"

"No," she said. "But don't shoot."

"I ain't going to Pen," he said.

"You won't have to go to Pen," she said. "Don't shoot!"

"I'm going to shoot," he muttered.

And straightaway he kneeled and took very careful aim. The Princess sat on in an agony of helplessness and hopelessness.

The shot rang out. In an instant she saw one of the horses on the pale grassy slope rear and go rolling down. The man had dropped in the grass, and was invisible. The second man clambered on his horse, and on that precipitous place went at a gallop in a long swerve towards the nearest spruce-tree cover. Bang! Bang! went Romero's shots. But each time he missed, and the running horse leaped like a kangaroo towards cover.

It was hidden. Romero now got behind a rock; tense silence, in the brilliant sunshine. The Princess sat on the bunk inside the cabin, crouching, paralysed. For hours, it seemed, Romero knelt behind this rock, in his black shirt, bare-headed, watching. He had a beautiful, alert figure. The Princess wondered why she did not feel sorry for him. But her spirit was hard and cold, her heart could not melt. Though now she would have called him to her, with love.

But no, she did not love him. She would never love any man. Never! It was fixed and sealed in her, almost vindictively.

Suddenly she was so startled she almost fell from the

bunk. A shot rang out quite close from behind the cabin. Romero leaped straight into the air, his arms fell outstretched, turning as he leaped. And even while he was in the air, a second shot rang out, and he fell with a crash, squirming, his hands clutching the earth towards the cabin door.

The Princess sat absolutely motionless, transfixed, staring at the prostrate figure. In a few moments the figure of a man in the Forest Service appeared close to the house ; a young man in a broad-brimmed Stetson hat, dark flannel shirt, and riding-boots, carrying a gun. He strode over to the prostrate figure.

"Got you, Romero!" he said aloud. And he turned the dead man over. There was already a little pool of blood where Romero's breast had been.

"H'm!" said the Forest Service man. "Guess I got you nearer than I thought."

And he squatted there, staring at the dead man.

The distant calling of his comrade aroused him. He stood up.

"Hullo, Bill!" he shouted. "Yep! Got him! Yep! Done him in, apparently."

The second man rode out of the forest on a grey horse. He had a ruddy, kind face, and round brown eyes, dilated with dismay.

"He's not passed out?" he asked anxiously.

"Looks like it," said the first young man, coolly.

The second dismounted and bent over the body. Then he stood up again, and nodded.

"Yea-a!" he said. "He's done in all right. It's him all right, boy! It's Domingo Romero."

"Yep! I know it!" replied the other.

Then in perplexity he turned and looked into the cabin, where the Princess squatted, staring with big owl eyes from her red blanket.

"Hello!" he said, coming towards the hut. And he took his hat off. Oh, the sense of ridicule she felt! Though he did not mean any.

But she could not speak, no matter what she felt.

"What'd this man start firing for?" he asked.

She fumbled for words, with numb lips.

"He had gone out of his mind!" she said, with solemn, stammering conviction.

THE PRINCESS

" Good Lord ! You mean to say he'd gone out of his mind ?
Whew ! That's pretty awful ! That explains it then. H'm ! "

He accepted the explanation without more ado.

With some difficulty they succeeded in getting the Princess
down to the ranch. But she, too, was not a little mad.

" I'm not quite sure where I am," she said to Mrs. Wilkieson, as she lay in bed. " Do you mind explaining ? "

Mrs. Wilkieson explained tactfully.

" Oh, yes ! " said the Princess. " I remember. And I had
an accident in the mountains, didn't I ? Didn't we meet a
man who'd gone mad, and who shot my horse from under
me ? "

" Yes, you met a man who had gone out of his mind."

The real affair was hushed up. The Princess departed east
in a fortnight's time, in Miss Cummins' care. Apparently she
had recovered herself entirely. She was the Princess, and a
virgin intact.

But her bobbed hair was grey at the temples, and her eyes
were a little mad. She was slightly crazy.

" Since my accident in the mountains, when a man went
mad and shot my horse from under me, and my guide had to
shoot him dead, I have never felt quite myself."

So she put it.

Later, she married an elderly man, and seemed pleased.

The Re-Creation of Poetry.
The Use of " Negative " Emotions.

An effect of the triumph of the romantic movement in the last century has been to separate the poet from the subjects which abound in ordinary social life, and particularly from those emotions engendered by the clash of personality and the hostility of circumstances. A distinct bias has been created against the expression of particular grievances, which are supposed to offend against the proper attitude to poetry. This convention is as dangerous as the distinction which the French classicists draw between noble and vulgar emotions, and has a similar reflection in its effect on the poet's vocabulary —the erection of a literary language. Certain words become sacrosanct and are repeatedly invited to contribute, not for themselves but for the prestige they bring with them. The same prejudice towards a definite poetic suitability accounts for the contemporary preponderance of "nature" themes and imagery drawn from the back-garden of the week-end cottage. Under the pressure of this romantic theory per- sonality and, still more, personalities have been squeezed out of contemporary verse. This is partly caused, no doubt, by the extension of the audience. It is doubtful if subjective poetry (that is, poetry which is not communal like the epic, drama, or narrative) is, by its own nature, capable of being stretched over such a wide area as that covered by the modern publisher. In fact, it demands an audience homogeneous in culture, and to some extent in its attitude to life, otherwise the difficulties of communication cannot be overcome, and the poet must fall back on commonplace, coarse reactions, or invest his small genuine discovery with a theatrical grandeur in order to get it a hearing.

The modern poet is to his audience an author, not a man. It is interested in his more generalised emotions, not in his relations with the life and people round him. Yet to himself the poet should be in the first place a man, not an author.

He should not be conscious of a distinction between the sensations he gets from his immediate contact with things and the sensations he uses as the material of his art. At present he is inhibited from expressing a set of emotions (those we call negative emotions) because of a prejudice against them which is based on a temporary social queasiness. With what consternation would the critics and the public receive from a reputable poet such furious but measured invective as that with which Churchill attacked the dying Hogarth! I shall not quote that passage on Hogarth's physical ruin, which begins:

With all the symptoms of assur'd decay . . .

since it is fairly well known. An assault from another direction shows exactly the kind of subject from which the modern poet is cut off, though not because he is unfamiliar with it:

Oft have I known Thee, Hogarth, weak and vain,
Thyself the idol of thy awkward strain,
Thro' the dull measure of a summer's day,
In phrase most vile, prate long long hours away,
Whilst Friends with Friends all gaping sit and gaze
To hear a Hogarth babble Hogarth's praise.

Churchill has little verbal delicacy and none of the fatal wit of Pope; he stuns his opponent under the cumulate blows of the obvious. But he is also capable of varying the tone of his anger, and the impression we receive from the whole of the Epistle to Hogarth is not that of a small dog snarling at a big one; it is really sensitive, and so poetic, indignation. Apart from the political issues involved, such as Hogarth's antagonism to Churchill's hero, Wilkes, it is a poem of the repulsion one personality may exert on another, the expression of the emotion with which one sophisticated social being may regard another, and made more poignant by the exploitation of Hogarth's decrepitude. Such material is taboo to contemporary taste; the artist is unable to approach it with an unprejudiced mind, since a low sort of agreement to universal solicitude has been reached by the modern community. In this respect the world of the eighteenth century is almost as remote from us as that of the Satyricon. Could we tolerate the innocent opportunism of the Matron of Ephesus except in the licensed playground of the classics?

Churchill is not pre-eminently a satirist; he has not sufficient detachment. He is a poet of invective, passionately absorbed in his subject. He cannot forget the miserable condition of Hogarth, and the thought of the venom which this almost extinct monster had the audacity to breathe out, stirs him to fresh indignant eloquence:

> I dare thy worst, with scorn behold thy rage,
> But with an eye of pity view thy Age ;
> Thy feeble Age, in which as in a glass,
> We see how Men to dissolution pass.
> Thou *wretched Being*, whom on Reason's plan,
> So changed, so lost, I cannot call a Man,
> What could persuade thee at this time of life
> To launch afresh into the sea of strife ?
> Better for thee, scarce crawling on the earth,
> Almost as much a child as at thy birth,
> To have resigned in peace thy parting breath,
> And sunk unnoticed in the arms of death.

Verse like this, though not often so fine as this, formed a not negligible part of the reading-matter of the eighteenth century ; to-day it has no survivors, and by some canons of criticism it would seem that we are well rid of it. It would most commonly be censured as unpoetic, since the term "poetry" tends to be narrowed down to expressions of certain kinds of experiences. Blake, who is qualified as an authority here, drew without immediate discrimination on his mundane comprehensions as well as on his celestial apprehensions :

> When Sir Joshua Reynolds died
> All Nature was degraded ;
> The King dropped a tear into the Queen's ear,
> And all his pictures faded.

There is no doubt that literature suffers from the absence of a socialised medium to carry off these reactions, explosions of the spleen or long-rumoured fulminations, and bring about that relief and cleansing of the mind which is one of the functions of expression. Such "negative" responses, which religion has exiled in forms of demons, are essential components of any fully satisfying work: So long as they are ignored we may continue to have a poetry fit for adolescents, but not for men, and the judgment of the common person, that poetry is "sloppy," will be quite justified.

Emotion acts not unlike such a fluid as the early scientists invented to explain the effects of electricity; it has really one continuous circular movement, but to the subject it appears to have two, parallel and in opposite directions. That is to say, it has a positive and a negative pole; it can be orientated, at its extreme, in either of two ways: as delight in, or disgust with, an object. Romantic poetry is always the expression of one of these extremes, but, since reactions are rarely so pure as to be fit to be represented as ecstasy, or complete revulsion, a great deal of the poetry based on this convention fails to satisfy modern sophistication. We need a poetry in which the moods are more subtly balanced. But, the more discordant the elements of a poem and the more freely they are associated, the greater becomes the difficulty of creating an aesthetic entity to bring about the catharis which is the function of a poem. In the romantic convention this is achieved by an assertion transcending the values of ordinary emotional experience, and very effective it may be, but, like all phantasmal satisfactions, in its continued employment it leads to impotence; the abused nerves are stretched beyond the limit of responsiveness.

The poetry of the negative emotions, of those arising from disgust with the object, provides the means for a whole series of responses in parts of the mind which have been lying fallow for nearly two hundred years. This contemporary value is greater than its absolute value, for it shares with the romantic lyric the paucity of the too-sharply differentiated response, the facile catharsis. Even, since delight is more valued socially than disgust, an aphrodisiac more than an anaphrodisiac, it is likely to be always under estimated by criticism; but this natural prejudice should not be allowed to obscure, as it too frequently does, the perfection of expression the negative poem may achieve, as for instance in the concluding lines of the *Dunciad*.

Swift is a great master of this kind of poetry. His verse has no pleasure-value beyond that of its symmetry and concision, but it is the most intricate labyrinth of personality that any poet has built round himself, not excepting Donne. It is characteristic that the study of " negative " emotions in poetry should tend to centre particularly in the fact of personality. That Swift was morbid is a commonplace; his verse would supply a text-book of psycho-pathology with as much material as it could use. The interest for the literary critic lies in Swift's success in transforming this material into forms of art. As a preliminary, we may examine the conclusion of one of his most repugnant descriptions, " The Lady's Dressing Room " :

> When Celia all her glory shows,
> If Strephon would but stop his nose . . .
> He soon will learn to think like me
> And bless his ravished eyes to see
> Such order from confusion sprung,
> Such gaudy tulips raised from dung.

After the long and exhaustive inventory which precedes them, these lines produce an expansion which is of the nature of a catharsis. It is effected by the sudden breaking of the monotonous revulsion with the introduction of a mass of irony and the final completely satisfying plastic image. Without sacrificing the integrity of his disgust he draws up the blind on a landscape towards which the mind may leap with justified delight, since the idea of erecting order out of chaos is an absolutely valuable one, whatever the implication in this particular instance. After this momentary concession Swift brings down the shade again with the last word, rhyme-enforced, but the image floats on in the consciousness. A similar process of expression, more complex æsthetically, and with the positive bias uppermost, may be observed in such of Baudelaire's poems as the " Hymne à la Beauté " or in " L'Amour du Mensonge," which concludes :

> Qu 'importe ta bêtise ou ton indifférence ?
> Masque ou décor, salut ! J'adore ta beauté !

Catharsis is a term which should perhaps be limited to works in which the emotion is objectified in characters and action. Yet an analogous process is the essential of success in a poem. A poem must, at some point or another, release, enable to flow back to the level of active life, the emotions caught up from life and pent in the æsthetic reservoir. Otherwise the poem is an artifice, a wax effigy in a glass case, a curiosity. In a poem there may be several such points of release, or of partial release, and it seems necessary that the predominant release should take place sufficiently near the end of the poem to be held in the consciousness till the poem is concluded. It need not take place in the last lines of a poem, though in fact it often does, but this is an effect which becomes mechanical and may be tiresome to sophisticated readers. The final couplet of the Shakespearean sonnet imposes this localisation on a poet ; it is a demand which is sometimes disadvantageous to Shakespeare himself. All fully-evolved formalistic structures, like the heroic couplet and the ballade, are susceptible to this automatism ; lacking the element of surprise, their effectiveness as agents of the release is quickly diminished.

It seems that an early step to be taken, if poetry is to be liberated so that it may become a natural form of expression in the modern world, is an examination of the kinds of effect which have been employed to bring about the essential release.

E. R.

(To be continued.)

Comments and Reviews

Mr. Eliot's Criticism

HOMAGE TO DRYDEN. By T. S. ELIOT. The Hogarth Essays.
(Hogarth Press, 3s. 6d.)

The title of this volume is misleading, for the two more important
of the three essays included are devoted to the metaphysical poetry
of the seventeenth century. Though short, these essays contain
probably the most penetrating body of observation on the metaphysical poets that has yet appeared in English, and it is nothing
less than a calamity for literature that Mr. Eliot should have been
compelled to discontinue the book, "beginning with Chapman
and Donne, and ending with Johnson," which, he tells us in the
preface, he once projected. He was admirably fitted for the work
both by his gifts and his predilections ; and the book, had it been
completed, would not only have enriched the literature of criticism,
but would also have stimulated, by making it more conscious of
its aims, the poetry of to-day.

Mr. Eliot's diagnosis of the increasing psychological debility
of English poetry since the time of the Elizabethans and their
immediate successors is sufficiently well known, but here it may
be briefly stated again. The poets of these eras, he says, " possessed a mechanism of sensibility which could devour any kind of
experience." Afterwards—Mr. Eliot attributes the evil to Milton
and Dryden—" a dissociation of sensibility set in." Poetry
occupied itself only with certain classes of experience, not with
" any kind of experience." Of the verse of the eighteenth century
poets, Pope, Collins, Gray, Johnson, and that of the romantic
poets, Shelley, Keats, Wordsworth, Tennyson, this was equally
true. From this poverty of the poetic spirit, this failure of poetry
to deal completely with experience, sentimentality, among many
other evils, arose. The main problem of the poet now is to re-
integrate this poetic consciousness which for two centuries has
been split up, and to deal with experience completely again. But
this he will do successfully only if, among other things, he
knows and steeps himself in, and does not imitate, the poetry in
the English tradition in which this has already been done.

This bald summary does small justice to a very notable analysis
of English poetry, but it may serve to indicate what a wealth of
application, not only to the poetry of the past, but to that of our
day, would have flowed from the analysis had Mr. Eliot written
his projected survey. That this analysis is accepted as a truism
by intelligent people to-day is due chiefly to Mr. Eliot ; the trouble

is that it is very loosely accepted, too loosely to be of effectual use to the poet. Mr. Eliot has always striven to make as exact as possible the implications of his theory. He has tried to show the necessary connection with a sensibility capable of devouring any kind of experience, of a habit of mind in a certain sense philosophical—or, at least, intellectually curious—and of that with a poetry which will be at need " simple, artificial, difficult, or fantastic." He has reiterated that " the possible interests of a poet are unlimited ; the more intelligent he is the better " ; and this, as he is careful to demonstrate, is not merely a pious opinion, but a fact which may be deduced from a study of great poetry. He has shown admirably that poetry which dispenses with these qualities —with what might be called psychology—is bound sooner or later to become sentimental. But, best of all, he has not demonstrated all this on the plane of general ideas ; he has been interested rather in the actual ways in which this more complete poetic sensibility works and can work, showing how and in what terms the unlimited interests of the poet have been and may be again translated into poetry, and what have been the uses and possibilities for the poet of the " simple, artificial, difficult, and fantastic." Were the body of Mr. Eliot's criticism larger—three or four times larger—than it is, its influence on contemporary poetry would perhaps be decisive. It is, one feels, a misfortune that it has not been decisive.

The danger of criticism such as this, which has its eye disinterestedly on possibilities of the English poetic tradition which have been overlooked or unfulfilled, is that it tends to exalt poets, however small, who have expressed some of those possibilities, at the expense of others, however great, who have not. Mr. Eliot's criterion of poetry becomes insensibly a pragmatic one, and the poet who is more stimulating than another to this age becomes to him not only stimulating but sometimes, one feels, great. This fault is more injurious than it seems : it gives an effect of derangement of values. For example, the excellent essay on Marvell in this volume would be calculably more important if it did not contain a depreciatory reference to Milton. Such things throw a critical judgment out of proportion, the last thing, one imagines, that Mr. Eliot desired. But after one has encountered in all of the three essays in this volume an exasperated sentence on Milton, one begins to wonder if Mr. Eliot is in reality capable of appreciating the greatness of Milton's poetry, and although the doubt is dismissed as unjust, a certain feeling of insecurity has been given. It is bound to be intensified when one reads, " I have long felt that the poetry of the seventeenth and eighteenth centuries, even much of that of inferior inspiration, possesses an elegance and a dignity absent from the popular and pretentious verse of the Romantic Poets and their successors." Wordsworth, the greatest of the Romantic poets, is neither popular nor pretentious, and at his best he has a dignity far less assailable, because his own, than that of

Johnson or Gray, even if in his case it is incompatible with elegance. Mr. Eliot's failure—perhaps through impatience—to acknowledge things such as these, lessens the weight of his judgments, and lessens it needlessly. His criticism is more comprehensive and more sound than that of any other writer of this generation, but it would be infinitely better if it were compatible with an appreciation of the importance of Milton as well as of Marlowe, of Wordsworth as well as of Dryden, in the English poetic tradition. Until it is, it will have a faint but damaging, and altogether misleading, resemblance to the criticism of a school.

EDWIN MUIR.

PHYSICO-CHEMICAL EVOLUTION. By CHARLES E. GUYE. Methuen. 6s. net.

It is only comparatively recently that the conventional character of scientific concepts has been thoroughly realised. During the nineteenth century, and particularly in England, scientific men were, for the most part, naively realistic. Matter, for example, was regarded as an ultimate reality. The same may be said of the Newtonian space and time, and also, in many cases, of the Newtonian "forces." Such assumptions were always open to philosophical criticism, but it is the progress of science itself which has brought about a radically different estimate of the function and validity of science. A branch of science, such as physics, is essentially an attempt to bestow order and coherence upon a certain region of experience in terms of certain fundamental entities and principles. The difference between the modern scientific outlook and that of the Victorian age is due to our realisation of the fact that these entities and principles are largely arbitrary. In terms of the Newtonian outfit, absolute space and time, inertia, mass, force, and so on, a very good description was given of a certain region of experience. It was, perhaps, natural that scientific men should regard these entities, not as logical fictions invented by the mind to enable it to handle the material of experience in a congenial manner, but as constituents of the independently existing external world. The invention of electron theory and of relativity theory enable us to dispense with the Newtonian outfit, and to describe the same region of experiences more conveniently in terms of quite different fundamental entities. The status of these entities has now, therefore, become clear. They are logically arbitrary logical fictions. A science is, as it were, a game played according to certain rules, or a work of art obeying certain conventions. That science should be successful appears, therefore, to be a miracle. But relativity theory suggests that the universe we discover is the universe we have created, so that the marvellous subjection of nature to our intellectual tastes becomes less paradoxical.

COMMENTS AND REVIEWS

Such is the general outlook on science from which Professor Guye's speculations arise. He is interested to know whether a universal science is possible—that is, whether such primary entities and principles could be logically constructed as would suffice to describe the phenomena of life and mind as well as that of matter. He does not think that electrons, atoms, molecules, as at present defined in physics, are sufficiently richly endowed to play convincing rôles in biological and psychological phenomena. If they are dowered with a few more properties than those now attributed to them they may, without hindrance to their occupations in producing purely material phenomena, also serve to " explain " life and mind. There seems to be no objection to be made to this suggestion. The primary entities of physics have become more and more enriched as needs have arisen. In this way the atom, for instance, has developed from a homogeneous incompressible sphere into a highly complicated " miniature solar system." If it has also got to become " living " or " conscious," doubtless the matter could be arranged. But we doubt if science will go that way. It seems more likely that biology and psychology will proceed to develop in considerable confusion until some great genius explains away both " life " and " consciousness," perhaps merging them both into some higher unity, together with that continuum in which Einstein has already merged space, time, and matter. In speculating about a universal science, one is permitted to be fanciful. Professor Guye, however, is not particularly fanciful, but quite sober and thoughtful. To those who like to speculate with decorum, his work may be commended.

J. W. N. SULLIVAN.

TROY PARK. By EDITH SITWELL. Duckworth. 5s. net.

Miss Sitwell's technical skill is such that it compels, first of all, attention to her unusual vision, and, secondly, interest in her point of view. " Troy Park " does little to enhance one's opinion of the former, and leaves a feeling of dissatisfaction that the latter has not a greater value. It is a disappointing book, for though it contains the most interesting work Miss Sitwell has yet published, it reveals her as a lesser poet than one would have been before justified in pronouncing her.

Her qualities are very definite, but not obvious. In the first place she has stated her sensory reactions in a manner fitting and particular to her own perceptions, refusing the ready-to-hand, accepted means of sensuous metaphor and using instead a method of psychological correspondences. The danger incurred was two-fold : the lesser, that of obscurity, the greater that, in increasing the suggestiveness of her epithets, she should too much relax her grip on the reader's imagination. To avoid this she limited her field, so that by the repetition of almost identical processes in slightly varied contexts, she might develop a consistency of meaning. So Admiral Yang's face " is as flat as the notes of pianolas," and " The child that lies upon the sand Has a face as pastel flat As mechanic piano's notes:" she writes,

> " Like country clouds of clouted cream
>   The round and flaxen blond leaves seem,"

and

> " The clouds are bunchéd roses,
>   And the bunches seem
>   As thick as cream."

Yet, though in this way Miss Sitwell has succeeded in giving to her poetry freshness and malleability, in doing so she has been obliged to restrict herself and tends to become monotonous. It is undoubtedly an achievement, but to what extent more than a technical one could only be judged intuitively until the publication of " Troy Park," and now not definitively.

In her earlier work her insistence on, and the limited use of, her individual manner of writing, suggested a doubt on her part as to its æsthetic validity. Here she is as successful as before only when she writes in the mocking, fantastic vein of *Clown's Luck, Four in the Morning*, or " *I do like to be beside the Sea-side.*" Even then she is sometimes dependent on old themes and too apt to be carried away by the facility of rhyming very arbitrarily connected words and of associating ideas by their face-value. When her tone becomes elegiac, however, her manner is seen to arise not from the originality of her point of view, but from a technical perversity which strives to forge a vision that is not æsthetically justified by the content. This does not, of course, imply that Miss Sitwell is insincere. It means that the originality of her vision—a limited one—is purely sensory and does not enable her to see the harmony which creates poetic value. There are passages of great verbal sensitiveness in *The Child Who Saw Midas, Colonel Fantock, The Pleasure Gardens* and elsewhere, but they are usually rhetoric unessential to the development of the theme. Without them the poems appear in the commonplace nudity of sluggishly trite concepts, as elaborations of such *clichés* as :

> " a thousand legends
>   Of unseen beauty that will never die."

or

> " A world that is yet undreamt, unborn,
>   Where never a shade is of cruelty or scorn."

Such passages as the opening of the first poem, or as :

> " When night came sounding like the growth of trees,
>   My great-grandmother bent to say good-night,
>   And the enchanted moonlight seemed transformed
>   Into the silvery tinkling of an old
>   And gentle music-box that played a tune

COMMENTS AND REVIEWS

Of Circean enchantments and far seas,
Her voice came lulling as the splash of these,"

are so immediately pleasing as to blind one to the hollowness which
they screen, but one's judgment after reading the whole book
can only praise Miss Sitwell as a virtuoso.

DOUGLAS GARMAN.

FIRST POEMS.   By EDWIN MUIR.   Hogarth Press.   4s. 6d. net.

There is little in this first book of poems to arrest the attention,
and yet behind the measured beat of the verse one feels a dignity of
thought that refuses to be hustled by the conflicting violences of
the moment.   Mr. Muir writes coolly and without strain, urbanely,
sometimes dully, and his thought moves at the same level.   His
limitations are not dissembled under a pseudo-brilliance or pretentious technique, and this straightforwardness is a quality setting
his work apart from much that is noisy opportunism.   Almost all
the poems are written in conventional decasyllabic metre, and,
with the exception of the ballads, one feels that this form is as yet
the most suitable for Mr. Muir.   His attempts to write in free verse
do not come off ; they lack a definite and individual rhythm.   In
the poem " Horses " his imagination works clearly and forcefully :

> " But when at dusk with steaming nostrils home
> They came, they seemed gigantic in the gloam,
> And warm and glowing with mysterious fire,
> Which lit their smouldering bodies in the mire.
>
> Their eyes as brilliant and as wide as night
> Gleamed with a cruel apocalyptic sight.
> Their manes the leaping ire of the wind
> Lifted with rage invisible and blind."

or in *Reverie*, where he writes of lovers,

> " . . . those two, who, in half-dumb talk,
> With broken gestures, and half-shapen speech,
> In unintelligible rapture walk,
> Too far for vain and longing thought to reach."

This latter poem is the most effective in the book for the reason
that, without a direct statement, it determines a very definite
attitude.

Of the ballads the one " Of Eternal Life " has taken too much
from " The Ancient Mariner," but " Hector in Hades " is a very
apt fitting of the form to the content, and, in the " Ballad of the
Flood," written in dialect, there are signs of a much freer manipulation of language, which, if it were developed, would greatly increase
Mr. Muir's power.

D. M. G.

PARALLAX. By NANCY CUNARD. Hogarth Press. 3s. 6d. net.

Miss Cunard's title is aptly chosen. Her poem is an attempt to express an attitude without recourse to the conventional method of *trompe-l'œil*, which subordinates the adjunctive processes to a unity of perspective that is psychologically inaccurate. She realises that an idea is not perceived in isolation, and, instead of using her art in trying to isolate it, she accepts the contingent emotive and mental currents it sets up, allowing to them their original force undiverted by preconceptions. She is not, of course, original in this—Laforgue and Mr. Eliot, to mention only two, have already proved the poetic value of her method—but sometimes she writes vigorously and individually. It is difficult to show this by quotation, for her vigour is in the action of the poem rather than in its parts. One feels an intensity which, on analysis, breaks down into echoes of other voices and pastiche.

> " I that am seed, root and kernel-stone
> " Buried in the present, I that exact fulfilment from every hour
> Now tell you :
> Accept all things, accept—if only to *be aware*."
> " I am most surely at the beginning yet.
> If so, contemporaries, what have you done ? "

The idiom is Whitman's, and the thought. Miss Cunard has accepted much and is aware, but she has not yet reduced her awareness to coherency. One feels that, and also that the discipline she needs must be exercised by her own personality and not by the influences to which she submits. In imitating—the word is not too strong—" The Waste Land," Miss Cunard has followed a good, but dangerous model too slavishly.

> " In the rim of the tide along Commercial Street
> You meet one like you for an hour or two "—

and

> " And along the Strand, up Queen Victoria Street.
> O City, City, I can sometimes hear . . . "

or,

> " By the Embankment I counted the grey gulls . . .
> . . . .
> In Battersea I drifted, acquiescent . . .
> . . .
> At Wimbledon . . .
> In Gravesend . . .
> . . .
> Kew in chestnut-time, September in Oxford Street "

and the end of Part III in Mr. Eliot's poem, are too close parallels to escape the accusation of plagiarism. One does, however, admire Miss Cunard's intention of using an idiom that is not worn out nor divorced by association from experience.   D. M. G.

COMMENTS AND REVIEWS

AN INDIAN ASS. By HAROLD ACTON. Duckworth, 4s. 6d.

There is in this second volume of Mr. Acton's poems the same crudity of thought and expression which was noticeable in " Aquarium." It is an utterance of boredom and disgust by one who would dissemble these ruins under a fantastic pleasure-dome in which to exercise the strange modes of his imagination. As an inscription to one of the poems he quotes from " The Duchess of Malfi " :

> *Talk to me somewhat quickly,*
> *Or my imagination will carry me*
> *To see her in the shameful act of sin.*

These lines might well have served as a motto for the whole book. Mr. Acton talks quickly, and often at random, in an effort to achieve a positive point of view in the face of the disillusion which ensues from his glances at a world sinning against his limited æsthetic ideal. The cursoriness of these glances robs his satire of force and often detracts from the value of his imaginative statement. About the former there is a coarseness of perception which singles out the obvious, as when he writes :

> *And pleasures, money, all are volatile,*
> *For after belching Pol-Roger the bile*
> *Will wreak revenge.*

or, as in the poem " After " :

> *They do not cower*
> *Before the charabancs' toot toot a toot*
> *And men who bring their sandwiches to boot,*
> *And break beer-bottles where men's souls were torn*
> *By invisible billion hands . . . where agony was born.*

As a descriptive writer Mr. Acton is not frequently more successful. He falls back on such bizarre expressions as :

> *. . . beautiful in death*
> *As one that stumbles on a slumber, falls*
> *On downy-wingéd doze of braided air.*

or destroys an effect by incoherent sequences of qualification. When he says :

> *Death clanks his rusty mail and flaps his wings*
> *And ogling, draws the man into a dance,*

one cannot with certainty reassemble the disparate parts of the image. In poems dependent on exotic imagery he is at his best, when he is " dangling a silly mandrake root," but the thinness of such matter is revealed by the necessity under which one feels him to be, of throwing to reality a prosaic life-line, as :

> *' I do not care a damn,' the train replies.*

D. M. G.

THE TWELVE SAINTS. By Ruth Manning Sanders.
Christophers. 7s. 6d.

It is quite proper that the young novelist should perplex himself and his readers with a number of insufficiently considered ideas, since, so effective is success upon the prematurely successful, if he begins with a small thing done neatly, he is unlikely to improve in future work upon anything but the neatness. "The Twelve Saints" is rather confused. It would have been a better book if, regardless of all else, Miss Sanders had contented herself with portraying a number of artists and art-mongers. She has a rich sense of character, unforced humour, and a fresh, bold mind. But the extraneous material which clogs the comedy assures us that she will develop. What matter that she has this once failed in her attempt to show reflected in the world of ideas the conflicts of the world of phenomena ; that her symbolism is incoherent, her imagery dull and her treatment of the more powerful emotions comparatively superficial ?

Faith but not, I think, history, supports the suggestion that in the middle ages the relations of the artist with his public were untroubled, and that what the one wrought for no vulgar profit from the fulness of his heart was by the other joyfully and reverently appreciated. A pretty suggestion, true or false. And a useful criterion whereby to judge the artist who compromises with commerce as well as the artist who, in despair of attaining a wider recognition, studies the whims of a small coterie. These and other types might be seen in the town of St Judd's, and be depressed by the examination of the Abbey cloisters, whose magnificent statuary recalls noble devotion. Even Gregory Dunn, dealer in artistic furniture, detects something offensive to him in the sculptured saints, his sensibilities perhaps sharpened by the fact that his father had been one of those upright craftsmen who used pegs instead of glue, to the great detriment of his declining trade. It may be also that Ann's ineffective religiosity and Elizabeth's simple paganism should be regarded as fragments broken from a vanished whole. But about this some doubt is necessary. The author's interest in living creatures becomes too vigorous for her idealism, and the saints and stars and so on are perfunctorily treated.

What Miss Sanders has done conspicuously well is to work out, for her own use at least, an alternative to the irony with which so many modern authors assure us that they find the emotions of their characters faintly ridiculous, and to the exhortations of the elder novelist that we should mingle our own tears with their puppets. Simon and Bone are both fools, both irritating. The deepest grief of the one is obviously to be ascribed to wounded vanity, and most of the other's tragedy is due to a physical disease, with the result that we recognise their rhetoric to be emotionally insincere. But this recognition is not made to kill our sympathies. It does not even confine pity to the facile exclamation : " Poor little men ! " For amid the collapse of Miss Sanders' symbolism, her preference for the real over the phenomenal stands true.

It should be added that Miss Sanders' style, though occasionally inflated by passages of conscious prettiness, proves her respectful intimacy with the English language.   H. C. HARWOOD.

THE PAINTED VEIL. By SOMERSET MAUGHAM. Heinemann. 7s. 6d.

Much of what is called cynicism is merely the obverse of an exuberant sentimentality. Its exponents seem once to have believed that life is planned for the pleasure of imbecile children by a creator experienced in the production of slush films, and in losing that faith to have reacted into discrediting all things but lust and greed. Really it is hard to understand how some cheap wit could be found amusing if it were not regarded as the sole alternative to a cheap emotionalism. The audience that laughs to-night at a revue playlet cried the night before at the cinema, and is not aware that the criticism of life can be conducted by any other formula than one of these two, now seeking an unreal comfort in a monstrous misrepresentation of human nature and now relaxing from this effort in the silly-smart mockery of its own delusions. But there is a more serious kind of cynicism, treating actual conduct, yet deficient in truth or beauty because it has not attained to, or has declined from, cognisance of the principles whereby the inconsistencies visible in its material may be reconciled and a unity presented for intellectual enquiry or artistic representa-tion. Mr. Somerset Maugham's cynicism is of this more interesting class.

Kitty of " The Painted Veil," who has been trained, according to the Thackerayan tradition, for a brilliant marriage, blunders into one of no great profit ; and no doubt, whatever the wealth or social position of her husband, would be unable, her life work accomplished, to find any career but the pursuit of trivial amuse-ments, amid which she reckons adultery. She is detected in her first intrigue, and for some time wonders whether her husband, Walter, will condone her infidelity for the sake of his official advancement, or whether he will set her free to make a better marriage. But Walter is an extremist, and carries Kitty off to a cholera-ridden city in the hope that she will meet with an un-pleasant death. And now the novel becomes interesting. So far Mr. Maugham has been expending witty but commonplace satire on a pair of casual amorists, and threatens to show us a Kitty, dignified by suffering, regaining her husband's confidence. But while it is true that Kitty begins to grow up, begins to understand the nastiness of what she did, the incidents of the cholera epidemic impress upon her that her husband has been and is making a ridiculous fuss about his private affairs. Against this awful background of disease her sin looks as petty as herself. The cynicism is carried one stage further when Kitty discovers herself to be after her awakening as easily tempted to animal indulgence as before. Beyond that Mr. Maugham cannot go, though the closing pages illustrate not only his limitations but his consciousness of them. To give a climax to this episode he asks us to believe that five minute's conversation is sufficient to put into sympathy persons who have lived together for decades in misunderstanding and in- difference approximating to dislike. And the object which Kitty proposes for her future is to bring up her daughter to be frank, and free to seek something more than matrimony ; which moral is defective in that it evades a problem by charging the next generation with its solution, and ludicrous in that if Kitty's child has Kitty's temperament she will substitute pre-marital for post-marital unchastity.

The setting of this novel will be tiresomely familiar to readers of " On a Chinese Screen." Mr. Maugham has added no new picturesque detail, and the strong irony of the earlier volume is weakened when repeated in this less rigid form. Moreover, in many places Mr. Maugham has brightened his dialogue by the introduction of romantic or witty phrases alien to the supposed speaker and out of key with the narrative's prevailing tone. The contempt of a resident in South Kensington for a resident in Earl's Court is a perhaps excusable caricature of snobbery ; not, however, in itself more amusing than the lusciousness with which the author explains the Mother Superior's aristocratic connections. On the whole " The Painted Veil " is unlikely to increase Mr. Maugham's reputation, though it will, notwithstanding its imaginative langour, delight admirers of his wit, and interest students of his shrewd and honestly sceptical curiosity.

H. C. H.

Among New Books

POEMS AND FABLES. By R. C. TREVELYAN. Hogarth Press. 3s. net.

Mr. Trevelyan writes smoothly and sincerely, but without distinction. His imagery is thin and worn :

> " Beauty had I pursued,
>   As a child a winged bird, vainly."

Here the epithet is unnecessary ; the possibility of a child's pursuing a wingless bird is, in the context, too ludicrous to need elimination.

" O soul," I cried, " the cage is open : spread thy wings," he writes, and of his life,

>   " Nought now but a barren wilderness did it seem ; "

and of Pleasure,

>   " It is like a flame
>
>   .   .   .
>   Vanishing in smoke,"
>
>   or
>   " A fugitive scent
>
>   .   .   .
>   Laden with memories
>   Of childhood hours."

The effect of such poetry is soporific. It can make no impact on the reader's consciousness, because the original impulse can only be faintly perceived through layers of accumulated literature. The most successful of the poems is the last, composed " On a theme from Chuang Tzu."

THE SHADOWGRAPH. By EDWARD SHANKS. Collins. 5s.

Mr. Shanks, in this volume, reveals himself as a very clumsy writer, with little delicacy of thought or sensitiveness to language.   He writes very gustily of women, horses, trees and sentiment, but is rarely more invigorating than in this apostrophe to the wind :

>   " Blow louder, wind, about
>   My square-set house, rattle the windows, lift
>   The trap-door to the loft above my head
>   And let it fall, clapping.   Yell in the trees
>   And throw the rotted oak-bough to the ground,
>   Flog the dry trailers of my climbing rose—
>   Make deep, O Wind, my rest ! "

or more profound than :

>   " It was not you I loved, it was not you !
>   It was your beauty was the flickering fire
>   That, on the wall I watched so eagerly, threw
>   A gibing shadow of my own desire."

In neither quotation is Mr. Shanks obscure, though his demand in the first case follows somewhat inconsequently so loud a racket, but in neither case is the significance at all increased by the fact of its being in verse.   He is not, however, always so explicit.   When, in a sonnet, he writes of two hearts burning one into the other :

>   " As do the cold, unmoving elements
>   When to their joy the chemist's will consents
>   " And from that flame some residue endures "

one is at a loss to understand the cause of the element's joy—unless it be in a chemico-mystical coitus—nor is it clear whether " *that* flame " refers to the chemist's will or an assumed bunsen-burner. Such laxity of expression is to be condemned, not only for its own sake, but also because the idea that poetic effects are obtained by the conjunction of high-sounding words and vagueness of meaning is far too current.

HILL FRAGMENTS. By MADELINE MASON-MANHEIM. Palmer. 6s.

There is the clearest evidence in this volume, to which Mr. Arthur Symons contributes a preface, that the state of mind which is the aim of mysticism is fatal equally to the production and the appreciation of poetry. A transcendent aim precludes the possibility of reference to other experience,and the joys of Nirvana, to which any detachment from the object of contemplation is a hindrance, are incommunicable in proportion to their genuineness. But the pre-condition of art is just such experience as is worthless to the consistent mystic; and art's first principle is communication. True "mystical" poets, such as Vaughan and Traherne, describe their ecstasy in terms of life, of differentiation, indicating the ineffable unity by a poetic definition of the parts. Miss Mason-Manheim's verses come out of a general emotion in which words are used superstitiously as an instrument of revelation, as a quality rather than an accessory of vision. And Mr. Symons sanctions the muddle when he states his belief that

> "Music, in itself, is not a representation of the world, but an immediate voice of the world . . . the ecstasy of music can be maintained indefinitely and at its highest pitch, while the ecstasy of verse is shortened by what is definite in words."

It is small wonder that, with such a theory for encouragement, Miss Mason-Manheim's free-verse should be so confidently banal and fluid, and that her critic should so blindly misjudge its quality. "Her preference for the homeliest words, and for the rhythms in which the art—as I have said—consists in a seeming disregard of art, is in her favour; for with those unadorned words that come to our lips when we speak to one another, she obtains effects . . . of abstract passion and depth of thought, of unrestrained emotion, of a sense of mystery, of tragic ecstasy," etc., etc.

Under this dispensation the language of poetry is progressively meaningless, and the function of the critic is to use it as a springboard for a plunge into ineffable feeling. Such adventures rapidly become auto-generative, and then there is no need for the springboard at all.

ON LIFE AND LETTERS (3rd and 4th series). By ANATOLE FRANCE. The Bodley Head. 2s. 6d. each.

These volumes complete "La Vie Litteraire," his literary criticism, in the Bodley Head's excellent half-crown series of translations from Anatole France. M. France probably reads less well in English than any great French writer. It was making the best of a bad job to translate him, as Mr. Miall has done, as literally as possible, and expect that the reader would know enough French to sense the original. To read him again in our hard language is to become almost painfully aware of how little of a critic he was, being always so supremely himself. All poets, most novelists (all, indeed, except the school of M. Zola), and the greater number of even the merely literary men of whom he treats, become dissolved in the great bland oil which he sheds upon them. But then it is the most wonderfully refined oil in the world.

LETTERS FROM ENGLAND. By KAREL CHAPEK. Geoffrey Bles. 7s. 6d.

The beautiful irony of "The Insect Play" and the menacing, though intermittent, strength of "R.U.R." are not present in this book. Mr. Chapek is now just extremely observant and gently humorous, with every now and then a burst of poetry, unmistakable even in its second-hand prose guise. He sometimes pauses before our greensward and such traditions to wish that he were even a Czechish poet, and yet he can say of our trees

AMONG NEW BOOKS

that "suddenly there is a sort of mumbling within them, they make a grotesque remark, a fork of pixie-like humour flies out of them, and once more they have the solemn appearance of old leather armchairs." He loves our policemen, hates our Sunday, and obviously tends to worship our Shaw. He is awed in our University towns, delighted in our countryside, and, at Wembley, frightened of our machines. All these emotions are described in a quaint, bright English which betrays the verbal genius of the original Czech, and reflects great credit upon his translator, Mr. Paul Selver. Mr. Chapek's drawings, crude as they are, admirably assist his air of what one would, perhaps, in the end, call "child-like enquiry" if one had not heard of his plays and did not know that he is deeply read in the pragmatic philosophers.

LONDON LIFE IN THE 14th CENTURY. By CHARLES PENDRILL. Allen and Unwin. 10s. 6d.

An industrious and very readable book, particularly useful for reference on matters of trade in the century which saw the birth of trade unionism. The chapters on the street life and topography of London, its pageants, processions and civic organisation, are supplemented by descriptions of the activities of the bravos, "men of straw" (professional perjurers recognisable by wisps of straw in their shoes), swindlers, cut-throats, bogus pilgrims and sorcerers who, by keeping life dangerous, helped to preserve those qualities of individual initiative which are the sole sanction of a group movement. There is an amusing story of the lady who saved the burghers of Calais. In 1329 Edward III, preparing for a great jousting in Chepe, ordered a noble archway in the form of a tower to be erected across the street, so that the queen and her ladies might view the passage of arms. "Unfortunately, when they ascended the archway it collapsed in the middle, letting them down in most undignified fashion on the knights below, several of whom were injured, though none seriously. The carpenters who built it were on the point of becoming victims of the king's wrath when the gentle Queen Philippa, with her usual magnanimity, interfered and saved them from punishment. To avoid such accidents for the future, the King built beside Bow Church a great house of stone from which to view the tournaments." Mr. Pendrill's use of anecdote is discreet; it illuminates the actual narrative, from which it contrives a relief for the reader's attention.

THE BEST POEMS OF 1924. Small, Maynard & Co. $2.00.

Unless one were thoroughly conversant with the English and American magazines of the day it would be impossible to say how satisfactorily Mr. Strong has carried out his task. The number of poets represented, however, would suggest that he has been catholic in his choice, with a bias, acknowledged in the preface, towards Irish writers. An anthologist of contemporary work—Best Plays, Best Short Stories, Best Films or Best Poems—is in a difficult position. His work, if it is to be representative, must, in the present state of literature, necessarily lack unity, and Mr. Strong's undoubtedly does that. Again, if such an anthology is to serve any valuable purpose, it would seem necessary to give more than a single poem, whenever possible, of any poet, or perhaps, to exclude the poetry of those writers whose work is published periodically in books. The beauty of the individual poem is, of course, justification for its inclusion, but at present it is often necessary to read a poet at some length, until acquaintance with his mode of expression enables one to understand him. Too often this anthology only stirs an intuition as to the beauty of a particular poem. Knowing Mr. Hardy we can fully appreciate his poem "The Missed Train," while a very slight acquaintance with Mr. Kreymborg leaves us uncertain as to the significance of the interesting poem "And She Said and I Said."

The poems which, at a first reading, stand out from the others are, in addition to the two mentioned, those by Miss Cunard, Mr. Freeman, "King's

THE CALENDAR

Ransom," by Miss Wylie, " Emily Hardcastle, Spinster," by Mr. Ransom and the first of Mr. Frost's.

THE COMPLETE POEMS OF EMILY DICKINSON.   Martin Secker.   21s.

Emily Dickinson died at Amherst, New England, in 1886.   Her life was extremely secluded and she had no pretensions to publicity.   It is only since her death that, except for one or two poems, her work has been printed at all. She was undoubtedly a personality of unusual force and integrity, and her verse reflects these qualities.   It will be discussed at length next month.

MILTON : MAN AND THINKER.   By DENIS SAURAT.   Cape, 15s.

This book is devoted to a lucid exposition of Milton's ideas and of their influence on the structure of his poems.   It will be reviewed at length shortly, but in the meantime we may say that the view of Milton therein represented is one which the modern mind will find much more congenial than the one generally current.   It should assist that revival of the poet's prestige which is rendered necessary by the diminishing effect of the usual pietistic criticism.

MYTHOLOGY.   By JANE ELLEN HARRISON.   Harrap.   5s.

This little book is an addition to the series called Our Debt to Greece and Rome.   Miss Harrison does not attempt to calculate very fully the actual debt, but her book is a contribution to the study of the origin of gods and goddesses.   Her idea is that a people makes its gods in the image of what it desires.   This theory is worked out most fully, and brilliantly, in the case of Poseidon.   Miss Harrison's writings are always fertile in suggestion : " It was the supreme genius of the Greeks as contrasted with the Romans that they were image-makers, *iconists.*"   The contrast might be extended to the whole of modern Europe, unfortunately.   Our gods, or our idols, have no concrete forms, so that the imagery of our arts is predominately derivative. Archæology is the basis of Miss Harrison's arguments, which are always illuminating, if on the whole too consistently genteel completely to account for the tremendous vitality of a world of myth.   The assistance of psychology has to be invoked to reveal the origin and meaning of many of the attributes of divinity, which have their root in deep-lying and not always reputable fastnesses of human desire.

The CALENDAR
of Modern Letters

VOLUME I
NUMBER 4

JUNE
1925

The Later Life of Theseus, King of Athens.

(From the Memoirs of Menestheus, the Erecthid.)

BY MARY BUTTS.

WE were all without illusion that any good was to be expected from these affairs. From the first they appeared deplorable; now that the worst has happened, I can only repeat that it was expected, foreseen, foretold, and that, as so often occurs, now it is over, the situation is left very much as it was before.

Now that the late Government in Athens has changed, as it was bound to change, it can be seen that the activities of the late king were no more than the wind ruffling the unstirred halls of Ocean, where sit, if I may say so, those dumb and flexible powers who reigned before him, and have been shown to survive him. I mean that I, after these years of exile and observation, have come back into my place. Or, it would be more prudent and more cautious to say that a place has come back and been filled by me.

Theseus has gone. He was not legitimate—not one of those earth-sprung princes created to rule because in some sense they are this piece of land. He had no business in Athens here at all, though he might have done well enough in Troezên. When he chose to come and lord it here, he should not have been surprised if, though the people applauded him, the air and the stones did not accept him; and that in time the people of this ancient situation were persuaded, not by him, but by the stones and the air.

Theseus went. During his reign I watched his efforts, I and others, and knew that all we had to do was wait and watch the spending of his energy, and even admire its furious turns. It passed. When it was over, I took my place and my turn. The land had sighed, turned over, and now sleeps again.

But what a time we had! New laws, new drains, new wives. I remember as if it were yesterday the day Phædra arrived in her Cretan ship. The daughter of Minos and of Pasiphaë. She seemed a staring, silly maid. A little sub-normal, I thought, a freak of over-breeding. She was very quiet in the palace, though I was rather pleased at the shrine she built to a featureless but peculiar Aphrodite.

There is nothing I deplore more than the effort made by men like Theseus to abstract and beautify the gods. At the same time to make them into men. I and my friends know that they are neither abstract, human, nor necessarily beautiful. So I welcomed the gesture of Theseus' wife, but, again, I may have idealised it. She was probably homesick for some Cretan daimon, a furtive, indoor, woman's goddess.

Well, the Cretan neurosis soon found its expression. As is usual in these affairs, it was the talk of the place before the actors or sufferers knew what was happening to them.

What no one foresaw was the appeal to Poseidon. Nor the immediate response in circumstances when a god such as Theseus conceived might well have counted seven. In half-an-hour the matter would have been explained. Artemis should have seen to that. Personally, I wish Poseidon had let Hippolytos be, promise or no promise. Only I know that the divine element must always work like that. It is an automatic quality, and the gods when they act are so much stored power released. In the same manner, Artemis did not come until Hippolytos' extremity compelled her. A racing goddess, but a woman?

But it is little use to speculate on what ought to have

happened. Theseus, our late showman, gave us an exhibition that will not soon be forgotten. It was not the first. It proved not to be the last.

His energy in passing new laws in the first months of his widowhood is impossible to describe. It became difficult, before the feast of Anthesteria, to catch sprats, to draw water between sunset and midnight from the public fountains, and forbidden to invoke Poseidon on any account at all.

It became possible to marry one's aunt, and there were regulations as to the destruction of fish-heads in hot weather for which I think there is something to be said. At the same time, the war he made almost immediately on the Lapiths was evidence that his character was weakening.

We did not oppose it. There are worse things than a small war, fought in one's own place so as not to interfere with the harvest. I was not curious about the Lapiths; but when a community is ruled by a man like Theseus, kept in a constant state of excitement, with nothing to do but neglect its business to talk not even about his ideas but about him, I considered their arrival was reasonably well-timed. Personally, I believe he invited them; but I will describe, as I saw it, the result of the first and only battle in the campaign.

Indeed, it is well known how they met. Theseus and that old scoundrel Perithoös. How they craned over their chariots to observe each other, and Theseus countermanded the charge, and how they walked out between the lines and examined one another till Theseus kissed him. The city knows how they came back, arm in arm, both sides straggling behind them; and the noise they made opening up the palace for a foreign army to get at the wine. It had always been more of an inn than a gentleman's residence. The little queen Phædra had tried to introduce the Cretan formality. Theseus had played at that, but not for long. But there was no ceremony that night when they roared their songs and rang their cups, and lit cressets whose light danced on the marble in the wind and lit the palace right out to sea.

At dawn they went roaring down to the Piræus. I thought of the wonderful luck of the man, to whom the next event was always kind. There is a kind of compensation for the man who uses life, who gets into trouble and into pleasure as a boat runs from tack to tack. He had better remember, though, that he is used, and not so honourably, as the man who submits to life's using of him. I might have been a Theseus.

But there they were that night, Theseus and Perithoös the heroes. He sent his Lapiths home, but he stayed; and they went riding together, went drinking, went talking, until the town began to say " The end of this will be a new queen."

It must be remembered that he was not a man to act upon design, and one who would as lightly offend the Dioscuri as he would have taken Heracles into his house when that hero had just murdered his own children. The fool never knew that blood will more than out, that blood will have blood. He has been praised for what he did then, for his friendship with a man so close to him in temperament that he could despise his madness and the pollution of blood; keeping him with him till his wits came back, and telling him that the sole evil of his act was his fear of it. I heard that said, and saw Heracles comforted at last. I smiled. I do not know what blood is, but it is not so easily got rid of as that. The earth wins at last. We shall go down to the house of Hades, and there will be no more of these swaggering Olympians and the heroes they have so jovially begot. And I mean to be on the side that must win, if it means a lifetime of quiet.

Besides, I saw Perithoös chewing a twig of buckthorn last March, for a purge, I suppose, not uneasiness, before they began the scandalous entertainment we witnessed when they stole the immortal sister of the Dioscuri, Helen-of-the-Egg, the daughter of Zeus and the Swan.

I do not doubt that people were right when they said that it was Perithoös' suggestion. He would have done anything for Theseus. Theseus must have put it to him in this way : I can hear him say : 'Those Cretan sisters were both a mistake. One to hang herself, the other to go off with a god. Hippolyta was too much the other way. We were too like each other. I was unfair to her, and I'm sorry for it now. I did not treat her as I would have been treated, and it is a shame to me. There are only Phædra's children left ; I don't like the breed. I must have another choice of heirs. But a pure Greek this time, Perithoös'.

Then Perithoös suggested, without an idea but to get his friend what he wanted: "Why not a goddess this time, Theseus?"

I suppose they discussed it a little, but I am sure that, after a hundred words, they were asking "Which one?" and when I consider their difficulties I do not wholly reject their choice.

Every far-seeing and observant man has had his eye on the nursery of Tyndareus. The girls were born to be queens in Hellas. Queens have come to no good lately in this city; but there was no harm in Theseus asking. Only, when he asked for her, he was refused on the count that she was a child.

The reason was not only sufficient, it was true. But Theseus and Perithoös left the city at once. A month later they came back, arm-in-arm, roaring, and told the town they had stolen her. To marry her? No. For ransom? Not at all. But to leave with his mother for three years till she should be old enough. Anyone could see that this would not do. What did he suppose her brothers would have to say about it? The Dioscuri were a notable pair of young men. Far better to have married her at once, child or no child; but that is the sort of thing Theseus did not do.

Immediately I retired to my country estate, where they would know when to find me.

Theseus made no excuses. I cannot suppose that he had any. He is reported to have said that the marriage would make for peace in Hellas, and one of the Fates would cut her throat when she heard about it; but that he could not touch a child. His position seemed contradictory. I suppose he was vain enough to want her conspicuous beauty, at his age, who had had Ariadne, Hippolyta and Phædra. I waited with impatience for her brothers, hoping to hear a piece of the divine mind, and watch a contest between an old hero and the young. I am not a hero. I and my house were before this fashion for law-givers and unfortunate husbands; and I shall be here when some funeral games, getting cheaper every year, are all that is left of them. I should not be surprised if it is I who will insist on some small decencies being preserved, and an offering of at least a minimum of honey and hair. All the same, since ceremonies round holy graves are a part of public life, why not have the body in the grave practically anonymous, and the sacred snake ? It is known what the sacred snake is there for. At the same time it is not known. Certainly I would have Theseus forgotten as Theseus.

I will now describe what happened. There was an attempt made to hide the girl. Theseus had brought her to his mother; but this was not generally known. I was looking for her myself in a strange place, when I came upon the brothers, Castor and Polydeuces, doing the same thing. I offered them my reflections, nothing more. They were too innocent to use and too proud to influence. One was a king's son and the other a son of Zeus, but my position was less equivocal than theirs. Not that they recognised it, blown as they were with these new splendours; but they were boys enough to be glad of any company, and to explain why they were found among the cliffs at Scyros in a cave.

Their objections to the marriage were obscure and mostly untrue. They said that Helen was too young ; but Theseus had agreed with them. They said that Theseus was too old : which did not matter. They said his former marriages had been unfortunate : which is immaterial. Then they implied that Theseus had fore-knowledge, and was deliberately going against what was bound to happen : which is impossible. They showed no love for their sister, but an acceptance as though she were a part of nature. Not as men speak from pride of race. They took her away, I was told, in silence. Afterwards, Theseus and Perithoös were seen on the terrace, looking out to sea, together and also silent.

I did not pretend to understand. The life of the girl Helen has been worth attention. I felt that she was of the same stuff as myself, put to the uses of those new heroes. The uses to which she has put them we are beginning to learn. They have forgotten that there were potencies here before Zeus. But this affair began with the jovial theft of a pretty child and some inconsistent behaviour. It ended with the return of the child, and it was plain to see that Theseus did not think that he had lost any of his dignity. Knowing that he was soon likely to attempt an even more conspicuous adventure, I had a time of indecision when I questioned myself, not for the first time, as to what I had gained by the part in life that I had played.

Before the Argo's voyage and the hunt of the Calydonian Boar, life moved quietly in this land, arranged on certain antique forms. These I have upheld against the innovating heroes. There are dark spots in nature. Let them stay dark. Man need not try to illuminate them. His business with them is to keep harmony by due propitiatory sacrifice to the infernal powers. I would offend no sacred snake. Omit no libation of honey, milk or blood. Especially not blood. It is, when you think of it, the cheapest of the three.

That there are powers propitious to man I do not deny. That the unpropitious can be disregarded I hold to be the belief of an idiot child. Hard, pliant and astute man must be, observant of birds and the prohibitions of his folk.

That is what these men are not doing. In the place of nature they have put their own wills. The minotaur died; but the Cretan curse returned. I was sorry for Hippolytos, the son of a virago our hero king made a martyr of.

What has the Golden Fleece done for us? Gold will go back the way it came. I have seen this in the sky.

With three queens under the earth and one refused him, with heirs of a kind to succeed him, the ruler of a people who cheered him and twittered at him, in the late middle years of his life Theseus decided that he had not dared enough, and that the time had come for a yet more outrageous enterprise. He had lost the young Helen. Well and good. This time he would have a goddess.

It was said that Pallas Athene was his first choice. I wondered mildly what she would have thought of Phædra's small white palace after her Olympian house. Of course, I remembered that in earlier days her life had been simple, and she had exacted from us no more tendance than was customary when our lives were simple too. That was before these goddesses had gone up in the world, and become daft on heroes. Jealous, also, of each other. Artemis attended Hippolytos' death, and swore to Aphrodite that she would kill Adonis in revenge. That, I suppose, is going on somewhere. But would they allow themselves to be stolen? Anyhow, Theseus changed his mind. He and Perithoös went away, side by side, in two small chariots; and no one knew where they were going. They did not return, and slowly the tale came round that two handsome men of middle age had been seen going down to the House of Death and Persephone. They went through the mountain. They came to the place. They crossed Acheron, Cocytos, Styx. I do not know how they managed Cerberus. To end it, they got inside.

They had come to steal Persephone.

They stole Persephone. I am telling you what happened. I do not know how they did it. Nor what they said to her. It is a long time since she lost her habit of reappearing among us with the spring. Also, there is something about the house of Hades that is agreeable to women. Most of the conspicuous ones there are men, but a woman sits on the throne of that house and distributes its poppies. It is all Persephone, and Eurydice that a man put back. Only it seems certain that she was willing to go. It is a terror to me to admit it, but certainly, since these events, the House of Hades has lost much of its prestige. I can no longer see it half-lit, smelling of dark flowers and blood. It has become one of other places. I wish I knew how they persuaded her. Unless he was lying, and Theseus did not lie, she said she would come and live with him in his Athenian house, and be a queen to this city. What did they offer her? What did she ask? It happened quickly, I imagine, but she came away between them.

Then Cerberus caught them at the door, and all I know is that Persephone herself was turned back, and Theseus stuck to a rock, and of Perithoös nothing was said.

It was then that opportunity found me, and I became king again in Athens, and did something to restore old ways and discourage conversation. I was in the full interest of my negative experiment when they came back, first Perithoös, then Theseus.

They seemed to take more pleasure in my society than they had done, and were good enough to say that they found me unchanged. I could not say that of them. They were older. They were fatigued. There is one thing certain about these heroes, that they wear themselves into their graves. And they do not wear well. However, I thought it becoming to give up the kingship at once.

We were back where we had started, nearly a lifetime

ago; and time was now our common enemy. If I had realised
it then, I should have grieved to have given up that for which
I had waited for so long. But it had always seemed to me
that he was mortal, and I the immortal, for I come of the
life that rises and flowers and passes down into the earth again.
From uncountable ages my fathers were the earth-kings of
this place, and for them the earth's luck held, and they were
re-born in their sons for ever. Only I have no son. In me,
for the last time in direct line, Athens has returned to her
kings, seeds of the Erecthidæ, sprung-of-the-soil. So I conquered Theseus the hero, who did not understand these things.

I have striven to alter nothing.

It was not I who threw Theseus over the cliff. We were
walking one day and talking, and I noticing how he was
ageing, though proud and angry like a king-bull. The thought
of bulls recalled my mind to Crete, and Crete to Minos—a
square throne, tight-waisted women, pinched Phædra,
a grinning, black Aphrodite-at-home, the north wind that
came ruffling our sea, loud voices, men with gold hair.

Then, as I was thinking, his foot slipped, and he was over
the cliff's edge ; and if I trod on his hand as it clung, well,
I was king again.

Only, to quiet all tumult in the city, I established his young
children by Phædra at Scyros, and gave him the mound,
the games, the libations and cut tresses for a hero, even to
the sacred snake.

But it was I who put them there. Things may be equal
between us. I leave that as I have left other things.

Poems

By DOUGLAS GARMAN.

Retrospect.

*" Sweet friends, what shall become of Faustus,
being in hell for ever ? "*

Earth, the old earth, is wan with shreds of winter
Torn by gusty winds from a silent sky,
And caught, as straws in trees, by stark hills wounding
Heaven with their hands, outstretched to azure fields
Where the birds sing. Spring has been dead so long—
Hyacinths fragrant in the window-pots
And the white surf of snow ebbing from the meadows—
And summer followed spring with cruel feet,
Leaving a trampled corpse beneath the trees.

Are your arms empty, Paris ?   And your cheeks
Wrinkled ?   The golden cups where Priam drank
Are dusty shrouds for the white bones of Greeks,
And the wine is spilt.
Flutes all night sighed in the cedar-groves
Beneath the moon, and the doomed palace hung
A giant flower in the perfumed gardens,
Swayed by the gusty light of torches held
By home-sick slaves.   Andromache's proud hands
Twined laurel with yew for Hector's drunken brow,
While Paris, the Trojan pierrot, woman-eyed,
Smiled at the sleepy boy that poured his wine.
Unheeded, through deserted corridors,
Naked Cassandra crept, wailing her grief
In answer to the owls : and when the flutes
Were mute, dawn, like a pale consumptive, woke
And coughed the blood-stained pellet of the sun.
Then I, unwanted stranger at their tables,
Fled from Helen's bed through the Grecian camp
And put to sea.

O earth is sad !—yet man's impatient soul
Clings to his body like the withered leaf
That a mad wind flutters and spares and flutters
On a dead branch. The eloquence of streams
Is stunned with frost's bright hammer, and the ponds
Hold in their gelid depths no secrets hid,
But dreams of summer, golden-footed summer,
And spring with silver feet. They too have forgotten
Their youth and the life stirring in the mud ;
They, too, feed on visions and forget
That worms grow busy when the soul has fled.
O the smoke of leaves piercing through the tree-tops !—
It is more solemn than Death in a great city.

And she is always there.
Why she ?—when that other reflected fair
Image is brighter and
More constant, though I cannot stretch my hand
To touch her hair.
Beyond the fires the wind in the pine-trees moaned
Like Death's shroud rustling in an empty house,
And the spilt flames were blood on the grey rock.
There smiling Lillith wooed her youthful lovers
With evil lips and secret perilous eyes,
Which mirrors held in swift uncouth reflection
The grave's most horrible shapes, and broken dreams,
And moons adrift in a distracted sky.
But in the tones of that too gentle voice
Were Margaret's tears and rumour of her love—
And I, Walpurgis-night's buffoon and fool,
Turned from the spectre that smiled behind that face,
For Death's fine scarlet thread was round her throat.

In the city, winding through the mist,
Creep Death's unlovely crowds with noiseless feet :
And none of them smile or look back at me,
None of them weep.
It is no slight thing to have escaped Death !

Where have the birds all flown ?   What voices spoke
Of langorous foliage and slow-winding rivers ?
I, too, have dreams behind my eyes : but here
Is only mud, and rain dripping from the house-eaves,
And long brown valleys leaning to the sea.

When I have drawn the curtains and my lamp
Is lit, I pay no attention to the rats
Or the wind tearing at the window-joints,
But I remember the ruins of old cities
And the birds flying to the south—
And I, Faustus, who have foretasted life
In Trojan love-draughts and on Margaret's lips,
Weep that those heedless ghosts should pass me by—
It is no slight thing to have escaped Death !

[*This poem is the introduction to, and the following a part of, a longer poem.*]

The Lovers.

Over the way
They beat that same insistent time,
Whacking the ivories, stepping on the gas . . .
O, she can play . . .

The ripple of the music fills a pause,
Flowing in through the window, ruffling the calm
Of conversation's twilit, cultured lake :
But when the oil of supercilious smiles
Has stilled those waters, unexpectedly
The room is filled with the impatient ghosts
Of dancers, and the shaded lights are swung
In extravagant agitation, stirring the blood.

Yet, though my eyes are dulled with dreams, I smile
And thank my hostess for a second cup ;
Admiring the whiteness of an arm which bears
African bangles and green Chinese jade—

Too placid ostentation of that wit,
That gathers heterogeneous beauty fast
On a single thread, and as adroitly moves
Down smooth encyclopædic ways of thought,
From Buddha's lap to Dante or the Film.
Anthropomorphic Babel of worn souls,
That, built with words, sways in the darkening room,
Sways, but stands firm, buttressed with many tears
Unshed.

But there is laughter over the way.
A blonde girl leaning to her lover's arms
Backward glances through dishevelled hair,
Sighing love's tremulous sighs, commingled with
Tears for uneasy days and treacherous nights.
Her fingers falter as his fingers glide
In feigned indifference to explore her throat—
And she smiles, until too aptly curious he
Stirs louder laughter in her sleepy veins,
Whose throbbing warns her of submission and
Ensuing sneers of a less credulous world.

Through the close-woven evening urban air
The shrill cacophony of her pursuit
Pierces. Then there is silence and I turn
From that inscrutable shut door, that hides
The strange enactment of a guessed-at love,
To watch, fearfully, the other guests depart,
Who leave me lonely, an unwilling lover.

Re-crossing the Bridge Alone.

The wistful music of departure floats
In opalescent seas—
A fugue of ghostly trees
Responding to wan lights of lifeless boats,
Shimmering mutely in a lustrous stream.

Where she has gone to does not matter much—
The leafless branches dip
Griefgentle hands to touch
Reflexions—soon, of course, she'll come again,
Shadowy footsteps echoing in a dream.

A tree, one taller than the others, lifts
A beckoning fingertip ;
But she has gone, a ship
Without a wake, that like a sad cloud drifts
Through opalescent seas and leaves no stain.

———

Antithesis.

Dark streets with bloodshot eyes
Run to a river of fire—
Strings of a passionate lyre,
Where curious fingers wandering, in surprise
Wake melodies to glut the soul's desire.

A sailor he, or monster from the sea
With stars spilt from the necklace of the moon,
Caught in his seaweed-tangled hair ; and she
A dockside whore, or shrine of chastity
Whose white flame gutters in life's dark lagoon.

With drunken hands he fumbles at her dress,
Wrackclouded foam of separating waves
That dims his sight : she bends to his caress
Lips pale with sale of kisses ; mute with stress
Of chanting requiems at lovers' graves.

Fearing his arms she draws the tattered blind—
Black veil, with whitebranched coral damascened,
Between the fact and seeming intervened—
And smiles her hate, loathing the rough limbs twined,
A sinuous shroud about a corpse demeaned.

Satiety by lust in crumpled sheets
She sleeps—pale priestess by illicit throes
Of passion shamed. Her hair's stream greedily flows
To lick death-pallid breasts, whose lipless teats
Burn like the fallen petals of a rose.

Dark streets with bloodshot eyes
Run to a river of fire—
Strings of a passionate lyre
Where curious fingers wandering, in surprise
Wake melodies to glut the soul's desire.

October.

Like an old woman, very tired, you smile
Sad month, and all the while
Minutes and weary leaves fall from Time's tree.

I shall not hear again the moan of ships,
At night mist-bound upon a moonless sea,
Nor feel the slow tide's lips
Lazily wandering to kiss my feet
At night.

No one moves in the street,
No one stirs in the woods, and by the sea
Only dead boats are waiting for the dawn.

Now mistresses forlorn
Mourn in deserted squares for lovers dead,
And tears are shed
By fountains buried under fallen leaves
For languid hours that will not come again.

The sun's pale leper in a grey bed grieves
In sullen anger at the world's dull pain—
And we cannot go out
Without galoshes and an overcoat
Because of the rain.

THE CALENDAR

O mist of sadness stretching to the sea,
And silences of sorrow in the street,
And smoke of burning leaves !

There is no longer splendour at mid-day !
But suns, like moons that wander out at noon—
Pale whores awake too soon—
Wearily sway
To slow, embittered rhythms of disgust
That low winds play
On rusty strings of desiccated trees.

O golden, withered leaves, and empty seas,
And wasted hours !

Introspective Filigree.

My soul is the white stone where water drips
From old impassive fountains of the mind.
There languid women stoop lascivious lips
Smiling, and in the mute reflection find
Bones of dead lovers.

A flute of constancy slips amber notes
Between the folds of interwoven sighs :
And in the limpid fountain-water floats
Ophelia's ghost, staring up with sweet eyes
At Hamlet her lover.

Unheeded patience of concentric waves
Shiver their suave circumference at the brim.
The mirror trembles ; and the white soul craves
Strange limbless fishes with bright scales, and dim
Retreats of still shadow.

Where moonlight silvers twisting shapes of girls
The sun has snored upon a golden bed.
Music of dripping water strings sleek pearls
With crashing splendour of emeralds on a thread
Of tremulous anguish.

Sleep rustles irridescent furious wings
In the white flame of glacial cascades—
Sad moth, whose dirge a sorrowing swan sings
Dying, while sound dies and radiance fades
Like dreams of young lovers.

Sonnet.

If I were dead still Love would follow me
Into the grave, and quarrel for my flesh
With worms, peer in my lustreless eyes and see
Herself mirrored there, smile, and start afresh
To woo me. Love would lay her lips on mine
And find the stench of my decay still sweet,
My bones soft to her breast ; and she would twine
Gaily fairest flowers for my winding-sheet.

But Love dead, her ghost would unceasingly
Haunt the paths of my life and anger me :
So in this intermission between tombs
Where the soul, dazed with woken dreaming lingers,
Love's phœnix bird is dearer with her plumes
Of fire, than ashes drifting through my fingers.

Beggars and Brigands.

By STELLA BENSON.

WE Europeans are always busy trying to reform established facts by quoting proverbs and the classics at them—like saying Avaunt to a ghost. " Honesty is the best policy," we say, splashed as our honest waistcoats are with mud from the wheels of the Rolls Royces in which the successfully slick go by. " Beauty is only skin deep," we teach the plain pig-tailed daughters of fathers who are away taking lovely ladies to Brighton. " You can't keep a good man down," we good men say to one another as we sell matches side by side in the gutter. " Kind hearts are more than coronets," is our reply to dinner invitations we don't get. The bottom is knocked out of most of our morality—and yet we pretend our morality still holds water. Ours is a shut-eye culture.

But the Chinese—whom we sometimes call " mystic "—are much more prosaic. In China nobody would pretend for a moment that honesty was the best policy—indeed it does not rank as a practical policy at all. In China there is no choice—no coy pretence of virtuous choice between two masters ; those who serve Mammon become governor-generals, and those who don't remain coolies. But only the half-witted would deliberately choose not to. It is no use telling a beggar or a brigand that honesty is the best policy if begging or the possession of a rifle has put three thousand dollars in the bank for him. Which of us would trouble to water the city streets with the sweat of our honest brows if, by tying a piece of raw meat round our calves to represent an open sore, we could earn a handsome fee at every door in our suburb ?

Begging and brigandage pay so well in China that I often wonder why everyone does not embrace one profession or the other. Of course, they require different temperaments ; the artist nature should devote itself to begging, and persons of a tougher fibre should tread the easy path of brigandage. Recruits to brigandage, I suppose, are limited by the fact that there are not quite enough rifles to go round, though this difficulty will soon be removed by enterprising war-lords. And as for beggars—every time I see a beggar I realise that not everyone could bring that rich and dramatic art to perfection. To be a beggar you have to possess individuality and the rare power of arresting attention. The small town of Mengtsz can show four distinct styles in beggars. There is the large, insolent young beggar who carries on his back an unhappy old woman, theoretically, but not actually, his mother, and expects to be paid for this exhibition of filial devotion. There is the passive beggar who, with areas of raw meat skilfully half-displayed through exiguous rags, stands mutely shivering at doors until kind housewives fill his bowl. There is the blind— or theoretically blind—musician, hardly, perhaps, to be classed as a beggar. Sawing an interminable series of plaintive notes out of a one-stringed fiddle and dressed always in a neat blue robe, he walks briskly along, cocking his eyes at the sky, and is from time to time jerked out of the jaws of danger by a little attendant boy. And there is the beggar who sits on the ground with one of his legs hooked round the back of his neck, sobbing out a hysterical confusion of words and frightful hiccoughs of agony. The strange position of the leg is for some reason supposed to represent incurable paralysis. All these beggars, I am told by those who know, are wealthy capitalists and live in luxury. I saw a group of them coming out from a feast which some inane philanthropist had provided for them. They walked out upright, joking and rubbing their stomachs, but when they saw us they all collapsed in the street and began shuffling along on their sit-upons, using their arms as crutches—the usual beggar method of progress— and they all began practising the different varieties of their art for our benefit. Certainly, if you have the temperament for it, the vocation of beggary should be seriously considered. But it needs genius. Money earned in this way is not everybody's money.

No, I will be a brigand when I take out my Chinese naturalisation papers. I shall play Ma-Jongg in mountain caves, wear jade bangles and rich silk turbans, clatter through respectful villages on horseback to the stirring sound of gongs and rifle fire—and end up a war lord.

THE CALENDAR

Even a quite ordinary brigand, a beginner, the equivalent, say, of an O.B.E., can afford to smile at governors and magistrates, who—even in China—are paid to pretend that honesty is the best policy. For instance, we are contemplating a trip to a cave some fifteen miles from here. The Chinese district superintendent will not let us go without an escort of eighty soldiers at fifty cents a day per man. But we are advised by a good authority that a tactful gift of a bottle of champagne or a roll of silk to the brigand chieftain who has his headquarters in the cave in question would be a safer protection than all the soldiers in Mengtsz. The chieftain, thus wooed, would, we are assured, entertain us hospitably in his cave. I daresay he would enroll us in his band. Or perhaps the premium for membership would be rather high. A second bottle of champagne—a cigar. We brigands are a kindly, easily-pleased lot, as long as you don't quote proverbs at us.

The Reminiscences of Mme. F. M. Dostoevsky.

TRANSLATED FROM THE RUSSIAN BY S. S. KOTELIANSKY.

These reminiscences are translated from the rough drafts of Mme. Dostoevsky's manuscripts which found their way to the Caucasus during the Civil War in Russia. The Archives of Georgia (Caucasus) managed to get hold of all Mme. Dostoevsky's manuscripts in August, 1922, and handed them over to the Moscow Central Archives.

The manuscript consists of over thirty separate notebooks of different sizes and served Mme. Dostoevsky as the basis for the final and polished text of her Reminiscences now kept in the Moscow Historical Museum.

THE EVE OF MY ACQUAINTANCE WITH F. M. DOSTOEVSKY.

ON the third of October, 1866, about seven o'clock in the evening, I arrived at the Sixth Grammar School (by the Tchernyshev Bridge) to attend Professor P. M. Olkhin's shorthand class. The lesson had not yet begun. I sat down in my usual seat, and had just started arranging my exercise books, when our professor came up, sat down on the bench near me, and said : " Would you like to undertake some short-hand work ? I have been asked to find a shorthand writer, and it occurred to me that you might like to take on the work." I answered him that I was longing to find work, but doubted if I knew shorthand well enough to undertake any responsible work. Mr. Olkhin said that the work in question would not need greater speed than I possessed (100 words a minute), and that he was sure that I should be able to manage it satis-factorily. Then I asked who was to give me the work. "Dostoevsky, the author. He is now writing a new novel and wants to write it with the help of shorthand. Dostoevsky thinks that the novel will contain about seven folios of large

size, and he offers fifty roubles for the work." On my expressing my consent, Mr. Olkhin gave me a folded piece of paper
on which was written Dostoevsky's address, and said to me :
" I'll ask you to be at Dostoevsky's to-morrow at half-past
eleven sharp, not earlier and not later. This is how he put
it to me to-day. I am only afraid that you won't make
friends with him : he is such a gloomy, stern man." I gave an
involuntary smile, and said to Mr. Olkhin : " But why should
we be friends ? I'll try to do my work as well as I can.
Dostoevsky, the writer, I respect so much that I am even
afraid of him, and this somewhat frightens me."

Mr. Olkhin looked at his watch, went to the chair and began
his lecture. I must confess that this time his lecture was
wasted on me. My thoughts were occupied with the conversation that had just taken place, and I was filled with happy
thoughts. My cherished dream was to be realised : I had
got work. If Olkhin, so strict and exacting, found that I knew
shorthand, and wrote quickly enough then it must, indeed,
be so ; otherwise he would not offer me the work. Olkhin's
recognition of the progress I had made delighted me and
raised me in my own eyes. I think that to everyone the first
independent work in any branch whatever must have a great,
perhaps even an exaggerated importance. Of such importance
was to me, too, my first work. I felt as if I were advancing
along a new road, that I could earn money with my own labour,
that I was becoming quite independent ; and the idea of
independence to me, a girl of the sixties, was the dearest
of all. But still more pleasant and important than the work
itself was the chance of working with Dostoevsky, of getting
to know the writer personally. Indeed, he was my father's
favourite author, and the name of Dostoevsky had been
familiar to me from my childhood. I myself was enraptured
by his works and had cried over *Memoirs from the Dead House.*
And, all at once, the happiness, the luck—not only of making
the acquaintance of the famous novelist, but of actually helping
him with his work ! My agitation was intense, I wished to
share my joy with someone. I could not help telling it all
to my colleague, Alexandra Ivanovna I., who had just come
into the class room. She was much older than myself, quite
clever, extraordinarily bold, sharp-tongued and very capable,

but she often missed her lessons. Hearing of the work offered to me, she was a bit shocked that Olkhin had offered it to me and not to her, for she considered herself the best pupil. She congratulated me on the commencement of my shorthand career, and began asking me questions ; but I did not answer them, for I knew that Olkhin did not like the students to talk during the lessons. But when the lesson was over, Mlle. I. had her curiosity satisfied. . . . I walked with her as far as her house, and then took the coach, and in half-an-hour's time I was at home. I told my mother all the particulars, and she, too, was very glad : we talked for a long time of my luck. From joy and excitement I scarcely slept the whole night, picturing Dostoevsky to myself. Considering him a contemporary of my father, I imagined him as a quite elderly man; now I imagined him as a stout and bald-headed old man ; now as tall and awfully thin, but always stern and gloomy, as Olkhin had described him. Above all I was agitated as to what I should say to him. He seemed to me so learned, so wise, that I trembled beforehand for every word I might say. I was also upset by the idea that I did not clearly remember the Christian names and surnames of his characters, and I felt sure that he was bound to talk of them. Never having met authors in my circle I imagined them as different beings, who had to be spoken to in quite a special way. Recalling to my mind those days, I see what a child I was then, in spite of my " respectable " twenty years.

My First Meeting with F. M. Dostoevsky.

On October 4, the momentous day of m, first meeting with my future husband, I awoke cheerfully, happy and excited by the idea that to-day my long cherished dream was to be realised : from a school girl and undergraduate I was to become an independent worker in the field chosen by myself.

I left the house a little earlier so as to call at the Gostiny Dvor to get a fresh supply of pencils and to buy a little portfolio, which, in my opinion, would give my youthful appearance a more businesslike look. By 11 o'clock I completed my purchases, and in order to get to Dostoevsky's at the appointed time, "neither earlier nor later,"* I walked with slow steps along the Bolshaya Meschanskaya and Stoliarny Pereulok, continuously consulting my watch. At twenty-five past eleven I came up to the house, and asked the concierge, who stood at the gate, where flat No. 13 was. He pointed to the right, where, by the very gates, was an entrance to a staircase. The house was a large one, with a great number of small flats, inhabited by small shopkeepers and artisans. It at once reminded me of the house in *Crime and Punishment* in which Raskolnikov, the hero of the novel, lived. Flat No. 13 was on the third floor, reached by an ugly staircase, from which at that moment were coming down two or three men of a rather suspicious appearance. I rang the bell, and immediately the door was opened by a middle-aged woman, with a green, checkered shawl thrown over her shoulders. I had read *Crime and Punishment* recently and well remembered the Marmeladovs' checkered " family " shawl, so that the identical shawl of Dostoevsky's servant involuntarily struck my eyes. To her question whom I wanted to see, I said that I came from Mr. Olkhin and that her master knew that I was coming.

I had not yet had time to undo my scarf when the door into the hall opened wide, and in the background of a bright sun-lit room there appeared a young man, quite dark, with dishevelled hair, with an open chest and in slippers. On seeing an unfamiliar face he cried out, and instantly disappeared behind a side door. The woman asked me into a room, which was the dining-room. It was quite modestly furnished ; near the walls stood two large trunks covered with carpets. A chest of drawers stood by the window and was covered with a white, knitted cloth. Along the wall stood a sofa and over it a clock. I felt great relief when at that moment I saw the clock showing half-past eleven. The woman asked me to take a seat, saying that her master would come in presently. Indeed, in a couple of minutes Dostoevsky appeared and asked me to come into his study on the right, and himself went out, as it turned out later, to order tea.

---

* This was Dostoevsky's usual expression. In order not to lose time in waiting for someone he would fix the exact time, always adding "neither earlier, nor later."—A.G.D.

REMINISCENCES OF MME. F. M. DOSTOEVSKY

Dostoevsky's study was a large room with two windows, which was very bright that day, but at other times it produced a gloomy impression : it was rather dark and still ; one felt oppressed by that strange stillness. In a far corner of the room stood a couch, covered with a brown cloth, rather worn, and in front of it was a round table covered with a red cloth ; on the table stood a lamp and a couple of albums, and round it were easy chairs and stools. Over the couch in a walnut frame hung a portrait of a very thin lady, in a black dress and a black bonnet. " This is probably his wife," I thought, as I did not know anything about his family life. Between the windows was a large mirror in a black walnut frame. As the space between the windows was much wider than the mirror, the latter was nearer to the right window, which was unsymmetrical and ugly. Two large Chinese vases of a beautiful shape stood on the window sills. Along the wall was a large divan of green morocco leather and near it a little table with a jug of water. Against the back wall, across the room, stood a writing table, at which I always sat afterwards when Dostoevsky dictated to me. The furniture was most ordinary, similar to what I had seen in the houses of not too prosperous people. I sat and listened, thinking that I should presently hear the voices of children, or the noise of a child's drum, or that the door would open and there would come into the study the unusually thin lady whose portrait I had just recently been examining.

Mr. Dostoevsky came in. To start a conversation he asked me how long I had been working at shorthand. I replied that I had been learning it for the last six months. " Has your teacher, Olkhin, many pupils ? " he asked. " At first there came over one hundred and fifty applicants, but there remain now only about twenty-five." " But why so few ? " he asked. " Many of them thought that it was quite easy to learn shorthand, but when they saw that it could not be done in a few weeks they gave it up," I said. " With us," he said, " it is always like that in every new thing : many start ardently, but cool down quickly and give it up. They see that application is needed, and who wants to work now ? "

Dostoevsky seemed strange to me.

At the first glance he looks rather old, but presently one

can see that he is not more than thirty-seven. He is of middle height, erect. His face is worn, sickly. Bright brown, even slightly reddish hair, well greased and strangely smoothed. His eyes fail to match.* One is an ordinary brown eye, the pupil of the other is very much dilated, and the iris cannot be seen. This dissimilarity gives his face a mysterious expression. Dostoevsky's face appeared very familiar to me, probably because I had seen his portraits before. Dostoevsky was dressed in a rather old, blue jacket, but his shirt was snow-white. To tell the truth, at first sight I did not at all like Dostoevsky.

Five minutes after my arrival the woman came in and brought two glasses of very strong, almost black tea. On the tray were two rolls. I took a glass, and although I did not want tea, and even felt hot, I began drinking it so as not to make a fuss. I was sitting by the wall at the little table near the writing desk ; and Dostoevsky was now sitting at his table, now pacing the room, smoking all the time, frequently putting down his cigarette and starting a fresh one. He offered me a cigarette. I refused it. " Perhaps you refuse out of politeness ? " he asked me. I said that I did not smoke, and did not like to see women smoking. A conversation by fits and starts began, and Dostoevsky kept on turning from one subject to another. The longer it went on the stranger Dostoevsky seemed to me : crushed, exhausted, ill. It also appeared strange to me that almost at once he declared that he was ill, that he had epilepsy. Of the work to be done Dostoevsky spoke vaguely. " We shall see how to do it ; we shall try ; we shall see if we can manage it." It seemed to me that our working together would hardly come off. It even occurred to me that Dostoevsky doubted the possibility and convenience of that way of working, and was perhaps going to give it up. To help him out I said : " Well, let us try ; but if you find it inconvenient, tell me frankly then. Rest assured I shall not regard it as a grievance if our work does not come off." Dostoevsky asked my name. I told him ; but he forgot it immediately, and asked me again.

---

* During one of his epileptic fits he fell down and stumbled on a sharp object, and so injured his right eye. Professor Yunge who treated him prescribed atropine, owing to which the pupil of his eye was dilated.—A.G.D.

REMINISCENCES OF MME. F. M. DOSTOEVSKY

The time was passing in conversation. Finally, Dostoevsky dictated to me from the *Russky Vestnik* and asked me to copy my shorthand into ordinary writing. He began dictating very rapidly, but I stopped him, and asked him to dictate with the speed of ordinary conversational speech. Then I began translating my shorthand into ordinary writing, and I did it rather quickly ; but Dostoevsky hurried me all the while and was surprised that I copied out so slowly. I observed to him that as I should be making the copy at home, not here, it ought not to matter to him how long the work took me. Looking through my copy Dostoevsky found that I had omitted a full stop and the hard sign in one word, and he remarked on it sharply. Altogether he was strange : either somewhat rude, or evidently too frank and outspoken. He was evidently too irritable and could not collect his thoughts. Several times he would ask me something, and then he would pace the room, pace it for quite a long time as though forgetting my presence ; and I sat without stirring, afraid to disturb his train of thought. At last Dostoevsky said that he could not possibly dictate to me then, but if I could come to him that evening at eight o'clock he would then start on his novel. Although it was very inconvenient for me to come the second time, I promised to come, as I did not wish to put off the work. When I was leaving Dostoevsky said : " You know I was rather glad when Olkhin proposed sending me a girl shorthand writer, and not a man. You are probably surprised, perhaps it seems strange to you ; you may ask why." " Why, then ? " I asked. " For this reason, that a man is sure to have a drinking bout, and you, I hope, will not." The idea of me " having a drinking bout " seemed to me so funny that I burst out laughing, and said : " Most certainly I shall not, you may be sure."

When I left Dostoevsky I was in a very depressed mood. I did not take to him, and he left a painful impression on me ; it also seemed to me that we should not be able to work together and that my ideas of independence would come to nothing. This was the more painful to me because last night my mother and myself were so delighted at the starting of my new career. It was about two o'clock when I left Dostoevsky. It was too far away to go home, and I decided to call on my relations, the Snitkins, who lived in the Fonarny Pereulok, to have dinner there, and to return to Dostoevsky in the evening. Besides, as I was young, I wanted to boast to my relations that I was already beginning " to earn a living." More than once they let drop a hint that " it was easy for me with my mother behind me, that it was time I did something." But when I began learning shorthand they made fun of my " art," and said that I was only wasting my time. My relations were intrigued by my new acquaintance, and began asking me about Dostoevsky. The time passed quickly by, and by eight o'clock I was at Alonkin House. It was very unpleasant for me to enter that house : there were so many people there in the street and near the gate, and all of them such common people. The door was opened by Fedosya (she was quite pleased when, leaving in the afternoon, I gave her 20 copecks), and she went to announce me to Dostoevsky. I waited a few minutes in the dining-room, then entered the study and, after exchanging greetings with Dostoevsky, I took the same seat as in the morning, at the little table by the wall. Dostoevsky proposed that I should sit at his table, assuring me that it would be more convenient for me to work there. I must say that I felt highly flattered by his suggestion that I should sit at the table at which had been written such talented work as his recent novel *Crime and Punishment*. We changed seats, and began talking. Dostoevsky asked me again my name, and my father's name, and inquired if I was a relation of the gifted young writer Snitkin who had died recently. Dostoevsky made further inquiries about my family, of whom it consisted, where I had studied, what had made me learn shorthand, etc., etc., and why had my studies been so successful. In answer to his questions I had to tell him many particulars of which I shall speak later on in my story.

I told Dostoevsky that my father was a civil servant who had died in the spring. My mother was alive ; my sister was married to G. Svatkovsky, the censor, and my brother studied at the Petrovsky Agricultural College. I had finished my studies at the Grammar School with honours, and had been awarded a large silver medal. Then I had entered the Teachers' Classes, only just founded by Prince Peter Oldenburgsky. There I had no luck ; I took up natural science, but my heart was with literature, and during the hours when according to the professor I had to make chemical experiments in crystallising salts, I was so much absorbed in reading my favourite authors (and above all, by the novels of Dostoevsky, which fact, of course, I did not mention to him) that all my tubes and retorts, left unattended, burst, and I myself became the laughing stock of my sweet colleagues. And when at the lecture of Professor Brandt I saw the dissection of a dead cat, I felt sick with disgust, and decided that a scientific career did not suit me. I left the classes for good.

To Dostoevsky's question what made me take up shorthand, I answered that my family was well-off, and that there was no need for me to earn my living. But, like most of the younger generation, I set a great value on complete independence, which could only be achieved by those who have work to do which compels them to rely on their own efforts. Dostoevsky said, seeing that Olkhin had selected me from all his pupils, I must possess brilliant ability if I was the only one quite prepared for that work. I said it was not a question of brilliant ability, that my success in shorthand was due to a special reason. Dostoevsky wished to know what that reason was, and I had to tell him. The courses commenced in the beginning of April, 1866. I immediately started on them, but after five lessons I was in complete despair : shorthand appeared to me a regular abracadabra, which I could not grasp, so obscure and unintelligible it seemed. I wanted to leave the classes, but my father, whose days were numbered, persuaded me to give up the idea. He assured me that if I worked hard I should overcome the difficulties. And his words indeed came true.

On April 28, 1866, my father died, and I was terribly upset by his death. It was the first real sorrow of my life ! I was distressed, I cried, and could find no peace. My mother, to distract my thoughts from this great calamity, advised me to work, to stick to my shorthand. I wanted so much to justify my father's belief in my abilities, so I made up my mind to work hard and to achieve my purpose of becoming an efficient shorthand writer. The kind Olkhin came then to my assistance. Learning of my desire to work hard at shorthand, he suggested, for the sake of practice, that I should copy pages of a certain book in shorthand and send him my exercises by post. He corrected them, sent them back to me ; I learnt by my mistakes, and, of course, avoided making similar ones in my further work. The shorthand correspondence with Olkhin made it possible for me to make progress in the practice of shorthand, and a daily two hours dictation helped me to achieve a speed of 100 words a minute. When in the beginning of September Olkhin's lectures commenced, it was found that the great majority of the pupils, over three-fourths, had given up shorthand altogether ; the rest did almost no work during the summer months ; so that it turned out that I was the only one quite prepared for independent work.

To all questions put by Dostoevsky I answered simply and seriously. On the whole, I behaved seriously, almost sternly, as Dostoevsky told me later on. I had made up my mind beforehand that if I had to work for private people I would establish my relations to them on a serious footing, avoiding any familiarity, so as no one should dare to address to me an unnecessary word, or to make a joke. It seemed to me that such behaviour on my part would be the best : for surely my object was to work, and not to make acquaintances ; why then take part in trifling conversations ? It would be much more becoming to behave strictly. Dostoevsky told me later on that he had been pleasantly struck by me : I was so young and yet behaved so well. No one who talked to me would think of using an unnecessary word—such an effect would my reserved manner produce. I believe I did not laugh once as I talked to Dostoevsky. He told me afterwards that my capacity for establishing my relations with people on a cold, respectful footing had pleased him very much. He had been used to meeting many nihilist women and to seeing their behaviour, and had expected the girl recommended to him to be like them ; therefore he was pleased to find in me the complete opposite of the prevalent type of young girls of that time.

During our conversation Fedosya prepared the tea in the dining-room and brought us two glasses and two rolls ; also a lemon. Dostoevsky asked me again if I wanted to smoke. Then he went to the window and took two pears from a paper bag and gave me one. Being used at home to good manners, such lack of ceremony on the part of a man who scarcely knew me appeared somewhat strange to me. But Dostoevsky offered the pear so good-naturedly that the lack of ceremony pleased me ; I took the pear and ate it then and there with my young teeth, which needed no artificial appliances.

We went on talking, and, owing to his sincere and good-natured tone, it suddenly seemed to me that I had known him for such a long time, and I felt at ease and happy.

For some reason our conversation turned on the Petrashev-sky revolutionary group and on capital punishment, and Dostoevsky told me that when he was standing on the Semionov Drill Ground among the others sentenced to death he knew, by the preparations which were going on, that he had only five minutes left to live. But it seemed to him that his life would last not five minutes, but five years, five centuries. White death shirts were put on them. The group was divided into batches, three men in a batch. Dostoevsky was in the second batch. The first three men had already been conducted to the pillar and tied to it. In a minute they would be shot, and then would come his turn. Oh, Lord, how much he wanted to live ! How sweet life seemed to him—what a lot of good he could do ! He remembered then his whole past life, the not at all good use he had made of it, and he wished so strongly to try again, and so strongly did he wish to live, to live long, long. But suddenly the retreat was sounded, and he felt cheered up. The first three were untied from the pillar and led back ; and a new sentence was read. Dostoevsky was sentenced to four years' hard labour in the Omsk Fortress. He was happier that day than he had ever been before. He paced his cell all day long (in the Alexeyev Ravelin of the Peter and Paul Fortress), singing all the time, singing loudly, so happy was he at the life given back to him. Then his brother was admitted to see him before his deportation, and on Christmas Eve he was despatched into that remote region. Dostoevsky told me that he had in his possession the letter* written by him to his brother Michael on the day the sentence was pronounced ; that he had recently recovered it from his cousin. Dostoevsky told me a great many things that evening,

* The letter here referred to has been published in the book "Dostoevsky : Letters and Reminiscences." (Chatto & Windus.) Translated by S. S. Koteliansky and J. M. Murry.

and I was extremely struck by the fact that he was so deeply and sincerely frank with me, a young girl whom he had seen to-day for the first time in his life, and whom he did not know at all. He seemed so reserved and stern, and yet he was telling me so much and giving me so many details, all so frankly and sincerely, that I could not help being surprised. Only later on, when I got to know him, as well as his family relations, more closely, I understood the reason of his frankness and confidence. Dostoevsky was at that time spiritually lonely and he felt too acutely the need of sharing his thoughts and feelings perhaps even with perfect strangers so long as they were not hostile to him, and so long as he could discover in them a sincere and attentive attitude towards him. As for myself, his frankness and confidence pleased me very much, and left a wonderful impression on me.

I was a bit uneasy and annoyed that he did not begin dictating to me. It was getting late, and I had to go home. I had not seen my mother since early morning. I had promised her to come home after my morning interview with Dostoevsky, and now I was afraid that she might worry. I had no wish to spend the night at the Snitkins house. It would have been awkward to tell this to Dostoevsky, but, to my great pleasure, he himself said he was going to begin dictating. He started pacing the room with long strides, from the fireplace to the door, and every time he reached the fireplace he invariably knocked twice on it. He was smoking cigarettes all the while, taking a fresh one and throwing the unfinished one in the ash tray on the desk. After he had dictated to me for some time he asked me to read to him what I had written, and at the very first sentences he stopped me. " From Roulettenburg ? Did I say Roulettenburg ? " he asked. " You dictated that name," I answered. " Impossible ! " " But is there a city of that name in your novel ? " I asked. " The action takes place in a city where there is a casino, which I must have called Roulettenburg," he replied. " If there is such a place you must have dictated its name, otherwise how could I have known it ? This geographical term is perfectly new to me," I said. " You are quite right," Dostoevsky admitted. " I must have muddled things up." I must say I was a bit put out, thinking that I had made some mistake. But I was glad that the misunderstanding was cleared up. Dostoevsky was evidently absorbed in thought and troubled, or perhaps he was too tired.

Then Dostoevsky said that he could not dictate any more, and asked me to copy out what I had got down in shorthand, and to bring it with me to-morrow at twelve. I promised to do so without fail. It struck eleven, and I said that I must go home. Dostoevsky asked me where I lived. Learning that I lived in the Peski suburb, he said that he had never in his life been in that district, and did not know where it was. But if it was far he would send his servant with me. As it was far away and D. insisted that the woman should see me home, I had to say that I was going to spend the night with some relations who lived quite close to him. Dostoevsky saw me to the hall, and called the servant to light me down the stairs. As Fedosya and I were going downstairs I asked her what was her master's patronymic. I knew, from his novels, that his Christian name was Fiodor, but I did not know his father's name.

In the Stoliarny Lane it was quite noisy : drunken people were coming out from the public-house ; and I felt alarmed. Happily I soon came across a cabman and he agreed to take me home for 40 copecks. I urged him to drive quickly, and as he turned out to be a good-natured old fellow we began talking, just to kill the time, and he told me all about his village. At last I reached home. I had to wait a long time till the concierge woke my people. My mother had thought that I was going to spend the night at the Snitkins', and she had told the servant to bolt the door and to go to bed. I gave mother a full account of my day, and told her with rapture of how Dostoevsky was frank and nice. But not to grieve mother I did not tell her of the painful impression I have taken away with me—an impression more unpleasant than any I had hitherto experienced—and this despite the interesting way in which the day had passed. And the impression was indeed painful : for the first time in my life I had seen a man unhappy, deserted and badly treated ; and a feeling of deep compassion and sympathy was born in my heart.

(To be continued).

Scrutinies

(4) Arnold Bennett.

By EDWIN MUIR.

THE three representative novelists of the age which ceased so suddenly and so completely with the beginning of the War were undoubtedly Mr. Wells, Mr. Galsworthy, and Mr. Bennett. Twelve years ago Mr. Bennett would have been generally considered the least conspicuous of the three ; to-day he is, on the whole, the most conspicuous. In a world alien to his way of thought he is respected ; and our respect for him is, perhaps, chiefly a tribute to his personality. For he has immense vitality ; he is never daunted ; he gives always, and takes delight in giving, a sense of capability. These are qualities which equally in a confident and optimistic era such as that which preceded the War, and in a doubting and pessimistic one such as we live in now, would be bound to be welcomed. They increase our sense of power if we feel strong, and temper our sense of impotence if we feel weak. They are biologically useful ; they inspire confidence. The question whether Mr. Bennett's vitality is the artist's vitality, his courage the artist's courage, and his competence the artist's competence, has been generally overlooked in the satisfaction which his positive qualities, artistic or not, have given us. Yet it is an important question. The competence of the practical man to deal with the section of life which his will encounters is something quite different from the competence of the artist to deal with experience imaginatively. To the man of action this practical competence is so real that its reality is nearly unconditional ; it is the ground, conscious and unconscious, of his actions ; it is axiomatic. To the artist, on the other hand, it is largely an illusion ; he sees that it is based on negative as well as on positive qualities ; that, for example, it implies a limitation of vision, useful biologically, but injurious to the artist ; that it starts with all the utilitarian illusions from which art alone, now that religion is in a state of suspended animation, can give us freedom. A book written by a man of practical capacity, if that capacity extends to the art of writing, will be always interesting. But its virtues will be the virtues of a practical personality, not those of art. Whether Mr. Bennett's novels belong to this category is the main critical question that can be asked concerning them. Provisionally let us hazard the judgment that he is a practical man who has chosen to express himself through the art of the novel; that he is an imaginative writer whose imagination is limited to such intuitions as can come to one who is determined to master the machinery of life rather than to see.

Take, for instance, Mr. Bennett's indomitable sense of his capability. It is disquieting that this is hardly to be paralleled in literature. Balzac, it is true, had some of it, but we recognise it in Balzac not as a virtue, but rather as a defect of his qualities, as his chief illusion about himself, the touch of vanity which falsifies his work. Now in Mr. Bennett this invariable competence to deal with all sorts of situations and all classes of experience on an excessive note of confidence is not a defect of his qualities; it is his characteristic quality. And we become conscious that this competence is simply the *savoir faire* of the practical man who *must* master the situation, and to do so must see no more in the situation than he can master, rather than the courage of the artist, who must see the situation in itself, whether it can be practically mastered or not. How clear and definite Mr. Bennett is when he is describing states of mind which his characters as successful people will remember later with profit; and how vague and incompetent when he writes about states of mind which will be of no conceivable utilitarian value to them ! As Hilda Lessways led Sarah Gailey home from the scene of the attempted suicide,

" She was not extremely surprised. But she was shocked into a most solemn awe as she pressed the arm of the poor tragic woman who, but for an accident, might have plunged off the end of the groin into water deep enough for drowning. She did really feel humble before this creature who had deliberately invited death; she in no way criticised her; she did not even presume to condescend towards the hasty clumsiness of Sarah Gailey's scheme to die. She was overwhelmed by the woman's utterly unconscious impressiveness, which exceeded that of a criminal reprieved on the scaffold, for the woman had dared an experience that only the fierce and sublime courage of desperation can affront. She had a feeling that she ought to apologise profoundly to Sarah Gailey for all that Sarah must have suffered."

This is admirable ; it describes the reaction of a practical young woman to an experience she has never encountered before. We see her cataloguing her sensations ; she will learn from them ; they will make her in some way more competent. But then follows her imaginative reaction :

" And as she heard the ceaseless, cruel play of the water amid the dark jungle of ironwork under the pier, and the soft creeping of the foam-curves behind, and the vague stirrings of the night-wind round about—these phenomena combined mysteriously with the immensity of the dome above and with the baffling strangeness of the town, and with the grandeur of the beaten woman by her side ; and communicated to Hilda a thrill that was divine in its unexampled poignancy."

The transition is astonishing. The situation passes from the intensely practical, where Mr. Bennett's mastery is complete, into the intensely human ; and at once his mastery falls from him ; he takes refuge in the vaguest of rhetoric. The moment which Hilda will remember all her life, when the sea, the sky, the city before her and the woman by her side, are changed, and become part of one universal experience—this moment Mr. Bennett cannot describe ; he can only make us feel that he is impressed by it, a little theatrically. He is vague here, as every practical man is when he is faced by something on which his will cannot operate.

The predominance of the practical in Mr. Bennett's novels is shown still more strikingly in their descriptive passages. There have been few writers who have described so fully as he, and yet have avoided describing visually. Conrad, perhaps an equal slave to description, used all his powers to make the scene visual ; Mr. Bennett uses his to tell us all about it. Conrad does sometimes make us see what he wishes us to see ; Mr. Bennett, at his best, describes something which, if we happened to see it, we should recognise. His directions are like those of a man in the street who tells us how many turns we must take to reach a certain place, and by what signs we may recognise a shop there which we wish to find. We should have to pass through a street under repair, and then he would proceed to say that the gas main had burst a week before, and dozens of windows had been smashed. But after passing the street we should come to a square, and he would say that one side of this square was blocked, and why, and soon we should be well into the middle of a history of the square. Nevertheless, we must ignore the square and turn to the left into a short narrow street, and the shop would be the fifth on our right ; there would be three stone steps leading down into it. All these things, because they had a bearing on practice, would interest our guide, and finally we should find the shop. And in Mr. Bennett's novels we always find the shop ; but we do not go into it to see it, but always for a different purpose, and the consequence is that we never see it, we only know what is in it. We begin to have a sense, perhaps, that here a whole drama of buying and selling, of tear and wear, of credit and cash, is being worked out, and as practical men we are thrilled. We feel at last that if we chose we could run the shop ; for the practical man likes to think there is nothing he cannot manage, and that is the secret of his curiosity about all practical undertakings, even when they are outside his scope.

Thus in Mr. Bennett's novels we are always brought back to the illusions of the practical man. The mass of machinery which keeps urban civilisation going, the means of transport, of profit, and of pleasure ; our chairs, our fireplaces, our baths ; the beds we sleep in and the bells we ring ; all these are of supreme interest to the practical man, because to him they are not merely pieces of dead convenience, but instruments upon which he impresses his power. They are of supreme interest, too, to Mr. Bennett. They are not merely the environment amid which his characters live ; they are the *media* through which his characters express themselves. They bring people together ; they become integral parts of friendship and of love. In this benevolent working of the mysteries of machinery Mr. Bennett finds a certain romance which to the less practically-minded will for ever seem a little naïve. A mechanical part of our environment, a telephone or a tramcar, heralds a love affair, or becomes part of one. Is it not marvellous ?

Mr. Bennett seems always to be saying; but we are never quite sure that it is marvellous. Hilda Lessways is about to meet Edwin Clayhanger after a long absence.

" When she was going down the stairs, she discovered that she held the *Signal* in her hand. She had no recollection of picking it up, and there was no object in taking it to the breakfast room ! She thought : ' What a state I must be in ! ' "

So a newspaper reveals Hilda's state of feeling, and so furniture, houses, property, clothes, express the minds, morals, and passions of Mr. Bennett's characters.

This mode of presentation is, of course, perfectly valid, for obviously the accessories of modern life are enormous in their sheer weight, and obviously they have become part of our expression as well as of our experience. But obviously, too, they are not such a great part of experience as Mr. Bennett implies. He tries to make his environments do too much ; he over-emphasises them, and gives them a false impressiveness—a sign, perhaps, that his conscience is not without a suspicion of guilt. In the unnecessary description of St. Andrew's Church in " Riceyman Steps "—unnecessary, for the church appears only to be described, and disappears after that—we can see Mr. Bennett's style in acute distress, becoming embarrassed, and sinking into journalese, in an attempt to conceal the fact that the church is really unimportant. He begins self-consciously : " St. Andrew's Church, of yellow bricks with freestone dressings, a blue slate roof, and a red coping, was designed and erected in the brilliant reign of William IV., whose Government, under Lord Grey, had a pious habit, since lost by governments, of building additional churches in populous parishes at its own expense. Unfortunately its taste in architecture was less laudable than its practical interest in the inculcation among the lowly of the Christian doctrine about the wisdom and propriety of turning the other cheek. St. Andrew's, of a considerably mixed Gothic character, had architecturally nothing whatever to recommend it. Its general proportions, its arched windows, its mullions, its finials, its crosses, its spire, and its buttresses, were all and in every detail utterly silly and offensive."

That, it must be admitted, is Mr. Bennett at his worst. Yet the emptiness and calculated verbosity of the second

sentence tell us a great deal about him ; they always appear
when the inspiration fails. They fall like a judgment on Mr.
Bennett when he is writing about the artistically irrelevant,
when he is padding. Perhaps it is an uneasy conscience which
makes him pad the style at the same time, and leads him into
the bad taste of periphrases like " in the inculcation among the
lowly of the Christian doctrine about."

There is more padding in Mr. Bennett's later novels than
in his earlier. The plots are constructed, one might almost
think, to make the padding necessary. In " Riceyman Steps,"
the hero is the owner of a second-hand bookshop ; he is also an
antiquarian interested in the streets and history of Clerken-
well ; and, in addition, he is a miser. In other words, his interest,
his passion, is for things, not for people. " Elsie and the Child "
shows us still more clearly the limitations of the practical and
capable view of life. What a mass of machinery, of hotels and
yachts, what a disproportionate interest by all the characters
in the furnishings of existence, what a poverty and difficulty
of human reaction amid this waste of machinery ! In perusing
Mr. Bennett's optimistic pages, a weariness of the spirit sometimes falls on one ; one is saddened by the pleasure which
these characters have in using that vast mass of machinery,
which to most is not a means of pleasure at all, but a bleak
necessity.

It is his delight in all the properties of modern life that
fixes for us Mr. Bennett's spiritual era. That era is Late Victorian ; it comprises the few decades which saw the complete
triumph of machinery and had not yet realised the barrenness
of that triumph. The fight against machinery, waged by
Carlyle, Ruskin, and Arnold, was over ; the time of weariness
in the midst of machinery had not come. Meanwhile, the
industrialisation of England had marvellously increased one
thing which, more than the growth of knowledge or the decay
of religion, was modifying everyday life : it had marvellously
increased property. Mr. Bennett would be inconceivable in an
age which did not believe religiously in property, either as a
thing bringing happiness, or as a thing which will bring happiness in the future, through a more equitable distribution of its
resources. He would be equally inconceivable in any age when
property was relatively scarce ; in England before the industrial

revolution. He is the representative of an era of almost universal and absolutely naïve optimism, which is now past. And more than any other writer of that era, he has its limitations and its simplicities. His work as a novelist is dated. But the qualities which make him an anomaly as an artist make him also a very interesting and original literary personality. He has brought into literature qualities which are seldom found there, qualities which perhaps should not be found there, but qualities which, nevertheless, are interesting as well as admirable. They marshal themselves into a unity, and we see behind them a character of weight and integrity, and of a thoroughness which once more takes us back to the happy times of Victoria. And it is perhaps the possession of this character, this personality, which makes Mr. Bennett so interesting to the present generation.

A Death.

By J. F. HOLMS.

AFTER the doctor had gone the pain in his head increased. If he asked again for morphia he would be able to sleep. But sleep meant, and for a week had meant, the possibility of not waking up. If he asked for morphia now he would have to prepare himself. The painful sweat gathered and broke out on his temples; it trickled into his left eye, and with a clumsy movement he turned his head and smeared it away on the pillow. He was more frightened this time than he had been before; for each successive agony of fear seemed in its turn the first he had suffered, inescapable as life; and the other times he had been afraid floated in his mind as memories of safety, passed now for ever, when he had been afraid, it is true, but afraid only in his imagination, afraid as a person in security may suddenly be afraid that he will some time have·to be afraid. As he lay his gaze rested on a naked branch that stirred beyond his window against the whitish sky. And, while he watched the branch, he sought again, as he had done before, since this was the position he customarily found least uncomfortable, to realise that it was he—he who had lived the forty years of which his memory told him, the forty years that had brought him to this moment in which he watched the branch moving outside the window— that it was he, his life, that within sight of that branch would soon end. But between him and the comprehension of his death he felt an obstacle which, as a fly on a window-pane, he could neither see nor penetrate, and in which seemed to him to lie the cause of his fear. Could he make his death real his fear would go. But, while he struggled to reach it, the thought of death eluded his grasp as a figure in a mirror. His death was without meaning to him. Only his fear of it, and that only while he felt it, was real. For each day resembled the last. Each day, when he awoke, the days that were past became indistinguishable in his memory, and it seemed to him that now for the first time he was face to face with his fear, as it had seemed to him on the day before. He was not ready yet ; another two or three days and what he felt must happen would happen, and his soul would open, the scales fall from his eyes, and fear from his heart. To-morrow was too near, almost to-day ; the day after to-morrow perhaps.

His agony subsided and the pain in his head absorbed his consciousness. He remembered himself walking, a little boy, along a country road on a hot summer afternoon. The white dust lay half-an-inch deep. The words *the Lady on the Ball* formed themselves in the air, and the smell of dust and crushed nettles filled the room. In the circus there had been a trick cyclist. The wheels of the bicycle rose and fell, bumping round the stage. If the pain in his head did not stop the fever would increase. He had heard the doctor tell the nurse that any rise of temperature was dangerous ; if necessary he was to be given morphia. But the doctor knew he was going to die. So did everybody. They knew that in two, three days, a week, he would be dead, and in his bed would be lying someone else, alive when he was dead. They knew it all the time they talked to him and washed him. They knew that they would have to die too some time, it didn't matter. And though they knew he was going to die in a week, they washed him and looked at him as if he were someone like themselves, who was going to die some time, it didn't matter. But he knew more than they. Some time didn't mean never. And when they looked at him he looked back accusingly, threateningly, as if he were God, to tell them that they must feel some time, not never, exactly what he was feeling now. But they looked in his eyes and their faces bore the same calm, solicitous and kindly expression. No one could have told that they knew that in two, three days, a week he would be dead and that in the bed from which they had lifted his body would be another patient, whom they would wash and look at and talk to with the same firm gestures and the same solicitous expression. With pain not their own, once seen, they could sympathise ; to-morrow or to-day one of them might have toothache. Pain was always present in their lives and his pain became in a way their pain. But death happened some time, never. His death they could see, but they could not feel. If they felt his death as he was feeling it, if only in the vague way they felt his pain as he was feeling it, they would feel their own death and could not bear to look at him. They knew that morphia dulled his pain, but they did not know what it was like to prefer torture to the possibility of dying before one was ready. He thought of his body lying in his bed after he had died ; he could see them straightening and pulling out his limbs. He supposed he was washed naked all over. He was a dark man, and the thought of others looking on his naked, flaccid and dead body filled him with disgust and nausea ; but the images formed in his mind and his fear was forgotten.

He determined to try to sleep without morphia. He tried to imagine himself a month ago, a normal, irritable man suffering from a severe headache. And to soothe the pain he tried to imagine a woman's hand stroking his forehead with a cool, regular and caressing touch. The hand moved gently and his breathing grew easier. That was enough ; he could sleep now. But the hand continued stroking his forehead. Each touch dragged and tore his nerves. He made a noise in his throat to attract the attention of the nurse. She came across the room and began to stroke his forehead. He recognised her at once. He had known for some time that Frances had come to the home as a nurse. She looked at him kindly and sadly, and, seeming not to notice his convulsed features, continued passing her hand from the centre of his forehead up towards the crown of his head with a slow, monotonous movement. Her eyes never left his, and, tortured with agony and hopeless lust, he felt her hand rubbing its way through flesh and skull, which peeled and shredded like blotting-paper under the friction of his wet forefinger on his desk at school. She stooped to kiss him, but the pain burnt in his grooved skull like white-hot iron, and, turning his head on the pillow, he saw the grey distempered wall and a white curtain moving. Someone had opened the window.

He touched the bell at his bedside and asked for morphia. The pain left him and the room began to grow dark. He could sleep now. But before he could sleep he remembered something he had to do at home. For years he had meant to do it, but he had kept putting it off from year to year till he had got used to the pain of knowing he had not done it, and to the shadowy, unreal and hopeless life caused by the know-ledge that the pain was there, even when he did not feel it, just as a man gets used to cancer. Of late years, in fact, he had almost ceased to feel the pain, and the knowledge that it was there had become as profound, familiar and little-considered a part of his life as the appearance of his own features or the sound of his wife's voice. His memories came thick and clear. After he had ceased to feel the pain at all at other times it had long persisted immediately on waking up in the morning. All the early years of his marriage he used to wake heavy with pain and fear. But that life and that pain, those mornings and the memory of them were so long past that they rose new before him as though he were reading a book. He could not remember when that part of his life came to an end, but at some time or other his life had become as he knew it now—or had known it a month ago. He had settled down, made money, and the quarrels with his wife had grown rarer and rarer till they too became first memories and were finally forgotten. The climbing anguish rose through his heart, but his soul felt free and light. He got out of bed and dressed himself, his gaze fixed on his moving hands that trembled slightly. He met no one as he went out. It was almost dark outside and the streets were wet. A long straight road led up hill to outlying suburbs. On each side were square houses, each in its garden. Though nearly dark there was no light visible in any house, nor had the street lamps been lit. Pavement, trees, the mould in the gardens, the bricks in the walls, the iron railings were soaked and rotten with soot. After he had walked for some time, at the corner of each side street he felt on his face a breath of cold air that smelt of rust and empty spaces. He was near the edge of the city now, and he turned to the right. He had some difficulty in finding the house he was looking for, into which he had not been for twenty years. Unlocking the side door he went in; he tried to lock it after him, but the key would not fit, so with difficulty he pushed the rusty bolt across and, suddenly convulsed with terror, shook the door softly to see if it would hold. It held, and not daring to shake harder, which he knew would start the socket, he turned and saw

through the small cobwebbed window that the moon had risen
and was shining on the figure of a policeman standing silent
and motionless among the garden trees, his round cheek
gleaming in the sad moonlight like wax.   Silently he turned
away, and, older than he had been as a child, recognised and
struggled with the fear that was beginning to stifle him.
He came to the large bedroom.   The red-shaded electric lamp
by the bedside burned dully, and getting into bed he settled
himself to read.   The light flickered, went out, flickered again ;
he tried quietly to screw the bulb more firmly into the socket,
but the glass crumpled stiffly under his hand like papier mâché.
A dull red glow, however, persisted.   It was nearly time now.
Slowly he forced his legs over the bedside.   Nothing moved,
and he strained his eyes to penetrate the gloom and to see
what he had come for.   The light began to burn brighter,
burnt white and strong, and he saw at his feet the white,
naked and waxen figure of a little boy, whose wide open eyes
stared at him with triumphant malice.   But now the malice
faded and in its stead dawned sweet shame, fear, and fawning
expectance.   The chains fell from his soul and limbs ; rage
streamed red-hot through him ; leaping out of bed he seized
the stiff small body, and, whirling it above his head, repeatedly
crashed its skull against the brass bed rail, which quivered
noiselessly at each blow.

His face and limbs distorted, he struggled up to consciousness.   Minutes passed of an extremity of fear that obliterated
thought and humanity.   Slowly the mist passed from his
eyes, beside him the night-light burned dim and steady, and
reality spread its long habit of safety solid around him.   Truth
and substance faded from his horror, withdrawn, laden with
a thousand memories, thither whence it had come, leaving its
empty recollection as a toy for thought.   I haven't had such
a nightmare since I was a child, he thought.   But beneath
the security that enfolded him grew an uneasiness that became
pain.   It slid into his consciousness, and reality, familiar,
permanent and secure, reminded him that he was going to
die.   His trapped soul turned in the net.   Whether awake or
asleep he had suffered that anguish of fear.   Even if he had
never felt that terror before and might never feel it again ; if
he lived and forgot it ; that he had felt it once meant that it

existed in the universe, that it existed and might exist again for him. Only in life could he be safe, and in a hundred hours or so he would die. " God help me, God help me ! " His features were hideous, but no tears came from his burning eyes. " Almighty God, let me live and not die! " But pang upon pang rose bursting through body and brain, lifting his stiffened body till he sat upright in bed, his arms, naked to the elbows, round which clung the crumpled sleeves of his pyjamas, stretched out before him rigid as crowbars. His eyes ceased to implore, and, seeming to grow larger, fixed on the wall opposite a look of blank and astonished anger. From his mouth gushed blood and a muffled clamour ; a nurse hurried in, and putting her arms, with their white starched cuffs, round his body, eased it carefully back on to the bed.

Poetry and the Absolute: the Case of Rimbaud.

By SAMUEL HOARE.

THE problem presented by Rimbaud's abandonment of poetry at the age of nineteen and his silence for the remaining eighteen years of his life has generally been considered rather in relation to the facts of his life than to the nature of his poetry. What manner of man he was appears clearly enough from his history—the successive dashes from his home in the Ardennes to Paris, the participation in the insurrection of the Commune, the roving partnership with Verlaine and the subsequent vagabondage through Europe, the long years as merchant, trader, gun-runner and explorer in Africa. The force, the hardness, the indomitable will and irreconcilable pride displayed at every stage of this history are invoked to explain the supreme renunciation of his career: when the ideals on which he has based the whole weight of his energies—the revolution of society, the inauguration of a new era of emancipation for humanity, and of a new poetry emancipated by *l'alchimie du verbe*—crumble successively beneath him, he has the strength to face his disillusionment, to turn his back for ever on all the objectives towards which his life has hitherto been directed, and withdraw, in a proud silence, from Europe and the literary scene. More precise enquirers have endeavoured to assign to some definite event in this history the function of a turning point—it has thus been suggested that his final abandonment of literature dates and originates from the rupture of his relations with Verlaine.

These explanations, so far as they go, contain some truth. The abandonment *is* in the nature of a disillusionment, there *is* here something like the failure of a strong man who still remains unbeaten.* And we must add, before leaving this aspect of the matter, that for us, surfeited with more questionable heroisms, there is something admirable in this thwarted career : the effort of Rimbaud remains heroic and Promethean, as he envisaged it himself. Here, as in his poetry, he is hard, diamond-like, flawless even : for about the violence of his most devastating gestures there remains always an essential nobility, and the harshest of his jeering cries are dignified by the accents of passion and of suffering.

But the real interest of the problem—an interest that remains unsatisfied by the theories summarily indicated above—is that we have here a unique case of a poet of the first order who ceases creative activity at the height of his creative power. Its analysis should throw some light on poetry in general and Rimbaud's poetry in particular, for it belongs rather to the field of psychology than to that of history. The enormous force and vitality of Rimbaud suggest that his career is less than anyone's to be explained in terms of the impact on him of external events, and the extraordinary prococity of his genius suggests that we have to deal with a character, an attitude to life, already fully formed, and little likely to be subject to a progression of enthusiasms and disillusionments. It seems more profitable therefore to disregard " the facts " altogether, to treat the question purely as one of literary psychology. On this basis we must take it that Rimbaud's abandonment of poetry was *inevitable*. We assume, just as the scientist assumes the uniformity of nature, a uniformity of Rimbaudian nature : the forces which produced the poetry must be those which have led to its abandonment ; the poetry itself involves the existence of what must render its production impossible. The subject of the investigation is not now the activity of the man but the nature of the poet's mind, and for the knowledge of this there is ample material in his works.

Rimbaud is a free spirit : an antinomian and a nihilist,

---

* On se demande souvent la raison pour laquelle Rimbaud quitta les lettres. Le doute est impossible. Seul, évité par la race de ceux-là même qui cherchent a réparer l'injustice et la recommencent envers d'autres, écœuré des cafés, trouvant que ce joli monde ne méritait pas son suicide et que le suicide était un peu ridicule, il choisit le seul dénouement possible.— Jean Cocteau : " Le Secret Professionel."

he denies everything. This attitude is generally taken to be common to all the poets termed *maudits*, including, for instance, Verlaine, who was, I think, the inventor of this description. But there is a great difference between the cold intellectual ferocity of Rimbaud's revolt and the naïf perversity, punctuated by bouts of self-commiseration, of Verlaine. Rimbaud's attitude is not, like Verlaine's, emotional in its origin ; it might rather be defined as an intuitive perception of the inadequacy, for any absolute purpose, of the structure of values on which civilisation is built. It is a fiercer, more militant form of the refusal of Ivan Karamazov, who wanted to hand God back the ticket. And it is not without significance that this spirit should enter European literature almost simultaneously in Dostoevsky's novel and in the poetry of Rimbaud, for it is an entirely modern discovery, the product of a new form of consciousness, as distinctive perhaps for its own period, which is still ours, as the eighteenth century rationalism of Voltaire or the sentimental humanitarianism of the early Romantics is for theirs. Generally it has been rather watered down and subjected to compromises—in Dostoevsky, for instance, it is put up for demolition (though against Ivan Karamazov and the magnificent fable of the Grand Inquisitor Father Zossima makes a poor showing). We find it again in Laforgue, here much diluted by irony and a self-conscious and amusing sentimentalism. In our own day it has had a remarkable flowering in the shape of Mr. James Joyce's " Ulysses." In Rimbaud it exists, one may say, in the pure state.

This has important consequences for his poetry : the world as well as the spirit of that poetry is nihilistic. The substance of this strange world is, indeed, identical with that of our familiar—all too familiar—universe, whose objects and ideas are rendered with an astonishing hardness and brilliance ; but their relations have been entirely revolutionised.

It may be said that the aim of all poetry is the establishment of relations. We live in a world whose phenomena are all tagged and labelled, ranged ready in categories in the mind ; disregarding the labels and contemplating the reality, the poet perceives relations between the labelled things ; by expressing these relations he makes us, who had hitherto been content to read the labels, aware of the realities which they represent. The nature of the relations perceived depends upon the poet's mental make-up; they form a system, and it is therefore justifiable to speak of the world or universe of the poet, an individual world, which these relations characterise. In its intervention between us and the world of actuality the mind of the poet is a prism distorting phenomena into forms of significance, but always in accordance with certain laws of refraction determined by its own structure. Now the peculiarity of the relations which Rimbaud establishes is that they have no finality and form no system. In this universe there are no laws ; nothing is imposed of necessity ; the relations to be established are limitless, and the poet's choice is free among an infinity of possibilities. It is, in fact, a universe in a state of chaos, over whose arrangements in patterns of an arbitrary and exquisite beauty the poet presides with the detachment of a god. Its elements are so denuded of reference to their functions in the actual world that they can be built like little coloured blocks into these strange mosaics ; curious transpositions are possible :

> *Une mosquée à la place d'une usine, une école de tambours faite par des anges, des calèches sur les routes du ciel ; un salon au fond d'un lac.*

The one fixed thing, the *point de repère* in this flux of interchangeable forms, is the poet himself. About the movements of his mind the world shapes itself like iron filings about a magnet. At the height that he has reached the only important fact about the universe is his contemplation of it. He exists : he is aware of the universe : the universe of which he is aware is therefore justified ;

> . . . *j'y suis, j'y suis toujours.*

The " problems " of the universe belong to a lower plane, for in *his* universe the significance of anything is measured solely by its capacity to be used for the purposes of his poetry, to be flung into the crucibles of his mind for *l'alchimie du verbe* to work on. All other values than this are abolished, they are simply non-existent. Only as material for his superb poetry has the universe any value at all. His poetry is therefore profoundly non-moral : it is quite literally beyond good and evil.

POETRY AND THE ABSOLUTE

In this attitude there is a kind of mysticism ; one remembers Claudel's designation of Rimbaud as a mystic in the savage state. It has its analogies in English poetry—in the poetry, such as that of Wordsworth or Blake, which takes advantage of momentary perceptions of a world that has become completely unified. But these momentary perceptions seem, in their case, to be achieved unconsciously and as if by miracle, in the course of an effort towards some other aim, whereas with Rimbaud the abolition of all values allows him to start consciously with this absolute vision as his point of departure.

The universe regarded as material for poetry and nothing more : this is surely *pure* poetry. It seems, indeed, too pure to exist. Like certain chemicals, poetry cannot long exist in the absolutely pure state. The complete detachment which makes it possible is an attitude that cannot be maintained indefinitely.

For though, for the purposes of poetry, the universe is in Rimbaud's power, for the purposes of existence it is not. As a god, as a creator, he is free ; as a human being he is in chains. Every poet is in some degree involved in a dichotomy of this nature, but since the values by which he lives are those which his poetry affirms, the transition from the creator to the human being becomes possible ; there is simply, in the forward flow of existence, a continual movement from one level to another and back again. But in Rimbaud's case there is a complete severance ; the poetry can only exist by a denial of all values, and the denial of all values renders his own human existence valueless, without purpose or meaning. It reduces him to existing merely on the unorganised series of his reactions to the external world. Now it is possible for an individual, perhaps even for a poet, to exist hand-to-mouth on his sensations in this way, but only if he is not sufficiently intellectually interested to be concerned with the problem of values ; the intellect, on the contrary, which denies all values, demonstrates by its denial a preoccupation with the problem, and for it, therefore, such an existence is impossible. Having accomplished its work of demolition it must go on, past denial. It has the choice of acceptance, or of the affirmation of a new value. There is no middle way, short of abandoning intellectual activity altogether.

At a certain stage in Rimbaud's development he is faced

with these alternatives. That the problem did not pose itself earlier, that Rimbaud's poetry exists at all, is no doubt because, for all its maturity in the literary sense, his is the poetry of adolescence, of the period when the universe can be regarded with the detachment proper to one not yet inextricably involved in it, the period of the considerable mental clearances that precede construction. With him this period synchronises with a natural bias of his mind, and perhaps this conjunction of time and temperament explains—if miracles can ever be explained—the extraordinary perfection of his art. Set free by his Satanic spirit from the labour of abstracting and grouping the elements of the outer world into a fixed framework of his own, he can turn all his forces on the problems of formal expression. He thus reverses curiously the normal progression of the poet, who, coming to terms almost unconsciously with life, spends years of labour on the construction of an art ; with Rimbaud the art is complete almost from the outset, and it is in the attempt to come to some terms with life, to give his activity some direction, that he is defeated.

At the stage when the problem becomes insistent the reflection of his spiritual perplexity becomes evident in his poetry. Towards the close of *Bateau Ivre* there appears something that has never before intruded into his hard, objective world—a vague nostalgia, an uneasy regret, the personal confession of a poet who has hitherto been able to include himself, like any other object, in the detached indifference of his vision—

> *Or, moi, bateau perdu sous les cheveux des anses, ...*
> *Je regrette l'Europe aux anciens parapets.*

and further on,

> *Mais, vrai, j'ai trop pleuré. Les aubes sont navrantes,*
> *Toute lune est atroce et tout soleil amer.*

He is tired of the enormous waves of his imaginary sea, his leviathans and giant serpents ; all that he desires now is an expanse of still water where in the twilight a solitary child launches a paper boat. Uneasiness, a gaze turned upon himself and upon his own past, characterise the few remaining poems he is to write ; even technically considered they mark a change. Take this for example :

Peut-être un soir m'attend
Où je boirai tranquille
En quelque bonne ville,
Et mourrai plus content
Puisque je suis patient.

Si mon mal se résigne,
Si jamais j'ai quelque or,
Choisirai-je le Nord
Ou le pays des vignes ? . . .
Ah ! songer est indigne,

Puisque c'est pure perte ;
Et si je redeviens
Le voyageur ancien,
Jamais l'auberge verte
Ne peut bien m'être ouverte.

This pure and slender melodic line is utterly different from the heavily orchestrated harmonies of his earlier work. The poetry of his past is for him over and done with ; he has come to a dead end. His rebellion has become renunciation, his pride withdrawn into melancholy.

For the movement of the mind which has produced this change and which will ultimately lead to his complete abandonment of poetry we have the evidence of *Une Saison en Enfer*, written precisely at the period of crisis, and difficult and contradictory because it is the faithful reflection of an internal conflict.

It is impossible to over-estimate the value of this book : it ought to be regarded as the Bible of the modern consciousness. In the few pages of a confession of the year 1873 there is put on record a certain agony of the spirit which has never found expression in literature before, and which is, in all essentials, that with which our own generation half-inarticulately struggles. Its only literary analogy is with certain inward dialogues of Villon, a spirit with whom Rimbaud has much in common and whose poetry we know to have been one of the formative influences upon him.

In one aspect this colloquy of a mind divided against itself is the record of a search for an absolute value. For Rimbaud, as we have seen, the choice is acceptance of those values which he has denied or the affirmation of a new one. Acceptance for him is impossible . . . *quant au bonheur établi, domestique ou non, non, je ne peux pas.* And his search is equally abortive, for the intellect which has denied so strenuously is completely immobilised by its own previous activity. When all values have been destroyed there is nothing left to build with. When denial has closed all the exits there is no way out. Nevertheless he tries vainly to lay hold on something firm in the meaningless flux in which he is involved. He envisages solutions, to reject them almost at once. Tired of regarding humanity with the contempt it deserves, he will try charity :

> *j'ai songé à rechercher la clef du festin ancien, où je reprendrais peut-être appétit.*
>
> *La charité est cette clef.—Cette inspiration prouve que j'ai rêvé !*

And again :

> *Je bénirai la vie. J'aimerai mes frères.*

The spectacle of Rimbaud blessing life and loving his brothers is a strange, almost comic, fantasy. *N'aime pas ses frères qui veut.* And he is aware that it is impossible. His search for an absolute value is bound to end in failure, for his nature cannot accept any value as absolute. And yet his intellect finds it impossible to function on negatives—it keeps demanding, like Archimedes, somewhere to stand. So that we find him ready to believe in anything at all, if only he could believe :

Ah ! je suis tellement délaissé que j'offre à n'importe quelle divine image des élans vers la perfection.

Sometimes he seems to envisage some kind of miracle ; a light will appear in his darkness, a new way of life will become possible, and a sudden conversion or change of nature will solve his problem by abolishing it. But the *éclair* with which he is illuminated turns out always to be some derisory ideal—religion, or *le travail humain*—which he has little difficulty in disposing of.

Meanwhile his retreat back to the emancipated universe of his creation is already cut off. That creation was only possible while his spirit was completely free ; and the search for something which would give some direction to his activity constitutes in itself a limit on its freedom:

Moi ! he exclaims, *moi qui me suis dit mage ou ange, dispensé de toute morale, je suis rendu au sol, avec un devoir à chercher et la réalité rugueuse à étreindre ! Paysan !* The endeavour to grapple with *la réalité rugueuse*, the intrusion of its fixed forms, the admission of a judgment of value, shatters the universe of his creation. He is aware of this :

Eh bien ! je dois enterrer mon imagination et mes souvenirs ! Une belle gloire d'artiste et de conteur emportée ! And thus at the close of one of the prose poems of *Les Illuminations*, evocative of a city of a fabulous and nightmare-like reality, he exclaims :

Quels bons bras, quelle belle heure me rendront cette région d'où viennent mes sommeils et mes moindres mouvements ? And elsewhere in *Les Illuminations* is the same sense that he is exiled from the universe in which his spirit was at home, the country of tents of red meat, arctic flowers which do not exist, prairies of steel and emerald, prodigious plantations where savage gentlemen chase their newspapers under a created light. Some of these *Illuminations* are simply a constatation of his position—*Vies*, for example :

. . . A présent, gentilhomme d'une campagne maigre au ciel sobre, j'essaye de m'émouvoir au souvenir de l'enfance mendiante. . . . Je ne regrette pas ma vieille part de gaiété divine : l'air sobre de cette aigre campagne alimente fort bien mon atroce scepticisme. Mais comme ce scepticisme ne peut désormais être mis en œuvre, et que, d'ailleurs, je suis dévoué à un trouble nouveau,—j'attends de devenir un très méchant fou.
. . . Mon devoir m'est remis. Il ne faut même plus songer à cela. Je suis réellement d'outre-tombe, et pas de commissions.

The poetry of his past is therefore left behind him ; he has been driven out of his garden of Eden and cannot return. There remains the further question whether another poetry is not possible, and why civilisation too has to be abandoned in favour of the deserts of Harrar. To this *Une Saison en Enfer* gives a perfectly definite reply. Since he has reached an intellectual *impasse*, since on the plane of the intellect his problem is insoluble, the energies that were employed in the

creation of an emancipated universe out of the raw material
of the world are now to be devoted to another end, to a construction in existence. He puts his trust in what nowadays
we should term the unconscious, letting himself go without
further questioning on the current of life, abandoning all
attempt to attain finality by way of the intellect:

    . . . *C'est la veille. Recevons tous les influx de vigueur
et de tendresse réelle. Et, à l'aurore, armé d'une ardente patience,
nous entrerons aux splendides villes.*

If he is to possess truth it is to be a different truth, and
in a different way ; the last words of the book announce the
new aim :

    posséder la vérité dans une âme et un corps.

But his problem arose out of his conflict with the values
of Western civilisation, a civilisation which is itself a construction of the intellect, in which the intellect is supreme,
and in which, if he lives at all, he must live by the intellect.
He states this clearly :

    *L'esprit est autorité, il veut que je sois en Occident. Il
faudrait le faire taire pour conclure comme je voulais.*

It is this authority of the intellect, working at lower levels
than his own, that has made it impossible for him to make
the best of two worlds, to exist in the modern Western world,
conforming to the dictates of its civilisation, and at the same
time retaining, as a private habitation of the spirit, that free
created world of his which he calls in contrast the East, or
the Garden of Eden. The philosophers say :

    *Vous êtes en Occident, mais libre d'habiter dans votre Orient,
quelque ancien qu'il vous le faille,—et d'y habiter bien. Ne
soyez pas vaincu.*

To this his reply is simple :

    Philosophes, vous êtes de votre Occident.

The abdication of the life of the intellect involves, therefore,
withdrawal from the life of the West. He had never com-
promised with the bourgeois civilisation that he hates : now
he need no longer even combat it. Discarding it once for all
he disappears into Africa. Poetry, even poetry based on
denial of it, is part of that civilisation ; he writes not another
line.

Pioneers, O Pioneers!

By EDGELL RICKWORD.

THE boy turned in bed and put up his hand to the switch. As he pressed the button from him he saw the colours fade off the backs of his books. In the faint light which came from the window they stood out like rocks against the snow of the walls. His mind yearned towards them, not so much for their buried ore as with a friendly sentiment, such as one feels for the clothes and habits of a person more familiar than exciting.

But as he fell asleep he thought most of their potentiality; of the next day, when he would dig in them, and of all the following days when he would steep himself in them and wade through them and stride over them, to further half-seen peaks of knowledge and power; to a mythical future whose attributes he conceived, not in details, but vastly, as a golden heroic age of nobility, generosity and command.

"Les régions polaires," says Dictionnaire Larousse, "connaissent une nuit de plusiers mois." As he stumbled along the darkness appeared less thick and a spark here and there in the snow flamed and went out. At first he could see no sun, but later a dull crimson disc swelled like a boil in the grey skin of the sky. In its subdued glow the transparent Arctic flowers were faintly visible. Their slender crystal stems were fluid green like deep water, their blossom a bare grey outline in the air like wine-glasses under water. No sound came there, no wing. The reindeer stood far off in herds. There were no shadows, only the lichen, sombre green and red, bearded the faces of old rocks.

So the year-days passed over slowly. Utter darkness became filled with shadowy masses of cliff and boulder. The dull sun rolled heavily over the horizon and shapes were absorbed again in the thick of night. He felt the panic of an explorer separated from his carriers. He lost count of days and a little thought expanded to a mania. Like a berg drifting south, the transparent temple of sun-life dissolved in the warm stream of night-life. Flesh and flower exchanged their forms. The distance was illimitable, the confusion ultimate.

Presently a gigantic cromlech, the Ritz-Astoria, reared a thousand storeys ; foursquare honeycomb, oozing rich light from clammy cells overbrimmed by the summer of prosperity. Millionaires, atonied of all functions, whizzed by in bed-chairs fitted with wireless telephones. The poets of the Celtic twilight had all been gathered into one hall for an evening's entertainment, or was it the soughing of thirty express elevators ? In the Palm-Court the little nieces of the millionaires, as once the nieces of cardinals, waited to be summoned from their lipsticks and their cocktails.

There were no chamber-pots in the bedrooms, which explained the vast sewer dwarfing the St. Gothard, through whose acrid darkness he stumbled towards a distant illumination.

On stately terraces magnified from the Trianon of Versailles, exquisitely tailored as American girls, they stared arrogantly at the reindeer herds massed like a forest against the flickering horizon (inclusive terms). Slim, cold yet provocative in their slender suits trimmed in a last ironic gesture with monkey-fur, they eyed the impotent glamour of the moon. In one of the closed balconies for the coloured races a pregnant negress dreamed of moon-eaten swamps and yearned for the mangoes the fast cargo-plane was hurrying from the experimental farm behind Lagos. He threaded the extensive drying-grounds, through the bleached glare of linen. Ten thousand towels were employed nightly.

On a raised platform men thrust and pounded on instruments of brass. No tune came to him, but it was as if he looked down a pink whorled shell, spirals of mother-of-pearl flung out from the beating stick of a little man at the focus of sound. He moved towards a street of booths, mingling unnoticed with the crowd, past glittering fountains of sarasparilla, where young men sat gravely drinking. By chance into a booth.

"It's a dime to touch, dame." The show-women's squawk.

"Nothing doing." A girl as lovely as a Lyceum heiress,

standing in front of the rank crowd, her gloved hand poised like a butterfly over the painted fruits on the fat lady's thigh.

"Aw, come on now, yer ken have a finger in the pocket-edition for a nickel, darling." Pushed forward a wicker cradle where a babe lay in drugged silence, blown pneumatic limbs testifying its genuine parentage.

The girl fingered her own rich sack, flushed, conquered. She stared insolently at the men round her. None offered. At last she leaned sumptuously forward and whispered to a scraggy youth in a high stripped vulcanite collar. Patrician and Gladiator. Baudelaire's nightmare of democratic degradation—dans le berceau, elle songe à se vendre un million—outpaced by reality.

He was still dazed when he found himself in front of a large stucco hall. It stood at the end of the fair, its entrance so placed that it might be the stomach of which the lane of booths was the throat. At the mouth of the sac a turnstile extracted alimentary juices from undigested throng. Here he paused a moment while out of the broth of sound of hucksters, and balls flopping against the canvas backs of shies, and the corrosive melody of the merry-go-round, a trickle of blobs of living meat found its way to this gate. They came neither swiftly nor reluctantly, but with the earnest stare of those who know that they are doing their duty. The girls, vivacious before, set their faces in a stupid expression such as he remembered having seen on the faces of women in picture galleries.

LIVING WAXWORKS.
PRACTICAL IDEALS.
Ancient Art purified for you
and your daughter.
Cleansed of mysticism and eroticism
by a purely Arctic process
invented and practised by citizens
of the
Confederated States.
Masterpieces of the Dark Era are now
presented that will inspire
every member of the family.
Art leads the Race.

THE CALENDAR

The hall is divided into a number of compartments, and in each is a group of life-like figures set in various scenery, the colouring, composition and grouping of the figures recalling certain pictures seen in European galleries ; but the details are all novel. The legends are in Gothic lettering.

Sacred and Profane Love. A stenographer sitting at a knee-hole desk, with typewriter, dictaphone and filing cabinet.

The Annunciation. A surgeon in white uniform hands to a girl who has just turned from an electric cooking-range, a medicine phial containing less than a spoonful of spawny fluid. A half-open window shows Joseph hard at work making entries in a ledger. The meaning of this was obscure till he moved near enough to read the lettering on the phial, which ran

> Et puis décantez lestement
> L'homuncule dans la bouteille,

or words to that effect.

He passed many others which had no meaning for him, and only paused for a glance at a Raphaelesque " Ascension," in which the typical citizen was elevated above an adoring group on a cloud shaped like a manager's roll-top desk. The last compartment was fronted with a placard, on which he read :

> Original work by the biggest living artist.
> Life-size group of the Brunswick Martyrs
> Commemorating 300th Anniversary of lost expedition
> which opened the route to the Arctic.
> Escublio, Paxton, Trepan, Asluphor and Narcissus
> Pioneers of Civilisation
> As they were found frozen in their last camp
> On the site of the hotel Ritz-Astoria.

That world crumbled in the fracas of a passing milk-cart, and he curled closer in the warm bed, wondering if his slow and painful exploration of the intellectual Polar Circle was also preliminary to the spread of banality. The yellow morning sun smeared itself on the oaten walls of his room, and the door through which he must enter the real world looked like the bite in a slice of bread and butter. The sweet familiar taste was strong in his mouth, so that he did not know whether to swallow or to spit.

Comments and Reviews

COMPLETE POEMS OF EMILY DICKINSON. Secker.
21s. net.

Amherst in 1830 must, as far as one can judge, have been an intellectual kitchen-garden, where all the plants were cultivated primarily for domestic use. Yet it was there that the delicate, exotic flower of Emily Dickinson's mind blossomed and flourished, unknown to her great contemporaries—Poe, Melville, Hawthorne —and but little influenced by them. Her poetry is intensely personal, and, by the lengths to which she carried it, she made her philosophy of individualism also peculiarly her own. The two most important facts of her life are her sequestration after the three years (1853-56) spent in Washington and Philadelphia, and the puritanical atmosphere of her home. Apart from this, we know little, save for the evidence of a few published letters and her poetry. But though the latter has now appeared in a complete edition, one cannot agree with her biographer, Mrs. Bianchi, that " explanation of her is as impertinent as unnecessary " ; one would wish for a further revelation of her personality than her poetry affords.

This is, indeed, a quite legitimate curiosity, for in Emily Dickinson's case poetry was but a part of the temple which she built for the protection and development of her soul. It is almost a condition of the mystic individualism which she practised that her poetry should not express her whole personality. Withdrawing more and more completely from the world, she was careless, sometimes contemptuous, of their understanding, and if one desire that understanding, one must take into consideration the letters, which serve as complement and commentary to her poetic works.

The two, in fact, are often but arbitrarily distinguished, for though, according to her statement to Colonel Higginson, she wrote but little poetry before she was thirty, one can trace in the correspondence prior to that time, the development of that epigrammatic brilliance of mind which is her most personal characteristic. Of her only sister she wrote when she was twenty-five : " Sisters are brittle things ; God was penurious with me, which makes me shrewd with Him." Already she was distinguishing *her* God from the dour, uncomfortable deity whom her relations worshipped tediously in the Amherst meeting-house. This was the beginning of her revolt. And it is probable that about this time some emotional shock, translated by her mystical nature into a spiritual revaluation, occurred to hasten her withdrawal into herself in an effort towards stability. From then on the habit of seclusion grew on her. It

THE CALENDAR

is as though some fundamental weakness, a lack of spiritual initiative, restricted her search for truth to her own soul ; for it was not fear that drove her to shun people—her exploration is, indeed, remarkable for its boldness. She could write :

> " Heavenly Father, take to Thee
> The supreme iniquity,
> Fashioned by Thy candid hand
> In a moment contraband.
> Though to trust us seems to us
> More respectful—' we are dust.'
> We apologise to Thee
> For Thine own duplicity."

It is in such poems of negation that the trenchancy of her mind is most clearly revealed.   When she comes to make the statement of her faith, an animistic belief in nature, her vigour is replaced by charm, and her force is often dissipated in quaintness.

For this reason Emily Dickinson is a stimulating, rather than a satisfying poet. Her positive ideas or emotions are too often weakened by a timidity in the face of realisation. Life was to her an exhilarating and passionate experience, but though it was " a pang, sweeter to bear than to omit," it was also a " spell so exquisite that everything conspires to break it." It was not that she feared death, but that the awe with which she contemplated eternity made her enjoyment of life tremulous, her reactions to it ultimately a little dubious.   Her point of view had no place for the general. Always she was whittling her consciousness down to fit the limits of her own subjective experience, and, since that was extremely restricted in its scope, her attitude is very intense but at the same time æsthetically bigoted.

The power of her verse is largely due to her cultivation of an unusual and personal angle of vision, which strips objects and concepts alike of their conventional attributes, revealing them clearly and arrestingly by an individual process of re-assimilation :

> " There is a solitude of space,
> A solitude of sea,
> A solitude of death, but these
> Society shall be,
> Compared with that profounder site,
> That polar privacy,
> A Soul admitted to itself :
> Finite Infinity."

The terseness of her style, which she uses sometimes with the greatest effect, is often disappointing. She pursues an idea from what is apparently a shred of observation, but stops short of its full development ; and this is her greatest weakness, arising from her inability to poise concepts in an inevitable balance. But when

318

all is said, Emily Dickinson remains as a virile, stimulating personality who frequently gave in her poetry the true expression of herself. The restrictions which she imposed on her experience reacted on her verse, leaving it sometimes dry and colourless, but more often with the incisive force of her ascetic mind.

DOUGLAS GARMAN.

MILTON. By DENIS SAURAT. Cape. 15s. net.

The difficulty in dealing with Milton has always been that few or none of those who admire his spacious and sunlit verse have had the patience to consider his politico-religious opinions, while few who did consider his opinions had any feeling for his verse. Milton was a revolutionary. So, for that matter, was Shelley. But Milton had the luck to see, as poor Shelley did not, his revolution translated into politics. What Milton hated, the men of the class then governing England also hated. What Milton loved was loved by the best men of his time. Milton, in short, was no lonely eccentric like Shelley, but a successful politician. The Commonwealth collapsed around him, and he returned to poetry. But, beyond the slightest doubt, he would with unction have exchanged all the eternal fame given by the poems he dictated in his blindness for the knowledge that he could still serve the Commonwealth.

M. Saurat does not quite, for all his admirable learning, understand this. He appears to approve those American critics who protest against Milton being called a Puritan because to their imaginations the word " Puritan " suggests a bleak New England farm. " Milton," they exclaim, " knew several languages ; lived in London ; drank beer and pipes of tobacco. He could not, then, have been a Puritan as old Aunt Agnes was. He was too well educated. He must have been a child of the Renaissance, a Humanist." But Milton was a Puritan, and, *pace* M. Saurat, a typical Puritan, at a time when Puritanism signified not merely a ritual of abstinence and profession, but a devouring flame of godliness.

The nearest, I suppose, that anyone living to-day got to the understanding of Milton was in the first weeks of the German War. Then, and then only, we all of us did more or less distinctly imagine a clean conflict of right and wrong, of black and white. The emotion nourished by those times has died, and we no longer accept the simple antithesis which made those times endurable. And that, after all, was a national war. But Milton's was a war of ideas. The Commonwealth might have become Christ's Kingdom. It did not. Instead it dribbled into failure. And Milton was blind, an ex-bureaucrat, just saved by his unimportance from the scaffold. Time moved on. In utter defeat, out of a humble cottage, a blind man, whose private life was scarcely less squalid than his public, a blind man casually pardoned for sedition, sent out " Paradise Lost," " Paradise Regained," and " Samson Agonistes." Pungent poets like Marvell, mellifluous poets like Cowley, were his contemporaries. If Milton stands so high above them, it is not by reason of his studies, his talents, or even his life-long nourished ambition to be a great poet. His character made him great, and the times in which he tested it. Hard, humourless, egotistic ; quite unamiable and certainly magnificent, he fertilised the talents of Tennyson with the genius of Gladstone.

To this aspect of Milton, M. Saurat directs but a little of his attention, and he is certainly justified in ignoring the obscure history of the Commonwealth, which Gardiner has scarcely done more than Guizot to illuminate, which is still bescummed by Carlyle's froth, since the critic is not enjoined to take on the duties of the historian. M. Saurat uses the modern method, two modern methods ; he ascribes Milton's intellectual development to his emotional experiences and his expression to his library. On the former procedure little need be said. It is true that Milton wrote on divorce because his own experiments in matrimony made him unhappy, and on the liberty of the press because he had cause to dislike the censorship, but it is not the whole truth, for occasions should not be confounded with causes. What is really questionable is M. Saurat's treatment of the way in which Milton was influenced by what he had read. The classics, the Italians, Jonson, Shakespeare are subordinated to the Kabbela and Robert Fludd. Now, M. Saurat's conjectures are very interesting, and his discovery of passages in the first and nineteenth books of the Zohar parallel with passages in " Paradise Lost " highly important. But is Milton, " Man and Thinker," pinned down thereby ? Was not Gifford in his insistence on Milton's debt to the Jonsonian phrase more illuminating ? It is not what we read but what we select from our reading that is important. M. Saurat's unfortunate appendix on the chances of Milton being a victim of hereditary syphilis suggests that subtlety rather than adequacy in Miltonic criticism interests him.

H. C. HARWOOD.

THE COMMON READER. By VIRGINIA WOOLF. (Hogarth Press, 12s. 6d.)

There is no explicit link between the literary essays which make up this volume and to be just to Mrs. Woolf it would be necessary to criticise each of them separately, the longer ones at any rate, for it is a great virtue in these pieces to stimulate a sort of private discussion in the reader's consciousness. If however the reader is of the sort that finds discussion harsh and unprofitable, the picturesque is sufficiently in evidence to enable him to ignore very comfortably the deeper implications of Mrs. Woolf's criticism. The essay called " The Pastons and Chaucer " is to our mind the most substantial in the book and it shows as clearly as any what is constantly the subject of her inquiry, the influence on a writer of the society in which he lives—the relation of artist and audience.

Analysing the freedom with which Chaucer absorbs into his verse every kind of experience, ignorant of our uncomfortable distinction between the poetic and the unpoetic subject, Mrs. Woolf says

" He could sound every note in the language instead of finding a great many of the best gone dumb from disuse, and thus, when struck by daring fingers, giving off a loud discordant jangle out of keeping with the rest."

And of course, this freedom from any necessity of verbal compromise is simply the reflection of an unprejudiced relationship to experience, of an " unconscious ease " . . . " which is only to be found where the poet has made up his mind about the world they (his women) live in, its end, its nature, and his own craft and technique, so that his mind is free to apply its force fully to its object."

This happy state has been, in some considerable degree, the lot of the writers of any age remarkable for its literature, the Elizabethan, the Augustan, and the Victorian. In spite of internal dissension, the writers of these periods had a solid stratum to which finally they could refer to give value to their emotional utterances. For the Elizabethans it was the passionate life, for the Augustans the social life, the " honnête homme " of polite scepticism replacing the chivalrous knight of the literature of religious idealism. The Victorians, of course, lack the serenity of their predecessors ; the protestations of Carlyle and Browning are symptoms of the insidious ravages of the will to believe which replaces in-bred conviction. Still, they took advantage of the lull before the storm and produced the last examples of the literature which retains its expressive value along the whole scale of group-sensibilities. Since then, the reading-public has split. We have the small body of educated sharp-witted readers from whom a small spark of intelligence sometimes flickers, but being passionate, if at all, only about values and not experience, ultimately uncreative; and themselves so frequently practitioners as to be unsatisfactory even as audience. Beyond lies the vast reading-public which is led by the nose by the high-class literary-journalist-poet type and its tail tweaked by the paragraphist with pretentions not rising above personal gossip. Mrs. Woolf sketches this gloomy scene with a restraint and delicacy which we cannot emulate. But her essay " How it strikes a contemporary," coming as it does at the end of a volume which begins with Chaucer, flings the contrast of then and now into unmitigated light and shade. Mrs. Woolf concludes that as all the signs point to this as an off-season, the best thing the critic can do to fill in the time is " to scan the horizon ; see the past in relation to the future ; and so prepare the way for masterpieces to come."

This is advice which the middle-aged will perhaps welcome ; but we doubt if these studious evangelists are of much use as path-straighteners for the Messiah. If the past is any guide, he will come with none of the signs of grace and perhaps attempt to borrow five pounds from the ladies and gentlemen scanning the horizon. For what, in fact, does all the present fuss about literature amount to ? It is the disease of an age which has no proper outlet for a great deal of its energy and so directs the surplus into forms which retain a certain amount of prestige from the time when they were the ornaments of the life of educated aristocrats. It should be clearly understood that creative literature has nothing whatever to do with the mass of material which in books and periodicals is produced as literary criticism. The public has never been so confused and debased in its tastes as during the fifty years in which the discussion of literary questions has become general. The only useful criticism must be technical, but the stuff the public swallows now is, like the pap the mother-monkey provides for its young, a masticated product easy of digestion ; only the parent monkey does not extract all the nourishment.

If the discussion of literature is of little help towards the production of masterpieces, in itself not an inspiring aim, the admission of boredom from the public might lead to better results. In its present tendencies literature is far too destructive, too anti-social, or at least enquiring, to be appreciated by those whose appetites are sufficiently keen, or gross, to enable them to approve the contemporary spectacle. Modern work appeals necessarily to a restricted audience, of no particular class but with a common sensibility, and there is no object in trying to expand this audience artificially. It is certainly to the advantage of literature, now, to fall below commercial standards of value. If the common reader could really be identified with the author of these essays we should not have been able to make them the excuse for a tirade. Unfortunately the sensitiveness which is common to them is a quality with which we rarely meet in contemporary criticism. Perhaps we may hope it is a property of the inarticulate, who silent and un-named, form the real modern audience. Whether or not Mrs. Woolf's title be an appeal from the self-styled *illuminati* to the anonymous throng, at any rate she may claim the attribute which is the most valuable of those in Johnson's definition of the common reader, one whose sense is "uncorrupted by literary prejudices."

E. R.

THE DEATH OF CHRISTOPHER MARLOWE. By J. Leslie Hotson. Nonesuch Press. 7s. 6d.

By a piece of research in which chance and ingenuity most happily collaborated, Dr. Hotson has discovered for us the true circumstances of Marlowe's death. The traditional story, with its sentimental bohemianism, is completely discredited, but the new one, by bringing the affair into closer contact with Marlowe's personal conduct and character, leaves us with a more important and more troublesome riddle.

The absolute value of the documents which Dr. Hotson presents is apparent, because they include the actual text of the pardon which was granted the man who killed Marlowe, and the coroner's inquisition, in which the fatal quarrel is described by eye-witnesses, on oath. The fact is that Marlowe was killed in a room in a Deptford inn early in the evening of May 30, 1593, by a man named Ingram Frizer. The only other men present were Nicholas Skeres and Robert Poley, with whom both Marlowe and Frizer were associated, since all had done secret service work for the Government, and Frizer and Skeres were probably connected with Marlowe as well through the service of Walsingham (see "The Death of Marlowe," by Eugénie de Kalb, *Times Literary Supplement*, May 21, 1925). If, then, there is any question of foul play, the company was well chosen, and there were no other witnesses. If there was any need to throw dust in the eyes of the coroner's jury they were men who would not find it difficult to agree upon a story. Dr. Hotson has unearthed various fragments from contemporary records which show that Marlowe's companions were unambitious cheats and their oath not worth more than a pound or two.

The story told at the inquest is this. The four men met about ten in the morning, passed the time together and dined. After dinner they walked in the inn garden "in quiet sort" and went indoors to supper about six. After supper Marlowe and Frizer had words about the payment of the bill. Marlowe was "lying upon a bed" and Frizer was sitting at a table, with his back to Marlowe, between Skeres and Poley, "in such manner that the same Ingram ffrysar in no wise could take flight." Marlowe, "on a sudden and of his malice," drew Frizer's dagger from where it hung at his back and gave him two wounds on the head with it "of the length of two inches and the depth of a quarter of an inch." Frizer, in fear of his life, and unable to get away, struggled with Marlowe for his dagger, "and so it befell in that affray that the said Ingram, in defence of his life, with the dagger aforesaid of the value of 12d., gave the said Christopher then and there a mortal wound over his right eye of the depth of two inches and of the width of one inch, of which mortal wound the aforesaid Christopher Morley then and there instantly died."

We may suppose Frizer to have seized the wrist of the hand in which Marlowe held the dagger and to have turned the point away from himself. Then, if he were the stronger man, he might certainly have wounded Marlowe in the face, but, if one may judge from one's own brow, it would need a very strong and well directed blow to pierce two inches through the bone *over* the eye, unless, indeed, Marlowe were still lying on the bed and the weight of Frizer's body forced the blade down. But in this case the excuse that he was in fear of his life and unable to get away from Marlowe would be hardly good enough. Vaughan's account, written seven years after the affair, conflicts with the coroner's report at several points and does away with this difficulty of the strength of the blow, for he says that Ingram, with his own dagger (but in self-defence), "stabbed this Marlowe into the eye, in such sort, that his braines comminge out at the dagger's point, hee shortlie after dyed." Vaughan, however, was not present, and his virtuous imagination may have added this picturesque detail, since he comments " thus did God, the true executioner of divine justice, work the end of impious Atheists." Still, the coroner should have confirmed the position of the wound *over* the eye. The inquest appears to have been summary. No comment is made on the passive attitude of the other two men, and the jury found that Marlowe was killed in self-defence.

The possibility that Marlowe was murdered should be neither seized upon nor ignored ; on the present evidence we cannot tell. But even in those days, which Dr. Hotson describes as Italianate, it is not likely that men like these fought to the death for the price of a couple of meals ; there is no suggestion of drunkenness. If there really was a quarrel between Frizer and Marlowe it may have been not over the bill, but over a larger transaction in which he had cheated Marlowe, for Dr. Hotson has caught Frizer in some shady affairs. Speculation is useless, but at this point we must mention another discovery of Dr. Hotson's which may point the direction for future research. It is a certificate of good character from the Privy Council to the University of Cambridge, showing that even before he was 23, Marlowe had acquitted himself well in secret missions, so well that the Government wished his good name to be vindicated against popular rumours by the conferring of his M.A. degree at Commencement of that year 1587. Six years later though—in fact, a fortnight before he was killed—he was summoned to appear before the Privy Council on an unknown charge. Had he, in the interval, become obnoxious to his masters ? Many subversive opinions were attributed to him, and even pamphlets, in which, Beard says (1597), he affirmed " our Saviour to be but a conjurer and seducer of the people, and the Holy Bible to be but vaine and idle stories, and all religion but a device of policy."

If the Government was privy to Marlowe's death, it would be interesting to know how much or how little Sir Thomas Walsingham, at whose house he had just been staying, knew about it. The death of Marlowe made no difference, apparently, to a sort of small business relation between himself and Frizer, and it may be noted that Chapman dedicates the continuation of " Hero and Leander " to Audrey, his wife.

It will be seen that Dr. Hotson's discoveries raise as many questions as they answer, and we can only hope that the same skill and knowledge will clear still more of the same path.

For this academic publication the Nonesuch Press has not declined from its high standard of design and production. Its appearance is very pleasing, and it contains facsimiles of two of the important documents.   E. R.

LE BAL DU COMTE D'ORGEL. By RAYMOND RADIGUET. (Bernard Grasset, Paris, 7fr. 50.)

When Raymond Radiguet died in 1923, he had already written a book of poems, *Les Joues en Feu* (yet to be published), and two novels, *Le Diable au Corps* and *Le Bal du Comte d'Orgel*. Yet though he was only twenty when he died, his last book shows no signs of that usually irritating anomaly, *l'enfant prodige*. As he wrote of Rimbaud : " L'âge n'est rien. C'est l'œuvre et non l'âge auquel il l'écrivit qui m'étonne. . . . On fait toujours mieux. Mais que les timides qui n'osent pas montrer leurs œuvres en attendant de faire mieux ne trouvent pas ici une excuse à leur faiblesse. Car dans un certain sens, plus subtil, on ne fait jamais mieux, on ne fait jamais plus mal." It is in this subtle sense that one perceives the value of Radiguet's work.

Le Diable au Corps is the story of a young boy's precocious love for a woman older than he and married, but the vigour and sincerity with which it is told rid it of the mawkishness that was to be expected. It is not a really remarkable book but it shows great promise and, in *Le Bal du Comte d'Orgel*, that promise is in great part fulfilled. How well Radiguet understood what he wished to do may be realised from his note apropos of *Le Bal :* " Roman où c'est la psychologie qui est romanesque." For this is his achievement—to have written a novel dependent for its success, not on its plot, but on the *romance of the mind*. He is not concerned, as are so many of his contemporaries, with the sophisticated exploitation of intricate, unusual psychology, but writes with the candour of an assimilated sophistication, only possible to the great. The ingenuousness which at first strikes one, does not affect " ces profondeurs que notre esprit ne visite pas, où se forment les vrais pressentiments." He is sure of his content : only in his expression of it is he sometimes naïvely uncertain. There is nothing strained about his writing, none of the *préciosité* of, for instance, M. Morand, whose brilliance so often dissembles an emotional and psychological hysteria. Radiguet's tendency to be sententious is essentially a youthful fault. When he writes of the insipid, worldly Paul Robin, " Ne pas vouloir être dupe, c'était sa maladie," he utters an astute criticism, but it should not have been necessary to add, " C'est la maladie du siècle." To do so detracts from the force of his remark, and in the same way his generalisation of the characters in the admirable scene on *le train des théâtres*, dulls the vivacity of his portraiture.

For the rest, *Le Bal du Comte d'Orgel* is a slight, but remarkable, novel. The scantiness of *décor* is justified by its effect—calculated by Radiguet—of accentuating the drama of the two personalities, Mahaut and François. It is regrettable that French literature, in its present state of somewhat unhealthy, in-bred sophistication, should have been deprived of such an invigorating influence, but there is no doubt that Radiguet has already made himself felt, and his book should certainly be read by those English people who wish to understand contemporary French mentality.

D. M. G.

THE SEVEN DAYS OF THE SUN. By W. J. TURNER. (Chatto and Windus. 5s.)

There is always a shade of impertinence in attempting to analyse the problems of expression with which a poet is faced, but it is necessary to do this in order to criticise. In the case of Mr. Turner it would seem that he is doubtful as to the integrity of his poetry, and that he is striving to adapt it to a closer relationship with experience by introducing satire. In this he fails because he lacks the wit necessary for its execution. At best his humour is blunt : at worst it leads him to the clumsy, and rather self-conscious, elaboration of a *jeu de mots*—exclamation marks are scattered thickly through his poem.

After his last book of verse, " Landscape of Cytherea," one had looked for a development of the lyrical qualities which he there showed, but in " The Seven Days of the Sun " his method is entirely different. His rebellion against scientific positivism has led him to satirise science, and to do this he assumes the character of an undergraduate, for whom

" Reality is bewilderment."

But he never gets to grips with his subject. He fidgets about its surface ; as, for instance,

" What is the Evolutionary Theory ?
Does anybody know ?
No doubt women are all descended from cats
Psychologically !
But bodily they appear to be imitations of the Greater Apes
Like ourselves.
It is by examining the teeth
That we discover who are our relatives.
Do not look a gift horse in the mouth ! "

The great defect of the poem is that Mr. Turner pretends to an agility of mind, a skittishness, which is foreign to him. The result is that his sword is often turned against himself :

326

" O the clever !
The clever, clever, clever !
Who are mere waste-paper baskets
Of one another's epigrams ! "

It is as though, committing the sin against the Holy Ghost, he would exculpate himself by jeering at—for he cannot altogether deny—the Holy Ghost, so that his final apostrophe to the " voice of Light " falls quite flat.

One looks forward to Mr. Turner's return to his own poetry (of which there is here but a pale reflection), for one cannot believe that " The Seven Days of the Sun " owes much to his personal inspiration.

D. M. G.

ST. MAWR. By D. H. LAWRENCE. Secker. 7s. 6d.

One of these two novelettes—as the publisher with ironic pedantry terms them—has already run through these pages, and need not be closely studied here. The other, and longer, is less known in England. Neither, however, can be reviewed without reference to the rare genius of Mr. Lawrence, as elsewhere expressed in fiction, poetry, or criticism. Not " St. Mawr " itself, nor " The Princess " is an independent work, and Mr. Lawrence never has written an independent work. He proffers commanding beauties, and now and again he seems to have translated his black, subtle philosophy into art, but to many admirers it must seem that the work matters less than the man, that his fiction is not a series of lovely or startling adventures, but the authentic autobiography of a lonely soul engaged upon a rare quest. Mr. Lawrence, by no trickery of technique, suggests to the reader that anything will happen, and something quite tremendous may. He excites, always and everywhere. He satisfies that excitement too rarely. In point of fact, " St. Mawr " is more exciting and less satisfactory than any of his recent work. There are passages where man's kinship with the lower animals is made so plain that we can only and weakly gasp our admiration, but there are passages of pure bosh. On the whole, the bosh predominates. " St. Mawr " is one of Mr. Lawrence's halting places. He halts there, half bewitched by the past, half summoned forward by the future. He piles up rhetoric, but cannot, as yet, disengage the future from the past. It is chaos ; and Mr. Lawrence, while able to ride, is unable to govern, the storm.

To come to particulars. " St. Mawr " is the story of a woman disgusted by the etiolated intelligence of her husband, and fascinated by the full-blooded nobility of her horse. But the horse, carried across the seas, neighs after a long-legged Texan mare, and the woman goes out into the wild, up the Rockies, to seek the solitude upon which she may burn, as on a vestal altar, her spiritual virginity. She is annoyed by—symbolically speaking—the Prince of Wales and his replicas in Canadian butter. She is contemptuous of the Zane Grey heroes, those natural Tom Mixes Somewhere in the wild, where alfalfa for want of water cannot grow, where the rat eats humanity out, she may live. Or may she not be able to live ? Mr. Lawrence cannot say. The lurid phantasmagoria of his imagination streams by, but the Thing Behind he has not handled.

" St. Mawr " is not a good story ; ill-shaped and stiffly-jointed. " The Princess " is a good story, but better in its incidents than in its theme. Re-reading it, one cannot fail to be impressed by the power of Mr. Lawrence. But . . . to read it is to walk in the track of lightning. Here a tree is cleft, there a vista demoniacally illuminated. Mr. Lawrence's genius is destructive and appalling, and one knew that before. The creative Mr. Lawrence has not in these novelettes been busily enough occupied.

H. C. H.

THE TRAP. By DOROTHY RICHARDSON. Duckworth. 7s. 6d.

Probably no one has done more than Miss Richardson to transform modern fiction. She popularised, if she did not invent, the subjective novel, and genius, beside which her own meagre talents insignificantly fade, has been expended upon it. Once, and not very long ago, Miss Richardson's novels, or rather the instalments of Miss Richardson's novel, were reckoned as quite important. She was parodied, discussed, esteemed. But now . . . it would be meiosis to say that Miss Richardson has failed to fulfil her earlier promise. The bleak truth is that Miss Richardson perfected a way of saying things without having anything to say. The bleak truth is that Miriam Henderson gets steadily duller and more verbose.

" The Trap " must be very close to Miss Richardson's nadir. Miriam, flopping like a sickly frog from one marsh pool into another, has landed herself into the company of Miss Holland, who is efficient and gentlewomanly, but an esurient fool. Miss Holland perplexes Miriam. Hypothetically, Miriam should be interested to meet the vicar's daughter, to taste a new slice of life. But Miss Holland has false teeth of vulcanite, which she slops down into a saucer every night, and Miriam hears it through the curtain. Then Miriam doesn't mind windows rattling, and Miss Holland does. And then Miriam is, or after all might have been made, more intelligent than Miss Holland. She took Miss Holland out to an Italian restaurant, and Miss Holland was shocked by the presence of prostitutes.

All the time, too, Miriam is hating men. They are so complacent, so . . . fatuous, so altogether unlike nice girls of twenty-nine. It annoys Miriam so much. Complacently fatuous men, fatuously complacent men, always misunderstand. But what do they mis-

COMMENTS AND REVIEWS

understand ? Miriam can hardly tell. It would be so nice if men were pleasant at first sight. Women are. Then women begin to go off. They take out their vulcanite dentures, and put them into saucers ; you can hear them through the curtains. Nothing is left, because, perhaps, all these nice doctors and Russians are quite as unpleasant as women heard undressing the other side of the curtain. Everyone is so silly. Everything is so silly. Thus far Miriam.

Miss Richardson, though knowing better, takes us no further. To the associations of her early youth she attaches so much importance that she vomits them on her public. It is so crude, and it is so dull. The other day Miss Richardson protested with some passion against the poor way her books sold. Do they deserve to sell better ? Is there anything there but an excellent manner execrably applied ?

H. C. H.

———

DISCURSIONS ON TRAVEL, ART AND LIFE. By OSBERT SITWELL. (Grant Richards, 21s.).

The usual travel-book is dull, especially if written with literary pretensions. It is filled with facts which appeal to the memories only of the encyclopædic maniacs who express themselves in that communal art medium, the correspondence column ; and its description of the foreign scene, though propped by frequent photographs, never reaches the imagination, because the details are arranged according to no æsthetic principle. The latter criterion is one by which every travel-book must be judged which aims at more than the practical serviceability of Baedeker. Mr. Sitwell's *Discursions* easily survive the test ; the successive pictures of Southern Italy, Sicily and Bayreuth presented there are continuously readable and vitally evocative ; the casualness of their presence together is subordinated to the unity imposed by a very individual pictorial sense. The lustrous decorative art of Tiepolo, which he elucidates in his final chapter, has many points of sympathy with his own imagination, which is at once representational and consciously stylized. A good example of this is the description of Acireale, an architecturally grotesque town in the shadow of Etna, which destroyed it in 1693 :

"With the streets and squares thus hastily thrown up, like the scenery of an improvised theatre, the life of the town could continue as before. In the daytime an orator could address the market-place with bold words and gestures from one of the balconies, while the masks below reflected the democratic feelings of surprise, horror, and laughter. At night, however, the masks would be hidden, and the balconies would become floating rafts in the air, from which cool music would drip down into the hot ways below, or barges, moored high among the fresh play of the young winds, from which, for once, reversing the usual order, the ladies, masked by darkness, would serenade the men waiting below, or, themselves silent, watch the life flowing beneath them and hear the snarling voices and deep braying of the piazzas carried up by eddies of warm, flower-scented air."

The great deal of information imparted is enlivened by intelligence, sarcasm, and (a quality in Mr. Sitwell not usually stressed by his critics) good sense. *Discursions* is a book whose limitations are implied in its title, but it is such a good one of its kind that it deserves to be distinguished from the slovenly and amateurish productions with which it might be associated under the heading of "Travel."

B. H.

SELECT DIALOGUES OF LUCIAN. Translated by FRANCIS HICKES. (Guy Chapman. 3s. 6d.)

Peregrinus the Cynic once resolved to prove the sincerity of his beliefs by burning himself to death in public at the Olympic Games. First, however, he made a speech to the crowd, hoping perhaps that they would forcibly prevent him from carrying out his design. But the majority shouted, "keep your promise." On this the old man "grew pale, trembled and was silent." Lucian, who was present, describing the incident afterwards to a friend, remarked, "You can easily understand how much I was diverted by him." Respect for suffering is, to some degree, a modern development, but Lucian's insensibility seems to be not so much a consequence of his age as a personal deficiency of temperament which put large tracts of reality outside his comprehension, and so invalidates his occasional pretensions to universal satire. For that, a coherent view of life is necessary, and a coherent philosophy is outside the scope of a mind whose capacity for experience has never proved itself equal to the task of synthesis. Lucian's method and style, in this seventeenth-century translation, is continuously suggestive of Swift's ; but who will dare to say that "Gulliver's Travels" is invalid as an interpretation of life ? The profundity and spirit of such art are not in Lucian ; his constructive vision goes no further than that of Sextus Empiricus :—" He who is of the opinion that anything is either good or bad by nature is always troubled. . . . But he who is undecided about things good and bad by nature neither seeks nor avoids anything eagerly, and is therefore in a state of tranquility." But the literary equipment of his satire has never been surpassed. To the dramatic power shown in "Timon," the narrative power of "The True History," and the argumentative wit of "Charon," he added a supreme pictorial fancy which enabled him to destroy the gods in the con-

COMMENTS AND REVIEWS.

vincing setting of their own abodes. The publisher deserves thanks for making accessible to moderate pockets and Greekless readers this classic rendering of some of Lucian's most brilliant work.

B. H.

THE LITTLE CHRONICLE OF MAGDALENA BACH. Chatto and Windus. 6s. net.

There seems to be a conspiracy on the part of biographers, novelists and painters to idealise great musicians out of existence. It is permissible to represent any other kind of artist as he really was ; the musician alone must be represented, physically and spiritually, as an angel descended from Heaven. Why this should be so it is impossible to imagine, since in actual fact he is not merely as fallible as other mortals, but often a person of the most reprehensible moral tendencies. Indeed, " if music be the food of love," what else can we expect ? Euterpe, moreover, has long been notorious for being the most thirsty of the Muses.

In view of all this we must confess to having approached this book with many qualms, and forebodings which in the reading happily proved to have been groundless. It certainly presents an idealised picture of Johann Sebastian Bach, but this is largely justified on several grounds. Firstly, it purports to be the journal of a loving and devoted wife, written long after the object of her devotion had been dead. Secondly, we know so little about him that there is not the usual irritating discrepancy between the man as we know he was or must have been, and the portrait with which we are presented. Thirdly, if there ever was an exception to the general rule indicated in the preceding paragraph, it is surely Bach, who, even judging from the little we know about him, must have been as near to being an angel as any man who ever lived ; an angel, though, not of the soft, sentimental variety of our childish imaginings, but a veritable Angel of the Lord on whom it is not possible to look without fear and trembling. And it is because the anonymous writer of this little book has felt this—in his music rather than in the facts of his life as we know them—that we may say that it is a good book. The best things in it are probably those passages in which awe and fear are stronger even than the great love of Anna Magdalena for her husband.

" I have had awful moments when I looked at him, seated in his armchair, with the children and myself all round engaged on our various pursuits, and yet I felt that he was all alone—above us, beyond us, and lonely. Sometimes the feeling was so strong and painful that I would upset my sewing or my music copying and run to him, and, kneeling by his side, put my arm round him."

" I never quite got used to him in all the years of our marriage : I would have queer stabs of astonishment at the something so big

331

in him which I never quite understood or could explain, which the people of Leipzig, which even his own sons and daughters, in spite of their admiring respect, never seemed to perceive. But to me it was always in the background of my mind, it was like a faint fear, and even our love never entirely cast it out. He was always bigger than I could reach to."—

That is very much what we all feel about Bach. Our awe and fear are sometimes greater even than our love for him. There are moments when we feel he is almost as inhuman as one of Mr. Shaw's Ancients in the last part of " Back to Methuselah."

The writer shows himself, or herself, to be a fine musician, with a thorough knowledge and understanding of the music of the master. The book is singularly free from the irritating inaccuracies, due to ignorance, which most authors commit when writing on musical subjects, and, finally, it is well written without detracting from the artlessness of character with which the imaginary writer is invested.

CECIL GRAY.

COMMENT.

Der Neue Merkur for May contains a very interesting and exquisitely written study by Wilhelm Hausenstein of the life of Rembrandt's son, Titus, who served as a model for so many of the paintings. This study is an excerpt from Herr Hausenstein's book on Rembrandt, which will shortly appear in Germany. The author treats with remarkable imaginative insight the life of the queer Rembrandt household, and its influence on Titus, whose fate was to be always a son, " nothing but a son." It is an admirable psychological study. In the same issue there is a very up-to-date but rather unilluminating survey of the English stage by Rudolf Nutt. The monthly review of European events, in politics and literature, is as usual very able.

The most noteworthy items in *Die Neue Rundschau* for the same month are a translation of an essay on Hamlet by the Danish writer, Johannes V. Jensen, which has already, we believe, appeared in English, a translation of one of Mr. Bernard Shaw's many pronouncements on civilisation, a vivid account by Alfred Döblin of a journey into Poland, and a very short, but illuminating and characteristic, note on Novalis by that admirable writer, Hermann Hesse. The short stories are by Leonhard Frank and Benvenuto Hauptmann. In both reviews the speculative and critical articles are, on the whole, better than the stories, but both maintain a high standard.

E. M.

COMMENTS AND REVIEWS

POETIC UNREASON. Robert Graves. Cecil Palmer. 6s.

The objections to the introduction of psychoanalytic theory into the criticism of poetry are obvious, and most of them are accurately illustrated in Mr. Graves' book. Psychoanalysis, in its present state, is as much a matter of taste as poetry, and is more popular, since it leaves the individual free to exercise his personal discrimination unembarrassed by commonly accepted standards. Mr. Graves has a concrete, lively and ingenuous intelligence, and in a previous book he explained his adherence to Dr. W. H. Rivers' Church of England compromise with the conflicting Continental dogmas of the unconscious. In place of the Freudian wish-fulfilment theory Dr. Rivers substituted an unconscious conflict as the essential significance of dreams ; he denied the uniformly sexual contents of the unconscious ; and emphasised the comparatively conscious character of dreams occurring in light sleep, as opposed to the archaic dreaming of heavy slumber. These are the principles on which Mr. Graves conducts his examination of poetical theory and practice.

One or two quotations will make his position clear. " For the poet, the writing of poetry accomplishes a certain end, irrespective of whether the poem ever finds another reader but himself ; it enables him to be rid of the conflicts between his sub-personalities. And for the reader, the reading of poetry performs a similar service ; it acts for him as a physician of his mental disorders." " Every age has hitherto thought it possible to find a touchstone by which to judge poetry absolutely, and further, every age has thought it has found such a table of absolute values which it was only a matter of time before every one would accept." Whereas, " all that I am insisting on is that no poetry has hitherto appeared, and no poetry can hope to appear, to which an absolute permanent value may legitimately be accorded." The definition of poetry is the statement or solution of a conflict more or less unconscious, and since one man's conflict differs from another's, the conflicts of one age from those of another, the only criterion we are left with is pragmatic : " Does it work in this particular case ? " Certain poets, such as Shakespeare, resume a greater number of contemporary conflicts than do others, and are consequently more widely read. Since we have an inclination towards absolute valuations, they are called geniuses by an age that finds such conflicts relevant ; by an age that does not they are forgotten, as was Shakespeare in the century 1650-1750, and will be again.

Mr. Graves' general theory of relativity is not new, but it contains some truth and is expressed with spirit. It is in his particular theory that he gives himself away. Excited, for example, on reading Edward Lear's Nonsense Songs, by the just supposition that " the adoption of this pseudo-infantility of expression must surely denote suffering in an extreme form," he continues : " Francis Thompson's Sister Songs and Lear's Nonsense Rhymes are apparently the same sort of escape from the same sort of conflict ; strange that Lear is treated less seriously. And who will say that the foolery in Edward Lear is less worthy of our tragic imagination than the terrible foolery at the crisis of King Lear ? " Lear's poems have considerable force, of a kind that psycho-analysis makes more readily explicable ; but Mr. Graves does not use these terms inconsiderately. In the course of the book he analyses a number of poems of varying merit ; and having uncovered some or other of the underlying conflicts, he adduces the personal suffering of the poet as evidence of the poetical value of his work. The psychological implications of this attitude run through the book and prejudice Mr. Graves' treatment of every subject of importance. Beides the conflict theory, Mr. Graves makes use of Dr. Rivers' distinction between the dreams of light and heavy sleep, as a definition of classical and romantic poetry. " Classical poems are written in a mood in which the poet is preoccupied, perhaps, but aware of the conventional waking view of reality ; when the emotional (romantic) kind of poem appears, it rises either from actual deep sleep or from a ' brown study ' trance, disturbance in which will affect the poet with the same shock

THE CALENDAR

as if he had been actually asleep." And the greater part of " Poetic Unreason " is a defence of the illogical, symbolic and unaware processes of thought that distinguish what Mr. Graves calls our " lower level " dreams and romantic poetry. The subject has inspired him to some acute and entertaining criticism ; but since justification, not enquiry, is his concern, he suppresses at will any portions even of Dr. Rivers' mild and home-brewed psychology that cause him uneasiness. The result is worthless as a contribution to serious criticism, but has considerable value as the psychological confession of an interesting poet. Up to a point Mr. Graves' honesty is exceptional and his evasions have consequently genuine interest. But the correlation of criticism with modern psychology is an unavoidable development, however dangerous ; and it is unfortunate that Mr. Graves, while he avoids none of the dangers, should have found nothing of importance to say on it.

J. F. HOLMS.

Among New Books

DAY OF ATONEMENT. By Louis Golding. Chatto & Windus. 7s. 6d.

Of all the fatalities which have pursued the Jewish race the most curious, though not the least explicable, is that, while it produces many great artists, great art cannot be made out of it. It is, for instance, impossible to make a tragic figure out of an orthodox Jew. Causation is too rigid and simplified in Jewry to allow any strict Hebrew soul to stand nakedly at the mercy of circumstances in even its most desperate moment. Again, to make a tragic figure from a proselyte, by virtue of his proselytism, is hardly easier, for the entirely opposite reason that religious conversion is the most hysterical of human acts. Mr. Golding writes of an apostate Jew who commits the ultimate sacrilege of preaching Christ in the synagogue and is murdered by his loving, but devout and conservative wife—a *dénouement* which, though magnificently prepared, quite fails to excite pity. Mr. Golding must be tired of being reminded of his promise, but that is still the best of this novel. Its sceneries and incidental philosophies are excellently composed, and its prose is always adequate and sometimes beautiful.

MOUNTEBANKS: A PLAY IN THREE ACTS. By Frank Birch. Chatto & Windus. 5s.

This play is vigorously written, but the central emotions are over-expressed. The situations, which centre round the fatal passion of a monk for a girl in a travelling show, and have for background the clashes between the monastic idea and the rich medieval lay life, are familiar and have lent themselves advantageously to novelistic treatment. Mr. Birch modernises his characters after the manner of "Saint Joan," and they have a clear-cut if unmemorable life in action. But when the action is delayed by dramatisation of general ideas, the dialogue touches fustian.

LONDON LIFE IN THE EIGHTEENTH CENTURY. By M. Dorothy George. (Kegan Paul, 21s.)

The material condition of the poor in the eighteenth century was notoriously low, and historians describe it according to one or other of two unreconciled economic theories. Until recently the Industrial, like the French Revolution, was accepted as an event so radical and influential that lesser causes of cleavage from the *status quo* were either neglected outright or perverted from their proper semblance into ramifications of the principal movement. Mrs. George's conclusions from the unrivalled mass of evidence she has collected are, to some degree, a timely and convincing modification of that view, but she refrains from making it her main thesis, and wisely, for London was less affected than any of the great towns in the immediate consequences of the industrial upheaval. She shows clearly, however, that much of the social misery usually ascribed to that event was really due to the collapse of trade after the Napoleonic wars, though in that relation, too, the capital "to a great extent escaped both the torrent of pauperisation which deluged the greater part of agricultural England and the catastrophic fall in wages which occurred in many places." The history which will disentangle the evidence as a whole and establish the causes in their right proportions remains to be written. Meanwhile Mrs. George has given us a detailed and admirably presented picture of the vast slum which produced and carried the culture by whose refinement we are nowadays abashed. The scene she describes is too multifarious to be touched on in a short notice, and in its general lineaments is well known. One of the most interesting chapters is that on vital statistics, in which she discusses at length that extraordinary riot of gin-drinking between 1720 and 1750, whose ravages stripped off London's civic decoration for Hogarth's vision.

THE TORTOISESHELL CAT. By NAOMI ROYDE-SMITH. Constable. 7s. 6d.

If for nothing else, and in any case for this especially, Miss Royde-Smith deserves congratulation ; she has caught adolescence in its decline, without brushing the bloom from its wings. Gillian is neither, on the one hand, nymphomania masked as innocence, nor, on the other hand, the pole-star by guidance of which all masculine barks must steer. She is just a nice girl, very pretty . . . and all that, but not wondrous, and her remarkable innocence, after amusing the reader, begins to bother *her*. She very nearly sails into an unholy mess. And she herself is not to be congratulated on the way she got away from it. With the same competence the author handles secondary figures.

Very much more might have been done with the theme, good as the treatment is, and one still desiderates from Miss Royde-Smith something sharper. This is all great fun. Miss Royde-Smith might be quite as funny and ten times more important. She is, in short, too good to make us content with her smoothly clever but slightly unenterprising commentary upon life.

MANIFESTE DU SURRÉALISME. POISSON SOLUBLE. By ANDRÉ BRETON. Kra. 7 frs. 50 c.

M. Breton's definition of the process or faith of which he is the prophet is as follows :—

SURRÉALISME, n.m. Automatisme psychique pur par lequel ou se propose d'exprimer, soit verbalement, soit par écrit, soit de toute autre manière, le fonctionnement réel de la pensée. Dictée de la pensée, en l'absence de tout contrôle exercé par la raison, en dehors de toute préoccupation esthétique ou morale.

Young's " Night Thoughts," says M. Breton, are surréaliste from beginning to end ; Shakespeare only " dans ses meilleurs jours." His arguments are based on the theory of the unconscious and the association of images which holds the field at present ; he is dogmatic where he should be tentative. His effort is in the direction of what M. Benda has described as the hatred of general ideas, the feminisation of art, the sole enjoyment of the concrete and the particular ; the emotionalisation of literature. It ignores altogether the constructive effort in poetry, the organisation of the *whole* into something significant. It is the lack of this organisation which makes so tedious the reading of M. Breton's prose poems *Poisson Soluble*. The concatenation of imagery is sometimes stimulating, but it leads nowhere. The poem and the day-dream are not identical, though they make use of the same mental processes. Perhaps M. Breton will agree when he has carried his analysis a little deeper. At least, he ought not to let his evident gifts rot in the slough of his present enthusiasm.

TRISTAN CORBIÈRE. By RENÉ MARTINEAU. Le Divan. 12 frs.

Corbière is a remarkable poet, who, although he died in 1875, is still not so well known as many lesser writers. M. Martineau's biography, which was first published some twenty years ago, is in this edition fuller and more precise, thanks to documents and information supplied by relatives of the poet.

The CALENDAR
of Modern Letters

VOLUME I   JULY
NUMBER 5   1925

Return *

By LUIGI PIRANDELLO.

BACK again in the dreary hill-top village where he was born, Paolo Marra understood that his father's ruin must have begun at the moment when he had left off building houses for other people, and begun to build one for himself. The thought came to him when he looked at the house, no longer his, where he had lived for a while as a boy—a house planted in one of those high and narrow ancient streets, all running down the hillside at the same precipitous angle, like the dried-up beds of torrents, paved with cobbles.

All the desolation was embodied in the spectacle of the arched and doorless doorway, that stood between the walls that were once to have shut in the great courtyard, over-topping them by nearly a yard—ragged red stone walls, old, and still unfinished. Through the arch was the courtyard, sloping and cobbled like the street, with a great well in the middle. The iron bar upholding the pulley was still in place, but the paint on it, once of a reddish colour, was now almost entirely eaten away by rust. A sad thing to see, that crumbling iron hoop, that seemed sick beneath its scars of paint and decay ; sick, too, of the melancholy creaking of the pulley-wheels, when the wind at night moved the bucket-rope, and above the empty luminosity of the courtyard overlaid with dust hung, as though fixed there for eternity, a luminous square of sky, misty and filled with stars.

---

* From the volume of short stories "Tutt'e Tre," Florence, 1924.

His father's wish had been to build this courtyard between the house and the street ; then, seeing the uselessness of the scheme, he must have abandoned it, leaving the empty door-frame and the unfinished walls.

At first no passers-by had tried to enter, because the earth was still strewn with stones ready for laying, and it seemed that the building was only interrupted for a little, and might be taken up again. But as soon as grass began to sprout between the cobbles under the wall, these stones all at once took on a look of being crumbled and old. Some of them had been carted away when, after his father's death, the house had been sold to three separate owners, and the courtyard left a kind of no-man's-land ; and the rest had become seats for the gossips of the neighbourhood, who now looked on the courtyard and the water of the well as their own, and used to wash there and spread their clothes to dry, and, when the sheets stretched out on the stones and the shirts flapping from the lines showed glaring white in the sunshine, would loosen their hair, shining with oil, upon their shoulders and painstakingly search their heads, one for the other, as monkeys do.

The street had, in fact, absorbed the courtyard, which had no door to shut it out.

And Paolo Marra, seeing the invasion for the first time, and the doorsill under the arch worn down, and the pilasters chipped, and the paving destroyed by the wheels of carts and ploughs that had been stabled in the once clean and airy barns beside the house (reduced long since to the occupation of filthy tenants)—Paolo Marra, oppressed by the reek of garbage and rotten straw, with a foul black stream of rinsing water running between his feet as it trickled over the cobbles into the street, felt rise in him a surge of pain and revulsion in place of that secret and voluptuous sense of fear, which in the distant memory of his childhood had clothed the courtyard, when at night it was empty and deserted, with the deep star-filled sky stretched over the livid whiteness of the cobbles, and the well in the centre a mysteriously splendid thing.

Women and urchins gathered round him to stare, gaping at the old trailing coat he wore, which together with his clumsy spectacles and ragged fringe of hair reaching almost to his humped shoulders, seemed to him consistent with his calling of a schoolmaster, but which in reality gave him the appearance of a strange and rusty evangelical pastor from overseas. And when they saw him turn away with all his disgust stamped on his pallid face, they broke into titters and guffaws of laughter.

Standing there, his anger urged him to stride back into the courtyard, of which he was still rightful master, and drag these women, one after the other, from the piles of stones, and drive them out before him, into the street. But used now to reflect before his actions, he paused. If they saw in him merely a stranger, somewhat grotesque perhaps, a man grown old and ugly before his time through a life of painful study and misfortune—but still a stranger, and not the boy he had once been and that some of them might still remember, he would do better to renounce his rights over the place they had usurped than stir up for himself all the pain of his old memories. One of these memories alone sufficed to quench his impulse to fling himself against these women—the memory, still burning, of his mother, leaving this house for ever, holding him by one hand and with the other drawing over her face a fold of the black handkerchief that covered her head, to hide her crying and the fearful bruises from her husband's blows.

He, as a boy, had been the cause of those bruises, and of the irremediable breach between husband and wife that had followed, and of his mother's death, of heart-break, scarcely a year later; he who, in his folly, had set himself up, then fourteen years old, as his mother's champion against his father, who had betrayed her; for he had not understood, as now, as a man, he understood, that his mother, horribly disfigured from her babyhood, by a fall from a window, was obliged to bear this betrayal if she was to continue to exist in the same house as her husband. To him, her son, she had naturally embodied what was Mother. He could not have conceived another or a different one. He felt himself enwrapped and caressed by the infinite tenderness that shone forth from those eyes, which might still have been beautiful, jet-black as they were, had they not been edged with a bloodless red that showed above the underlids dragged down, together with the whole sockets and the cheeks, into the scarred and ruinous cavity of the frightful wound, from which only the end of the nose emerged. And all the mother love, animal and spiritual, he heard in her voice, without caring that it seemed to come, half-stifled, from her nostrils, rather than from her poor monstrous mouth. He knew that his father, risen from the gutter, had become lord and master to her ; and it maddened him to see her not only renounce every shred of claim to gratitude, but actually ready and willing to lay her face—that scarred and tragic face—where he had set his foot. It maddened him to see his father use her as a slave, while she showed in every act and every movement the tremulous gratitude of a tamed and broken beast, always afraid of not being quick enough to anticipate his every need and wish, or to clutch to her some absent-minded crumb of kindness as though it were a blessiug far beyond her deserts. He was only six years old, and still he revolted, and tore himself away in a passion when his mother would have shown him to this woman or to that, who upbraided her for her too great submission. He would thrust his fingers into his ears, so as not to hear from the next room the words that always accompanied the gesture cut short by his flight —the explanation that she had a son, and that, considering her calamity, was an undreamed-of blessing for God to have vouchsafed to her.

He was too young still to understand that she put forward and dwelt upon her son in order to hide perhaps from herself, as well as others, the indescribable misery of her flesh that had had to beg love from this man, though she well knew him to be owned and possessed by another woman, and though she missed no whit of the repulsion with which, every once in a while, the tremendous charity was conceded. She felt that in the sight of all she must justify herself, and be cleansed of this degradation suffered for her son.

Finally it came to his knowledge that his father had taken up with a widow, a woman of the people, a certain Nuzza La Dia, who had once been his betrothed, but whom he had abandoned in order to marry a girl of higher standing than himself, and with a good fortune—endurable, if hideous, since she was the daughter of the engineer who had helped him to make his way, and who, having had his collaboration for so long, had finally made him a partner in all his concerns.

He knew that every Sunday morning the pair of them used

to meet in the little parlour of the Convent of S. Vicenzo, where an aunt of theirs was abbess. They used to pretend to go and visit her, and the old abbess, who was content to find in their relationship sufficient cause for the tender intimacy between them, used to enjoy the sight of them sitting opposite each other at the little table before her double grill—he, become a gentleman, with his blue Sunday suit that seemed always stretched to bursting by his great shoulders, and the hard collar that threatened to strangle his purplish throat, and a red tie ; and she, brimming with obvious sensual delight, but quiet and placid with satisfaction, dressed in some black stuff gown, all twinkling with bits of gold in the severe and churchlike gloom of the little parlour. Mouthful by mouthful, one for him, one for her, they nibbled at the innocent confections of the convent, and drank, a sip for her, a sip for him, little glasses of the convent's pallid red wine. And they laughed together until even the old abbess aunt, planted like a wax-work behind her grating, was melted into smiles.

One of these Sundays he went to take them off their guard. His father had just time to hide behind a green curtain that covered a side-door, but the curtain was short, and under the hem, still swinging slightly, stuck out his great shining Sunday boots. She sat where she was, beside the table, with the little glass still between her fingers, in the act of raising it to her lips. He had planted himself in front of her, and drawing his head well back, had spat full in her face. His father had not moved behind the curtain. Nor, when he got home, had he spoken a word to him, nor touched a hair of his head. He had taken his revenge upon the mother—beaten her till she bled, and driven her from the door ; then he had taken the whore publicly into his house, and had done with the mother and the son for ever. The mother had died a year after, and he had been put to school in another place. He had never seen his father again.

Now, on this homecoming, after all these years, he had not been recognised by a soul. Only one human being had spoken to him, of whose identity he had no idea—a tiny man muffled up in a huge cloak, so small a creature as to be almost laughable in that great shroud. Very mysteriously this being had beckoned him apart and begun to speak, scarcely above a whisper, of the house and of his right to possess the court-yard, or, if he did not want it himself, to relinquish it in favour of a certain poor woman whom it would be God's own charity to repay for the love and devotion she had lavished on his father, and for the care she had shown him right up to the end when, paralysed and dumb, he had been reduced to want ; a certain Nuzza La Dia she was, and in the end she had begged his bread ; and now, homeless, she dragged herself here every night, to sleep in a cellar under the stairs.

Paolo Marra turned and gazed at the little man as if he had been the devil incarnate. And the little man, in response to his look, had suddenly screwed his features up into a grin and winked in a manner that was actually diabolical—as if he had been the devil in person who had thrown the mother from the window as a child, to deform her, and made this Nuzza La Dia beautiful for the temptation of his father, and led him, as a boy, to spit in her face and so bring destruction upon them all.

And the devil, when he had winked, wrapped himself up with much furling and unfurling in his crazy cloak, and went away.

Paolo Marra knew that this fancy of his was nothing but his imagination, prone to work easily because now, for some time past, he had felt a twinge of remorse at having let his father die in desperation, without a word from him. Now, standing there, he felt the twinge again ; but he drove it from him with a spasm of hatred ; and the hatred, too, he knew not to be all real, but mixed, within him, with some other feeling which he had always shrunk from defining to himself, for fear of hurting the most grievous of all his memories—the memory of his mother. Now, even about this too, hitherto a thing of purest misery, was woven and intertwined a sense of uttermost degradation and shame ; for no sooner did he call up the wretched and tortured face of his mother than there rose up automatically beside it the face of the other woman, un-sullied and beautiful, and the unescapable memory of how she had looked on that morning, with his spittle still hanging on her cheek—a little uncertain smile of surprise and happiness about her parted lips, with the white teeth showing between, and all the sorrow, all the sorrow in the world in her eyes.

Translated by ADA HARRISON.

Poems

By EDMUND BLUNDEN.

By Road.

Who knows not that sweet gloom in spring,
    That waiting gloom, that grave delight
    In coming bloom,
    In the first flight
Of bird, or thought, so wild of wing ?

Now when round hedgerow's earthy claws
    And painted shells that blanch near by
    The dark grass swells
    And from the eye
In buds each old black nest withdraws.

I well might go to my old haunt
    And find the green brook brushing down
    By celandine
    And sedges brown
And hopper's-houses grimed and gaunt.

I well might go where the burnt ring
    And rusty kettles year on year
    Show life has yet
    Her freedoms dear—
And I will go, another spring.

THE CALENDAR

It may be, I shall then unfold
    Why with such thrill and venturous joy
    I crossed that rill,
    A hurrying boy,
One Lenten Sunday ages old.

The mild mysterious spring was there,
    The silk palm glowed, the vole peeped shy
    Beside the road
    Where you and I
Went on and blest the orchard air.

Then coming to the timbered cot
    Of your good friends, how deep it strook
    That he would lend
    His longed-for book—
Old Walton, which forthwith he got

And by the window gave to me.
    The apples in the window-sill,
    His humorous chin,
    I see them still,
I see his good wife getting tea.

But where's the mystery ?   There it was ;
    And is it there ?   And can I find
    Spring's dusk so fair
    Now that my mind
Looks far beyond such floating floss ?

O look not out : the young spring broods
    So wondering-warm on nest and bough,
    Her dark eyes charm,
    Her babe leaps now,
And godhead glistens in those woods.

" Thy Dreams Ominous."

Blest is the man that sees or hears
   The shuttles of the eternal weaver,
And shrieks not, sobs not savage tears,
   Burns not with fever.
He is a tree that's firmly planted
   Where a plunging cataract blanches,
Spreading there as though enchanted
   His lucky branches.

But what if I, whose different thews
   Scarce bear the dawning light unwincing,
Discovered in some curious clues
   Vision commencing ?
I should be drift wood, moon and sun
   In gulping, groaning water-gorges
Sucked down, shot high and snatched and spun
   Through timeless orgies.

Shepherd's Calendar.

When lambs were come, who could be slow and sear ?
When lambs were come, and each black thorny rod
Lit up with seraph birth and budded clear
Fresh as the lambs and clouds, and smiled at God ?
The clay-green from the river solved away
Till all was crystal ; who the crystal conned
Saw where blue pike with their wild lemans lay,
And by old ragstones the new waving frond.

And many a girl by tinkling pastures stood
With primrose brow toward eve's single gem,
And waited in the bright ethereal mood
For one who then would kiss her garment's hem,
Some don and darling of our rural sphere,
That now, this soon-come spring, goes slow and sear.

Misunderstandings.

In the bright shallow of this broadened dyke,
   Whose willow-wood, late chopt, gives now
     Not one sweet shading bough,
See in the sun the two young mating pike
   With golden strakes and dapplings fine
    In mutual love themselves align ;
Where he and she together bask and dream,
There is no time but that, no other theme.

The flooded river hurled and flurried hoarse
   With lashing branches and brown scum,
     And yet the time was come.
These following love up a still lonely course
   Reached this imagined bower, nor knew
    The dwindled river far withdrew.
And now in unsuspicious love they lie
In the bright prison where they soon will die.

The mild wood-pigeon looked, and look she might,
   For last year's willow-wood : 'twas gone !
     She rose and floated on
To one near by ; and there in April light,
   Her thin twigs set, sat warming two
    Sweet eggs, that shone like roses through.
Man came, she startled ; he but looked and learned,
But to her frost-cold eggs she ne'er returned.

James Joyce : The Meaning of "Ulysses"

By EDWIN MUIR.

NO other novelist who has written in English has had a greater mastery than Mr. Joyce of language as an instrument of literary expression, and no one else, probably, has striven so consciously to attain it. "Dubliners" was an ideal apprentice piece for an artist ; in it Mr. Joyce set himself to describe accurately the things he saw, attempting at the beginning what most writers achieve towards the end. "The Portrait of the Artist as a Young Man," marked a further stage. That book was as much a recreation of language as a record of experience. The marvellous dialogue which appeared first in it was not like the transcriptions of ordinary talk in "Dubliners "; it was a second language which was used consciously to vary and complete the lingual pattern of the work. That pattern of speech seemed complete in itself, a thing of different nature from, but as real as, the events and experiences, many of them sordid, which it described. There were thus two values in the novel, separate, yet necessary to each other : the value of language and that of life, the value of art and that of experience. To Mr. Joyce the first of these is pure, the second mixed. Art must descend into life, the word must seek out all it can and enter into it ; yet, having entered into it, it returns and remains pure in the consciousness of the artist. Life cannot soil it, but only a disobedience of its own laws.

In the "Portrait of the Artist as a Young Man " Mr. Joyce acquired the mastery of language, the knowledge of and reverence for its mysteries, which prepared him for "Ulysses." He learnt, too, for the second time, the strict realism which, because it demands perfect exactitude in the rendering, is valuable as a discipline, makes an intensive demand on the artist's powers of expression, and by putting a strain on them enhances them. In embracing this realism he discarded the facile sensibility of his time, which was occupied only with the secondary phenomena of consciousness—with the psychological effect of the object rather than the object, with distinctions rather than with things—and which in that preoccupation while seizing the shadow lost the substance. " The Portrait of the Artist as a Young Man " not only left Mr. Joyce with a greater command over English than any other novelist had possessed ; it was as well a sort of self-inoculation against a sensibility grown burdensome. Without either of these " Ulysses " could never have been written. For in " Ulysses " the dual values of " The Portrait," the values of life and art, of reality and imagination, are developed side by side until each attains its maximum of expression, and the discrepancy between them issues in a form of humour which through its intellectual profundity becomes universal. It is a humour not of fashion, nor of character, but of the processes of life, those processes which create history and produce religions and civilisations while leaving the great part of the human race, the average sensual man outside us and within us, spiritually unchanged and apparently spiritually unchangeable. It sets forth the dreams of religion, the magic of language, the splendours of the intellect, the revolutions of history, over against the simple facts : the naïvety of physical desire, the functions of the body, the triviality of the floating thoughts the body sends up into our minds. A theme so tremendous could only be expressed in great tragedy or great comedy, could only in one of these two ways be lifted into a plane where it no longer overwhelms us, and where having passed through it we are freed from its worst oppression. Had Mr. Joyce not inoculated himself against sensibility by an overdose of realism he could never have attained this emancipating comic vision of the entire modern world. Had he not been so sensitive that he suffered monstrously from his sensibility his comedy would have had no driving power behind it. One feels again and again in " Ulysses " that the uproariousness of the farce, the reckless-ness of the blasphemy, is wildest where the suffering of the artist has been most intense. A writer whose sufferings were so great and so conscious needed a more elaborate technique than most writers do, as much to put a distance between himself and his sufferings as to express them.

" Dubliners " and " The Portrait " were a necessary preparation, an apprenticeship strengthening the artist against life. They were exercises working out a part of Mr. Joyce's problem ; but in " Ulysses " the whole problem is faced and to the extent of Mr. Joyce's present powers resolved. That problem must needs have been the problem of all the things from which he suffered, for the sincere artist is distinguished from the rest by the fact that his essential concern is with the things which make him suffer, the things, in other words, which stand between him and freedom. There is thus a necessary and an organic relation between him and his work, to create being, as Ibsen said, an act of emancipation. But when, as in " Ulysses," the creation is encyclopædic, when it attempts to gain freedom not from one but all the bonds, all the suffering, of the artist's soul, the impulse from which it started becomes a part of the autobiography of the book as well as of the writer. What Mr. Joyce suffered from in writing " Ulysses " was obviously in its completeness the life he had known ; our modern world in all its intellectual manifestations as well as in its full banality ; in its beliefs, its hopes, its charities, its reverences ; its religion, patriotism, humanitarianism, science, literature, politics ; its illusions as well as its realities. How could the full volume of all those burdensome hopes, theories, sensibilities, banalities, cruelties, meannesses, sensualities, be rendered in a work of art ? Obviously not in a story, an action having a beginning, a development, a climax and an end, but rather in a record of the most obvious unit of time in which all these could manifest themselves, in that unit of time which begins with something recalling birth and ends in something resembling death : in a day. " Ulysses " is a complete course, a set banquet, of the modern consciousness. And being that no other unit could have served ; the author could not have got into the record of a year what he has got into the record of a day.

But this banquet of the modern consciousness was to be a comic summing up as well as a banquet ; it was to be not only abundant, but so burdensomely, absurdly abundant that all the courses would be made to appear ridiculous, as Rabelais made the courses of the medieval banquet ridiculous. And as Mr. Joyce's encyclopædic plan justified the time unit of his chronicle, so his comic intention justified the minuteness of his portrayal, his huge accumulation of imaginative material. His humour is one on side, like that of Rabelais, a piling up of one burden on the mind after another until the breaking point is reached—the breaking point of laughter. It operates by oppressing us consciously with all the things which oppress us unconsciously, and by exaggerating all this until it seems ridiculous that we should bear it, or more exactly that it should exist at all. A sense of this or that anomaly in social relations, the sense which finds expression in polite comedy, is far too light to shift this immense weight. To do that comedy must include as many factors as the greatest tragedy; it must embrace not only man, but all that he believes in, the whole anthropomorphic cosmos. But even when the absurdities of the spirit are piled up in this way they are still not in the realm of universal comedy : the last touch is still wanting. That is given by a running contrast between the vast symbols invented by man and his simple earthy reactions, between the extravagance of belief and the simplicity of fact, the decency of civilised life and the unseemliness of instinct. That was the mainspring of Rabelais' humour, and it is also that of Mr. Joyce's. The more absurd and minute the description of physiological reactions, the greater obviously the effect. On the one hand an infinite immensity, on the other an infinitesimal smallness ; the intellectual dreams and spiritual struggles of Stephen Dedalus in the one balance, the vagaries of Leopold Bloom's instincts in the other ; around us the phantoms our minds have created, and within us the utilitarian functions of our bodies. And as the intellectual shapes which man has conceived to be first a release and then a burden are exaggerated, so his physical idiosyncrasies, his trifling thoughts, are refined upon. There is in Mr. Joyce's obscenity as in that of Rabelais an intellectual quality, as if in searching the recondite secrets of the natural processes of the body he were trying to penetrate to an unconscious humour of the cells, of those elementary principles of life which have built up not only the body but all this phantasmal structure which we call thought, religion and civilisation. His emphasis on the unseemly, on what, in other words, we have surpassed, depend upon, and wish to forget, is, at any rate, a necessary element in this kind of humour and an essential part of the plan of " Ulysses." It is perverse, that is to say, intellectualised deliberately, but so it had to be to achieve its purpose.

The vision of the world whose mainspring is in this radical sense of contrast is one which, if it did not issue in humour, would be nightmare. In " Ulysses " it does not always issue in humour. The brothel scene is horrible partly because it is a mis-shapen birth, because, conceived as a grand example of the humour of horror, it attains, through its failure, an atmosphere of horror which because it is unintentional is strictly monstrous, and incapable of being resolved either into art or into human experience. This scene is a work of genius ; it is more astonishing than anything else Mr. Joyce has written ; but it has the portentous appearance of something torn from the womb of imagination, not the completeness of something born of it. We derive from it a vivid notion of the monstrous suffering through which the artist is passing ; but here he has not passed beyond it ; and we suffer equally as participators in the horrors of a raw experience and as spectators of a heroic but unavailing attempt to escape from it and set it in the realm of freedom. Had Mr. Joyce succeeded with this gigantic scene he would have produced something supreme in literature and not merely something supremely astounding and terrifying. It was obviously designed to be the climax of the work ; in it the last resources of the theme were to be brought on the stage ; the unconscious desires which up to now had been allowed only a chance or oblique expression were to come nakedly to the surface and attain freedom. They do not attain freedom. The brothel scene is not a release of all the oppressions and inhibitions of life in our time ; it is rather a gigantic attempt to attain release.

But if we grant this crucial failure in the book, and a number of minor failures, there remains more comedy in the grand style than has appeared in our literature since the Elizabethan age. The last chapter has been much praised, but there are others only less admirable. The scene in the pub. where Bloom is routed by the Citizen produces by an openly mechanical technique Mr. Joyce's sense of contrast between an ordinary happening in all its banality and richness, and the fantastic and etiolated symbols which the desires of men and the conventions of literature discover for it. Here it is the obviousness of the means, the mechanical ease with which the simple event assumes conventional or lofty forms in the fancy that is at the root of the humour. We seem to see the illusions at their normal work. The banal fact and the fantastic interpretation are both present before our eyes, are both obvious and credible, the one arising spontaneously from the other, and are both ridiculous. The chapter of parodies, which has been so much criticised, is still more remarkable. There we see the figure of Mr. Bloom passing, as it were, through a comic pageant of the English spirit. In his progression he assumes a sort of absurd universality ; he is a man " of Israel's folk . . . that on earth wandering far had fared " ; he is " childe Leopold " and " sir Leopold that had for his cognisance the flower of quiet," and " Master Calmer," and " Leop. Bloom of Crawford's journal sitting snug with a covey of wags," and " Mr. L. Bloom (Pubb. Canv.)." He is a type, and a succession of types through history, and a multi-plication of types in space ; one person in himself and many persons in time and in the minds of men. In this scene Mr. Joyce's comic imagination is at its height ; it raises Mr. Bloom into a legendary figure and gives him history and the world for his stage. But in doing that it fulfils once more the requirements of Mr. Joyce's humour, for to squat Mr. Bloom on the centre of that stage was to attain a comic vision of the world and of history.

What is it that through this use of contrast, this breaking of our resistances by accumulation, Mr. Joyce tries to set in the plane of low comedy ? First of all, professional seriousness of all kinds, and secondly the objects about which people are serious in this way : religion, to which the comic reaction is blasphemy ; patriotism, to which it is little less ; literature, to which it is parody ; the claims of science, to which it is an application of anti-climax ; sex, to which it is obscenity. When comedy attempts to become universal it has perforce to include blasphemy and obscenity, for these are the two poles of this comedy just as the soul and the body are the two poles of human existence. To see religion with the eyes of comedy is not, of course, to laugh it out of existence, any more than to see sex comically is to destroy it. All that comedy can destroy is strictly the second-rate, everything that is not in its mode the best, everything less genuine than the genuine—a class of thoughts and emotions which make up the preponderating part of the experience of most people and of all ages, and is a permanent burden which at times may become unbearable. Books such as " Ulysses " and " Gargantua " can only be written out of an almost insupportable feeling of oppression ; for humour on this scale the sense of oppression is needed as a driving power. The load of oppression which Rabelais cleared away we can see now clearly enough ; it is more difficult to realise, although it is easy to feel, what it is that oppresses in our age a creative writer like Mr. Joyce. But when the reverences of any time are taken very seriously and not very intensely, when a belief in enlightenment, progress and humanity becomes habitual, and men act and think with a fearful eye on it and on the most mediocre of its priests, it has already become as injurious to the creative impulse as the strictest obscurantism could be. It is a weight of second-rate sentiment and thought, and the time comes when the only thing to be done is to clear it away.

To destroy so completely as Mr. Joyce does in " Ulysses " is to make a new start. Or more exactly, the new start must have been made before the destruction began, for the new thing destroys only that it may have room to grow in freedom. But what is new in this sense in " Ulysses " it is hazardous to attempt to say yet ; for the things which are most new in it have a breath of an antiquity which seems to antedate the antiquity of classical literature, and to come out of a folk rather than a literary inspiration. Mr. Joyce's prostitutes in the brothel scene exist neither in the world of literature, as that world has been conceived almost since its beginning, nor in the world of fact. They are rather figures in a folk-lore which mankind continually creates, or rather carries with it, creations and types in the dream in which sensual humanity lives, and which to humanity is the visible world. This folk-lore, which is the aesthetic utterance of the illiterate classes, and of the illiterate parts of our nature, which co-exists with literature, but in a separate world, is not inarticulate ; but it expresses itself anonymously, and is such a constant attribute of human life that it rarely feels the need of the more permanent, the more specialised, expression of art. It attains its perfection from day to day by means which are as suited to its purposes as the means of literature are to the purposes of literature. Yet from it literature arose, for like literature, it is aesthetic, and has the freedom of perception which can only come when men are delivered from their utilitarian prejudices. And to it accordingly literature must periodically come back, as much to test as to renew itself. This is the world to which Mr. Joyce has in part returned, in part striven to return, in "Ulysses." He has seen, as only a profound theorist on art could have seen, that the sources of art lie here, that here is the primary division in our consciousness from which flow on the one hand the laws of art, and on the other the laws of the practical world in which we live. The great categories of literature, such as the pathetic, the tragic, and the comic, which with the interior development of literature tend ever to become more pure, more formal, Mr. Joyce has related to the loose and undifferentiated categories of popular imagination, and, starting from these, has set out to attain a more essential pathos, a more complete comedy, than the conventions of modern literature could have given him. He has not escaped the dangers of such an ambitious attempt. In "Ulysses" there are passages of unassimilated folk-lore which we feel do not belong to literature—diurnal phrases of Dublin talk which should not have survived the day, which, perfect in their time and place, get a false emphasis when set deliberately into the frame of a work of imagination. But where the attempt is successful, Mr. Joyce's imagination has a unique immediacy, a unique originality. In one glance we seem to see the life which he describes immediately before and immediately after he has set his seal upon it, and the transformation of reality into art takes place, as it were, under our eyes. Then we feel sometimes that in sweeping aside the aesthetic sense of three centuries, Mr. Joyce has penetrated to the aesthetic consciousness in itself, the aesthetic consciousness, that is to say, before it has become selective and exclusive, as the more it is developed and refined it tends to become, and still includes everything. It is, of course, obvious that the totality of the responses of that consciousness cannot be rendered in literature, of which selection is not merely a virtue, but also the condition. Yet in the history of literature, as has often been shown, the principle of selection sometimes becomes a conventional, an arbitrary one, and, indeed, continually tends to do so ; and, therefore, it is at rare times necessary for the artist to put himself in a position where a fundamental act of selection becomes compulsory, and where he feels that every decision, whether to include or to reject, is significant not only on traditional grounds, but is made by his own unconditional volition and as if for the first time. " Ulysses " not only raises the problem of selection again ; in part, it answers it by bringing into literature things banished from it, as we now see more clearly, on moral and conventional rather than essential grounds In doing that, Mr. Joyce has both enriched literature and potentially widened its scope

Poems

BY BENJ. GILBERT BROOKS.

Mid-Victorian Rhapsody.

The grandee, prim, magniloquent
Parades the foursquare London street :
Top hat tall as an ebony scroll,
Golden ostrich-plumes his whiskers . . .

. . . Snaky rocks
Shudder into the heavens : mid swaying pines
Blue limelight sweeps the pale sad countenances,
Passionate lovers, poised,
Stiffened like mediæval miniatures
Pre-Raphaelite, a-swoon.

The female set square slyly flaunts
White cap, frail shawl, black velvet coat ;
Her skirt, be-bustled, flowered and frilled,
(A silk trapezium) glides beneath.

Yet, hand in hand,
With cold moist lilies pacing
The forest's magic gloom, they gaze through depths
Of pool-like eyes and with sweet-bitter lips
Bewail their thwarted destinies :

While oriental domes conspire
To bless with mild benignities
Tall chimneys whose black billowing wads
Wave semaphores to mushroom trees.

Love blared and flared, wind-shrill, with rattling drums,
Pennons like flaunting skies, fifes burning bright
Like autumn moons ; blared, flared, and with the tramp
Of the feet, throb of the blood and foam-like shout
Of lips, marched, whirling through: and left a desolate
    land . . .

Limp birds like broken aeroplanes,
Tottering over drear blanched plains.

Give me again red skies : carmine flashing on grey,
Like veins through old men's faces ; burn black vapours
Like passionate hair : ah me !

Pale boats, drifting across green glass :
Calm sea like icefields hung in vacuums.

" The Lord of Terrible Aspect."

Night, swarthy and frail amid strange flowers,
Brooding on seas like unsmooth glass,
Seas that lick flatly at the crashing pebbles,
Weakling and dumb. . . .

Strident from sombre, bale-born mists
A yelling red moon harrows up the sky,
Swinging his leash of light,
Hounding the pitiful waves against the sand,
With dire and amorous hand.

Oh ! see him rend the flower-like stars,
Blaze red to white, and dwindle
(Poor, insane, once potent Lord of Love)
Dwindle to pale flakes, withered autumn leaves,
Blown in the rifts of dawn.

An Historical Bride

By IRIS BARRY.

BASIL RIDDING'S tastes were in no way accidental. A long and costly process of education had fixed hereditary traits developed through the course of twelve hundred years.

He often meditated on the quality of his mother's personality. He would reflect, from time to time, on the atmosphere of that room in which he had for the last time seen her, whence she had made a delicate departure for another, surely equally well-ordered world. Lady Ridding had quitted the British Empire with all the assurance of Royalty, so well illustrated by the story of the great Queen whose eyes never turned to see if a chair were present ; who just sat down, when it was her will to be seated, as though the air itself would thicken into an obsequious seat if nothing more substantial were there. She was convinced that precedence is perpetuated, and that arrangements had been made on the astral plane for her punctual and polite reception.

She had seen Basil grow up calmly, and died satisfied. He had romped, more priggishly than eagerly, on the playing-fields where Waterloo was won ; breathed the dust of the sirocco, poked his long nose into a gaming-room or two, slid down an Alp and been drawn up a funiculaire, looked for crackelures in Amico di Sandros, used the word hyperæsthesia, read Flammarion on the Lido, Disraeli on a Cunard liner. He had felt most at home, out of England, in Boston and Provence.

Like many of his generation, Basil was a poet. This man of cultivation, of such birth and so rich, was something of a lion. Hostesses appreciated this. He surrounded his leisure with fairly beautiful and very old objects : French pictures, Sinetic jade. He roamed among these precious goods, showing them to interested visitors, keeping his one Poussin till last. He had an occupation, the bureaucratic one. At thirty-five he prepared to wed.

This, however, was one of the most difficult problems with which life ever presented him. He must, it was evident, marry beauty, race, culture. But the marriageable girls of his period seemed sadly out of their rôle. Not for them the dignity, the ineffable charm of the past to which they owed so much. Cruder strains of healthy blood imported by actress mammas, in fact a fastness, a bourgeois brightness and eagerness, rendered totally unsuitable for Basil's purpose such young females as circulated in his immediate neighbourhood.

Sometimes as often as every other day he strolled into the family picture-gallery and scrutinised with a blameless but reminiscently-incestuous zeal the serene and admirable features of his great-aunt Clotilda. That was the sort of wife he would like to find.

Back in London he prepared himself to devote all of what energy he had to this pursuit.

" Have you ever thought of Connemara, Grisel ? " he asked his sister, who was pouring out his tea in the Elers drawing-room during the temporary absence at Dax of his great-aunt, president of his town establishment. " The West of Ireland provides, or should do, the necessary conditions. The middle-ages have entrenched themselves in the bogs of Connemara, so I hear, although I have never been there. Do you think it would be dangerous to go there just now ? The inhabitants, I believe, are particularly inflamed against us at the moment. What do you think, Grisel ? "

" Someone there might perhaps do, my poor Basil," she agreed. " But I'm a great believer myself in America. I believe all the best English stock is there, hidden away, but beautifully preserved. Colorado, the Mississippi, Richmond, Virginia : why not go and lecture on poetry in the Southern States and mix freely with some unsuspecting families ? "

" I think I might do worse than scour Ireland first," he replied, selecting a cigarette from the unique four-handled tyg at his elbow, " for it is, I feel quite sure, the repository of vast stores of romance. You have only to read Yeats ; Joyce again ; Shaw too, I feel is nothing but a perverted romantic. All that may have influenced someone, somewhere, to be as I would have them. No ? "

" It may be. Let us hope it has. But beware of pouring

your proposal into the wind-tanned ear of some sad-eyed peasant arriviste. For even in Ireland they are not quite all the daughters and sons of kings, you know."

"You do not understand me," Basil said a little crossly, "or the trouble I am prepared to take. It is not that she would be Irish. It is the clinging to tradition . . . "

"That is why I advise you to scour America," Grisel said. "They cling enough. There is no immediate hurry. Why tumble into a bog ?"

"I think I might go and look round," he said. "My future marriage appears to be not without difficulty. I must leave no stone unturned. First the rural parts of England. Scotland I strike out. The mists make them hoarse, and those who are not hoarse I have seen in town. I do not even boggle at a penniless miss, but she must have, oh, you know so well, Grisel, what she must have besides the appearance ; a restfulness, a suitability." He broke off.

Grisel picked up the woolwork firescreen she was engaged in embroidering. She felt she had said enough.

Basil disappeared into the gizzard of oldest England next day : visited half-forgotten collaterals and friends of the family, seeking among the dowagers, squires, even rectors (of high degree) for the woman destiny doubtless reserved him. Age-eaten carriages were brought out to sun themselves once more, and bear ladies for his scrutiny. Letters on costly paper written in crabbed script by withered white hands went this way and that, borne by page-boys : even by post. Lower than his own heaven he swam awhile among the impoverished-genteel. But here as elsewhere the old blood had paled.

Back in London he threw himself into necessary activities, attended councils, signed memoranda, sometimes attended to charities and organisations for keeping alive the moribund gratitude of the poor.

Then, one day, when he had almost decided to go to America, he went to a little tea-party at the house of the last but one Viennese ambassador's wife, an aged daughter of some vanished barony, on whose rheumatic left was seated a young person. As Basil advanced his hand to make contact with the claw of his hostess, he dropped a glance at the lady beside her.

"*So* good of you to come. *Too* charming," said old Lady Foksey, laying bare the long tusks of her race in a terrifying smile. "You do not know my little friend Aminta," she continued, seizing the stranger's wrist. "This is Sir Basil Ridding, pet," she said, "an old friend of mine. Talk to her, Ridding."

Basil gave one of his celebrated bows, which possessed all the best qualities of an eighteenth-century reverence without its blatancy. The girl, ever so languidly, raised her head, which was hidden by a rather shabby but elegant enshadowing hat of horsehair interwoven with jet. Her face became visible : lamb-white eyelids fringed in deep black lifted up to disclose brown eyes, quiet and mournfully vacant as a doe's. She smiled. Basil's heart experienced an unwonted irregularity of beat. He sat beside her, sipping tea and nibbling at a cinnamon cake, prepared to hope.

"Lady Foksey did not tell you my name," she said, gazing at him with those untroubled eyes. "It is Aminta Courtenay Przalika." She gracefully smoothed down some complication of her costume. The slowness and magnificence of her movements pleased him. She was tall, had a Gobelin face, long slender hands, pointed feet, and sat erect without stiffness. And, as they talked together, he found, too, that she was too much the real thing to chatter. Her conversation was distinctly restful.

Basil took his departure after an hour, and conveyed to Lady Foksey a desire on his sister's part to be allowed to visit her.

"A ravishing creature, Miss Przalika," he murmured before saying adieu to his hostess.

"She is the daughter of Countess Przalika, the morganatic wife of old King Caryl," Lady Foksey breathed : was it with menace ?

"So ! " exclaimed Basil, and made his way out. Miss Przalika's origin was more than he had reckoned on.

"Grisel," he said to his sister on entering his home, "I believe that I have at last met the future Lady Ridding." He related the encounter : she approved. Two days later she called on Lady Foksey, and, by a series of fragments of conversation with the old woman, contrived that Basil should take Aminta in to dinner at a not inconsiderable function the following week. Lady Foksey understood perfectly. She was, indeed, able to congratulate herself on what had been, actually, her little scheme. Everything was prepared for Basil's further acquaintance with the heaven-sent bride.

The evening of the dinner-party arrived, Basil led Aminta to the dining-hall among the other guests invited by the famous political Duchess of —— to meet some almost important plenipotentiary. Aminta was robed in silver, which artfully conveyed a perverse assurance at once of her youth, her beauty and her distinction. After all, was she not some sort of royalty ?

" Yes," and " Oh, *yes*," she said to Basil during the first course. He noticed her appetite for *hors d'œuvres* was a little pronounced. Soup, fish, she accepted, entrées, roasts, game, sweets, ices and dessert went the same way, and she drank what must have amounted to a bottle and a half of wine. He was divided between surprise at her capacity for food and admiration for her indifferent, almost dreamy way of disposing of it. The Duchess, who, of course, had hardly eaten anything, already had a heightened colour, a strand of her hair had wandered from its jewelled bandeau. But Aminta looked as serene as before. And she did not attempt to interest him, or give him quick eye-glances : she did not gabble of the latest plays, or make epigrams with obvious enjoyment of her own wit, as girls he had met recently had done. She knew, thoroughly, in a royal way, that she *was* interesting. If she spoke more than to agree musically with him it was of far-off things, olden times. He was touched and delighted to find that she ignored the ingredients of the English cabinet, hardly seemed aware of a Republic in France. Gawaine and the Medicis, Charlemagne and Helen were more real to her than Ford or General Lawrence. She quoted John Suckling ; had never heard of, still less dipped into, the execrable Edwardian divagations of Proust. Some miracle had preserved her from any knowledge of events later than the middle of the nineteenth century : she had read nothing since Stendhal, whom she dubbed a flunkey. If one said " the Russians " to her, she fancied it was an allusion to the retreat from Moscow. The preoccupations of his stomach appreciated this back-reaching perspective. Heaven he felt had most abundantly blessed him in causing his orbit so propitiously to cross that of the historical creature at his side.

Dinner over, he followed her out on to the balcony over-looking Carlton Terrace, where she stood looking aloft at the stars.

For a moment he wondered if she were real, or an ancestral apparition : until the recollection of the food she had ingested flashed into his mind. He conversed with her, expressed his admiration. Turning, she gave him a slow, gracious smile, but said nothing. He ventured to place a kiss on her arm. No doubt Lady Foksey had prepared her. She touched his hair with her other hand.

"You are unlike the Englishmen I have met," she said.

"And you are Queen of all the romance in the world," he replied, and enfolded her in his high-born arms. Although this was only their second meeting there seemed nothing for it but for them to unite their destinies. He placed a kiss on her perfectly turned, perhaps a trifle Hapsburgian, lip.

Some days later Basil's great-aunt Ridding, Lady Foksey, Grisel Ridding, and a very potent representative from the kingdom of Aminta's father foregathered, with solicitors hovering near, to discuss the approaching nuptials. Everything was arranged, the month for the marriage fixed, when Basil joined them. The great-aunt mentioned the word " portion."

" Ah," sighed the noble envoy, " that is a troubled question. His late Majesty did his best for the Countess : but extravagant habits, y'know—Mademoiselle has little."

" Mademoiselle," interrupted Basil, " is a treasury in herself. I snatch at her, even penniless."

" Ah ? " queried the envoy, casting a shrewd look at Basil. " But Mademoiselle has resources. She has written for some years," he continued.

" Written ? " Basil cried, aghast. " Written books ? For money ? " It was almost as though he had discovered she kept a boot-shop in Piccadilly. The envoy made a gesture, deprecatory, tradesmanlike. Old Lady Foksey blew a snort of disgust down her flaccid nostrils. But Grisel said quietly :

" Of course, once married, she would feel no necessity to pursue such a vocation ? "

Lady Foksey cut in furiously : " Aminta is *too* romantic. Of course, her mother—still, we needn't go over all that. But the result is, Aminta seems to take our ancient associations too . . . well, crudely."

Basil let out a quick sigh. Was there a blight on the bride ?

" She writes romances, you mean ? "

" Oh, continually," the envoy replied. " A sort of Chaucerian prose, you know, allowing for the difference of language, something more than Morris and quite saleable."

" Ah ! " This put a slightly better complexion on the journalistic habit.

" And of course, once married, I feel *sure* dear Aminta would not dream," remarked the envoy's wife, who had sat quietly by.

Other questions relative to the union were discussed. Great-aunt Ridding signified that she was prepared to retire. She had said little, as she was very deaf, and preferred not to meddle and make people shout.

Aminta was summoned.

Basil placed on her left hand a ring which Jane Seymour had given to a Ridding. She received the relic coolly, bent to kiss Grisel, her future sister-in-law. In spite of her appetite and her journalism, Basil felt almost certain that she was the most suitable woman he had ever met, or was ever likely to find.

Great-Aunt Ridding arranged a reception to announce the engagement. All the uncontaminated aristocracy, all the gravest and oldest gentry, the flower of foreign ambassadorial magnificence, and, with the easy ampleness of those who have nothing to fear, two " king-making " editors of newspapers, were bidden. Closed rooms of the town house were unshrouded, heirlooms brushed up, and some supernumerary domestics culled from outposts. Decorations of stiff early-Victorian bouquets in white paper-lace frills were chosen, as, through some little oversight in general training, no one remembered how Saxons, Stuarts and even Georgians had arranged such matters.

The hour approached : Great-Aunt Ridding took up her

station at the head of the Piedmontese staircase leading to the reception rooms, seated herself in an Elizabethan chair with petit-point seat, disposed her satins and ordered her Cluny headdress. Basil stood beside her.

Aminta was almost late for the ceremony, but her costume explained the delay. A mediæval gown fresh from Hanover Square (none of your French dressmaking for the chosen of the Riddings, dear no, why, that only dates from the Regency) : a long sheath of marvellously preserved or imitated Spitalfields brocade enfolded her, spreading at the ground to hide her pointed morocco shoon : a square-cut neck, long hand-shadowing sleeves of green : an embroidered lawn handkerchief in the left hand, and a coronet of her own abundant brown hair, dressed very high and full.

The guests mounted to greet the central figures of the group. Aminta received all congratulatory murmurs with great calm, just sufficiently suggestive of maidenly reserve. When everyone had arrived Great-Aunt Ridding began to rise from her chair : the guests remained stationary in elegant groups inside the first drawing-room, waiting for the old lady to indicate, on completing her surrection from the chair, that the hour had arrived to move towards a sort of Roman feast spread on porphyry tables in the third drawing-room. The old lady rose, slowly, stiffly. Basil stooped to offer a bended elbow. The guests, who were slightly thirsty, stood momentarily silent and motionless, all eyes focussed on the Riddings and Aminta. And then Aminta made a step forward to assist Great-Aunt on the other side. Her peculiar shoes hampered her a little, she caught one foot in the hem of her robe, made a rapid pace with the other foot to free herself, but stepped instead on the trailing fullness of her skirt, and, throwing up her arms like a suicide, plunged down the marble staircase. Breaths were caught, eyebrows rose, hands trembled a little, and Aminta continued to fall.

It was a terrible moment for Basil. Nothing like it had ever happened before in the whole twelve centuries of his family's history. The bride-elect was falling downstairs. His limbs froze, Great-Aunt, deprived of his assistance, dropped back heavily on the embroidered seat of her throne. The bride-elect was falling into the arms of two footmen.

THE CALENDAR

Those costly and decorative machines had stepped smartly forward and presented themselves as buffers. Long experience in the clumsy stumblings of pantrymaids had prepared them for accidents of the kind. They caught Aminta neatly, and placed her, on her feet, on the mat. A loud groan burst from the moist lips of Basil, and he rushed down the stairs in pursuit.

"*Most* unfortunate," snapped Lady Foksey in the background.

"To be disregarded," retorted Great-Aunt firmly, rising unaided this time, under the stress of the moment.

"We will have some supper," she pronounced. *Noblesse* triumphed once more : the personages, without showing any particular emotion, stalked into the third drawing-room, and, secretly vowing it was *too* tiresome for the girl, spoke of hounds, of the Riviera, or of recent sales at Christie's.

Meanwhile Basil had swept Aminta impetuously into the empty breakfast-room, and, after assuring himself that she was unbroken, placed her in a saddle-bag chair and knelt at her feet. She looked pale, leant back, turning away her magnificent head. She knew too acutely what she had done. No commination had ever been prepared for an action like hers, so monstrous was it. It was impossible that people could fall downstairs, publicly. She leant back, closed her eyes, and waited for what Basil would say.

He read her thoughts.

"Aminta," he said, from his position on the hearthrug, "Aminta, I love you!"

The robust tones in which he made this singular remark were so unfamiliar, it seemed so unusual a thing for him to say, that she pushed back the white lids of her eyes and gazed at him in amazement.

Some incredible emotion had him by the throat. It almost unnerved him, for, while he realised with the utmost clarity that her precipitation down the stairs had certainly been mistaken and almost sinful, he also had to admit that the danger which she had momentarily run had ignited a strange and rather uncomfortable fire in his bosom. No, blame Aminta he could not. He gazed into her pale face, in which he was pleased to trace a likeness to her royal parent, with something that appeared positively to be adoration.

AN HISTORICAL BRIDE

Had he not almost lost her ?

Had perhaps his family been only ever so little less distinguished, the footmen consequently a degree less automatic and trustworthy, she must certainly have been dashed to the ground.

Something of the old knightly fervour, dissipated though it was by generations of in-breeding, swept through him.   Not his admiration for her magnificent total immersion in the Past, which hitherto had been her chief charm, could rival her loveableness just now immediately after the hour of danger. His eyes filled, he attempted to gather her in his arms fiercely and rapturously.

" I love you, dear, dearest Aminta," he cried.   " When I saw you falling I realised it.   Had it been another woman " (he shuddered at the idea) " who knows, I might have been shocked.   But, I love you ! "

He seemed quite unlike himself, a little like a sentimental commoner.   Even the shade of a likeness was revolutionary. She gazed at him for a moment.   Instinct came uppermost, got the better of her, commanded her to make the most of her very feminine hour, and gave her a shove into reality.   She made a little murmuring sound, and, bending forward, attempted to hide her face on his shoulder like any dairymaid.

A moment or so later the pair ascended the Piedmontese staircase, and, her arm resting in his, entered the banqueting room.   The tiniest suspicion of a coo of admiration rose from the entire gathering.   Aminta was entirely unruffled, serene. The recollection of her unpremeditated flight was erased, thereupon, from human memory.   Eating began.

The wedding took place some weeks later, appropriately enough in the 11th century chapel of Riddingsdale House. The rectors and dowagers, the tall equine daughters and over-dentated sons of allied families, and two personages sent to represent the successor to Aminta's great father (the successor was delighted to have her off his hands and had paid for the trousseau) filled the carved stalls of the antique edifice.   A bishop presided, royalties sent gifts, the *Times* described it with dignity.   Aminta, like a pillar of ivory in her parchment-coloured velvet gown and Mechlin veil, half swooned at the conclusion of the ceremony, a little compliment much appreciated by the bridegroom. The honeymoon at the Ridding Dower House in Cheshire passed like the action of a stately dance. Aminta walked on the keep, fed the peacocks, and conversed gently, gently with her husband. They returned to London. Grisel and Great-Aunt had vacated the town-house, and the pair took up residence. Aminta proved a born hostess.

Basil never had to speak to her on the score of her former literary activities. They had ceased, vanished like the recollection of her accident. The passage of time proves it in every way a shrewd union. It is said, indeed, that Aminta will be the wife of a Governor-General before many years have elapsed.

The Reminiscences of Mme. F. M. Dostoevsky.

Translated by S. S. KOTELIANSKY.

My Second and Subsequent Visits.*

ALTHOUGH there was comparatively little to copy out of the work dictated yesterday, I so wanted to write it in a clear hand that I arrived half an hour late. I found Dostoevsky in great agitation. " I was beginning to think," he said, " that you found work with me difficult, and that you would not wish to come any more ; I did not write down your address even, and was afraid that what I had dictated to you yesterday might be lost." I apologised for being late, and said that if I were to stop working with him I should certainly let him know beforehand and return the dictated original. Dostoevsky began telling me that it was incumbent on him to finish the novel by November 1. " Meanwhile," he said, " I have not yet decided on the plan. I know that the length must be not less than seven folios of Stellovsky's editions ; but what the novel is going to be like I don't know." To my question as to whether the novel was to appear in a monthly magazine, Dostoevsky gave me a detailed account of his business relations with Stellovsky, the publisher. The story was, indeed, a revolting one. It must be said that Dostoevsky owed much money ; debts taken over by him after his brother's death and after his review *Epocha* had stopped publication. The debts were in bills, and the creditors worried Dostoevsky terribly ; they threatened to seize upon his property and to put him in prison. The urgent debts he had to meet amounted to three thousand roubles, and he had been trying to find the money, but with no result. When all attempts to persuade the creditors to wait some time longer

* Continued from Vol. 1, No. 4.

had failed and Dostoevsky was driven almost to despair, then the publisher Stellovsky came forward with the offer to buy the copyright of all Dostoevsky's works to be published in three large volumes. For the copyright Stellovsky offered to pay 3,000 roubles, on condition that Dostoevsky gave him a new novel, of seven folios large size, in a two-columned page. Dostoevsky's position was critical, and he agreed to all conditions, only to save himself from the debtors' prison. The agreement was made in April, 1866, and Stellovsky deposited 3,000 roubles with a Notary Public to be paid to Dostoevsky's order. The three thousand roubles Dostoevsky handed over the very next day to the creditors. . . . Thus of 3,000 roubles obtained for his copyright Dostoevsky received no ready cash at all. But the most revolting thing was this : quite soon it became clear that the 3,000 roubles had passed again into Stellovsky's pocket. Having bought up for a mere trifle Dostoevsky's bills from the creditors, Stellovsky forced him to accept extremely bad terms. The price for the copyright of all Dostoevsky's works, three thousand roubles, was in itself scandalously small, in view of the success of Dostoevsky's novels, especially after the publication of *Crime and Punishment*. But the cruellest thing of all was the clause requiring Dostoevsky to deliver the new novel by November 1, 1866. In case of non-delivery Dostoevsky was to pay a heavy fine ; and should the novel not be delivered by December 1 of the same year he was to lose his copyright, which would pass then to Stellovsky in perpetuity. That man was a cunning and astute exploiter of our authors and musicians (as, for instance, of Pissemsky, Krestovsky, Glinka). He was always looking out for people who were in a difficult position and used to catch them in his net. I think that by stipulating for the delivery of the new novel at a fixed date with a heavy fine for non-delivery, Stellovsky was certainly calculating on appropriating the copyright of Dostoevsky's books. Dostoevsky at that time had been absorbed by his work on *Crime and Punishment* (running as a serial then), and in view of the great interest aroused among the public, he wished to complete it to the best of his ability. And then to write ten folios of a new novel ! Knowing the sickly state in which Dostoevsky nearly always was, Stellovsky counted on the chance that

he would not have the time nor the energy to exe-
cute two works simultaneously, and then, according to the
agreement, he would acquire the copyright of Dostoevsky's
works for ever. And it would certainly have happened had
not God given Dostoevsky the strength to finish his new novel
in time. That was the state of Dostoevsky's affairs then.
He also told me that, as it seemed almost impossible to write
the novel during that one month of October, his friends—
Maikov, Milyukov and others—suggested that Dostoevsky
should give them the plan of his novel, and each one of them
would write a part of it, so that the three or four of them could
manage to have it done in time. But Dostoevsky preferred
paying a fine or even losing his copyright to signing his name
to a work which he had not written.

However little I knew the world and its affairs at that time,
yet that business of Stellovsky astonished and revolted me.

As usual, tea was brought in, and Dostoevsky began
dictating. But he seemed to find it difficult to settle down.
He often stopped, thought, asked me to read over what I had
written, and after an hour he declared that he was tired and
that we had better have a rest. We began talking, but
Dostoevsky was perturbed and passed from one subject to
another. He again asked me my name, and forgot it instantly ;
twice he offered me cigarettes, although I had told him that I
did not smoke. Then the conversation turned on the Russian
authors who always interested me. Replying to my questions,
Dostoevsky as it were put aside the thoughts that were besetting
him and spoke calmly and even gaily. He spoke of Tourgenev
as of a man of great talent ; he was only sorry that the latter
lived for long intervals abroad, and therefore had forgotten
Russia and Russian life. He spoke of Nekrasov, as of a friend
of his young days, and placed his poetic gift very high. About
Maikov he said that he considered him one of the wisest and
best of men.

Dostoevsky began dictating, and became again irritable
and perturbed. Evidently he found it hard to settle down to
work. I explained it by his not being accustomed to dictating :
hitherto he had written his works himself without the help of
others. After four o'clock I was making ready to go home,
and promised to bring a fair copy of that day's work. When

THE CALENDAR

I was leaving Dostoevsky surprised me very much. He said :
" What a large chignon you wear ; are not you ashamed to
wear false hair ? " I said that I had no chignon, only my own
thick, nice hair. Such a remark of his seemed to me strange
and unceremonious. That day Dostoevsky gave me a ream
of the thin mail paper with hardly visible lines, on which
he usually wrote, and showed me what margins to leave.

Thus began and continued our work : I used to come at
twelve and stay till four, and during those four hours he dictated
to me for three half hours, sometimes more, and between the
dictations we talked. With joy I began to observe that
Dostoevsky was more and more getting used to the new way
of writing, and that every day he seemed quieter. Especially
was this seen when I counted the number of my written pages
and compared them with a printed page of Stéllovsky's edition ;
after which I could say definitely the number of pages dictated
to me. The growing number of pages greatly cheered and
pleased Dostoevsky, and he would ask impatiently : " How
many pages did we do yesterday ? " Our talks were many,
and every day he unfolded before me a sad page of
his life. A deep sympathy was stealing into my heart at his
accounts of painful circumstances, of which he seems never
to have been free, and from which he cannot free himself
even now.

It also seemed strange to me that I never met any one
of his family. I did not know of whom the family consisted
(he did not speak of it, and I could not ask Fedosya, as Dostoevsky himself always saw me to the door). Yet one member*
of his family, whom I took to be his cousin, I met,
I believe, on the fourth day of my visits to Dostoevsky. I
was just coming out of the gate when a young man stopped
me. I recognised in him the dishevelled youth whom I had
seen in the house during my first visit. Close to me he seemed
more ungainly than at a distance : he had a swarthy, almost
yellow complexion, black eyes with yellow pupils, thick curly
hair and tobacco-stained teeth. " You don't recognise me,"
he said familiarly, " I saw you at my father's. (" So that is

---

* This was Pasha,—Dostoevsky's stepson, by his first marriage.

his son," I thought.) I do not want to come in during your work, but I am curious to know what shorthand is like, the more so as I myself am going to start learning it. Please," and without any ceremony he took my portfolio, opened it, and there in the street began examining my notes. I was so confused by that familiarity that I let him rummage among my papers. " It is a curious game," he said, as he handed back my portfolio.

During my three visits to Dostoevsky he appeared to me so kind and sympathetic that it seemed strange to me that such a nice man could have a son who was so free and easy and almost impudent. . . .

Between the dictations our conversations were quite lively. I ceased to fear the " famous author," and spoke to him frankly and freely, as I would talk to an old friend, or to my father. I asked him about various events in his life, and he readily gratified my curiosity. He told me fully of his imprisonment in the Peter and Paul Fortress, how he communicated with the other prisoners by knocking on the walls ; he spoke ot his life when he was serving his term ot hard labour, and ot the convicts he had known there. Sometimes he complained of his difficult position, of his burdens, of his debts. He spoke of foreign countries, of his travels, of his meetings with various people. He told me of his Moscow relations, of whom he was very fond. He also told me that he had been married, that his wife had died two years ago, and he showed me her photograph. To tell the truth, I did not like her very much : she looked so old, terrifying, almost dead. Yet, as he told me, the photograph had been taken a year before her death.

But it turned out that all the stories told by Dostoevsky were sad ones. I was grieved that his life had been so bitter and hard. I once asked him : " Why do you recall only unfortunate events ? Why not tell me of your happiness, of how happy you have been ? "

" Of my happiness ? But I have never experienced happiness, I have always been waiting for it. I recently wrote to my friend Baron Wrangel that in spite of all the misfortunes that had befallen me I still dreamed of happiness ; that I dream of beginning a new life."

It was painful to hear that such a good and gifted man had never yet been happy, and now in his almost old days was dreaming of happiness !

He told me of the court he had paid to Anna Korvin-Krukovsky ; how she had given him her word to marry him, and how he had released her, for he found that, with their different convictions, they could not be happy. And he spoke of her a great deal as of a sensible, kindhearted and talented girl.

Once Dostoevsky told me that he was on the point of making one of these three decisions : to go to the East, to Constantinople and Jerusalem, and perhaps remain there for good, to marry someone, or to go abroad to play roulette and become a gambler. The attempt to solve these problems gave him a good deal of trouble, and he asked me what I thought would be the best solution. I said that if he had to make a choice between those three decisions the best thing he could do would be to choose marriage. " And do you think I could marry ? " he asked, " Or perhaps you think that nobody would marry me ? But whom should I choose : a sensible or a kind woman ? " " Certainly, a sensible one," I answered. " No, if I am to choose, I'd choose a kind one, so that she should love and cherish me," said Dostoevsky.

As we talked of marriage in general the conversation turned on my own case, and Dostoevsky asked me why I did not marry. I said that two men were paying me attentions, but I did not love either, I only respected them, and I should like to marry one whom I could love. Dostoevsky ardently supported my view that one ought to marry " for love," and that for a happy marriage " respect " alone was not enough.

Once, in the middle of October, when Dostoevsky was dictating to me, A. N. Maikov suddenly appeared in the doorway of the study. I had seen his portraits, and therefore recognised him at once. Entering, he remarked jocularly on the patriarchal way in which Dostoevsky lived : the door into the flat was half open, there was no servant about, and anyone could come in and take away the whole flat. Dostoevsky seemed to be pleased at Maikov's coming, and he introduced me at once as his zealous assistant, saying : " A. N. Maikov ; my zealous collaborator, Anna Gregorievna Snitkin."

REMINISCENCES OF MME. F. M. DOSTOEVSKY

I must not conceal the pleasure it gave me to hear Dostoevsky admitting and valuing my assistance. Hearing my name Maikov asked me if the late Snitkin was a relation of mine. Maikov was in a hurry to leave and said he did not want to interrupt our work. I suggested an interval for rest, in which I could copy out the dictation. Dostoevsky accepted the suggestion, and they both went into the next room, and stayed there talking about twenty minutes. Coming in to say good-bye to me, Maikov asked Dostoevsky to dictate something to me. Dostoevsky complied with his wish and dictated to me half a page of his novel. Immediately I read my notes aloud. Maikov examined the notes, and said : " No, I can't make that out."

Maikov produced a very pleasant impression on me. As a poet I had loved him before, and Dostoevsky's praise of him only strengthened my impression.

The longer the time went on the more Dostoevsky got into his stride. He no longer dictated to me monologues thought out at the time, as he did at the beginning. He worked at night, and dictated to me from his notes. At times he managed to write so much during the previous night that I had to sit at home late after midnight to copy out the dictation. But then with what triumph would I announce next day the growing number of pages ; and how pleased I was to see that my assurances that the work was progressing and would be ready in time, made Dostoevsky smile happily. Both Dostoevsky and myself entered into the life of the heroes of the new novel (*The Gambler*), and both he and myself had favourites and bugbears among the characters. My sympathies were with the grandmother who had gambled away a fortune, and also with Mr. Astley [the Englishman], and I despised Pauline and the hero of the novel, whom I could not forgive for his faintheartedness and his passion for gambling. . . . Dostoevsky, on the contrary, was on the side of the Gambler, and said that he himself had experienced many of his feelings and sensations. He assured me that one might possess a strong character and manifest this all one's life, and yet not have strength enough to conquer in oneself the passion for roulette. The characters of the novel became living people to us, and we argued about them. I often wondered at my courage in expressing my views, as well as at the extraordinary indulgence with which the talented writer listened to my childish remarks and opinions. His indulgence to my words I attributed to his extraordinary kindness, and I felt deeply grateful to him.

During the three weeks of my work with Dostoevsky all my former interests had receded to the background. With Olkhin's permission I no longer went to his lectures, I saw very little of my friends. For the all important thing to me was the work for Dostoevsky and those most interesting conversations which we had during the intervals between dictations. I compared our conversations with the talks of the young people of my circle, and how empty and insignificant those talks appeared to me compared with the ever new subjects discussed in the conversations of my favourite author. Each time I left him I was under the impression of ideas new to me ; at home I felt sad and dull, and I lived in the expectation of my coming next meeting with Dostoevsky. I thought with sadness that our work was nearing completion, and with it would end our daily meetings. I realised what a blank my life would be when those interesting and animated conversations would be no longer open to me. And how surprised and delighted I was when Dostoevsky gave expression to the same idea that was worrying me.

Five days before the end of our work Dostoevsky said to me as I was leaving :

" You see, Anna Gregorievna, we have got to know one another ; we have met on friendly terms every day and got quite accustomed to talk together ; and now, when the work is over, all this will come to an end, and we shan't meet one another. Indeed, I shall be sorry ! I shall miss you. Where could I see you ? "

" But, Fiodor Mikhailovich," I said, " two mountains never come together, but two human beings may."

" But where ? " he asked.

" Well, in society, at the theatre, at concerts," I replied.

" But you know," he said, " that I go very rarely into society or to the theatre ; and what is the good of meeting in society when one sometimes can't say a word to another. Why don't you invite me to your house, to your family ? "

REMINISCENCES OF MME. F. M. DOSTOEVSKY

"Please do come, we shall be glad to see you. I only fear that you may find mother and myself uninteresting company.'

"When may I come ? " he asked.

"Well, we can fix the time when we have finished our work," I said. "Surely the work is the most important thing now."

One day, coming to Dostoevsky, I found him agitated. He had a fear lest Stellovsky, in order to put into operation the clause respecting the fine, might, on some cunning pretext, refuse to accept the manuscript. I began to reassure Dostoevsky, and promised him to inquire what was to be done in such a contingency. That same evening I asked mother to go and see a friend of hers, a lawyer. The latter advised that the manuscript should be delivered either to a Notary Public or to the police inspector of the district where Stellovsky resided, and that an official receipt should be taken for it.

On October 29 the last dictation took place : the novel *The Gambler* was finished. Thus, from October 4 to 29, in twenty-six days, a novel of seven folios, two-columned, Stellovsky edition, had been written.

Dostoevsky was very glad, and said that he wanted, on the safe delivery of the manuscript, to give a dinner at a restaurant to his friends (Maikov, Strakhov, Milyukov), and asked me to take part in the feast. He asked me if I had dined before at a restaurant. I said I had not. "But you will come to my dinner ? " he asked. "I want to drink the health of my dear collaborator. Indeed, without your help I could not have finished the novel in time. So you will come, won't you ? "

I said I would ask mother ; but in my own mind I decided not to go. I thought that with my shyness and lack of social experience I should cut a dull and silent figure, only spoiling the general merriment.

Next day, October 30, I came to Dostoevsky—not to work, but to hand over the copy of the dictation done the day before. Dostoevsky met me with particular warmth. When he saw me he got up to greet me, and I noticed that he even blushed. As usual, we counted the pages and were glad that there were so many. Dostoevsky wanted to go through the novel to-day to get a general impression of it, to make a few corrections, so as to take it to Stellovsky next day. He then gave me the fifty roubles for my work, and shook my hand several times, thanking me for my collaboration. Then we talked a great deal and with animation.

I knew that October 30 was Dostoevsky's birthday, and therefore I decided to put on my silk lilac dress instead of the ordinary black costume. Dostoevsky, who had always seen me in mourning, was flattered by my attention, and said that lilac suited me very well, and that, owing to my train, I looked taller and more graceful. How pleased I was to hear his praise ! But my pleasure was spoilt by the visit of Emily Dostoevsky, the widow of Dostoevsky's brother, who came to congratulate him. Emily Dostoevsky behaved to me in a dry and haughty manner, which surprised and even hurt me. Dostoevsky was displeased with the tone of his sister-in-law, and he became more cordial and attentive to me. He offered me a book that had just come out, and himself led Emily Doestovsky aside and began going through some papers with her. At that moment A. N. Maikov came in, He bowed to me, but evidently did not recognise me. Maikov asked Dostoevsky how the novel was getting on, but Dostoevsky, engaged in conversation with Emily Dostoevsky, gave no reply. Then I resolved to answer for Dostoevsky, and said that the novel was finished yesterday, and that I had just brought the last pages of the copy. Maikov then came up to me, held out his hand, and apologised for not having recognised me at once. He explained it by his being short-sighted, and also by the fact that in my black dress I had seemed to him shorter. Maikov began inquiring about the progress of the novel, and asked my opinion of it. I was fascinated by the new novel, which had become so dear to me, and I said that there were in it three characters (the grandmother, Mr. Astley and the enamoured General) extraordinary alive and good. I must have talked for quite twenty minutes so easily and freely to that dear and nice man. Emily Dostoevsky was somewhat surprised and even shocked that Maikov showed me so much attention and cordiality ; yet she did not alter her dry tone, considering it beneath her dignity to regard with decent feeling a mere shorthand writer.

REMINISCENCES OF MME. F. M. DOSTOEVSKY

Maikov went away, and I was making ready to go, wishing no longer to contemplate Emily Dostoevsky's sour looks or to endure her haughty tone. Dostoevsky tried to persuade me to remain ; and wishing to smooth over the unpleasant impression caused by this meeting with his relation, he saw me to the hall and reminded me of my promise to invite him to our house.

I confirmed my promise. " When can I come to you—to-morrow ? " he asked.

" No, to-morrow I shall not be at home ; I have an engagement at my sister's," I replied.

" The day after to-morrow, then ? "

" No, I have a shorthand lesson."

" Then on the second of November ? "

" On Wednesday I am going to the theatre."

" Christ ! All your evenings seem to be occupied. Do you know, Anna Gregorievna, I think you say so on purpose, simply because you do not want me to come to see you. Tell me the truth."

" I assure you," I said, " we shall be glad to see you. Come on November 3, on Thursday evening about 7."

" Thursday ? What a long time to wait. I shall miss you ! " he said.

I took his words for a sweet compliment.

(To be continued.)

Right Readers and Wrong Readers.*

My Experiences with " Martin Arrowsmith."

By VERNON LEE, Litt.D.

I HAVE strung together these notes in answer to a request for more studies like those in my *Handling of Words*. This is not a review of *Martin Arrowsmith* in the sense of an account, for I take it that by this time everyone able to appreciate will have read Mr. Sinclair Lewis's amusing but also disconcertingly serious new book. Still less is this a criticism. For criticism, as hitherto practised, starts from the implicit assumption that the critic can tell the artist what he ought to have done and even what he intended to do ; works of art and literature being judicable according to a code applied by the particular critic, all other codes being erroneous and responsible for the worst aberrations, indeed deduced from such. Now, rightly or wrongly, I am convinced that, except for a dozen or so precepts old and solid as the hills, against confusion, redundancy, anti-climax and similar wasting of the reader's attention, there can be extracted from this sort of criticism only one instructive item, namely the unintentionally conveyed information about the critic himself, his likings and dislikings. This, however, has considerable interest. Since, recognised for what it is, analysed and classified as such, it may help us to penetrate the *raison d'être* of all literature, by showing how various kinds of readers respond to various kinds of writers. For unless I have gone entirely astray in my *Handling of Words*, when the writer treats a subject, treats also sentences and parts of speech, let alone metaphors, and illustrations, in the way which is *his* way, referable to his temperament and habits, he is manipu-

---

lating the reason, experience, emotions and imagination of his readers, each of whom (and the same is true of the artistic beholder or musical listener) will answer to this treatment according to *his* temperament and habits. Hence it becomes interesting to know how a given reader responds to a given writer; at all events it is the only kind of criticism which interests me. So, whenever I shall imply " Mr. Sinclair Lewis ought to have done this or not done that," this should be understood to mean " ought in order to meet the wishes and elicit the happiness of readers who happen to be *like me.*" While his having done something by which I have been disappointed or annoyed, is a proof that (lack of skill being ruled out in this case) there are other people with likings and dislikings different from mine ; at all events there is one such person of different literary wants and aims, namely Mr. Sinclair Lewis himself. And, should these preliminary remarks shock anyone as a nihilistic falling back on " De gustibus non est disputandum," I would answer that it is no good disputing (still less legislating !) about tastes before you have accounted for tastes, which you can do only after finding out what tastes there are. And the taste easiest for me to describe and understand is, at present, my own. So I set out to describe, and, if possible, understand, what happened to me, or rather *in me*, in relation to *Martin Arrowsmith*.

In this personal experience what strikes me first and last, is my difficulty with the chief, the only dramatic, incident in the book, namely the experiment on the plague-stricken islanders. This is not a sentimental, humanitarian difficulty ; that would require my taking the business seriously. My difficulty is just that I feel it to be entirely cock-and-bull. I cannot swallow a scientific expedition which purposes to test an alleged antidote by giving it to only half of the islanders and seeing whether the other half will die for lack of it. I cannot swallow scientific men who solemnly believe that plague can be finally abolished by, and *only by* such a statistically exact experiment ; scientific men who forget that the hope of escaping the plague would induce the majority of mankind to use even the most scientifically discredited, let alone imperfectly tested, specific, while the minority, the temperamental anti-vaccinationists, would go on and pooh-

pooh the test, questioning the statistics and ascribing even their own eventual death of plague not to lack of the antidote, but to dozens of other possibilities and impossibilities. Scientific men would never believe this nonsense about the test. And what concerns us at present, I refuse to believe in their believing it. Indeed, I should be all the better pleased if someone would write to say that the episode under discussion, so far from being an invention is taken with barely an alteration from p. 37 of *Beitrage Zur U.S.W. Jahrgang* XII, and that my venturing to call it " cock-and-bull " just shows, etc., etc.

What it *does* show is that I happen to feel it to be cock-and-bull. And my persistingly feeling it to be cock-and-bull (and not the greater or less credibility to other people) is part of my experience with *Martin Arrowsmith*; and will lead to some curious facts about the relations of Readers and Writers which are my sole concern at this moment. *Cock-and-bull*; please remark, and moreover suspected of having been invented solely to bring about a certain dramatic situation which the author did not see his way to bring about otherwise. And here I must remind you that the element of the *cock-and-bull* is plentiful in the literary masterpieces of all languages and not unknown elsewhere. Everyone who has written stories must be aware of several unwritten ones, plots and situations, of incomparable interest, pathos, humour, etc., which had to be reluctantly abandoned because they wouldn't hold water. Moreover, a number of other subjects so irresistibly tempting that we try to disguise their points of leakage ; or recklessly embark on them without so much as bunging the holes (like some adventurous boys on a certain lake) with stolen apples. We trust to the friendly Reader baling out the water or being so entranced by the scenes we show him, as not to notice that a little more of improbability will submerge what Dante, when setting forth on a rather doubtful voyage, called *the little skiff of our mind*. Like Dante, we trust to the Reader's wish to believe. For however that may be in matters theological, there is among the fundamental facts of literary and artistic experience the certainty that we shall acquiesce whenever we greatly enjoy what we are being told or shown. Plenary indulgence is accorded whenever our sympathising interest has been excited, and our admiration awakened ; whenever a work of art or literature (or a human creature re-fashioned by hero worship or love) offers release from the boredom of real life and admission into a seventh (or demi-semi !) heaven of unreality. When this has come to pass, and to make it is the artist's and poet's especial mission, we brook no interruptions to that bliss, and automatically push aside, " close our apprehension up " to anything which could check our interest or spoil our pleasure. Hence the very essence of a masterpiece is that, fulfilling as it does our heart's desire, what faults it has shall be unnoticed, or transfigured by our forgiveness into additional graces. And, as concerns novelists and playwrights, we invariably accept the hugest *cock-and-bulls* for the sake of what is made of them : think of all Shakespeare's damsels in male attire never once suspected by their nearest relations, his exchangeable pairs of lovers and entirely convertible villains ; think of that one and only pocket handkerchief (and never to be sent to the wash!) deciding poor Desdemona's doom. . . Has not the whole world and four centuries of it forgiven, swallowed these, not gnats, but full-fledged chimaeras ? Quite similarly, returning to Mr. Sinclair Lewis, two great empires-full of Readers and Reviewers, have swallowed like milk that episode of the statistical experiment practised (or not) on those plague-stricken islanders; while there it is, still sticking in my throat, whenever I so much as think of *Martin Arrowsmith.* Now why ? For this *why* will be found to contain not merely an isolated fact concerning one Reader, to wit, myself, but the general law governing the relations of all Readers with all Writers.

The inquiry will be helped by comparisons with what is taking place in my case about another recent novel. I happen to be up in arms against my friend the *Affable Hawk* for daring to call attention to what he calls (forsooth!) improbabilities, *faults*! in *The Constant Nymph.* Out upon thee! Thou purblind critic, pedantically bent on the too-too natural blackbeetles and potato peel of realism ! Desist from breaking in on my perfect enjoyment of these lovely queer young people and lovely uncomfortable places (not Tyrol only, but that Genoese village) ; leave me to the enchantment of this blend of tenderness, drollery and pathetic youthful tragedy, romantic, musical, Mozartian . . . Respect, O thou who art named *Affable*, this meeting, full of gratitude and forgiveness, between the Right Reader and the Right Writer. Instead of which, in the case of *Martin Arrowsmith*, I am manifestly the Wrong Reader, the one who strains at a gnat ; the Reader who cannot forgive because he has not found what he expected.

What I did expect in *Martin Arrowsmith*, a novel described as having Science herself for sole heroine, was a renewal of the special imaginative emotion, possible perhaps only in the heart of an ignoramus, awakened by certain biographies of men of science, say that of Duclaux or Metchnikoff : very human figures, but, as I see them, watching by the loom of life with the archangels' song in their mortal ears. . . . Also, when I opened the parcel containing *Martin Arrowsmith*, there crowded reminiscences of what Besnard has painted in the *Ecole de Pharmacie* : his field naturalists in the spring woods and geologists on the glacier; moreover, the drugs and the knowledge elaborated in laboratory and lecture-room shown symbolically in the doctor reaching tensely for the glass into which the drops are counted out by the nurse, while his other arm props the girl fainting on her pillows ; and in the companion fresco the first outing of the convalescent, tottering beatific. Nor any less those visions of worlds remote in place and time which flit across the mind of his students of modern science : the sea-swamp whence all life has arisen, the jungle river where our forbears swung from tree to tree, the trampling mammoths and huge saurians playing in unnavigated seas. This was what, however vaguely and confusedly, I expected from *Martin Arrowsmith*. Instead I have been shown only pauper " cadavers " being dissected ; and trays of test tubes whose contents are but so many chemical formulæ except when we are told it is ulcerous pus fresh from the hospital. Even such things as these might awaken the emotion, solemn, *Lucretian*, left by the books of say, Loeb and Bateson, if the microbiology of *Martin Arrowsmith* dealt like them with the mysteries of life's origin and transmission. But nothing of the kind ! In order (I suspect) to lead up to the cock-and-bull business of the plague-stricken islanders and the statistical test, the researches of Martin (and his rather schematic, allegorical teacher Gottlieb) are allowed to deal only with toxins and anti-toxins; and these latter, severally austerely unapplied by the true man of science. But applied, misapplied of course, only by disgraceful grotesque quacks. And it is with such potential quacks and mercenary *boosters*, at best with rowdy sawbones cramming for exams. between bouts of drunken horseplay, that, rather than with Besnard's audiences of grave youths fit for the *School of Athens*, Mr. Sinclair Lewis has peopled his American University.

Well, some other Reader of *Martin Arrowsmith* may here interrupt me : " Suppose that is exactly what an American University *is* filled with; nine-tenths at least of its inmates and the remaining tenth, personified by Martin Arrowsmith himself and his friend Terry in nine-tenths of their life and thoughts, namely when they are *not* absorbed in microbiology. And is it not rather splendid to think that from out of just such dull, ' boostful ' or rowdy creatures as these real ones, science is ceaselessly elaborated in its healing purity, even as are the anti-toxins out of the cagefulls of inoculated guinea-pigs and the test tubes filled with pus ? "

The reader who speaks like that is the Right Reader for *Martin Arrowsmith.* I am the wrong one. Wrong, because as I have been at such lengths to explain, the book has not given me what its subject had led me to expect : a sense of the greatness, the fascination of the particular science which Martin Arrowsmith preferred to love, ease and worldly advantage. And that this, as I would call it, this *Besnard-fresco*, or *Lucretian*, aspect of microbiology, should not have been shown by Mr. Sinclair Lewis's book, depends also upon something more essential than his choice of personages and *mise-en-scene* ; upon yet another characteristic doubtless connected therewith in his scarcely conscious preferences. I mean his *style*. For unless I was mistaken in those studies of mine on the *Handling of Words*, every—shall we say heaven-born ?—writer has an individual and, I believe, temperamental, hence unalterable manner of saying things. Moreover, and here is my point, a manner allowing him to treat some subjects so as to develop their full stature and significance, but inevitably distorting, withering up, other subjects. Whence I conclude that even had Mr. Sinclair Lewis wished to fulfil

THE CALENDAR

the expectations of Readers as queer as myself and my kind, he could not have done it. Short of being a second Whitman, he could not have brought home to us the majestic attractiveness of science, its emotional appeal like that of mountain-peaks under the starlight, or of a Bach prelude on a great organ, while, as is the case in this new novel, he used up not the personages and background only, but also the language, all *boost* and *pep*,which had enabled him to make a masterpiece of *Babbitt*.

The Laugh

By BELLA COHEN.

MEYER lay on the bed, the covers drawn up over his mouth. His thin, long nose projected over the quilt seemed very long and wax-like ; and his eyes were closed. His feet stuck out beyond the edge of the bed, for Meyer was a tall man, and illness seemed to have stretched him out.

Hannah, his wife, stood near the bed, looking down upon him sorrowfully, her fingers patching her mouth.

" A man who has never been sick in his life to fall so sick. And he only fifty years old—the best years," she thought.

She turned from the bed and silently began to clean the rooms she and Meyer had lived in for the last eight years. Every now and then she stopped to look at the man in the bed.

" It seems so strange for him to be in the house with me and yet not say a word to me." Hannah spoke to herself. " I don't like that white sheet over the quilt."

Hannah carefully placed the broom in the corner near the stove and pattered over to the wooden trunk where she kept her red shawl. A close, layer-like smell of moth balls and unaired clothing lifted itself sluggishly and receded. The red shawl was near the top. It had white stripes and was made of sheep's fleece. Hannah had knitted and dyed the shawl when she was still young and wore a black plait down her back.

She placed the red shawl over the sick man's feet, but they persisted in sticking out—their long, misshapen toes digging into each other with soles as hard as leather. They stood up stiffly perpendicular.

Hannah looked at them and a strange terror gripped her. Her Meyer was sick. Her Meyer was very sick ! Desperately, she thought of the House. Perhaps she had better call Mrs. Brandt. Someone . . .

A knock sounded.

Hannah hurried to the door and opening it softly, looked up into the ruddy, round face of her sister Brahne.

" You ! " she cried delightedly. For a moment, the sadness left her eyes. She was no longer alone—all alone—for now, if only for a few moments, she had her sister with her. Someone of her own blood.

" Yes, here I am ! " And Brahne stepped into the room. Everything in it became dwarfed, for Brahne was large, large of feet, hands, head, mouth, teeth, and voice. By lifting her hand she could have flattened its palm on the ceiling as easily as she carried her twins on each hip.

The two looked at each other, for they had not seen each other for a year. Brahne had moved her bakery, her husband and children into a suburb, and Hannah, who could not ride in cars because it made her dizzy, did not visit her.

" Meyer is sick, very sick," Hannah finally said. Her hand went up to her mouth again.

Brahne turned to the bed and looked at the man.

" He doesn't seem so bad," she decided. " What is it, a cold ? "

" No, it's something more. The doctor wouldn't tell me. I think it's his heart."

" Heart ! That's how much you know about men."

Brahne seated herself and discoursed in bellows.

" Men are children. They don't know how to bear even a scratch on the finger. They get a little cold and right away they want to go to Coloraydo and get consumption. They want to be petted and fondled like a month-old baby. The more attention you give them the more they want. Many times I think to myself, why do they send men to fight in the wars when they are such weaklings ! "

Hannah listened meekly, her hand on her mouth.

" Maybe that's true what you say, Brahne," she offered timidly, " but Meyer is now laying like this the third week. And, you know, he's never been sick since we've been married."

The tears formed in her eyes and dropped down her cheeks.

Brahne's large, limpid eyes wandered from the sick man's face to his feet. The red shawl threw a new light into her eyes.

THE LAUGH

Hannah wiped the tears away as she mumbled :

" God should spare him for me. If he should die—"

" Die ! " scoffed Brahne, with difficulty shifting her eyes from the shawl to the man's face. " People don't die so fast."

The sick man stirred and the cover moved down from his mouth. He was smiling.

Brahne rose from her chair and walked heavily to the bed. She beckoned her sister.

" See ! " she said. " He's not sick. He's smiling A man who sees Death doesn't smile, hah Meyer ? "

The sick man did not open his eyes nor move at all at the sound of his name. But the smile was still there.

" I could make him laugh ! " Brahne wagered.

" Laugh ! " her sister repeated, sadly. " What wouldn't I give to hear him laugh again ! "

Brahne looked at the red shawl, lips drawn in, one eye half shut.

" Well," she said finally, " would you give me the red shawl if I made him laugh ? "

Again the hand went up to the mouth, and Hannah considered. Brahne had always wanted that red shawl she knew.

She nodded.

" Yes," she finally assented. " But you must make him laugh."

Brahne leaned over the bed and tickled the soles of those stiff feet. A broad smile already stretched across her face.

" Hah, Meyer," she called out, " don't think you can fool me ! "

Again she trailed her large, square fingers over the calloused feet. A slight trembling took hold of the man. His toes began to wriggle stiffly—creakingly.

" Well, Meyer, how about a little laugh ? " Brahne called cheerfully. Hannah stood over her husband, her hand almost hiding her mouth. Now and then she looked at her sister.

Brahne bent to her task with determined lips. She no longer smiled. She wanted that red shawl. This time she played on the soles as if she were playing the piano. Then she changed to a quick tattoo. A weak, little gurgle issued from the parted lips of the man, but his eyes did not open.

"Well, Meyer," shouted Brahne. "You can do better than that!"

She tickled those stiff feet with the full vigour of her strong fingers. And, suddenly, the covers flew back and the red shawl dropped to the floor. A ringing laugh cut the silence of the room. The sick man laughed again and again like a hysterical girl, but his eyes never opened.

Brahne, her hands on her hips, joined in lustily, and even Hannah smiled tenderly and without sadness.

Suddenly the laugh broke into two and the man stiffened from head to toes. The lips drew themselves together slowly and painfully, and then they were still. The soul of Meyer had fled on the back of a laugh.

"Brahne!" Hannah screamed. "Brahne!"

"What's the matter?"

But Hannah had already fallen on her knees beside the bed, moaning:

"He is dead! My husband is dead! My husband is dead!"

Brahne, big and powerful, looked down upon the dead man and the weeping woman with a puzzled look in her stupid eyes.

"But anyway I made him laugh," she said. "The red shawl is mine."

———

Comments and Reviews

The Hudson Memorial.

Every now and then the envy of the mediocre finds an outlet in the persecution of some artist or writer of more than average intelligence. Mr. Shaw long ago beat the journalists into the cringing sanctimoniousness with which they now regard every word he utters, but two other of our most representative artists, Mr. Joyce and Mr. Epstein, either do not possess or do not wish to exploit that genius in controversy which is the life-blood of Mr. Shaw's art. It is, then, particularly agreeable to find Mr. Shaw lending the weight of his formidable dialectic to the side of the artist in the recent controversy over Mr. Epstein's panel in Hyde Park. It is to be hoped (it is in fact incredible that it should be otherwise), that his letter to *The Times* of June 19 should not restore sanity to the argument and that the editors of the popular daily Press, if they are not susceptible to a sense of personal decency and public responsibility, will at least fear to pronounce further on a question in which they have clearly made themselves ridiculous, and if the passage of time had granted that freedom of speech which is allowed to the historian commenting on the reviews of Endymion, we should add, infamous. "Fair comment" is an elastic term, but it must be clear to any fair-minded reader that the journalists would not have dared to comment on the reputation of a business man, a lawyer, or a medical specialist, with the scurrilous vulgarity of the recent campaign. But an artist is fair game to any sentimental ignoramus or copy-hunting reporter. The journalists, of course, are not alone to blame. Certain members of Parliament offended the dignity of the House by remarks of a startling imbecility. Natural obtuseness, though, is only to be pitied, and in technical criticism, we agree, a real artist neither expects nor desires any mercy. But, in a popular discussion, the parties being innocent of all technical knowledge, the debate necessarily descends to irrelevancies, and at its worst to personalities. In signed work, personalities bring their own responsibility ; anonymously, they are unpardonable. It is against these aspects of the affair that we trust everyone will lend their influence. The responsible bodies of artistic opinion should use their support to counteract this attempt to diminish the reputation of an artist whose work does honour to whatever individual or institution which may be happy enough to possess an example of it.

THE CALENDAR

MR. WOLFE'S EXHIBITION.

The exhibition of drawings and water-colours which Mr. Edward
Wolfe is holding at the Mayor Gallery, 18, Cork Street, contains
some very interesting work. His studies of café scenes and one or
two of the landscapes have great qualities of movement and colour,
but it is his drawings, perhaps, which show the more originality.
In " The Garden " (41) he uses pen and ink very effectively, and
the two drawings " Zara " (30) and " Study for Portrait " (35)
show a strong sense of character. Mr. Wolfe is already known
as a contributor to the London Group, but it is to be hoped that
before long he will have an exhibition of his paintings.

CHEKOV THE DRAMATIST.

" The Cherry Orchard " has at last been put on the English
stage (it was produced by the Stage Society at a couple of matineés
some years back), and the venture seems to have taken well. Those
who were unable to see the play at the Lyric Theatre, Hammer-
smith, may remedy the omission now that it has moved to the
Royalty Theatre, and there, no doubt, those who have seen it will
go to see it again. For no other modern play demands and is
worth such sustained and repeated attention. Chekov is not an
" easy " dramatist, and the difficulty of catching his delicate shades
of meaning was not lessened by the manner of this production.
Individually, the Oxford Players gave us sound, and at times
imaginative, renderings of the characters. But, though the strings
were all right, the instrument did not, to our mind, respond in an
entirely satisfactory tone. There was a tendency to emphasise,
perhaps even to mis-create, a conflict between romance and reality
which is the most obvious reading of the dramatic situation. By
this means, pathos is directed towards the romantic lady who
owns the cherry orchard, and the exquisite harmony of the play
is upset. The conventional emotional reactions are as remote from
Chekov as the corresponding *clichès*. The importance of his
innovation in technique is that it is his means of breaking with the
" theatrical " play, so that his drama is all sensibility. Hence the
danger of allowing the conceptions of the theatre, the most sentimental of training-grounds, to blur the simply poetic representation
of Chekov the writer.

TROTSKY ON LITERATURE.

In spite of a good deal of rodomontade about the future, when
" the average human type will rise to the heights of an Aristotle,
a Goethe, or a Marx," Trotsky's " Literature and Revolution " (Allen

393

COMMENTS AND REVIEWS

and Unwin, 8s. 6d.) tells us a lot about contemporary affairs which is very much to the point. "It is silly, absurd, stupid to the highest degree, to pretend that art will remain indifferent to the convulsions of our epoch. The events are prepared by people, they are made by people, they fall upon people, and change these people. Art, directly or indirectly, affects the lives of the people who make or experience the events. This refers to all art, to the grandest as well as to the most intimate. . . A profound break in history, that is, a rearrangement of classes in society, shakes up individuality, establishes the perception of the fundamental problems of lyric poetry from a new angle. . . " This explains the profound boredom which afflicts the reader of so much modern work which is technically competent ; it simply is not alive in the world we are living in. Trotsky is a harsh critic of much so-called revolutionary art ; he does not let his doctrine or his faith blind him to the real questions of literary achievement. Of course there is much more propagandist comment than real criticism, but the book is lively reading and a good informal introduction to the politics of contemporary Russian literature.

THE PIRANDELLO SEASON AT THE NEW OXFORD.

The production of Pirandello under his own direction, at the New Oxford, for which Mr. Cochrane is to be thanked, will be over by the time this note appears. During the fortnight four plays were staged, "Six Characters," "Henry IV," "Naked," and "Right you are if you think so"; and this order denotes justly enough their respective values. It is unnatural to see acting as competent as that of the Compagnia del Teatro d'Arte di Roma on a London stage. Signor Ruggero Ruggeri's Henry IV was the most distinguished individual performance ; his talent is of the first order. "Henry IV" is a play of remarkable qualities, but Pirandello is liable in it to lose momentary command of his theme in vital passages, and the unity of effect in its presentation was largely due to the genius of this actor. The general acting of the company, however, is on a plane to which we are unfortunately unaccustomed. The "Six Characters" is one of the best stage plays of the generation, and it was given its full effect last week. It should become a popular classic when a year or two has sterilised it for British consumption.

A NEW POEM BY RIMBAUD.

Every now and then, out of somebody's heap of manuscripts, a new poem by Rimbaud is dragged into the light to astonish us with the proof that in his brief spell of creative activity he was as remarkable in productiveness as he was in intensity.

THE CALENDAR

" Ce qu'on dit au Poète à propos de fleurs," which is the name of the latest discovery, was sent by Rimbaud to Théodore de Banville (among whose papers it was found) in July, 1871—that is to say, it precedes " Bateau Ivre " by a month or two at most. Already his disgust with " ideals," represented by the conventional flowers, finds an outlet in savage mockery. And is not the whole problem of his life summed up in the question asked by this stanza ?

> En somme, une Fleur, Romarin
> Ou Lys, vive ou morte, vaut-elle
> Un exrément d'oiseau marin ?
> Vaut-elle un seul pleur de chandelle ?

We have not yet been able to examine the facsimile of the manuscript included in the limited editions of the volume which contains this poem (AU CŒUR DE VERLAINE ET DE RIMBAUD, by Marcel Coulon. Le Livre. 12 frs.), but it is undoubtedly genuine. The author also discusses the authenticity of " Poison Perdu," a sonnet frequently attributed to Rimbaud but excluded, justly we think, from the definitive edition of his works published by *Mercure de France.*

A SCOTTISH PUBLISHING ENTERPRISE.

THE PORPOISE PRESS, Edinburgh, hopes to assist the " cultural reawakening " of Scotland by a series of accurate reprints of the national classics. Besides accuracy, these editions will aim at tasteful, but not elaborate, production, and the first two volumes to be issued may certainly be commended for their appearance. These are : Henryson's *Testament of Cresseid* and Robert Ferguson's *Scots Poems* and they are reasonably priced at six and nine shillings respectively.

PAMPHLETS.

As we go to press we receive a batch of pamphlets from the HOGARTH PRESS—" Histriophone. A Dialogue on Dramatic Diction," by Bonamy Dobrée ; "Contemporary Techniques of Poetry," by Robert Graves (3s. 6d. each) ; " The Character of John Dryden " by Alan Lubbock ; " Fear and Politics," by Leonard Woolf. (2s. 6d. each) These represent an admirable endeavour to break the tyranny of the big book and avoid the disjunctiveness of volumes of reprinted articles. For the thrashing out of contemporary problems the pamphlet is of course the ideal form, and we hope that we may see the time when answering pamphlets follow thick upon each other's heels.

394

COMMENTS AND REVIEWS

COUNT KEYSERLING SURVEYS THE WORLD.

THE TRAVEL DIARY OF A PHILOSOPHER. By Count
Hermann Keyserling. Translated by T. Holroyd Reece.
Cape. 2 Vols. 36s.

By Bertrand Russell.

Count Keyserling is a man of some eminence in post-war
Germany, where he has a considerable following as a philosopher.
He is one of those who are weary of European civilisation in its
most modern form, and anxiously surveying the world for something
less disgusting. In Germany, since the war, the number of these
has grown enormously, and most of them turn to Asia for inspiration. In this Diary they can find much that harmonises with
their mood, in spite of the fact that it was written before the outbreak of the war. The later part, it is true, was somewhat·revised
during the war, but there is no noticeable difference of tone. It
says much for Count Keyserling that his reflections before the war
do not seem like echoes from a bygone age ; this is more than can
be said of most writers of general reflections on life and civilisation.
It is necessary to appreciate his personal circumstances in order to
understand his reactions ; for, though he aims at philosophic impartiality, complete success in this pursuit is not given to mortals,
as he is quite aware. Until the aftermath of war dispossessed him,
he was one of the German aristocratic landowners who formed a
reactionary garrison in the Russian Baltic Provinces, now Esthonia,
Latvia, and Lithuania. This position ensured on his part a
neutrality of feeling in the war, together with a singular blend of
German culture and the Asiatic conservatism of the old Russian
autocracy. This blend of East and West makes him unusually
capable of understanding intimately the different civilisations of
the world. In his travels, his method is to make himself always
sympathetic and receptive in each new country. He tries to soak
himself in its atmosphere until the thoughts that would be thought
by a native arise in him spontaneously. This is certainly the right
way for a philosopher to travel ; criticism should never be allowed
to arise until after dramatic sympathy has been exercised to the
full. In Ceylon, India, China, and the Pacific Islands, he practised
his method without much difficulty. On his way from Honolulu
to San Francisco he exerted himself to the utmost to produce a
mood in which he would like America. In the Yosemite Valley,
the Grand Cañon, and the Yellowstone Park, he was quite successful ; but at last a test came which was too severe :

" My friendly feeling has gone. Chicago is awful. All life is
given over to mechanical regulation to such an extent that even
the visitor surrenders himself unconsciously to it out of fear of
perishing otherwise. And his instinct does not err ; the man who
cannot, or will not, be an apparatus for a special function in Chicago,
who is not ready to pledge the whole of his being to it, must perish.''

It should be added that he got over this mood by the time he reached New York, which he admired as it deserves. Chicago alone, in the whole round world, was too much for his powers of sympathy.

While on the Pacific he analyses his feeling of hostility towards America, with a view to getting rid of it :

" It is not possible without loving surrender to understand anything at all ; as long as the slightest inclination to criticism remains in the centre of consciousness, it is hopeless to do justice to what is strange. How can I manage to change my attitude fundamentally in the course of a brief week ? I must undertake something like a psychological analysis. When I have found this out, and thereby the insufficiency of my aversion—for there is nothing which could objectively justify subjective contrariness— then I will no doubt be master of my undesirable mood."

The conclusion at which he arrives is that it is not America, but the West generally, that he really dislikes ; and that the basis of his dislike is " the circumstance that all forms have become fluid to the Westerner." I think this is a just analysis of the most usual ground for preferring the East to the West. It leads to two reflections : one, that forms are rapidly becoming as fluid in the East as in the West ; the other, that the love of fixed forms is essentially aesthetic, and belongs to the spectator's view of life. As to the first : I met in Peking a Hindoo who was Professor of Economics in the State University of Iowa ; he was indignant at the usual view that India is a very religious country, and maintained that most of its inhabitants were materialistic rationalists. He was an extreme instance, but the West is producing more and more of his type among educated Indians. In China, there are more and more men and women whose culture is American, who regard the Confucian code of manners as we should regard that of a mediæval court. In Japan Western fluidity dominates the whole middle class ; sooner or later revolution will make its domination universal. Therefore one who admires the East for the fixity of its forms, is like one who admires the West for its piety, or its aristocratic chivalry ; he is admiring something which is rapidly disappearing, and which all the most vigorous elements in the countries concerned are doing their utmost to abolish.

With regard to the second point, that the love of fixed forms belongs to the spectator's view of life, this is only partially true. The aristocrat loves fixity because nothing else can secure the prolongation of his special privileges. Such motives, however, have not much influence upon the traveller. What he demands of a country is that it shall be intellectually interesting, and aesthetically satisfying. This is not what the inhabitants demand of it ; they want it to be such as to give them personal happiness. This shows why the Asiatic admires America, while the European traveller admires Asia. Asia is superior to America as a spectacle ; America is superior to Asia as a machine for producing happiness in the inhabitants. This point of view is not developed by Count Keyserling, who, for all his dramatic sympathy and imagination, apparently despises *human* sympathy, by which I mean the desire that others should find the happiness they seek. If he felt this kind of sympathy, he would not rest so contentedly in an aristocratic outlook.

Count Keyserling is an advocate of the modern tendency to place psychology, in many respects, above physics. The most influential form of this tendency at the present day is psychoanalysis, concerning which he has not much to say. But his readiness to accept Indian magic and other Indian manifestations which most men of science would regard as superstitions, is explicable as springing from the same source. So is his comment on the exceptional capacity of Englishmen to resist tropical heat. Speaking of Ceylon, he says :

" It is interesting that Englishmen flourish pretty well here, in spite of the fact that they retain the British mode of life, which, as such, is the most unhealthy that can be imagined for the Tropics. The explanation, and at the same time a new proof of it, is, that the Britisher possesses, of all Europeans, the most concentrated powers of imagination."

This is a most surprising statement. My own view would be that the British flourish best in the Tropics owing to their habit of physical self-discipline, which is a product of Puritanism and public schools. The result is that they are more apt than other Europeans in the Tropics to take sufficient exercise, and to abstain from excess in alcohol—both far more important in hot climates than at home. But such an explanation is too homely for the modern mystic.

In other passages, the English are treated less politely. For instance :

" Whenever I meet one of the representatives of this people, I am shocked by the contrast between the dearth of their talents, the limitation of their horizon, and the measure of recognition which every one of them exacts from me, as from everybody else. Even the more eminent Englishmen (the really eminent remain, as everywhere else, beyond the confines of generalisation) can hardly be taken seriously as intellectuals. . . . They all think, feel, and act alike. There are no surprises in the inner life of any one of them. . . . The infinitely richer nature of the German has not yet found its form, and on this account he is not accepted anywhere unless there be some compelling reason."

Aristocratic feeling is a very vital element in Count Keyserling's reactions to the world. He considers Buddha superior to Christ, and attributes his superiority to the fact that he belonged to a ruling house. He is very happy with the rulers of Japan, for whom he has an unqualified admiration. He loves the knightly virtues of Old Japan. While in Kyoto he says :

" A feeling which ' resembles sorrow ' steals over me. It is explicable enough : no matter how much I may be an intellectual, I feel, nevertheless, the fundamental instincts of the knight very vitally in me, and they no longer fit into this age. The days of the nobleman are numbered. What folly to see in this fact a sign of unqualified progress ! "

Nostalgia for the past is the basis of his love of Asia ; the things he loves in Asia will soon be as dead as the things he loves in mediæval Europe. In post-war Germany, love of Asia is often associated with politically radical opinions, because Asia is supposed to stand for pacificism and freedom from bureaucracy. These, however, are not the things that attract Count Keyserling ; he finds the pacificism of Indian and Chinese sages slightly distasteful, and Japanese bureaucracy in no way repulsive. Intellectually, he apprehends what is good in Western ideals ; temperamentally, it leaves him cold. Like the Neo-platonists, he struggles to preserve a dead excellenee in a world which has decisively moved away from it. However just may be the standard of values of men who attempt a task of this sort, they are doomed to futility. Whether we like it or not, America stands nearest to the future of the world. To improve the world, it is necessary to develop through American ideals and organisation. Every age has its own merits, just as every country has ; it is as impossible to transplant in time as in space. Industrialism and democracy may be barbaric for the moment ; so was Christianity in the eyes of Marcus Aurelius. But it is the barbarism of growth, which time will cure. And the cure will not come through an attempt to keep alive what is moribund in the world of to-day.

A JAPANESE CLASSIC.

THE TALE OF GENJI. By LADY MURASAKI. Translated from the Japanese by ARTHUR WALEY. Allen & Unwin. 10s. 6d.

BY BERTRAM HIGGINS.

" The Tale of Genji " was written in Japan at the beginning of the eleventh century. This is the first English translation, and Mr. Waley expects the whole novel to occupy six volumes ; a final volume will contain the authoress's Diary and a critical essay on her work and period.

The nine chapters given here introduce us to the boyhood and adolescence of the hero of this extraordinary tale. Genji is the son of the Emperor (" he lived it matters not when ") and his concubine, Kiritsubo. The first chapter ushers him in, rather conventionally, with the slightly ironic hyperbole and mystifying " asides " of the courtly style in vogue at the time of Murasaki. His mother dies during his early childhood, her delicate spirit broken by the jealous persecutions of the Court ladies, and Genji the illegitimate is cherished by the Emperor as his favourite son. " This, too, incurred the censure of many, but brought no enmity to the child himself ; for his growing beauty and the charm of his disposition were a wonder and delight to all who met him.   Indeed, many persons of ripe experience confessed themselves astounded that such a creature should actually have been born in these latter and degenerate days."   The chronicle-cum-fairy tale mannerisms end with the chapter, and never reappear : henceforward the narrative blends an individual and most pointed description of the external event with a subjective method which anticipates many of the technical experiments of the European novel seven— indeed, nine—centuries later.   But that initial encomium of Genji is in perfect tone with the development of his biography, which, for all its analytic sophistication and disillusioned appreciation of motive, is suffused with a peculiar entrancing idealism.   Such a tone may be found in a few Western novelists, accompanying a similarly mature outlook on life ; but it will be found only in those novels, like " The Idiot " and " The Brothers Karamazow," which are based on a conception of the heroic in human character.   Genji is as far as maybe from the heroic ; Lady Murasaki's sympathies are thoroughly socialised, her interest is in the amiable qualities. The convincing power of her idealisation of Genji can perhaps be partly accounted for by the exclusively aristocratic setting in which he is placed ; there is no clash of social values in that community, and the insinuating artistry with which it is represented has the power to make its standards as absolute for the reader as for the inhabitants.   Again, it is possible that the Oriental mind, obeying a logic which is at some points incomprehensible or antipathetic to the Occidental, has a different integrity from ours, and that romanticism there can exist with realism in relations that we should consider contradictory.   But the most likely explanation, and one which would define the unique charm of the tale, is this : Lady Murasaki's treatment of life and character subordinates all curiosity about their value to an exploration of their beauty, and the choice being maintained with far less compromise than in the great literature of the West, the idealisation appeals to a part of the mind which is comparatively fresh to such an experience.

It is in this atmosphere of strange beauty that Genji thrives ; and all the other figures in the book profit by it, in their degrees. Rapt from it into another climate, into the frame of English life, he would be as " caddish " as Dostoevsky's Myshkin would be maudlin.   The ethics of Lady Murasaki's people are negative ; the two tragic scenes of her story—the sudden death of Yugao at the moment when Genji's love is likely to atone for her past unhappiness, and the simultaneous humiliation of his mistress Rokujo and death of his unapproachable wife Asi—are ascribed to supernatural influences.   (Mr. Waley says that " it is a fundamental thesis of the book that hate kills.")   Genji acts entirely from impulse, but his ingenuousness is guided by an admirable sensibility. The delightful scene in Chapter 2, where he discusses anecdotes of sexual experiences with his young friends, shows his plain-spokenness in intimacy : his conduct on more formal occasions is marked by an extraversion so refined and creative that its most frequent expression is the allusiveness of a quotation or an extempore poem. His love affairs, with which this first volume is mainly concerned, are varied with great subtlety, with the result that we get an introductory idea of the versatility of the writer's literary skill and at the same time an all-round impression of her subject's adolescent personality. Genji's enthusiastic temperament makes his loves eventful, and his profound natural sincerity, annotated by the unprejudicial worldliness of Murasaki, keeps the reader's interest in even his brief, wine-flushed encounter with the betrothed of the Heir-Apparent.

Mr. Waley's translation, from the bilingual point of view, is beyond the ordinary reviewer's criticism ; from the literary, it is almost beyond praise. His English adapts itself flawlessly, often brilliantly, to the demands of the narrative. He has purposely refrained from giving any information about Genji's future. Speculation has only the last chapter of the present volume to work on, in which there seem to be indications of a sterner purpose in Genji, and perhaps of a corresponding change of tone in Murasaki herself.

PICTURES OF EXPERIENCE.

THE METAPHYSICAL FOUNDATIONS OF MODERN SCIENCE. By E. A. BURTT. Kegan Paul. 14s. net.

BY J. W. N. SULLIVAN.

Nearly every kind of sustained and purposeful intellectual activity at the present day is influenced by that body of assumptions and theories that make up modern physics. Perhaps it would be better to say the assumptions " associated with " modern physics ; for it is these assumptions, regarded as metaphysical conclusions rather than as scientific tools, that influence modern thought. These assumptions may be variously described. We may say, for instance, that the universe may be completely described in terms of material particles moving about ; that everything that does not immediately present itself as that can be associated with it as an " effect," or as what Mr. Bertrand Russell calls an " outcome," when he says of man that " his origin, his growth, his hopes and fears, his loves and his beliefs, are but the outcome of accidental collocations of atoms." Or we may refuse, as any modern physicist would, to regard atoms as fundamental, or even, perhaps, space and time as fundamental, and substitute whatever final entities our analysis has reached at the moment. But all such descriptions are, as it were, but local embodiments of the one great persistent assumption on which this philosophy, so far as it is connected with modern science, is based. That assumption may be described by saying that ultimate reality shall only be ascribed to entities capable of being treated mathematically. This assumption may, at times, issue in materialism—as long as particles of matter are the last terms of our analysis. It may, as it would for a philosophy based on relativity, issue in something not at all materialistic, as when space and time, as well as matter, is derived from an indefinable relation, the "interval" between indefinable "point-events." But the "interval" and "point-events" may be treated mathematically.

It has occurred to Professor Burtt to investigate the origin of this assumption, of this criterion of "reality," and the history of its steadily increasing popularity and prestige. This task is an important one, for this assumption, as we have said, influences every branch of thought. Even amongst scientific men, it is true, there are some who doubt whether the criterion is universally applicable ; there are some biologists, for example, who regard "purpose" as a necessary conception in explaining the phenomena of life, and "purpose" probably cannot be treated mathematically. But when we find critics concerned with the deepest problems of art regretting our incomplete knowledge of the "nervous system," we see that the ideal of mathematical description, doubtless in a more or less vague form, does correspond to a very general aspiration. Yet there is no logical necessity for supposing that ultimate realities must be susceptible of mathematical treatment, and many minds find themselves able to dispense with this assumption. The whole outlook has a history ; there have been periods when it did not exist, or, at least, was not general.

Professor Burtt thinks that the modern period began with Copernicus. Besides the dominant Aristotelianism of the later Middle Ages, there was also a neo-Platonism, a philosophy which considered mathematical harmonies of the first importance as a key to understanding the universe. Copernicus was definitely influenced by this dissenting movement. His avowed object in taking the sun instead of the earth as the centre of reference was to give a mathematically more harmonious description of the motions of the heavenly bodies. But there can be no doubt that he regarded this as more than a pleasing mathematical device. In obtaining these simple mathematical expressions, he was also unveiling the plan on which God had constructed the universe. But Copernicus probably did not rise to Kepler's conception of mathematical harmony as the *cause* of the observed facts. In refraining from making this step, Copernicus was nearer to the modern scientific outlook than was Kepler. A modern would agree that, other things being equal, the simplest mathematical description of the facts is the truest, but in saying this he would also probably be aware that he was accepting a certain theory of truth. He would not agree that there is any *a priori* reason why mathematical harmonies should be discoverable in nature at all. But for Kepler not only was the only true knowledge the knowledge of mathematical relations, but the real world was a world of quantitative characteristics only. Such a man might easily have spent his life in inventing empty mathematical fantasies, and, as a matter of fact, he did invent a good many. But he was fully scientific, in the modern sense, in his insistence that mathematical hypotheses must be verified by observation. This criterion enabled him, out of a large number of wild speculations, to hit on his three laws of planetary motion.

The work, both of Copernicus and of Kepler, was geometrical; they did not give *dynamical* descriptions of phenomena. This was, indeed, impossible with the primary entities at their disposal. The notions of "mass" and "force" had first to be isolated. This was done by Galileo. A complete mathematical description of matter in motion now became possible. It might be thought that all that had now been accomplished was to show that the universe had an aspect that could be mathematically described. But for Galileo this aspect was the real world. Hence the emphatic distinction he made between primary and secondary qualities. Masses, velocities, forces, existed in a sense quite other than did sounds, sights, odours. These latter existences, according to Galileo, are "subjective," but figure, weight, motion are things that would remain "without the living animal." Professor Burtt takes us pretty thoroughly through the subsequent developments of this point of view. It is the point of view which leads to the theory that man's hopes and fears, etc., are somehow the result of "accidental collocations of atoms," and it has given rise to some of the most celebrated questions in philosophy. But, although the theory was developed, it can hardly be said to have become clearer. Some of the well-known enormous difficulties which attend it are pointed out by Professor Burtt in his concluding critical chapter. But it may be that the progress of science itself will make much of this criticism unnecessary. For the mathematical description of phenomena, in the terms adopted by Galileo and Newton, has been replaced by a more satisfactory mathematical description in terms of quite different entities. In the Newtonian philosophy mass, space, and time are fundamental. In the theory of relativity they are not fundamental. In relation to point-events and intervals they become, as it were, "secondary" qualities.

It is important, in relation to this discussion, to notice that, by taking a sufficient number of special hypotheses, Newton's general scheme can still be preserved. The great merit of Einstein's theory is its simplicity, and those who accept it are obeying the same impulse that led men to accept the Copernican theory. But if, like some of our older physicists, one experiences an unconquerable aversion to the theory, one may still build up an equally comprehensive scheme in terms of the old entities. It would be a vastly more complicated scheme, and it would be deficient in aesthetic charm. But complexity and ugliness are not logical objections. It would appear, therefore, that a scientific theory involves logically arbitrary elements. Certain entities are selected, certain principles are adopted, and an orderly and coherent description, in these terms, of a certain region of experience, is attempted. It is open to anyone to endeavour to give a description of the same experiences in other terms. Which description we adopt will depend upon our mental habits and tastes. There seems to be no reason whatever why the appetite for mathematical simplicity should be taken as the key to ultimate reality. If, as mathematicians, we find that men are the outcome of accidental collocations of atoms, and if, as men, we find this conclusion intolerable, then we are simply reminded that we have other appetites than a yearning for mathematical simplicity. That the world has a mathematical aspect is almost certain ; that this aspect is somehow more " real " than any other there is no reason to believe.

The materialistic philosophy current until about ten years ago, and against which Professor Burtt's criticisms are directed, has no longer any scientific justification. Modern physics is not materialistic. This being the case, there seems to be no reason for clinging to a theory which, if not unintelligible, is at least open to the most formidable philosophic objections. The outrage done to our feelings by this theory is also an objection to it. It is not sufficient to attribute this sense of outrage to man's mistaken feeling of self-importance. The assumption is that man's feeling of self-importance is a mistake. But malicious interpretations are somehow supposed to be scientific by many people. There is supposed to be something hard-headed and robust, for instance, about explaining a work of art as a product of anal erotism. And professors of materialism, in expounding their extraordinary faith, lay great stress on their own unyielding and undaunted courage. All other men, by implication, are of softer stuff, and take refuge in cheap consolations. It is a relief to know that this unconvincing pose is not now required by science. We may conclude that our suspicion is justified that insensitiveness plays quite as great a part as the passion for truth in making materialism acceptable. With the decline of the materialistic philosophy, we may expect also a decline of the prestige now enjoyed by the cynical view of human nature. We may expect also a growing indifference to the findings of the common-sense school in the criticism of works of art. We shall probably be permitted to believe that the world is as wonderful as it seems to be. As helping to bring about this desirable result, Professor Burtt's book is to be commended.

MRS. DALLOWAY. By Virginia Woolf. Hogarth Press. 7s. 6d.

Mrs. Woolf has culture and intelligence ; she writes from a strong and genuine productive impulse ; her sensibility, when she does not force it, is fresh, individual and admirable in its kind ; for its expression she has developed a fastidious and accomplished technique ; and finally, in " Mrs. Dalloway " it is clear that what she intended to do, she has done, in the sense in which this statement holds truth. These are uncommon merits, they have gained Mrs. Woolf the reputation of what is called a distinguished writer, and their possession entitles her to criticism on her own standards.

" Mrs. Dalloway " is considerably the best book she has written ; in it her gifts achieve their full effect, and her capacity to say what she wants to is almost complete. How then, one asks, as the tide rises through her pages, can such talent coexist with a sentimentality that would be remarkable in a stockbroker, and inconceivable among educated people. Sentimentality is an interesting term, more liable to misconstruction than most ; and it is perhaps clearer to say of this novel that it is impossible to believe that if its author were asked directly whether the thoughts that pass during an hour through the head of any man of fifty bear any resemblance whatever to the soliloquies of Peter Walsh and other characters that fill her pages, her answer could differ from our own. This, however, is what we have to believe, with the result that in spite of, or on account of Mrs. Woolf's talent, her writing conveys an effect of automatism that is curious, and æsthetically corrupt. " Mrs. Dalloway " has the design, apparent intensity, and immediate aspect of a work of art, and it is an interesting problem of æsthetic psychology to explain so self-subsistent a mirage entirely unconnected with reality. This is not to say that falsity is inherent throughout Mrs. Woolf's writing. Her natural and unvitiated talent springs immediately from sensation, and her sensibility of this kind is rare and valuable. When she resists the virtuoso's temptation to expanded bravura pieces, her transcriptions of immediate sensation have the freshness, delicacy and vitality of direct perception, a quality that is not relative, and is sufficient in itself to distinguish her work from intelligent novel-writing. But here Mrs. Woolf's talent stops, in more senses than one. For this quality of direct sensational perception is precisely that of a child's, undisturbed by thought, feeling and other functions to be acquired in the course of its development as a social organism. And Mrs. Woolf is by no means entirely a child ; she is thoroughly involved in human relationships, which form moreover her subject matter as a novelist. But her essential reactions to them are a child's automatic reactions, who believes what he reads in a book, who believes life is what he is told it is, that some people are good and others bad—though bad ones are not to be found among persons he knows—who believes,

COMMENTS AND REVIEWS.

in short, in the absoluteness of his first social impressions as a group member. Together with this more essential Mrs. Woolf exists an intelligent, experienced and sensitive adult, whose business it is to justify her to the world. But these are unhallowed partnerships whose offspring, as I have said, are sentimentality and æsthetic corruption. When she leaves immediate impressions of experience, Mrs. Woolf's treatment of character and human relations is almost ludicrously devoid of psychological and aesthetic truth ; as soon as she touches them she is as false as her rendering of impressions is true. The motives, thoughts and emotions she attributes to her characters have precisely as much and as little relation to the truth of life as the motives, thoughts and emotions postulated of the ideal person who forms its public by the daily paper. There are one or two exceptions to this, in particular the character of Septimus Warren Smith, where Mrs. Woolf rather shakily approaches imaginative truths ; but most of the book, despite its pure and brilliant impressionism, is sentimental in conception and texture, and is accordingly æsthetically worthless. Such judgments, as is evident in this review, cannot be expressed in terms of purely literary criticism, which, indeed, is an instrument not applicable to the valuation of contemporary literature, as should be clear from experience and history.

J. F. HOLMS.

MY HEAD ! MY HEAD ! By ROBERT GRAVES. Martin Secker. 5s.

Mr. Graves has succeeded very well in writing his first prose romance, for he has given real movement and life to his conception of the two Old Testament stories of Elisha and the Shunamite woman and of Moses' leadership in the wilderness. In the former case the original framework is so slight that Mr. Graves has been able to use it truly, without coercion, to fit his needs, and his assumption that Elisha was the father of the woman's child is justified by the treatment. His further assumption, that the Shunamite woman was an intelligent, rather sceptical, but amicable critic of the Mosaic tradition is necessary for the interpolation of his rendering of that tradition. She is made to question Elisha as to the truth of the story told in the Pentateuch, in order that, with his replies, Mr. Graves may build up his own interpretation of the character of Moses, supposing quite plausibly that " Elisha . . . had the secret tradition of what took place at Sinai and Kadesh and elsewhere, in a direct line of confidence from Joshua."

The characterisation is straightforward and sufficient for the purpose of the tale, and the two principal figures, Moses and Elisha, though losing something of their heroic qualities, are represented fairly as types of practical men working in the interest of their faith. Their own belief in Jah is unquestioned, and, being by nature leaders, it justifies them in the use they make of their intelligence and magical powers to govern and advise the people. It is with the problem of these magical powers that Mr. Graves is largely concerned, and here the vigour of his story sometimes fails. For, in spite of the discussion of the problem in the " Argument," he has not made the very necessary decision as to whether he shall treat the miracle rationalistically or with faith. He says there that " mere rationalism does not take one far " ; and, after telling, from the rationalist point of view, the story of the Israelites who impiously lifted the veil of the ark and were punished with the plague, he adds that this presentation of the story does not satisfy him, and insists that the Israelites died because they knew they had committed sacrilege. He maintains that in cases of violation of taboo the offender, wherever he does not choose self-destruction, *does* die, " not by ' auto-suggestion,' or some such comfortable means," but by an accident connected with his offence. He then continues : " So in the case of Moses ; to say, as the rationalists do, that his miracles were all mere tricks or lucky accidents unconnected with Jah is manifestly false, because Moses obviously believed in Jah, and was more loyal to him than to his friends and relatives, and with one exception . . . performed all his miracles in Jah's name. . . . Jah in the wilderness was a reality : Moses had seen him with his own eyes and had in turn passed on the vision to the congregation." This reasoning is weak, for there is no evidence that Moses had seen Jah (unless we accept the incident of the burning bush with the proviso that Mr. Graves makes in a foot-note), and it is further weakened by the narration of the trick which enabled Moses, with the help of petroleum springs, to show Jah to the people.

Mr. Graves's usual method, however, when confronted with a miracle in the original, is to treat it rationalistically and then to fit in this explanation with his own idealistic theory. But though he fails to do this in the instance referred to and in the case of Elisha's restoring the child to life, he does not spoil the effect of the story, for that depends rather on its total æsthetic coherence than on its philosophical content.

Douglas Garman.

PIANO QUINTET. By E. Sackville West. Heinemann. 7s. 6d. net.

One of the least fortunate results of popular education is that fiction has become popular too, and therefore both pretty and erotic. The fault lies in the fact that the emotional experiences of uneducated persons are universally associated with a desire for intimacy with a member of the opposite sex, while at the same time the confusion into which at the moment the ethics of inter-sexual relationship are plunged makes it impossible for the artist who seeks immediate rewards to regard his anyhow important theme frankly or treat it exhaustively. On the one hand we have the optimist who flatters the Boy with tales of the Perfect Flapper or the Flapper with tales of the Perfect Boy. On the other hand, we have the more cynical sensationalist who, knowing that the appetite to which he panders is diseased, offers to his female readers the prospect of lustful Sheikhs, girl-beaters and artists, to his male sinful women miraculously redeemed by honest affection, or children initiated with no less pain than delicacy into knowledge of the symptoms of philoprogenitiveness. To the girl, Douglas Fairbanks with a darkened face. To the hobbledehoy, a choice between Mary Pickford and Pola Negri. At such a crisis of taste anyone who can find something to write about other than Love will be sure of a respectable welcome. Mr. Sackville West has attempted a theme even more troublesome than the sheerly non-erotic. He has tried to describe the relations of a strongly sexed woman with the other members of a musical party in which she is on tour, to give free expression to her lusts, and to reduce this . . . Libido . . . to its proper dimensions. One reading of "Piano Quintet" persuades one that Mr. West, had he only had more experience of novel writing, might have achieved a small, but brightly distinct, triumph. A second reading proves that Mr. West, however much better he might have been if he had been differently educated, is already good enough to command serious attention ; and *that*, happily, has been awarded him. How far the speculations concerning Mr. West's meaning approach the truth is one question. What is wrong with Mr. West's art is another. It is the latter question that is the more important.

It seems as if Mr. West, with a very good story up his sleeve, had been afraid to let it out. The woman loves Aurelian, and Aurelian, like others of the quintet, loves the woman. But neither Aurelian nor anyone else is capable of the entire self-surrender which she in her pride demands. In two powerfully and exquisitely arranged conversations this antagonism—*amor contra mundum*—is discussed. In the rest of the book Mr. West imitates anything and anybody. Now he plays with the Pathetic Fallacy, striving to lend importance to accidents by assuring his readers that inorganic matter throbbed, thrilled, winked, blushed, flinched or smiled at what was happening in a way which Charles Dickens more entertainingly exhausted. Now he gives us scenes, such as that of the military tattoo, which bear no relation to his theme. He is terribly on tiptoe to be up to date. It would just be a joke if he therefore fell into the neo-Gothic manner of the seventies but the damage does not end there, for he has by his old-fashioned devices seriously impeded the progress of his tale, so that the reader is more surprised than pleased to discover behind all this scaffolding ideas of real importance and rare poignancy. The best advice for the reader to take is to read " Piano Quintet" with patience, and the author to strive not again to try his readers' patience so far.

H. C. HARWOOD.

FISHMONGER'S FIDDLE. By A. E. COPPARD. Cape. 7s. 6d.

Of all contemporary short-story writers, Mr. Coppard is the most refreshing, for the simple reason that he takes less interest in himself than in what goes on round him. More often than not, a short story is written to release a mood or to put forward a thesis, and the subject matter is selected and made to fall in. Moreover, in a brief tale, the preservation of unity is a very ticklish affair ; art abhors a compromise and prefers monotony to diversity. Joy is notoriously fleeting, but sorrow abides and is easy to convey ; the moods of sorrow, disappointment and disillusion impose a ready-made unity in which all thought and objects of all thought appear coloured grey, like cats at night. Irony, too, is a great leveller, as are all the non-participating moods which look aslant upon or away from life. Just as melancholy means for the sufferer primarily a falling-off in diversity of interests, so for the melancholy-minded writer the manifestations of life lose their proper quality and become invested with dreariness or horror.

Mr. Coppard's resilient temperament is one of his chief assets ; he will always be a good writer and some time, perhaps, a great one. At present he suffers from the defects of his qualities ; he lacks intensity and the personal conviction by whose help writers much his inferiors in general level of achievement have here and there produced more memorable stories. Mr. Coppard realises, as many writers do not, that however much individuals suffer, the world goes on ; that to insist upon an emotion is often to weaken its effect and tire the reader, and that ninety-nine times out of a hundred what passes for tragedy is either morbidity or sentimentality. We do not for a moment suggest that Mr. Coppard is always trying to achieve tragedy and failing. One subject may suit him better than another, but he has no failures. Nor has one any fault to find with the quality of his emotion. Only it is at times a little light in weight, a little diluted, wine mixed with water ; at worst, it thins away into facetiousness, whimsicality, or into echoes of Hibernian English, that familiar substitute for the language of emotion. His stories drag their anchor, so to speak ; their very buoyancy makes them stray, and though they are never garrulous, they do from time to time flirt with triviality.

But it would be misleading to press this criticism. For the few contemporary writers who might make Mr. Coppard appear trivial, there are scores whose work seems heavy to the point of unreadability beside his. He can make a soufflé out of the most unpromising ingredients ; he can be comic without being artificial, farcical without being mechanical. He understands the lives of poor people, and portrays them from a central position, without prejudice and without sentimentality. Neither their goodness nor their badness comes as a shock to him ; he has no axes to grind, social or moral. Well served by an acute ear for the curiosities of provincial speech, he is at his best in sketches of the countryside, *Willie Waugh* and *Dumbledon Donkey*, their humour, sympathy and playfulness are delightful. In the longer pieces, he has the air of feeling his way ; they are excellent in detail, but they tend to hang fire. But when most exuberant and unrestrained, there is always a core of life, a creative stir in the heart of Mr. Coppard's stories.

L. P. HARTLEY.

THE DAY OF ATONEMENT. By LOUIS GOLDING. Chatto and Windus. 7s. 6d. net.

Brief mention was made in last month's issue of this surprising book, and more especially of the difficulties inherent in the theme adopted by Mr. Golding. But no apology should be required for returning to the discussion of a novel which, whatever its defects, is likely to survive in popular esteem ninety-nine per cent. of contemporary fiction, and which is intended to illustrate nothing less than the collision in modern times between Judaism and Christianity and the effects of that collision upon the son of its victims. Mr. Golding is himself a Jew, but, unlike many Jews and many Gentiles, neither sentimentalises nor despises his race. Simply as a historian of an English ghetto Mr. Golding shows himself here, as he did in ''Forward from Babylon,' to be unequalled. If we remain unconvinced that he is yet able dramatically to illustrate the full extent of his thought upon a less limited theme, we must admit that his very failures are interesting. He has all the qualities of a first-rate novelist. What he has yet to attain is the technical ability wherewith to put these qualities into perfect balance.

The scene in which Eli confesses to his wife—that stern daughter of Israel—his apostasy is as nearly good as it could be made. It fires the reader's imagination, while it satisfies his intelligence. The quaint and crabbed ritual of Sabbath Eve is bathed in a really poetic beauty. Leah's tenderness to her husband, and his own forebodings of the wreck that his confession will cause, are delicately interwoven with the homely details of the feast. There is humour, too—not mere comic relief, but the humour that is the fruit of a sense of proportion ; and the indignation of the Gentile servant at Eli's conversion to something approximate to her own creed—at a respectable God-fearing Jew who went to synagogue as regularly as if it were to Mass, thus lowering himself to a blackly Protestant repudiation of ritual—brings upon the scene both refreshment and illumination. Here, and here perhaps only, Mr. Golding attains to a serene mastery of his material and allows his readers the pure æsthetic pleasure to be derived from the contemplation of great art.

Elsewhere, however, Mr. Golding is less successful. The same qualities are there, but they are not happily wedded. The earnest excitement provoked in him by his imagination is thrown too crudely at the public. Consider, for example, these three passages : (1) " Hapless youth and maiden in your sequestered village upon the river bank, among your green meadows, under the lee of the pine woods, the years contract, the months are fewer, time is a chain of inexorable hours dragging as from a pit of doom the doleful day, the Day of Atonement." (2) " Lo, I have been in Aceldama " (Eli says)," even unto the potter's field, the field of blood. Go from me. Go from my side." (3) " Eli, the incomparable scholar out of Krovno by the Dneiper, became a carpenter for many a month and year—till a more potent preoccupation called him from his bench, as it had called another of the same race and mystery to the agony of the brickcroft and the spitting faces at street corners." These passages are not casually selected, but belong to definite crises in the narrative. More like them might be found. And what with all this apparatus of Jacobean tautology and Biblical reminiscence do they do except register, without communicating to the reader, the author's private emotion ? They are not art. They are attempts to replace art by rhetoric. And the sacred parallel to the sufferings of Eli—who in fact never claimed to be the Messiah—might more properly, one thinks, have been left to the reader's gumption.   H. C. H.

STREAMERS WAVING. C. H. B. Kitchin. Hogarth Press. 6s. net.

" Your garden, Mr. Homfray, is so lovely that it hardly seems quite genuine."

" It is not genuine. It dates . . . . from Tuesday, when Winckworth's installed it."

This novel, too, has the air of brand-new installation. The arrangement is aggressively brilliant, but external, and lacks the easy inevitability of natural growth. In particular, the catastrophe, though extremely effective in itself and in the opportunity it provides for a display of virtuosity in the final chapter, is not a solution of the situation that has been created, but a highly spectacular demolishment of it.

There would be no complaint if, in the earlier chapters, Mr. Kitchin had not appeared to promise so much, or if Lydia Clame, the history of whose decline this book is, were less distinctly and sympathetically realised. That spinster of thirty years lives in Bloomsbury, but is " just the tiniest bit West, both spiritually and geographically." Possessing sufficient, though not ample means, she " always seems to have just been doing something, or to be just going to do something. Never actually to be doing anything." In default of other occupation, she has cultivated a wit and a fastidious self-consciousness that are compensation for the sense of inferiority provoked by people of more animal vitality. Nevertheless, she must perish from spiritual starvation unless she can draw the necessary nourishment from a rather inaccessible Geoffrey. Probably she would not have succeeded, but then the story of her gradual decline *vers une mer glaciale*, would have been intensely interesting, and might have been tragic. Mr. Kitchin does not face the issue. With the same thunderbolt he destroys Miss Clame and the coherence of the attitude to life he had until then expressed.

The book is exhilaratingly written in a clear bright prose that only suffers from a redundance of thin epigram when Miss Clame's thoughts are being followed. The minor characters are seen and felt, and the *mise-en-scéne* is swiftly indicated. If Mr. Kitchin can write with less of an eye to immediate effect, his next novel should be thoroughly good.

C. H. R.

THE CRUISE OF THE NONA. By H. BELLOC. Constable. 15s.

Mr. Belloc emphasises his conviction that books, " save here and there a piece of lyric verse, and here and there a good run of rhythm in half a page of prose," are not worth " one day's riding upon a horse or sailing upon the sea." Yet with surprising complacency he has just written another, of 347 pages, for no better reason than that this task had been set him. Such statements necessarily destroy one's belief in their author, for if a man have a boat and prefer sailing it to writing, he were better at sea than here pursuing " the most abominable of all trades." But one suspects that Mr. Belloc's intention is to sway his readers favourably by suggesting that he is, after all, a plain straight-forward man, one who enjoys life, and a sportsman, and for that reason to be trusted as a writer and a thinker. It seems probable that he counted on some such reaction in order to establish a pleasant, familiar relationship between himself and his reader—his " dear Maurice " or another—which would pass off his dogmatism as plain-speaking, his love of exercise as mental healthiness, the exploitation of his personality as literature.

This latter confusion is an increasing evil. The Johnson myth is swollen every publishing season with some new elaboration of " the Doctor's " personal idiosyncracies—his stockings become more wrinkled, his waistcoat dirtier—until Johnson the writer is eclipsed by the grotesque and fanciful conception of Johnson the Man of Letters. Such a transposition is a godsend to the hack writer, for in this way he is no longer obliged to concern himself with ideas, but may content himself with loosing his *convictions* on the flood of a genial bluffness. It is something of this kind that Mr. Belloc does. The voyaging of the Nona leads him from subject to subject on which he wishes to pronounce, and there is always a storm, or Portland Race, or an unexpected breeze ready at hand to divert his attention and the reader's whenever it shall suit him. Thus no question is discussed fully and few interestingly. It is already common knowledge that Mr. Belloc is a Catholic, dislikes the Prussians, believes in aristocratic government, and looks upon politics as a dirty game. These convictions—it is his boast that he has no opinions, only convictions—gain nothing from being displayed discursively, and the manner in which they are expressed leads often to banality and sometimes to contradiction. At one moment when he is denouncing the " prolonged hesitation among the politicians, men by their petty trade unused to and unfit for tasks of magnitude," he says that war would not have come save for their lack of virility, but later he writes, " It is to the Dreyfus case that we owe the four years of war, 1914-1918." These two statements are typical of Mr. Belloc's manner of thinking ; unless he proves some connection between them their value amounts to nothing.

It is so throughout the book. The haze of generalisations is occasionally pierced by an arbitrary conclusion or a half-statement bombastically proffered as a conviction. Those who admire Mr. Belloc will read him with pleasure, for they will be ready to associate themselves with the reiterated " I " and to accept the easy flow of his writing as a suave and able style. But others will be irritated and bored by the diffuseness, prolixity and tedium of the mind reflected faithfully in this prose.

D. M. G.

AXEL. By VILLIERS DE L'ISLE ADAM. Translated by H. P. R. FINBERG, with a Preface by W. B. YEATS. Jarrolds. £3 3s.

In making so sumptuous a shrine for this idol of declining romanticism there was the danger of drawing attention to the more perishable qualities in Villiers' work. He is not in the first rank of the writers of gorgeous passages ; he added nothing, in that particular vein, to what had already been done by Chateaubriand, Hugo, the exotic Flaubert, even Gautier. His eloquence borders on the precious, like his social eccentricities, and though each is no doubt a perfectly genuine expression of his character, to the spectator the pose seems to be sustained at the cost of grace. " The fine gesture, at all events," was Villiers' reply to the insinuations of life and death, and what is best in " Axel " springs from that root. His fame is most likely to be assessed on the strength of " Axel " with a few *contes* and anecdotes as out-riders to his more elaborate triumph.

COMMENTS AND REVIEWS

The play is certainly made to be read. As Mr. Yeats records in his preface, it was acted with effect in Paris in the early nineties, but its dramatic devices are so simple that their weight can be realised in the reading, and, on the other hand, there is a good deal of dialectic in the text which could not be fully appreciated in the theatre.

There is an essential difference between the drama of ideas, in which the characters and action illustrate or symbolise the author's conception of life, and the drama in which the dramatic quality is inseparable from the idea, is the idea itself. " Axel " belongs to the former kind, for we can imagine other ways in which the conflict between idealism and realism might be expressed, though not so well expressed. But there are no alternative renderings for " Hamlet," or even the " Cherry Orchard," since these are not made up of concepts, but are individual conceptions. The great merit of " Axel " is the vigour with which the characters and the dramatic situations to which they move, express the ideas from which they are born. Villiers' ideas are intelligent and disputable. His natural pride forced him to deny a world in whose affairs he could play only a menial part. In the post-Kantian idealistic philosophy, re-inforced by an older but similar current through Kabbalism and Rosicrucianism, he found a perfectly impregnable stronghold from which to defend his supreme gesture. " Live ? Our servants will do that for us."

It is a Gothic ruin, in which certain pieces of fine workmanship —the initiation ceremony and, with reservations, the final scene—still command admiration but it is no longer habitable. Mr. Sturge Moore's decorations have a hieratic dignity which is in keeping with the spirit of the text. Mr. Finberg's rendering is faithful and, though a trifle stilted, more readable than many translations we have seen. One would have thought, though, that it was the three shilling and not the three guinea public which would be in need of translations from the French.   E. R.

Among New Books

ESPALIER. By SYLVIA TOWNSEND WARNER. Chatto & Windus, 5s.

Miss Warner's poems are emancipated and clean in diction, perceptive and witty, slight in substance but firm in texture. There is only one quality which her pleasing intelligence is unable to encompass and apply in this volume, and that is poetry's one thing needful, imaginative sincerity. No artifices or substitutes, however cunning, can make up for its lack ; this second form of life is exclusive to those who can pay it the homage of an unqualified belief in its reality. The auxiliaries to Miss Warner's will to poetry are sometimes formidable, for she can ward off with neat idioms and a tasteful selection of tried expedients the periodical crises of inflation consequent on an equivocal compact between mind and language. But they mount later on, more blatant for the repression. " The Image," an attempt to recreate and modernise the ballad " Lord Rendell,'' jars on the reader's sensibility because, no fresh emotion being infused into the version, it alternates between parody and imitation.

> " Take out, take out my winding sheet
>   From the press where it lies,
> And borrow two pennies from my money-box
>   To put upon my eyes."

Isolated, that can be enjoyed as legitimate parody, but not in conjunction with the changed intention and flat virtuosity of this :—

> " Why do you speak so loud, Mother ?
>   I was almost asleep.
> I thought the church bells were ringing
>   And the snow lay deep."

Miss Warner's talents as a writer make one hope that she will undertake the reorganisation of inner processes required of her as a poet.

HANG ! By FRANK PENN-SMITH. Chatto and Windus. 6s.

The figures in all these tales (including the animal fables) are recognisably human. Though nothing very fundamental about them is revealed by the stress of circumstances, they are seen, against clearly suggested Australian or African backgrounds, sufficiently concrete and differentiated to engage the reader's sympathy. But sympathy—and words—Mr. Penn-Smith squanders recklessly in the attempt to extract from a situation more meaning than it contains. Lacking the ability to invent really significant incident, he is driven, whenever his story arises from the interplay of personalities, or the reaction of character to environment or event, to blur the effect by explanatory padding. Even the humorous stories suffer from prolixity. Yet Mr. Penn-Smith has a knack of genuinely comical observation that would benefit considerably if the writing were tighter.

GUITAR AND CONCERTINA. Poems by GUSTAV FRÖDING, translated by C. D. LOCOCK. Allen and Unwin. 5s.

In his renderings of a selection from the work of the modern Swedish poet most popular in his own country, Mr. Locock shows very considerable agility. He has retained the original metres and the often complicated rhyme-schemes—really he over-translates his original, which is the least common of translators' weaknesses. Though much of the " poetry " has inevitably disappeared, these very readable translations show that Fröding had a vigorous and responsive mind, and a thorough command of both his instruments.

CONTEMPORARY FRENCH LITERATURE. By René Lalou, translated by W. A. Bradley, Cape. 18s.

Names, reputations, and general tendencies are discussed in a way which is at least exciting. The reader cannot fail to be impressed by the tremendous literary activity which the book reflects, even if that activity seems to some extent a feverish one. Such a catholicity of response, from the poetry of Mallarmé and Valéry, as well as that of Romains and Claudel, from Bergson as well as Benda, Henri Bordeaux as well as Jean Giraudoux, indicates a sensibility which does not feel very deeply. None the less, if used with caution, the book may be found useful for those who wish to fill in gaps in their reading of the French literature of the last fifty years.

THE POEMS OF JOHN MILTON. Volume 1. Edited by H. J. C. Grierson. The Florence Press, Chatto and Windus. 12s. 6d.

This edition of Milton's poems has three points which commend it : its editor, its type, paper, and other details of production, and its very reasonable price.

Professor Grierson has adopted the arrangement which is common to the Florence Press editions of the poets, the absolute chronological order according to date of composition. The advantages of this plan in enabling us to follow the development of the poet's mind do not need to be underlined. The inclusion of Milton's Latin, Greek, and Italian poems in this order is, of course, essential, for they contain personal references which we do not find in the English poems. The type used throughout this series is one of the finest that has been designed for the printing of poetry.

The present volume contains all Milton's poems except " Paradise Lost," which will be issued separately in the autumn.

THE MOTHER'S RECOMPENSE. By Edith Wharton. Appleton, 7s. 6d.

It has become a commonplace of criticism to say that the art of Henry James tended continually to melodrama. Miss Edith Wharton, the most earnest and literal of his disciples, suddenly vindicates this theory. " The Mother's Recompense " is as gaudy as its title, though it contains the usual little circles of bright intersecting consciousnesses, still leaves no mildest emotion undescribed, and is written throughout with the old beautifully bland air. The plot hangs upon a threat of technical incest—the engagement of Kate Clephane's old lover to her daughter—and various attempts are made to make tragedy out of the alarm of the womenfolk as, in turn, they come into touch with the realisation of this central horror. A less able writer than Miss Wharton might, by giving less reality to his characters, or by contenting himself with one settled " viewpoint," have made a more credible novel. As it is one feels that she has wasted her excellent full-length portrait of Kate Clephane, and her brilliant snapshot of the New York clergyman-magnate.

SELECTED POEMS. By Siegfried Sassoon. Heinemann, 3s. 6d.

This 75-page volume contains no new poem by Mr. Sassoon, and it is rather a disappointing selection. There are examples from many periods of his work—two poems are dated 1908—but it is difficult to understand the principle on which he bases his choice. If it is historical, it would have been well to arrange the poems in chronological order ; if, on the other hand, Mr. Sassoon's intention was to include only his best work, we must venture to disagree, by the argument of comparison, with the exclusion of such poems as " The Imperfect Lover," " The Kiss," " Sporting Acquaintances " and " Prelude to an Unwritten Masterpiece." Mr. Sassoon was the most effective satirist in verse that the war produced ; he must be credited with the invention of an original satiric style. Since then he has elaborated another form for the same purpose, and when these later poems shall have been collected out of the periodicals it ought to prove a very good occasion for a review of the whole urgent matter of satire—in particular, of the effects on the satirist of the changed beliefs about individual responsibility since the time of Pope.

THE WEEK-END BOOK. Nonesuch Press, 6s.

The second edition (eighth impression) of this original anthology, containing certain additions and improvements in the arrangement.

BETWEEN THE OLD WORLD AND THE NEW. By M. P. WILLCOCKS. George Allen & Unwin. 12s. 6d.

Mr. Willcocks supports his opinion that the theory of Evolution was the rock on which the tide of human consciousness split into two currents, by deductions from literature. The three " prophets of the will," Goethe, Balzac, and Shelley foresaw a change, the working out of which was to find expression in the work of Butler, Whitman, Dostoevsky, and Hardy. Between these two groups are the typical Victorians—Tennyson, Eliot, Carlyle, etc.— who fixed their eyes on the glorious promise of what was to be ; those who escaped this complacency, Browning, the Brontës and Meredith ; and those who wrecked this complacency, Tolstoi, Chekoo, Ibsen and France. Mr. Willcocks sees in this changed attitude towards experience, " an attempt to gather into one expression the whole universe of manifested life," an effort to build " the future religion of humanity, which will concern itself entirely with the unfolding of the Life Force, or Immanent Will."

If one could penetrate behind the palisade of hyperbole one might find Mr. Willcock's ideas more interesting, but his continual over-emphasis detracts from the value of his thesis and the arguments with which he supports it.

HERBERT TRENCH. *Notice sur sa Vie et ses Oeuvres.* Par ABEL CHEVALLY, *avec texte et traduction de son poème,* " La Bataille de la Marne." Oxford University Press and Les Presses Universitaires de France. 1s.

In a three-page introduction to this pamphlet M. Chevally makes one of those bursts of lyrical journalism with which the French are apt to salute writers whom they cannot commend with their minds. He has made the translation because Trench expressed a wish that it should be done, but also because " L'hommage enflammé que Trench a rendu par ce poème a la France et ses destins . . . mérite en tout cas, à défaut d'admiration littéraire, un témoignage de reconnaissance et d'appréciation." M. Chevally has not succeeded in adding to Trench's reputation as a poet, but he has given a faithful translation which occasionally improves on the original in point of diction.

The CALENDAR
of Modern Letters

VOLUME I   AUGUST
NUMBER 6   1925

Breughel.

By ALDOUS HUXLEY.

MOST of our mistakes are fundamentally grammatical. We create our own difficulties by employing an inadequate language to describe facts. Thus, to take one example, we are constantly giving the same name to more than one thing, and more than one name to the same thing. The results, when we come to argue, are deplorable. For we are using a language which does not adequately describe the things about which we are arguing.

The word " painter " is one of those names whose indiscriminate application has led to the worst results. All those who, for whatever reason and with whatever intention, put brushes to canvas and make pictures are called, without distinction, painters. Deceived by the uniqueness of the name, aestheticians have tried to make us believe that there is a single painter-psychology, a single function of painting, a single standard of criticism. Fashion changes and the views of art critics with it. At the present time it is fashionable to believe in form to the exclusion of subject. Young people almost swoon away with excess of aesthetic emotion before a Matisse. Two generations ago they would have been wiping their eyes before the latest Landseer. (Ah, those more than human, those positively Christ-like dogs—how they moved, what lessons they taught ! There had been no religious painting like Landseer's since Carlo Dolci died.)

417

These historical considerations should make us chary of believing too exclusively in any single theory of art. One kind of painting, one set of ideas are fashionable at any given moment. They are made the basis of a theory which condemns all other kinds of painting and all preceding critical theories. The process constantly repeats itself.

At the present moment, it is true, we have achieved an unprecedently tolerant eclecticism. We are able, if we are up-to-date, to enjoy everything, from negro sculpture to Lucca della Robbia and from Magnasco to Byzantine mosaics. But it is an eclecticism achieved at the expense of almost the whole content of the various works of art considered. What we have learned to see in all these works is their formal qualities, which we abstract and arbitrarily call essential. The subject of the work, with all that the painter desired to express in it beyond his feelings about formal relations, contemporary criticism rejects as unimportant. The young painter scrupulously avoids introducing into his pictures anything that might be mistaken for a story, or the expression of a view of life, while the young *Kuntsforscher* turns, as though at an act of exhibitionism, from any manifestation by a contemporary of any such forbidden interest in drama or philosophy. True, the old masters are indulgently permitted to illustrate stories and express their thoughts about the world. Poor devils, they knew no better! Your modern observer makes allowance for their ignorance and passes over in silence all that is not a matter of formal relations. The admirers of Giotto (as numerous to-day as were the admirers of Guido Reni a hundred years ago) contrive to look at the master's frescoes without considering what they represent, or what the painter desired to express. Every germ of drama or meaning is disinfected out of them; only the composition is admired. The process is analogous to reading Latin verses without understanding them—simply for the sake of the rhythmical rumbling of the hexameters.

It would be absurd, of course, to deny the importance of formal relations. No picture can hold together without composition and no good painter is without some specific passion for form as such—just as no good writer is without a passion for words and the arrangement of words. It is obvious that no man can adequately express himself unless he take an interest in the terms which he proposes to use as his medium of expression. Not all painters are interested in the same sort of forms. Some, for example, have a passion for masses and the surfaces of solids. Others delight in lines. Some compose in three dimensions. Others like to make silhouettes on the flat. Some like to make the surface of the paint smooth and, as it were, translucent, so that the objects represented in the picture can be seen distinct and separate, as through a sheet of glass. Others (as for example Rembrandt) love to make a rich thick surface which shall absorb and draw together into one whole all the objects represented, and that in spite of the depth of the composition and the distance of the objects from the plane of the picture. All these purely aesthetic considerations are, as I have said, important. All artists are interested in them ; but almost none are interested in them to the exclusion of everything else. It is very seldom indeed that we find a painter who can be inspired merely by his interest in form and texture to paint a picture. Good painters of " abstract " subjects or even of still lives are rare. Apples and solid geometry do not stimulate a man to express his feelings about form and make a composition. All thoughts and emotions are inter-dependent. Our faculties work best in a congenial emotional atmosphere. For example, Mantegna's faculty for making noble arrangements of forms was stimulated by his feelings about heroic and god-like humanity. Expressing those feelings, which he found exciting, he also expressed—and in the most perfect manner of which he was capable—his feelings about masses, surfaces, solids and voids. His hero worship made him, by stimulating his faculty for composition, paint better. If Isabella d'Este had made him paint apples, table napkins and bottles, he would have produced, being uninterested in these objects, a poor composition. And yet, from a purely formal point of view, apples, bottles, and napkins are quite as interesting as human bodies and faces. But Mantegna—and with him the majority of painters—did not happen to be very passionately interested in these inanimate objects. When one is bored one becomes boring.

Inevitably ; unless I happen to be so exclusively interested in form that I can paint anything that has a shape ; or unless

THE CALENDAR

I happen to possess some measure of that queer pantheism, that animistic superstition which made Van Gogh regard the humblest of common objects as being divinely or devilishly alive. "*Crains dans le mur aveugle un regard qui t'épie.*" If a painter can do that, he will be able, like Van Gogh, to make pictures of cabbage fields and the bedrooms of cheap hotels that shall be as wildly dramatic as a Rape of the Sabines.

The contemporary fashion is to admire beyond all others the painter who can concentrate on the formal side of his art and produce pictures which are entirely devoid of literature. Old Renoir's apophthegm, "*Un peintre, voyez-vous, qui a le sentiment du téton et des fesses, est un homme sauvé,*" is considered by the purists suspiciously latitudinarian. A painter who has the sentiment of the pap and the buttocks is a painter who portrays real models with gusto. Your pure aesthete should only have a feeling for hemispheres, curved lines and surfaces. But this "sentiment of the buttocks" is common to all good painters. It is the lowest common measure of the whole profession. It is possible, like Mantegna, to have a passionate feeling for all that is solid, and at the same time to be a stoic philosopher and a hero-worshipper; possible, with Michelangelo, to have a complete realisation of breasts and also an interest in the soul or, like Rubens, to have a sentiment for human greatness as well as for human rumps. The greater includes the less; great dramatic or reflective painters know everything that the aestheticians who paint geometrical pictures, apples or buttocks know, and a great deal more besides. What they have to say about formal relations, though important, is only a part of what they have to express. The contemporary insistence on form to the exclusion of everything else is an absurdity. So was the older insistence on exact imitation and sentiment to the exclusion of form. There need be no exclusions. In spite of the single name, there are many different kinds of painters, and all of them, with the exception of those who cannot paint and those whose minds are trivial, vulgar and tedious, have a right to exist.

All classifications and theories are made after the event; the facts must first occur before they can be tabulated and methodised. Reversing the historical process, we attack the facts forearmed with theoretical prejudice. Instead of considering each fact on its own merits, we ask how it fits into the theoretical scheme. At any given moment a number of meritorious facts fail to fit into the fashionable theory and have to be ignored. Thus El Greco's art failed to conform with the ideal of good painting held by Philip the Second and his contemporaries. The Sienese primitives seemed to the seventeenth and eighteenth centuries incompetent barbarians. Under the influence of Ruskin, the later nineteenth century contrived to dislike almost all architecture that was not Gothic. And the early twentieth century, under the influence of the French, deplores and ignores, in painting, all that is literary, reflective or dramatic.

In every age theory has caused men to like much that was bad and reject much that was good. The only prejudice that the ideal art critic should have is against the incompetent, the mentally dishonest and the futile. The number of ways in which good pictures can be painted is quite incalculable, depending only on the variability of the human mind. Every good painter invents a new way of painting. Is this man a competent painter ? Has he something to say, is he genuine ? These are the questions a critic must ask himself. Not, Does he conform with my theory of imitation, or distortion, or moral purity, or significant form ?

There is one painter against whom, it seems to me, theoretical prejudice has always most unfairly told. I mean the elder Breughel. Looking at his best paintings I find that I can honestly answer in the affirmative all the questions which a critic may legitimately put himself. He is highly competent aesthetically ; he has plenty to say ; his mind is curious, interesting and powerful ; and he has no false pretensions, is entirely honest. And yet he has never enjoyed the high reputation to which his merits entitle him. This is due, I think, to the fact that his work has never quite squared with any of the various critical theories which since his days have had a vogue in the aesthetic world.

A subtle colourist, a sure and powerful draughtsman, and possessing powers of composition that enable him to marshal the innumerable figures with which his pictures are filled into pleasingly decorative groups (built up, as we see when we try to analyse his methods of formal arrangement, out of individually rather flat, silhouette-like shapes standing in a succession of receding planes)—Breughel can boast of purely aesthetic merits that ought to endear him even to the strictest sect of the Pharisees. Coated with this pure aesthetic jam the bitter pill of his literature might easily, one would suppose, be swallowed. If Giotto's dalliance with sacred history be forgiven him, why may not Breughel be excused for being an anthropologist and a social philosopher ? To which I tentatively answer : Giotto is forgiven, because we have so utterly ceased to believe in Catholic Christianity that we can easily ignore the subject matter of his pictures and concentrate only on their formal qualities ; Breughel, on the other hand, is unforgivable because he made comments on humanity that are still interesting to us. From his subject matter we cannot escape ; it touches us too closely to be ignored. That is why Breughel is despised by all up-to-date *Kunstforschers*.

And even in the past, when there was no theoretical objection to the mingling of literature and painting, Breughel failed, for another reason, to get his due. He was considered low, gross, a mere comedian, and as such unworthy of serious consideration. Thus, the *Encyclopaedia Britannica*, which in these matters may be safely relied on to give the current opinion of a couple of generations ago, informs us, in the eleven lines which it parsimoniously devotes to Peter Breughel that "the subjects of his pictures are chiefly humorous figures, like those of D. Teniers ; and if he wants the delicate touch and silvery clearness of that master, he has abundant spirit and comic power."

Whoever wrote these words—and they might have been written by anyone desirous, fifty years ago, of playing for safety and saying the right thing—can never have taken the trouble to look at any of the pictures painted by Breughel when he was a grown and accomplished artist.

In his youth, it is true, he did a great deal of hack work for a dealer who specialised in caricatures and devils in the manner of Hieronymus Bosch. But his later pictures, painted when he had really mastered the secrets of his art, are not comic at all. They are studies of peasant life, they are allegories, they are religious pictures of the most strangely reflective cast, they are exquisitely poetical landscapes. Breughel died at the height of his powers. But there is enough of his mature work in existence—at Antwerp, at Brussels, at Naples, and above all at Vienna—to expose the fatuity of the classical verdict and exhibit him for what he was : the first landscape painter of his century, the acutest student of manners, and the wonderfully skilful pictorial expounder or suggester of a view of life. It is at Vienna, indeed, that Breughel's art can best be studied in all its aspects. For Vienna possesses practically all his best pictures of whatever kind. The scattered pictures at Antwerp, Brussels, Paris, Naples and elsewhere give one but the faintest notion of Breughel's powers. In the Vienna galleries are collected more than a dozen of his pictures, all belonging to his last and best period. The Tower of Babel, the great Calvary, the Numbering of the People at Bethlehem, the two Winter Landscapes and the Autumn Landscape, the Conversion of Saint Paul, the Battle between the Israelites and the Philistines, the Marriage Feast and the Peasants' Dance—all these admirable works are here. It is on these that he must be judged.

There are four landscapes at Vienna : the Dark Day (January) and Huntsmen in the Snow (February), a November landscape (the Return of the Cattle), and the Numbering of the People at Bethlehem which in spite of its name is little more than a landscape with figures. This last, like the February landscape and the Massacre of the Innocents at Brussels, is a study of snow. Snow scenes lend themselves particularly well to Breughel's style of painting. For a snowy background has the effect of making all dark or coloured objects seen against it appear in the form of very distinct, sharp-edged silhouettes. Breughel does in all his compositions what the snow does in nature. All the objects in his pictures (which are composed in a manner that reminds one very much of the Japanese) are paper-thin silhouettes arranged, plane after plane, like the theatrical scenery in the depth of the stage. Consequently in the painting of snow scenes, where nature starts by imitating his habitual method, he achieves an almost disquieting degree of fundamental realism. Those hunters stepping down over the brow of the hill towards the snowy valley with its frozen ponds are Jack Frost himself and his crew. The crowds who move about the white streets of Bethlehem have their being in an absolute winter, and those ferocious troopers looting and innocent-hunting in the midst of a Christmas card landscape are part of the very army of winter, and the innocents they kill are the young green shoots of the earth.

Breughel's method is less fundamentally compatible with the snowless landscapes of January and November. The different planes stand apart a little too flatly and distinctly. It needs a softer, bloomier kind of painting to recapture the intimate quality of such scenes as those he portrays in these two pictures. A born painter of Autumn, for example, would have fused the beasts, the men, the trees and the distant mountains into a hazier unity, melting all together, the near and the far, in the rich surface of his paint. Breughel painted too transparently and too flatly to be the perfect interpreter of such landscapes. Still, even in terms of his not entirely suitable convention he has done marvels. The Autumn Day is a thing of the most exquisite beauty. Here, as in the more sombrely dramatic January landscape, he makes a subtle use of golds and yellows and browns, creating a sober yet luminous harmony of colours. The November landscape is entirely placid and serene ; but in the Dark Day he has staged one of those natural dramas of the sky and earth—a conflict between light and darkness. Light breaks from under clouds along the horizon, shines up from the river in the valley that lies in the middle distance, glitters on the peaks of the moun-tains. The foreground, which represents the crest of a wooded hill, is dark ; and the leafless trees growing on the slopes are black against the sky. These two pictures are the most beautiful sixteenth-century landscapes of which I have any knowledge. They are intensely poetical, yet sober and not excessively picturesque or romantic. Those fearful crags and beetling precipices of which the older painters were so fond do not appear in these examples of Breughel's maturest work.

Breughel's anthropology is as delightful as his nature poetry. He knew his Flemings, knew them intimately, both in their prosperity and during the miserable years of strife of rebellion, of persecution, of war and consequent poverty which followed the advent of the Reformation in Flanders.

A Fleming himself, and so profoundly and ineradicably a Fleming that he was able to go to Italy, and, like his great countryman in the previous century, Roger van der Weyden, return without the faintest tincture of Italianism—he was perfectly qualified to be the natural historian of the Flemish folk. He exhibits them mostly in those moments of orgiastic gaiety with which they temper the laborious monotony of their daily lives ; eating enormously, drinking, uncouthly dancing, indulging in that peculiarly Flemish scatological waggery. The Wedding Feast and the Peasants' Dance, both at Vienna, are superb examples of this anthropological type of painting. Nor must we forget those two curious pictures, the Battle Between Carnival and Lent and the Children's Games. They, too, show us certain aspects of the joyous side of Flemish life. But the view is not of an individual scene, casually seized at its height and reproduced. These two pictures are systematic and encyclopaedic. In one he illustrates all children's games ; in the other all the amusements of carnival, with all the forces arrayed on the side of asceticism. In the same way he represents, in his extraordinary Tower of Babel, all the processes of building. These pictures are handbooks of their respective subjects.

Breughel's fondness for generalizing and systematizing is further illustrated in his allegorical pieces. The Triumph of Death, at the Prado, is appalling in its elaboration and completeness. The fantastic " Dulle Griet " at Antwerp is an almost equally elaborate triumph of evil. His illustrations to proverbs and parables belong to the same class. They show him to have been a man profoundly convinced of the reality of evil and of the horrors which this mortal life, not to mention eternity, holds in store for suffering humanity. The world is a horrible place ; but in spite of this, or precisely because of this, men and women eat, drink and dance, Carnival tilts against Lent and triumphs, if only for a moment ; children play in the streets, people get married in the midst of gross rejoicings.

But of all Breughel's pictures the one most richly suggestive of reflection is not specifically allegorical or systematic. Christ Carrying the Cross is one of his largest canvases, thronged with small figures rhythmically grouped against a wide and romantic background. The composition is simple, pleasing in itself, and seems to spring out of the subject instead of being imposed on it. So much for pure aesthetics.

Of the Crucifixion and the Carrying of the Cross there are hundreds of representations by the most admirable and diverse masters. But of all that I have ever seen this Calvary of Breughel's is the most suggestive and, dramatically, the most appalling. For all other masters have painted these dreadful scenes from within, so to speak, outwards. For them Christ is the centre, the divine hero of the tragedy ; this is the fact from which they start ; it affects and transforms all the other facts, justifying, in a sense, the horror of the drama and ranging all that surrounds the central figure in an ordered hierarchy of good and evil. Breughel, on the other hand, starts from the outside and works inwards. He represents the scene as it would have appeared to any casual spectator on the road to Golgotha on a certain spring morning in the year 33 A.D. Other artists have pretended to be angels, painting the scene with a knowledge of its significance. But Breughel resolutely remains a human onlooker. What he shows is a crowd of people walking briskly in holiday joyfulness up the slopes of a hill. On the top of the hill, which is seen in the middle distance on the right, are two crosses with thieves fastened to them, and between them a little hole in the ground in which another cross is soon to be planted. Round the crosses on the bare hill top stands a ring of people, who have come out with their picnic baskets to look on at the free entertainment offered by the ministers of justice. Those who have already taken their stand round the crosses are the prudent ones ; in these days we should see them with camp stools and thermos flasks, six hours ahead of time, in the vanguard of the queue for a Melba night at Covent Garden. The less provident or more adventurous people are in the crowd coming up the hill with the third and greatest of the criminals whose cross is to take the place of honour between the other two. In their anxiety not to miss any of the fun on the way up, they forget that they will have to take back seats at the actual place of execution. But it may be, of course, that they have reserved their places up there. At Tyburn one could get an excellent seat in a private box for half a crown ; with the ticket in one's pocket, one could follow the cart all the way from the prison, arrive with the criminal and yet have a perfect view of the performance. In these later days, when cranky humanitarianism has so far triumphed that hangings take place in private and Mrs. Thompson's screams are not even allowed to be recorded on the radio, we have to be content with reading about executions, not with seeing them. The impresarios who sold seats at Tyburn have been replaced by titled newspaper proprietors who sell juicy descriptions of Tyburn to a prodigiously much larger public. If people were still hanged at Marble Arch, Lord Riddell would be much less rich.

That eager, tremulous, lascivious interest in blood and beastliness which in these more civilised days we can only satisfy at one remove from reality in the pages of our newspapers, was franklier indulged in Breughel's day ; the naïve ingenuous brute in man was less sophisticated, was given longer rope, and joyously barks and wags its tail round the appointed victim. Seen thus, impassively, from the outside, the tragedy does not purge or uplift ; it appals and makes desperate ; or it may even inspire a kind of gruesome mirth. The same situation may often be either tragic or comic, according as it is seen through the eyes of those who suffer or those who look on. (Shift the point of vision a little and Macbeth could be paraphrased as a roaring farce.) Breughel makes a concession to the high tragic convention by placing in the foreground of his picture a little group made up of the holy women weeping and wringing their hands. They stand quite apart from the other figures in the picture and are fundamentally out of harmony with them, being painted in the style of Roger van der Weyden. A little oasis of passionate spirituality, an island of consciousness and comprehension in the midst of the pervading stupidity and brutishness. Why Breughel put them into his picture is difficult to guess ; perhaps for the benefit of the conventionally religious, perhaps out of respect for tradition, perhaps he found his own creation too depressing and added this noble irrelevance to reassure himself.

Poems

BY BERTRAM HIGGINS.

Ulysses in Ithaca.

Now that I've come to you by storm
Of geyser-steaming brine and hail,
I find your lips, love, scarcely warm,
    And the world's face gone pale.

Barbarian in this leisured land
Of soon-built cities and safe joy—
An import nerveless and unmanned
    As our false horse at Troy,

I am pulled passive through quaint streets
For alien ritual with hushed breath,
Whose soul's a crater that secretes
    Action and arms for death.

Rapt in its sandy palaces
Your soul is abstract as blown glass,
Where, stripped of depth and fantasies,
    My mirrored exploits pass

Like a long caravan beset
By glossy Bedouins of the sun,
Pierced in its tegument of wet
    And discrete on a dune.

I watch your strange limbs breathe or move
Noiselessly across clouded rooms,
Less durable than those you wove
    On night-unravelled looms.

POEMS

How can I, silvering in such air,
Bequeath firm sinews to this race
Sprung from a dream you would not share
    And a misjudged embrace?

Prepare, nymph of the anchored prow,
Your salt-dried breasts for ceaseless foam!
O temperate gods, forget the vow
    That made my bourn my home!

The mists of my young breath still float
On billows I must cleave again,
And the blithe voice that launched my boat—
    That echo shall remain

Highest of all heartrending cries
From memory's seamews in the wake
Until my landless enterprise
    Puts in at the Low Lake.

Now hope's unsprung enchantless ears
Can muffle syrens' tongues in waves,
And, happy with my former fears,
    Storm will not leave his caves.

Magic Despair shall make my sails
Furl like a tendril-necked tall swan
Or fill with spiced ethereal gales
    Wafted by me alone.

O bitter dungeon whose green hand
Has chained my friends in weeds and cast
Their bloodless images on sand,
    Your gates have fallen at last:

Wasting beneath my reckless stare
The porous ocean sheds its oil
Till gods and dolphins choke with air
    Upon its bony soil.

The mirage hoisted by black tides
To flash with fins and coral isles
Now bares its marrow—here subsides,
    Hissing with all its reptiles.

I see Adventure's bright ensign
Fall-fading on horizon ships . . .
Ah, dip in distance and steep brine,
    Forsaken lovely lips !

I've won from that old siege and storm
Whose unseen death-mask was your face,
A kiss too constant to be warm,
    A freezing true embrace.

Doom and Steadfastness.

O friend of affliction, freely choose your path !
My mind, mured between the animistic wrath
Of a dead dispensation and dawn's slab
Of solid cold, sighs for a lightning stab
To come quell quickly, here and forever. Kind heart,
Which way will you turn ? What wonder if we part ?
Your vow vouchsafed in hope is vain, for now
Duty-dissolving Doom undoes my vow,
And all our amity, immune from ill,
Sinks at a stroke of suicidal will.
Be bold in bereavement. Beckon up no shade
From the underground where once our youth was played,
Chiding you to companion me in chains,
But let my lost life leap within your veins,
Transfused entire to travel in distress
Still by itself, yet share your steadfastness.

The Saint.

(To the L.'s.)

Saint Sosostrian once, while wandering
With his mother, Mirica,
Praying loud and pondering,
Chanced upon the Afric village
Where, in his wild youthful day,
He had committed fornication
With a woman of the Nubian nation.
The artless niggers, when they heard
Of his arrival, left their tillage,
(For his double reputation
Stirred wonder and pride in his own village)
Thronging the sandy market-place
To hear his words of wit and grace.
He, man of the world and saint,
With his saint's sincerity
Fortified his oratory—
Sermon and scandal mixed, to win
By twin appeal to lust and law
Souls that no other bait can draw
In a land of sun and sin.
Over the mob his wild eye ranges
Reminiscential and prophetic,
Seeing God's hand in all pathetic
Aboriginal facial changes
Since his boyhood. So he drivels
Over the past till . . . God's hand shrivels !
There in the crowd, prepared to pray,
Was the woman with whom once he lay.
No Abyssinian damsel with
A dulcimer, he saw before him :
Stained were the lips he kissed, and puffed
The eyes that then adored him.
Courage, Sosostrian !
Motionless as a monument, the saint stood in the sand,
Marvelling at the Lord's high purpose when He led him to that land ;
Not one sin absolving,
In his mind revolving
Delicate problems of conduct between mistresses and sons and
      mothers,
Such as have earned the patient thought of Emerson and many
      others.
Distracted with these modern worries,
Statuesque, tongue-tied,
He seemed so stern and holy a figure

THE CALENDAR

That all the people cried,
" O mighty man of heaven, descend,
From Heaven, which hath no need of thee,
Soon to our sinful earth, and tend
Us sinners, numbering seventy-three ! "
Primed for a visionary evasion,
The saint returned to his duties :
Baptised and blessed,
Confirmed, confessed
All but the woman whom he had possessed.
Then, raising high his hoarse, God-gifted
Organ voice of Africa,
His leman from the crowd he sifted,
Hastening, nevertheless, to say :
" I trust you all respect my grave intention
In singling out this Nubian for a text ;
My brief career with her calls for no mention
From this gay world, nor happily, from that next.
Such trivial divine excesses
As youth forgetfully dabbles in
Are but the thousandth of a thousandth
Fraction of a venial sin !
No beatific vision can be gained
Before innumerable cups are drained,
A man's whole substance wasted, wantons kissed :
That is the meaning of the Eucharist.
Does any doubt me ?   By the faith that's mine,
I hereby call upon the desert for a sign ! "
He paused, the people prayed, until
The tardy desert whirled its sand
Into a spiral on his head
And a tame dune at either hand.
But the persecuted Nubian
Was not the least impressed :
Though Heaven itself had proven his theories,
Pragmatism seemed the best.
So, in the reverent hush,
She stirred, the woman who had paid ;
Contrived to lift a blush
Above her ardent natural shade,
And, with small effort, straight she stood,
A figure of fine womanhood,
Armed with an excellent brief and sustained by histrionic mood :
" I cherish no dubiety
Re the functions of true piety,
Though you'll need more than piety
To cope with life's variety.

432

Nor would I trouble your repose
But that the Holy Ghost enjoins
On me the duty to disclose
This product of your earlier loins :
Come forth, Khaliba-Cheeta ! ''
The population stared, the saint
Blenched, Mirica fainted
To see the grinning youth who came,
Shamble-limbed, flesh-tainted
With the vice that the white man gives to the black
In fair exchange for the rights of the shack,
The hold on the gun, position on the fence,
Herb-coloured calicoes and spheres of influence . . .

Sosostrian lingered in that town no longer,
But fled precipitately into the desert,
Feeling the need of mystical communion
With One of more refinement than plain Nature.
There he dwelt in a secret rich oasis,
Nourishing himself on pears and pomegranates
And all the facilities that goats afforded ;
And when, after the usual forty days,
He issued forth rotund, the simple villagers,
Exclaiming on the miracle of his fasting,
Once more did ample penance for their sins.

But first, that their state of grace might be known,
After choosing their text from the end of St. Peter,
They crucified the Nubian upside down
And burned Khaliba-Cheeta ;
Not tarrying in these pious pauses
But hurrying back to their tillage,
Happy in the consciousness
Of having soothed a saint,
Subsidised his righteousness,
Relieved his slight embarrassment
By eradicating its causes—
Though a stench stayed in the village.

The Visitation of the Hero.

Out of a land where cries of death and birth,
Rattle and wail unceasing as earth's winds,
The summoned Hero hailed us and came riding
With marble face and eyes steadily staring.
Aware, in thudding hinterlands of æther
Of snowy hoofs and the heraldic neighings,
The sky let down a drawbridge of gold rays
With a block of its own bluestone for a pathway,
Whence, sunken image of a windy morning,
He fell expanding, binding with bright shadow
The bitter-fenced allotments of our myriad islands.
Here the monistic clamour of the surf
Sounds its one tone of meaning but no message
Through limpid days,
And Memory stakes its claim in wildest nocturnes,
Deducing tenants from transparent tombs
Crowded from dawn and dangled in men's minds
By white webs from the broad breast of the sun.
These are the Hero's friends, their festival
Is on blood's daily death and funeral
When sleep retiring like a tide from under
Washes our waiting half.   The hot corpse laid,
They break from being lulled on each small shore
Whose last gesture was lonely and met numbness.
Their loose-limbs blend, wisps of a resurrection,
And chuckle in union, reckless of the sad poise
Of realms relaxing with snatched herbs of hillocks
With pulp of dusty trees, printless garbage of flowers
And egoist strays of flesh now netted in abandon—
A sliding jumble on earth's tilting cable
Of humble brick-brack to amuse the moon.
That visiting all-Sky's bride on usual midnights
Tempers her undress to the heat of stars,
Declining silver with climatic justice
On these mid-air events and the visiting Hero,
Who loathe to begrudge or school his monsters' frolics,
Considerate as wind, curves then in his communion.
But now this wonder came with waxing sun

As if our keen need blinded light and fitness
Or Time reversed the colour of his moods
Just before mid-day.
So matching sometimes clever with dense clouds
The Seasons grapple for an hour of sky,
And then the red-mouthed ape and the mild gnu
Mix elegies side by side in the striped air—
Tremble to see each other's tactful dreams
Blenching and blanching in that madman's eye.

What eager newfoundland foresees him now
Whose soul's in the restoration of our sighs ?
We live arcane, relapsed and numerous
As parasitic saints on Christ's sick tree,
Clasping ourselves on sapless recollection
And falser than before in a packed semblance.
I see my failure frozen on my friend's faces
Hushed to their depths ; an icy badge of sameness
Binding our brows with irony and silence
To stem the hæmorrhage of each broken vision.
We cooled his lightning into type for texts—
His impulse cowled to minister to three
Impulsive Fates in mind's plutonian caves,
Blind baleful weavers of inactive knowledge.
This was your last endeavour, lost Eurydice !
—She was the thought first found in twisted shades
Small and pale, soft-fluttering in fumes.
We moved to the pit-head, equipped and listening :
The spiry lamentation breathed our names.
We were roped down one man, as one man lifted
Through chasms of fixed fear, through barking darkness,
The scorched head fainting on our arms' cool fibres . . .
Expedient against dark, that unison
Prolonged in day, holds us in inner darkness,
Come back, twice ghostly, to earth's neutral playground,
The fading forfeit of old aspiration—
Far as Eurydice in her gassy jungle
From Sun redoubling in his unscaled prairies
Energetic delight, a future harvest.

A Country House.

By DOROTHY EDWARDS.

FROM the day when I first met my wife she has been my first consideration always. It is only fair that I should treat her so because she is young. When I met her she was a mere child with black ringlets down her back and big blue eyes. She put her hair up to get married. Not that I danced attendance on her. That is nonsense. But from the very first moment I saw her I allowed all those barriers and screens that one puts up against people's curiosity to melt away. Nobody can do more than that. It takes many years to close up all the doors to your soul. And then a woman comes along, and at the first sight of her you push them all open, and you become a child again. Nobody can do more than that.

And then at the first sight of a stranger she begins talking about " community of interests " and all that sort of thing. I must tell you we live in the country, a long way from a town, so we have no electric light. It is a disadvantage, but you must pay something for living in the country. It is a big house, too, and carrying lamps and candles from one end of it to another is hard. Not that it worries me. I have lived here since I was born. I can find my way about in the dark. But it is natural that a woman would not like it.

I had thought about it for a long time. Not that I know anything about electrical engineering ; but there is a stream running right down the garden, not a very small stream either. Now why not use the water for a little power-station of our own and make our own electricity ?

I went up to town and called at the electrician's. They would send someone down to look at it. But they could not send anyone until September. Their man was going for his holidays the next day. He would be away until September. Now I suddenly felt that there was a great hurry. I wanted it done before September. They had no one else they could send, and it would take some time if I decided to have it done.

I asked them to send for the electrician. I would pay him anything he liked if he would put off his holiday. They sent for him and he came in and listened to my proposal.

At this point I ought to describe his appearance. He was tall, about forty years old. He had blue eyes and grey hair brushed straight up. His hair might have been simply fair, not grey. I cannot remember that now. He had almost a military appearance, only he was shy, reserved and rather prim. His voice was at least an octave deeper than is natural in a speaking voice. He smiled as though he was amused at everyone else's amusement, only this was not contemptuous. Do not think for a moment that I regard this as a melodrama. I do not. I saw at once that he was a nice fellow, something out of the ordinary, not a villain at all.

He smiled when I asked him to put off his vacation. Nothing could be done until he had had a look at the place, and he was perfectly willing to come down that evening to see it. If it were possible to start work at once something could, perhaps, be arranged. I was pleased with this and I invited him to stay the night with us.

At five o'clock he was standing on the office steps with a very small bag, which he carried as if it were too light for him. He climbed into the car and sat in silence during the whole long drive. When we reached the avenue of trees just before we turn in at my gate—although it was still twilight, under the trees it was quite dark, because they are so thick—he said : " I should imagine this was very dark at night ? "

" Yes, as black as pitch," I said.

" It would be a good thing to have a light here. It looks dangerous."

" No. I don't want one here," I said, " nobody uses this road at night but I, and I know it in the dark. Light in the house will be enough."

I wonder if he thought that unreasonable or not. He was silent again.

We turned in at the gate. My wife came across the lawn to meet us. I do not know how to describe her. That day she had a large white panama hat and a dress with flowers on it. I said before that she had black hair and blue eyes. She is tall too, and she still looks very young.

The electrician, his name was Richardson, stood with his feet close together and bowed from the waist. I told her that I had brought him here to see if it was possible to put in electric light.

"In the house?" she said. "That would be lovely. Is it possible at all?"

"I hope so," said Richardson, in his deep voice. I could see that she was surprised at it.

"We don't know yet," I said, "we must take him to see the stream."

She came with us. The stream runs down by the side of the house, curving a little with the slope of the garden, until it joins the larger stream which flows between the garden wall and the fields. We followed it down, not going round by the paths, but jumping over flower beds and lawns. Richardson looked all the time at the water, except once, when he helped my wife across a border.

"There is enough water," he said, "and I suppose it is fuller than this sometimes?"

"Yes, when it rains," said my wife. "Sometimes it is impossible to cross the stepping stones without getting one's shoes wet."

Now I will tell you where the stepping stones are. Where the stream curves most a wide gravelled path crosses it, and some high stones have been put in the water. When we came down as far as that Richardson said : "This is the place where we could have it. We could put a small engine-house here, and the water could afterwards be carried through pipes to join the stream down below, forming a sort of triangle with the hypotenuse underground."

I asked him if he was certain that it could be done.

"I think so," he said seriously.

My wife smiled at him eagerly.

"I hope the building will not be ugly ; it would spoil the garden."

Richardson smiled in the amused way, and answered :

"It will, but it will not be high. We must have it at least half underground, with steps to go down to it. Would it be possible to plant some thick trees round it ? Yews, as long as they do not interfere with the wires."

"Oh, yes, thank you," she said, "I believe we could have that."

Richardson looked about him a bit more, and he took some measurements with a tape measure from his pocket. Then we went back to the house. At dinner I asked him where he meant to spend his holiday.

"I am not sure," he said seriously. "I thought perhaps the Yorkshire moors would be a good place."

"You won't find anything better than this," I said. "Put off your holiday until September."

My wife moved to the door.

"Would you have to stay here during the work?" she asked.

"Or somewhere near here, Madam," he said.

"Yes, of course, here," she said, and walked out of the room. Richardson bowed from the waist again.

We arranged it easily. He would not put it off, but he would make this his holiday. He would bring his motor bike here and explore the country around. He could be here always when there was anything for him to do, and he considered our invitation to him to stay here more than enough compensation for the change of his plans.

Afterwards in the drawing-room he asked my wife if she was fond of music.

"That is what she *is* fond of," I said. "She plays the piano."

What can anyone do with a strange man in the drawing-room but play the piano to him? She played a Chopin nocturne. Now I could watch girls dancing to Chopin's music all day, but to play Chopin to a stranger that you meet for the first time! What must he think of you! I can understand her playing even the nocturnes when she is alone. When one is alone one is in the mood for anything. But to choose to play them when she is meeting some one for the first time. That is simply wrong. Chopin's nights are like days. There is no difference except that they are rounded off. That is nonsense. Night does not round things off, night is a distorter. Those nocturnes come of never having spent his nights alone, of spending them either in an inn or in someone else's bedroom. No! How do I know what Chopin did! But I tell you they are the result of thinking of darkness as the absence of the sun's light. It is better to think of it as a vapour rising from the depths of the earth and perhaps bringing many things with it.

But he liked it. That is, Richardson liked the nocturne. He asked her to play another. While she turned over the pages I said aloud :

" Night isn't like that. Night is a distorter."

My wife looked into the darkness outside the window.

Richardson looked at her, then he looked at me in uncertainty. She began to play, and he, for a moment pretending to be apologetic, studied her music with concentration.

Why didn't they ask me what I meant ? I could have proved it to them. In any case, it was an interesting point.

She played a lot of Chopin. Then as she came from the piano she said :

" You are fond of music, too. Do you play ? "

" No," he said. " It was my great ambition to be a 'cellist but I never learnt to play it well, and I haven't one now. It is my favourite instrument."

" It is only the heavy father of a violin," I said. But I said it only because all that Chopin had annoyed me. I like the 'cello very much.

" I have never liked anything better than the piano," said my wife. " I am sorry you do not play."

" He sings," I said.

He smiled with amusement.

" Do you ? " she asked, eagerly.

" Yes," he said, half bowing from where he sat.

" I knew by your speaking voice," I said. " Please let us hear you."

" I will bring some songs with me if you wish it," he said. " That is very kind of you," and he leaned back in his chair and cut off all communication with us. We sat in silence until my wife left us. Then we talked a little about the electric light and then went to bed.

The next day the work began. Until the small building was up and the pipes laid from it back to the stream Richardson could do nothing more than see that the measurements were right. He carried a small black notebook and kept looking at it and then looking up at us and saying :

"This is no work at all, you know ; it is simply like a holiday."

He brought his motor bike down, but he went for few rides. Most of the time he spent looking at the first few bricks of the building, or crossing and re-crossing the stream over the stepping stones, with no hat on, and his black note-book open in one hand, as though he were making some very serious calculations. I do not suppose he was for a moment.

As I said before, I do not regard this as a melodrama. I do not consider him a villain, but, on the contrary, a nice enough fellow, but it was irritating to me the way he wandered round in a circle looking for something to do.

In the daytime he could look after himself, but in the evening we treated him as a guest.

The second day he was here, after tea, I suggested taking him for a walk. He bowed with one hand behind his back, and he kept it there afterwards. I noticed it particularly. My wife came too. We walked down the garden, Richardson still with his hand behind his back, walking just behind her, talked to her about the work, and he said the same things over twice.

When we got to the bottom of the garden and through the door which opens on the bank of the stream she gave a cry of horror. And I will tell you why. It was because I had had the grass and weeds on the banks cut.

She turned to Richardson.

"I am so sorry," she said, "you should have seen this before it was cut. It was very pretty. What were those white flowers growing on the other side ? "

"Hemlock," I said. "It had to be cut."

"I don't see why," she said. "It is a pity to spoil such a beautiful place for the sake of tidyness." She turned to him petulantly.

Now that is all nonsense. A place must be tidy. There were bulrushes and water lilies as it was. What more must she have ? A lot of weeds dripping down into the water ! There is a difference between garden flowers and weeds. If you want weeds then do not have gardens. And I suppose

THE CALENDAR

I am insensible to beauty because I keep the place cut and trimmed. Nonsense! Suppose my wife took off her clothes and ran about the garden like a bacchante! Perhaps I should like it very much, but I would shut her up in her room all the same.

We walked along in silence over the newly-cut grass. It was yellow already with having been left uncut too long. I went first across the bridge, and my two friends who admire Chopin so much came after. We were in the cornfield now, and I will tell you what it is like. There is a little hill just opposite the bridge and the corn grows on top of it and on its slopes. It is a very small hill, but the country around is flat, and from the top of it you can see over the trees a long distance. We began to walk up the path to the top. The corn was cut and stood up in sheaves. That is what I like. When we reached the top Richardson took his hand from behind his back and looked around him. There is a lake a few miles away, and on either side of it the land rises and there are trees. Beyond that again is the sea. And from the hill the sea looks nearer than it is and the lake like a bay. Richardson thought it was a bay. I thought so too when I was a child.

" I did not know the sea was so near," he said.

" It isn't near," I answered. " That is a lake. There are even houses in between it and the sea, only you cannot see them."

He took a deep breath.

" You know it is very kind of you to let me stay here. It is very beautiful. I have not seen a place I like better. I am most grateful. And the work is simply nothing. It is a real holiday."

At this point he fingered the black note-book which stuck out of his pocket.

If things had not happened as they did he might have come down often ; he might have spent his week-ends here. He was not a bad sort of fellow.

He did not want to leave the hill, but my wife did not like walking about on the stubble in her thin shoes. We walked back by the path which leads between a low wall and some small fir trees to the back of the house. I had the path made for her, because she prefers that walk.

A COUNTRY HOUSE

After dinner Richardson sang. His voice was all right, deep like his speaking voice, only not so steady. She played for him, and he stood up at attention, except that, with his right arm bent stiffly at the elbow and pressed to his side, he clutched the lapel of his coat. He sang some Brahms. It was quite nice.

I went to write some letters, and afterwards I walked about in the garden. When I returned they had left the piano and were talking. He was very fond of Strauss. She had not heard the *Alpine* symphony. We were so far from everywhere here.

The time went on. Richardson grew more restless every day. And yet he was lethargic too. He hardly left the house and garden, and he still wandered back and forth by the work. He did not interfere with the men by giving unnecessary orders, but he still studied his note-book as though there were important calculations there. I know all this because I watched him as if he were my brother.

My wife used to go down there to sit sometimes in the mornings. But he hardly spoke to her then. It is natural that a man would not care to talk about music and all that when the men were working in the sun. It was curious how much interest we all took in the little building and the pipes and the water, and yet when we thought of the electric light in the house, which was to be the result, all the romance was gone out of it. This is not simply my experience. It was so with my wife and Richardson too. I know by my own observation of them. The minute the building was finished we went down to see it. Nothing but a yellow brick hut with steps to go down and an opening like the mouth of a letter box in the wall nearest the stream.

" The water is shut off now," said Richardson. " We have to put a grating in it before the water comes through."

There was a hole in the concrete floor too, and from that the pipes would lead back to the stream. The first pipe was there with a big curve in it. It was nice to see it getting on.

After that they dug a ditch and put the pipes down. He helped them to dig.

Every night he sang and my wife played, but I did not always stay in the drawing-room. One night, though, I remember particularly, he sang a song by Hugo Wolf about a girl whose lover had gone, and while the men and women were binding the corn she went to the top of a hill and the wind played with the ribbon that he had put in her hat. It was something like that ; I have forgotten it. I asked him to sing it again. I suppose they were pleased that I liked something. He sang it.

an dem Hut mein Rosenband, von seiner Hand
spielet in dem Winde.

Now I should think that the hill that she climbed in that song was like the hill in our cornfield, and the girl sat there for hours " like one lost in a dream."

The days passed, and everything remained the same except the work, and that went on quickly. We walked about together sometimes. One evening we went again through the door to the little river where the grass had been cut. We were going along the bank talking when we heard a splash and there was a boy swimming in the water. I shouted to him and told him to come out and not swim there again. His white back flashed through the water to a bush on the other side, and he began to dress behind it. When I turned back she said :

" Why did you send him away ? It looked so nice."

" He can go somewhere else to swim," I said.

Richardson said nothing.

" He does no harm here, surely ? " she said.

Bulrushes and water lilies are not enough for her. She must have weeds and naked boys too. And do you think she ever bathed in a river when she was a child, and hid behind a bush when someone was coming ? No, of course not. And does she think the boy wants to be seen bathing ? And if he is not to be seen, when he is here, he might as well go somewhere else.

We never talked about anything except the work, and he talked about music with my wife. They never said anything illuminating on the subject though. It is a funny thing that you can spend days and weeks with a man and never mention anything but water pipes and electricity. But, after all, you can't talk about God and Immortality to a man you hardly know. Anyhow, it is nice to see someone so much interested

in his work. No. That is nonsense. He was not interested
in his work. When the engine came we were enthusiastic
and he was as miserable as sin. What business has an electrician to get excited over yellow bricks and water pipes ?
He was restless. He could not settle to anything. If he read
a book, half the time it would be open on his knee and he
looking away from it. I noticed him very particularly.

The day before everything was finished and he was to go—
he was not waiting to see the light actually put in the rooms—
I was chalking out a garden bed just at the bottom of the
garden by the door. It is a shady place, and I meant to plant
violets there, especially white violets—not in August, of course,
but it was better to get it prepared while I thought of it. I
heard them coming along on the other side of the wall. She
was saying :

" Before I was married I stayed with my music master in
London. He had two sons, but no daughters. His wife
was very fond of me. That was the happiest time of my life.
One of the sons is a first violin now. I went to a symphony
concert when we were in London once and saw him play. I
don't know what happened to the other one."

" Let us sit down here," said Richardson. I knew there
was something wrong with him by his voice, I detected that
at once.

I suppose they sat down on the large tree stump outside.
They were silent for a moment. I suppose she was looking at
the water and he was looking at her. Then he said, beginning
as though he were talking to himself, and yet apologising too :

" Please forgive me, I ought not to say it. I have never
been to a place which has given me such pleasure as this. I
had never noticed scenery or nature much before. When
one likes a place it is because one went to it in childhood or
something of that sort. But this has been so very beautiful
while I have been here. I suppose from the beginning I knew
I could not come here again. It is impossible. Forgive me
saying so." His voice became deeper as he went on, I
noticed that.

" Oh, but you must come here again," she said, anxiously.
" There is no one here at all, and we have so many tastes in
common."

"No," he said, "you think I don't mean it. I walked up and down in the garden just now and I came to a decision. At first I thought I would not speak a word to you, but afterwards I decided it would not make any great difference if I did. People do not change their lives suddenly. That is, they don't except in literature. And now I feel at peace about it. No harm at all—none. I do not mean that literature is artificial you know, only that it is concerned with different people."

Now, what word had he spoken that a husband could not listen to ? And yet we would have looked very interesting from an aeroplane or from a window in heaven.

And do you suppose she wanted to know what he was talking about ? All she said was :

"Oh, but my husband has asked you to come here himself. You must come often and bring your songs. There is no one to talk about music to here. And I cannot go to any concerts, we are so far from everywhere."

He was silent. They stood up, and I waited for them to come through the door. I suppose nobody could expect me to hide behind a tree so as to cause them no embarrassment. "Excuse me, I was just passing at this moment. Please go on with your pleasant conversation."

However, they chose to go back by the other way along the bank of the stream.

We spent dinner very pleasantly. Nobody spoke a word. Richardson was not fully aware that we were in the room. He looked at the tablecloth. I did not go away to write letters after dinner. I never left the drawing-room. I suppose no one could expect me to do that. After the music we sat round the empty grate and said nothing, and we went very late to bed.

The next morning, after breakfast, I went up to the flagstaff. If you climb up the steep bank at the left of the house and walk along until you come to a narrow path with trees growing there, you come to a ledge, and the flagstaff has been put there, because it can be seen above the trees. I was standing there disentangling the rope to pull the flag up when he came up to me.

" What time are you going ? " I asked, and pulled out my watch.

" At eleven," he said.

" I suppose you think it funny that I should be putting the flag up on the day that you go ? "

" I did not know you had a flagstaff," he said. " I suppose it can be seen even from the sea ? "

" Yes."

He was silent, and he looked across at the house.

" Where is my wife ? " I asked.

" In the drawing-room, practising."

" I hope you will send in your bill as soon as possible."

" Oh, yes," he said. " It will come from the firm, you know. They pay me. I wanted to walk round the corn field before I go."

I pulled up the flag and fastened the cord.

" I'll come with you," I said.

We walked in silence to the top of the hill, and he stood and looked all round, at the house and at the sea. Taking leave of it, of course.

" In the village down there," I said, " there is a very nice girl called Agnes. She isn't pretty, but she is very nice."

Now Agnes was the name of the girl in the song by Hugo Wolf, but I knew he would not see that. He looked at me in surprise. Then he took out his watch and said he must go. There was no need for that. If you go away on a motor bike why go exactly at eleven ? He had to keep himself to a time, that is what it was. We turned to go down the hill.

" I put up the flag because it is my birthday," I said, though that was not true.

He looked at me without listening to what I said.

When we got back to the house his motor bike was standing outside the gate ready. He went into the house to fetch his cap and my wife came out with him. Half way to the gate he turned to her and thanked her. He had never experienced such pleasure in a holiday before. Then he shook hands with me and said nothing.

" Come down to see us often," I said. " Come whenever you like, for week-ends."

" Oh yes," said my wife, " please come and bring your music."

He looked embarrassed. I was watching him. I knew he would be. He looked at the ground and mumbled :

" Thank you very much. Good-bye." Then he turned and went out through the gate, and in a few minutes he drove away under the trees.

She went into the house. She thinks he will come again, call and listen to her play Chopin.

I went to sit down by the engine house. The engine was working, and it throbbed and shivered noisily, while there was hardly any water in the curve of the stream. It has made a great difference to the garden. Up above the flag waved senselessly in the wind.

———

Petrarch, d'Annunzio, Solitude, and other matters.

A DIALOGUE
BY
ROBERT NICHOLS.

SHADE.—You breathed my name.

READER.—Is it you, Messer Francesco Petrarca ? Yes, by the purple mantle and the apple-green leaves of spring laurel twined about the grizzled locks, by the earnest eyes and musical voice, it must be. I scarcely expected to have the good luck to behold you in this narrow house of mine only too closely overhanging one of the most noisome cities in the world. Do not let the real estate boosters get wind of your whereabouts, or they will capitalise on your shy presence.

SHADE.—I come only to those who need me and love my spirit. The gentry you mention have not heard of me and would not love me, for I come to treat with you concerning the book* that lies open before you, my *Solitude*, a word detestable and, indeed, incomprehensible, to them. You smile. But there are traces of tears about your eyes.

READER.—Well there may be. It is but a few days since I thought my lonely self reconciled to Multitude in digesting the work of another humanist, Erasmus, his *Praise of Folly*. I have just discovered I am not old enough to become reconciled to folly.

SHADE.—Do not be too sure you will ever be reconciled. " As one grows older," says Goethe, " the ordeals grow greater." No truer word was ever spoken, and few can better appreciate that truth than myself. What is of importance is not reconciliation, but the manner in which we support the want of it. And perhaps the business of the true poet is precisely this—

---

* The Life of Solitude, by Francis Petrarch, translated with Introduction and Notes by Jacob Zeitlin, Associate Professor of English in the University of Illinois. University of Illinois Press. An excellent rendering with a lucid and discerning Preface.—R. M. B. N.

to provide us with material suitable to aid us in affecting a reconciliation to life. My poems to Laura abound in sorrows, but they are a record of sorrows which enriched and fortified life, not of miseries which degraded it.

READER.—Milton affords some support to this contention.

SHADE.—"To justify God's ways to Man," yes. And so does Goethe, with whom I have had of late much conversation. He avers that the function of poetry is "to make man contented with the world and his condition."

READER.—Does he say that ? We English do not read him.

SHADE.—How extraordinary ! Montesquieu remarked that the English demand above all things "that a man be at all points a man." Goethe is most a man of any that have visited this planet. And you assert the English do not read him !

READER.—Forget the English. They read neither Goethe, nor Montesquieu, nor you. They do not even read their own Milton and Shakespeare. They read the sporting, finance, and divorce news. But I am amazed. You speak thus of Goethe with Dante at your elbow ?

SHADE.—I do. Had it been granted me to develop beyond the bounds appointed me, that development would have been rather toward Goethe than Dante. Goethe is at once nearer the Ancients, whom I admired, and the Moderns, whom in my person I foretold. As to Dante, he abides in a place apart, far from the Ancients, from myself, and far from the Moderns.

READER.—I think I understand you. He is the only great poet who has ever shocked me. I must admit I find him extremely unsympathetic to my temperament.

SHADE.—And, therefore, largely incomprehensible. For, as Goethe has observed, we can only appreciate what is akin to us. But we have wandered far from my volume and your distress.

READER.—Ten years ago a friend introduced me to the great proletarian leader of a suffering nation. "Monsieur Vandervelde," he said, "let me introduce to you a young English poet of profound melancholy and a natural genius for disillusion." Secretly flattered, I nevertheless rather resented the terms, which seemed to me excessive in implication. I need not have resented them. War could bruise, but not break a spirit which peace has broken. Cast derelict from the battle,

A DIALOGUE

I discovered in Solitude the virtues which even universal murder could not wholly blemish : the hell man had created he could transcend—flowers of pity, of fortitude, of aspiration blossomed amid the blood and flames. To-day among Multitude I comprehend with terrifying clarity the words of Bacon : *Certainly virtue is like precious odours, most fragrant when they are incensed and crushed : for prosperity doth best discover vice, but adversity doth best discover virtue.* That war transformed men into tigers, but this peace has conjured them into swine.

SHADE.—And the same philosopher avers, *Whosoever is out of patience is out of possession of his soul.* Once more seek solitude and it shall return you that possession. It was this possession of the soul for its own sake which I sought, and so doing, I became the First Modern.

READER.—Far be it from me to bandy words with one so eminent, but have you not overlooked the Taoist poets of China, for instance Lu Yun and T'Ao Ch'ien ?

SHADE.—These poets were metaphysical. Lu Yun, singing of " living in retirement," concludes :

> *My spirit is tuned to the Spring Season :*
> *At the fall of the year there is autumn in my heart.*
> *Thus imitating cosmic changes*
> *My cottage becomes a Universe.**

The small admixture of the metaphysical in me was the least important part, and the most dissolvent of my true nature. The leaves of the laurel hid my tonsure. To follow St. Augustine required a certain effort of my spirit, which the graceful volubility of Cicero did not demand, since I was primarily an Italian, a rhetorician, a pagan, and a poet.

READER.—Like d'Annunzio.

SHADE.—I am delighted that you observe the similarity. There is an opinion abroad that I was largely a glittering pedant, that the workmanship of my poems surpasses the material ; that there was in me something cold and eupheuistic: It is even asserted that my Laura, in her green dress sprigged with violets and her silver wreath, is a fiction, an extravagance as irritating as that which discovers in the " friend " of your Shakespeare's sonnets cosmic consciousness, or the Established

---

* Waley's translation. From *One Hundred and Seventy Chinese Poems.*

Church, or the Male Directorate for the Home of Strayed Cats. These are absurdities which the introduction to the volume before you may do something to correct, provided its readers appreciate the slightly submarine humour therein indulged by our professor. Yes, d'Annunzio and I have much in common though I am his superior, as the ancient poets are always superior to the modern.

READER.—Pedant !

SHADE.—Not at all. d'Annunzio is superior to me as a man of action, and perhaps as a rhetorician. I too knew love—

READER.—Has d'Annunzio ever known love ? I doubt it.

SHADE.—Love has always been what the poets have made it ; and forasmuchas the poets of different peoples, times, and climates differ, so does the character of this their fairest and most ambiguous creation. You are of the north and the twentieth century. I and d'Annunzio are of that south which seems, like all that is very ancient, peculiarly tenacious of its character. For you love is perhaps as the pervasive light of that sun you see so seldom ; for us, children of the sun, it is the sun itself. But we are discussing not Northern or Southern ideas of love, but d'Annunzio and the Petrarch that was. My passion for Laura served as an occasion for poetry and became magnified thereby. Nor ought those who are not artists to proclaim d'Annunzio or myself insincere on this account, since the artist is most thoroughly, harmoniously, and lastingly himself when the quill is between his fingers. As I am, so d'Annunzio is voluble, volatile, impressionable. He is concerned with temperament, particularly his own, wherein again he resembles me. The Renaissance cultivated personalities and I mine, even as to-day d'Annunzio, altogether a Renaissance personage, cultivates his, and simultaneously practises the arts of love, of war, and of poetry.

READER.—Not unsuccessfully.

SHADE.—Success, however, is concerned as an end in the case of the art of poetry only. For in love, perhaps, we love most fully the woman we do not gain. Posterity knows not even the name of the girl or girls by whom I had a son and a daughter. All the world has heard of Laura. I envy d'Annunzio his defeat.

A DIALOGUE

READER.—You do ? I am delighted. That defeat has been my secret consolation. Nor did I by any means regret it for Europe's sake.

SHADE.—I am sorry to hear that.

READER.—And yet more did I rejoice for d'Annunzio's. Had he succeeded, he would perhaps have lost something in his own eyes, and certainly he would have lost nearly all in mine, though this last would, I admit, have weighed nothing with him had he known of it.

SHADE.—How lost ? As a man of action or as a poet ?

READER.—Separate them in his case if you can ! Ah, how I envy d'Annunzio at Fiume ! Of all hours lived by any man since this handful of dust, known as I, has perambulated an unquiet planet, those hours of the man d'Annunzio in that beggarly little city I have envied most ! His cause was disgraceful—

SHADE.—By heavens, no !

READER.—Permit me. In my opinion, his cause was disgraceful and his means unjustifiable. But he had the honour of feeling his back to the wall and modern Europe for once united (was she not battling with a poet ?), leagued against him. All hung upon him and him alone. His legions were bound together by the frailest thing in the world—his words. During days of extreme peril and riot, during nights of anguish and of doubt, he came to terms with his spirit. I envy him, how I envy him ! His cause was unworthy, but he suffered greatly for it. In his overthrow he at last possessed all that was heroic in his spirit, and came to know what he was worth.

SHADE.—Be not too sure that he cared so much about the cause. To him, perhaps, the whole episode was but the creation of a poem.

READER.—That was why I challenged you to separate in his case the poet from the man of action.

SHADE.—I did not accept the challenge, for I am well aware that we poets, especially we rhetorical poets, seek any excuse for having life more abundantly, whereof war (like poetry) is only one among several means. In such an episode the poet may be seen living his life as if he were creating a mighty strophe, the design whereof is the pattern the poet imposes on life, its pulse, the pulse of his quickened and imperilled blood, its "dying fall" the supreme peripeteia described by the soul in immeasurable triumph or defeat.

READER.—Above all in defeat!

SHADE.—You of the North delight more in defeat than we.

READER.—The Saga heroes are all defeated.

SHADE.—On one point, however, we are entirely agreed. We seek the same epitaph.

READER.—Which is?

SHADE.—One that few in these days, if I am to judge by their miserable countenances seen afar off, as the figures limp wearily out of Charon's cockle, deserve: *I have lived.*

READER.—Words which cause no little supercilious merriment in the East.

SHADE.—I have little acquaintance with the Orient, albeit I have passed pleasant hours with certain of the Chinese poets. The Orient and its ideas appear to me barbarous.

READER.—And coincides with its opinion of us. Yet I would suggest you cultivate the Eastern poets. For you need expect no future shades during the next two centuries to seek your society, if, indeed, they are permitted to encroach upon those groves wherein you wander, a permission that I trust will not be granted.

SHADE.—You seem to be very discontented with your age, yet doubtless you are no exception to the general rule. Every man is born in the age most appropriate to him, or so I have come to think since I crossed the Shadowy Waters.

READER.—A comforting belief when life is over: because forsooth I wore the coat that I lost yesterday it must indubitably have fitted me.

SHADE.—You are sharp tongued.

READER.—I am sharply used.

SHADE.—I would your wits were as sharp as your tongue. Yes, our age is appropriate provided we are resolved to cultivate any aptitude we may possess for using what we find. And that which we would find is always present have we the eyes to discern and the understanding to make it our own. *Thou wast not born,* says Epictetus, *but when the world had need of thee.*

READER.—A very convenient belief. I wish I could share it. But I doubt if any of us are needed by the world. I have yet to meet the man with whom the world could not dispense without so much as noticing it. This crass world needs nothing that would be of any true service to it.

SHADE.—Well, then, seek your satisfaction in obstinately being what you are. That is a resource fortunately denied to none of us. Nor is it negligible. For me to be in love and to be composing poetry about it, or to be solitary and to be inditing a high and sententious prose thereon were sufficient. I practised the art of enjoying this or that state or activity as an end in itself, and not for the satisfaction of service, or for the sake of any conclusion to which my immersion or activity might conduct me. Therein d'Annunzio and I are at one : both absolute artists. The absolute artist is interested in the presentation to himself and others of What-Is, for the sake of the pleasure to be had in creating that presentation, and not for any idea of service, or any conclusion to be drawn from that presentation when complete.

READER.—With that few artists—

SHADE.—I said the absolute artist.

READER.—It is well you limit this brutal statement to absolute artists, a genus which—

SHADE.—I overhear hints of outrage in your voice, and being of what you call this genus, I hasten to add—that is perhaps why the absolute artist is often (and more especially by you Northern peoples) considered immoral. But he is not immoral. He is ammoral as the Nature whence his reverie of presentation springs is ammoral. This is also one of the many reasons why charges of inconsistency, if not of downright insincerity, are preferred against him, when, forsaking the chisel, the quill, or the brush, he sets to work in the direct material of life itself. It has been accounted to me for an inconsistency that, a fervent Republican, I yet associated and delighted to associate with princes. Our d'Annunzio, with the constitution of Fiume, in many ways so revolutionary, among his papers, accepts the title of prince. There is nothing inconsistent in this : we stand together, both absolute artists.

READER.—And pagans.

SHADE.—And pagans. Certainly. Why not ? Have I not declared the leaves of the laurel hid my tonsure ? And I was very willing that they should. I became a priest the more

THE CALENDAR

conveniently to become a pagan, and I believed (with every other pagan) that to the men of stature belong the spoils.

READER.—A belief not uncommon among men of stature, and one, so I have heard tell, to which the prince, who was d'Annunzio, subscribes. I regret that those concerned have displayed so little imagination as to offer him the title of prince, and I consider he degraded himself by consenting to become one. Is it not sufficient to be a poet ? I could find it in my heart to wish he had celebrated whatever his princedom was intended to celebrate by returning to that original name that was his before he became d'Annunzio.

SHADE.—You are not an Italian, and in so far as you are a rhetorician (and I begin to suspect you of being one), you are a rhetorician of an inverted habit.

READER.—I am an Englishman. Englishmen like their heroes to be called Smith, Brown, or Robinson.

SHADE.—Do not try to persuade me that this is to be attributed to democratic feeling. They like it because to them the barbarity of nomenclature makes the heroism more remarkable and conspicuous, even as to a foreigner it makes it more outrageous. Northern races do not understand the meaning of what is fitting. It is not *convenable* to be a hero and to be named Robinson. You are the proudest and most perverse people on earth, for you carry the pedantry of your snobbism even into the pantheon. I suspect even so particular a youth as yourself, however you may prate of enjoying the spectacle of d'Annunzio's warlike exploits, for a very similar reason—

READER.—Such as ?

SHADE.—That you consider him an amateur at the game of war. You are a lazy nation, and you make the glory of the amateur's occasional triumph an excuse for your laziness.

READER.—No, we are sceptics. We distrust experts.

SHADE.—Which is the very reason why certain of you would like, if you dared, to object to my poetry, and do object to d'Annunzio's prose. You feel that it is too good to be, in any sense of the word, true.

READER.—A certain exuberance of temperament—

SHADE.—Come ! You talk like a stay-at-home chattering after an evening at *Lucia*. The fact is you are dazzled, and as you hate the sun in your land of fog, and scarcely believe it is

456

the sun when you see it, so you dislike every form of brilliance, and when that brilliance is obviously founded on that sort of hard work of which you are quite incapable, why then, you are indeed scandalised !

READER.—There is something in what you say. I must acknowledge I can never quite understand how it is that we, a sceptical nation, are so easily shocked.

SHADE.—Precisely because you are sceptical. It takes faith of the simplest and grandest kind to act as d'Annunzio acts, or write as he writes.

READER.—But you told me not to be too sure that—

SHADE.—A cause and the possession of faith are different matters.

READER.—If I am being English, assuredly you are being Italian.

SHADE.—Perhaps. You will at least acknowledge the presence of the hard work.

READER.—I must. And therein d'Annunzio resembles you.

SHADE.—Certainly. No less than I, d'Annunzio is an incessant worker, an erudite scholar, an impassioned philologist. He, again, is an artist superlatively preoccupied with sonority and pattern. In his novels, too, as in my poems, there are no stories, only states of mind and pictures. I observed that he is my superior as a man of action. I spoke true—for he has succeeded in a procedure after the proper conduct of which, even at Vauclose, I only groped : for him the living of his life has become the fashioning of a work of art. Five years after receiving the Laureate crown in the Capitol, I indited at Vauclose the volume before you. To-day d'Annunzio, five years after the fantastic triumph in defeat of Fiume, issues from his villa this pronouncement, " I have become again the solitary proud artist of nineteen hundred and eleven."

READER.—Amid the jeers of the rabble press.

SHADE.—I was at least spared that ! A humanist, I nonetheless never championed the cause of reading matter for the masses. How could I ? I was a pagan, and, therefore, believed that only a noble man can be virtuous greatly, know wisely, perceive and feel finely. Doubtless your lower and middle classes are industrious and respectable, but they have no notion of greatness, nay, they have even an instinctive hatred of it.

THE CALENDAR

READER.—Accordingly, they see in d'Annunzio only a poseur. They adore Consistency because it accords with the tameness and flatness of their lives and spirit. The unfamiliar scares them. From aeon to aeon the artist advances toward them with outstretched hand—" I am come," cries he, " that you may have life and have it more abundantly ! " But they reject him and, should he turn away to live that more ample life for himself and to create it, partly out of envy, partly out of fear, they spit at him. Multitude, I abominate you !

SHADE.—Do not be too hard on Man. He invariably fears what he does not understand. The poet is a chameleon. If it be true, as Napoleon asserted, that " Imagination rules the world," let us remember the Sovereign Imaginative, the Poet, is also the creature of his own imagination. That role which imagination posits to us as suitable to the circumstance of the moment, we assume as if by second nature. The spectacle profoundly disturbs the multitude, which attributes a want of sincerity to this instability, because Multitude hates to doubt, and this spectacle invites it to scepticism. I, too, was a sceptic.

READER.—A somewhat embryonic sceptic.

SHADE.—Owing to my circumstances.

READER.—So our professor would seem to indicate. I admire the perspicacity with which he has demonstrated your relation to Montaigne. I have only one quarrel with him, and I pick it with the utmost reluctance. He appears to me insufficiently to have stressed this point, upon which you have just now insisted, namely, that you were an artist, a rhetorical artist at that, and as such the creature of Imaginations, whether your own or others, becoming by turns troubadour, republican, diplomat, disciple, humanist, according to whether you had your eyes on Laura, your foot upon the Capitol, your ear at the ante-chamber, your finger between the leaves of St. Augustine, or your nose in Quintillian.

SHADE.—Ha ! ha ! ha !—a devil's advocate, young man ! You deny me any personality whatever ?

READER.—Far from it. I attribute to you a succession of lives more fabulous than those of the phœnix. You resumed whole civilisations. A man such as yourself is chiefly a minting machine. All his knowledge, moral, philological, and aesthetic,

A DIALOGUE

uniting with the virgin ore of all that he has seen and felt, is transformed in the furnace of his creative intelligence, and issues as a new currency, stamped on the reverse with the character of the age, and on the obverse with the unique personality of the creator.

SHADE.—A brilliant if not very poetical comparison. Young man, my suspicions were well founded—you are quite the rhetorician. Then I have a personality after all.

READER.—I accept your gentle raillery, for my comparison stands. The poet always has a personality—at the moment all his forces focus upon creation.

SHADE.—Only then ?

READER.—Perhaps not only then, though then most of all. When alone and ignorantly browsing among the possibilities of what he next will be, then, too, he exists. Our professor has understood this and strongly emphasised your figure at Vauclose. Indeed, ere I read this, I had not imagined you so pagan a figure.

SHADE.—I had also other aspects. I was alone save for that strange companion Solitude, who restores us to ourselves. And being, then, most myself, the apex of the forward thinking wedge of my age, I became also, as the great poet always is, a prophecy. I wandered whole days upon the sunny mountains and through valleys and in dingles fresh with dew. I thrilled to the silence of a vast forest, and arose at midnight to walk alone under the diffused light of immense heavens, or, accompanied by my shadow, watched the moon lift the crags a visage charged with equivocal dream. Oftentime I remained erect in contemplation, silent and with eyes fixed, communing with myself of many, many things and taking small account of all earthly interests. Unknown to myself, I became the first Romantic.

READER.—You loved silence, you whom any sound but the rippling of the brook, the light breeze among your papers, or the sweet murmur of your own poetry could disturb.

SHADE.—My most fundamental self was, however, pagan. I delighted in suspended judgment. Not seldom did I rehearse to myself the words of the Epicurean poet : *Sed nihil dulcius—*

READER.—Lucretius. How does it go ?

459

THE CALENDAR

Sweeter by far on Wisdom's rampired height
To face serene the porches of the light
And thence look down—down on the purblind herd
Seeking and never finding in the night
The road to peace—the peace that all might hold,
But yet is missed by young men and by old,
Lost in the strife for palaces and powers,
The axes, and the lictors and the gold.

SHADE.—A not wholly inadequate rendering.

READER.—Mallock's. But the possibility to indulge this passion for solitude and suspended judgment is passing. The aeroplane—

VOICE.—Mr. Jas. Brown an' his Jazz Babies will now sing you *Flat-tire Momma, Poppa's gwine to give you Air*, after which the Reverend Judd will lecture on *The World as a Happy Family*.

SHADE.—Horror ! What voice is that ?

READER.—The radio next door : the voice of Progress itself.

SHADE.—My songs were sung in the streets, but not thus was it that I celebrated Laura. Pleasure then was neither dismal nor vulgar. I regret that I must bid you an altogether instantaneous adieu.

READER.—Alas, not even the companionship of an illustrious phantom is permitted me, but the solitude I prize must be peopled with voices I detest. O future age wherein do you imagine that you are superior, since the temple from which you have driven the diety is become with your entire approbation an habitation for devils ?

California, 1925.

Thoughts on the Poetic Discontent.

BY JOHN CROWE RANSOM.

NOT many poets are satisfied with dualism. Mr. Goreham B. Munson, in a remarkable and brilliant analysis, has apparently succeeded in making a dualist out of Mr. Robert Frost, but only by a considerable simplification of Mr. Frost's mind, which may or may not be relished by the owner.

A dualist is a practical man whose mind has no philosophical quality. It may be that we begin our intellectual lives as dualists, but under the logic of experience (if our minds entertain the logical categories) we soon find that the largest problem in our lives is to effect an escape from dualism. The dualist sees himself as one, and the objective world as another ; this world is not sympathetic, not even sentient, but still fairly plastic to his will, and capable of being made by hard work to minister to his happiness : a wilderness which may be transformed into a garden, a habitat which has the makings of a home. His problem is purely the physical one : the application of force at the point where it will do the most good.

Philosophy and metaphysics take their rise most naturally when one perceives that the object, which is the world, is too formidable to be controlled altogether by the subject, which is oneself. Defeat humbles the proud spirit of a mortal. He cannot impose his will upon Nature, and self-respect will not permit him to deceive himself through the illusion of work, the debauchery of " practical " life. Insisting upon his own independence, he is forced to conclude that his personal identity is a tiny thing fighting a precarious and inevitably a losing fight against annihilation by superior forces. Then he consents to surrender the idea of his own dominating personality in exchange for the more tenable idea that he is in some manner related by ties of creation to the world, and entitled to some share in the general patrimony. The second step in his intellectual career is to discover somehow this community. It is a mystical community, capable of a great variety of definitions. So he finds God appointing to Nature and to himself appropriate places in a system where not a sparrow falls without effect and the hairs of his own head are numbered. So he is quick to note every sign of understanding on Nature's part, and his songs are filled with " pathetic fallacies." He is persistently trying to escape from an isolation which he cannot endure.

These efforts may or may not bring contentment. The romantic constructions of his mysticism are generally obnoxious to the sober observations of his science, and frequently they fall. The romantic poet comes to the point of puncturing his own illusions, objecting to his own romantic treatment of Nature, and cancelling the line which his own creative fancy has projected. He has advanced at this point to a third position which is later and further—though not all would say higher—than the position he has just vacated. Certainly it is not merely a return to his first position, though it is an affirmation of dualism. For too much history has intervened, he is a dualist with a difference—reluctant, speculative, sophisticated rather than ingenuous, and richer by all the pathetic fallacies he has ever entertained. There is a naïve, unqualified, strictly-business sort of dualism, and there is a matured and informed dualism which though critical is also romantic and poetical—and his is now the latter. It may be that most poetry is composed wholly from the point of view of the second, the purely romantic position. Nearly all the poetry of the Nineteenth Century, for example ; Byron returned in great bitterness to dualism, but Worsdworth, Shelley, Tennyson, and Browning continued indefinitely (with few lapses) to find sufficiency in their romantic escapes. But the earlier and greater poets (Chaucer, Spenser, Shakespeare, Donne, Milton) along with or following their own share of lovely romantic adventures, turned back to the stubborn fact of dualism with a mellow wisdom which we may call irony.

Irony may be regarded as the ultimate mode of the great minds—it presupposes the others. It implies first of all an honourable and strenuous period of romantic creation ; it implies then a rejection of the romantic forms and formulas ; but this rejection is so unwilling, and in its statements there lingers so much of the music and colour and romantic mystery which is perhaps the absolute poetry, and this statement is attended by such a disarming rueful comic sense of the poet's own betrayal, that the fruit of it is wisdom and not bitterness, poetry and not prose, health and not suicide. Irony is the rarest of the states of mind, because it is the most inclusive ; the whole mind has been active in arriving at it, both creation and criticism, both poetry and science. But this brief description is ridiculously inadequate for what is both exquisite and intricate.

Mr. Frost's poetry is anything but pretentious, it is trim and easy, and sometimes apparently trifling, yet it contains plenty of this irony. It is modern in one of the common senses of modern : its spirit transcends the Nineteenth Century mind and goes back to further places in the English tradition for its adult affiliations. It is immensely metaphysical, as Mr. Munson does not seem to admit. When this poet sees the bent birches in the wood, he " likes to think a boy's been swinging them," a hypothesis which would immediately put man and nature into a sodality of merry play. But he is too sceptical to believe that : he is forced to consider that ice storms have bent the birches, and thereupon his romantic impulse, baffled but not yet defeated, takes a new tack and begins to personalise the trees, imagined under their ice-coating. This is not dualism. Whenever he dwells on Nature, he is the same ; as when he finds the rotting timbers attempting to warm the forest with the " slow smokeless burning of decay." It would indeed seem that Nature never otherwise puts in an appearance in human art—whether poetry or painting. Always the natural processes are personalised, and art consoles us with its implication of far-flung analogies between our order and the natural order. Mr. Frost is more than ordinarily delicate in making this implication. And sometimes he is at pains to deny the truth of the more obvious implication which we would like to make. We would like to believe that the phoebes were sorrowful when the master's house burned, but he assures us they were not :—

> One had to be versed in country things
> Not to believe the phoebes wept.

This is irony, and rather brutal if salutary. But like all inveterate poets, he commits this irony in a context sprinkled with sly romanticisms.

The Reminiscences of Mme. F. M. Dostoevsky.

TRANSLATED FROM THE RUSSIAN BY S. S. KOTELIANSKY.

DOSTOEVSKY'S TWO VISITS TO OUR HOUSE.

SO the happy time passed, and dull days came to me During the last month I had got used to hurrying cheer-. fully to my work, to meeting Dostoevsky with joy, and to carrying on our animated conversations, so that now it had all become necessary to me. All my former habitual occupations lost their interest for me, and seemed to me empty and futile. Even the promise of Dostoevsky's visit did not give me any joy ; on the contrary, it weighed heavily on me, for I realised that neither my good mother nor myself could be interesting company for such a talented and clever man. If interesting conversations had taken place between Dostoevsky and myself, it was due, I thought, to the fact that they turned on a subject which occupied us both. But now Dostoevsky would come to us as a visitor, who was to be " entertained." I began thinking of subjects for our talks on the evening of his visit. I am afraid that the impression of a wearisome journey to such a remote place as we lived in, and of a dull evening spent in our company, would efface in so impressionable a man as Dostoevsky the memory of our previous meetings, and that he would resent being burdened with such a tedious acquaintance. Longing to see Dostoevsky, I was, however, quite willing that he should forget his promise and not come to us.

But, being a person very much alive, I tried to occupy myself and to distract my gloomy mood. I went off to my sister's for the day, played with her child, and in the evening told her and her husband of my work and of my visits to Dostoevsky during the whole of October. Working in the afternoons with Dostoevsky and copying out in the evenings,

REMINISCENCES OF MME. F. M. DOSTOEVSKY

I had little time left, and could only see my sister now and then by snatches ; and, therefore, I had many stories to tell, the more so as she, curious to know all about Dostoevsky, asked a good many questions. When I had answered her questions, my sister remarked : " You are wrong in getting infatuated with Dostoevsky. Indeed, my dear Netochka, your dreams cannot be realised, and the Lord be praised for it ; particularly as he is so ill, and so burdened with debts ! "

I replied hotly that I was not " infatuated with Dostoevsky," that I did not dream of anything in particular, but that I was glad to talk to a clever and talented man, and that I was grateful to him for his constant kindness and attention to me.

On my way home I turned over in my head what my sister had said to me, and I asked myself : " Am I really infatuated with Dostoevsky ? Is it indeed the beginning of love ? If so, it is a mad idea ! . . . No ; evidently my sister has exaggerated ! "

Next day I went to the shorthand lesson. At school I was told that the doctor had forbidden Olkhin, in view of his illness, to go out of doors, and that Olkhin had asked his pupils to come to his house. I went there. Olkhin congratulated me on the successful completion of my work. Dostoevsky had written to thank him for recommending a shorthand writer. Without my assistance, he said, he could not have managed to finish the work in time. He added that he had found working with the help of shorthand quite convenient, and he hoped to use it in the future. Olkhin said that he was satisfied with this opinion on the first pupil of his who had undertaken successfully independent work. I gave Olkhin five roubles, the stipulated 10 per cent. of my salary, and I gave his children two pounds of sweets.

To my great surprise, I noticed a certain feeling of hostility towards me on the part of my colleagues. Evidently, most of them considered themselves quite competent in shorthand and were hurt by the preference shown to me. Miss Alexandra I., as the boldest, made it quite clear to me, and declared rather sharply that she would *demand* the next work that came in, and would not give it up to anyone. I assured her that I made no claim on future work ; that I rather wished to go on with my studies so as to catch up my colleagues. She had just heard from me about Dostoevsky's coming visit, and she announced that she would come to me on Thursday for the whole evening. Apart from her desire to make the acquaintance of the famous novelist, she was going " to ask Doestoevsky to find work for her either as a shorthand writer or as a translator. He knew all the reviews and with his introduction she could get work anywhere." Her contemplated visit was terribly unpleasant to me. Dostoevsky would not have only to spend a tedious evening with us, but, thanks to Alexandra's insistence, he would also have to take upon himself the business of finding work for her. And besides (I must confess) I was afraid that Alexandra, with her cleverness and audacity, would produce on Dostoevsky a too favourable impression, as compared with me, and somehow I did not desire this. Added to which, my desire to see Dostoevsky again and to talk to him was becoming more ardent every day, and it seemed to me that the talkative Alexandra would spoil our conversation. But how to get rid of her, seeing she had invited herself ? I thought for a long while and was greatly worried about it, and then I decided on a feminine stratagem : to call on her on Thursday morning and to tell her that Dostoevsky had paid us his visit the previous night, on Wednesday, and so was not coming on Thursday. That little lie was disgusting to me, but what could I do if I feared her rivalry so much ?

On Thursday I bought excellent pears, of the sort Dostoevsky liked, and various other things with which he used sometimes to treat me. I arranged the tea-table, and at seven o'clock I began waiting for him. It struck half past, then eight o'clock, but Dostoevsky did not come ; and I decided that he had either forgotten or changed his mind. At half past eight he arrived. I met him with the question : " How did you manage to find us ? "

" That is all right," Dostoevsky replied. " You speak as if you were sorry that I had found you. And I have been trying to find your house ever since seven o'clock ; I have driven round and round. Everyone knows that there is a Kostromskaia Street, but how to get there no one could tell. So that I drove about enquiring in all the little shops.At last I found a kind fellow who stood on the step of the cab and showed the cabman where to drive."

My mother came in and I introduced Dostoevsky to her. He kissed her hand gallantly and told her that he was greatly obliged to me for my help with his work. While mother was preparing the tea, Dostoevsky told me of the troubles he had met with in delivering the novel. Stellovsky was not at home, he had left for the country, and his people could not say when he would return. Then Dostoevsky took the manuscript to Stellovsky's office, but the manager flatly refused to accept the novel, as he had had no instruction or order from his employer to that effect. To the Notary Public Dostoevsky came too late, and the office was closed ; at the district police there were no chiefs present in the afternoon, and he was told to call later on. He spent the day in anxiety, and only at ten o'clock in the evening he managed to deposit the manuscript with the inspector of the police, and received a formal receipt. And Dostoevsky took it out of his pocket and showed it to me.

We sat down to tea and began talking as pleasantly and unrestrainedly as ever. The topics of conversation I had prepared had to be put aside, so many new and interesting ones had come up. Dostoevsky quite fascinated my mother, who was so shy of the " famous author." Justice must be done to Dostoevsky, he knew how to " fascinate " people. He could be enchanting, and many a time afterwards I saw people who were even prejudiced against him fall under his influence and charm.

We began talking of how he had passed the last four days. He was having a rest, and was going to rest for another week, and then he would start on the third part of *Crime and Punishment*. " I want to ask your assistance, my good Anna Gregorievna," he said to me. " I found it so easy a way of working that I am going to dictate my further writings, and I believe you will not refuse to be my collaborator." I replied that I should be pleased to help him, but I wondered how Olkhin would regard it, if I was to take on fresh work, which he had perhaps intended to give to some other pupil of his. " But I have got used already to your way of working, and am perfectly satisfied with it. It would be strange if Olkhin wished to recommend someone else whom I do not know, and who may not suit me. But perhaps you yourself do not want to work with me, then, of course, I shan't insist." Dostoevsky was obviously annoyed that I had not agreed at once. I began saying that Olkhin would probably find no objections to my continuing to work for Dostoevsky, but as a mere matter of politeness I must ask him. And then I told Dostoevsky that many of my colleagues were looking askance at me for the preference shown me by Olkhin, and one lady had even made a few biting remarks on the subject.

"Who dared do that ?" Dostoevsky said. "A young lady, Alexandra I., but I have revenged myself on her by not introducing her to you." And I told him of my "feminine stratagem." "Why did you do it ?" he asked.

"I was afraid she would make too favourable an impression on you" I had to confess, "and also I wanted to talk to you, and to ask you many things, and I should hardly have been able to do it in the presence of a young lady unknown to you."

Dostoevsky was evidently pleased with my confession.

About eleven o'clock Dostoevsky said good-bye, and took my word that at the next lesson, on Monday, I would talk over the matter with Olkhin, and let him know the result. We parted on the most friendly terms, and I returned to the dining room quite enchanted with an evening marked by such animation and friendliness. But ten minutes later our maid came in and told us of an unpleasant incident. The cabman whom Dostoevsky had engaged for the evening had left his cab for a few minutes to go into a shop. While he was away the cushion of the seat had been stolen. The cabman was in despair, saying that his employer would deduct five roubles from his wages, but Dostoevsky promised to pay him the money.

I was so grieved and upset. It seemed to me that that annoying incident would affect Dostoevsky's attitude to us, and that he would no longer want to come to see us, at such a remote place, where he could be robbed, seeing that his cabman had been robbed. At the thought that the impression of that wonderfully spent evening might be effaced by this annoying incident, I almost cried.

The sixth of November was a Sunday, and I was to go to a birthday party given by my godmother. She lived a long way off, and I began to make ready quite early. To pass the time, I sat down to play the piano, and did not hear the bell ring ;

but hearing steps in the next room, I guessed that someone must have called. I looked round and suddenly saw Dostoevsky standing in the doorway. I instantly shut the piano and walked towards him. " You know," he said, " I have been missing you all this time, and this morning I was wondering whether I should come to see you or not. Would it be convenient ? Would not your mother and yourself consider my speedy visit too strange : he was here on Thursday, and he comes again on Sunday ? Well, I decided after all to come to-day, and, as you see, I am here ! " I said that mother and I were not society ladies, and that we were glad to see him. But this time there was no animated conversation : I only answered Dostoevsky's questions. I was annoyed that the drawing room was not sufficiently heated, and that it was very cold. Dostoevsky observed : " How cold it is here to-day, and how cold you yourself are to-day."- I was also somewhat vexed that, owing to Dostoevsky's visit, I should be rather late for my godmother's.

Seeing me in a bright silk dress, Dostoevsky asked if I was going out. Learning that my godmother lived near Alarchin Bridge, Dostoevsky suggested that he should take me there in his cab. On our way, at some turning, he put his arm round my waist to support me. But, as a girl of the sixties, I had a prejudice against all such marks of attention as the kissing of a woman's hands or the putting of an arm round her waist in helping her to get out of a cab. I said to Dostoevsky, " Please do not trouble : I shall not fall out." Dostoevsky was hurt by my refusing such a trifling service, and said, " How delighted I should be if you *did* fall out ! " I burst out laughing, and peace was restored. All the time we talked cheerfully. Saying good-bye to me, Dostoevsky grasped my hand and made me promise that I would come to him on Tuesday to talk over the work on *Crime and Punishment.*

Anna Gregorievna Snitkin, as seen from the first part of her Reminiscences, published in The Calendar, became Dostoevsky's stenographer in October 1866. In November Dostoevsky proposed to her, and they were married on February 15, 1867. Two months after their marriage, on April 14, 1867, the couple left for abroad, where they remained until the spring of 1871. During those years abroad Dostoevsky wrote "The Idiot" (1867-8), "The Eternal Husband " (1870), "The Devils " (1871),

The following chapters are taken from the original Russian volume " Reminiscences of Mme. Dostoevsky " just published (Moscow, 1925).

THE CALENDAR

Fiodor so often spoke of the certain " ruin " of his talent, if we remained any longer abroad, and was so tormented by the thought that he would not be able to keep his family, that as I listened to him I, too, was driven to despair. To relieve his anxious mood and to disperse his gloomy thoughts, which prevented him from concentrating on his work, I had recourse to the device which always helped to distract his mood and to amuse him. As we possessed then about three hundred thalers, I said that it would be worth while to try once more our luck at roulette ; I pointed out that as he had occasionally happened to win, there was no reason why we should not hope that our luck would turn this time, and so on. I certainly did not entertain any hope of his winning at roulette, and I also was very sorry to part with a hundred thalers, which it was necessary to sacrifice, but I knew by the experience of his former visits to the tables that, after receiving new and exciting impressions, after satisfying his craving for risk, for gambling, Fiodor would return home calmed, and realising the futility of his hopes of winning at the tables, would sit down with renewed strength to his novel, and in a couple of weeks would make good his losses. My idea of his going to play roulette pleased my husband very much, and he did not oppose it. Taking with him 120 thalers and stipulating, if he lost them, that I should send him money for his return fare, he left for Wiesbaden, where he stayed for a week. As I had supposed, his playing resulted disastrously, and his travelling expenses included, Fiodor spent 180 thalers—quite a considerable sum of money in our circumstances. But the cruel torments which he experienced during that week, as he blamed himself for robbing me and our child, had such an effect upon him that he decided *never* again in his life to play roulette. And this is what my husband wrote me on April 28, 1871 : " A great thing has happened to me ; the filthy fancy, which has *tormented* me for ten years (or truer, since the death of my brother, when I found myself suddenly crushed by debts) has vanished. I kept on dreaming of winning ; I dreamt seriously, passionately. Now it is all over and finished. This was actually the *last* time. Do you believe me, Anya,

that now my hands are untied ?   Gambling was a tie on me :
but now I shall think of work and shall not dream of gambling
for nights on end as I used to do."

I, of course, could not all at once believe in such a great
happiness as Fiodor's indifference to roulette.   Surely he had
promised me not to play so many times before, and yet he
had not found the strength to keep his word.   But this time
the happiness was realised, and indeed that was the *last* time
he played roulette.   Later on, during his travels abroad (in
1874, 1875, 1876, 1879) Fiodor never once went to a casino.
It is true that roulette was soon forbidden in Baden, but
roulette tables were to be found in Saxony and in Monte Carlo.
The distance would not have prevented my husband from
going there, if he had wished to play.   But he was no longer
drawn to it.   It was as though Fiodor's "fancy" of winning
at roulette was a sort of diabolical suggestion or disease, of
which he suddenly and for ever cured himself.   He returned
from Wiesbaden cheerful and calm, and immediately sat down
to the continuation of his novel *The Devils*.   He foresaw that
our going back to Russia, settling in a new place and the
expected increase of our family would not allow him to do
much work there.   All my husband's thoughts were turned
to the new period opening before us, and he speculated on
how he would find his old friends and relations, who, according
to him, might have changed considerably in the last four
years.   In himself he was conscious of a certain definite
change of views and convictions.

(To be continued)

The Returning Hero.

By EDGELL RICKWORD.

THE representation of the Hero, and of the heroic in action, is the achievement towards which great poetry has always moved. Is it possible, in the absence of pathetic elements from the Universe, as we see it now, to project such a figure ? Perhaps, for the purposes of this metaphysical poetry, the anthropomorphic is obsolete.

Mr. Wyndham Lewis suggests that there is a similar hold-up in the plastic arts :

" As already his body in no way indicates the scope of his personal existence (as the bear's or the barnacle's indicates theirs) it cannot any more in pictorial art be used as his effective delimitation or sign."

It was with the invention of language that man's capacity outgrew his physical form, and in poetry we find continually the purpose to represent him as other than he looks ; fundamentally, as more powerful than he is. Wistful literature is simply this desire turned upside down (as certain Orientals will say, " Oh, what a beautiful child ! " and in parenthesis, " The ugly little brat," to deceive any maleficent, jealous spirit that may be eavesdropping), primarily under the influence of christian ethics. But, at bottom, creation is the attributing to a suitable figure of extraordinary powers our super-animal vitality demands, which are inhibited from physical expression under present biological conditions. From Ulysses to Don Juan and Hardy's Napoleon this mechanics holds good, only with the de-humanization of nature it becomes more and more difficult to represent the vehicles of power in concrete forms. Hardy's Spirits share the modern fate. In the poignancy of the actual fables there is nothing to choose between the Odyssey and the Dynasts. Where are we to find, or how tap, that immense fertility of invention which makes the ancient poem so eminently superior ?

THE RETURNING HERO

We can at least be sure that even if the Odyssey were *composed* by one man, the labour of *creation* was by no means his alone. His labour was an æsthetic choice out of the mass of folk-imagination, so that most of his energy was spent simply in arrangement, to which a very great part of art may be reduced. The trouble for our modern poets is not any lack of sensibility or technical gifts, which several possess in high degree, but the necessity of creating entire any mythology they may want to use. The only living mythology is that of the nursery, and though one or two poets have relapsed on this, the result cannot deeply affect a healthy adult community. Since poetry should give the illusion of control over circumstance, in one obvious activity these childhood-fantasies baulk us—in the realisation of sex.

As far as the texture of verse is concerned, the actual descriptive imagery, the modern poet could be very well off. The sciences, industry and engineering, the habitual activities of common life, are all waiting to be drawn from, and provide a variety of material not surpassed by any period. The effort which still seems to hang fire is that of conceiving the poem itself in a modern metaphor, as Marlowe seized on the broadsheet reports of a case of German charlatanism to embody his lust for absolute power. In this he was helped by the race consciousness, or sub-consciousness, and we must look to this elaborately grotesque tailor of deep-seated desires to provide the costumes for our Hero and his Antagonist. It is none of the poet's business (the attempt is fatal to his art) to supply the Cosmos with mask and cod-piece.

The literature of disillusionment is reaching the last stage ; it is becoming popular with the reading-public. Mr. Strachey and Mr. Huxley have replaced Ruskin and Carlyle. No doubt, too, all young men of poetic ambition have their version of *The Waste Land* in their wash-stand drawer. If this is not quite the same thing as popularity it means at least that Mr. Eliot's inspiration was not merely personal ; in its coarser manifestations, if not in its ultimate delicacy, it tuned in with an emotion common to the best spirit of the age, a fastidious and anguished rejection of the various forms of satisfaction offered by the Spirit of Historical Culture. The passion for sophistication is only one of the forces of life. The determination not to be fooled is, a young Frenchman said, the disease of our time. But that is no reason for taking the first turning back to divine simplicity. The hefty heroism of Mr. Masefield's narratives is meretricious. The stoicism of Mr. Eliot's middle-aged lover is as tense heroics as the material of his art will bear.

Though we are not likely to cut any more ideals for a good many years, being hardly convalescent from the wholesale extractions of the last century, we cannot imagine the poets remaining content to cultivate the drugget-fields of genteel discontent. A Hero would seem to be due, an exhaustively disillusioned Hero (we could not put up with another new creed) who has yet so much vitality that his thoughts seize all sorts of analogies between apparently unrelated objects and so create an unbased but self-consistent, humorous universe for himself. The form of him is naturally still in question, but we can be pretty sure that he will not be a Watts horseman in shining armour. Possibly he will be preceded (I should say that he is being preceded) by some tumbling, flour-faced harbingers to the progress (for we cannot grow serious all at once) just as the death-facing wire-walker in the circus is led into the ring by clowns who mime his tragedy. Perhaps the Hero will be one of these loons himself, for the death-defying gesture is a demoded luxury in the modern State. So long as the social mind has no coherent expression like that given it by a super-natural explanation of the Universe, the fantastic and the comic, disintegrating forces, will continue the most reputable of styles. They need by no means be inimical to heroic poetry, to which not dignity is essential, but a conception of power: and the further this can be removed from conventional erotic, ethical, or other social values, and the more deeply it can be resolved into its abstract elements, a diagram or skeleton of impulses (like the bare tremendous Sign of the Hero of the Dance of Death), the nearer it will approach a reality underlying the surviving fabric of the old culture.

———

Reviews.

THE IDEA OF GREAT POETRY. By Lascelles Abercrombie. Secker. 6s.

It has been Mr. Abercrombie's intention in the five lectures
here reprinted simply " to enquire what *are* the qualities most
noticeable in the poetry which has, as a matter of acknowledged
fact, been recognised as great." As was to be expected of a critic
so sensitive to poetry, he has written much in appreciation of
certain great poets—Dante, Shakespeare, Milton and Wordsworth
—and has occasionally been original in his praise, but he has done
little to make clear the main thesis of his book. He fully realised
the chief difficulty which presents itself in such a discussion
when he wrote " Too often the poetry which is accepted as great
has been praised for its ideas, its passions, its characterisation,
without any appreciable regard for the conditions which enable
these (or any other) qualities to exist *as poetry*." To obviate this
he adds that, he hopes " it will be allowed, during the later stages
of our discussion, that nothing which is there said to make for
greatness has been admitted except under the conditions which
make it *poetry*, though these conditions may not be expressly
mentioned : for they will, in fact, have been mentioned once and
for all as the foundations of everything else." With this proviso
much of what Mr. Abercrombie says may be accepted, but it is
only in continually showing its truth that his book would be of
value.

It is, indeed, not at all clear what Mr. Abercrombie means by
" great," for he speaks of the *Decameron* as " one of the first poems
in the world " when he is actually concerned with showing that
it is not great. Or of Wordsworth he says, " What we miss in
him is the supremely great *poem*," and yet of the *Ode on the Intimations of Immortality* that it is " the height of modern poetic art
in English." If then, as it would appear, poetry does not depend
on greatness for its pre-eminence *qua* poetry, it is important to
show if, or in what degree, the poems chosen to illustrate greatness
are also great poetry. But Mr. Abercrombie when he is writing of
Paradise Lost, or the *Iliad*, or *Hamlet* says little of their poetry :
much of what he says would be equally applicable to *War and Peace*
or *Moby Dick*. What he is really doing is to discuss greatness
and not great poetry, and this confusion of intention leads to a
confused kind of criticism, for it tends always to obscure the value
of craftsmanship—the first condition of poetry for the critic.

There is poetry and non-poetry—there is good poetry, but there is no point at which it breaks off into great poetry. It is much more satisfactory to base the scale of values on subject matter, but this point of view Mr. Abercrombie has only hinted at. When he makes a distinction between the poetry of *experience* and the poetry of *escape*, he is much nearer the root of the matter, but he only glances at this distinction.

The fault of such an attitude towards the critical function as Mr. Abercrombie exploits is particularly noticeable in one instance. He says of the great range of matter in *The Dynasts*, " and as this is compacted into tremendous unity of final impression by a singularly potent idea of life, the result is a poem which can only be compared, and will only be compared by the criticism of the future, with the great poems of Europe " : and later, " perhaps no better instance could be found of the greatness of poetry coming from the vigorous mastery of an idea over the whole unruly fact of life." It is this insistence on vastness of subject instead of perfection of expression as the criterion of poetry which tends to weaken criticism, and it is this attitude towards poetry which Mr. Abercrombie stresses.

There are, however, other causes for the disappointing effect of the book. The language throughout is at a high tension of romantic eulogy, so that unless the reader enter fully into Mr. Abercrombie's enthusiasms the questions at stake will frequently be obscured by rodomontade. One feels with Johnson that, " We must confess the faults of our favourite, to gain credit to our praise of his excellencies. He that claims, either in himself or for another, the honours of perfection will surely injure the reputation he designs to assist." This attitude of sustained admiration is deadening : the more so that Mr. Abercrombie, by setting forth his point of view in terms of positive achievement, does not attempt to make his criticism applicable to the conditions of modern poetry.

DOUGLAS GARMAN.

ASHE OF RINGS. By MARY BUTTS. Three Mountains Press : Paris. 3 $.

Miss Butts is a short-story writer of ability ; in " Ashe of Rings," she essays the novel with much the same technique as she used for the short story. This raises the question of technique. A short digression is, therefore, necessary.

By technique is generally meant the various means which a writer uses to express his vision. As such it is in every period a collective as well as an individual thing ; the expression on the one hand, of what people call the spirit of the age, and, on the other, of the personality of the writer. And as in the political realm, as indeed in human life generally, there is here, too, a conflict between the individual and the mass, between the *Zeit Geist* which, if it could, would make us impersonal and undistinguishable vehicles of its expression, and ourselves as individuals desiring absolute utterance for our personal visions. No absolute freedom of this kind exists, in literature or in life, as we know ; and so the writer who tries to escape the spirit of the age (an attempt which must always be hopeless in any case) is likely to attain less freedom than the one who, recognising it, wrestles with it for the prize of his personality. For the spirit of the age is not only a thing which limits the writer's expression (though that it does so we can recognise when we look back even upon such a recent era as the 'nineties) ; it is also the thing which gives most immediately what life may reside in what he says. But that life, it almost appears, can only be tapped at its living source, as Mr. Joyce tapped it in " Ulysses," when one has struggled against the spirit of the age ; for in the struggle, the deceptions, superficialities and fashions of the age are stripped away until, if the writer is fortunate or honest, the point is reached where the age and he come into immediate contact, not by a conscious act merely, but through a kind of final necessity. The writer who does not resist his age, defending himself against a'l its claims crowding in upon him and overwhelming him, will belong to the literature of fashion. The writer who refuses to realise his age is not likely to belong to literature at all. The apparent exceptions to this rule, such as Blake, are not exceptions at all ; for no one was more painfully concerned with his age than Blake. This brief generalisation, which could only be supported in a much longer argument, I must leave for the moment as it is.

" Ashe of Rings " is a striking example of the literature of fashion. Its technique is not essentially personal, as is the technique of writers so various as Mr. Joyce, Mr. Strachey, and Mr. Eliot ; it is a technique which might at different moments belong to almost anyone who writes in the idiom of the time. It is a generalised technique and, therefore, never quite fits the situation or the emotion it is enlisted to convey ; and so the general effect is always a little false. For it is only a technique which a writer has gradually perfected, not as an exercise, but always for specific and concrete ends, which will render at last his specific vision. Miss Butts' vision, one feels, is sometimes individual ; but it is as if she translated it continuously into something which has scarcely anything to do with her or with it. The fault is a common one, though seldom illustrated with such brilliance as in " Ashe of Rings " ; its prevalence is what makes it interesting. It is the fault of a large class of writing in which the inspiration is seen by the writer as one thing and the literary effect as something totally different ; the first being susceptible of transposition in quite an arbitrary way into the second. When this transposition takes place, the inspiration, which is personal, becomes mere raw material to be manufactured into effects resembling other effects of the time : the unconscious error here, a very elementary one, being that if this process does not happen, the result will belong neither to the age nor to literature.   This perennial error is betrayed in bad writing of all kinds ; in melodrama, the West-end comedies of our time, the novelette, journalism ; but it infects sometimes work which in happier circumstances might have been good.   When this occurs it can only be a sign that in a particular writer the spirit of the age is manifesting itself with hesitation, for no writer would take the trouble to secure the outward signs of the age in his work if the influence of the age were felt overpoweringly by him.   Miss Butts has made the mistake of trying to express the age instead of herself, which means that the *Zeit Geist* is not immanent in her, and has to be treated as subject-matter rather than expressed as content.

All this being so, it is not surprising that the story itself should turn out to be as old-fashioned as the style is modern.   Miss Butts' characters are not merely good and evil ; they are conventionally good and melodramatically evil.   She is consistently on the side of virtue, a policy good in itself, but artistically a bad policy, for it inevitably makes the good characters appear prigs ; and she does not even try to comprehend evil, again a bad policy, for the more comprehensible evil is made the more interesting aesthetically it becomes, as we may learn from Shakespeare, as well as from Dostoevsky.   All this is elementary, yet Miss Butts' imagination ignores it, even if her style does not.   That she has talent both her technique and her imagination, sentimental as it often is, tell us.   If that talent were integrated, it might produce something above the ordinary.   But at present it is not integrated, and from that fact flow all the main faults of the book.

EDWIN MUIR.

THE POLYGLOTS.   By WILLIAM GERHARDI.   Cobden-Sanderson. 7s. 6d.

A year or two ago Mr. Gerhardi wrote a novel which was so delightfully funny that it was generally commended to, and even read by, thousands ignorant of the conventions of Russian fiction therein half imitated, half satirised.   A second novel is notoriously difficult to write.   The merits of the first only increase the obstacles in the way of the second.   The unhappy novelist is asked to choose between imitating himself and risking his young reputation by doing something different.   Mr. Gerhardi, I suspect, was fully aware of the dilemma.   Was " Futility " to be succeeded by still greater futility, or was his humour to be let loose in a new field ?   Mr. Gerhardi has composed a compromise which is probably the worst on which he could have tumbled.   By a pale imitation of " Futility's " merits he solicits the suffrages of the ninety and nine reviewers who simultaneously and with some pride discussed him. " You expected something like this," he murmurs, " and here it

REVIEWS

is." At the same time he adventures into English vulgarity. For the present he is safe. He is carried on the wave of fame. One of the noisiest of his flatterers is a gentleman who in praising " Futility " admitted that he did not know whether its humour was deliberate or unconscious, and who now cannot find enough to say about the subtlety of " The Polyglots." Mr. Gerhardi, in short, is established as an authority on the aftermath of the Russian revolution, and has only to write " Nasha " or " Katya " to send us into shrieks of laughter. But what has he in store against the days when this joke wears thin ? Only, I regret to observe, jokes about lingerie.

In so far as " The Polyglots " is not an attenuated imitation of " Futility " it resembles one of those large draper's sheets in the interstices of which are printed *The Observer* and *The Sunday Times*. The popular voice has decided that under-garments, like kippers and lodgers and mothers-in-law, are inherently comic. Perhaps they are. But the best of jokes, as for example the joke about the curate's egg, cannot sustain infinite repetition. How often Mr. Gerhardi plays with lingerie cannot be estimated without reducing this notice to the precision of a laundry list. The Russian general presented sets complete to ladies he admired. One of the most nearly sympathetic characters committed suicide in his sister's set. And there is a small girl with a weak bladder whose knickers have frequently to be adjusted ; oh ! there is no end to the exquisite comedy of this. But it won't do. When the stage was much more innocent than it is now a big laugh could be won by the hero— Charles Hawtrey, I think—ejaculating " Damn ! " Next came " Bloody." Worse words have still to be mentioned. But lingerie is almost exhausted. You come very soon to a garment next the skin. And Mr. Gerhardi has only combinations in reserve for his next novel.

To render his humour fertile Mr. Gerhardi must give up looking for formulæ. His keen sense of the illogical is a real asset to him, and in the farcical application of Slavonic frankness to ethical problems he is scarcely, if at all, surpassed by Tchehov. But he must no longer go about in second-hand clothing. Russian reach-me-downs might be passed off as, at least, unusual. In the cast-off garments of the late Ally Sloper he is almost pathetic. Let us hope that " The Polyglots " marks a stage in his development where he will not long abide.

H. C. HARWOOD.

NOAH'S ARK. By A. WILLIAMS-ELLIS. Jonathan Cape. 7s. 6d.

Mrs. Williams-Ellis's subject is the manner in which a sophisticated and highly self-conscious young woman comes to terms with life, effecting the reconciliation of her intelligence and her instincts. Frances' difficulty, both before and after marriage, was to discover

how she and Edward could live in harmony without it being necessary for them to cut themselves down to this small common
denominator. For a long time she is too civilised to succeed, but
at last, being unable to work at her modelling, yet needing adventure
more than her husband, who finds his in his work, she remembers
" what the creatures went into the ark for." "A child . . .
Breeding . . . That's what it wants with us next."

Such a theme can only be made capable of supporting a work of
art, and so convincing, on condition that it is exploited in terms of
character. Though character-drawing in the conventional sense
is unnecessary, it is important, if the reader is to be persuaded
of the story's truth and so moved by it, that the individuality of
the actors' intelligences should be realised. This Mrs. Williams-
Ellis never quite accomplishes. Frances introspects at considerable
length and holds long conversations about herself with her father-
in-law, but her ideas, though copious and good, without being
first-rate, lack any characteristic timbre. Nor are her copiously-
annotated actions particularly revealing. As a result, the reader,
though learning much about Edward and more about Frances,
cannot be said to have experienced either of them.

Whether Mrs. Williams-Ellis, through lacking the novelist's
peculiar gift of self-projection, is unable to transpose her experience
into the keys of imagined character, it would be rash to determine
from a first novel. Probably, however, she fails artistically not
because of her inexperience, but because her impulse was fundamentally not æsthetic but sententious. Though her intelligence
prevents the suspicion of deliberate allegory, her heroine ultimately
is not Frances, but Mrs. Everyman. Nevertheless, her book, being
written animatedly and intelligently, is to be recommended as a
tract that is both amusing and pertinent to the times.

C. H. RICKWORD.

A STORY-TELLER'S STORY. By SHERWOOD ANDERSON. Cape,
7s. 6d.

Mr. Sherwood Anderson is a baffling writer, baffling because
baffled. The conscientious flatness of his style (of which the title
of his latest book affords an excellent example), its pedestrian
movement, its air of groping after the obvious, its un-rhetorical
reiteration of unimportant words, continually leaves us in two
minds, puzzled and irritated. Clearly it is Mr. Anderson's intention
to say what he has to say as plainly as possible, without frills and
affectations, looking his meaning squarely in the eye. He thinks
that in much modern writing the means of expression have gone
astray and suffered corruption, obscuring rather than illuminating
what is vital in life ; and it is his mission to bring expression up-to-
date, restore it to its function, make it correspond to the things that

REVIEWS

really take place inside us.   As often as not this rehabilitation seems
to consist in perversely putting in what other writers would leave
out.   When others would be content with saying a man walked
along the street, Mr. Anderson would go further.   His amplification
of the simple movement is easy to imagine.   " The man walked
along the street.   He used his feet in walking, setting one foot
carefully in front of the other.   The foot that was coming down
would press upon the ground, and a little later the man would do
the same with the other foot.   The man would go on doing this
until he was tired and then, perhaps, he would sit down."
     This is not an unfair parody : Mr. Anderson is often more unkind
to himself.   Part of his intention, it seems, is to make the conscious
and the unconscious mind change places ; we are made aware of
difficulties in the management of the body and limbs—difficulties
with which we were familiar in infancy but which we have long outgrown.   Conversely, in Mr. Anderson's world it is possible for a
man to discuss with a woman whether he should take off his clothes
in her presence.   To be sure the man was a little drunk ; but this
condition Mr. Anderson scarcely considers such a divagation from
true normality—the normality he is searching for—as ordinary
sobriety.   People to him are like houses.   It is a metaphor to
which he continually returns : their outsides convey nothing to
him, but sometimes through a door or window he gets a glimpse of
what is within : and it is at these critical moments, when he has
found himself, so to speak, that he seems least of all to be writing
about human beings.   In the stress of emotion his characters
neither talk nor behave credibly ; they are a law unto themselves,
mouthing and gesticulating in the flawless isolation of a synthetic
world.
     Mr. Anderson is disgusted with industrialised America.   His
pilgrimage through it is the subject of " A Story-Teller's Story,"
and he brings it vividly before our eyes, fusing the real and the
imaginative life.   It is a record of successive dissatisfactions, of
occupations thrown up, of casual friendships, of literary beginnings,
aspirations and achievements, of years of disappointment and
moments of ecstasy.   It is convincing because, here, Mr. Anderson
is writing about himself : the amazing strength of his personality
survives his presentation of it, the fact of his enthusiasm sublimates,
as it were, the objects of his enthusiasm (though they are respectable
enough) and makes us like him more and more.   " Like " his
characters is a thing we can rarely do, even if (which is uncertain)
he means us to like them.   And it is in this connection that we feel
warranted in imputing a fundamental falsity to his reconstruction
of life.   The first question the reader asks himself about a character
is, Do I like him ?   One cannot go on living with a person, either
in fiction or in life, uncertain whether or not one likes him.   That
its hero was an unmitigated cad must be most people's recollection
of *Many Marriages*.   Yet Mr. Anderson, in narrating his history,

entirely ignored such a preoccupation, treating a situation that had no interest except for its rights and wrongs as though they did not exist. The demoralisation that is implied by the contemporary American doctrine of " uplift " is a thing to deplore ; but it is no remedy to invent an arbitrary human consciousness from which the moral sense and all its implications are excluded. Mr. Anderson does not quite exclude them : he finds substitutes in the relation between the workman and the materials of his craft, in the sensation of " cleanness " that comes of turning out a good piece of work. But that is to confuse morality with æsthetics. He wants all men to love each other ; but they are not, apparently, to accept any responsibility for the outcome of their loves.

Is it Mr. Anderson's seriousness that is at the root of all this ? He wants to write, but still more (the despised Puritan working in him) he wants to be serious. " What a man wants," he in an unguarded moment confesses, " is to be able to justify himself to himself." Precisely ; and we recommend the statement to Mr. Anderson as the theme of some future novel, begging him not to twist the meaning of the term " self-justification " into " self-realisation." But " self-justification through Art " is not a good maxim for a writer, and it will not add to our enjoyment though he save his soul in every line.   L. P. HARTLEY.

CONTEMPORARY TECHNIQUES OF POETRY : A POLITICAL ANALOGY. By ROBERT GRAVES. Hogarth Press, 3s. 6d.

A pamphlet war might do a good deal to improve the modern race of poets ; at least there is room for a literary analogy to Bernhardi's too-abused theory. Toleration or indifference has gone so far, and so prostituted the terms of praise, that it is impossible to tell from an ordinary review whether a book of poems contains really original work or if it just avoids the more obvious commonplaces. Under this wadding the feebler shoots are protected from the contempt which would naturally cut them off, and live to blossom in collected mediocrity—absorbing so much sun and air from the healthier growths. The task of pruning is such a delicate one that autocratic statements are not to be recommended ; it is by personal evaluations, such as this essay of Mr. Graves's, backed up by the knowledge of practice, that some order may be introduced into the present muddle. Only, if pamphlets are to be as useful as I think they can be, they must be of a price that allows them unrestricted circulation.

Mr. Graves draws his analogy from contemporary politics by dividing the poets into three parties—Conservatives, Liberals, and Left-Wing reformers, revolutionaries and exiles. His comments on the techniques of the two constitutional parties are mischievous and mildly destructive ; they have the wisdom-in-humour, the disarming smile which always saves his prose divagations from

REVIEWS

becoming portentous, even in the treatment of final problems, but opens a path for casual evasions which does not always tempt him unsuccessfully.

" I am the historian merely ; but having regard to the enormous dead-weight of prestige behind the Conservative view, and to the popular success of the Central Party, I shall possibly find myself making out the clearest case for the party which is least vocal, the Left Wing."

A most courteous assassin, and we have no desire to quarrel with the means that lead to so admirable an end. But is it simply the desire to champion the oppressed which enables Mr. Graves to make out the best case for the less-appreciated of the younger poets ? Do not their merits entitle them not merely to an equalitarian, but to a preferential judgment ? To get itself said, any new thing has to break up, more or less, and re-model, the old forms of expression. All the poets lumped together as the tradition were innovators in their time and none of the new modifications of verse technique quoted by Mr. Graves seems to us incapable of being absorbed into the English tradition. It is rather too much of a sacrifice to surrender to merely conventional versifiers the title of traditionalists, so that those who have real vigour of expression must be branded, though honourably, revolutionaries. The blood of Donne and Milton is more likely to be found in these apparent throw-outs than in the approved stereotypes which crowd our more sumptuous anthological mausoleums.

We differ rather in approach than in conclusions from Mr. Graves, and must commend his essay as a timely and valuable piece of propaganda. His chapter on " Structure " is most suggestive, though condensed. The psychological basis of verse is a subject which has occupied him before and led to interesting statements. Changes in the physiology of verse, diction and rhythm, are manifestations only of the more elusive renovation of the core of the mind.

The outlook for poetry, if it can find its audience and assert true values, is certainly more encouraging than it was twenty years ago. Many powerful conventions have been realised to be demoralising, and experience is seen to be pretty well autonomous within the conditions of successful expression. The war of attrition against critical inertia still needs speeding up, and for this short raids into the opposing trenches are most efficacious.

E. R.

TOM MOORE'S DIARY. *A Selection edited by* J. B. PRIESTLY. Cambridge University Press. 6s.

One agrees with Mr. Priestly that this Diary, so largely concerned with affairs of transitory interest, " gains from being compressed.' It would, perhaps, have gained more had the compression been more stringent, or had what remains been more fully edited. In places the interest flags owing to a lack of information about the people concerned, and one easily loses the thread when, after a lapse of several weeks, there is no indication as to when the next entry was written. A selection, however, is certainly justified by the light which the Diary throws not only on the social and literary activities of the time, but also on Moore's personality—though it does not reveal the latter so favourably as Mr. Priestly implies.

As a retailer of gossip Moore was admirably qualified. His knowledge of literature and his fame as a poet allowed him to meet with most of the contemporary writers and artists, while his attractive person, fluting voice and social charm gave him the entry to the houses of the cultured nobility. As a result his Diary is full of amusing incidents and witty anecdotes. He heard Wordsworth affirm to a large party of people that he had published the "White Doe" in quarto "to show the world his own opinion of it," and he writes amusingly of several ladies who insisted on kissing him while crossing the Irish Channel in spite of his efforts to get away and be sick. From this point of view the Diary is full of interest, but the portrait it gives of Moore himself is distasteful. His merits are obvious: he did not bear grudges, he sang prettily, he was generous and entertaining, and very affectionate with his wife ; indeed, had his profession been other than an art, he would remain for posterity a good-natured, rather insipid character. But he was a poet, and since he was unable to dissociate social from literary values, his work is almost worthless. He is an early specimen of a type now common—the social-artist and social-critic. Writing was valuable to him only as a passport into good society or as an activity in which he indulged as in a ball or a dinner party. His approach to literature was fundamentally as frivolous as his social conduct.

D. M. G.

WORDS AND IDIOMS : Studies in the English Language. By LOGAN PEARSALL SMITH. Constable. 7s. 6d.

Of these five interesting and learned essays on aspects of English, " Four Romantic Words " and " English Idioms " are, perhaps, the most immediately suggestive. For the old question between the romantic and the classical has been raised again during these last few years, and the importance of idiom as a prospective fertiliser of a literary language grown poor is being more and more clearly recognised. The causes of the present impoverishment of literary language are defined with admirable clarity in " English Idioms." There has been a " remarkable and modern growth of idiomatic phases in our speech," the author says, and this may be explained " as a reaction against the deadness of much contemporary English —the increasing use of life-forsaken words in that jargon of science and abstract thought which is so characteristic of the present age.

REVIEWS

. . . . The truth is that learned languages, having for their main object the naming of concepts, naturally tend to colourless abstraction. Representing the triumph of reason over the incoherence of immediate sensation, they embody the results of science in their vocabulary, and the laws of thought in their grammar. For the purpose of order and abstraction, they reject much of the illogical but psychological element of experience, the bodily sensations and the lively feelings which accompany sensation, and all those reasons of the imagination and the heart of which, in Pascal's phrase, ' the reason knows nothing.' " With this admirable summary by an acute student, it is difficult to disagree. But if Mr. Smith is right, if language has in the last few generations become a better vehicle for thought and a worse medium for imaginative literature, the further conclusion must follow : that the main stream of vitality in the age which has preceded ours and in our own has gone and is going into science and abstract thought rather than into literature. This has been asserted by Mr. Bertrand Russell ; and the immense vitality of modern science, the comparative poverty of modern literature, must, indeed, be self-evident. The interesting thing is the effect this has had on language. It is not that language has been modified merely by the inclusion of new scientific and abstract terms ; it has been used so long in a particular way that now a philosopher like Mr. Russell can handle it easily and beautifully, as if it were an instrument which completely satisfied him, while an imaginative writer like Mr. Joyce has to distort it as the only hope of amplifying it, and in addition has to fall back freely on idiom (whose function, Mr. Smith asserts, " is to bring back ideas from the understanding to the sensations from which they were originally derived "), in order to achieve imaginative and psychological solidity. It may be that the habit of the age and the language has become so strong that the imaginative artist is unable to seize impressions and emotions immediately ; and has rather to work back to them from the concept and thus to attain deliberately what some ages have started with. This is as much as to say that we live in an age of enlightenment, but also that there is an imaginative revolt in train against it.

All these deductions from Mr. Smith's premises find indirect support in his interesting essay on " Four Romantic Words." These words, " romantic," " originality," " creation," " genius," have certainly less power now than they had a century ago, perhaps because they are no longer felt imaginatively, as the artist feels them, but formulated for the purposes of thought. But, formulated, they are found to contain very little. For the moment the genius of the language has left them high and dry, counters for the use of scholars and rhetoricians. Thus the word " romantic," which gradually grew in power in the eighteenth century until it became the symbol of the revolt against the eighteenth century, is no adequate symbol for the revolt of our time against the tyranny of an enlightenment on a far greater scale. It rose as a specific response to a specific human need ; and what we lack is a symbol for a very different need, that of out own time. No doubt that symbol will sometime arise. **E. M.**

PREJUDICE AND PROMISE IN XVᴛʜ CENTURY ENGLAND. C. L. KINGSFORD. Clarendon Press. 15s.

In his treatment of the subject in the series of six Ford Lectures delivered in 1923 and put together with five useful appendices in this book, Mr. Kingsford has succeeded in giving us a very presentable picture of XVth Century England. Whether the title is well chosen or the apologetic vein in which he introduces his theme, as if he really did think that everybody would be bored, is open to question. Only if one approaches the XVth Century as an interlude between the questionable glories of the Edwards and the equally expensive pomp of the Tudors does it appear to be dull and without interest.

No one who has witnessed the trial scene in "Saint Joan," with its dramatisation of the central struggle of the period when the Middle Ages were passing and the Renaissance coming in, can ever again excusably speak with a certain patronising tolerance of the XVth century. The incidents and the events of the Hundred Years War and of the antagonism of the Houses of Lancaster and York are mere corks that show us the way the currents are flowing. Feudalism collapsing, nationalism arising—these two facts in themselves are enough to make the century fascinating.

In the first two lectures one does not feel that Mr. Kingsford quite grips his subject. They are interesting, but one has the impression that it has all to do with that most unreal and utterly superficial history of Courts. Perhaps it is necessary to uncover the dead monarchs of the dynastic arguments and wars of the dead rose leaves and dried dung with which the prejudice of the later age strewed them.

In his lectures on "Social Life and the Wars of the Roses" and "West Country Piracy" he has succeeded in whetting one's appetite. There must be a fire of economic activity and of social pressure underneath this smoke of banditry and piracy in Devon and in Cornwall. Opportunity obviously there was for loot and more profit therein than in honest exchange and peaceful intercourse with the merchant cities of Spain and Italy.

Still, the English seamen are at that very primitive stage at which, for the most part, they are lying in wait for the great galleys and carracks which the hand of Providence in the guise of the Gulf Stream and the South-West Wind has driven against the rocks of the Cornish coast.

Fowey, Plymouth, Dartmouth and Poole, it is evident from what Mr. Kingsford shows us, became nurseries of seamen because

REVIEWS

the elements allowed them more easily to grow rich as " sea-beggars " than as hard-working artificers or patient fisher-folk.

Here we have another race and a new generation of Vikings—pirates all. In the map of Fowey Estuary which he gives us we are able to see at a glance in this one instance what becomes apparent to the visitor who observes the inlets of Devon and of Cornwall. Up these stretches of deep water with their narrow entrances across which, as at Dartmouth, bowmen could command the entire fairway, enemies even when better equipped and more heavily armed found it hard to pass. So at an early date Bristol and Totnes, Southampton and Exeter were able to develop as communities with a commerce, and behind that commerce an industry undisturbed in its growth. These factors had much more to do with the success of Peupous and Drake, of Pay and Granville than is generally recognised. One has only to contrast the home-keeping habits and the backward economy of the gentry of Glamorgan with that of the no more hospitable " West Wales " to see how important was this factor of geography in the development of the Devon seamen.

Hakluyt gives us many hints, and that " Libel of English Policie," written in the XVth century (in many ways one of the most significant writings of the age), affords us many more, of those stirrings behind the incidents recorded in this book. Quite the most noticeable omission is any reference to the " Libel," despite the mention it makes of Fowey and of other West Country ports.

J. T. W. NEWBOLD.

CONTACT COLLECTION OF CONTEMPORARY WRITERS. Three Mountains Press, Paris. 3$.

It is not at all understandable what intention governed the collection of these stories, poems and articles into one volume, unless it were an open-minded but uncritical catholicism. Good work is mixed with bad, modernism with conservatism. On the one hand Miss Stein would seem to be elaborating, tediously and very boringly, a small point of consciousness; on the other Miss Sinclair tells a long ghost story with the conventional aids of local colour and objective discussion—even of an epilogue beginning, "A year later . . ." The poetry is not interesting. Mr. Marsden Hartley has a certain sense of rhythm, but in the single poem here printed shows no other quality ; Miss Mina Loy's sixty pages, despite her idiosyncratic spacing of type, is doggerel; and the two poems by Miss Sitwell have previously appeared in the volume " Troy Park," already noticed in THE CALENDAR.

The best stories are those by Miss Butts, Mr. Ford, and Miss Barnes. The very amusing extract from " Work in Progress " by Mr. Joyce cannot here be seen in true perspective. Messrs. Hemingway, Herman, and McAlmon write naturalistically of youthful American life in small towns, and amongst other contributors are Mr. Havelock Ellis and Mr. Norman Douglas. Mr. W. C. Williams's critique of Miss Marianne Moore's poetry is enthusiastic but not very explicit.

It is to be hoped that if another Contact Collection is to appear it will contain more work by fewer authors, for at a time when there is so little uniformity of method one needs more than a single example of an author's work if one is to form an opinion of it.

D. M. G.

Among New Books

THE CHARACTER OF JOHN DRYDEN. By Alan Lubbock. Hogarth Press. 2s. 6d.

The side of Dryden's character which Mr. Lubbock justly emphasises is his conservatism, for it was this that gave him the mental leisure to pursue his personal endeavour of helping on the perfection of language, whether in prose or verse. In a remarkable degree he accepted the ideas of his age—or at least such of them as were useful to him—and his aim was not to increase their range, but to give them the benefit of lucid expression. Mr. Lubbock's suggestion that " his conservatism came not from timidity, not from laziness, not from snobbish conceit or suspicion, but from intense and passionate gusto, from ardent enjoyment of life as it was, from anxiety to seize and incorporate into himself all his surroundings," should be qualified : it was not only these reasons that prevented him from attempting " to say anything new," but also a fundamental lack. His was not a large mind, in the sense that he had not, and therefore could not develop, an original or personal attitude to life. This accounts for the neglect which Dryden suffered from the nineteenth century. So much Mr. Eliot has already remarked (in another of the " Hogarth Essays "), but the amplification of this criticism which Mr. Lubbock implies is important as serving to show Dryden's achievement in a fairer perspective with that of other poets and of Milton in particular. Mr. Lubbock himself does not attempt the comparison, but his essay has a bearing on Mr. Eliot's judgment and its apparent denigration of Milton in favour of Dryden.

Mr. Lubbock's Essay is interesting as far as it goes, but there are other qualities in Dryden's character which he might have discussed, and which would have instilled a more lively blood into the rather plethoric figure with which he presents us.

SENLIN : A BIOGRAPHY. By Conrad Aiken. Hogarth Press. 3s. 6d.

In this long poem Mr. Aiken has failed technically to avoid monotony, and for this there are several reasons. The metre he has used is a free penta-metre (with occasional three foot lines), but his habit of alternating weak and strong endings and of rhyming usually the latter, robs his verse of the elasticity of blank verse and does not allow it the full possible vigour of rhyme. Then, too, the frequent repetition of lines and phrases with no, or but slight, variation is wearisome and tends to distract the mind in the second context without throwing new light on the statement. Again, the reiterated interrogations are very unsatisfying, and suggest that Mr. Aiken is uncertain as to his own intention, but hopes by this means to pass off his uncertainty as intentional. The texture of the poem is often spoilt by the use of rather precious metaphorical language in which the imagery does not appear to be sustained by the meaning, but to be appended fancifully. These defects are such as to weaken the movement of the poem and frequently to obscure the author's meaning.